BUSINESS STRATEGY

AN ASIA-PACIFIC FOCUS

BUSINESS STRATEGY

AN ASIA-PACIFIC FOCUS

Irene Chow PhD
Chinese University of Hong Kong

Neil Holbert PhD
The American College in London

Lane Kelley PhD
University of Hawaii at Manoa

Julie Yu PhD
Chinese University of Hong Kong

PRENTICE HALL
Singapore New York London Toronto Sydney Tokyo

First published in 1997 by
Prentice Hall
Simon & Schuster (Asia) Pte Ltd
317 Alexandra Road
#04-01 IKEA Building
Singapore 159965

 © 1997 Simon & Schuster (Asia) Pte Ltd
A division of Simon & Schuster International Group

All rights reserved. No part of this publication may be reproduced, stored in retrieval system or transmitted in any form, or by any means, electronic, mechanical, photocopying, recording or otherwise, without prior permission in writing from the publisher.

Library of Congress Cataloging-in-Publication Data

Business Strategies: an Asia-Pacific focus / Chow Irene ... [et al.].
        p.   cm.
    Includes bibliographical references and index.
    ISBN 0-13-525858-8
        1. Corporations—Asia—Case studies.   2. Industrial organization-
-Asia. I. Chow, Irene.
HD2891.85.B874   1997
338.7'095—dc20   96-9086
                                                                       CIP

Printed in Singapore

5   01 00 99

ISBN 0-13-525858-8

Prentice Hall International (UK) Limited, *London*
Prentice Hall of Australia Pty. Limited, *Sydney*
Prentice Hall Canada Inc., *Toronto*
Prentice Hall Hispanoamericana, S.A., *Mexico*
Prentice Hall of India Private Limited, *New Delhi*
Prentice Hall of Japan, Inc., *Tokyo*
Editora Prentice Hall do Brasil, Ltda., *Rio de Janeiro*
Prentice Hall, Inc., *Upper Saddle River, New Jersey*

CONTENTS

Foreword by Alan M. Rugman	vii
Preface	ix
Chapter 1: Strategy and Strategies: With an Asian Perspective	1
Chapter 2: Analyzing the Environment	27
Chapter 3: Analyzing a Firm's Internal Environment	47
Chapter 4: Strategy Formulation	70
Chapter 5: Strategy Implementation and Control	89
Country Profile: Japan—The Post-Bubble Environment	111
Case 1: Toyota Motor Corporation in 1994	124
Case 2: Sony Corporation	162
Case 3: According to Honda, an American Legend Faces the 1990s	180
Case 4: Matsushita Electric Industrial Company	207
Country Profile: Hong Kong	225
Case 5: Jardine Matheson Holdings Limited	239
Case 6: Chinese Entrepreneurs—The New *Hong*: Cheung Kong (Holdings) Limited	249
Case 7: Cathay Pacific Airways Limited	272
Case 8: Splendid Duesseldorf Production Limited	285
Case 9: Hongkong and Shanghai Banking Corporation Limited	297
Country Profile: China: The Evolving Economic Force	309
Case 10: Nike, Inc.	327
Case 11: The Caishikou Barbershop	354
Case 12: Goldlion Holdings Group: A Hong Kong Company Enters China	366

Case 13(A): The Nugent Company: Strategic Options for Marketing a High-Tech Product in China	378
Case 13(B): The Nugent Company: Developing a Bridgehead for Marketing a High-Tech Product in China	387
Case 14(A): Kentucky Fried Chicken in China	395
Case 14(B): Kentucky Fried Chicken in China—Expansion and Consequent Problems	407
Case 15: Exporting Pollution to China	416
Case 16: Exporting US Business Ethics to China	419
Case 17: Foster's Brewing Group Limited	425
Case 18: The China Strategy: A Tale of Two Firms	435
Case 19: Acer Incorporated	450
Country Profile: South Korea	461
Case 20: Daewoo: The Favored Korean *Chaebol*	*475*
Case 21: Ssangyong Cement Industrial Company Limited	492
Case 22: Samsung Electronics Company Limited	510
Case 23: Lucky-Goldstar International Corporation—Diversification and Globalization	527
Country Profile: Singapore: Asia's Brave New World	551
Case 24(A): Singapore Airlines: In Pursuit of Excellence	565
Case 24(B): Singapore Airlines—An Update	585
Case 25: Kao in Singapore	594
Case 26: Haw Par Villa Dragon World	613
Index	633

FOREWORD

In teaching strategic management a common viewpoint is that the conceptual foundations of strategy are universal, that there is a common theory of strategy that is not culture bound. At the same time, it is argued that the applications of strategy need to be adapted and made relevant for different countries and cultures. This is achieved by using local cases, instead of the North American ones that are used in most of the well-established major textbooks on strategy.

As the authors of this book demonstrate, this academic attitude is not good enough. Not only do the cases have to be made relevant for Asian students, the content of strategic management also has to be reconsidered. In particular, the "process" by which strategy is implemented will differ in an Asian context compared with a North American one. There are tremendous differences between the implementation of North American business concepts and Asian ones because implementation depends on people. Asian managers and workers will perform and behave in a distinctive manner in comparison with North American managers and workers. Thus, the teaching of strategic management needs a deep awareness of cross-cultural management issues since the implementation process (the structure of strategy) is just as important as the formulation of strategy.

The paradox is that such process differences matter even though we now live in a globalized world economy. The globalization of production has not harmonized world consumption. Instead, local differences still matter, and successful multinational enterprises have to reconcile economics-based globalization pressures with the need to be nationally responsive. The concept of national responsiveness means that firms need to be in tune with the different voices of consumers and also be aware of local government regulations and policies. These well-known propositions in international business have been slow to catch on in US-written strategy textbooks. Fortunately, this book is extremely strong on the international dimension of strategy and this strength will reinvigorate the teaching of strategy concepts as well as processes for students in the Asia-Pacific region.

Today, in a world of triad competition, North American, Asian and Eruopean multinationals are competing for world market shares. In this globally competitive system, strategic advantage can be obtained by both pure globalization strategies (cost, differentiation, focus) but also by national responsiveness. In the Asia-Pacific region, there are three important influences on organizational structures and the process of strategic management. These are: the role of government; the role of the family; and the role of historical and cultural factors. Strategy teaching must take these into account. It is not so much that business practices differ, as that the context matters. Even multinational enterprises need to be close to the customer, manager and worker. As a result, there are no universal principles of strategic management that are culturally exempt. Rather, each concept needs to build on the process by which it will be implemented. Given the wonderful variety of Asian cultures, the teaching of strategic management for Asian students becomes a great challenge. It is one which this book helps to meet.

Alan M. Rugman
Professor of International Business
University of Toronto
Canada

PREFACE

Asia is the world's economic engine.

Historically, influences have flown from the West to the East. In the course of colonialism and would-be colonialism have come Western ideas, Western technology, and Western people.

Today the flow is also the other way. The phoenix-like rise of Japan to world prominence has marked the post-World War II world, as have the economic successes of the "Four Little Dragons": Hong Kong, Korea, Singapore, and Taiwan. And in the wings are China, Indonesia, Malaysia, Thailand, Vietnam, and others.

In this book, we seek to look at the universals of management with the magnifying glass on the economies of Asia, each of which has its own special look. The cases too focus on Asia ... on companies indigenous to the region, and on multinationals who have looked to Asia for further growth.

This book is a start. While there can never be a true finish to anything in the world of business, our strategy in doing this strategy book is clear: to open the way for new visions and to help direct those visions to the East.

After all, East *is* East....

Irene Chow
Neil Holbert
Lane Kelley
Julie Yu

CHAPTER 1

STRATEGY AND STRATEGIES: WITH AN ASIAN PERSPECTIVE

Introduction

In this chapter we seek to develop a framework for an understanding of business strategy as a whole, by seeing it as a part of a chain of events, and then look at some of the elements that make it strategy and not something else.

But before that and throughout the chapter, we will address our special concern: business strategy in a narrow as well as a wider Asian perspective, with observations about the West. Our ideas about business in general and strategy in particular have to some extent come from Europe but mainly from the USA. One is tempted to speak in general terms about these Western ideas on the one hand, and about Asia on the other. There are, of course, problems with this. The West in this context means the USA and Europe. Within Europe too, history and tradition reveal great diversity among the nations—nations that have been at war as much as they have been at peace for a thousand years! Some of the obvious differences are:

- Within Christendom, the Catholic, the Protestant, and the Orthodox (e.g., Serb, Greek, and Russian)
- An open, informal, and secular attitude often identified with the Protestant lands as against a conservative, family-oriented and "religious" tradition among the Catholics and the Orthodox Christians
- A class-bound society (especially in Great Britain) and a more egalitarian social structure in many other countries
- A confident, aggressive stance of most Europeans versus the defensive mentality of groups like the French peasantry, Northern Ireland Protestants and Serbs from the former Yugoslavia, who give the impression to the outside world, of feeling threatened

Though in many ways, European integration is progressing and tastes are becoming similar, historic memories, cultural identities and ethnic exclusivity remain and may be promoted and even become more pronounced as counterpoints to homogenization.

As for the USA, it too is a vast tapestry of many cultures within one nation nonetheless, it has one language and has had a common market since 1789, and certain characteristics of America which reflect the American thinking about strategy are quite obvious. The USA is proclaimed as the land of the "all", the "now", the "all now", the "quick fix", and of the live-wire vitality of competition and contentiousness. In the business arena, specifically, the theme persists of business and government at odds with each other, of the need for short-term profits to satisfy shareholders and please security analysts, on whose recommendations often rests the value of the stock and thus the value of the manager's options; of short-term vistas for managers (especially in marketing) whose jobs frequently depend on this month's or this quarter's results. This short-term outlook, nervous and explosive, reflects in many ways the nervous and explosive nature of America itself. All of this tends to leave little for basic Research and Development (R & D) and the implementation of all the business sense that had been the making of the country.

East and West: Gulfs and Bridges

Yet, all the differences among Europeans (and their longer histories) and the United States of America (and its shorter history) notwithstanding, as far as Asia is concerned, there do remain obvious cultural divides ("fault lines") between the "East" and the "West".

East	West
• Focus on the family (in Japan, the "family" also includes the company and the country)	• Focus on the individual
• Indirectness	• Directness
• *Guanxi* (personal connections) are considered overwhelmingly important	• Personal connections important, but individual drive and merit (regardless of origins) are also vital
• Acceptance	• Determination to overcome
• "Public" focus of life: the market, the street	• "Private" focus of life: the home, the car
• Face: saving, giving, having	• Face: taking, slapping, "in your face"
• Order: stasis	• Order: dynamism
• Harmonization	• Combativeness

The notion of the success of the East deriving from a "Neo-Confucianist" (or "soft authoritarian") orientation (order, respect, place, harmony) is the one which is widely if not universally accepted. The sacrificing of personal freedom for the perceived greater good is almost a cliché, but like so many clichés, it bears much truth.

The next round of East-West tension will be a fight over first principles: whether "democracy" promotes social stability or erodes it; whether free speech is worth the cultural trash it produces in the West; whether the health of the extended group, at the end of the day, matters more than the unfettered freedom of the individual ...

... These "Neo-Confucianists" make no secret of their disdain for Western assumptions about what makes "the good society." The prize they seek are the hearts and minds of 1.7 billion East Asian citizens who have been on a three-decade economic roll and are now groping to define their place in the world ...

... Most Americans reflexively believe that individual freedom and democratic political systems are prerequisites to economic success. It is time, the Asians are saying, to think again. As Lee Kuan Yew, the former prime minister of Singapore and the intellectual father of Asia's Neo-Confucianists, has put it, many Asians have come to reject "the American view" that "out of contention; out of the clash of ideas and ideals, you get good government" and a healthy economy. "That view," Lee says, "is not shared in Asia."[1]

And yet, exchanges between East and West are of course legion, and belie any attempt to build neat conceptual walls between the two. Take the notion that is currently being drummed up as Total Quality Management (TQM), based on the perceived Japanese notion of quality control. Of course, it wasn't that at all, having been brought to Japan by the American statistician W. Edwards Deming. He had long urged US corporations to treat their workers as associates rather than adversaries. His theories were based on the premise that most product defects resulted from shortcomings of management rather than from carelessness of workers, and that inspection after the fact was inferior to designing for better quality.

Deming was an obscure statistician in the United States in 1950 when he was asked by some Japanese industrial leaders, to deliver a series of lectures on his quality-control principles based on his research in World War II. He and his message were eagerly embraced by the Japanese, who believed that, without many natural resources or a colonial empire, they would prosper only if they sold products in world markets.

His success in Japan made him the leader of a generation of specialists on product durability and reliability who were then sought by American companies trying to catch up with their Asian counterparts. But his renown in the United States never matched the success he achieved in Japan.[2]

Many Japanese noted the irony that Deming received such immediate acceptance in Japan while being ignored in his own country for decades. It was only in the 1980s, they remembered with a touch of pride, that the Japanese economic miracle encouraged American companies such as Ford to call Deming out of retirement as a management consultant.[3]

Strategy and Government

Closer to the realms of government and business is the fact that in Asia, in general, effective participatory political democracy *is* subdued or absent. Indeed, writes Beck, there is an "authoritarian nature (to) most of (the region's) political systems. This, of course, is an asset, because it frees the economic decision making process from democratic political pressure."[4] This generalization about the long shadows of States in the business arena is correct (except for Hong Kong, of which more below). We may look at states that can be called *supportive* (Japan: where the government identifies with business whose essence it created), or *exhortative* (Korea, Taiwan: where business growth has derived from State policies and where economic growth has led to increased openness in authoritarian regimes), or *paternalistic* ("Neo-Confucian" Singapore), or even *autocratic* (China, whose Communist Government encourages the increasing prosperity that they know only capitalism can bring). Whether these stances by these states are "assets" (as Beck believes—see above), or negatives (because they are antithetical to freedom as known in the West) is, as noted, debatable. As Fukuda observes about Japan:

> *While the individual may be sacrificed sometimes for the benefit of the state, most Japanese wonder whether they would rather choose total freedom and poverty over limited freedom and a higher standard of living.*[5]

Asian Country Focuses

Spotlights on individual countries can sharpen our understanding, and just a few examples are now offered.

In Japan, the emphasis remains on harmony (*wa*). The two main characteristics of Japanese society are groupism and vertical relations. Many Japanese identify their native characteristics as stemming from the Tokugawa era—a period of Japan's self-imposed isolation from the rest of the world which lasted more than 250 years. During that era and thereafter, the Japanese had come to believe that:

1. An individual receives a continuous flow of blessings that establish obligations within groups.
2. Social, political, ethical, and religious norms are of value only as they are valuable to groups.
3. Values are achieved in groups.
4. All the values are best implemented by, or in the name of the symbolic head of family-style groups.[6]

Lifetime employment and the *keiretsu* system (interconnected webs of manufacturers and suppliers and banks) may be fraying a bit, but, compared to the West, notions of loyalty and cooperation and long-term goals for company and country are still well-developed. While the government wants people to take more leisure, and while there is growing awareness that the average Japanese doesn't live as well as his income should allow, the notions of seriousness and self-sacrifice are also strong. Banks are still relatively patient and loyal to their customers who historically have been favoured with capital at lower interest rates than were extended to American companies, and banks don't readily foreclose on besieged properties, like many Japanese investments in Hawaii and California. Companies' suppliers are also not compelled, or are even allowed, to compete with each other to the benefit of those companies. In fact, the suppliers often hold the companies' stocks, as do the banks, more or less through good times and bad as a sign of loyalty.

In short, the Japanese picture has always looked like a hand with management, labour, suppliers, banks, and government as its fingers rather than like bitterly contentious separate entities.

Things are changing, but this basic picture is still viable and it is apparent that in a country like Japan business and business strategy work differently from the normative American model of competition within and without the company. With the close links between business and government, and within business itself, it is apparent that share-of-market and other long-term objectives can be a real goal for Japanese business, and that in Asia it is impossible to understand a company and its strategy without reference to the role of the government of its country of domicile.

In Korea, to cite another Asian powerhouse, the government can significantly affect the life of its great business combines, the *chaebols*, by putting pressure on banks to lend or not lend to them. Since the chaebols are heavily debt-financed, government views of the moment (like many Asian countries, Korea has a government of laws and *also* of men) must be understood if strategy is to be understood.

As already mentioned, in other Asian countries such as India, Indonesia, Malaysia, Singapore, Taiwan, and Thailand as well, government casts long shadows on business: business and politics interlock in often unpredictable ways, but those shadows *are* great, real, and permanent.

And finally Hong Kong, one of the four little dragons—along with Korea, Singapore, and Taiwan—that are linked to the big dragon, Japan.

> *Japanese economists use the metaphor of a "flying geese" pattern ... Japan leads the flock, followed by (the) four (little dragons) and (others behind) bringing up the rear. All are flying in the formation of "modernization", picking up industries sloughed off by the one in front.*[7]

Even in Hong Kong, where the government remains aloof, it is vital to understand the relationship (or non-relationship) between business and government.

In Hong Kong, the great business combines, the *hongs*, virtually *are* the government of the colony (now called a "territory" so as to not offend China), at least until China regains sovereignty from the United Kingdom in 1997. In Hong Kong, freewheeling competition (probably the freest in the world) sees equity offerings of staggering sizes and deals that often seem inscrutable (buying and selling parts of each other and doing things that look anti-competitive). Business strategy in Hong Kong, then, exists mostly not with an eye on the shadow that the government may cast (the present government proclaims a policy of positive non-intervention) after the 1997 handover. Will China kill (or even wound) the goose that lays the golden eggs?

Chapter 1

The Persistence of Background

As with any country, the countries of Asia will progress or not depending on their competitive advantages both given and created: natural resources and historical circumstances and reactions to them all, and also the policies and laws of the government.

The ideas about business and business strategy that have come out of the West may or may not seem relevant when we look at strategy in Asia. It is not that the Western background is not important; it is, but it must always be seen as a backdrop or as a frame of comparison ratner than as a standard that should be followed everywhere.

Different Countries: Different Goals

Can we quantify these diverse ideas with some quantitative data? A study of managerial goals of business in the USA, Japan, and Korea can help put some of our observations into sharper focus. Managers in three countries rated each goal shown, from 0 (low in importance) to 3 (high in importance). The results are provided in Table 1.1 with ranking of items for each country in parentheses.[8]

Table 1.1 Rating of Goals in Three Countries

Items	USA	Japan	Korea
Return on investment	2.43 (1)	1.24 (2)	1.23 (3)
Stockholders' gains	1.14 (2)	0.02 (9)	0.14 (8)
Market share	0.73 (3)	1.43 (1)	1.55 (1)
Product portfolio	0.50 (4)	0.68 (5)	0.19 (6)
Operational efficiency	0.46 (5)	0.71 (4)	0.47 (5)
Financial structure	0.38 (6)	0.59 (6)	0.82 (4)
Product innovation	0.21 (7)	1.06 (3)	1.24 (2)
Corporate image	0.05 (8)	0.20 (7)	0.12 (9)
Working conditions	0.04 (9)	0.09 (8)	0.15 (7)

As can be seen, nothing involves US firms more than return on investment. This is important in Japan and Korea too, but to a much lesser extent. For those countries, market share comes first, underscoring our comments about Asian focus on the longer term, vs. US focus on the more immediate. In line with this note too is the greater emphasis on product innovation in Japan and Korea (the longer term again), and the relatively low importance accorded in those countries to stockholders' gains as compared to the USA.

In the broadest terms, the differences between the **Asian** countries as a whole (longer-term emphasis, working *with* rather than *against* government, seeking harmony rather than confrontation) and **America**, read the **West** (shorter-term emphases, combative, individualistic) can begin to offer insights into business strategy. Will the continuing economic gains in Asia lead to continuing political loosening and continual drift to the individual rather than the collective? Will history, culture, and imperatives of circumstances bring Asia closer to the ways of the West (especially the West's more enviable aspects of liberty, openness, and the freedom of choice)? And whatever the answer, will there be a continuing drive towards what has been called the Pacific Century, to coincide with the coming of the third millenium?

The Strategic Imperative

And now to planning, and, in particular, *strategy*. It is a word that has been taken from the science of warfare, and has become fashionable to a fault in both the academic and the business worlds.

Simply put, it really isn't difficult to understand what the core of "strategy" is—a vision, a road map, an idea of where we were, are, and want to go and want to be—part of a chain of events that seeks to ensure that we *will* get there.

Strategy is surely a universal imperative for enterprises: whether in developed, developing, or underdeveloped countries; large or small; operating in one country or multinationally; focusing on goods or services; consumer or industrial; whether successful or (especially perhaps) not-so-successful; whether Western or Asian.

But without a deeper look at what strategy really is, we can neither understand it nor profit from it.

The "Chain"

As noted already, strategy is first of all a Part of a "Chain". It does not exist by itself, but follows from higher-level planning (deep and basic), and leads to action (execution and evaluation), then looping back to start all over again in an eternal cycle of thinking and doing.

We can look at the steps as follows:

1. Mission
2. Scenarios
3. Strategy I   : Strategic philosophy
4. Strategy II   : Strategic goals
5. Tactics I   : Tactical framework
6. Tactics II   : Tactical objectives
7. Execution
8. Evaluation I   : Feedback and control
9. Evaluation II : Reappraisal

This "chain", this "process", *is* universal. To repeat, it exists for *any* planning needs, large or small, sooner or later, East or West. Each step involves internal (micro) and external (macro) considerations, often crazily interacting (or getting tangled up) with each other. Further chapters will focus on each of these considerations.

It is quite likely that a normative Asian conciliatory mode of planning will involve more people in various stages of the process than in the West, at least for the sake of face. But even though some of the nine steps can be skipped if we think the results of those steps are known, it is perilous to skip any step because we didn't know it was there.

And finally *with* all the participative emphasis in Asia, the final decision will still have to be made by someone at the top, someone who was probably the instigator of it all anyway and who has sought in the course of things to get lower rung participation to try at least to help engineer consent.

Such leadership, such "the-buck-stops-here" thinking, may be softer (as in Japan) or gruffer (as in China), but it exists, for decision making cannot be as democratic as is often viewed by those who have never lived the organizational life—East or West.

Finally, it must always be remembered that the "chain" is a process; it is something *we* devise and use; it has no life of its own and should always be a subject of constant attention and questioning. Does such a more-or-less "formal" way of thinking suit as well? Is it perhaps becoming an icon or a fetish, subject to hardened rules that only serve to atrophy matters? Are we perhaps just paying lip service to it? It needs to be reviewed and constant improvements sought, even as we do the same for more physical and technical processes. Indeed, these latter need to be incorporated into our chain of planning as much as possible, so long as they (the things on the technical side) don't become ends in themselves.

> *Continuous improvement is a theme heard throughout the halls of manufacturing firms today. Another theme prevalent in manufacturing is the elevation of the information systems (IS) function beyond a basic data processing environment. Because of the combined interest by senior manufacturing managers in both, continuous improvement and enhancing IS with information technology (IT), firms are rapidly pursuing business objectives that focus on deriving strategic value from information. These managers have taken the view that a properly designed approach to information systems will positively impact the ability of the firm to generate real gains from continuous improvement programs and therefore enhance the firm's ability to compete successfully in the global marketplace. A true customer focus demands that this take place.*[9]

Mission

Let us now look at each step in the chain. The chain starts with the notion of "mission". What is the Company in business for? Obviously to make profits and to ensure its own continued existence. For example, is it determined to be a leader in all things—seeking always to take the "first bite" out of a market, the lion's share of the fresh kill as it were, or is it more orientated to watch and wait, learn from others and take a "second bite", like the smaller creatures that accommodate themselves to live in the lion's shadow? Is it a company whose focus is on one country, or does it operate in a broader field?

DHL, the US-based courier company that is solidly entrenched in Asia too, sees the World as its mission. Here is its "Worldwide Mission Statement".

Strategy and Strategies: With an Asian Perspective

DHL will become the acknowledged global leader in the express delivery of documents and packages. Leadership will be achieved by establishing the industry standards of excellence for quality of service and by maintaining the lowest cost position relative to our service commitment in all markets of the world.

Achievement of the mission requires:

- *Absolute dedication to understanding and fulfilling our customers' needs with the appropriate mix of service, reliability, products, and price for each customer.*
- *An environment that rewards achievement, enthusiasm, and team spirit and which offers each person in DHL superior opportunities for personal development and growth.*
- *A state-of-the-art worldwide information network for customer billing, tracking and management information and communications.*
- *Allocation of resources consistent with the recognition that we are one worldwide business.*
- *A professional organization able to maintain local initiative and local decision-making while working together within a centrally managed network.*

The evolution of our business into new services, markets, or products will be completely driven by our SINGLEMINDED COMMITMENT to anticipating and meeting the changing needs of our customers.

To cite just two more examples of worldwide companies with strong presence in Asia, the apparel maker Benetton has long made it known that it seeks attention by going far beyond clothes to social issues, that "the company's philosophy (is) not to push a product but to attract attention to its name by addressing social issues."[10] Indeed, its advertisements showing young people of different races embracing, a young priest kissing a young nun, coloured condoms flying about, and the agony of a terminal AIDS sufferer and his family, all have been used (in a way that has been called variously sincere and cynical) to break through category clutter and reinforce the simple theme of the "United Colours of Benetton".

Disney also has stated the idea of its mission quite clearly as it contemplates the Asian scene. While Disney's president of feature animation, Peter Schneider, is convinced his product can be doing better here, he is aware of the Asian taste for sex and violence when it comes to cartoons. He said he admired the technology of the Japanese work but believed animated films should have a broader appeal. According to him,

Japanese animation is so successful. Why isn't ours? There is no real answer other than that they are different movies. We take another tack. Our films are less violent but still adult entertainment. They are family oriented, and not just cartooning. They are a movie. Aladdin *is the most successful movie this year, not just of animated films but also of cartoons and live action movies. Disney has no intention of tailoring its work to make it more acceptable to an Asian audience, according to him. "We make the movies for ourselves. We tell stories that are interesting in the telling. If people like the story, it will make money."* [11]

Chapter 1

Mission statements emanating from Asia with their sometimes large helpings of mysticism that often sound both self-serving and promotional may especially surprise us. Yet, there is nothing unworldly about the actions of Kazuo Wada, head of the Yaohan Department Store empire, the first retailer to set up a major branch (in the satellite town of Shatin) outside of Hong Kong's traditional shopping areas, and the first Japanese company to redomicile in Hong Kong—seen to be a gateway to China.

This is what Wada writes of his Company's mission as he sees it, in a spirit typical of the "leader" figure in Asian business—the kind of businessman who sometimes seems like an anachronistic Asian emperor-poet or a philosopher-king out of Plato.

The days of doing business solely for the sake of making profits are over. Formerly, the single-minded pursuit of profit alone was acceptable, and what is more, Japan developed into an economic power as a result of this, but doing business in the 21st century cannot be conceived of without thinking about contributing to the world. "To be provided for by means of providing for others." We are now about to enter into the days when this philosophy prevails.

We are constantly striving to demonstrate that Yaohan is a company which implements this philosophy. One of the methods employed is the "Yaohan Group Declaration". In Japan, of course, this is done in the Japanese language, but in all overseas stores English is employed for making the staff become aware of it. I would now like to introduce the English version, entitled "The Declaration of Yaohan Group":

"By studying and practising the truth of life's philosophies, the Yaohan International Group of Companies strives to create a company which will render better service to people all over the world and in so doing, hopes to become a model for other companies."

In 1965 I was participating in the training programme for newly recruited staff at the "Seicho-no-Ie" training centre when I was suddenly inspired. It was revealed to me that the business philosophy of Yaohan was not wholehearted devotion to the pursuit of profit but to serve all people in the world. This revelation was duly announced in 1965 as "the Yaohan Department Store Declaration", and at present is adhered to as the basic philosophy of our company by all staff in the form of "The Declaration of Yaohan International Group".

Advancements of Japanese companies to foreign lands have been subject to severe Japan-bashing, especially in the United States. Since Yaohan's philosophy is not wholehearted pursuit of profit but to contribute to all people in the world and to become a model company, however, we have never been the target of Japan-bashing. Rather than that, numerous approaches have been made from overseas asking us to set up stores, and we have been welcomed with open arms.

During the coming 21st century, it is important for Japanese companies to discard the idea of wholehearted pursuit of profit and to switch to a philosophy of serving the human race. Naturally profit constitutes an important yardstick when evaluating the merits and demerits of a company. It would be impossible for a company to survive by disregarding profit. Nevertheless, the days when companies were evaluated solely by their ability to derive profit are gone. It is now the time for participating in the international society of business with a new yardstick.

Notions from Sony about its mission seem similarly mawkish but perhaps instead, genuinely springing from an Asian consciousness that has seen itself submerged by the West, and which now seeks to call upon all the best it sees in itself, seek to blend Asian groupism with a certain Western do-it-yourself spirit. Whatever it may be, it is worthwhile to read the Sony sentiments.[12]

Never follow others; blaze a trail and open up new areas where no one has ventured.
Sony leads, others follow.
We do what others don't.
Study yourself, think yourself, judge for yourself, and carry things out yourself.
There may be a limit to a man's ability but there is no limit to his efforts.
Nothing is happier for a man than to do work that he enjoys.
It is your own task to wake up your sleeping talent.
Each person should be conscious that a man's worth lies in his ability.
Everyone has a desire to do some creative work. Presenting a theme for study, fostering interest, and encouraging true ability are jobs for the executives.
A right man in the right place is a slogan for yourselves, not for your boss. You should find the right place yourselves.

Surely all mission statements inevitably contain elements of hype but it is also true that many contain real clues as to what the organization is up to, or *thinks* it's up to as it proceeds along its way. Often, one can intuit real urgency and authenticity, suggesting underlying notions that indeed lie close to the surface of management thinking. It would be naive to believe that mission statements are not also self-serving, and imbued with shadow as well as substance. The very willingness to proclaim these ideas to customers and markets both inside and outside the organization suggests nonetheless that they are useful guideposts to the shaping of strategy.

Let's look East once more.

National character—formed by history and embedded in culture—has an impact on mission, and, as noted again and again, it is important to always keep in mind the nations of the West and the East, and, also the differences among the nations in the East. For Korea, for example, the sense of adversity and the challenge of overcoming it, has always been a basis of national character, a sense no doubt derived in modern times from Korea's decades as a Japanese colony as also the bitter Korean War of 1950–1953 and its aftermath. Notes Warnoff:

Chapter 1

> ... the Korean people have never really liked easy tasks. They usually pick a goal, sometimes an ambitious one like changing from one of the most hopeless and backward economies to a dynamic, industrialized one ... Unlike others, the fact that things are harder than ever may not deter them. It could just as well spur them on.[13]

This way things are derived not only from national character, but also from the results of the exigencies of history. Japanese and American business raise money through private banks and stock markets. By contrast, Korean *chaebols* have tended to rely on Government-controlled banks or financial institutions. In Korea,

> The ... government ... had to raise capital for a selected group of successful and loyal entrepreneurs and nurtured them with low-interest loans, preferential taxes, import-export licenses, and acquisitions of government properties at below market price.[14]

All of this interest in Korea (not dissimilar to the formation of Japan's zaibatsu) has not been an unmixed blessing of course, as the chaebols have had to *face outwards*, always an imperative in strategy and a difficulty for those weaned in a supportive cocoon.

> The lack of separation between business ownership and management, government involvement in business [leading to difficulties in succeeding without such protection] and the authoritarian Confucian culture are limiting factors in continued growth, which requires wider participation.[15]

In Japan, it is the notion of interdependence that permeates the very life of every business organization, and the search for harmony (*wa*) that both feeds into, and from it. One of the missions of any Japanese company is to foster this.

What *is* this web that is constantly being spun?

> With regard to stockholding (in a sogo shosa [Japanese trading company] who is a client) it is true that the (main) bank does not by itself have a controlling share, but when the holdings of member companies (of a bank's network) are included, the voice of the main bank is influential on many issues ...[16]

And what *is* this notion—so Japanese but still so seemingly mystical—of harmony as it relates to the Japanese company? In Japan,

> Top management is a group, not a single individual. Any person who makes important decisions or participates in a meeting to make such decisions may be considered a member of top management, and exactly who constitutes the top management is often not clear-cut.[17]

Research has been undertaken to study influence—both *direct*, where sanctions, etc. are threatened; and *indirect*, where requests are involved—of US suppliers on their Japanese channel partners. Findings suggested "that Western channel partners may enjoy little success influencing Japanese channel partners, in general, no matter what strategy they use."[18]

Whether described as the preference for interdependence (over dependence or independence), or the search for harmony, or the imperative of indirection, it is clear that these Japanese ways are not echoes of the Western urgencies, and that their playing out is inherent in mission and all that follows.

But to return one last time to the theme of 'differences within similarities' in Asian business, the mission for companies in Japan while sharing a Confucian underpinning, obviously will reflect national differences as well.

Just looking at Japan, Korea, and Taiwan—although obviously firms differ widely from each other in *any* country in terms of size, history, philosophy, etc.—one can readily see the basic thrusts that affect corporate missions in those countries and everything that derives therefrom: In Japan the emphasis on the group (yet buttressed by Government); in Korea on the State; in Taiwan (again buttressed by Government) on the smaller, family, pattern.[19]

Scenarios

From mission, there ultimately emerges strategy. But before strategy come *scenarios,* the "what-ifs". One need not focus here only on "futurism" and "futurists", although that should not be overlooked. We *should* ponder about "megatrends". Will "knowledge" really become the most valued currency of organizations as they become flatter, leaner, meaner, greener, and even more protean in shape; will they continue going from "'cottage industry' to 'cottage industry'", at the offices at home in the cottages of the 21st century, as the notions of giant factories and giant office building (with huge numbers of workers) become archaic; will the world be getting bigger (with more opportunities) or smaller (with hard blocs), or both?

And yet beyond those megatrends, managers everywhere, not least in Asia, need to ponder long and hard on still other scenarios. What if the Japanese economic miracle is finally petering out; what if China proceeds along its course of adopting capitalism while retaining power in the hands of the Communist gerontocrats; what if it *doesn't;* what if Hong Kong continues to shine as a beacon of free trade and economic power after the 1997 reversion to China; what if it doesn't; what if those "soft-authoritarian" states like Singapore, Taiwan, South Korea, Thailand, Malaysia, and Indonesia prove to be continuing models of success, rather than the pluralist democracies of the West?

Broad futurist scenarios, then, and narrower schemes focusing on power and potential, must be considered by businesses as they move down a step from their seminal missions to contemplating scenarios, and then on to strategy.

Strategic Philosophy

Strategy—strategic thinking—starts now. The mission and scenario sessions dealt with poetry, looking at possibilities and probabilities through layers of imagination.

Those sessions are not intended to collect results and then go ahead and do what you want to do. If they are treated that way, it is better not to have them. Rather, the ideas derived from those sessions set the stage for the first of the two strategy steps: *the construction of the strategic philosophy.*

As we construct, deconstruct, and reconstruct this strategic philosophy, we must always ask: will it work? Czepiel[20] suggests four questions for consideration. Does the strategy fit the changing environment? Is it internally consistent, including matching the objectives set for the managers who will implement the strategy? Does the strategy fully exploit the firm's resources and distinctive competencies? Are the strategy's risks consistent with its rewards?

It is built of vision and is designed for practicality. It is crafted rather than prefabricated from many materials, and constantly worked and reworked as we go along.

It can be a straightforward statement, such as this one by the British retailer Marks & Spencer, which has been successfully operating in the Hong Kong market:

> *The principles on which Marks and Spencer was founded proved sound cornerstones for the building of today's company. But they did not stand alone. Each generation added to them and moulded them into today's principles. These are:*
> 1. *To offer customers, under the Company's own brand name, St. Michael, a selective range of high-quality, well-designed and attractive merchandise at reasonable prices.*
> 2. *To encourage suppliers to use the most modern and efficient techniques of production provided by the latest discoveries in science and technology.*
> 3. *With the cooperation of these suppliers, to enforce the highest standards of quality control.*
> 4. *To plan the expansion of M & S stores for the better display of a widening range of goods and for the convenience of our customers.*
> 5. *To simplify operating procedures so that the business is carried on in an efficient manner.*
> 6. *To foster good human relations with customers, suppliers and staff.*

Or it can be an idea like the suddenly blinding light of the possibility of pan-Asian advertising and promotions. Multinational companies are chasing this Asian rainbow more eagerly than ever. Spurred by the growth of the international media and the subsequent emergence of a pan-Asian consumer class, advertisers are increasingly trying to consolidate brands and strategies to carry across national borders. More importantly, they want to mould Asia's massive, growing markets into a single mass entity.

> *"I have seen a staggering change in the last three to five years in favor of finding regional synergies,"* says Alan Fairnington, regional chairman of the J. Walter Thompson advertising agency. *"Even though I had seen a trend toward global advertising, it surprised me because the Asian markets are so different."*
>
> Admittedly, not every company can communicate a single message across Asia's

numerous cultural divides but the number of products going pan-Asian is expanding from a clutch of luxury items to a broader array of consumer and packaged goods. Worldwide marketers like Coca Cola, Pepsi Cola and Nike have embraced Asia as part of their global ad campaigns, with modifications for local appeal. Consumer products giants Procter & Gamble and Unilever have launched some of their myriad brands throughout the region but are still scrambling for more pan-Asian candidates.[21]

It can be an idea like the "world car" come alive again in a time when strategic alliances are playing ever-increasing roles in world business. As automobiles go, it's about as close to a hi-tech, high-margin Mercedes as ape is to man. But this squat, nondescript vehicle built by Suzuki Motor Corp. is more than just a $6000 economy car. It's a symbol of today's auto industry: Sold in Japan as the Cultus, the same car is a Ford in Taiwan and a Chevrolet in America.

Call it burden sharing, a "borderless" or simply a confusing product, but for automakers the world over, cross-marketed cars resulting from a spate of strategic alliances are a fact of life. The main reason is the high cost of development, manufacturing and marketing—up to $2 billion per car—spread over the three mainstay markets, the US, Europe and Japan. Ohara Ken, a board member at Mazda Motor Corp., says: "Joint ventures are the threads that hold the car business together today."

Tie-ups promise to become even more common by early next century. That's because the globe, now split into three main car markets, is making room for a fourth: Asia. According to Mazda, Asians will demand 5.2 million cars a year by 1995, roughly equal to Japan's market today. "The region will be the world's fastest-growing car market by the 21st century," says Nishiyama Hitoshi, an auto analyst at Nomura Research Institute, a Tokyo think tank.[22]

Or it can be the sudden realization that the notion that "one size fits all" may need to be re-examined. Although the jeans market in Hong Kong is both saturated and highly competitive, market studies and trade audits revealed a gap in the market. According to the studies, no established brand had yet offered denim wear which had the following four product characteristics:

1. Female-based image
2. Specially styled and cut for Oriental women
3. A strong European connotation
4. Medium price range

After further studies to obtain representative sizing of Asian women, Fornari Jeans was introduced in the market as the only product which were cut to fit the Oriental woman from hip to ankle.[23]

With its emphasis on conclusions drawn from heavy preliminary thinking, "Strategic Philosophy" often leans heavily on paradigms, looking at a lot of things in a compact way, and putting names on them. This one (Exhibit 1.1) from the famous strategist, Kenichi Ohmae—focusing in on perceived corporate strengths (from left to right) and on our perception of the attractiveness of the market (from top to bottom)—is quite typical.[24]

Exhibit 1.1 Nine Strategy Options

MARKET ATTRACTIVENESS			
High	*Serious Entry into the Market* — Opportunistic position to test growth prospects; withdraw if indications of sustainable growth are lacking.	*Selective Growth* — Select areas where strength can be maintained, and concentrate investment in those areas.	*All-out Struggle* — Concentrate entire effort on maintaining strength; if necessary maintain profit structure by investment.
Medium	*Limited Expansion or Withdrawal* — Look for ways of achieving expansion without high risk; if unsuccessful, withdraw before involved too deeply.	*Selective Expansion* — Concentrate on investment, and expand only in segments where profitability is good and risk is relatively low.	*Maintenance of Superiority* — Build up ability to counter competition, avoiding large-scale investment; emphasize profitability by raising productivity.
Low	*Loss-minimizing* — Prevent losses before they occur by avoiding investment and by lowering fixed costs; when loss is unavoidable, withdraw.	*Overall Harvesting* — Promote switch from fixed to variable costs; emphasize profitability through (analysis) of variable costs (in terms of design, function and product price).	*Limited Harvesting* — Reduce degree of risk to a minimum in several segments; emphasize profit by protecting profitability even if loss of market position is involved.
	Low	Medium	High

———— CORPORATE STRENGTHS ————▶

Strategic Goals

Once the strategic philosophy has been established as a framework, it is time to move on to strategic goals. They share certain characteristics with *tactical objectives* (see section on Tactical Objectives). The basic difference is that while *tactical objectives* are expressed mostly in numbers (and thus have a "hard" look and feel), our strategic-based goals are more like further crystallized *ideas*, broad brush rather than pinpoint.

Earlier we looked at some of the underpinnings of *mission* in various Asian countries and suggested that government intervention, familism, and a search for harmony rather than conflict, for suggestion rather than directive, and for indirectness rather than directness were all observable phenomena.

In setting goals, this less formed, less hardened, less direct Asian approach, compared to the West, is probably also present. As an American writer noted:

> *The Japanese view the emphasis we place on "strategy" as we might regard their*

enthusiasm for Kabuki or sumo wrestling. They note our interest not with an intent of acquiring similar ones but for insight into our peculiarities. The Japanese are somewhat distrustful of a single "strategy", for in their view any idea that focuses attention does so at the expense of peripheral vision. They strongly believe that peripheral vision is essential to discerning changes in the customer, the technology, or competition, and is the key to corporate survival over the long haul. They regard any propensity to be driven by a single-minded strategy as a weakness.

The Japanese have particular discomfort with strategic concepts. While they do not reject ideas such as the experience curve or portfolio theory outright, they regard them as a stimulus to perception. They have often ferreted out the "formula" of their concept-driven American competitors and exploited their inflexibility ...[25]

Attributions about Asian views on business (and on the world) could be spun out endlessly. Ideas such as challenge, harmony, indirectness, and interdependence have all been offered. Without becoming compulsive about it, each of these could be counterpoised to Western complacency, contentiousness, directness, and independence.

A further and final element, common to all of the East, and not least to Japan, is persistence. After all, with such a long way to go to catch up and with limited natural resources but unlimited discipline, who could doubt it? Asks Turpin:[26]

Is persistence another stereotyped value of the Japanese? Why should Japan be singled out as the country where persistence is so cherished? ... Japanese leaders of the late 19th century recognized that Japan had to industrialize to avoid Western domination. Resistance (gambare) was closely linked with the idea of survival (ikinokori) and catching up (oitsuki) with Western powers. In strong contrast to the West where the mercantile class had, over time, displaced the aristocracy, Japanese public policy deliberately bred social entrepreneurs from the samurai (i.e., military) class. Strongly influenced by its Confucian values of patience, loyalty, determination, and endurance, the samurai class was given the formal mission of establishing Japan in the modern industrial world.

Goals may include studying new opportunities uncovered in discussions on mission, scenarios, and strategic philosophy, say in future niche marketing where now we're strong but not all-pervasive. Or they might centre around detailed study of EU, NAFTA, APEC, ASEAN, and other current and emerging blocs to merge and meld our presences in all of them, both now and up ahead. Or even to redefine the company itself, as in the case of corporate identity work in Japan:

When Asahi beer was first launched in Japan, its market share of the beer industry rarely reached beyond the nine per cent level. It took a drastic change in its image (as "New Asahi Beer") and an overhaul in its flavour and processing to boost the brewery's share to 24 per cent.

Chapter 1

> *When deregulation forced mutual savings banks to compete with commercial banks, the Sanyo Mutual Savings Bank adopted the name and corporate symbol of Tomato Bank. While the new name may seem to be an incongruous choice for a financial institution, it nevertheless successfully communicated the bank's new, fresh and cheerful image, a message that was not lost on the Japanese housewife, the bank's target audience....*
>
> *Corporate identity in Japan vastly differs from corporate identity as it is practised in the US where it is still centred on the creation of a visual identity system, i.e., graphics and logo design. In Japan, it extends to redefining a company's business domain, using design as a valuable management strategy rather than just as a symbol of the company name.*[27]

While such goals may sound limp rather than limpid, in reality they represent a sharp coming to grips with the world that can only be essayed *after* mission and scenarios have been explored and absorbed.

Most of all, it must always be remembered that goals, like tactical objectives, must share the common traits of *all* sound objectives. They must be *doable* (and not mere pipe dreams); *realistic* (and not hysterical to frighten employees into doing something—it doesn't matter what); *focused* (that is, focused on the business and not on the shrill egos and black recesses of the minds of top management); *concrete* (and not airy-fairy and harebrained); *horizon-specific* (short-term, medium-term, long-term); *reviewable; flexible*; and *measurable*.

As already noted, it is down the line in tactical objectives that we will put numbers to these objectives, but for now we are still in the realm of vision (*not* "visions"!): of possibility, probability, and potential; if not still poetry, then also not quite yet prose.

Tactical Framework

Tactics follow strategy; vision leads to method; the road map leads into the vehicle.

Obviously, in the world of business it isn't always, or probably ever, as neat as that.

In the successful company, it's more like a flow, organically moving down the trail (the "chain"). The pieces and the steps must *interrelate*: They must have something to do with one another, and not be just idle disconnected noodlings that are interesting, but bear no relationship either to each other or to the broad purpose of the business. They must then *interweave*, fitting together like an intricate carpet woven on a loom to form a pattern. And then they must *interlock*, hold together so they don't fly apart and split into a thousand fragments the moment they have been assembled. Metaphors are plentiful, but there must be glue, and that glue, the focused thinking of management, an inherent part of the process and not put on later. Finally, the pieces, the steps in the chain, must show *synergy*; the word though overused, is nonetheless apt. The whole of the planning process must produce results greater than the sum of its parts. Good early "mission" thinking that leads to vague "scenario" writing can only lead to fuzzy strategy; and strong strategy that is translated into confused tactics is likewise futile.

Never is the notion of transition from step to step in the chain more important than when we move from strategy to tactics. It needs to be seamless and logical, rather than mindless and mechanical. If thinking breaks down here, we can end up with *Grand* Strategy (for the company as a whole) built up not SBU (strategic business unit) by SBU from each individual *Brand* Strategy (a thinking about what each item in the portfolio was, is, and can be), but from each individual *Bland* Strategy ("Oh my strategy? Well it's to move ahead and keep on top by heavy television commercials that are fun to watch and appeal to everybody."). (See also below.) Of Bland Strategy we need say no more now, except that it is really, at best, only tactics and then not especially well thought out at that, and often much less even than that.

Tactics, therefore, must flow from strategy if they are to have any bite. Tactics that are constantly panicky and ad hoc, rather than drawing life from strategic thinking, will just turn the company into an "adhocracy".

Tactical Objectives

Tactical framework leads to tactical objectives. Like strategic goals, they too must be doable, realistic, focused, concrete, horizon-specific, reviewable, flexible, and measurable. They must derive from what has been done before, hold together, and serve to impel us organically down the chain.

Indeed, if strategic development can't produce a good tactical framework and solid tactical objectives ("a share of X% by such and such date, based upon Y% distribution and Z% advertising awareness"; or "A work force that comes in with such and such minimum and average levels of literacy and numeracy that will rise to such and such levels following career path movements and technical and humanistic training in the organization"), then all that has gone before has failed.

And again here, as everywhere in the "chain", there will be meaningful work done only if people feel they won't get punished (reprimanded, demoted, fired) for expressing honest opinions. Like for example, for noting that the tactical objectives which have been conveyed to them (and in the formulation of which they may have played no part) are fanciful and irrelevant and are designed to "hang" people rather than move the process along. If we do not forcefully state the need for *faith and trust* in organizations that may be running instead, on envy and slyness, then we fail to do our job of trying to expain what the organization needs above all else.

In some companies and industries in the US, the workers have always had the faith and trust that their companies would do the right thing by them. There was a time when the banks, insurance companies and public utilities there never fired anybody. Once, neither, for example, did IBM; however, global competition, succession and the steamroller of computer-led organization flattening technology have taken their toll of this faith and trust.

Manufacturing firms are also experiencing restructuring programs which often result in corporate downsizing and the direct or indirect termination of numerous white and blue collar employees. Many of the employees who were both promoters of continuous improvement programs, and even championed the changes taking place within the firm, found themselves out of work and bewildered by the process that resulted in their exodus from the work environment. One only has to look at General Motors, IBM, Eastman Kodak, and a host of other firms, to witness tens of thousands who were downsized in the name of continuous improvement. Not to be restricted to the US, downsizing and restructuring is becoming increasingly common in both Europe and Japan.[28]

Execution

Tactics leads to *execution*. Till now, we have only talked, nobody has actually *done* anything yet. We now go for it but if what we go for (and maybe even do) isn't *worth* going for (or doing)—because there was no sound prior thinking in all the stages up to now—it won't mean a thing.

Execution means work, coordination, discipline, flexibility. As suggested earlier, if those who must execute (say, the salespeople) have not been brought into the planning process, then execution may be halfhearted. They may not be convinced that they will earn more by pushing the still unproven new product than by continuing to push the established winners. So you must ask in this execution phase: have you really "closed the ring" by effectively "selling" to your "internal customers"?

Feedback and Control

Feedback—the first of the two steps in the Evaluation stage tells us what the results of our actions have been. Are we getting better employees? Are they staying longer? Has the word of what we're doing gotten out? Has our corporate value been reappraised upward by security analysts? Has the product or service sold well, as determined by both sales results and survey findings—including the real bottom line: are they coming back for more? And what are we doing to ensure that the feedback is actually taking place—and constructively?

Reappraisal

The strategic planning chain ends, and loops back to start again, with the second step in Evaluation: *Reappraisal*.

There must be a will to look intelligently, even doubtingly, at what's happening, or not happening. Is what we know really being implemented? What's the trouble? *Who's* the trouble? What "constraints", either external or self-imposed, are holding us back and would we be willing to do something about them?

> *The theory of constraints is an evolving theory that, in its simplest form, asks the question: What is constraining the firm from making more profits now and in the*

future? For example, if the firm does not have sufficient manufacturing capacity for a certain level of sales, then sales promotion efforts may be a waste of time and resources if additional capacity cannot be added in a timely manner. On the other hand, if the firm possesses excess manufacturing capacity relative to sales level, then promotion activities to boost the level of sales, including market segmentation, is a rather obvious and fundamental response. One could make the argument that many firms with excess capacity, physical and/or human, have chosen to downsize the corporate structure, with a focus on cost reduction, rather than expand their markets, and therefore horizons, to include emerging economic areas of the world.[29]

The commitment to adopt the discipline of making and using strategy implies a willingness to reflect on what all the events in the chain have meant from a standpoint of the two vital "Corporate P's" that are the root of all pleasures and the joy of man's desiring: *profitability,* and, with it, *perpetuation*—of paychecks, perks, and privileges.

One can intellectually accept the need to review and measure one's objectives, but that is not sufficient. It is imperative at this point that we be willing to look at fundamentals beneath fundamentals beneath fundamentals, to look right into the very heart and soul of the enterprise, and see why things really are working—and more importantly, why they may *not* be working. (For in spite of our dedication to strategy-based planning, they just may not be.)

While the insights gained may be powerful, involving radical reassessment (literally going to the *root*) of pet ideas and of good friends and (horrifically) even of ourselves, such a radical reassessment is inherent in the process—it comes with rationality.

And so this last-step, last-stop, reappraisal must loop back, quite likely changing previous ideas of mission, scenarios, whatever. And it must go on all the time. To repeat, it is both the prize we wrest from, and the price we pay for, strategy-centred thinking.

Long-term Implications and Strategic Vision

Our first observation on strategy was that it is part of a "Chain", and our second is that strategy is not for tomorrow afternoon, but for the long term, involving many things but based always on "vision".

Vision quite clearly is seeing what isn't visible now. The notion of the constant assembling, disassembling, and reassembling of the corporation itself is one that marketers think about all the time as global competition and national recessions pose problems never thought of before. In one such vision, the corporation itself is sometimes seen as the "virtual corporation".

> *... Just like the recent successes and failures with Re-engineering and Total Quality Management, to name only a few, the notion of virtual corporations must be rooted in, driven by, or at least substantiated through new, visionary information technology in order to really become a vision of the future. The key is that a corporation must*

be able to separate its functional groupings of personnel, facilities, and other resources from their physical organizations—or, in other words, to form multiple "virtual organizations" simultaneously out of the same physical resources and adapt them without having to change the actual organizations. The justification is simple: there exists only one physical organization at any point in time regardless of how adaptive it is, and it is always subject to organizational inertia. Thus, for example, a design engineer at an auto manufacturer in Detroit can be an effective team member with industrial designers in Milan and manufacturing engineers throughout the Midwest, while at the same time being involved with other team of customers, dealers, suppliers, and other vendors vertically or horizontally associated with the enterprise. Only through information can this virtual organization become meaningful and only by employing a new generation of information technology can this vision be realized....[30]

"Vision"—as already suggested—must be distinguished from "visions". "Visions" are hobgoblins and "things that go bump in the night". "Vision" is indeed the precious gift of seeing what *isn't* as clearly as what *is*, and determining which "isn't"s we should try to bring to life. In vision is a large dose of *hope*.

British pharmaceutical giant Glaxo has joined the rush of drug firms eager to exploit the China market. "We put the emphasis on Hongkong and China because that is considered the engine for future growth in 2000 and beyond," said Mr. Neil Maidment, Glaxo China area director (North Asia Pacific).

He expected other international firms to appoint Hongkong-based staff to their boards, due to the mainland market's potential. "China's health consciousness is rising," he said, pointing to the inclusion of health issues in mainland newspapers. He attributed this to the country's growing economy and its vast number of consumers. Glaxo is planning to open a representative office in Guangzhou next year to organize functions for Chinese doctors and medical officials. It has similar offices in Shanghai and Beijing.[31]

In vision too is a large dose of *persistence*. In some respects, Ho Chi Minh City (Saigon) is a hospitality entrepreneur's dream: Occupancy rates at most hotels here range from 80 per cent to completely full. But the city can also be a hotelier's nightmare. Bales of red tape, virtually insurmountable barriers to land ownership, frequent power brownouts and the local Marxist-Leninist ideology—dying but still kicking—are just a few of the problems companies face when they decide to do business here.

Yet, in anticipation of huge profits, more and more foreign property developers—notably from Hong Kong and Taiwan—are plunging into the hotel business.[32]

And *reappraisal* (as suggested already):

American Telephone & Telegraph Co. appears poised to sprint past its competitors in the world's largest telecommunications market.

AT&T vice-chairman Randall Tobias announced on Tuesday that AT&T and China's State Planning Commission—which banned the US telecommunications giant *from the Chinese phone market just $3^1/_2$ years ago, signed a wide-ranging agreement that for AT&T could mean "billions of dollars in revenue over the next decade." ...*

Mr. Tobias said that once the State Council locates Chinese companies to serve as joint venture partners, AT&T could build several plants to manufacture such products as the company's 5ESS (R) telephone switches, microelectronics parts, optical transmission products, cellular communications systems and office phone networking systems. He said the company will also establish a program for training Chinese telephone company personnel....

The agreement is the result of a remarkable mix of luck, skill and timing that placed AT&T amid a constellation of political and economic pressures....

In 1979, China invited AT&T to build the first joint venture plant in China for telephone switches. AT&T, then still a monopoly in the US, rejected the deal because China wanted more advanced switches than AT&T was willing to provide.

Since reconsidering and coming to China in 1985, AT&T has established joint ventures to build fiber optic cable and transmission equipment but it found itself cut of the lucrative switching market by NEC, Alcatel and Siemens, all of which have established switch factories in China.

It is a market AT&T could hardly afford to miss. China currently has 30 million phone lines. (A switch is equivalent to a phone line.) The Government's goal is to reach 100 million lines by the year 2000. This means that China will be installing an average of 10 million switches a year. With switches averaging $120 each, the potential sales revenue is some $1.2 billion annually.

Such companies as Northern Telecom, a Canadian concern with extensive manufacturing operations in the US, and Telefon AB L.M. Ericsson of Sweden have been more successful than AT&T in selling imported switches to China. Both companies, which often get concessional financing from their governments for the sales, are now vigorously trying to get permission to set up switch plants in China.

But AT&T is likely to beat them because of two additional advantages: last year's $18 billion US trade deficit with China, and China's fears of the new Clinton administration.[33]

In vision too, is the acceptance of *uncertainty*. In a dynamic region like Asia especially, full of stable and unstable governments, a future that is probably bright but still filled with clouds and storms, and a reluctant dependence on the outside world to keep the furnace stoked, vision must be a priority, but the imponderables must also go to the head of the table of contents of any strategy-based planning.

The economy beyond Asia still drifts, not yet able to shake off recession. In Asia, however, signs are more promising. Japan, the region's great motor, seems ready to stage a comeback ... China, our auxiliary engine of limitless promise, acquires *ever-increasing horsepower in coastal and border zones and south of the Yangzi river ... New Europe struggles to give birth to a $6 trillion market of 345 million people. The European Community's arrival is proving more difficult than most expected ... And then there's Russia. Asia's northernmost reaches remain a polar mystery.*[34]

Strategy, then, demands a long hard look into the future, an exercise of vision that indeed extends beyond tomorrow afternoon. For strategy is "time-binding". Awesome decisions that we make based on strategic thinking bind us not only now but down the corridors of time, and they bind not only us, but our successors too, as the "learning curve" yields its secrets, its fruits, and its disappointments. For, from strategy flow fundamental directions, aimed at long-term change and long-term commitment. What comes out of this process is *impact, fundamental shifts in thinking*, and *momentous moves* involving (say) relationships with governments (to support, oppose, ignore, embrace, etc.) or financial markets (to finance through equity, say, rather than debt, involving greater emphasis therefrom on short-term earnings and dividends rather than on longer-range focus). Be that as it may, strategy takes the long road. Not so much here, perhaps, of "*How do I get from A to B?*" (taking either the proverbial shortest straight line or a better, maybe circuitous route), but "*Why do I really want to get from A to B at all?*"

Hamel and Prahalad have used the term "Strategic Intent" to suggest also such a radical rethinking of strategy. They believe that looking at things outside of the usual way can help an organization to achieve success. This could include a broader and deeper vision of not only now (and competitors that we know) but also tomorrow (and competitors we haven't *yet* met); and of not only here, but everywhere. As they put it: "Assessing the current tactical advantages of known competitors will not help understand the resolution, stamina, and inventiveness of potential competitors. Sun-tzu, a Chinese military strategist, made that point 3000 years ago. 'All men can see the tactics whereby I conquer,' he wrote, 'but what none can see is the strategy out of which great victory is evolved.'"[35] (Again, a voice out of Asia that we might wish to listen to, and which, indeed, is being increasingly cited as one that we *should* listen to.)

It follows that strategy also involves high-echelon thinking by the high-stakes players in the organization. This doesn't mean that the ideas of lesser ranks (the "lowerarchy" of the "hierarchy") shouldn't be solicited. To repeat, it merely means that, ultimately (however uncomfortable we feel about it in the normatively egalitarian West) it is the top and the top only who will make the moves flowing from strategy, moves that will shape and shake the organization. It also means that those on the top shouldn't be spending their time on making strategic decisions on whether to use opaque or transparent folders to file correspondence in.

Not all companies would agree with this thought, but most would, or should; and in our Asian focus there is no question that the "top" business and/or government people do indeed call the shots, whether in Confucian Singapore, Communist China, or even nominally consentual Japan.

Review Questions

1. With the advent of the European Union, which essentially eliminates barriers to trade between its members, do you think European nations will become more alike, less alike, or both? Why?
2. What are the overarching dimensions that seem to separate the "European" and the "American" outlook in business?
3. What are the overarching dimensions that seem to separate the "Western" and the "Asian" outlook in business?
4. In the United States, government and business seem often to be at odds with each other. What is the relation between government and business in various Asian countries?
5. Discuss the differences in views presented among managers in the United States, Japan, and Korea.
6. Discuss the "chain", and suggest additions and variations to it.
7. Do you think the "Nine Strategy Options" paradigm is useful or not? Why? Suggest alternatives.
8. Explain the notion of "strategic alliances" and discuss its strengths and weaknesses for businesses.
9. What can a company do to achieve real sustainable competitive advantage?
10. What does "time-binding" mean? Give examples from the world of strategic business thinking.

Endnotes

1. Powell, Bill, Who Needs Democracy? *Newsweek*, November 25, 1993, p. 25.
2. Holusha, John, W. Edwards Deming, Management Expert, Dies at 90, *International Herald Tribune*, December 22, 1993, p. 2.
3. God of Quality Control, *International Herald Tribune*, December 22, 1993, p. 9.
4. Beck, Simon, Rare Look at Miracle Economics of Asia, *South China Morning Post*, September 20, 1993, p. 8.
5. Fukuda, Kazuo John, *Japanese Management in East Asia and Beyond*, Hong Kong: The Chinese University Press, 1993, p. 45.
6. *Ibid.*
7. Fukuda, Kazuo John, 1993, *op. cit.*, p. 5.
8. Chung, Kae H. and Hak Chong Lee (Eds.), *Korean Management Dynamics*, New York: Praeger, 1989, p. 172.
9. Weston, F.C., Jr., Constraints Theory Related to Information Systems and Continuous Improvement in Manufacturing, Paper delivered at the *First International Conference on Production and Operations Management and Management Information Systems*, Hong Kong, December 20, 1993, p. 1.
10. McCarter, Michelle, Benetton Condom Kindness, *Advertising Age,* February 25, 1991, p. 19.
11. Klapwall, Thea, Mickey Mouse Seeks Passport to the East, *South China Sunday Morning Post*, February 21, 1993, p. 3.
12. Lyons, Nick, *The Sony Vision*, New York: Crown Publishers, 1976, p. 99.
13. Warnoff, Jon, *Korea's Economy: Man-made miracle*, Si-sa-young-o-sa Publishers, 1983, p. 286.
14. Chung, Kae H. and Hak Chong Lee (Eds.), 1989, *op. cit.*, p. 3.

15. *Idem.*, p. 6.
16. Kunio, Yoshihara, *Sogo Shosha: The vanguard of the Japanese economy*, New York: Oxford University Press, 1982, p. 183.
17. *Ibid.*, p. 256.
18. Johnson, Jean L., Tomoaki Sakano, and Naoto Onzo, Behavioral Relations in Across-Culture Distribution Systems: Influence, control, and conflict in US-Japanese marketing channels, *Journal of International Business Studies*, Fourth Quarter, 1990, p. 651.
19. *See* Kae H. Chung and Hak Chong Lee (Eds.), 1989, *op. cit.*, p. 46.
20. *See* John A. Czepiel, *Competitive Marketing Strategy,* Englewood Cliffs, NJ: Prentice-Hall, 1992, pp. 451–452. For his four questions, Czepiel draws upon Seymour Tilles, How to Evaluate Corporate Strategy, *Harvard Business Review*, Vol. 41, No. 4, July–August 1963, pp. 111–121; and Richard Rumelt, The Evolution of Business Strategy, *in* William F. Glueck (Ed.), *Business Policy and Strategic Management,* 3rd ed., New York: McGraw-Hill, 1980, pp. 359–367.
21. Karp, Jonathan, Medium and Message, *Far Eastern Economic Review*, February 25, 1993, p. 50.
22. Katayama, Hans and Brian Nadel, Auto 2002, *Asia, Inc.*, September 1992, p. 54.
23. Focus: Marketing excellence awards, *Media*, August 1, 1992, p. 37.
24. Ohmae, Kenichi, *The Mind of the Strategist*, London: Penguin Books, 1982, p. 141.
25. Pascale, Richard T., Perspectives on Strategy: The real story behind Honda's Success, *California Management Review*, Vol. XXVI, No. 3, Spring 1984, pp. 47–48.
26. Turpin, Dominique V., The Strategic Persistence of the Japanese Firm, *The Journal of Business Strategy*, January–February 1992, pp. 49–50.
27. Romero-Schwartz, Sophia, Business Strategists Put Faith in Corporate Identity, *Asian Advertising and Marketing*, November 1990, pp. 108–109.
28. Weston, F.C., Jr., 1993, *loc. cit.*, pp. 1–2.
29. Weston, F.C., Jr., 1993, *loc. cit.*, p. 3.
30. Hsu, Cheng, Letter on the Virtual Corporation, *Business Week*, March 1, 1993, p. 7.
31. Lee, Carrie, Glaxo Joins Drug Firms Flowing Northward, *South China Morning Post*, February 22, 1993, p. 42.
32. Bow, Josephine J., Vietnam's Heartbreak Hotels, *Asia, Inc.,* December 1992, p. 36.
33. McGregor, James, AT&T Looks Poised for Success in China, *Asian Wall Street Journal*, February 24, 1993, p. 1.
34. Water Rooster, Watershed, *Asia, Inc.*, January 1993, p. 29.
35. Hamel, Gary and C.K. Prahalad, Strategic Intent, *Harvard Business Review*, Vol. 77, No. 2, May–June 1989, p. 64.

CHAPTER 2

ANALYZING THE ENVIRONMENT

*So in war, the way is to
avoid what is strong and
to strike at what is weak.*
—Sun Tzu

Introduction

In this and the next two chapters, a structure is provided for analyzing and assessing the strategy of a firm. It is very important to have a structure for this analysis because it becomes the overall conceptual, analytical framework. The approach, which is commonly used in strategy texts, is referred to as a functional approach. It is illustrated in Figure 2.1 which shows how the analysis is divided between the external environment and the internal environment. You should be familiar with many of the concepts because they are derived from functional disciplines in accounting, finance, economics, management, and marketing.

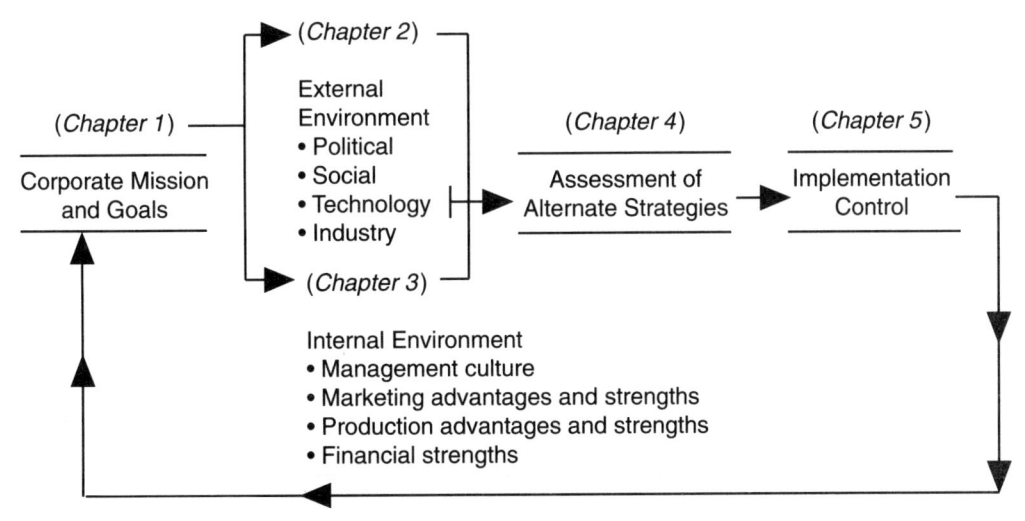

Figure 2.1 The Strategy Process

The next several chapters will describe and discuss the most relevant functional concepts for evaluating and determining strategy for the firm.

The Firm and its External Environment

The first requirement for understanding the firm is a thorough analysis of its environment which can be broken into two areas as depicted in Figure 2.1; its **macro environment** and its **industry**. Its **macro environment** includes the relevant forces acting on the firm from political, social, demographic, and technological factors. As we will see in this and the following chapters, these factors, especially the political ones, become extremely crucial for both local and foreign firms operating in the region.

Export Objectives

The economies of the East Asia region have relied on exports, especially to the US and other First World markets for their development. US citizens are used to the US government charging foreign firms—mostly Asian—with "dumping" their products into the US market, but a recent Asian newspaper carried stories about Japanese firms charging China with "dumping", the US charging Korea, the EU countries charging China, and India charging Korea. Everyone is concerned and everyone is trying to predict the course and outcome of the Clinton administration's position on trade and protectionism.

As illustrated in the preceding paragraph, understanding the environment in which the firm operates is one of its biggest challenges, and this challenge becomes more complex as its environment grows from a neighbourhood, to a region, to national, international and then global markets. Table 2.1 shows the size of countrywise imports and exports for 1981 and 1992. Nearly one-third of the US imports were from just five Asian countries: Japan, Korea, Taiwan, Hong Kong, and Singapore (GATT, 1992).

Political Forces

What is usually referred to as the firm's external environment involves the political, social, demographic and technological and industrial forces operating on the firm. Given the importance of international business to all of the countries that we are concerned with in this book, political forces in particular take on special meaning because of the great variance in the roles that the governments in this region play in economic affairs. Referring to political actions, the authors of a popular International Business text state that

> *The principles of the benefits of free trade are well known but are less widely accepted in practice. Yet every nation in the world acts to impede the free flow of trade.*[1]

The economies of the firms represented in the Asia-Pacific region represent a wide continuum of government involvement to support and to protect their businesses (Figure 2.2). In the region, as already noted, there are governments such as Hong Kong whose approach

Table 2.1 International Trade for 1981 and 1992 (Value in US$, billions)

Country/Territory	Exports Value (fob)	Share (%) 1981	Share (%) 1992	Country/Territory	Imports Value (cif)	Share (%) 1981	Share (%) 1992	Country/Territory	Total Trade (1992) Value	Share (%)
World	37,000			World	3,030			World	7,530	100.0
United States	447	12.7	12.1	United States	552	14.3	14.4	United States	999	13.3
Germany	429	9.6	11.6	Germany	408	8.7	10.7	Germany	837	11.1
Japan	340	8.3	9.2	France	240	6.3	6.3	Japan	573	7.6
France	236	5.8	6.4	Japan	233	7.5	6.1	France	476	6.3
United Kingdom	191	5.6	5.2	United Kingdom	222	5.4	5.8	United Kingdom	413	5.5
Italy	175	4.1	4.7	Italy	185	4.8	4.8	Italy	360	4.8
Netherlands	170	3.7	3.8	Netherlands	134	3.5	3.5	Netherlands	274	3.6
Canada	136	4.0	3.7	Canada	130	3.7	3.4	Canada	265	3.5
Belgium/Luxemburg	123	3.0	3.3	Belgium/Luxemburg	126	3.3	3.3	Belgium/Luxemburg	249	3.3
Hong Kong (a)	118	1.5	3.2	Hong Kong (b)	122	1.3	3.2	Hong Kong	240	3.2
China	85		2.3	Spain	100	1.7	2.6	China	166	2.2
Taiwan	81		2.2	Rep. of Korea	82	1.4	2.1	Spain	165	2.2
Rep. of Korea	77	1.2	2.1	China	81		2.1	Rep. of Korea	159	2.1
Switzerland	66		1.8	Taiwan	72		1.9	Taiwan	153	2.0
Spain	65	1.1	1.8	Singapore (b)	72	1.4	1.9	Singapore	136	1.8
Singapore (c)	64	1.1	1.7	Switzerland	68		1.7	Switzerland	132	1.8
Sweden	56	1.6	1.5	Mexico (d)	62		1.6	Mexico	108	1.8
Saudi Arabia	48	1.2	1.3	Australia	54	1.5	1.4	Sweden	106	1.4
Mexico (d)	46		1.2	Sweden	50	1.5	1.3	Austria	98	1.3
Austria	44	.08	1.2	Australia	45		1.2	Australia	87	1.2
Australia	42	1.2	1.2	Thailand	41	1.4	1.1	Saudi Arabia	82	1.0
Denmark	40		1.1	Malaysia	39		1.0	Malaysia	79	1.0
Malaysia	40		1.1	Denmark	34	.09	.09	Denmark	74	1.0

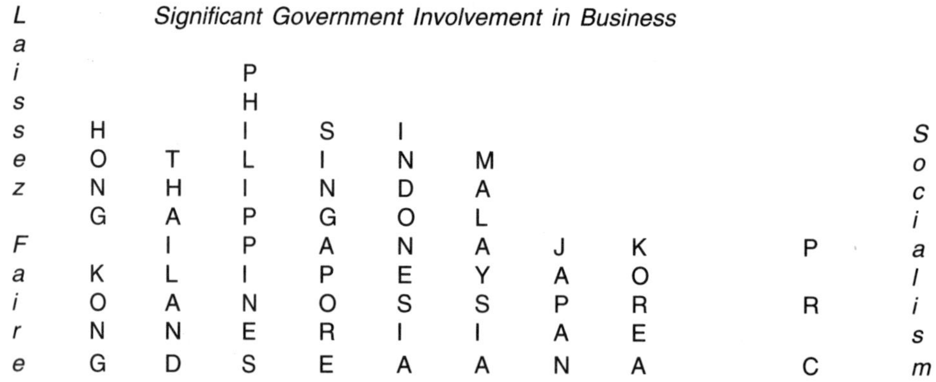

Significant Government Involvement in Business

```
Laissez                                                              Soc
 Faire  HONG KONG   THAILAND   PHILIPPINES   SINGAPORE   INDONESIA   MALAYSIA   JAPAN   KOREA   PRC   Socialism
```

Figure 2.2 Continuum of Political Involvement

is very laissez-faire (the business of Hong Kong is business!) to the other end of the continuum, the People's Republic of China (PRC) which Deng Xiaoping describes as socialist, even though he claims that the differences among the systems are neither the planning function nor the market. (As he asked one worker, to illustrate his point, is that a capitalist machine or a communist machine?) And so dealing with the "external environment" in this context means dealing with different institutions within the different economic systems. Table 2.2 describes the five-year economic plans of South Korea's Economic Planning Board (EPB). Given the authority of the board in the government hierarchy and the government's power in terms of the financial institutions, the EPB has played a major role in the development and structure of its industrial system; much more so than that of its Japanese counterpart, MITI. It has dictated the composition of industries—who and how many firms there will be, capitalization of those firms, providing financial assistance to export activities, and protection in its home markets. Today's industrial policy in South Korea is more liberal but it has already created extremely large, sophisticated firms that don't need protection at home and that have the state of technology and economies of scale to compete in international markets. Ten of the Korean chaebols were recently listed in the *Fortune* list of the 500 largest foreign corporations.

This section will detail some of the more significant impediments to trade that limit or constrain the strategy alternatives of firms in the region.

Ownership

Ownership can vary from fully private to fully government and all points in between. In the case of government ownership, the expectations of the organizations can also vary. The extreme case is that of the State Enterprises of the PRC. They are still a very significant part of the Chinese economy, and even though the goverment is encouraging a move towards a profit orientation, in 1992 approximately 30 per cent of the government's budget was used to cover their losses or to subsidise their operations. The South Korean government has other expectations of its steel company, Pohang Iron & Steel, which is profit-oriented and considered to be one of the most proficient steelmakers in the world. In 1992, it was picked

Table 2.2 Industrial Policy in Korea: 1982–86

Plan Title	The First 5-Year Plan (1962–1966)	The Second 5-Year Plan (1967–1971)	The Third 5-Year Plan (1972–1976)	The Fourth 5-Year Plan (1977–1981)	The Fifth 5-Year Plan (1982–1986)
Development Strategy of the Manufacturing Sector	Nurturing of basic industry and adjustment of social overhead capital (The establishment of the foundation for self-sustaining industries)	Capital goods import substitution and exportation of light manufactured goods (Outward-looking industrialization)	The build-up of heavy and chemical industries (Change in industrial structure)	Change in industrial structure and promotion of competitiveness (Realization of economic structure for self-sustaining growth)	Advance industrialization as seen in developed countries (Development of information intensive industries)
Rate of economic growth (Average per annum): Actual (Planned)	8.5% (7.1%)	9.7% (7.0%)	10.1% (8.6%)	5.5% (9.2%)	7.5% (7.6%)
Rate of growth in mining and manufacturing (Average per annum)	14.2%	9.8%	18.1%	10.3%	9.6%
Ratio of heavy and chemical industrialization to manufacturing sector (Target years)	10.2%	14.2%	29.8%	45.3%	
	Electricity, fertilizers, like refining, synthetic fibres (Nylon yarn), cement, PVC.	Synthetic fibers (polyester yarn), petrochemicals, electrical appliances (TV and refrigerator)	Iron and steel, transport machinery, household electronics (TV, transistor) shipbuilding, petrochemials	Iron and steel, industrial machinery and equipment, electronic appliances, components and parts, shipbuilding	Precision machinery, electronics industry, information industries

Notes: 1. Figures shown in parentheses are the set targets.
2. Figures for target year of each plan.
Source: Economic Planning Board, Republic of Korea, The Five-Year Economic Development Plan corresponding to Plan Period.

by Asian managers as being one of the best-managed companies in Asia. According to one economic analyst in an *Asian Wall Street Journal* article, it is one of the few Korean companies that Japan or the United States has to worry about. It is the third largest steelmaker in the world and is considered to be the cheapest producer.

Pohang was started as a stock company, even though the initial capital came from the government. This allowed the company to start operations at the level of economies of scale and technology to compete internationally from the very beginning. It is and has been in the process of privatization. *The Asian Wall Street Journal* recently reported that the Taiwan government was investigating complaints by their steel companies that South Korean steelmakers were "dumping" cold rolled steel in their market. This was denied by Pohang. During the same week, the same paper reported that Taiwan Aerospace (29 per cent owned by the government) was negotiating a joint venture with British Aerospace to be financed primarily by the Taiwan government). The seemingly obvious dichotomy between "government-owned" and "private-owned" may not be all that obvious in Asia after all!

At the other extreme are the economies in which there is strictly private ownership without government equity or subsidies. In the earlier stages of economic development in most of the countries in the region, many companies were government-financed or government-owned and controlled. This was especially true not only in the PRC but in the secondary industries of Taiwan and Korea. Many airlines such as Singapore International Airlines (which has also been consistently chosen as one of the *world's* best airlines) also started operations financed by the Singapore government. Even today, much of its stock is owned by the government.

Another important form of ownership that has political and economic ramifications is the joint venture in China, especially when the China partner is a political agency. This becomes very important in terms of doing business in that country because of the dealings that are necessary with regulatory agencies and the constantly shifting people who run (or seem to run) those agencies. This form of organization requires at least 25 per cent foreign capitalization, wage caps tied to local state enterprise rates, different roles for the Communist Party and worker organizations, and a required length-of-life stipulation. This organization type has, through the government agency MOFERT, guarantees in terms of supplies which can be especially crucial in a centrally planned economy. New ventures in China and at present in Singapore also enjoy tax holidays and/or tax reductions.

Market Entry

The governments of the region also vary in terms of entry of new firms, local or foreign, in various businesses ranging from retailing to manufacturing. South Korea has stipulations on foreign retailers in their country as far as the size (floor space) and number of stores is concerned. That government has also stipulated which and how many firms there can be in a specific industry. This has resulted in a market that is protected on both the production and the retailing sides, which has encouraged many of the manufacturers to also be involved in retailing.

In 1993 the Korean government announced that its market, which had been closed to a number of Japanese products, would be opened to them in the future. In 1974 the Japanese government enacted the "Large Scale Retailing Store Law" which was designed to protect small and medium size retailers by requiring location approval for new outlets—approval which could take years to get. The approval process might require up to eight years and approval may then be refused. A Japanese retailer and chairman of one of the largest retail groups in Asia, Kazuo Wada of Yaohan International Co., Ltd. (see also Chapter 1) has said of this legislation that "there is no more evil a law for consumers than the Japanese Large Scale Retailing Store Law"(see Table 2.3).[2] This law has already been amended. Again, at the other extreme is Hong Kong, which has few restrictions.

Table 2.3 Comparative Food Prices: Prices of goods in various countries

Items	Size	Japan	America	Singapore	Malaysia	Hong Kong	Costa Rica
Sugar (Granular)	1 kg	282	121	67	58	115	73
Nescafe Gold	100 g	748	273	336	270	526	320
Rice	1 kg	550	122	108	130	93	442
Coca Cola	350 ml can	92	48	49	47	50	72
Beer	350 ml can	210	82	154	125	74	102
Flour	1 kg	190	91	154	44	117	97
Butter	225 g	358	172	154	104	93	180
Milk	1,000 ml	242	82	231	205	232	52
Sirloin steak	100 g	580	88	161	233	464	57
Orange juice (100% pure fruit juice)	1,000 ml	355	114	153	205	256	137
Total		3,607	1,193	1,567	1,421	2,020	1,532
Index on taking the total Japanese prices as 100		100	33	44	39	56	42

Source: Wada, Kazuo, *Yaohan's Global Strategy*, Hong Kong: Capital Communications Corporation Ltd., 1992.

Tariffs

An import tariff can be defined as simply a tax on the price of a foreign-produced good. Its rationale is primarily to protect domestic producers who have a difficult time competing with foreign goods. It in effect increases the cost of that particular foreign item of goods. The tariff also can benefit the government because it collects the tariff, resulting in increased government revenues. The much discussed trade blocs—the European Economic Union (EU), the North America Free Trade Agreement (NAFTA), and in the region, the proposed ASEAN trade group—each has as a central purpose the reduction and/or elimination of tariffs and other barriers between members.

As a footnote to tariffs is the designation of the US Most Favored Nation Status (MFN) which provides the involved country the lowest tariff available to any country. This is a very important matter in the region for the People's Republic of China, who in 1993 is expected to have a trade surplus with the United States of over $20,000,000, and of Hong Kong which functions as a middleman for China. During the last several years the US government, especially its Congress, has threatened (because of human rights issues in China) to take away their MFN status which many believe would eliminate their competitive advantage, losing out to other countries such as Malaysia, Thailand, and Mexico. The MFN battle—in which the US seeks improvement in China's human rights policies in exchange for trade concession—appears to be an annual event.

The General Agreement on Tariffs and Trade (GATT) is an agreement among members to enhance and encourage trade on a worldwide scale. The major activity undertaken under the auspices of GATT is a series of rounds of negotiations to reduce trade barriers by multilateral agreements; i.e., involving all member countries and aiming that all members should be accorded MFN status.

The terms of GATT are administered by a permanent secretariat, located in Geneva, Switzerland. Its purpose is to resolve trade issues that are raised by the signatory members. When a member feels that a trade partner is not abiding by agreements, it can make an appeal to the secretariat, who will investigate the case, and render a ruling. The importance of trade and the concern with protectionist measures has been enough to insure compliance with GATT rulings. GATT can be credited with playing a very significant role in the successful trade negotiations which have resulted in more liberal trade policies around the world.

The present round of negotiations, the Uruguay round, was stuck for several years primarily because of differences concerning agricultural trade. France's agriculture, with its high subsidies, South Korea with its agriculture price supports, and Japan and its embargo on rice imports, are examples of very sensitive stumbling blocks to the resolution of these trade issues. (Both the Korean and Japanese people tend to support their government's protection of these programmes even though it results in rice prices in those two countries that are several times the international level.)

Environmental Issues: The Industry

Dynamic/Complex Markets

We can start to look at the firm's environment by focusing on two different dimensions, **how dynamic the market is**, and **how complex it is**. The degree of dynamism has to do with the rate and frequency of change. The telephone (telecommunications) industry is a good example of what in the past, at least, we could classify as an industry dealing with relatively low levels of uncertainty. Its market was very predictable. For a long time, it was a static environment with strong government controls because of its common monopoly status. At this particular time, this is changing dramatically with the new Electronic Highway which is still being defined but is clearly in the offing. The industry will change from a static one with bureaucratic organizations to one that is very dynamic requiring another organizational form.

The other dimension deals with the complexity which can be viewed in terms of *diversity* of environmental influences, the nature of the knowledge requirement, and whether the key influencers of the uncertainty are *interrelated*.

Simple/static conditions. To put it simply, a static condition means that the firm faces an environment that is relatively simple, and is not undergoing much change. Some of the best examples surprisingly, are in regulated industries such as telecommunications.

In the past it was fairly straightforward for a telephone company to forecast its future business and revenues. Population characteristics and trends would predict the number of households and together with family income forecasts these were good indicators for the number of residential phones demanded. Raw material suppliers often also fall in this category, especially where there are few suppliers and few substitutes. A final example illustrates this position quite clearly. The market demand for tricycles for toddlers can be reasonably forecast because it has historically been a relatively stable market of low complexity. If you know the birth rate and family income you can do a reasonable job of forecasting this market.

Dynamic conditions. Firms in this environment face continuous change. A good example is the garment industry, which is very dynamic because it is dealing constantly with change; in this case, changes in tastes and fashion. The *demand* for women's slacks can be forecast but it is very difficult to forecast the *styles* of women's slacks that will be demanded. Knowing this, when individual firms differentiate their product or service, they intensify the dynamic condition of the market. In this environment, the firm has to rely on expert opinion, consumer panels, market tests and similar techniques for their forecasts. It is obvious that this type of forecasting is not as accurate as in simple static environments.

Complex conditions. Complex environments are often the result of the diversities facing the firm which can come from numerous sources. For example, many smaller and middle size firms are now dealing with international markets, and each country introduces a separate set of environmental requirements such as basic market demand, government regulation, institutional structures, and cultural characteristics. Firms today are facing more and more complex environments which are also more dynamic. High complexity and high dynamic markets create an environment in which forecasting is more crucial but at the same time more difficult.

Implications. Figure 2.3 summarizes the possible environmental conditions and possible responses. The major points are: If a firm's environmental condition is fairly static and slow in terms of change, Stage I, considering past environmental conditions, is crucial for understanding the future. The more dynamic the environment, the more future-oriented the focus of forecasting using techniques such as:

1. Focus groups
2. Scenario planning
3. Delpphi technique

```
Complex
  ↑
           │  III  │  IV   │
           │       │       │
           ├───────┼───────┤
           │   I   │  II   │
           │       │       │
  ↓
Simple

Static  ←                    →  Dynamic
```

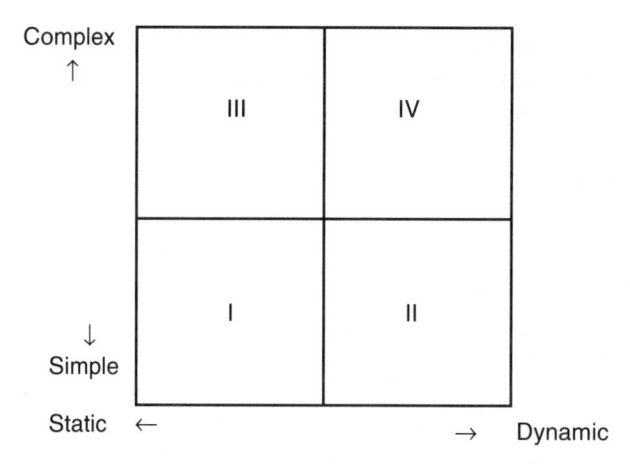

Figure 2.3 Dynamic-Complex Environments

In complex-dynamic environments, organizations will often take structural actions to make them less complex. For example, the firm might decentralize its product development and market research efforts to local markets to make those activities more sensitive. Japanese car manufacturers have located product design activities in North America to help insure that their cars reflect the taste of that market and also to help their parent from groups in the dollar-yen relationship. In the early 1980s, the Mazda RX-7 was built with enough headroom for someone under 5 feet 10 inches. In Japan this only eliminated a small portion of their market, but it eliminated a large portion of their North American market.

Industry Life Cycle

The Industry Life Cycle is a useful scheme for understanding the evolution of an industry. It is a concept derived from marketing, the Product Life Cycle. Both are based on the idea that products/industries pass through a series of well-defined *stages* from an initial point which has characteristics such as the nature and number of competitors, profitability, and demand, to a time of decline. It is an intuitively logical concept that integrates market conditions, market structure, and profitability.

In the initial or embryonic stage of industry, for example, when markets are not established and production is low, several things are predictable such as high production cost (low economies of scale), low company/product loyalty, high marketing cost, low profitability, and relatively low competition. This concept is based upon the following conditions:

1. Products have a limited life.
2. The industry's sales follow an S-curve until sales flatten when saturation of the market and eventually decline in sales occurs.
3. The stages are defined by the location of the sales curves inflection points. They are labeled as introduction, growth, maturity and decline. In the strategy literature, a fifth

stage is often added—the shake-out or competitive turbulence stage which starts at the point that sales are still increasing but at a decreasing rate.
4. The life of the product can be extended by finding new users or getting the present users to expand their consumption.
5. Profitability rises and then falls as the industry moves through the stages which correspond to the effect of the experience curve for recurring costs.

The life of an industry may be divided into five stages:

1. INITIAL or EMBRYONIC STAGE
2. GROWTH STAGE
3. TURBULENT STAGE
4. MATURE STAGE
5. DECLINING STAGE

These stages are illustrated in Figure 2.4.

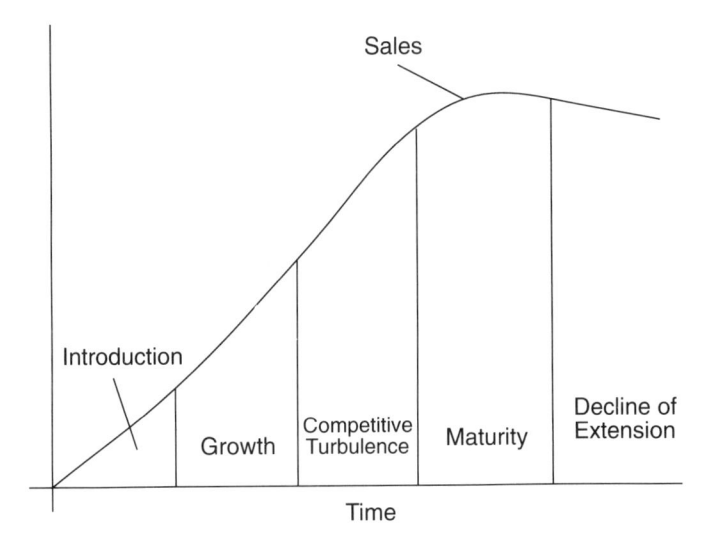

Figure 2.4 Classic Industry Life Cycle

The INITIAL or EMBRYONIC industry is one that is just beginning. There is low product acceptance, poorly developed distribution channels, potential consumers are unfamiliar with the product, there is no or low consumer loyalty, high prices, low competition, and high production cost and low profits.

As consumers become familiar with and accept the new product, sales pick up and we enter the GROWTH stage. Economies of scale come into play in both production and marketing, prices start decreasing, and profits start increasing.

In the third, the TURBULENT stage, sales continue to increase but at a decreasing rate;

the market is becoming saturated; there are few first time buyers and the market is moving towards simple replacement. Competition is strong as individual firms attempt to increase their sales by taking customers away from other firms.

In the MATURE stage, the market has often lost some firms and so, fewer firms share in the slowly increasing and then decreasing sales. The market starts contracting. Competition can be fierce as firms attempt to maintain sales levels and customers. During the early 1990s this has been the situation for the bulk of the consumer electrical appliance market, especially in developed economies. Prices of many of the products in this industry are lower today than twenty years ago.

The DECLINE STAGE. Eventually most industries enter a DECLINE stage, where growth becomes negative for a variety of reasons. This can be because of technological change (jet air travel), demographics (note an aging Japan), social change (health consciousness and related products), etc. These become Sunset industries.

For industries that follow the patterns of the industry life cycle, there are many strategy implications. Mickwitz[3] proposed that the response elasticity of various marketing tools changes during the movement through the stages. For example, advertising has the highest elasticity through the growth and decline stage, and price has the highest elasticity during the maturity stage. Levitt proposed "market stretching" activities to stave off decline. Others, such as Kerr and Kolb et al., propose different organization structures, management and leadership styles. For example, entrepreneurial style would be more appropriate for the early stages and bureaucratic in the later stages.

In reality, as emphasized in Chapter 1, firms are constantly trying to change the industry or to change their competitive position. Different firms in an industry can be experiencing different stages of the life cycle by positioning themselves in different markets. For example, the European and US automobile industry could be considered to be in the mature part of its life cycle, and Figure 2.4 on the stages of industry evolution is quite predictive in terms of industry growth, brand loyalty, overall rivalry, and scale economics but a low cost competitor enters this same industry and faces an entirely different market or looks for other markets where the industry is in an earlier stage of development. Daewoo of Korea seems to be using that strategy now by going into undeveloped markets.

Market Structure

From economics, we are provided with a categorization for market structure that provides an insight for understanding industries and the action of the managers of strategy. The first structure is *perfect competition*: a situation where there are many buyers and sellers, the products are homogeneous, there is perfect information about the products (price, quality, etc.), and there is free mobility of resources.

The other extreme from perfect competition is monopoly: a situation where there is only one seller of a product and for which there is no close substitute. In other words, where the firm and the industry are the same. A monopoly situation can be created by controlling a needed resource, or by government actions such as franchises (many municipal utilities) patents, regulations, tariffs, and quotas. In between these extremes, we have the most common market structures faced by firms: monopolistic (or imperfect) competition, and oligopoly. In monopolistic competition, developed conceptually by a Harvard economist, Edward Chamberlain, the market includes many firms in a highly competitive market, with extensive advertising and sales promotion and advertising, ease of entry and, most important, differentiated products. The purpose of differentiation, which firms constantly attempt to do, is simply to create and sustain consumer demand for their products in preference to those of their competitors. Compared to the horizontal demand curve that is a characteristic of perfect competition, differentiation causes a downward sloping curve.

The last situation, which actually is very common, is called **oligopoly**. It is characterized by a few large firms and because there are few, their activities tend to have major impact on each other. There are forces that tend to create this particular structure such as high entry costs, large economies of scale, mergers and acquisitions. Government policy in many of the Pacific Rim countries have actually encouraged oligopolies whereas other countries, such as the United States, have discouraged their formation with anti-trust legislation.

In an oligopoly, because of interrelatedness, there is a tendency to try and avoid price competition which can result in decreasing profits in the industry. This lesson was sharply demonstrated in the summer of 1992 in the US airline industry. One of the airlines attempted to increase their number of passengers by simplifying and reducing their fares, but this was immediately followed by reductions by the other airlines resulting in large profit losses throughout the industry. This particular structure tends to encourage price fixing or collusion.

The basic categorization of market structures from perfect competition to monopoly allows rigorous conceptualizations and theory building, but in fact most markets do not fit these pure types: rather they are composites. Government regulations, such as import quotas, can also introduce factors which make political considerations a very significant issue which also distort market forces for business decision makers. Composites require a different level of understanding.

One way of conceptualizing these composites is by identifying *strategic groups*. Usually within a basic industry there are several different groups of firms with the firms in a particular group having similar strategies. Figure 2.5 depicts one of these. In the lower price/number of segments served are firms such as Daewoo, Hyundai, and Yugo. Their strategy is to serve as the low cost, basic transportation segment of the industry. These firms compete mainly on price, therefore relying on finding cost advantages through economies of scale and cost of resources. Only fifteen years ago the Japanese car manufacturers were in this position, especially in terms of the US market, but as Japanese wages increased and there was trade pressure by the US government for voluntary export restraints, their strategy changed. The market niche filled by Toyota and Datsun (now Nissan) in the mid-1970s has been filled by a new set of firms that have the same comparative advantages. Toyota and Nissan have moved up to a higher quality and broader market segments to compete head-on with the likes of General Motors and Ford. The number of cars exported into the US did not increase as such but their revenue and sales volume did, as their prices increased. The firms that they compete with serve many segments of the market offering both low and high price automobiles, deriving their competitive advantages from economies of scale.

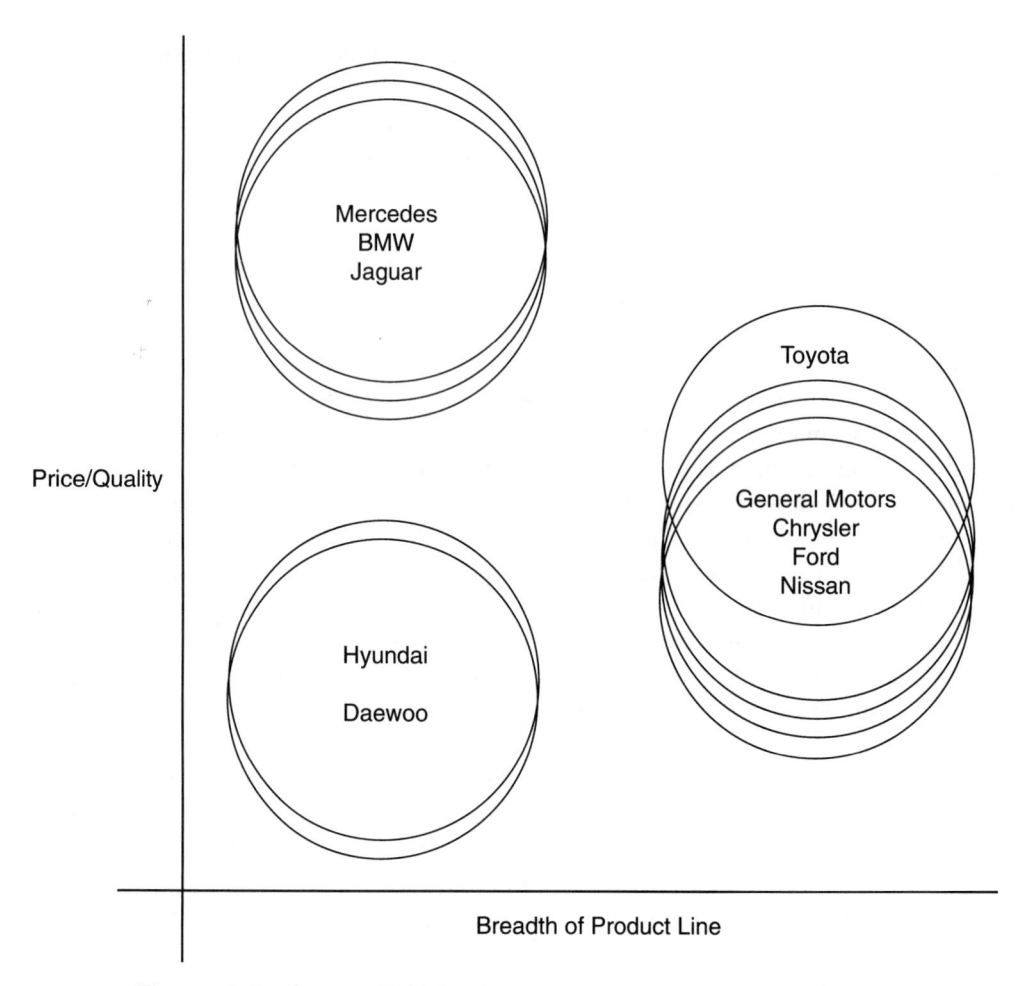

Figure 2.5 Competitive Positioning in the Automobile Industry

The third position identified in the figure is the market segment restricted for high price/quality only. This niche is characterized by Jaguar, Mercedes and BMW whose products represent the top end of the market, emphazing quality, performance, and status on the very top by Rolls Royce and Ferrari.

Implications of Strategic Groups

There are a number of important conceptual implications of the identification of strategic groups. It helps first of all to identify the firms which have similar and dissimilar strategies, the ones with similar strategies being the closest competition for the same intended consumers, e.g., fast food restaurants' closest competition is with other fast food restaurants. Second, some strategy groups are more attractive than others. Let's take the bottom end where the consumer is most concerned with price. Anyone offering a lower price can compete. And then there is the case of the firms offering/serving many market segments. Usually, they spend a lot of effort differentiating their products which affects their demand curves in economic parlance, i.e., through brand loyalty they can pass on higher prices than they could without brand loyalty. Third, different strategic groups have different mobility barriers. For example, it would be difficult for Hyundai to penetrate the luxury car market even if its product was of equivalent quality. It is perceived as an economy car and to make it a luxury car would require a change in that image. Ford Motor Company recently purchased Jaguar; its Ford line engine might be superior to the Jaguar engine, but if that was fitted in the Jaguar, it would take on the Ford image, one of lower quality, lower luxury.

The actual application of the concept is more complex than suggested here. First it is not two-dimensional but multidimensional. The figure also suggests that price and quality are congruent, but it is possible for firms to have high quality/low price strategies. The US stereo manufacturer, Acoustical Research, had a product line whose stereo speakers were classified with the very best but they used a low price strategy. They wanted their product to be affordable to a wide audience. Many times a firm with a high market share will use a low price strategy to make their market unattractive to potential competitors.

Porter's Five Forces Model

The work of Michael Porter (already alluded to in Chapter 1) has dominated the corporate strategy literature during the last decade. His approach to analyzing a firm's industry environment is to examine what he defines as the five basic forces in the industry. These forces are the threat of new entrants, the bargaining power of suppliers, the bargaining power of buyers, the threat of substitutes, and the rivalry among firms (the emphasis of the previous sections of this chapter).

Threat of new entrants. An industry might be attractive in terms of profitability and other factors but it may not be accessible to new firms because of various entry barriers. These can include factors such as:

- Necessity of economies of scale
- Proprietary product differences
- Capital requirements
- Brand loyalty
- Distribution channels
- Cost advantages
- Government policies
- Competitive strengths

Let's examine an industry that we are all familiar with, airlines, in terms of the above. To be a major player, the prospective firm would face all of the above barriers from government regulations to ownership of airport gates and computerized information systems. Airlines try to differentiate their services, but this is very difficult. A 747 is a 747 is a 747, although modifications can be, and are, made to it. An airline with extensive schedules and routes can differentiate itself, but this is usually done on only a regional basis leaving other markets for other airlines to do the same. Initially, the frequent flier programme tended to create stronger airline loyalty among its participants, but then all of the airlines followed suit, so it functions now as just another cost in an already competitive industry. This programme carried over into the Asia market as US airlines came into the region with their marketing programmes. Interestingly, three competing Asian airlines joined together to form their *own* frequent flier programme! New entries *are* possible in the industry but it is usually through niche strategies; i.e., using smaller planes, serving smaller markets. It is common for federal governments to use legal means to deter the entry of foreign airlines into their market. Several (most) countries in Asia have national airlines. It is common for government agencies to take actions to protect its country's airlines and even more so when it is a national airline.

Bargaining power of suppliers. This is a critical force for many Asian firms today, and is especially evident in certain industries. For example, the *chaebol* (large industrial corporations) of Korea (see also Chapter 1) are dependent on suppliers from other countries, especially Japan, for critical components in their electronic and automobile industries as well as on Taiwan in their electrical and high-tech manufacturing industries. In the extreme form, when there is only one supplier this is of course **monopoly**; a parallel to *monopoly* is **monopsony**, that is, only one buyer. The world economies were afraid that OPEC would be able to increase its members' economic power through a cartel arrangement. Its members were the suppliers of a major portion of the world's petroleum.

There are many ways and examples of supplier power. Some determinants of supplier power are:

- Presence of substitutes
- Concentration of suppliers
- Switching costs between suppliers

Power of buyers. The power of buyers is especially evident in economies where large retail chains dominate. These large retailers can become such major customers of manufacturers that they can dictate product specifications and prices. Sources of buyer power include:

- Buyer concentration versus firm concentration
- Ability to diversify backwards (becoming their own suppliers)
- Inability to differentiate among sellers
- Buyer volume

What appears to be a competitive advantage can become a weakness when a firm relies on one buyer. That one firm has monopoly, or rather monopsony power.

Power of substitutes. In a general sense, all firms in an industry are competing to substitute each other's products, but here we are concerned with the introduction of *new* products that compete with the traditional ones in the industry. Just fifty years ago, entertainment to many people meant the radio, or the movie theaters; television and its shows became the competition; today's new products are the VCR and movie rental tapes. Which is the next medium? What would you do to prepare for this coming medium if you owned a VCR tape retail/rental shop at the present? Developing a substitute that has advantages or increased values is a common way for outsiders to enter industries—for example, the new Kraft Company "non-dairy, non-cholesterol" ice cream.

Industry competitors and intensity of rivalry. The industry structure described in a previous section of this chapter can lead to predictable competitive strategies; for example oligopolies are conducive to having a price leader in the industry to avoid that form of competition. There are other factors that affect the intensity of the competition, including:

- Industry's growth rate
- Stage in the industry life cycle
- Fixed cost as a percentage of total cost
- Product differences
- Brand loyalty and switching cost
- Industry structure
- Exit barriers

The last factor, exit barriers, might not be as obvious as the others on the list in contributing to the intensity of the rivalry between the industry's members. When organizations simply want to stay in an industry because that is what they have always done and that is what they know how to do and when it is difficult to change and go into new markets and when it is very expensive to liquidate them; firms are more apt to remain in an industry. Those factors become exit barriers.

Summary

Having gone through this chapter, the reader may think that analyzing the external environment is a straightforward and common occurrence in organizations. In reality, it is not so. Aguilar, in *Scanning the Business Environment* (1967), found that firms made few environmental studies and that managers relied on oral and personal contacts rather than formal studies, for their information about their industry and its changes. In the classic work by Chandler, *Strategy and Structure; Chapters in the History of the American Industrial Enterprise* (1962), he suggested that the demand in the market was the stimulus for change. Aharoni (1966) found in his study of thirty-eight US firms in terms of foreign investment that strong forces were required to trigger external studies. Porter's study which dominates the discipline and the literature at present, found that studies of the external environment were usually focused on the acts of competitors. Stubbart (1982) researched formal environmental scanning systems and found that firms concentrate on "industry analysis" and not on "general environmental scanning" so that they are often too narrow in scope.

The external inpediments in the market by governments are crucial and of utmost importance to firms in the region. Tariffs, ownership, entry restrictions, and other activities are in continuous flux and have a significant impact on the success of individual firms. At present, there is a wide variance in income taxes in the region from Hong Kong's low 17.5 per cent to 27 per cent in Singapore and higher in Japan which means that in lower-tax economies, firms can be half as profitable as firms in other countries, but because of the lower tax rate, may in the end be just as profitable or more. There are many ways that governments assist and many ways they can create barriers to business activities. It is important that the firm analyzes not only its industry, and its competition but also the political, technological and social forces at work.

Questions for Establishing Industry Profile

- Size of industry.
- Scope of competitive rivalry (local, regional, national, or global).
- Industry life cycle—where is the industry in the evolutionary or life cycle stages (early development, rapid growth and take off, early maturity, late maturity and saturation, stagnant and aging, decline and decay) and are there any clues regarding how long it will be to the next stage?
- Structure and size of competitors—is the industry fragmented with many small companies or concentrated and dominated by a few large ones?
- The structure of the buying side of the market.
- Competencies of competitors.
- Ease of entry and exit.
- The pace of technological change as concerns both production process innovation and new product introductions.
- The extent to which economies of scale are present in manufacturing, transportation, or mass marketing.
- The extent to which high rates of capacity utilization are crucial to achieving low-cost production efficiency. Fixed and variable cost.
- Capital requirements.
- Industry profitability.

Industry Analysis Summary Profile

1. **Description of Industry, Structure and Competitive Mag**

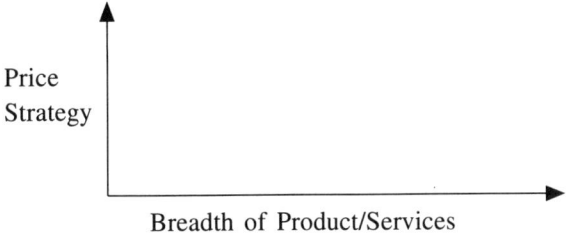

   Price Strategy ↑

   → Breadth of Product/Services

   - *Structure (Monopoly/Fragmented)*
     Implications _____

2. **Strategic Characteristics**
   - *Stage of Industry Life Cycle*
     Present _____
     Future _____
   - *Implications*
     Brand Loyalties _____
     Profitability _____
     Rivalry _____
     Key Success Factors _____

3. **Other Competitive Forces**
   Threat of Entry _____
   Competition from Substitutes _____
   Economic Power of Suppliers _____
   Economic Power of Customers _____

4. **Industry Prospect Factors**
   Very Attractive _____
   Attractive _____
   Neutral _____
   Unattractive _____

Review Questions

1. Give an example of how political-legal forces in another country affect business activities in your country.
2. Explain how changes in the value of your country's currency affect the international trade of businesses.
3. Give an example of how substitute products have impacted different market structures.
4. Identify an industry that has high entry barriers. What are the implications?

5. Identify an industry that has low entry barriers. What are the implications?
6. Give examples of exit barriers for firms operating in your local economy.
7. Create a Competitive Positioning Map for an industry. What are the implications of its particular configuration?

Suggested Further Reading

Boulton, W., et al., Strategic Planning: Determining the impact of environmental characteristics and uncertainty, *Academy of Management Journal*, September 1982.

Chandler, A.D., *Strategy and Structure: Chapters in the history of American industrial enterprise*, Cambridge, MA: MIT Press, 1962.

Diffenbach, J., Corporate Environmental Analysis in Large US Corporations, *Long Range Planning*, Vol. 16, June 1983, pp. 107–116.

Drucker, P., *Management: Tasks, responsibilities, and practices*, New York: Harper & Row, 1974.

Kotler, P., *Marketing Management: Analysis, planning, and control*, Englewood Cliffs, NJ: Prentice-Hall, 1980.

Leemhuis, J.P., Using Scenarios to Develop Strategies, *Long Range Planning*, Vol. 18, April 1985, pp. 30–37.

Leidecker, J.K. and A.V. Bruno, Identifying and Using Critical Success Factors, *Long Range Planning*, Vol. 17, February 1984, pp. 23–32.

Miles, R., *Coffin Nails and Corporate Strategies*, Englewood Cliffs, NJ: Prentice-Hall, 1982.

Moore, W.L. and M.L. Tushman, Managing Innovation over the Product Life Cycle, *in* M.L. Tushman and W.L. Moore (Eds.), *Readings in the Management of Innovation*, Boston: Pitman, 1982.

Penrose, E., *The Theory of the Growth of the Firm*, London: Blackwell, 1968.

Porter, M.E., How Competitive Forces Shape Strategy, *Harvard Business Review*, March–April 1979, pp. 137–145.

Porter, M.E., *Competitive Strategy*, New York: Free Press, 1980.

Porter, M.E., The Contributions of Industrial Organization to Strategic Management, *Academy of Management Review*, Vol. 6, No. 4, 1981, pp. 609–620.

Stubbart, C., Are Environmental Scanning Units Effective? *Long Range Planning*, Vol. 15, June 1982, pp. 139–145.

Endnotes

1. Rugman, Lecraw and Booth, *International Business: Firm and environment*, New York: McGraw-Hill, 1985.
2. Wada, Kazuo, *Yaohan's Global Strategy*, Hong Kong: Capital Communications, 1992.
3. Mickwitz, Gosta, *Marketing and Competition*, Helsinki: Centraltrycheriet, 1959.

CHAPTER 3

ANALYZING A FIRM'S INTERNAL ENVIRONMENT

*How to make the best of both
strong and weak—that is a question
involving the proper use of ground.*
—Sun Tzu

Introduction

Formulating an effective strategy requires an accurate assessment of the environment for market opportunities; a clear, precise definition of corporate mission; the establishment of objectives, and a thorough analysis of the resources of the firm. Given the dynamic nature of markets, the strategy of the firm must also be dynamic, evolving and changing with the requirements of its environment. At the same time, the firm's strategy must be matched with the realistic capabilities and potentials of its resources. One way that firms differ is that each has strengths and weaknesses in different areas and what is a strength to one is not necessarily a strength to another. The smallness of a firm can be used as a competitive advantage. At the same time, large size can also be used as an advantage in the same industry.

This chapter uses several conceptual approaches to assess the resources and potentials of the firm. These include determination of core competencies, a structured, functional approach, by SWOT analysis (strengths, weaknesses, opportunities, and threats), and value chain analysis. These will be defined and discussed in turn. The steps in the process are:

1. Identification of strategic factors and value-creating activities
2. Comparison of the factors and activities with historical information and internal standards of excellence
3. Comparison of the strengths and weaknesses with the capabilities and resources associated with key competitors
4. Comparison of the strengths and weaknesses with key requirements for success
5. Use of the results as input for formulating the appropriate strategies

Chapter 3

Identification of the Company's Distinctive Competence

To succeed, an organization must develop a *distinctive competence* or a set of competencies that differentiate it from its competitors. (Recall the discussion of sustainable competitive advantage in Chapter 1.) Distinctive competence refers to a firm's strength that cannot be easily matched or imitated by competitors. It represents the unique strengths of a company upon which it capitalizes to build its competitive advantage. This unique competence can build barriers to imitation. A company's distinctive competence lasts longer when barriers to imitation are high, the external environment is stable, and its competitors are slow to respond to the competitive advantage it creates. Such barriers to imitation are getting harder and harder to erect and defend, but organizations keep trying to erect and defend them nevertheless. Sony, Sanyo, JVC, and Panasonic all try to differentiate themselves from each other.

A company's distinctive competencies can be derived from its resources and capabilities. Resources include physical, financial, human, and intangible resources, such as brand name, patents, reputation, and technological know-how. These resources must be unique and valuable to a company. Capabilities refer to a company's skills at coordinating its resources and putting them to productive use. Although a company may have unique and valuable resources, it may not be able to create and sustain a distinctive competence unless it has the capability to use these resources effectively. Strategies are designed to capture a firm's strengths and minimize its weaknesses, turning weaknesses into strengths, and perhaps even into distinctive competencies.

Critical Success Factors

Critical success factors can be a mix of "hard" financial figures, such as sales growth, profits, return on investment, and features of a superior product, and "soft" indices of success, such as satisfaction, opinions of customers about service, employee morale, attitudes, and expertise.

Four major sources of critical success factors have been identified by a research team at MIT:[1]

1. Structure of the particular industry: for example, fuel efficiency, load factor and reservation systems are very important to firms in the airline industry.
2. Competitive strategy, industry position, and geographic location: e.g., Hong Kong is located at the centre of the Asia-Pacific region. It serves as a gateway to China and the economic hub for the Asia-Pacific region.
3. Environmental factors: GDP, political factors, economic development, inflation.
4. Temporal factors: internal organizational considerations, restructuring, organizational culture, top management turnover.

Prioritizing the critical success factors is necessary to assure that the most important indicators will be in focus. Three ways to approach the process of internal scanning will now be explored. They involve looking at *Organizational Structure*, *Corporate Culture*, and *Corporate Resources*.

Organizational Structure

Basic structures range from the simple structure of an owner-manager-operated small business to a conglomerate. A generic approach to organization structure would look at the progression from simple organizations to line, to line staff, to division type organizations, etc. It would also look at specialized types of structures including the matrix, the idea of the strategic business unit (SBU), and the conglomerate. These organization types are described in terms of strategy implications in Chapter 5.

The structure of the organization represents its attempts to divide up or integrate basic tasks and activities and the people who perform them. The whole structure is reflected in the organization's division of tasks for efficiency and clarity of purpose, and its coordination between departments to ensure organizational efficiency. Structure balances the need for specialization and the need for integration. Implementing a strategy successfully depends on selecting the right structure.

The relationship between structure and strategy was first investigated by Alfred Chandler. Chandler's study was based on four large American companies. He concluded that structure followed strategy.[2] Changes in strategy ultimately led to or resulted in changes in the organization's structure. Observations involved growth and the structural adjustments that were made to maintain efficient performance during market expansion, produce line diversification, and vertical integration. As an organization grows and succeeds, it tends to evolve into a more complex structure. Peters and Waterman found that many excellent companies have maintained a simple structure, with a lean staff.[3] Simple structure, with a lean staff, tends to be less bureaucratic and to better adjust to a fast changing environment, as well as being conducive to innovation.

Chandler identified four key growth strategies that are sequentially used with the development of the organization. He suggested appropriate structures for each state in the organization's development.[4]

1. Expansion of volume
2. Geographic dispersion
3. Vertical integration
4. Product or service diversification

Each strategy posed different administrative problems and, therefore, tended to lead to different organizational structures. The "fit" between an organization's strategy and the organization's structure is of vital importance if that strategy is to succeed.

The organizational structure varies across cultures. The typical organization structure in Southeast Asia tends to be low in complexity and formalization with a high degree of centralization, and tends to be a flatter organization. To a large extent, decisions would be retained by the owner of the organization or a small group of core members of the family or trusted seniors. Even with increasing size, there is a continued preference to retain this form. This is achieved by creating a loosely bonded molecular arrangement.[5] The large Chinese-owned organizations are loosely linked conglomerates. These diversified businesses are controlled through a central holding company. The *hongs** (such as Jardine Matheson and Swire) are foreign-owned corporations with their own distinctive organization structures. Other types of large organizations in Korea and Japan display different structural configurations. Exhibits 3.1 and 3.2 demonstrate the Japanese, Korean and Chinese business systems.

Exhibit 3.1   East Asian Business Systems

	Japanese Kaisha	Korean Chaebol	Chinese Family Business
Authoritative Co-ordination and Control			
Personal authority and owner domination	Low	High	High
Significance of formal coordination and control procedures	High	Medium	Low
Management style	Facilitative	Directive	Didactic
Employee commitment	Emotional	Conditional	Conditional
Business Domain and Development			
Business specialization	High	Low	High within firms medium within families
Evolutionary strategies	High	Medium	Medium
Inter-Firm Coordination			
Relational contracting	High	Low	Medium
Long-term intersector coordination	Strong through business groups and state agencies	Indirect through state	Limited and personal

Source: Whitley, R.D., The Social Construction of Business Systems in East Asia, *Organization Studies*, Vol. 12, No. 1, 1991, p. 3.

The Korean *chaebol* is highly diversified and tightly controlled by a holding company. The chaebol is different in nature from the traditional Japanese *zaibatsu*. In Japan, zaibatsus control the biggest banks and form an integrated financial power, together with support from government (through MITI), making it possible to achieve great and rapid adaptability.

---

* The terms *hong*, *chaebol*, and *zaibatsu* are similar to conglomerate, in Chinese, Korean and Japanese respectively.

Exhibit 3.2 East Asian Enterprise Structures

	Large Japanese Enterprises	Korean Chaebol	Chinese Family Businesses	US Diversified Corporation
Enterprise Specialization and Development				
Business specialization	High	Low	High	Low
Relational contracting	High	Low	Medium	Low
Evolutionary strategies	High	Medium	Medium	Low
Authority, Loyalty and the Division of Labour				
Personal authority	Low	High	High	Low
Enterprise loyalty	High	Medium	Medium	Low
Role individuation	Low	Low	Low	High
Enterprise Coordination				
Horizontal coordination	High	Low	Medium	Low
Vertical coordiantion	High	High	Low	Low

Source: Whitley, R.D., Eastern Asian Enterprises Structures and the Comparative Analysis of Forms of Business Organization, *Organization Studies,* Vol. 12, No. 1, 1990, p. 68.

Zaibatsu ownership had been separated from control, whereas the chaebol was controlled by the original founder. While zaibatsus were broken up after the war, they have re-emerged as *keiretsus*, interconnected webs of manufacturers, distributors, and banks. The organizations started from a profitable business in a single sector, and as a business proved successful, the entrepreneur began to diversify into new promising areas. Some family owners of chaebols who acquired considerable wealth may plow substantial proceeds back into their businesses. Ten of the Korean chaebols appeared in *Fortune's* International 500 list. Over 60 per cent of the chaebol chief executives are firm founders. Only 18.8 per cent are unrelated to the founding family. The rest are direct descendants and relatives of the founders.[6]

Corporate Culture

Organizational culture can be defined as "the shared meanings of organizational members—how things are done".[7] It is a collection of beliefs, expectations, and values learned and shared by members and transmitted from one generation of employees to another.[8] The functions of corporate culture include conveying a sense of identity, generating employee commitment, adding to organizational stability, and serving as a frame of reference. It is a pattern of basic assumptions developed by an organization as it learns to cope with its problems of external adaptation and internal integration that has worked well enough to be considered valid and to be taught to new members as the correct way to perceive, think, and feel.[9] It permeates into all functional areas. It has a significant impact on strategy formulation, implementation and evaluation activities.

The end product of organization culture will be reflected in an organization's values, beliefs, rites, rituals, ceremonies, myths, stories, legends, heroes, the way leaders react to crises, role modelling, allocation of rewards, systems and procedures, and philosophy. Organizational culture significantly affects business decisions.

Some scholars and researchers have tried to identify a set of values or traits that dominate strong organization cultures. The best-known attempt is Peters and Waterman's study on the culture values of successful companies.[3] These successful organizations have values promoting the following attributes:

1. A bias for action
2. Getting close to the customers
3. Autonomy and entrepreneurship
4. Productivity through people
5. Hands-on, value-driven activity
6. "Sticking to their own knitting"
7. Simple form, lean staff
8. Simultaneous loose-tight properties

The strong corporate culture can be a source of competitive advantage.[10] The well-known 7-S framework was developed by the McKinsey consulting firm. The 7-S framework views culture as a function of seven variables namely, skills, staff, style, systems, structure, strategy and shared values. *Skills, staff, style,* and *shared* values are the four "soft" S's while the three "hard" S's are *systems, structure,* and *strategy.* Exhibit 3.3 lists the strategic management tools, concepts, and techniques associated with the 7-S's. A strategy is considered successful when the other S's in the framework fit into or support it.

Wallach distinguishes between bureaucratic and innovative cultures.[11] Bureaucratic cultures are power-oriented, highly regulatory and structured, procedural and hierarchical. Government departments and public utility companies are examples of a bureaucratic culture. Innovative cultures may be characterized as dynamic, entrepreneurial, ambitious, creative, result-oriented and enterprising. Giordano (apparel) and Dickson Concepts (jewelry, etc.) are good Hong Kong examples of innovative cultures. Another approach for analysing an organization's culture is the Harrison and Stokes "four-petal" model for four organizational cultures: power, role, achievement, and support.[12]

Synthesized from other studies, seven characteristics have been identified that capture the essence of an organization's culture:[13]

1. Individual autonomy—degree of responsibility, independence and opportunities for exercising initiative
2. Structure—the extent of regulatory measures and control
3. Support—consideration and warmth experienced by the employees

Analyzing a Firm's Internal Environment

Exhibit 3.3 Integrating Strategy and Culture

Policy Concerns	Strategic Management Tools, Concepts and Techniqes
Shared values	Purpose and mission Hierarchy of goals and objectives Stakeholder analysis Critical success factors Corporate culture
Strategy	Environmental scanning Product-market analysis Competitive analysis SWOT analysis
Structure	Organization structure Strategy-structure linkage Centralized-decentralized responsibilities
Systems	Planning and control systems Resource allocation techniques Information processing methods
Staff	Skill analysis Organizational life cycle analysis Succession planning Employee relations
Skills	Critical success factors Capabilities Levels of resource support
Style	Value Decision making/power Leadership

4. Identification—the degree to which employees identify themselves with the organization as a whole
5. Performance-reward—the extent to which rewards are directly linked to performance
6. Conflict tolerance—willingness to be open and honest about differences
7. Risk tolerance—employees are encouraged to be aggressive, innovative and adventurous

In the preceding section we have discussed the basic terms and concepts used to understand organization culture but the organization forms of the region also are unique and different from those of the Western world. For example a very popular type of organization found in many Asian countries is the Chinese family business; the dominant form of business in Taiwan, Hong Kong, and many Southeast Asian countries.[14] In these family businesses, top management has absolute authority and power. The organization is highly centralized. They tend to use less formal planning and control systems. The reward system is not based on performance, but on seniority and loyalty.

One of the striking features of the Chinese family business is its highly personal nature. The internal coordination and control system is strongly associated with ownership and is highly centralized.[15] Family members fill the top management positions, and it is relatively rare for managers without strong personal ties to owners to become trusted members of the top management. Direct owner control of enterprises is linked to personal and paternalistic authority relationship.

Large Chinese organizations have adopted Western management practices, but still exhibit a strong family influence and dominance in their operations and decision making. Confucianism promotes self-control and dutiful conduct to one's superiors. The influence of such Confucian thought in maintaining harmony is very important, even at the expense of organizational effectiveness. Chinese entrepreneurs maintain more distance from their workers. Decision by consensus is not possible.

Formal positions and responsibilities are less significant in Chinese business than in Western organizations. Family-run management style tends to maintain control through personal ties and kinship. The family members are the core employees. The sons are the ones who will inherit the business. The next layer will be the more distant relatives and friends who owe their positions to their connection with the owners. The family relationship can be extended to include a network of relatives or kinfolk as well as people who are from the same place of origin, speaking the same dialect. The next outer layer are ranks of unrelated people who have worked for the company long enough and shown their loyalty. This layer may contain ranks of professional managers, technicians, supervisors and craftsmen.

The outermost layer includes unskilled wage workers. Personal connections have significant impact on one's career. Being treated as a member of the family has a significant effect on organization commitment. Non-family employees often regard employment as experience in preparation for starting their own business.[16] Loyalty among non-family employees is often low. Their career path of moving up to the managerial core is restricted. It is difficult to retain very competent staff. (This is unlike the chaebols in South Korea and the *kaisha* in Japan, where employees are guaranteed life-long employment.) This is the principal reason—indeed the controlling factor—why such firms typically do not grow beyond a certain stage. There are relatively few large corporations in Taiwan and Hong Kong. Other organization forms found in the region that will be described in Chapter 5 include the Korean chaebol, Hong Kong's hongs, and the state enterprises and collectives of the PRC. Each of these organizations deviate substantially from the prescriptive norms of organization theory but are very effective within the context of their local institutions—political, social, and cultural.

Corporate Resources and Capabilities

The strength of an organization, to a certain extent, depends on its available resources and capabilities. A corporation's resources include not only such generally recognized assets as people, capital and facilities, but also those analytical concepts, information and procedural techniques used within the functional areas.

Functional Analysis

Strategic management is a highly interactive process that requires effective coordination among all functional areas, such as human resource management, marketing, finance/accounting, production and operations, research and development, and information systems. This evaluation focuses attention on the firm's internal operations, especially its strengths and weaknesses.

For different types of organizations, such as manufacturing, hospitals, government agencies, etc., the functional business areas vary with different emphasis. It is not possible in this chapter to review in depth all the materials presented in these functional areas. A listing of the most crucial internal factors will be provided with a brief illustration of competitive advantage.

Strategic management requires inputs from all functional areas working together. Considerable amount of effort is required to coordinate and integrate all these functional areas. Relationships among the functional areas of business are presented in Exhibit 3.4. An internal audit of the functional areas provides an opportunity to discuss the issues related to the strengths and weaknesses, so that the issues, problems, and needs in all the functional areas are understood. Performing an internal audit requires gathering, assimilating, and evaluating information about the firm's operations. Critical success factors can be identified and their priorities decided.

Exhibit 3.4 Interrelationship among Functional Areas of Business

EXTERNAL ENVIRONMENT

- Production/Operation
- Human Resources
- Finance
- Purchasing and Material Management
- Strategic Plan
- Marketing
- Research and Development
- Management Information-system

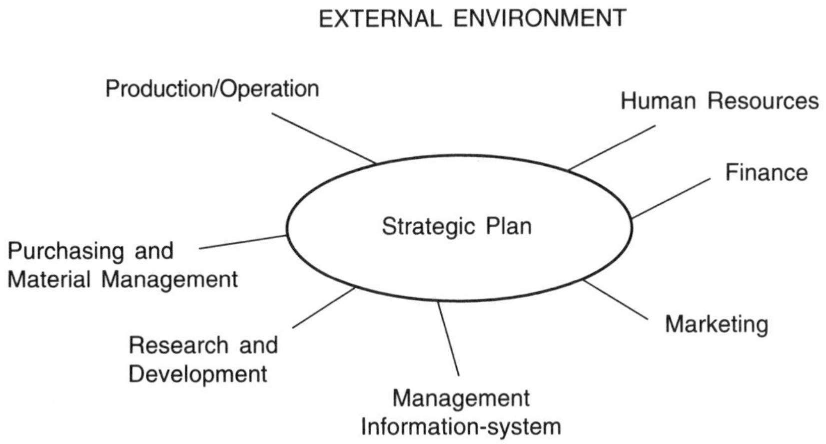

In the next section, the major functional areas will be briefly covered. Finally, all separate components should be integrated and summarized by using Michael Porter's Value Chain Analysis in order to gain competitive advantage.

Financial Position

The financial condition is an important indicator of a firm's competitive position and attractiveness to investors. An organization's financial condition can be reflected by analysing its liquidity, leverage, profitability, asset utilization, working capital and cash flow. Financial ratio analysis is the most commonly used method for determining an organization's strengths and weaknesses.

Financial analysis is an important function in strategic management decisions. The income statement and the balance sheet are two financial statements that show the financial situation of a firm and are useful for analyzing, controlling and planning the strategic financial aspects. The balance sheet is a summary statement of an organization's assets and liabilities. The income statement shows the income generated from an organization's operation during a period of time, usually one year. It shows the sales income minus expenditure resulting in profit or loss. Financial ratio analysis is a useful tool for investigating the overall financial condition of an organization. Financial ratio analysis is based on information provided in the organization's balance sheet and income statement. Exhibit 3.5 lists the definitions of some key financial ratios.

Here are the four basic categories of financial ratios:[17]

(i) Liquidity ratios. These measure the capability of an organization to meet its short-term financial obligations.

$$\text{Current ratio} = \text{Current assets} / \text{Current liabilities}$$

The current ratio varies greatly from industry to industry. A common rule of thumb is that the current ratio should be about 2:1. The liquidity situation in Japanese and Korean firms is different from companies from other Asian countries.

(ii) Leverage. This provides indication of a firm's financial risk, i.e., the relative proportion of its debt to its equity.

$$\text{Debt/Equity ratio} = \text{Total debt} / \text{Total assets}$$

The two major sources of funding are debt (loans) and equity (stock). The proportion of debt to equity reflects a firm's credit position. A good credit position, i.e., low level of current debt or having good prospects, enables a firm to expand by using borrowed funds.

(iii) Activity ratios. These reflect whether or not a firm is using its resources efficiently.

$$\text{Inventory turnover} = \text{Sales} / \text{Inventory}$$

If an organization is not turning over its inventory rapidly enough, it may create problems as a result of too much money being tied up in inventory.

(iv) Profitability ratios. These provide a measure of a firm's overall economic performance (effectiveness). Profitability is a common yardstick for assessing a firm's success. It is calculated by dividing earnings before interest and taxes (EBIT) by sales.

$$\text{Profit margin on sales} = \text{EBIT} / \text{Sales}$$

Exhibit 3.5 Ratio Definitions

Ratio	Ratio Formula
Liquidity Ratios	
Current	$\dfrac{\text{Current assets}}{\text{Current liabilities}}$
Quick	$\dfrac{\text{Current assets} - \text{Inventory}}{\text{Current liabilities}}$
Leverage Ratios	
Debt	$\dfrac{\text{Total debt}}{\text{Total assets}}$
Debt equity	$\dfrac{\text{Long term debt}}{\text{Equity}}$
Times interest earned	$\dfrac{\text{Earnings before taxes} + \text{Interest}}{\text{Interest charges}}$
Fixed-charges coverage	$\dfrac{\text{Income available for meeting fixed charges}}{\text{Fixed charges}}$
Activity Ratios	
Inventory turnover	$\dfrac{\text{Cost of goods sold}}{\text{Average inventory}}$
Average collection (period, days)	$\dfrac{\text{Average accounts receivable}}{\text{Average credit sales per day}}$
Fixed-assets turnover	$\dfrac{\text{Sales}}{\text{Fixed assets}}$
Total-assets turnover	$\dfrac{\text{Sales}}{\text{Total assets}}$
Profitability Ratios	
Gross profit margin (%)	$\dfrac{\text{Sales} - \text{Cost of goods sold}}{\text{Sales}}$
Net operating margin (%)	$\dfrac{\text{Operating income}}{\text{Sales}}$
Profit margin on sales (%)	$\dfrac{\text{Net income}}{\text{Sales}}$
Return on total assets (%)	$\dfrac{\text{Net income} + \text{Interest}}{\text{Total assets}}$
Return on equity (%)	$\dfrac{\text{Net income}}{\text{Stockholders' equity}}$

The Return on Investment is calculated by dividing earnings after taxes (EAT) by total assets. It examines how well the organization handles its assets.

$$\text{Return on Investment (ROI)} = \text{EAT}/\text{Total assets}$$

All these indicators (ratios) have important uses in evaluating the financial strength and weakness of an organization. Trends in its key financial ratios should be compared with those of its competitors or with industry norms.

Some other means of evaluating a firm's financial position include cash flow analysis, cost of funds, break-even analysis, ability to raise additional funds, relationships with creditors and stockholders, dividend policy, and appropriate use of funds and sources. The surplus of internally generated funds over expenditures enables a company to fund new investments without borrowing from outside sources.

Working capital refers to the current assets including cash, receivables, and inventories of a firm. Net working capital is defined as the difference between current assets and current liabilities. Working capital flows from cash to inventories, then to receivables and back to cash. It is important to maintain a smooth and rapid flow of fund in order to increase the efficiency of working capital and the firm's profitability.

Dividends compete with capital investments for the available cash flow. If earnings are not distributed to shareholders as dividends, they can be used as an internally generated source of funds. Companies that reinvest all of their earnings can be expected to grow at a rate equal to their normal return on equity.

The financial ratios are often misinterpreted and misused when applied to some Asian companies. This may be partly due to different accounting practices (financial reporting and disclosure practices in many developing countries are different from US practices) or the lack of understanding of the institutional, cultural, political and government tax considerations that influence the financial ratios. The liquidity situations in Japanese and Korean firms are different from those of companies from Western countries. The Japanese and Korean firms appear to be less liquid, solvent, efficient, or profitable than their US counterparts.[18] Through its tight control of the banking system, the South Korean government can determine which companies receive which loans and at what rate. The chaebol and zaibatsu simply increase the size of their companies to enable them to produce competitive goods on a large scale of economy, thus keeping out imports through market forces. However, if you calculate the debt/equity ratio for some of the large Korean chaebol or Japanese kaisha, you may find a very high leverage. A debt/equity ratio of 600 per cent to 800 per cent is common. The lower relative cost of debt that results from the tax deductibility of interest expenses is important in some Asian countries. In Korea, companies face severe supply constraints when it comes to equity financing. The government-supported debt financing was the only available source of funds. The relationships between the borrowing company, related companies, and their banks tend to be very close. The company may not run into liquidity problems or financial risks because of the high level of government support. Japanese organizations also tend to use an excessive proportion of debt in their capital structure. The proportion of debt to equity ratio of Japanese companies can be as high as 4 to 1, an amount considered dangerous or near bankruptcy by the US standard. The Japanese companies have been able to get by with this type of financing because of strong governmental support, the heavy saving patterns, and the long traditions of debt financing as opposed to the sale of stock. In Korea, state bureaucracies like the Economic Policy Board control domestic credit and favour certain export-oriented firms, and they mediate foreign credit through licensing schemes.

Analyzing a Firm's Internal Environment

Thus they have total control over access to investment capital. The chaebols are all structured with very low equity and huge debt components.[19]

Despite high debt and lower interest coverage ratios in Japan and Korea, the actual bankruptcy rate is very low.

Exhibit 3.6 displays financial statements of a typical Japanese firm.

Exhibit 3.6 Financial Statements of a Japanese Firm (in millions of yen)

	1990	1989	1988	1987	1986	1985
Current assets	2,201,555	1,433,798	1,143,371	922,308	974,130	966,128
Investment and advances	337,150	113,435	101,990	115,367	114,899	119,047
Plant and equipment	868,128	544,775	453,609	343,135	332,622	337,721
Other assets	965,274	272,766	746,477	30,520	28,494	74,365
Total assets	4,370,085	2,364,775	1,945,447	1,411,250	1,450,145	1,497,261
Current liabilities	1,995,891	1,119,031	1,003,018	586,950	828,295	647,518
Long-term liabilities	927,257	319,037	234,377	215,446	215,453	200,580
Minority interest	16,879	14,901	14,976			
Equity	1,430,053	911,816	646,076	608,834	606,392	599,163
Net sales	2,879,856	2,145,329	1,555,219	609,425	1,452,090	1,420,735
Operating revenue	65,336	56,143	32,742	9,922	21,543	18,372
	2,945,242	2,201,472	1,587,961	619,347	1,473,633	1,439,157
Cost of sales	1,938,016	1,475,352	1,147,014	451,681	1,086,659	982,198
SG & A	712,035	565,621	380,283	148,189	344,830	323,275
Operating income	295,191	160,499	60,664	19,477	42,144	133,684
Other income	91,553	60,018	57,147	23,52	76,011	42,967
Other expenses	159,315	55,001	45,975	17,333	34,027	34,740
Income before taxes	227,429	165,516	71,836	25,626	84,128	141,911
Taxes	126,976	95,176	41,465	16,105	48,802	78,023
Consolidated income	100,453	70,340	30,371	9,521	35,326	63,888
Affiliate equity	2,355	2,129	6,865	3,753	5,918	9,133
Net income	102,808	72,469	37,236	13,234	41,244	73,021

PIMS Analysis

Profit Impact of Market Strategy (PIMS) was developed by the Strategic Planning Institute. It is composed of various analyses of a data base containing about 100 items of information on the strategic experience of 3000 strategic business units throughout North America and Europe, for periods ranging from two to twelve years. PIMS research has identified nine major strategic factors that account for 80 per cent of the variation in profitability across the businesses in the data base. The results show that companies with a high rate of return had the following characteristics:[20]

- Low investment intensity
- High market share
- High relative product quality
- High capacity utilization
- High operating effectiveness
- Low direct costs per unit

The PIMS report can provide some clues for management action to be taken for improving profitability. It is useful in helping the strategic decision maker to identify key internal variables.

Marketing Capability: The P's

Marketing strategies are usually designed to increase sales and market share in order to increase long-term profits. Marketing can be described as the process of defining, anticipating, creating and fulfilling customers' needs for products and services. The marketing mix consists basically of product, price, promotion, and place (channels of distribution):[21] the so-called 4 P's. Exhibit 3.7 presents the elements of the 4 P's. Beyond the 4 P's are other P's also used by some marketing strategists: package, premiums, physical distribution, personal selling

Exhibit 3.7 Elements of the Marketing Mix

Product	Price	Promotion	Place
Quality	List price	Advertising	Distribution
Feature	Discount	Sales promotion	Direct selling
Brand name	Allowance	Packaging	Coverage
Design	Credit	Personal selling	Retailers
Product line	Payment periods	Publicity	Location
Reputation			Inventory
Warranties			Transport

and publicity/advertising. The marketing strategy audit tries to identify how well or poorly the marketing department is doing with the P's and beyond.

A market-driven company's mission is to try to provide what the buyer wants. All company activities are responsive to the customers' wellbeing. The marketing strategy must take into account the environmental forces, taking advantage of the firm's strengths while avoiding its weaknesses: it must be responsive to the competitive scene, recognize the meaningful consumer values, and include the distribution channels. The purpose of a strategy is to build a sustainable competitive advantage or competitive edge.

Customer analysis. Identifying the target or potential customers is an important starting point to find out who the customers are. Customer surveys, gathering and analyzing customer information, developing customer profiles, evaluating market positioning strategies, and determining optimal market segmentation strategies can all be used to advantage.

Marketing research. The marketing manager requires a lot of data; he must know the market and have relevant marketing information to make important decisions. Marketing research is a systematic gathering, recording and analysing of data about problems and opportunities relating to marketing of goods and services. Buyer intentions, surveys, sales force opinions, and experts are important sources of the needed information to produce and sell goods and services, evaluating alternative suppliers, and selecting the best among them.

The survival of the organization depends on the development and marketing of successful new products. Product decisions include quality, features, options, styles, brand names, packaging, size, service, warranties, and returns. Superior products, at least for a while, can be obtained through technological developments. Each product goes through different stages of the product life cycle. These stages are birth, growth, maturity, and decline. The marketing strategy is shaped by the passage of time. In the birth stage, launching of innovative products is most important. Product quality and advertising have the biggest impact on volume. In the growth stage, sales take off and expand. With the entry of new competitors and subsequent keen competition, there is as well an emergence of more mature buyers. Here pricing is critical. In the maturity stage, packaging is necessary to generate more sales. In the last stage, we try to develop new product uses and advertising assumes major importance, although we may elect ultimately to "harvest" the brand, let it be a "cash cow", and ultimately let it die.[22]

Many issues have to be considered when analyzing pricing strategies. Pricing strategy includes list price, discounts, allowance, payment periods, credit terms, initial price for new products, changes in short-term and long-term pricing strategy, penetration or skimming pricing strategy, cost of supply and value to the buyer, and price elasticity. Most companies in Asian countries adopt a low price policy in order to penetrate foreign markets. Japanese car manufacturers have successfully used rebates as a pricing strategy in entering the US market.

The major promotion tools include advertising, sales promotion, publicity, and personal selling. Each tool has its own advantages and disadvantages in attracting consumers. The cultural issue and local adaptation are important decisions in designing a promotional campaign.

Distribution decisions include warehousing, distribution channels, selective or extensive coverage, territories, retail site locations, inventory location, transportation arrangements, wholesaling and retailing. Various marketing entities, such as agents, vendors, distributors, brokers, serve as intermediaries in the distribution channel. Backward integration has the advantage of gaining control over suppliers. It is a particularly attractive strategy when suppliers are unpredictable, unreliable or not capable of meeting the company's needs. The distribution channel in Japanese companies is somewhat unique compared with the Western channel of distribution.

Japan's traditional distribution systems are controlled by network (*keiretsu*) that we have already cited. *Keiretsu* includes the country's trading companies (*sogo shasha*), manufacturers, wholesalers, retailers and banks.[23] Distribution channels in Japan are shown in Exhibit 3.8. Exporters have found the Japanese market hard to enter, but Japan's complex and exclusive distribution system has begun to break down. There seem to be growing roles for untraditional middlemen and other untraditional retail entities.

Exhibit 3.8 Traditional and Alternative Forms of Distributions in Japan

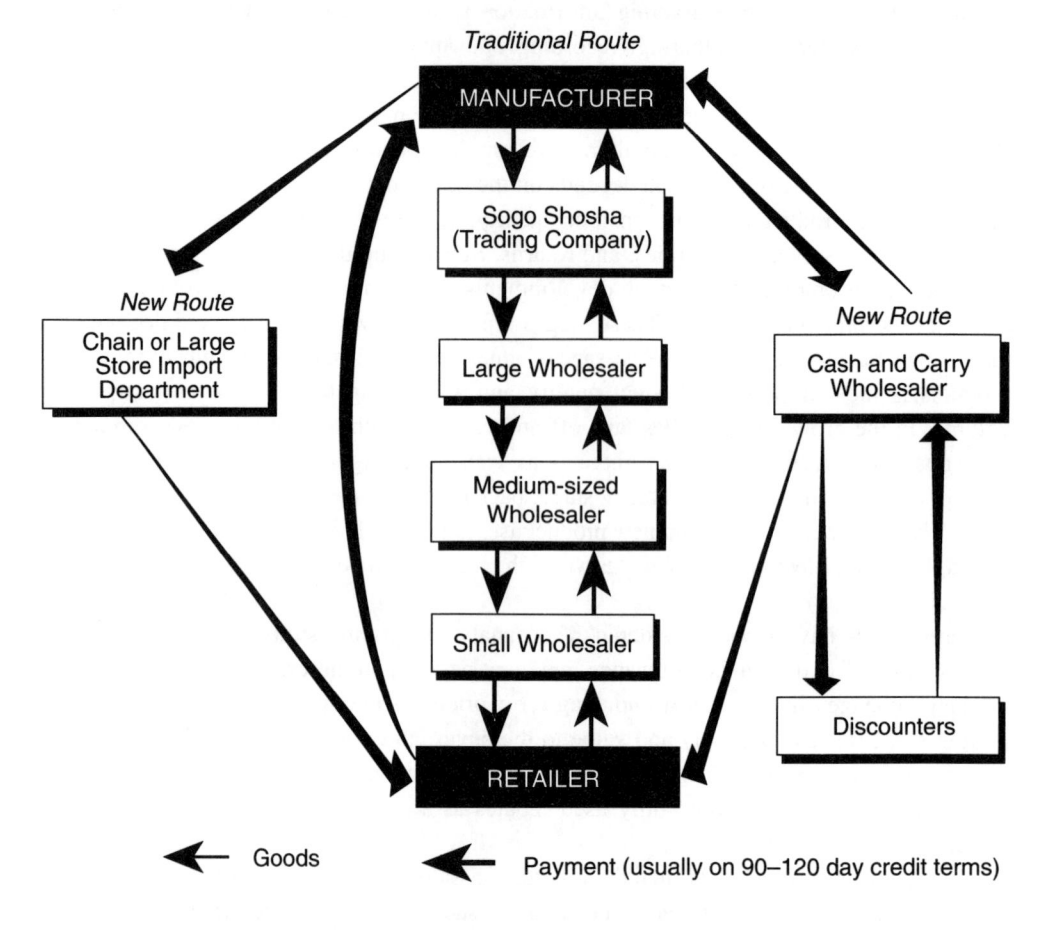

Traditional Route

MANUFACTURER → Sogo Shosha (Trading Company) → Large Wholesaler → Medium-sized Wholesaler → Small Wholesaler → RETAILER

New Route: Chain or Large Store Import Department

New Route: Cash and Carry Wholesaler → Discounters

← Goods ← Payment (usually on 90–120 day credit terms)

Source: *Asian Business*, February 1992, p. 24.

Human Resource Management

Human resource management helps gain competitive advantage through people. Managers are empowered to select, appraise, reward and develop personnel. It is important to try to encourage employee participation in the work process.

The quality of leadership at the top plays an important role in shaping the strategies. Leadership, a critical ingredient in strategy formulation and implementation, is based upon the skills and abilities of an organization's leaders. The board of directors are the integral part of an organization's leadership and can play an important role in strategy formulation and implementation, especially in overseeing the capitalization, resource allocation, diversification, setting the organization's mission, management philosophy, policies and strategies. The effective leader ensures that the organization's reward systems are consistent with its strategic direction. Business leaders in most of the Southeast Asian countries exert much greater power: subordinates are expected to comply and expect company loyalty to them in return. Under such a power structure (benevolent autocracy), it is easier to build and maintain harmony and a mutual reciprocal obligation.

Good people management increases morale, spirits and enthusiasm. Good procedures such as skills inventories, job descriptions, effective compensation benefits options, and motivational methods can bring out talent. Such people-based competencies are usually more difficult to sustain or transfer than product- or technology-based ones but, as suggested in Chapter 1, may be the only ones that can give a company a long-term edge.

The whole operation is significantly influenced by the quality and quantity of its human resources. An effective human resource system can give an organization a competitive edge in attracting and retaining high calibre people. Japanese workers are especially well-educated and well-trained. The development programme in Procter & Gamble is a good example of what can give a company a distinctive advantage over its competitors in Asia.

The relative importance of direct personal subordination to leaders as distinct from obedience to collective and positional authority is different even within Asian countries. Chinese enterprises give priority to those having family ties with the owners; Japanese companies expect employees to behave as family members. Traditionally, the Japanese company is a worker's "family" in a real sense. These management practices are common in Japanese and Chinese companies, and coupled with this commitment is a reliance on seniority-based promotion and salary increases.

Such a paternalistic ethos encourages relatively long-term employer-employee commitment and a seniority-based promotion system which rewards loyalty. In Japan, loyalty means complete, unconditional obedience to one's superior.[24] When filial piety to parents and loyalty to superiors are in conflict, the Chinese choose the former, while the Japanese choose the latter. Loyalty and commitment to organizational goals are encouraged in large Japanese companies. Loyalty and seniority are considered to be more important promotion criteria in Asian countries than in Western countries. Family or personal ties, for example, classmates or people who graduated from the same school, become important factors in promoting managers to high ranking positions. Outright nepotism in business has gradually faded away as organizations have become formalized, but, in general, a special relationship is still an important consideration in promoting managers to higher ranking positions.

Production/Operations

Production capacity is the ability to yield output. It is determined from a complex mix of organizational resources. Essentially, capacity is a description of the system's limitation. The four determinants of capacity are: manpower, machinery, materials, and money, the so-called "4 M's" of manufacturing. These are critical for the effective operation of an organization. Technology includes manpower and machinery, material acquisition, storage, and logistic distribution. Money refers to availability of capital. Technological strength can be obtained through cost efficiency, and uniqueness.

Just-in-time technique. The Japanese have been very successful in applying some operational techniques such as just-in-time (JIT) and flexible manufacturing. Flexible manufacturing technologies enable companies to produce small batches of high quality customized products at a cost that at one time could only be achieved through mass production. "Just-in-time" is an inventory control method for driving inventory down through improved control over capacity. A successful JIT programme results in reduced inventories through careful design of standard methods and procedures. JIT inventory systems help a company to closely monitor the quality of its inputs, generate cost savings from inventory reductions, and release cash for investment in plant and equipment. An effective material handling function can lower costs through tighter quality control.

Experience curve. The notion of the "experience curve" was introduced by the Boston Consulting Group. The underlying principle is that a reduction in per unit costs results as volume increases, since workers and management master the technique to produce the product more efficiently.[25] Small companies do not get the advantages of economy of scale and low cost of the large companies. They typically establish industrial networks, and try to develop contacts with domestic and foreign suppliers to find a niche for survival.

Total quality management. Total Quality Management (TQM) and ISO 9000 series are useful quality control tools that lower operating costs because of less rework, fewer mistakes, fewer delays, fewer snags, and better use of machine time and materials. *Kaizen*, the Japanese idea of quality control, means continuous improvement. Most of the factories in the Newly Industrializing Countries (NICs, like Hong Kong, South Korea, Singapore, and Taiwan) have lost their comparative advantage of low cost production. Manufacturing must move to higher-value-added products, and increase productivity to gain advantage. The Asian NICs try to upgrade their technology in order to gain competitive advantage. Management information system (MIS) applications include travel reservation systems, such as those installed in travel agencies for booking airlines tickets, hotel rooms and rental cars. In the banking industry, automated teller machines (ATM) and global transaction networks have been extensively used. MIS helps to streamline operations, and is used for critical strategic decisions. MIS also changes industry boundaries, and creates new business opportunities.

Company Analysis: The Internal Factor Evaluation Matrix

Internal analysis may be summed up with the Internal Factor Evaluation Matrix. This strategy formulation tool summarizes and evaluates the strengths and weaknesses in the functional areas. It provides a basis for identifying and evaluating relationships among those areas. Exhibit 3.9 shows a sample Internal Factor Evaluation Matrix.

Value Chain Analysis

Value Chain Analysis, as proposed by Porter, is a means of examining the nature and extent of the synergies that exist (or do not exist) between the internal activities of an

Analyzing a Firm's Internal Environment

Exhibit 3.9 A Sample Internal Factor Evaluation Matrix

Key Internal Factor	Weight	Rating	Weighted Score
Product quality	15	4	60
Channel of distribution	10	2	20
Plant facilities	10	3	30
Technological development	15	5	75
Profit margins	20	4	80
Quality control	15	4	60
Personnel quality	15	3	45
Total	100		370

Note: Numbers are arbitrary, and for illustration purposes only.

organization. The systematic analysis of individual value activities can lead to a better understanding of an organization's strengths and weaknesses. According to Porter, "Every firm is a collection of activities that are performed to design, produce, market, deliver, and support its products." All these activities can be represented using a value chain, as shown in Exhibit 3.10. Differences among competitors' value chains are a key source of competitive advantage.[26]

Exhibit 3.10 Value Chain

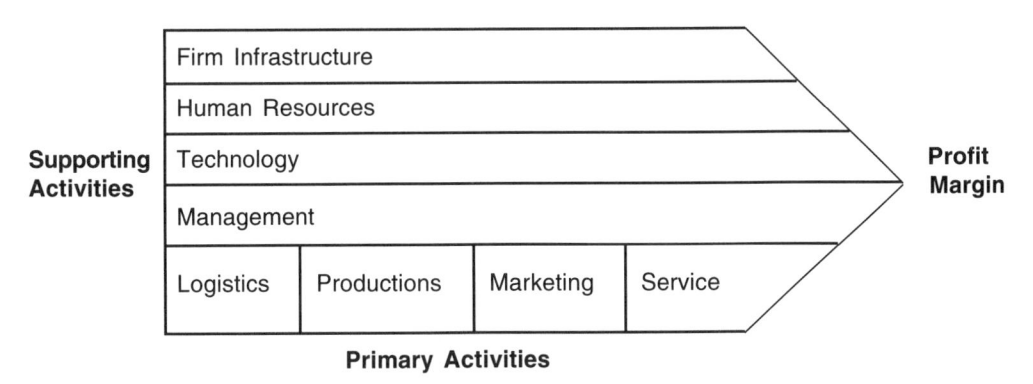

Supporting Activities: Firm Infrastructure, Human Resources, Technology, Management

Primary Activities: Logistics, Productions, Marketing, Service

Profit Margin

Source: Adapted from Michael M. Porter, *Competitive Advantage: Creating and sustaining superior performance,* New York: The Free Press, 1985.

Value chain analysis identifies a set of activities that add value. Each of these activities can be a source of competitive advantage for a firm. Primary activities contribute to the creation of a product. Secondary activities assist the primary activities. Porter identifies five primary activities that usually occur in any organization:

1. Inbound logistics of raw materials

2. Operations
3. Outbound logistics of the finished goods
4. Marketing and sales
5. Customer service

This results in cost reduction and increased productivity, quality, efficiency, and quicker response. The four secondary or support activities are: (a) the procurement process, (b) technology development, (c) human resource management, and (d) the infrastructure of planning, accounting, finance, legal, government affairs, and quality management. Each of these supporting activities may be further divided into a number of distinct activities. All these activities contribute to buyer value. Firms create value for their buyers through performing these primary and support activities.

Value chain analysis allows us to assess the strengths and weaknesses of a firm's primary and support activities. A firm gains competitive advantage by performing these strategically important activities better and cheaper than its competitors.

Gaining competitive advantage requires that a firm's value chain is managed as a system rather than a collection of separate parts. Coordination of the activities within the value chain is necessary. There are many potential synergies among the corporation's products and business units. We seek economy of scale wherein activities are conducted at the lowest possible cost per unit of output. Value chain analysis provides a valuable framework for integrating all the functional activities of a firm and studying a firm's strengths and weaknesses. In sum, this chapter focused on how to analyze the internal strategic factors in terms of strengths and weaknesses. These factors can be summarized by a checklist given in Exhibit 3.11.

Exhibit 3.11 Checklist for Key Internal Factors

Human resources
    Personnel quality
    Management quality
    Ability to attract and retain people
    Turnover
    Personnel policy
    Employees' skill and morale
    Employee relations
    Productivity

Financial
    Short-term and long-term capital
    Cash flow
    Profitability
    Capital structure
    Debt capacity
    Bank loan possibility
    Stock sales
    Tax situation

Exhibit 3.11 Checklist for Key Internal Factors (cont.)

- Leverage position
- Government assistance
- Financial planning
- Cost control

Marketing
- Product quality
- Service
- Market research
- Sales force
- Pricing
- Advertising/promotion
- Warranty
- Image
- Distribution channel
- Brand loyalty/goodwill
- Product line
- Concentration of sales
- Market share
- Growth rate
- Competition

Production, research and development
- Plant facilities
- Raw material
- New product designs
- Scheduling efficiency
- Quality control
- Basic research
- Equipment/inventory
- Product life cycle
- Research and development

Technology/Capability
- Technological development
- Patent development
- Innovation in products and processes

Management
- Organization structure
- Planning system
- Communication system
- Control
- Organization climate, culture
- Top management
- Responsiveness to change
- Social responsibility

Review Questions

1. Why is internal organizational analysis so important in the strategic planning process?
2. Outline some important areas that need to be analyzed in performing an internal organizational analysis.
3. In what way can a corporation's distinctive competence act as internal strengths or weaknesses?
4. Identify the critical success factors of the airline industry. What are the implications for strategic planning?
5. What is Strategic Business Unit? Select an organization and identify some of its strategic business units.
6. Do you agree with Chandler's notion "structure follows strategy"? Elaborate.
7. Try to find an organization which you are familiar with. Describe its culture.
8. Discuss how an organization can integrate its strategy and culture.
9. What is the basic concept behind Porter's value chain?
10. Describe the relationship between Porter's value chain and strategic management.

Endnotes

1. Rockart, J.F., Chief Executives Define Their Own Data Needs, *Harvard Business Review*, Vol. 57, No. 2, 1979, pp. 81–93.
2. Chandler, A.B., *Strategy and Structure: Chapters in the history of the industrial enterprises*, Cambridge, MA: MIT Press, 1962.
3. Peters, T.J. and R.H. Waterman, Jr., *In Search of Excellence: Lessons from America's best-run companies*, New York: Harper & Row, 1981.
4. Chandler, A.B., Strategy Follow Structure: Developing distinctive skills, *California Management Review*, Vol. 26, No. 3, 1984, pp. 111–125.
5. Westwood, R.I., Organizational Rationale and Structure, in *Organizational Behaviour: Southeast Asia perspectives*, London: Longman, 1992, pp. 93–117.
6. Cumings, B., The Origins and Development of the Northeast Asian Political Economy: Industrial sectors, product cycles, and political consequences, *International Organization*, Vol. 38, 1984, pp. 1–40.
7. Deal, E. and A.A. Kennedy, *Corporate Cultures*, Reading MA: Addison-Wesley, 1985.
8. Smircich, L., Concepts of Culture and Organizational Analysis, *Administrative Science Quarterly*, Vol. 28, 1983, pp. 339–358.
9. Schien, E., *Organizational Culture and Leadership,* San Francisco: Jossey-Bass, 1985, p. 9.
10. Barney, J., Organizational Culture: Can it be a source of competitive advantage? *Academy of Management Review*, Vol. 11, 1986, pp. 656–665.
11. Wallach, R., Individual and Organizations: The cultural match, *Training and Development Journal*, February 1983, pp. 29–36.
12. Harrison, R. and H. Stokes, *Diagnosing Organization Culture*, San Diego, CA: Pfeiffer & Co., 1992.
13. Robbins, S.P., *Essentials of Organizational Behaviors,* 4th ed., Englewood Cliffs, NJ: Prentice-Hall, 1984.
14. Whitley, R.D., Eastern Asian Enterprise Structure and the Comparative Analysis of the Forms of Business Organization, *Organization Studies*, Vol. 11, No. 1, 1990, pp. 47–74.

15. Redding, S.G., G.Y.Y. Wong, S.K.W. Tam and A.K.O. Yeung, Management Practices in Hong Kong, Ming Kwok Ping Data Bank Working Paper, University of Hong Kong, 1986.
16. Tam, S., Centrifugal Versus Centripetal Growth Processes: Contrasting ideal types for conceptualising the developmental patterns of Chinese and Japanese firms, in S. Clegg and G. Redding (Eds.), *Capitalism in Contrasting Cultures*, Berlin: de Gruyter, 1989.
17. Van Horne, J.C., *Financial Management and Policy*, Englewood Cliffs, NJ: Prentice-Hall, 1986.
18. Choi, F.D.S., A. Jino, S.K. Min, S.O. Nam, J. Ujiie and A.I. Stonehill, Analysing Foreign Financial Statements: The use and misuse of international ratio analysis, *Journal of International Business Studies*, Spring/Summer 1983, pp. 113–131.
19. Manson, E.S., et al., *The Economic and Social Modernization of the Republic of Korea*, Cambridge, MA: Harvard University Press, 1980.
20. Anderson, C.R. and F.T. Paine, PIMS—A reexamination, *Academy of Management Review*, Vol. 3, 1978, p. 603.
21. Kotler, P., *Marketing Management*, 7th ed., Englewood, Cliffs, NJ: Prentice-Hall, 1984.
22. Hayes, R.H. and S.G. Wheelwright, The Dynamics of Process-Product Life Cycle, *Harvard Business Review*, March–April 1979, pp. 127–136.
23. Stone, Eric, Tricks of the Japan Trade: Asian companies are learning how to sell to the Japanese, *Asian Business*, February 1992, pp. 20–25.
24. Morishma, M., Why Can Japan be Successful? *Critical Sociologist*, 1984, p. 12 (in Chinese).
25. Hax, A.C. and N.S. Majuf, Competitive Cost Dynamic: The experience curve, in A.C. Hax (Ed.), *Readings on Strategic Management*, Cambridge, MA: Ballinger, 1984, pp. 49–60.
26. Porter, M.E., *Competitive Advantage: Creating and sustaining superior performance*, New York: The Free Press, 1985, p. 37.

CHAPTER 4

STRATEGY FORMULATION

*The natural formation of the country
 is the soldier's best ally; but a power of
estimating the adversary, of controlling
 the forces of victory, and shrewdly
calculating the difficulties, dangers and distances,
 constitutes the test of a great general.*
—Sun Tzu

*What is of supreme importance in war is
 to attack the enemy's strategy. Next best
is to disrupt his alliances.* —Sun Tzu

Introduction

The strategic planning process, in order to be successful, must begin with the corporate mission statement, which defines the nature and scope of the business, as noted in Chapter 1. It should provide vision and direction for the organization for ten to twenty years ahead, while obviously being reviewable (and reviewed) all the time. The mission statement must be brief, clear, and understandable by everyone within the organization. One possible guideline for evaluation of a mission statement is that it should clearly specify the business by addressing three key elements—**what** it offers to the marketplace, **whom** it aims to serve, and **how** it intends to do so.

Strategic planning is dependent upon the gathering and assessment of information pertaining to both the external and internal environments. The former includes all macroenvironmental forces, such as economic, technological, political, and cultural/social forces. In addition, it is crucial that an industry and competitive analysis be performed to identify the opportunities for and threats to the firm. An assessment of the firm's internal environment, including its corporate culture and organizational resources, will help to identify its strengths and weaknesses. All of these findings should be synthesized into a summary of the strategic situation, so that an appropriate corporate strategy may be chosen.

Although planning activities may be conducted on different levels, specific attention should first be given to corporate strategic planning, which involves long-range planning undertaken by top management. Once the organization's mission and long-range goals have been set, they form the framework within which planning by different business units and functional departments may be undertaken.

This chapter addresses the formulation of organizational, business, and functional strategies. Generic corporate strategy alternatives and portfolio models will be presented first in the discussion of organizational strategies. The formulation of business strategies utilizing Porter's generic strategic approaches is then addressed. Finally, functional strategies are discussed. The strategic planning process should also address more specific issues related to the implementation, evaluation, and control of the chosen strategies. These aspects must necessarily be considered if the strategies are to be successfully implemented in the real world, and are discussed in Chapter 5.

Organizational Strategy Formulation

Generic Corporate Strategy Alternatives

A number of generic corporate strategy alternatives exist for the firm interested in building and managing a diversified portfolio. As mentioned, the alternative which proves to be optimal would obviously depend upon the assessment of the firm's strategic position. Each of these options will be described and supported by Asia-Pacific examples where appropriate.

(i) **Concentration.** A firm which undertakes a concentration strategy focuses on a single business, and develops its distinctive competence within one particular industry. The obvious advantages of such a strategy are directional clarity and unity, i.e., financial and human resources need not be divided among different strategic business units.

Concentration, however, also poses some risks; macroenvironmental forces may change, thus making the external situation unattractive for the firm. For example, changing customer needs or availability of product substitutes may lead to decreased demand levels. Thus, the risk of putting all one's eggs in one basket may be quite high.

McDonald's, which concentrates on the fast-food industry, benefits from its accumulated experience and distinctive competence on a global level. Seven of the top ten McDonald's outlets (with respect to sales) are located in Hong Kong. Its success in the Hong Kong market indicates the popularity of western food and the demand for high-convenience items. However, macroenvironmental forces such as the economy, cultural values, etc., could easily change, and thus present either opportunities for threats to McDonald's in the future.

(ii) **Growth strategies.** If an organization has a primary objective of growth with respect to sales, profits, market share, etc., then it may choose to use any number of growth strategies. Two strategies, vertical integration and horizontal integration, are discussed in this section. Diversification, another growth strategy, is addressed separately in the following section.

When a firm pursues vertical integration, it extends its competitive scope within the same overall industry. It may engage in backward integration by expanding its range of activities backward into its supply sources. For example, it may purchase a firm which supplies it at the present time, or build a plant to manufacture its own component parts. Alternatively, it may wish to move closer to the end users or ultimate consumers of its product, thus engaging in forward integration. The manufacturer which moves into wholesaling and/or retailing is an example of this growth strategy.

The establishment of effective and efficient distribution channels involves a balance between cooperation and conflict. Independent parties may have different objectives, which may lead to a great deal of conflict. Vertical integration allows a firm to secure more control, and perhaps greater competitive advantage.

Giordano Holdings, a casual wear retailer with operations throughout Asia, has been marked by strong earnings growth and share price increases.[1] The projected sales and profit increases for its home market of Hong Kong are more conservative, given its present distribution channel, which includes thirty-seven outlets. With eleven outlets in Singapore, it has reached close to market saturation. Contributions by its five outlets in Malaysia and nine in the Philippines are negligible.

Giordano's founder, Jimmy Lai, has recently entered into a joint venture (Tiger Enterprises) in order to develop wholesale and retail distribution throughout the People's Republic of China. Tiger has licences to manufacture, retail, and wholesale in China. Operations in China will focus on distribution and wholesaling. The wholesale business is expected to be double the retail operation as its products become more popular. Thus, Giordano's emphasis on a relatively narrow product line and its vertical integration have helped it to achieve economies of scale.

Horizontal (or lateral) integration involves growth through the acquisition of other firms in the same, or a similar, line of business and at the same level of the distribution channel. Organizations which integrate horizontally usually do so in order to increase sales or market share.

The use of both vertical and horizontal integration strategies allows the firm to stay within the scope of its existing product-market area, although in some cases the definition of its business may be slightly altered.

(iii) Diversification. When a firm chooses to move into areas other than its present line of business, a diversification growth strategy is undertaken. Concentric or related diversification is the acquisition of firms which have similarities to the existing business. Such commonalities may exist with respect to products offered, markets served, technologies utilized, etc. Thus, some strategic fit is maintained, and there is generally a sharing of costs and subsequently an increased competitive advantage.

Goldlion Holdings, a Hong Kong-based manufacturer of men's neckties, accessories, and apparel, has undertaken this strategy.[2] The company has recently diversified into the manufacture of men's garments and leather goods, as well as the manufacture and sales of men's shoes and ladies' handbags.

The acquisition of a firm in a totally new and unrelated line of business is referred to as conglomerate or unrelated diversification. This strategy offers many advantages, including minimal dependence upon any one business, risk minimization, and stable profitability. Organizations which engage in conglomeration will venture into any profitable business; this captures the essence of the truly diversified firm. Although such a diversification strategy may help to spread the risks undertaken by the firm, it also requires vast financial and management resources. Portfolio management may prove to be very challenging for organizations which choose to grow in this manner, and several portfolio models are described in a later section of this chapter.

Many firms have chosen this strategy in order to reduce risk. One industry which provides several good examples is that of women's undergarments. Competition has become extremely fierce during the last decade, and profits have dropped steadily since 1982.[3] The Wacoal company is the best-known Japanese manufacturer of women's underwear, employing 5000 people at home and embracing overseas operations in China, Thailand, Indonesia, and the US. The majority of Wacoal's sales is still generated by underwear, but it has diversified into other areas such as car design and health food production. Although Wacoal is considered to be geographically the most diversified of all Japanese undergarment makers, its overseas operations contribute less than 10 per cent of the group's profits and sales. The new non-core businesses are still losing money. Gunze, a traditional lingerie manufacturer, has moved into plastics and gardening products while another competitor, Atsugi Nylon, now makes textile machinery and houses.

Siam Cement Company is another relevant example. It is the largest cement producer in Southeast Asia.[4] Presently holding about 65 per cent market share in Thailand, it has been expanding the capacity of its existing businesses as part of its growth strategy. Siam Cement Company has also been involved in conglomerate diversification, venturing into areas such as television components and petrochemicals.

A final example is the Sembawang Group.[5] The management has plans of diversifying from its core business of ship repair into areas such as aviation and financial services. Its strategy is to continue to emphasize this core business, but launch new businesses to either complement it, or take advantage of profitable shipping routes in the Southeast Asia region.

(iv) Abandonment, divestiture, and liquidation.

When an organization finds that it is not operating efficiently or competing effectively, this category of strategies may be undertaken. If a particular line of business is no longer appealing, and the firm wishes to abandon it, then it should usually be divested as soon as possible in order to minimize the losses.

Divestiture, as a second strategy, involves either selling the business outright or setting it up as a separate corporation which may still be partially owned by the parent company. The divestiture of poor performers (or "dogs") often improves the organization's financial position.

In the event that a business seems irreparable, and beyond hope, liquidation may be the most appropriate strategy. The assets are sold, and the business is terminated. For a single-business firm, such a move may be very painful and unpleasant, but it is much less so for multibusiness firms. Liquidation is generally undesirable, since it results in losses for both employees and stockholders. In the long run, however, it may prove to be more beneficial than the alternative, i.e., bankruptcy.

Many Japanese companies made very significant investments in the US during the second half of the 1980s. However, the present recession, combined with the collapse of Japan's "bubble" economy, have forced these firms to reassess the growth potential of their US investment strategies.[6] MITI data shows that the earnings of Japanese companies in North America have decreased over the past few years, and the amount of foreign direct investment in the US has subsequently plummeted as well. Several foreign automobile manufacturers have pulled out of the US market, or have intentions of doing so shortly. Daihatsu Motor Company, Peugeot, and Rover have all withdrawn.

(v) Turnaround, retrenchment, and restructuring. Corporations which experience poor performance should first perform a thorough diagnosis of the situation in order to determine the underlying reasons for the lackluster performance. Once these have been identified, a number of turnaround strategies may be undertaken if the firm has not yet reached a critical stage. Turnaround strategies involve the trimming of operations in order to increase efficiencies, and may include different actions, depending upon the urgency of the situation.

Retrenchment is a strategy of pulling back and taking internal economy measures in order to ride out the storm of adverse conditions. This strategy typically results in an organization becoming less broadly diversified and thus operating within a narrower set of industry groups.

Japan's steelmakers (Nippon Steel, NKK, Kobe Steel, Sumitomo Metal, and Kawasaki Steel) are considered to be members of a "sunset industry" which has seen its day. They have been affected by a number of macroenvironmental forces including sluggish domestic demand, rising financing costs, and fierce competition. In order to retain their positions as the most efficient steel producers in the world, they have cut their labour forces dramatically and reduced their debts through new equity financing.[7]

When an organization makes radical changes in the mix or emphasis of its business portfolio, a set of restructuring strategies may be chosen. These strategies may involve both divestitures and acquisitions, which are often undertaken simultaneously. The resulting portfolio should display greater strategic fit than its predecessor. This strategy is very common at the present time, perhaps due to economic (i.e., recession) and other macroenvironmental conditions.

The US consumer electronics industry has been very depressed in recent years,[8] resulting in very noticeable restructuring. Toshiba has abandoned the manufacture of audio equipment, microwave ovens, and other goods to focus its efforts and resources on large-screen televisions. NEC Corporation has withdrawn from consumer electronics and shifted back to its core business, i.e., industrial electronics. Many firms, including Hitachi, Zenith, Samsung, and Bridgestone, have been involved in relocating and restructuring their operations.

(vi) Combinations. The strategy alternatives described above need not be used in isolation. Many large, diversified firms may find it most appropriate to implement a number of them simultaneously. Business portfolio models, introduced in the next section, may be employed to coordinate various business-level strategies and thus formulate a consistent overall corporate strategy.

Business Portfolio Models

Boston Consulting Group Growth-Share Matrix

The Boston Consulting Group's approach is a product portfolio model which uses the strategic business unit (SBU) as the unit of analysis.[9] An SBU is an organizational unit within a larger company which focuses its efforts on some product-market and is treated as a separate profit centre. The BCG matrix is composed of four quadrants, based on two variables—the relative market share and the industry growth rate (see Exhibit 4.1).

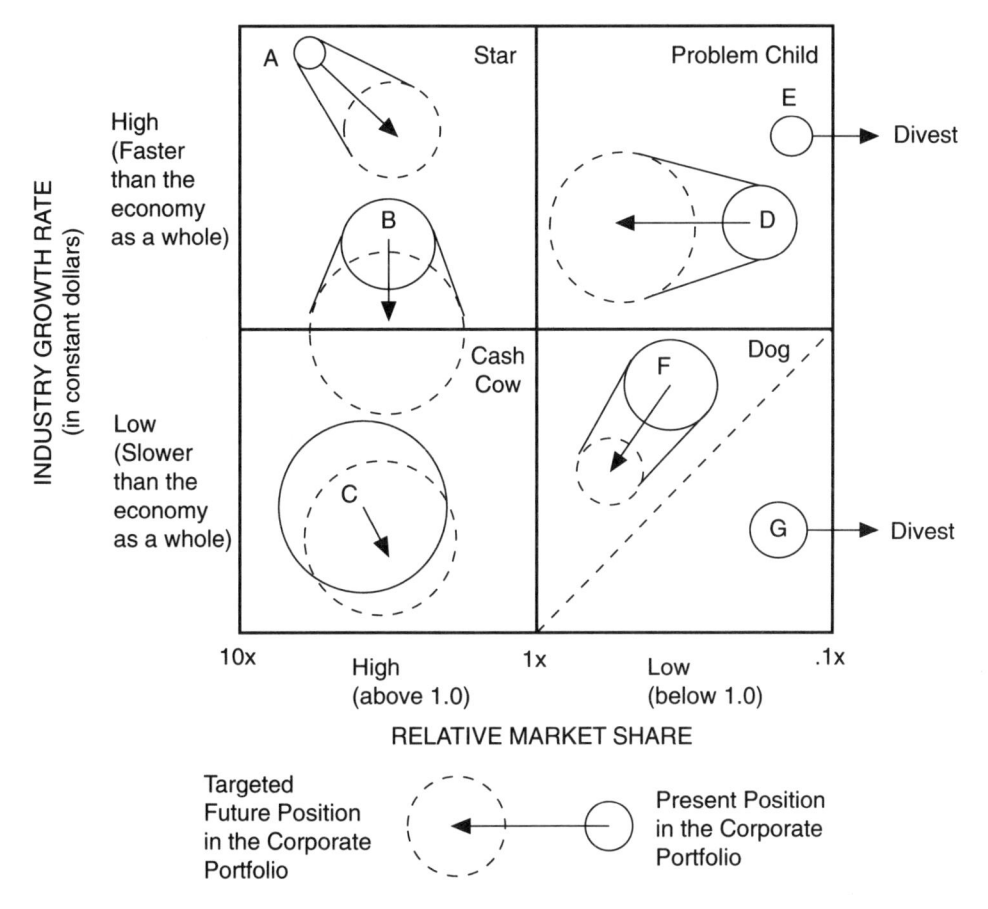

Exhibit 4.1 Boston Consulting Group Growth-Share Matrix

The first variable represents the SBU's market share relative to that of its largest competitor. Using this definition, the leader in its field has a relative share greater than 1.0, while that of followers is less than 1.0. The second variable, the industry growth rate, is corrected for inflation, and is divided into high and low levels.

In some cases, this may correlate with the growth and maturity stages, respectively, of the product life cycle. The distinction between high and low growth is arbitrarily set at 10 per cent. Each SBU's contribution to the organization in terms of dollar sales is represented by the area or diameter of the circle drawn. The product portfolio model often shows not only the present positions of its SBUs, but the forecasted positions as well.

Interpretation of the BCG matrix is based upon several rules of thumb. Margins and cash generated are a function of market share. Those firms with the highest shares tend to be most profitable, primarily due to economies of scale and experience curve effects. High market share, however, does not occur naturally; it must be earned or bought. Growth, on the other hand, requires cash input to finance added assets. No product market can grow indefinitely, so the strategist's job becomes very challenging at a certain point. Thus, it is obvious that relative market share is associated with cash generation, while industry growth rate is related to cash utilization.

Relative market share and industry growth rate are used to classify each SBU into one of four categories:

1. Cash cows. SBUs in this category use little cash due to their low growth rates, but generate a great deal of cash because of their strong market positions. Thus, they have a competitive advantage with respect to costs and profits.

2. Dogs. Both growth and relative positions of SBUs in this quadrant are low. They are competitively disadvantaged, and may often be cash traps, creating negative value for their organizations.

3. Question marks (problem children). Although the SBUs in this quadrant are faced with high growth industries, they have not yet achieved competitive advantage. Without the needed cash for growth, they could potentially slip into the dog category when industry growth slows.

4. Stars. These SBUs require a great deal of cash due to the high industry growth rate. However, their relative market shares are also high so they generate a substantial amount of cash as well.

Optimally, an organization should have a balanced product portfolio. The cash thrown off by its cash cows should be applied to question marks in order to improve their relative market shares. Once this has been accomplished, they become stars, which then ultimately fall into the cash cow category when the industry growth rates slow down. These products then become the support basis for new question marks. This cycle of cash flow is regarded as a success sequence.

The BCG approach is relatively straightforward and easy to use, but it has a number of drawbacks. The entire analysis is based upon two factors only, and neglects a number of other factors such as those considered in the General Electric strategic planning grid (see discussion below). Thus, it may wrongfully present an oversimplified situation. Although relative market share and industry growth rate may be quantitatively measured, the dividing lines between high and low levels of each variable are arbitrarily set. Once an organization's portfolio has been analyzed using this approach, management may use it to balance cash utilization and cash generation by its various SBUs. However, strategic implications may not be readily apparent to strategists using this tool.

General Electric Strategic Planning Grid

General Electric's strategic planning grid is yet another product portfolio model which has gained wide acceptance.[10] It is also used as a tool to assess the relative positions of the various SBUs within an organization's portfolio. The GE and BCG approaches have many similarities, but at the same time have some distinguishing characteristics as well. The GE stoplight approach, like the BCG approach, uses two factors for analysis, industry attractiveness and business strengths. Unlike the BCG approach, however, each of these is a complex combination of various individual elements, as suggested in Exhibit 4.2.[11] The variables used in the BCG approach, relative market share and industry growth rate, are also considered, but are given much less weight in this model. In addition to being more complex, this approach also stipulates three levels (high, medium, and low) for each factor, rather than the dichotomous levels used in the BCG approach.

Exhibit 4.2 General Electric Strategic Planning Grid

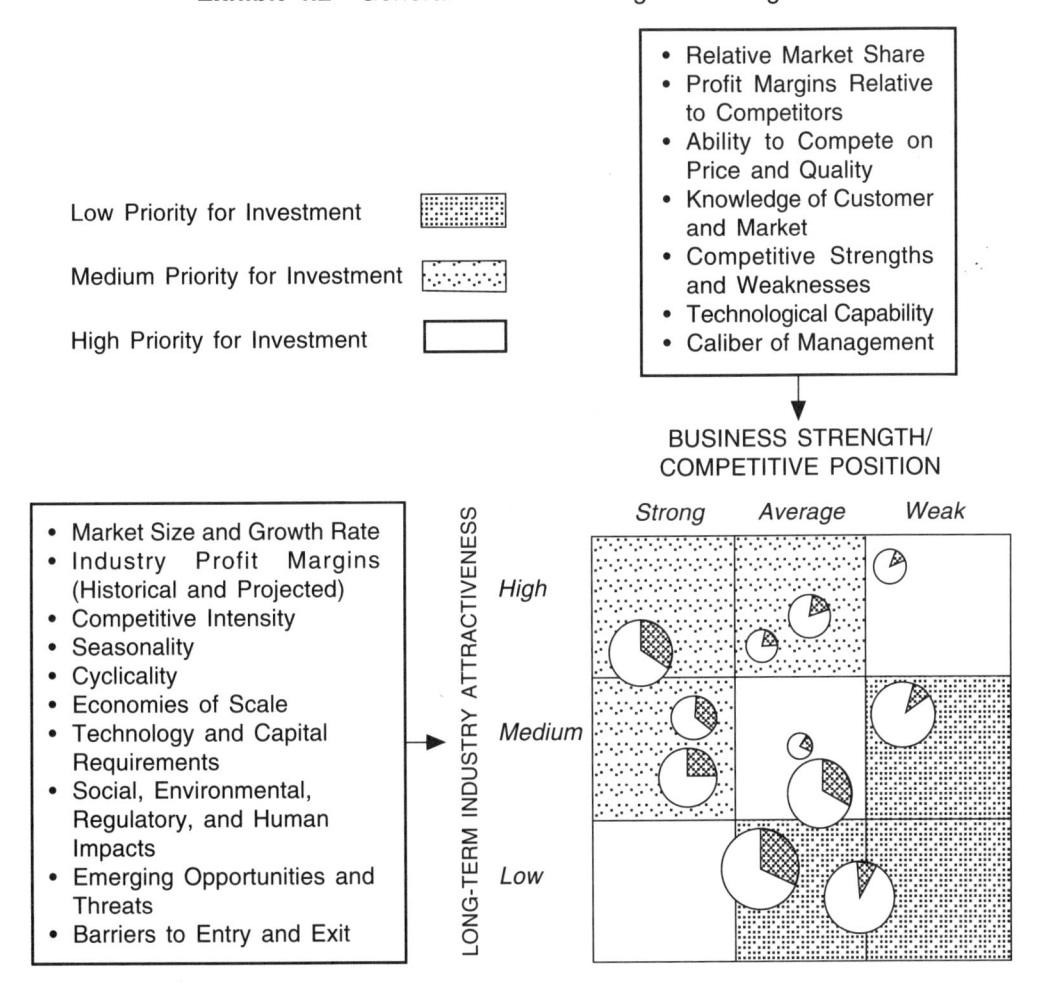

- Relative Market Share
- Profit Margins Relative to Competitors
- Ability to Compete on Price and Quality
- Knowledge of Customer and Market
- Competitive Strengths and Weaknesses
- Technological Capability
- Caliber of Management

Low Priority for Investment

Medium Priority for Investment

High Priority for Investment

BUSINESS STRENGTH/ COMPETITIVE POSITION

Strong   Average   Weak

LONG-TERM INDUSTRY ATTRACTIVENESS: High, Medium, Low

- Market Size and Growth Rate
- Industry Profit Margins (Historical and Projected)
- Competitive Intensity
- Seasonality
- Cyclicality
- Economies of Scale
- Technology and Capital Requirements
- Social, Environmental, Regulatory, and Human Impacts
- Emerging Opportunities and Threats
- Barriers to Entry and Exit

Although the additional variables do make this stoplight approach more reflective of the real world and thus more useful, the quantitative measurement of the variables is much more difficult. GE's strategic planning grid is more subjective in nature, and requires much more time and effort to analyze. Several rounds may be needed before consensus is reached by top management.

The positioning of an SBU on the GE grid, however, automatically indicates the strategy to be undertaken. If industry attractiveness and business strength are both high, then the organization is faced with a green light, and should expand. The same is true if the SBU is high with respect to one factor and medium with respect to the other. On the opposite extreme, low industry attractiveness and low business strength indicate that a red light exists, and the SBU should be harvested. The three categories along the diagonal of the grid represent a yellow light, and thus a maintenance strategy should be used. These strategic implications are obvious, and are perhaps the greatest advantage of this strategic planning grid.

Business Strategy Formulation

Once the overall organizational strategy has been formulated, attention should be given to the next level that is, specific business units. Michael Porter's competitive analysis is very useful here in assessing the situation faced by the organization.[12]

The five competitive forces—the threat of new entrants, the bargaining power of customers, the bargaining power of suppliers, the threat of substitute products or services, and the jockeying among current contestants—have been discussed in detail in Chapter 2.

In creating and defending its competitive position within a given industry, an organization may choose among three generic strategic approaches—overall cost leadership, differentiation, and focus. These three strategic approaches are shown in Exhibit 4.3, and are distinguished by their strategic advantages and strategic targets.[13]

Exhibit 4.3 Generic Strategic Approaches

	Uniqueness Perceived by the Customer	Low Cost Position
Industrywide	Differentiation	Overall Cost Leadership
Particular Segment Only	Focus	

STRATEGIC ADVANTAGE (columns)
STRATEGIC TARGET (rows)

Overall Cost Leadership

Cost leadership entails attention to cost control. Reduced costs may result from different aspects of the business, including economies of scale in production, lower raw material costs, reduced overhead, experience curve effects, and many others. Regardless of the source of its low cost position, however, management must not overlook essential issues such as product quality and supplementary services to be offered.

An organization which has a high relative market share may be most likely to pursue an over-all cost leadership strategy. The industry leader is generally more profitable, due to its higher level of efficiency in production. This strategy also allows a firm to protect itself to a certain extent from all five competitive forces mentioned previously.

Several skills and resources, as well as organizational requirements, are required for the successful implementation of this strategy.

Commonly required skills and resources are:

- Sustained capital investment and access to capital
- Process engineering skills
- Intense supervision of labour
- Products designed for ease in manufacture
- Low-cost distribution system

The common organizational requirements are:

- Tight cost control
- Frequent, detailed control reports
- Structured organization and responsibilities
- Incentives based on meeting strict quantitative targets

There are also some risks associated with overall cost leadership:

- Technological change that nullifies past investments or learning
- Low-cost learning by industry newcomers or followers through imitation or through their ability to invest in state-of-the-art facilities
- Inability to see required product or marketing change because of the attention placed on cost
- Inflation in costs that narrows the firm's ability to maintain enough of a price differential to offset competitors' brand images or other approaches to differentiation

Creative Technology Limited is a Singapore-based competitor in the sound card market.[14] It offers high-quality, value-added products to the mass market at low cost. Its strategy of minimizing unit costs has been accomplished through the use of in-house R&D, in-house chip design, vertically integrated manufacturing operations, and strict quality control. Creative Technology has also formed strategic alliances in order to shorten the product development cycle and broaden its product line.

Differentiation

Differentiation, the second generic strategy, involves the establishment of a unique position for a firm's product or service. It is important to point out that this uniqueness must exist in the minds of its customers, and may or may not be a true distinction from competitive products. Differentiation may be achieved through unique product attributes, distribution channels, or any other component of the marketing mix.

Japan's domestic consumer products market is already saturated, and the manufacturing technologies used by all competitors are more or less the same. Therefore, many Japanese manufacturers have begun to use design-centred strategies, selling looks rather than function or price.[15] As a differentiating factor, design may be a visual manifestation of product quality, and may even become the most essential part of the product itself, especially if this is a focus of the advertising and promotional effort. This trend is highly evident in the product offerings of firms such as Nissan, Sony, Canon, Yamaha, and Hitachi.

Another example of differentiation involves The Loft, a unique retailing concept introduced by Seibu Department Store, a Japanese retail giant.[16] Novel and creative displays of goods are presented in an open-plan warehouse design. Although many of the products are functional everyday items, the colourful and entertaining approach leads to volume sales. The shop in Hong Kong features five floors, each with a distinctive theme, such as "Planet Living" (kitchenware, home accessories), "Communicating" (gift items, greeting cards), "Moving" (games, luggage), "Brain Working" (stationery, office supplies), and "Art Working" (drawing equipment, magazines). Differentiation has been achieved through a concept of fun, and products are unique with respect to design, colour, shape, or material.

Once an organization has successfully differentiated its product, it may find that its customers' demand is relatively inelastic. Therefore, it may be able to charge a higher price, and thus increase its profit margin. In some industries, however, differentiation may entail a trade-off with costs, especially when the establishment of a unique position requires costly activities such as research and development or increased promotional efforts.

This may apply to competitors in the airline industry. Many companies are already making attempts to differentiate their inflight entertainment, as well as other services to be made available in the near future.[17] Northwest Airlines has made the largest commitment, and intends to spend US$450 million to improve services for all passengers. It has installed in its international fleet a sophisticated system called WorldLink which includes movies, video games, flight information, inflight shopping catalogues, and news broadcasts via satellite. Although the installation of such a system is very costly, it may also generate revenues through advertising spots in the programme material, and through inflight sales of duty-free items. Like all such differentiation efforts, however, competitors can copy it. There may, however, be a distinct advantage in being first, and there is always a definite need to think of the next step in the game, i.e., keeping one step ahead of the competitors.

The commonly required skills and resources and common organizational requirements associated with differentiation are listed below.[18]

Commonly required skills and resources are:

- Strong marketing abilities
- Product engineering
- Creative flair
- Strong capability in basic research
- Corporate reputation for quality or technological leadership
- Long tradition in the industry or unique combination of skills drawn from other businesses
- Strong cooperation from channels

The common organizational requirements are:

- Strong coordination among functions in R&D, product development, and marketing
- Subjective measurement and incentives instead of quantitative measures
- Amenities to attract highly skilled labour, scientists, or creative people

Differentiation, unfortunately, also involves a number of risks. Some of these are:

- The cost differential between low-cost competitors and the differentiated firm becomes too great for differentiation to hold brand loyalty.
- Buyers' need for the differentiating factor falls.
- Imitation narrows perceived differentiation, a common occurrence as industries mature.

Focus

Overall cost leadership and differentiation are strategic alternatives which are targeted at the entire industry. A focus strategy, on the other hand, is targeted only at a particular segment, and may incorporate either one or both of the previously mentioned approaches. This strategy focuses on the effective and efficient provision of a product or service. A firm which undertakes a focus strategy may wish to target a particular segment which has few competitors, and/or which is the least vulnerable to substitutes.

Pacific Island Club[19] is developing holiday resorts targeted at young, upwardly mobile Asian professionals. For example, its first resort on Guam catered mainly to Japanese tourists. Its packages are all-inclusive, and offer "casual yet chic hotel accommodation in exotic tropical settings, combined with unlimited leisure activities and fine dining". PIC's niche is different from that of Club Med, its French competitor which aims to attract twenty- to forty-year-old affluent Asians in the $3^1/_2$- to 4-star hotel bracket. While Club Med encourages its guests to participate in social and outdoor activities, PIC's approach is to let its guests do as they wish.

In the hotel industry, services and facilities offered by different competitors are very similar, so a focus strategy may be absolutely necessary for success.[20] At the lower end of the market, price is usually the most important factor. The further upmarket the hotel moves, however, the more easily it stands out. The Palace Hotel in Beijing was very successful in creating brand awareness among its potential clients long before it opened for business. This was accomplished primarily through the use of different promotional elements.

In November 1992, Choice Hotels was established as a joint venture between CDL Hotels International and Choice Hotels International of the US.[21] This Singapore-US group is focusing on the mid-range segment, i.e., three- to four-star properties. It believes that the desire for convenience and a fair cost, as well as an increase in the number of businessmen travelling around the Asian region, make this a very lucrative market segment.

Given that the focus strategy is a combination of the first two generic approaches, the skills, resources, and organizational requirements are simply combinations of those mentioned above for the previous strategies. The risks associated with the focus strategy include:[22]

- The cost differential between broad-range competitors and the focused firm widens to eliminate the cost advantages of serving a narrow target or to offset the differentiation achieved by focus.
- The differences in desired products or services between the strategic target and the market as a whole narrow down.
- Competitors find submarkets within the strategic target and outfocus the focuser.

The foregoing discussion seems to imply that every SBU within an organization should choose only one of the generic strategic approaches mentioned. There are, however, a number of dangers associated with specialization, i.e., the exclusive pursuit of a single generic strategy, be it cost leadership or differentiation. The disadvantages of strategic specialization include possible gaps or weaknesses in product offerings, oversight of important customer needs, ease of imitation by competitors, inflexibility, and narrow organizational vision.

Thus, firms should, whenever possible, seek to minimize these dangers by implementing mixed strategies. The combination of differentiation with cost-effectiveness gives a firm more flexibility, and makes it more difficult for competitors to imitate. Mixed strategies, however, may not be suitable for all conditions, but are preferred in the following situations:

- Customers are concerned about many product attributes.
- Competitors find it easy to imitate pure strategies.
- There is no conflict in achieving different aspects of the strategy.
- Fluctuating customer preferences and rival offerings demand a broader range of skills.
- The firm has become too narrowly focused around a single aspect of strategy and requires more openness and heterogeneity to ward off stagnation.
- Industries are relatively mature and differentiation by innovative products or economical processes is more difficult.

On some occasions, a pure, generic strategy may still be preferable to a mixed strategy. For example, a major market segment may have an overriding preference for a single feature such as price or quality. If the segments and preferences are stable and relatively difficult for competitors to serve, then a pure strategy may be best. Strategic specialization may also be necessary when multiple strategies are truly incompatible (e.g., high quality and low cost). Thus, managers should consider a number of issues in determining whether a single generic strategy or a broader, mixed approach would be more appropriate.[23]

Functional Strategy Formulation

Once corporate and business strategies have been developed, attention should be directed to the last level, that of functional strategies. Management must integrate the strategies of various functions, including marketing, finance, production, and R&D, in order to achieve consistency.

The marketing strategy must begin with a designation of the target segment and the specific needs to be met by the firm. The subsequent development of product, price, promotion, and distribution strategies will obviously have implications for the other functional areas. Product modifications, for example, may require more R&D or changes in the production processes. The pricing strategy will naturally have an effect on financial aspects.

Adequate financial resources are critical for success. Substantial sums are often required for research and development and the launch of new products. Intense competition may require great financial commitments, often just for survival. Firms which operate in international markets are also subject to foreign exchange fluctuations, which further complicate strategic issues.

The production strategy must take human resources and operations into consideration. An organization should try to produce high-quality products at low cost. As already mentioned, the industry leader is likely to be most effective and most efficient, due to scale economies and experience curve effects. However, every firm, regardless of its competitive stance, should strive to achieve a strategic optimum between quality and cost. This can be accomplished through attention to quality control and other aspects of production.

R&D provides the foundation for an organization's offerings. Although the benefits of R&D may not be obvious in the short term, it is an absolutely crucial activity for maintaining one's competitive position. Technological innovations must be integrated with the marketer's understanding of his potential customers' needs. Technological developments, per se, are not of great importance. It is the utilization and application of technology to address consumer needs which is the most critical.

This brief discussion aims to emphasize the need for coordination among all the functional strategies. They should all strive to achieve the same corporate goal, and be consistent with both corporate and business strategies developed at higher organizational levels. For a more detailed treatment of this topic, please refer to the discussion of the internal environment in Chapter 3.

Distinguishing Characteristics of Asian Strategies

The discussion in this chapter has concentrated upon the formulation of strategies from a western perspective. However, it appears that several Asian countries are faced with environments which necessitate the modification of traditional western strategies. A number of these countries are discussed below.

China

Demographically and economically speaking, China appears to be a very promising market for the future. Foreign investors have found that the PRC's political system, however, operates quite differently from the systems of other countries. McKinsey and Company, a management consulting firm, has conducted a survey of the top-performing multinationals presently operating in China.

The leading MNCs are moving into the PRC very aggressively in order to establish dominant market shares so as to preempt the entry of their big rivals. Having gone through the learning process, many MNCs are now moving into the second stage of involvement in China, i.e., managing local partners, keeping business systems simple, and laying the organizational foundations for a nationwide presence. Rapid expansion in both size and number of Chinese ventures will result in approximately US$200 million foreign-invested capital by 1997.[24]

Since the MNCs are operating in an environment which is foreign to them, it is vital that they find and cultivate good local partners. Part of the difficulty is that there may be conflicts between the objectives of foreign companies and those of their local partners. Foreigners generally seek assistance in securing plant space, staff recruitment, raw material sourcing, and product marketing. In addition, others may be looking for access to project opportunities, markets, flexible rulings on the use of foreign exchange or state funds, and sometimes even fiscal concessions. Most would naturally also look for *guanxi*, or special relationships with those in power, which is essential for getting things done in China.

Chinese partners, on the other hand, are generally more interested in gaining access to technology, know-how, foreign exchange, and new jobs. Unfortunately, the value which they are able to add with respect to the marketing, finance, and management functions often falls short of the foreign companies' expectations. Therefore, it is not surprising that many foreign companies have begun to dilute the influence of their initial local partners.

Rather than concentrate on establishing relationships with the individual firms themselves, MNCs are beginning to liaise directly with the ultimate decision-making authorities. The industry associations, commissions, and bureaus which sit above operating partners act like protective and powerful "mothers". For MNCs, these potential "mothers-in-law" represent the best and shortest route to the permissions, tax concessions, guaranteed customers, and central funding which they need.[25]

Some MNCs have even gone one step further and begun to deal directly with central government authorities. Such a move seems especially appropriate when the industry in question is primarily under central government control and is felt to be of strategic importance by the Chinese leadership, and the MNC can provide a clear value proposition. For example, both AT&T and Northern Telecom have signed agreements with the State Planning Commission to develop a nationwide, multiventure presence which encompasses all of their product lines.[26]

Japan

Japan's phenomenal business success may be attributed to a number of elements such as political, economic, and cultural factors. Lee Iacocca of the Chrysler Corporation attributes Japan's success almost entirely to its political and economic systems. He argues that Japanese industry is backed to the hilt by its close relationship with the government in the form of MITI (Ministry of International Trade and Industry).[27] The development of Japan's semiconductor industry illustrates this point well. As the semiconductor industry grew, it evolved in such a way as to promote linkages with other Japanese firms and prevent tie-ups with non-Japanese firms. In the mid-1970s Japan's MITI launched its VLSI (very large scale integration) projects, which involved preferential access to capital, government-sponsored research, strategies for licensing technology from foreign (mainly American) suppliers, and other means to help Japanese producers overcome the foreign lead in high technology production.[28]

Iacocca contends that Japan's economic destiny is not left to the free play of a laissez-faire economy. Its taxes are the lowest among all industrial countries in the world, owing largely to Japan's low defense spending. Time and again the visitor to Japan hears the phrases "confusion in the market" and "excessive competition"—shorthand for the dangers of letting market forces get out of control. While the American approach emphasizes getting prices right, the Japanese approach emphasizes getting enough money and getting the nation's money into the hands of its big manufacturing firms. Thus, this is a view of capitalism which depends on capital.

Japan has a system of goals and priorities which allows government and industry to work together in order to achieve its national objectives. The government determines which industries are critical to Japan's future and then helps out in R&D. Michael Porter also believes that Japanese chip-makers succeeded mainly because they were quicker moving than their American competitors. The important factor driving the semiconductor industry was not only private companies, but a network of government-business interactions as well. "Government policies have shaped the course of international competition in microelectronics virtually from the inception of the industry, producing outcomes completely different than would have occurred through the operation of the market alone."[29]

Many Japanese executives also identify cultural factors as important determinants of success. Says Akio Morita, former chairman of Sony, "No (economic) theory or plan or government policy will make a business a success; that can only be done by people. The most important mission for a Japanese manager is to develop a healthy relationship with his employees, to create a family-like feeling within the corporation."[30]

The starting level of Japanese and American semiconductor production was similar, but Japan improved much more rapidly, due perhaps in part to its culture. The Japanese are united as a single people or race. In the US there are various ethnic groups with different backgrounds and religions and races, making it much more difficult for them to work together in harmony.

Keiretsu, tightly knit groupings of companies, have been mentioned earlier as major contributors to Japan's success. They help to spread risk, development, and quality control responsibilities between a major manufacturer and its exclusive suppliers. The concept of "triple teaming" has also used the strong collective nature of its culture to benefit Japanese firms. Under such a system, trading, manufacturing, and financing firms work collectively to share resources such as information and expertise. In the business arena, triple teaming is most effectively implemented by the keiretsu. It may range from very small affiliations to huge horizontally organized corporate networks which include the nation's largest and best-known companies.

With respect to management theory, American and Japanese managers also display some significant differences. Among the 7-S's of management (Chapter 3), American managers favour the hard S's (strategy, structure, and systems), while Japanese managers pay meticulous attention to the soft S's (staff, skills, style, and superordinate goals, i.e., shared values).

Korea

South Korea's growth is a classic example of late industrialization which has been based upon learning, i.e., borrowing foreign technology rather than generating new products or processes. Learners, by definition, do not innovate, and must compete initially on the combined basis of low wages, state subsidies, and incremental productivity and quality improvements related to existing products.

There are four elements common to all late industrializing countries:

1. A high degree of state intervention to get relative prices "wrong" in order to overcome penalties of lateness. The state intervenes with subsidies to deliberately distort relative prices in order to stimulate economic activity. In exchange for subsidies, the state imposes performance standards on private firms.
2. Growth of large diversified business groups to transcend the hardships of having to compete without advantages of novel technology. Below the level of the state, the agent of expansion in all late industrializing countries is the modern industrial enterprise, which is large in scale, multidivisional in scope, and administered by hierarchies of salaried managers. In Korea, the modern industrial enterprise takes the form of diversified business groups, or chaebols, whose size and diversity are similar to those of the zaibatsu, Japan's prewar big business groups.
3. Emergence of salaried managers responsible for exploiting borrowed technology. Salaried engineers are a key figure in late industrialization because they are the gatekeepers of foreign technology transfers.
4. Focus on shop-floor management to optimize technology transfer. While a strategic focus on the shop-floor may be a tendency in late industrialization, this tendency may be stronger, depending on the country. Turning now to production workers, late industrializing countries have exceptionally well-educated work forces in comparison to their earlier counterparts.

As a special case of late industrialization, Korea differs from most others in the discipline its state exercises over private firms. Discipline exerted by the state and the rise of big business are interactive. Big business consolidates its power in response to government's performance-based incentives. In exchange for outstanding performance in the areas of exports, R&D, or new product introduction, leading firms are rewarded with further licenses to expand, thus enlarging the scale of big business in general. For entering especially risky industries, the government rewards entrants with other industrial licenses in more lucrative sectors, thus furthering the development of the diversified business group in particular. State discipline thus penalizes the poor performers and rewards only the good ones.[31]

Review Questions

1. Cite an example of an Asian firm which has used horizontal integration as a generic corporate strategy. Has its product-market domain been altered as a result of this move?
2. Abandonment, divestiture, and liquidation are often undertaken in order to minimize losses when businesses are no longer appealing. Describe a firm which has chosen to use this option.
3. The Boston Consulting Group's growth share matrix and General Electric's strategic planning grid may be used for purposes of opportunity analysis. Which one appears to be more useful for strategic planning? Explain.
4. Apply the BCG product portfolio model to an MNC which is doing business in Asia. State any assumptions made.
5. Industry leaders often pursue an overall cost leadership strategy. Give an example of a global marketer which has successfully implemented this approach. Does it have the skills and resources required?
6. Is product differentiation difficult to achieve in an industry which is faced with strict regulations (e.g., financial services)?
7. Describe a firm which has been successful in using a focus strategy in the past, but has since lost that advantage to its competition.
8. In the development of functional strategies, a number of conflicts may arise. What measures may be taken in order to maximize cooperation and minimize conflict among different functions within a given organization?
9. An American organization wishing to do business in China for the first time will obviously have to contend with local competitors who may have long-established and trusted relationships (*guanxi*). How can the US firm overcome this competitive disadvantage?
10. Traditional western strategies must clearly be modified before they are implemented in Asian cultures. Do you believe that one set of Asian strategies can and should be developed? Explain.

Endnotes

1. Giordano Strategy Stitches Success, *South China Morning Post*, Business Post, Vol. XLVIII, No. 235, August 24, 1992, p. 3.
2. Chinese Ties Help Thriving Goldlion, *South China Morning Post*, Business Post, Vol. XLVIII, No. 298, October 26, 1992, p. 3.
3. Frills and Spills, *Far Eastern Economic Review*, Vol. 154, No. 46, November 14, 1991, pp. 69–70.

4. Strength in Reserve, *Far Eastern Economic Review*, Vol. 149, No. 28, July 12, 1990, pp. 66–68.
5. Globalising Cautiously, *Asian Business*, Vol. 28, No. 9, September 1992, p. 8.
6. Survive, Relocate or Withdraw? *Tokyo Business Today*, Vol. 60, No. 6, June 1992, pp. 18–21.
7. Virtue is Its Own Reward, *The Economist*, Vol. 315, No. 652, April 28, 1990, p. 79.
8. Survive, Relocate or Withdraw? *loc. cit.*
9. Stalk, George, Jr. and Thomas Hout, *Competing against Time*, New York: The Free Press, 1990, pp. 9–17.
10. Allen, Michael G., Diagramming G.E.'s Planning for What's WATT, in *Corporate Planning: Techniques and applications*, New York: Amacom, 1979.
11. Thompson, Arthur A., Jr. and A.J. Strickland III, *Strategy Formulation and Implementation*, 5th ed., Illinois: Richard D. Irwin, 1992.
12. Porter, Michael, How Competitive Forces Shape Strategy, *Harvard Business Review*, Vol. 57, No. 2, March–April 1979, pp. 137–145.
13. Porter, Michael, *Competitive Strategy: Techniques for analyzing industries and competitors*, New York: The Free Press, 1980, pp. 34–46.
14. R&D Investments Improve Singapore's Competitive Edge, *Computer Products*, February 1993, pp. 500–504.
15. Sold on the Looks, *Far Eastern Economic Review*, Vol. 147, No. 8, February 22, 1990, pp. 34–36.
16. A Lofty Idea Taking Shape, *Hong Kong Business*, Vol. 12, No. 128, February 1993, pp. 28–29.
17. Things to Come, *Far Eastern Economic Review*, Vol. 155, No. 8, February 27, 1992, pp. 44–45.
18. Porter, Michael, 1980, *op. cit.*
19. Formula for Fun in the Sun, *Asian Business*, Vol. 28, No. 1, January 1992, pp. 12–13.
20. Standing Out in the Crowd, *Asian Business*, Vol. 26, No. 2, February 1990, pp. 54–55.
21. Hotel JV Aims to Fill Mid-Range Gap, *Asian Business*, Vol. 29, No. 6, June 1993, pp. 14–16.
22. Porter, Michael, 1980, *op. cit.*
23. Miller, Danny, The Generic Strategy Trap, *The Journal of Business Strategy*, Vol. 13, No. 1, January/February 1992, pp. 37–41.
24. Giants in China Build-up, *South China Morning Post*, Business Post, Vol. L, No. 45, February 16, 1994, p. 1.
25. China Projects Need "Mothers-in-Law", *South China Morning Post*, Business Post, February 16, 1994, p. 20.
26. Giants in China Build-up, *loc. cit.*
27. Fukuda, Kazuo John, *Japanese Management in East Asia and Beyond*, Hong Kong: The Chinese University Press, 1993, p. 36.
28. Fallows, James, Looking at the Sun, *The Atlantic Monthly*, Vol. 272, No. 5, November 1993, pp. 69–100.
29. *Ibid.*, p. 90.
30. Fukuda, Kazuo John, 1993, *op. cit.*, p. 39.
31. Amsden, Alice H., *Asia's Next Giant*, New York: Oxford University Press, 1989.

CHAPTER 5

STRATEGY IMPLEMENTATION AND CONTROL

If the sage wants to be above the people,
in his words, he must put himself below them;
If he wishes to be before the people,
in his person, he must stand behind them.
—Lao Tzu

Implementation of Strategy

> *When corporate leaders decide to do something about changing competitive conditions, too often all they do is reach in for the latest fad or fix-it; excellence, total quality management (TQM), benchmarking, just-in-time, zero-based budgeting, the learning organization, decentralization, or right-sizing. But none of these is designed to help a business organization manage the more radical forces that are dramatically reshaping the competitive capabilities of entire industries, not just individual companies.*[1]

In Chapters 1–4, we were concerned with the *formulation* of strategy which often turns out to be primarily an intellectual exercise with little effect on the organization and its culture. The next stage, *implementation*, does affect the organization and its prevailing culture. Often a perfect strategy fails because it is not implemented correctly. For example, in one of the cases in this text, a restructuring programme was undertaken without the input of the employees it would affect. There was resistance to the change, resulting in conflict which eventually led to a strike which cost the organization millions of dollars (Hong Kong) per day of lost revenue and, perhaps more important, its reputation as a top quality service organization.

Strategy implementation can be divided into two different parts: the first is dealing with the *culture*, and the second, dealing with the *structure* of the organization. Interestingly, both can be difficult and can result in failure of the new strategy but dealing with the organization *culture* is often the most difficult because of the resistance to change. We shall also look at three basic organization forms in the region: the kaisha of Japan; the traditional

Chinese organization, the Chinese state enterprise, and Korea's chaebol; and how they deal with change.

It is useful to look first at the degree of change that is required and how the structure and organization culture will be affected. The greater the change, the more the energy that must be expended on carefully designing an effective implementation process; also, the greater the change, the more complex the implementation. Let's look at this phenomenon as a *continuum*, and examine four circumstances.

A Continuation Strategy

This strategy simply means that the organization will continue the strategy that has been used previously. The advantage is that the staff members are familiar with its operation and require no new skills. This is like a stability strategy in which the firm attempts to maintain its growth rate in terms of its industry experience and to improve profit through improving efficiency, i.e., by being more cost-effective.

A Routine Strategy Change

This is similiar to the continuation strategy but minor changes may be made such as repositioning a product in terms of the competition. It is very attractive to firms for the same reasons as given above but it can substantially change their profitability. A good example of this is Giordano of Hong Kong, who previously attempted to compete as a high-price, high-quality, youthful apparel manufacturer and retailer. This was changed to a medium-priced product line geared for the middle class, which translated into lower margins but higher volumes and higher profits. The appeal of this strategy is that the firm can take advantage of its present skills.

A Radical Strategy Change

Radical strategy change often has major impact on both the structure and the culture of the organization. One of the activities that goes with radical change is the restructuring and downsizing going on at present in many large firms in Japan, North America, and Europe, forcing them to leave some markets completely and to redefine their products or services. Often the results affected by the organization's culture can have serious long-term repercussions. Think of the impact on the organization, manufacturing, development, career paths, and promotions, for a firm that goes through restructuring and downsizing (e.g., from mainframe to personal computers) at the same time. Often, organizations facing this situation will simply divest themselves of the unprofitable activities rather than go through the difficult process.

An Organizational Redirection Change

This type of change involves going into new industries, perhaps through acquisitions, mergers, or the firm's own development and entry. The governments of Japan and South Korea in particular have been very supportive of firms in declining or **sunset** industries, assisting them to move into more promising industries. One case in this book looks at the US$5 billion-plus acquisition of Columbia Pictures and Music Company by Sony. Is this change for a world leader in the electronics industry, a redirection, radical, or routine strategy change? The change process, the degree of change, can have tremendous effect on the organization and how it is implemented can often determine its success or failure.

Change and Organization Structure[2]

New strategies often require change in organization structure. In the following section we will describe a progression from simple to complex organization and then differentiate in terms of cultural types. Given the importance of the development of international markets, alternate organization forms for internationalizing are also described.

Simple/Small Organizations

There are many very successful organizations that are not characterized as having formal management practices, and are managed quite informally. One of the present authors is close to an organization which has resisted growing because it would have to change from a very informal organization at its present size (approximately 135 employees) to a much more formal management style at a larger size. It has remained relatively small and successful in a very competitive field—the garment industry. A second organization was so successful that it did not control its growth and did not introduce the management practices required for its more demanding and complex activities. The stress and pressures that came from not adapting the needed practices resulted in the founders leaving—actually, selling the business—without understanding what had really happened. Their conclusion was that it was very difficult to control success. In the smaller, informal organization, the "managers" were very effective; but they weren't in the larger organization.

Many traditional Chinese family organizations, which are informal in their approach to management, have been very successful and in many different economies of the world. There are distinct advantages (and disadvantages) for smaller, simple organizations. They tend not to have the rigidity often found in larger, bureaucratic organizations and, therefore, can be quicker in terms of change. The manager is often also the owner which means that decision making is simplified and that the management is more sensitive to operational problems, being themselves involved with the firm's operations. The advantages and disadvantages of simple organisations are shown in Table 5.1.

Table 5.1 Simple Organizations

Advantages	Disadvantages
1. Facilitate control of all activities.	1. Demanding on the owner-manager.
2. Possible rapid decision making and ability to change with market signals.	2. Increasingly inadequate as volume expands.
3. Simple and informal motivation/reward/control systems.	3. Does not facilitate development of future managers.
	4. Tends to focus on the owner-manager and not on future strategy.

Functional Organizations

As organizations grow, the need for formal organization and specialization increases. The small business may simply use its chequebook as its bookkeeping function but soon it will need better information, better control and decision making, and the simple organization will change to one with functional specialization of activities and expertise. The functions may be organized as production or operations, marketing, personnel, finance, or based on the particular activities of the business (housekeeping and catering departments in hotels, for example). Specialization is a chief advantage of functional organization; it brings expertise with it and tends to further develop expertise. It also brings with it coordination problems such as suboptimization, because functional experts tend to see problems in terms of their expertise, their function—from the viewpoint of a *subsystem*, rather than from a system or organizational perspective. The main advantages and disadvantages of functional organizations are shown in Table 5.2.

Table 5.2 Functional Organizations

Advantages	Disadvantages
1. Efficiency through specialization.	1. Narrow specialization and potential functional rivalry or conflict.
2. Improved development of functional expertise.	2. Foster difficulty in functional coordination and interfunctional decision making.
3. Differentiate management and operating employees.	3. Can occasion staff-line conflict.
4. Centralized control of strategic decisions.	4. Limit internal development of general managers.

Divisional Organizations

Again the dynamics of the firm and the complexities that it creates require another type of structure, primarily because of the inability of the functional organization to handle things and be efficient as the firm increases its products and/or services and enters into more markets. This calls for restructuring of the organization into divisions. The divisions can be formed on the basis of *product lines* (television, appliances, business machines), *markets* (retail, commercial), *geographic* (Northeast Asia, Southeast Asia), or *channels of distribution* (retail, catalogue). It is common for each division to have its own staff functions and that not only creates redundancies in the overall organization but also provides it with the functional expertise required for efficiency. The divisional organizational structure provides large organizations with a method of remaining close to their diverse markets. Divisional organizations have many advantages and some disadvantages as shown in Table 5.3.

Matrix Organization

This recently developed organization form integrates the characteristics of both, the functional and divisional structures. It is usually implemented for facilitating the development and

Table 5.3 Divisional Organizations

Advantages	Disadvantages
1. Force coordination and necessary authority down to the appropriate level for rapid response. 2. Place strategy development and implementation in closer proximity to the divisions' unique environment. 3. Free chief executive officers for broader strategic decision making. 4. Sharply focus accountability for performance. 5. Retain functional specialization within each division. 6. Serve as good training ground for strategic managers.	1. Create a problem with the extent of authority given to division managers. 2. Foster the potential for policy inconsistencies between divisions. 3. Raise the problem of arriving at a method to distribute corporate overhead costs that is acceptable to different division managers with profit responsibility.

execution of new products and programmes. This type of organization can provide functional authority and at the same time have, for example, a product structure that cuts across the functions with the possibility of an individual responsible, at least on a temporary basis, to both a functional and a product manager. This allows the product manager to cut across department lines providing the functions and the coordination expertise necessary for successful implementation. This type of structure has a basic disadvantage also in that the individuals involved are often confused in terms of their basic responsibility—whether it is to their function or to the "product" or to the "project" manager. The advantages and disadvantages are listed in Table 5.4.

Table 5.4 Matrix Organizations

Advantages	Disadvantages
1. Accommodate a wide variety of project-oriented business activity. 2. Maximize efficient use of functional managers. 3. Enhance coordination.	1. Can create confusion and contradictory policies by allowing dual accountability. 2. Necessitate tremendous horizontal and vertical coordination.

Starting International Operations

Going international is commonplace for small and large businesses in this geographical region but it introduces a new set of organization problems. A normal progression for companies in the region is to expand across national borders; international business is the way of business in the region. A good example is the use of the People's Republic of China by Hong Kong companies for both marketing and production of their products. Hong Kong manufacturing companies now employ more than 3,500,000 employees in China to produce goods primarily for international markets. For Hong Kong employers, business is international. Approaches can vary widely from wholly owned operations, to subcontracting, to original equipment manufacturers, to joint ventures (see Table 5.5).

Table 5.5

Stage I	Exports its products to foreign countries
Stage II	Establishes sales organizations abroad
Stage III	Licenses to foreign firms that make and sell its products to use its patents and know-how
Stage IV	Establishes foreign manufacturing facilities
Stage V	Multinationalizes management from top to bottom
Stage VI	Multinationalizes ownership of corporate stock

In Stage I, firms may use the services of trading companies to sell their goods in other markets. This approach was very popular in Japan and South Korea in the period when they were introducing their goods into the international markets. As sales increase in foreign markets, a point (Stage II) is reached calling for the company to contact and control its own marketing. It is important to note here that many firms use another route to enter new markets: subcontracting and OEM. In these activities, the firm restricts its activities to manufacturing and leaves the marketing to other firms who will most often sell the products as their own with their own brand names. These procedures are especially true of manufacturing firms in the People's Republic of China and Taiwan. Taiwan firms are the major manufacturers of laptop computers but they are manufactured for other computer firms all over the globe. This is done because of the technical abilities and cost efficiency of their operations. This places them at the mercy though, of their buyers. In the normal progression of economic development, these firms would be expected to establish their own brand names. It is interesting to observe that this has not tended to occur in Taiwan, a country known for its international exports and gigantic financial reserves but with few internationally established brand names.

Table 5.6 provides a means of categorizing different approaches to implementing strategy: the commander, the collaborator, and the crescive. (These labels also correspond to autocratic, participative, and collegial styles of leadership.) If the reader is familiar with the cultures of the region, the author recommends that an attempt be made to look at the particular approaches in terms of its being appropriate or inappropriate for a particular culture. According to Hofstede,[3]

> Both management practitioners and management theorists over the last eighty years have been blind to the extent to which activities like management and organizing are culturally dependent. They are culturally dependent because managing and organizing do not consist of making or moving tangible objects, but of manipulating symbols which have meaning to the people who are managed or organized.

Table 5.6 Comparison of Approaches for Implementing Strategy

Factors	Commander	Collaborative	Crescive
How are goals set? Where in the organization (top or bottom) are the strategic goals established?	Dictated from top	Negotiated among top team	Stated loosely from top, refined from bottom
What signifies success? What signifies successful outcome of the strategic planning/implementation process?	A good plan as judged on economic criteria	An acceptable plan with broad top management support	Sound strategies with champions behind them
What factors are considered? What factors or reasons are used in developing a strategy for resolving conflicts between alternative proposed strategies?	Economic	Economic, social, political	Economic, social, political, behavioural
What is the typical level of organization-wide effort required?			
During the planning phase	Low	High	High
During the implementation phase	N/A	Low	Low
How stringent are the requirements placed on the CEO for the approach to succeed?			
Required CEO knowledge: To what extent must the CEO be able to maintain personal awareness of all significant strategic opportunities or threats?	High	Moderate	Low
Required CEO power: To what extent must the CEO have the power to impose a detailed implementation plan on the organization?	High	Moderate	Moderate

Source: Adapted from David Brodwin and L.J. Bourgeois, III, Five Steps to Strategic Action, *California Management Review*, Vol. 26, No. 3, 1984, pp. 145–161.

In the classic work by Hofstede, *Culture's Consequences*,[4] the countries of the region have been generally classified as collectivist, power-oriented cultures but other writers have come to quite different conclusions. Table 5.7 lists some of these differences in respect of three countries/national cultures of the region. In this chapter, we are interested in how each organization deals with change. Western scholars have been the major contributors to the Organization Theory and especially to organizational development, a specialty in the discipline, which is concerned specifically with the change process. If you analyze the change mechanisms

Chapter 5

Table 5.7 East Asian Business Systems

	Japanese Kaisha	Korean Chaebol	Chinese Family Business
Authoritative Coordination and Control			
Personal authority and owner domination	Low	High	High
Significance of formal coordination and control procedures	High	Medium	Low
Managerial style	Facilitative	Directive	Didactic
Employee commitment	Emotional	Conditional	Conditional
Business Domain and Development			
Business specialization	High	Low	High within firms Medium within families
Evolutionary strategies	High	Medium	Medium
Inter-firm Coordination			
Relational contracting	High	Low	Medium
Long-term intersector coordination	Strong through business groups and state agencies	Indirect through state	Limited and personal

Source: Richard Whitley, The Social Construction of Business Systems in East Asia, *Organization Studies*, Vol. 12, No. 1, 1991, p. 15.

included, you will find the vast majority tend to use one strong behavioural tool: *participation*. There are dynamics inherent in the three organizational forms depicted in the following table which enhance or discourage participation. One of the most interesting is a process often used in large Japanese organizations—the *Ringi* system of decision making.

In terms of decision making, *ringi* (described in Figure 5.1) is a form of participation in decision making that involves both horizontal and vertical participation which does not require face-to-face interaction. The *ringi* method of decision making was presented as a distinguishing characteristic of Japanese management by a group of Japanese scholars in the late 1950s. (*Rin* means submitting a proposal to one's superior and receiving approval while *gi* means deliberation and decisions.) This process creates a working document (*ringi-sho*) which provides a means of participation without dealing face-to-face which can create a situation in which at least subordinates feel outside their role expectations. Note in Figure 5.1 how the document, the *ringi-sho,* is circulated both horizontally and vertically to parties who will be affected for review, revision, and approval. According to Fukuda,[5]

> The ringi process is generally characterized by its bottomup approach and collective decision making by consensus. It must be noted, however, that the ringi process

Step	Top Management	Middle Management	Lower Management and Staff

1. Identify and Define Problem
2. Analyse Problem → Generate Alternative Solutions
3. Select a Solution

RINGI PROCESS

Final Authorization — Inter-Unit Consensus — Intra-Unit Consensus (Ringi-Sho)

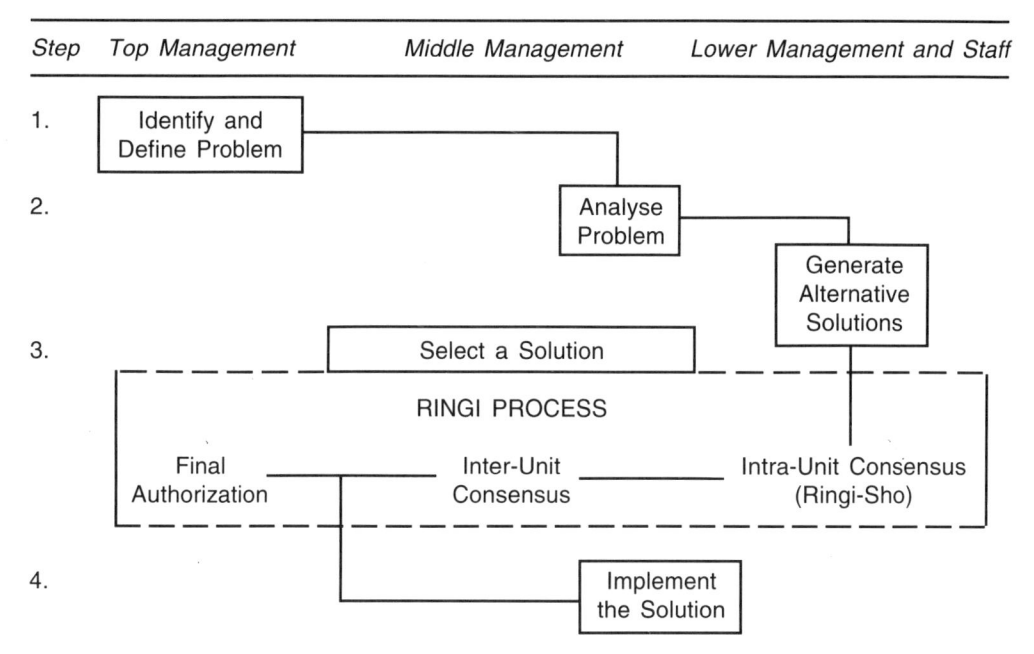

4. Implement the Solution

Figure 5.1 Ringi System of Decision making

alone does not constitute the total system of decision making. It is an integral part of the total system. Although the top management may not get directly involved in the problem analysis and the generation of alternate solutions, their instructions to perform those tasks are in fact communicated down progressively to the lower levels, following the top down approach.... it actually adopts both top-down and bottom-up approaches. Because of the high degree of participation through the ringi method and the use of consensus decision making, most students of Japanese management conclude that implementation and its changes tend to go smoother than in Western organizations.

The Chaebol

The *chaebol* of South Korea is a unique form of organization. It is very large both for the size of the Korean economy and for its stage of development. Whitley[6] describes it in Table 5.1 as having high authority and owner domination. Actually, the chaebols are now publicly listed firms but the families of the founders still own enough stock for control. They are very large in comparison to the size of organizations in the other Mini-Dragons. Even though Taiwan's economy has a GNP/capita over 50 per cent higher than Korea's, its largest business would rank number 7 compared with Korea's largest firms. Whitley describes its managerial style as directive but the style can be differentiated between the chaebol with successful and unsuccessful industrial relations. The style of the successful chaebol is not autocratic but paternalistic or benevolent autocratic. The successful ones are folk heroes of great status and are respected by the employees and the public which of course, wields, tremendous power. According to Hok Chong Lee, a past dean of the business school at Yonsei University, the career managers, the manager power groups, the *tobagi*, are often formed on the basis of common geographical and school ties. Most important, it is common for owners to bring their hometown or school friends into their organizations, the same as they do for family members and relatives. This form of *nepotism* fosters harmony, *inwha*, in the management structure. If it is based on friendship, it is called *hyul-yun*; if based on geographical background, *ji-yun*; on school background, *hahk-yun*.[7] Korean managers will attempt to have consultation with their subordinates even when using a suboptimal solution in order to maintain harmony in this group. Upward communication, especially critical or dissenting, is not common because of the deference to power and authority figures in the culture.[8]

The family concern is a popular organization type in Taiwan, Singapore, and Hong Kong. There are organizations, of course, in those economies that are not family organizations but this form is so popular and common that its peculiarities must be addressed. To understand this type of organization, it is imperative to understand the dynamics of the family in the Chinese culture. According to Whitley,[9] the primacy of family relationships and identities in Chinese society means that commitment to one's family overrides all other loyalties, and individual prestige is based on family status or standing rather than being organizational or occupational. Going further, he reports that in these economies, business success and wealth have become the major sources of family prestige, which is one reason for individuals who are not part of the "family" leaving the firm. Thus, commitment to employers among the expatriate Chinese and Taiwanese is always limited and conditional, unless there are very strong relationships with the business family. This means that there is no high commitment to employers, which in turn means that the owners are not able to trust the employees. This has major implications for many management practices such as delegation and participation in decision making which creates major constraints to expanding this organization type. The dynamics here are very different from those in the Japanese *kaisha* or the Korean chaebol.

The Equity Joint Ventures in China[10]

The equity joint venture organization type has been given a significant role in the "opendoor policy" of China which was initiated in 1978. This particular type is supposed to achieve different goals for the two sides. The goals for the Chinese are the transfer of technology and management techniques, and the earning of foreign exchange. For the foreign partner, it facilitates dealing with a multitude of government agencies, provides a source of low cost productive labour, and provides a means of entering the gigantic China market. It also creates unique strategy implementation problems.

Figure 5.2 depicts the major problems. The management system of joint ventures in China is characterized by the interlocking relationships between the joint venture management, state ministry, trade union and the Chinese Communist Party. The resulting complex organization form multiples the difficulties in strategic decision making and implementation.

Each of the above illustrations of management practices and organization forms in the region has distinct advantages and disadvantages for strategy implementation. The *ringi* method of decision making tends to facilitate implementation because of the high degree of participation it requires but with the Japanese penchant for consensus, the time requirements

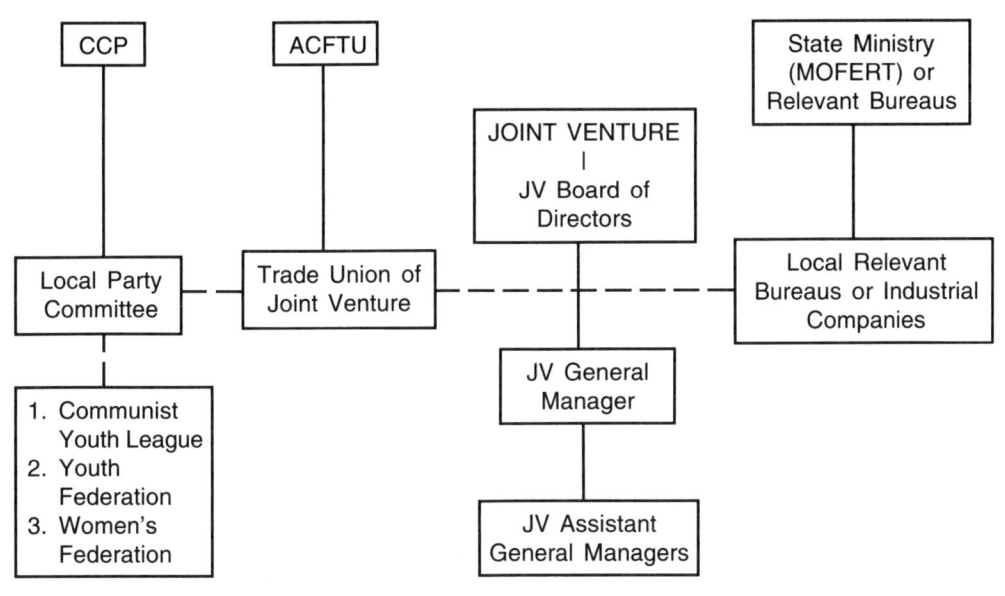

Figure 5.2 Joint Ventures in China

are often excessive. The Chinese family organization can be very effective because of its decisiveness and its singular focus of direction through the unity of the family—the inner circle—but its weakness is the alienation of employees outside the family—the outer circle. This creates the weak link in the chain of the process of implementation. The *chaebol,* **like the Chinese organizations, uses nepotism which creates harmony within the top management but again alienates other members of the organization.** The Chinese joint venture provides the political power of its constituents to facilitate change, but their numbers and role in the organization create a highly complex form of organization. Hofstede describes the countries of this region as high on his Power Distance and Collectivism dimensions. Even accepting his conclusions, it is obvious that their organization forms and practices have significant impact on the strategy implementation processes. In the second part of this chapter we will look at the process and procedures of evaluation and control of strategy.

Controlling the Strategic Planning Process

The strategic planning process that *assesses* the external environment and internal strengths and weaknesses, and then works on *implementation,* will not achieve its full potential unless it *monitors* the organization's progress along key strategic paths. The function of *control* is to bring about conformity to organizational requirements and achievement of the ultimate purposes of the organization. Strategic control is needed to ensure that the strategic plan is completed as planned. The strategic control process alerts the strategic planner to a problem or potential problem before it becomes critical. An effective control system helps to spot problems before they occur, and so can prevent financial disasters.

The Purposes of Strategic Control

Strategic control can be viewed as "the critical evaluation of plans, activities, and results, thereby providing information for future direction. It is the managerial function that ensures that actual organizational action corresponds to planned action." Juach and Gluck point out that strategic control is intended to see that implemented strategic choices result in the attainment of the objectives that gave rise to the process of choice.[11] Neale and Holmes perceive it as an advanced form of post-auditing of actual performance against planned performance with a particular emphasis on achieving long-range objectives within established time and cost constraints.[12]

Lorange conceptualizes strategic control as the top level totality of all control systems in the organization.[13] In his view, strategic control involves a continuous monitoring and measurement of: operating performance, strategic changes, programming activities, and changes in basic objectives. The control process is accomplished through the establishment and use of strategic checkpoints, which are benchmarks that may be used to evaluate progress towards the fulfilment of a given strategy. Strategic control thus focuses on the fit between the formulation of strategy and its implementation ensuring that the strategy is both on schedule and on target.

The Need for Strategic Control

Strategy evaluation is concerned primarily with traditional control processes which involve the review and feedback of performance to determine if plans, strategies, and objectives are being achieved. The need for strategic control is centred on the intrinsic nature of the overall strategic management process. It is intended to measure and evaluate the effectiveness of selected managerial strategy with a particular emphasis on the attainment of managerial objectives.

The control process. The strategic control process has three basic elements: objectives of the business, measure or evaluation of performance and feedback or corrective action. The purpose of control is to ensure that the corporation is achieving what it set out to accomplish. This process is viewed as a five-step process. Exhibit 5.1 illustrates these five steps of the strategic control process.

1. Determine what to measure. The first step of control is to specify what implementation processes and results will be monitored and evaluated. The process and results must be capable of being measured in a reasonable, objective, and consistent manner.

2. Establish standards of performance. Standards used to measure performance are detailed expressions of strategic objectives. The performance standards can be historical (past performance), industry norms (similar firms in the industry), or goals and/or targets for a particular period.

3. Measure actual performance. Measurements must be both qualitative and quantitative at the predetermined times.

Exhibit 5.1 Evaluation and Control Process

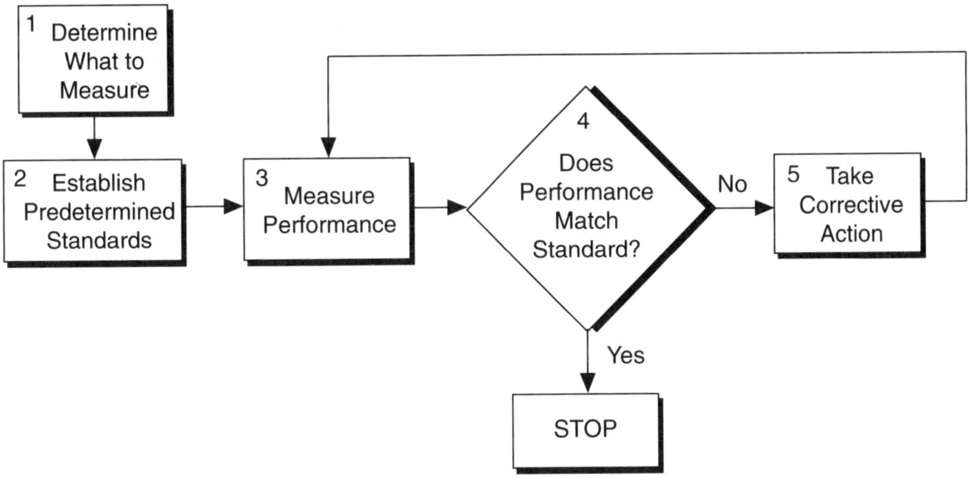

```
1. Determine What to Measure
2. Establish Predetermined Standards → 3. Measure Performance → 4. Does Performance Match Standard? 
   No → 5. Take Corrective Action (loops back)
   Yes → STOP
```

4. Compare actual performance with standard. This step compares performance against standards. If actual performance meets the desired tolerance range, the control process is complete.

5. Take corrective action. Finally, feedback is provided. If actual results fail to match the desired results, action must be taken to correct the deviation.

The simple model assumes that activities are controlled by establishing plans, normally based on an assessment of the future, which are then implemented and measured. The actual results are compared to the plan through feedback which leads to reaction, or "feedforward" which leads to the amendment of plans in the light of experience.

Very often, strategy implementation problems have stemmed from failures of control systems. The traditional approaches to control have emphasized the setting of predetermined standards, performing the work, getting feedback by measuring actual performance and comparing it with predetermined standards, and then taking any necessary corrective action. Several researchers have criticized the design and the feedback mechanism of strategic control. The major drawbacks of feedback control become readily apparent when controlling long-term strategies. Post-action control implies waiting for a strategy to be executed before getting any feedback on how well it was working. It may take several years before corrective action to alter strategic direction in the light of changes in internal or external circumstances is taken and the opportunities to benefit from such action would have been lost. Such post hoc nature of feedback control is particularly troublesome when environmental conditions are changing rapidly. There is a need for continuous assessment to make sure that the strategy is in accord with changing conditions.

Overcoming the traditional control systems of post-action nature requires using a feed-forward approach which involves anticipatory action or developing ways to minimize potential deviations from desired outcomes. Organizations are required to actively monitor the broad external forces and remain alert to respond to the external forces, such as government, societal changes, at the appropriate time, when they are controllable. That is, changes in internal and external circumstances need to be monitored on a continuous basis and strategic direction evaluated critically in the light of those changing conditions.

Adaptive control has to do with determining the quickest and most effective way in which to respond to changes. Strategic control involves anticipating or developing ways to minimize potential deviations from desired outcomes. Strategic control maintains actual performance close to a desired set of performance specification. Under the turbulent business environment, there is need for future-oriented strategic control. A forward-looking step to detect early signs of problems is to pay attention to changes in critical underlying environmental assumptions and in competitive positions, and then monitor these environmental factors to detect any significant deviation.

Schregogg and Steinmann (1987) criticized that the classical feedback control involves the comparison of actual performance with predetermined standards. Corrective action will be taken only if deviations from standards of performance have occurred. Due to the uncertainty and complexity in the strategic management environment, a three-step feedforward process is proposed.[14] The proposed model consisted of three distinct control activities: premise control, strategic surveillance, and implementation control. Premise control is designed to check systematically and continuously whether or not the premises set during the planning and implementation process are still valid. While premise control and implementation control are focused control, strategic surveillance is designed to monitor the full range of events inside and outside the enterprises which are likely to threaten the course of strategic action. Premise control is established at the point of initial premising, and simultaneously, strategic surveillance begins. When strategic implementation begins, implementation control is put into action. All three control devices work together counterbalancing the inherent risk in planning.

Gap analysis.   Another approach in measuring strategic results is strategic gap analysis, wherein we see whether the gaps between expected results and ideal outcomes are being closed, note internal and external changes, and take corrective action to get it all back on track. Evaluation and control processes are set up to ensure that the gap between expected and desired objectives will be closed according to the planned strategy.

Such gap analysis examines the difference between where the organization currently is and where it wants to be; assesses the relevance of the organization's strategy to its progress in the accomplishment of its goals, and ensures that when discrepancies exist, they are corrected. Where the gap is too great, either the objectives need to be revised or additional strategic alternatives need to be identified. The discrepancy or gap between the desired (ideal) outcome and expected (anticipated) outcome should be minimized. The gap must be perceived to be significant before any corrective action is taken. Strategists must be motivated to reduce the gap and believe that the gap can be reduced. If the organization is seen as incapable of reducing the gap, the gap may be ignored, and new perspectives sought. If extraordinary deviations occur, the firm should reassess goals, strategies, and plans, and formulate new strategies and implementation processes as needed.

The strategic management and control system are shown in Exhibit 5.2. The operating budget is used to set financial targets and record costs during the year. Periodical statistical reports are used to evaluate and monitor performance. To facilitate control, reports must be timely so that they provide feedback for corrective action. Performance appraisal and standard operating procedures represent behavioural and bureaucratic control mechanisms.

Exhibit 5.2 Strategic Management and Control Systems

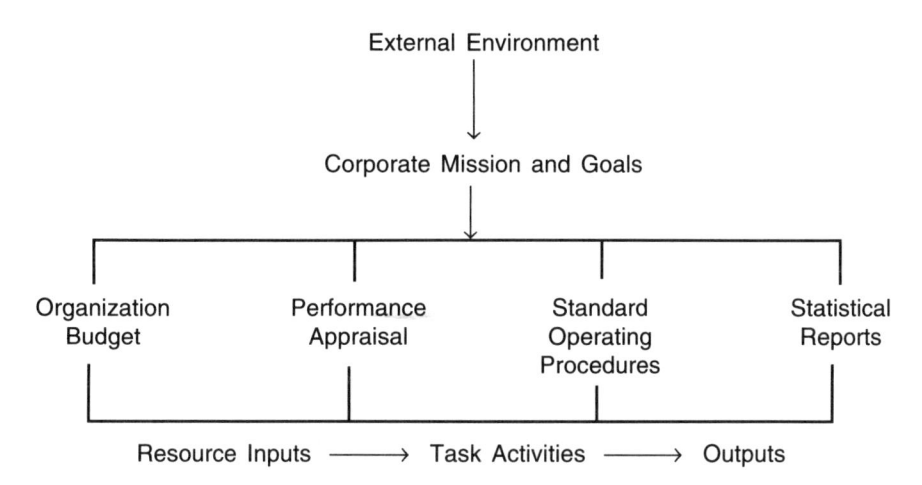

```
                    External Environment
                            │
                            ▼
                Corporate Mission and Goals
                            │
        ┌───────────┬───────┴───────┬───────────┐
   Organization  Performance    Standard      Statistical
      Budget      Appraisal     Operating      Reports
                                Procedures
        └───────────┴───────────────┴───────────┘

     Resource Inputs ──→ Task Activities ──→ Outputs
```

Source: Adapted from Richard L. Daft and Norman B. Macintosh, The Nature and Use of Formal Control Systems to Management Control and Strategy Implementation, *Journal of Management*, Vol. 10, 1984, pp. 43–66.

Incentive systems should be built in to improve strategic control. Are reward systems capable of recognizing and rewarding good performance? The emphasis should be on the rewards for meeting or exceeding standards, rather than punishment for failing to meet them.

Hrebiniak and Joyce identify five common control problems which in their view result in poor or unsuccessful strategy implementation:[15]

1. Poor objectives
2. Insufficient information processing capabilities
3. Management by negative exception and poor evaluation of performance
4. Poor performance appraisal
5. Avoiding and embracing error

On the other hand, Goldsmith and Clutterbuck[16] identify four recurring themes of *successful* cases in control:

1. Tight financial controls
2. Constant feedback of results

3. Close attention to business planning
4. Setting high standards and expecting people to stick to them

Requirements of a Control System

Many strategic planning processes have tended to become overly bureaucratic, mechanistic, unrealistic and out of touch with critical issues. Control should involve only the minimum amount of information needed to give reliable results. Too much control makes the whole system very rigid.

- Control should monitor only meaningful activities and results, regardless of measurement difficulty.
- Control should be timely so the corrective action can be taken before it is too late.
- Long-term as well as short-term controls should be used.
- Control should aim at pinpointing exceptions.

Other requirements of a control system include simplicity, consistency, flexibility and adaptability. Control must also be positive, fair and objective, prompt and exception-oriented, strategic and result-oriented, information-based and cost-effective.

The amount of control is dependent on the following factors:

- Objective/strategy
- Cost vs. benefit
- Acceptability
- Size of operation
- Technology
- Environment
- Power desired by top management
- Level of individual and group control (this will affect the amount of organizational control needed)

Barriers and resistance to control are:

- Too much control or over-control
- Aversion to accountability or loss of flexibility
- Inaccurate or arbitrary control

Using the market mechanism as a means of control amounts to allowing the market to dictate terms. Performance will be evaluated by output and productivity. Formal bureaucratic control relies on the use of explicit formal rules and regulations, and informal cultural control relies on the culture implicit within the organization. Bureaucratic control is the use of rules, policies and written documentation, and other mechanisms to standardize employee behaviour and assess performance. Clan control is the use of corporate culture, commitment, shared values and beliefs to control behaviour. Clan control is more effective in small informal organizations with a strong culture inculcating trust. Clan control is invisible yet can be very powerful.

In multinational corporations, the transfer of managers from subsidiary to subsidiary is a distinct control strategy. Such a process creates international, interpersonal verbal information networks. The use of clan control helps to create a sense of cooperation and shared values among organization members.

Means of Control	Criteria
Market	Profits, costs, competition, market share
Bureaucracy	Rules, standards, hirerachy, legitimate authority
Clan	Tradition, shared values and beliefs, trust

Major Criteria for Assessing Corporate Performance

1. *Profitability*
   Net profit
   Rate of return
2. *Market position*
   Market share
   Product leadership
   Sales force performance
   Sales per employee
3. *Productivity*
   Output per man-hour
   Cost per unit
   Capacity utilization rates
   Value added per employee
   Rate of innovation
   Order backlogs
4. *Personnel development*
   Employee satisfaction with promotion prospects
   Morale
   Cost of recruiting personnel
   Personnel turnover
   Ratio of indirect cost to direct cost
5. *Achievement of long-term corporate plans*
   Ratio analysis
   Variance analysis

Responsibility Centres

The conventional approach using the fundamental unit of analysis is the responsibility centre. The commonly used forms of responsibility centres are cost centres, revenue cenres, profit centres, investment centres, and discretionary expense centres.

Revenue centres measure the performance solely by output (i.e., the revenue brought in) while profit centres measure both input and output (i.e., revenue less expenses yields the profit). The bottom-line figure (profit) is the criterion to evaluate the efficiency of the whole corporation. Profit centres are self-contained units. Each unit contains its resource inputs and can be evaluated on the basis of profit or loss compared with other units. Such measures are valid only when the output of a unit can be clearly calculated. It is often not appropriate in the control of certain *service* departments, such as personnel, legal, computer, and information services departments. In the case of some state enterprises in the People's Republic of China, raw materials and other resources are controlled and allocated by the Central Government. The profit and loss may not reflect the actual performance of the unit or the organization, but may have political subtexts.

There are other problems in using profit centres as a measure of control. There is a tendency or an option to slack off on the dimension that is *not* being measured—either the output or the input dimension, e.g., processing less or incurring more costs, which are not measured, thus, making it easier for the manager to meet input goals (costs) or output goals (profits), respectively, whichever is being measured. One potential problem emerges in allocating costs to each centre: sometimes it is not possible to set up a fair formula for allocating joint costs, e.g., centralized computing system and other indirect costs.

Investment centres are concerned with the amount of assets employed to generate a particular economic result, and the effectiveness of using their assets (physical assets, such as plant, equipment, inventory, raw materials, etc.). The evaluation criteria are return on investment (ROI), payback period, and net present value (NPV).

The problem here is that there are different ways to measure fixed assets in terms of net book value, gross book value, current market value, replacement cost and economic value. The method of measuring depreciation also varies. The different measurements may yield different results.

Contingency Plan

Contingency plans consider events that are less likely to occur but that would require changes in the strategic plan if they *did* occur. Each type of organization or business is subject to different contingencies that should be planned for even though the ability to forecast accurately is limited. If contingency planning is done properly, it gives flexibility to the strategic plan and is invaluable during times of change and crisis within the organization. Strategy planning should integrate all these measures and approaches into a contingency-based system.

Teams should be formed by bringing together a cross-disciplinary group of both senior and junior managers, with different backgrounds and different experience to monitor the control process. Evaluation and control processes help strategists monitor the progress of a plan. They seek to answer a number of questions, such as the following:[17]

Consistency
- Are the decisions being made consistent with the policy?
- Is the strategy consistent with the environment?
- Are events in the environment occurring as anticipated?
- How are competitors reacting to our activities?
- Is the strategy internally consistent?

Appropriateness
- Are the resources and capabilities being used wisely?
- Is the strategy appropriate for available resources?
- Is risk in the strategy at the appropriate level?
- Does the strategy have an appropriate time horizon?

Workability
- Should we proceed with the plan as formulated?
- Is the strategy workable?
- Is the strategy feasible?

Timing
- When should results be evaluated?
- Are both short-term and long-term goals and targets being met?

Strategic Audit

The strategic audit is an examination of an organization's strategy to determine if the existing strategy has produced the desired results. The strategic audit is used to monitor closely those activities that affect overall corporate effectiveness and efficiency. To be effective, the strategic audit should parallel the corporation's strategic management process.

An organization normally undertakes a strategic audit if:

1. An existing strategy has failed to produce the desired results
2. A fundamental change has occurred in the organization's environment
3. A new management team would like to set its own course of action

Information technology, such as decision support systems, telecommunications, and networks are becoming less costly and more powerful tools for strategic control. For reference, Exhibit 5.3 provides a checklist for the strategic audit.[18]

Chapter 5

Exhibit 5.3 Strategic Audit of a Corporation

I. Organization's Goals, Performance and Governance
A. Performance
The overall corporate performance in terms of return on investment, market share, profitability trends, earnings per share
B. Corporate Mission Statement
Clearly stated mission, objectives, strategies and policies
C. Board of Directors and Top Management
The members of the board and CEOs
The calibre of top management team
The level of involvement

II. Environmental Analysis
A. External Environment: Opportunities and Threats
The macroenvironment: economic, sociocultural, political-legal, technological forces
The current situation or future opportunities and threats
Other key stakeholders: customers, competitors, creditors, trade associations, interest groups, local community, stockholders
B. Industry Environment
Competitive forces analysis: threat of substitute products or services, bargaining power of buyers, suppliers, rivalry among existing firms, the relative power of unions, government, business attractiveness, expected future growth pattern, overall industrial structure, number of competitors, the industrial analysis, etc.
C. Internal Environment: Strengths and Weaknesses
Corporate structure form—organized on the basis of functions, projects, geography, or some combination
Decision making style, centralized or decentralized
Corporate culture: the shared beliefs, common values, expectations

III. Corporate Resources and Functional Strategies
A. Marketing
Market position, sales, market share, marketing mix, i.e., product, price, place, and promotion
B. Finance
The financial analysis, i.e., liquidity ratios, profitability ratios, activities ratios, leverage ratios, capitalization structure, and currency stability
C. Research and Development
Technological competency
D. Operations/Production
Type and extent of operation capabilities of the corporation, cost of production, capacity utilization, timely delivery
E. Human Resources Management
Job analysis, performance appraisal, up-to-date job descriptions, training and development, attitude surveys, job design, quality of relationship with unions, turnover, absenteeism, and strikes
F. Information Systems
The corporation's IS performance and stage of development compared with that of similar corporations
Do its databases, system analyses, etc., help to implement interactive decision-support systems?

Exhibit 5.3 Strategic Audit of a Corporation (cont.)

IV. Critical Success Factors
Historical strategic factors
Short, intermediates and long-term factors
Assessing critical underlying success factors in different functional areas: marketing, production, finance, asset management, and human resource

V. Strategic Alternatives
Checking the basic strategies being pursued to determine whether they seem to be reasonable or normal relative to what one would expect
Are they in line with the norm, or do they deviate sharply from it?
Feasible alternative strategies available to the organization
Stability, growth and retrenchment as corporate strategies
Cost leadership and differentiation as business strategies
Functional strategic alternatives

VI. Implementation
Who is responsible for implementation?
Budgets
Standard operating procedures

VII. Evaluation and Control
Providing sufficient feedback on implementation activities and performance
Timely information and feedback
Adequate control measures
Standards and measures being used
Reward systems capable of recognizing and rewarding good performance

Review Questions

1. What are some of the behavioural reasons that make implementation of new strategies difficult?
2. How does the Japanese decision form, *ringi seido*, affect implementation?
3. Give an example of a firm with a global strategy. What are the advantages of its strategy?
4. In the traditional Chinese family organization, there is often an 'inside' and an 'outside' group. What are the implications in terms of implementing change?
5. How does the *chaebol* differ from the traditional Chinese family organization? Should the implementing of change differ? How?
6. Would the structure of the Chinese state enterprise affect implementation?
7. What is the role of control in achieving strategic objectives? Why is control needed?
8. Describe the key elements and basic steps in the control process.
9. What are the characteristics of effective strategic control systems?
10. How can strategic control be used to aid in strategic planning and implementation?

Endnotes

1. Want, Jerome H., Managing Radical Change, *Journal of Business Strategy*, 1993, p. 21.
2. Adapted from Samuel Certo and J. Paul Peter, *Strategic Management*, 3rd ed., Illinois: Irwin, 1995, pp. 116–121.
3. Hofstede, Geert, The Cultural Relativity of Organizational Practices and Theories, *Journal of International Business Studies*, Vol. 14, No. 2, Fall 1993, p. 88.
4. Hofstede, Geert, *Culture's Consequences: International differences in work-related values*, Beverly Hills, CA: Sage Publications, 1980.
5. Fukuda, Kezuo John, *Japanese Management in East Asia and Beyond*, Hong Kong: The Chinese University Press, 1993, p. 192.
6. Whitley, Richard, The Social Construction of Business Systems in East Asia, *Organization Studies*, Vol. 12, No. 1, 1991, p. 15.
7. Lee, Hok Chong, Managerial Characteristics of Korean Firms, in *Korean Managerial Dynamics*, New York: Praeger, 1989, p. 156.
8. *Ibid.*, p. 159.
9. Whitley, p. 15.
10. Adapted from Mee Kau Nyaw, Managing International Joint Ventures in China, in *International Business in China*, New York: Routledge Press, 1992, p. 174.
11. Juach, L.R. and W.F. Gluck, *Strategic Management and Business Policy*, 3rd ed., New York: McGraw-Hill, 1989.
12. Neale, C.W. and L.E.A. Holmes, Post-Auditing Capital Projects, *Long Range Planning*, Vol. 23, No. 4, August 1990, pp. 88–89.
13. Lorange, P., Strategic Control: Some issues in making it operationally more useful, in R. Boyden (Ed.), *Competitive Strategic Management*, Englewood Cliffs, NJ: Prentice-Hall, 1984, pp. 247–271.
14. Schregogg, G. and H. Steinmann, Strategic Control: A new perspective, *Academy of Management Review*, Vol. 12, No. 1, 1987, pp. 91–103.
15. Hrebiniak, L.G. and W.F. Joyce, *Implementing Strategy*, New York: Macmillan, 1984, pp. 114–123.
16. Goldsmith, W. and D. Clutterbuck, *The Winning Streak*, London: Weidenfeld and Nicolson, 1984.
17. Tilles, Seymour, How to Evaluate Corporate Strategy, *Harvard Business Review*, Vol. 41, No. 4, September 1963, pp. 111–121.
18. Wheelen, T.L. and J.D. Hunger, *Strategic Management and Business Policy*, 4th ed., Reading, MA: Addison-Wesley, 1992, pp. 52–57.

COUNTRY PROFILE

JAPAN—THE POST-BUBBLE ENVIRONMENT*

OVERVIEW

Japan's economic success since the end of World War II is widely regarded as a remarkable achievement for a resource-poor and densely populated country. As Japan dominated industry after industry, corporations worldwide were urged to adopt Japanese management practices. Quality management programs and "just-in-time" inventory control systems were frantically implemented as the panacea for organizational problems around the world. However, management is not an isolated process but occurs in the context of a country's environment.

Innumerable studies and theories have attempted to explain the reasons for the Japanese economic miracle by isolating specific and unique dimensions of Japanese management practices. Sharply conflicting opinions and studies have found some common ground of agreement but most studies neglect the impact of the country-environmental factors. The objective of this chapter is to provide a country-environment context for the reader to further delve into the areas of dissension and unanswered questions.

GEOGRAPHY AND DEMOGRAPHICS

The Japanese islands are relative in size to the State of California, and support an estimated population of 124.3 million which is growing at only 0.4 per cent per annum. Approximately 72 per cent of the land area is mountainous with 70 per cent covered in forest. Japan is the

---

* This country profile was prepared by Elaine K. Bailey of the Management and Industrial Relations Department, College of Business Administration, University of Hawaii, Manoa.

seventh most populous nation in the world with the ninth largest language community. The population of Japan is expected to reach 133 million in the year 2000 and then begin to decline.

The population is clustered in urban areas with more than 25 per cent of the Japanese population living in the greater Tokyo area and over 80 per cent living on the northern island of Honshu. The Japanese have a life expectancy of 76.09 for men and 82.22 for women, the longest life expectancy of any population in the world. The percentage of Japanese aged 65 and older will double to over 25 per cent by the year 2025, making it the oldest population in the world (Labor Trends, 1994). The issue of the aging population, with serious economic and social consequences, is one of the major long-term problems Japan must confront.

Proportion of the Elderly in Select Countries
% of population aged 65 or over

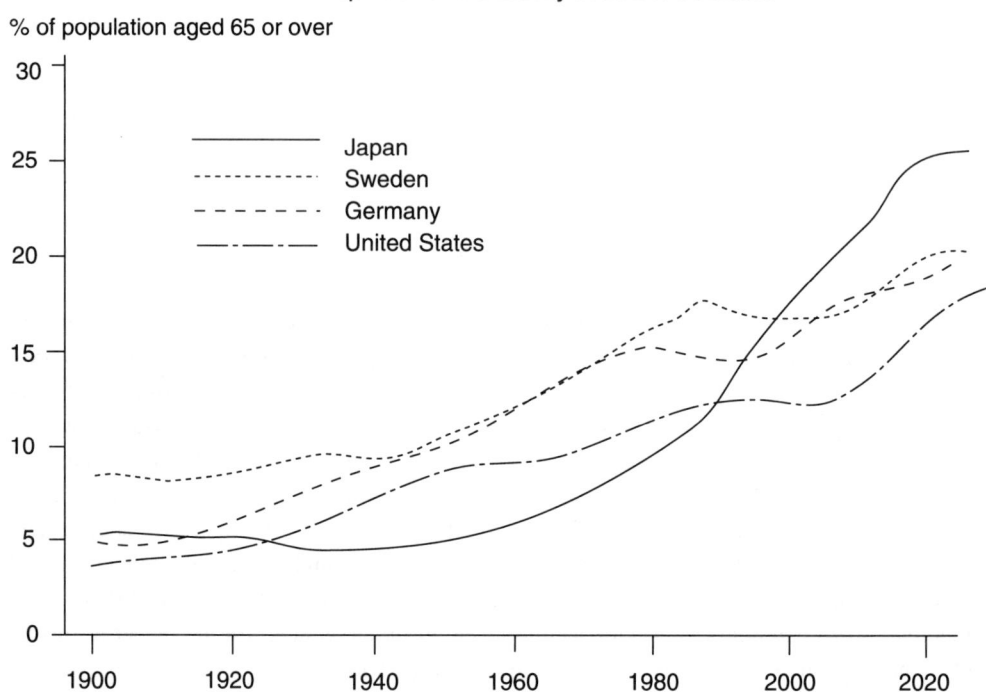

Source: *Jinko no doko* (Population Trends), Institute of Population Problems, Ministry of Health and Welfare, 1993.

The aging process is moving more rapidly and will last longer in Japan than other countries. The rapid escalation rate of the aging population is due to the increase in the life span of the Japanese, resulting from rising income standards, better diet, the widespread practice of annual physicals, introduction of universal health insurance, improvements in medical care, national and corporate safety programs, and high levels of public hygiene. The declining birth rate accentuates the increase in the number of the aging. The government

Total Fertility Rate in Select Countries

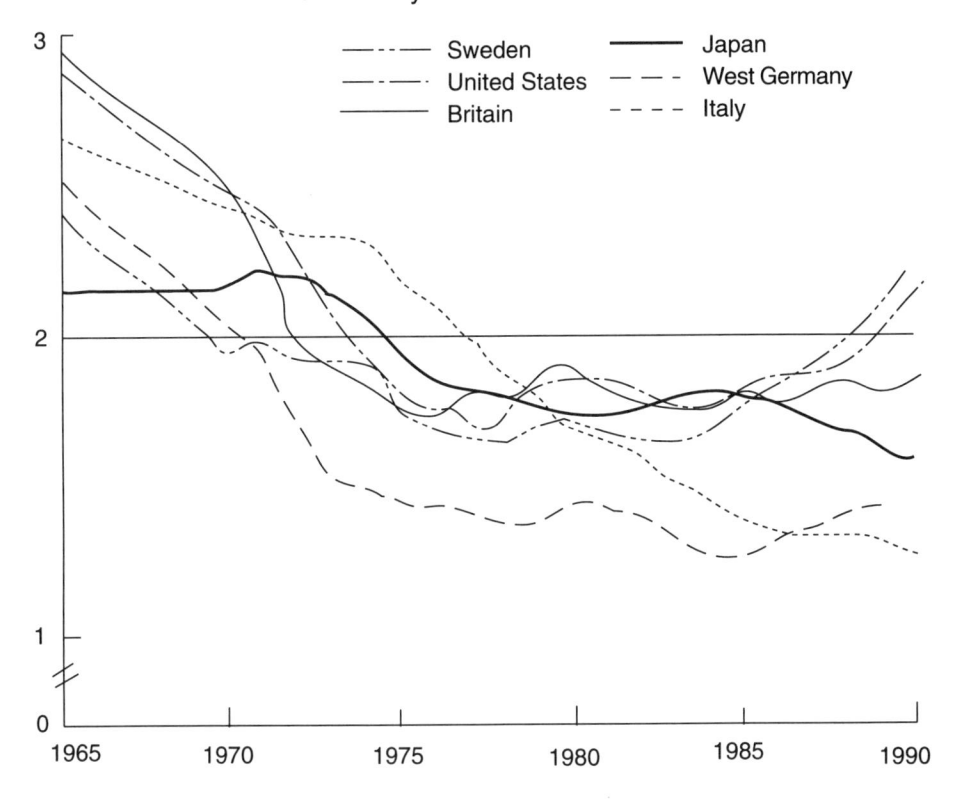

Source: Council of Europe, *Recent Demographic Developments in the Member States of the Council of Europe*, 1990, 1991.

implemented a small-family policy in 1949 and the fertility rate dropped to 2.37 in 1950 from the previous rate of 4.54 (Iwabuchi, 1994). The fertility rate continued to drop to 1.47 in 1993 resulting in a minus population growth situation.

A child-care law was enacted in 1992 in an effort to reverse the birthrate decline, and in 1995 coverage was extended to all businesses. The law requires employers to grant unpaid leave to either the mother or the father for one year following the birth of a child. New legislation proposes benefits amounting to 25 per cent of the wages of the parent on leave and continuation of health insurance and pension without the employee making the required contribution (Iwabuchi, 1994). Japanese women are delaying marriage or deciding to remain single with only 44 per cent of women aged 25 to 29 married according to the *Japanese Working Life Profile*, 1994.

The elderly, projected to be 25 per cent of the population in Japan by the year 2020, is creating an unprecedented workforce concern. The Japanese economy has been stimulated through an abundant, well-educated, technically trained, hard-working, and youthful workforce. However, with the older workforce increasing in number, and the gradual extension of the mandatory retirement age, older workers will remain in the workforce longer and retain more of the high paying positions. Workplace demographics are not necessarily directly correlated to differences in performance in consumer and labor markets but economic performance gaps may shift. The graying of Japanese society is an impetus for reform in pension plans, the medical system and social security funding. The Ministry of Health and Welfare released a reform agenda in 1994 projecting changes in both social security benefit levels and the ratio of total tax payments and social security contributions required. The government's objective is to hold the peak spending burden, which will occur in 2025, below 50 per cent compared to the current 38 per cent (Iwabuchi, 1994). Increased revenues required to maintain the elderly will require an increase in the consumption tax which generates revenue for social security or other equally unpopular measures such as the proposed national welfare tax which created a national cry of outrage.

HISTORY

The new government of the Meiji Restoration era beginning in 1868, implemented a national industrialization policy. The Japanese government announced open trade relations in 1874, and due to prolonged isolation, Japan was required to learn about modern commerce from the American and European merchants. The threat of Westernization accelerated the already existing government involvement in transforming and controlling the economy. However, the Meiji Restoration of the basic economic structure of Japan continued to limit production to agriculture, mining, forestry and livestock. Exports were limited to silk, copper, coal, tea, rice, and marine products while imports included textiles, metal products, equipment, and machinery (Ozawa, 1987).

Trading companies eventually evolved in response to the Japanese desire to manage their own business transactions. The absence of financial resources required to compete with outsiders resulted in the government's role in the economy to strengthen self-sufficiency. Government capitalized industries such as textiles, armaments, mining, shipbuilding and communication which were later transferred to selected private groups at extremely low prices. These Japanese trading companies increased their share to approximately 40 per cent of exports and imports by 1900 establishing the large financial and industrial organizations of the *zaibatsu* (Chen, 1995).

Government involvement in business was a mutually beneficial relationship as the overt support of government by big business in policy formation and implementation were critical to the success of government. The *zaibatsu's* vigorous support of the government's expansionist policies during both world wars mutually benefited government and business (Morikawa, 1992). Trading continued to increase to 70 per cent of exports and 90 per cent of imports by 1920 (Ozawa, 1987). Trading companies were more active and diversified during this era as a consequence of their accumulated knowledge of foreign trade.

The end of World War I resulted in the evolution of three active trading organizations: Mitsu, Mitsubishi, and Suzuki. The major trading companies implemented structural changes by diversifying their functions and activities following World War II (Ozawa, 1987). The vertically-linked, family-dominated *zaibatsus* were replaced by large horizontally-linked *keiretsus*. The new groups, although some retained their original names, competed against each other and were not monopolies but rather formed an oligopoly (Chen, 1995). The *keiretsus* primary direction became one of economic and technological dominance. Today, the *keiretsus* comprise one-third of the total economy, and Japan has over 4,000 trading companies dominated by a few large general trading concerns which manage approximately 70 per cent of the exports and 80 per cent of the imports (Chen, 1995).

Japan's leadership in industry and military power prior to World War II has been forgotten in the shadow of the rebuilding efforts and remembered for its shoddy 1950's products. In 1938, Japan was a world leader in Asian textiles, its steel production was greater than that of France and Italy and its industrial growth was faster than that of the United States (Prestowitz, 1988). The textile, shipbuilding, steel and consumer electronics industries were quickly re-conquered following World War II while other countries watched from the sidelines.

GOVERNMENT

Japan is a parliamentary democracy with a monarch, Emperor Akihito, as figurehead and a prime minister chosen by ballot of the Diet. The Prime Minister appoints a cabinet with the majority of the members being current members of the Diet. The Diet is a bicameral national legislature with a 511-member house of representatives elected every four years, and a 252-member house of councilors who are elected for a six-year term. The Japanese legal system is similar to the United States' with a supreme court which is appointed by the cabinet. There are four lesser court levels comprising a High Court, District Courts, Family Courts and Summary Courts. Japanese political style is based on consensus rather than confrontation and factions within the ruling party are as important as the opposition party.

The real power is exercised by politicians and bureaucrats through the numerous overlapping, semi-autonomous ministries which form the foundation of the Japanese government structure. The hierarchies include powerful groups of ministry officials, political cliques and clusters of bureaucrat-businessmen. This unique structure ultimately leaves no one in charge with no central governing body (van Wolferen, 1989). The ministries are controlled by autocrats and the government is the ministries which control the sectors of society under their authority (Prestowitz, 1988). The social and industrial structure of Japan is intricately interwoven with government processes and policies. In 1877 Tokyo University was founded specifically to prepare worthy successors to the civil service ranks. The civil service has always been the elite of the elite in Japan. The original officials of modern Japan were *samurai*, long members of the governing class (Prestowitz, 1988).

Development of industrial policy is a varied, sophisticated, and subtle process. The Industrial Structure Council of the Ministry of International Trade and Industry, the Telecommunication Advisory Council of the Ministry of Posts and Telecommunications and advisory groups to the other ministries are critical parties to the policy development process. Usually, fifty council members are chosen from leaders in business, consumer groups, labor unions, academia, government, and the press. The secondary level comprises subcommittees of similar composition organized along industry lines.

MINISTRY OF INTERNATIONAL TRADE AND INDUSTRY AND MINISTRY OF FINANCE

The Ministry of International Trade and Industry (MITI) conducts a variety of activities related to international trade and industry. MITI evolved out of the Ministry of Agriculture and Commerce (MAC) which was established in 1885, as the Ministry of Commerce and Industry. In May 1949 it was renamed and restructured with a mandate to formulate policies and regulations that promote the development of Japan's economy and industry with the objective of promoting economic growth and achieving a higher quality of life.

MITI historically targeted specific industries within the economy and was responsible for development of the framework for industrial relationships, distribution activities and management of raw materials. MITI is responsible for the economic sectors involved with consumer goods, machinery, information industries, high technology, international trade policy, environmental protection policy and energy resource management. Currently, MITI is involved with the deregulation policy and trade-related issues.

The Ministry of Finance (MOF) is responsible for the implementation of MITI policies. The MOF is the control agency for the budgetary process and the grantor of low-interest government loans. Various tax measures are implemented by the MOF which is a major rival of MITI (Magaziner and Hout, 1980). The government bureaucracy, business, and the political parties in Japan have intricate relationships and lines of communication which are often referred to as the tripod of economic development.

TRADE BARRIERS

Japan is not a major importer of manufactured products in monetary terms, as a ratio of GDP, or as a proportion of total trade, as compared with the United States, West Germany and all other EC countries. On the other hand, Japan imports more raw materials than any other industrialized country, including the United States. Japan is second to the US in crude oil and other fuel imports (Japan Institute for Social and Economic Affairs, 1994).

The World Bank concludes that Japan's low propensity to import manufactured and agricultural products is largely a result of informal barriers. Government procurement policies, complicated standards and certification procedures, differences in legal frameworks, protection of intellectual property rights and government regulation of retail barriers are examples of the government controls which present serious obstacles. The OECD notes that private business practices may be the biggest obstacle to the import of manufactures in Japan. The *keiretsu* presents the greatest challenge to entry into the Japanese market and exercises this control through government relationships (Leher and Murray, 1990).

The recent deregulation policies and measures to open markets are expected to impact only slightly as the measures are generally viewed as inadequate. Complaints from overseas officials and Japanese business leaders were expressed even though over 1,091 items were approved for deregulation. The World Trade Organization's investigation and report on the deregulation of markets and promotion of imports was generally favorable for future business relations (*EIU Country Report*, 1995).

ECONOMIC SECTORS

Demand trends in overseas markets have impacted on Japanese export volumes more than fluctuations in the yen's exchange rate. The demand is high for Japanese exports and transfer of manufacturing capacity throughout Asia. The strong yen results in lower prices for imports and counter the damage of the effects of the strong yen on corporate profits (*EIU Country Report*, 1995).

The mutually supportive relationship between Japan and the East and Southeast Asian economics provides a viable market for future develop and economic alliances. Japan is a source of capital, technology, human resource development and a potential market which provides a model for economic development and planning (Abegglen and Stalk, 1985). The current strength of the yen will reduce the risk of inflationary pressure increasing in Japan and will continue to lead to a radical restructuring of industry throughout Asia. The yen's appreciation has led to closer ties between Japanese firms and companies from other Asian countries (*EIU Country Report*, 1995).

The GDP is predicted to remain relatively stable due to the appreciation of the yen and the related increase in import volume. The labor market is expected to stabilize in 1996 which will likely result in increased private consumption. Corporate profits are expected to show modest growth over the next two years which will result in bonus payments. An increase in overtime hours and bonuses historically results in increase in household spending. A strong correlation exists between these variables (*EIU Country Report*, 1995).

Economic Structure

Economic indicators	1989	1990	1991	1992	1993	1994
GDP at market prices (¥ trn)	396.2	424.5	451.3	463.9	466.0	469.2
Real GDP growth (%)	4.7	4.8	4.3	1.1	− 0.2	0.6
Consumer price inflation (%)	2.2	3.1	3.3	1.6	1.3	0.7
Population (million)	123.3	123.6	124.0	124.5	124.8	125.0
Exports fob (US$, billions)	269.6	280.4	306.6	330.9	351.3	384.0
Imports fob (US$, billions)	192.7	216.8	203.5	198.5	209.8	238.2
Current-account balance ($ bn)	57.0	35.9	72.9	117.6	131.4	129.3
Reserves excluding gold (US$, billion)	84.0	78.5	72.1	71.6	98.5	125.9
Exchange rate (average) ¥:$*	138.0	144.8	134.7	126.7	111.2	102.2

*April 7, 1995: ¥84: $1

Origins of net domestic product 1993	Per cent of total	Components of gross domestic product 1994	Per cent of total
Agriculture, forestry & fishing	2.1	Private consumption	59.2
Mining & quarrying	0.3	Government consumption	9.8
Manufacturing	26.8	Private dwelling investment	5.5
Construction	10.3	Private plant & equipment investment	14.1
Electricity, gas & water	2.9	Government investment	9.0
Wholesale & retail trade	12.5	Change in inventories	0.3
Banks, insurance & real estate	16.2	Exports of goods & services	9.5
Transport & communications	6.3	Imports of goods & services	− 7.3
Other service industries	16.4	**GDP at market prices**	**100.0**
Government services	7.9		
Imputed rent, etc.	− 4.8		
NDP at factor cost (market prices, including others)	100.0		

Source: *EIU Country Report*, 2nd quarter, 1995 (© The Economist intelligence Unit Limited, 1995).

INDUSTRIAL

Aggressive efforts to restructure and diversify in both product and location of production has occurred throughout the manufacturing sector. Workers will continue to lose jobs in the industrial sector as manufacturing is relocated and organizations restructured but job generation in the service sector and part-time employment is expected to increase (*EIU Country Report*, 1995).

The current manufactured goods in other countries is only 20 per cent and is low by industrialized country standards. The manufacturing of high-technology goods is expected to continue in Japan. The market share of these companies in world markets can be controlled due to the Japanese monopoly in this field, thus the ability to manipulate prices as monetary markets fluctuate.

AUTOMOTIVE INDUSTRY

A modest increase in production of automobiles will not impact the continuing of the restructuring of the industry. Nissan alone is reported to be planning to reduce its workforce by approximately 7,000 over the next three years. Many companies are increasing overseas production and importing the finished products into Japan. Toyota opened a plant in Australia in March 1995, and plans to double production in the United Kingdom. According to a JETRO survey of 931 manufacturers operating in Southeast Asia, 38 per cent reported that their parent corporation will increase overseas production. A similar study conducted by the Bank of Japan reported that overseas corporations intended to increase production by approximately 10 per cent. The same corporations planned to increase domestic production by only 2.4 per cent (*EIU Country Report*, 1995).

CONSTRUCTION

Residential and commercial land prices declined for the fourth consecutive year as reported by the National Agency. Metropolitan residential prices are approximately 70 per cent higher than 1983, the beginning of the soaring asset inflation era. However, central Tokyo residential land prices plunged 15.3 per cent in 1994 and commercial land prices declined even more rapidly.

The Kobe earth quake increase construction in the Kansai area but resulted in a decrease of 5.6 per cent in the start of housing projects throughout Japan. The requirement to modernize and strengthen infrastructure and building throughout Japan in preparation for future earthquakes will result in an increase in the construction industry.

Housing starts and construction orders

	Housing starts		Construction orders*	
	'000 units	Per cent change	¥ bn	Per cent change**
1991	1,370.1	− 19.7	26,053.6	2.0
1992	1,402.6	2.4	24,123.3	− 7.4
1993	1,485.7	5.9	19,731.7	− 18.2
1994	1,570.3	5.7	19,198.3	− 2.7
April	135.8	11.6	1,131.0	− 7.8
May	130.1	13.5	1,045.5	− 16.9
June	147.9	10.6	1,406.1	− 2.9
July	145.4	5.8	1,392.8	17.8
Aug.	139.8	1.8	1,669.4	9.2
Sept.	132.6	− 2.7	2,193.4	− 7.0
Oct.	134.9	0.2	1,281.9	6.7
Nov.	137.0	4.5	1,584.5	20.8
Dec.	129.5	2.9	1,714.6	6.1
1995				
Jan.	100.2	− 5.6	n/a	n/a
Feb.	114.4	1.8	n/a	n/a

* From 50 major construction companies.
** On year-earlier period.

Source: Ministry of Construction.

AGRICULTURAL, FISHING AND FORESTRY

Agriculture, fishing and forestry account for about 2.7 per cent of the national income and 7.2 per cent of employment. Approximately 15 per cent of the land area is available for agriculture and stock-rearing. Agriculture is highly intensive, making considerable use of capital investment and technology. The forestry industry supplies the domestic market with timber and wood leaving 60 per cent of the requirements to be met through imports. Fishing contributes substantially to the domestic food supply and export earnings. Aquaculture is well developed, and there are inshore fisheries for crustaceans and shallow water fish (*The World of Information 1993/1994*).

FINANCIAL

The financial system continues in a weakened condition due to the volume of non-performing assets in land investment and stocks. The value of collateral against loans has eroded the capital foundation of financial institutions. The deflated values of real estate portfolios and rising yen rates have placed banking institutions in a tenuous situations and have become themselves a liability. The recent rescue of insolvent credit unions by government action is extremely controversial and has weakened the financial system. The government provided public funds to establish a special bank to rescue these financial institutions where widespread mismanagement and abuse of funds created many of the insolvent conditions.

Direct investment by Taiwan, China, Singapore and other Asian countries is rapidly increasing in Japan. Asian nations invested $464.4 million in 1993 compared to $98.5 million in 1992 (Takahashi, 1995). The majority of the money was invested in banking and service sectors, possibly with the intent to more easily access Japanese markets. Secondly, the yen's appreciation assists these countries in gaining more profit from exports. Finally, the fall in land prices has resulted in lower office rents and lower operating costs for foreign organizations in Japan. Combined with deregulation and simplified procedures for capital investment foreign investment is expected to continue to accelerate.

LABOR MARKET

Employment growth slowed due to the recession and the restructuring of organizations and relocation of manufacturing to overseas locations. New employment opportunities declined

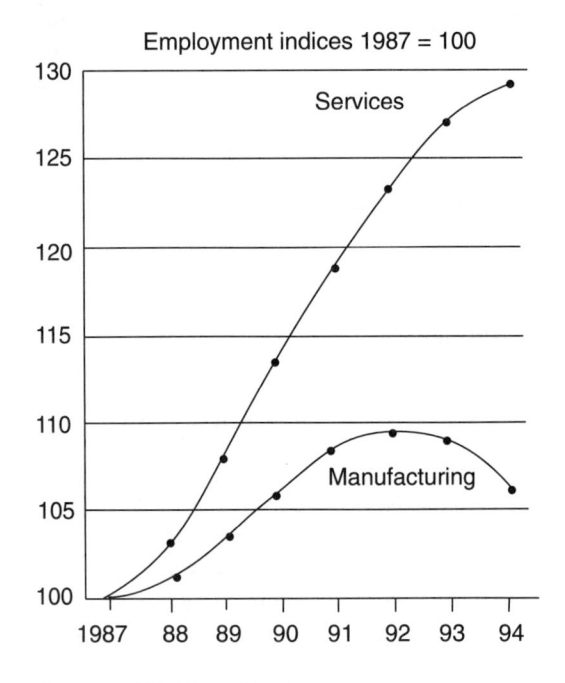

Employment indices 1987 = 100

Source: Ministry of Labour.

as large-scale reductions in employees occurred and graduate recruitment was reduced. The ratio of job seekers to job openings fell to 1.08 in 1992 for the first time and has continued to decline. The number of foreign migrant workers has declined and the policy of excluding unskilled migrant workers has been enforced. Unemployment for women and workers between ages 15 and 24 are higher than the average (Labor Trends, 1994).

Labor costs are high in Japan, and are continuing to rise as is labor productivity for the past one year. The current recovery in domestic demand has resulted in increased overtime hours. However, companies remain cautious and only half of the companies report intentions to recruit high-school graduates in 1995. The unemployment rate has remained constant since November 1994 and the labor market has remained stable since the beginning of 1995.

Employment trends (seasonally adjusted)

	Unemployment rate (%)	Ratio of active job offers to seekers*
1991	2.1	1.40
1992	2.2	1.08
1993	2.5	0.76
1994	2.9	0.64
April	2.8	0.66
May	2.8	0.64
June	2.9	0.63
July	3.0	0.62
Aug.	3.0	0.63
Sep.	3.0	0.64
Oct.	3.0	0.64
Nov.	2.9	0.64
Dec.	2.9	0.64
1995		
Jan.	2.9	0.66
Feb.	2.9	0.66

*Including part-timers and excluding new school graduates.

Source: Management and Coordination Agency, Ministry of Labour.

MANAGEMENT AND ORGANIZATIONAL BEHAVIOR PRACTICES

BUSINESS AND SOCIAL CUSTOMS

Gift giving, relative to the relationship is a traditional business custom and is more common than in other countries. The business card exchange is mandatory, and protocol requires time spent examining the cards received in a formal manner. Cards are so critical that major hotels offer quick printing services for cards with a Japanese translation on one side. Interpreters, translators and secretarial services can also be arranged through hotels in the large cities. Removal of shoes is a requirement before entering Japanese-style houses and restaurants. Restaurants are the usual site for private social entraining instead of homes and hotel suites.

NEGOTIATION STRATEGIES

Western negotiation style has disagreeable connotations of conflict, expression of strong emotion, and confrontation to the Japanese (March, 1988). Discussion of issues outside the formal meeting setting, working towards consensus and consideration of long-term interests are the integral dimensions of the domestic Japanese negotiating style. All parties' interests are heard before decisions are made (Sethi, Namaiki, Swanson, 1984).

A Westerner often views Japanese negotiations as oblique, indirect, lacking in openness, maybe even perverse (March, 1988). The Japanese sense of honor and mutual trust dictates that contracts remain verbal (Mitsubishi, 1988). This practice may not extent to international business transactions because of experience with foreign business practices. However, international negotiations require that all parties understand and respect cultural negotiation styles differences.

REFERENCES

Abegglen, J.C. and G. Stalk, Jr., *Kaisha: The Japanese Corporation*, New York: Basic Books, 1985.
Chen, M., *Asian Management Systems: Chinese, Japanese and Korean styles of business*, New York: Routledge, 1995.
Economist Intelligence Unit, *Country Report: Japan*, 2nd quarter 1995, New York.
Iwabuchi, K., Social Security Today and Tomorrow, *Economic Eye, A Quarterly Digest of Views from Japan*, Tokyo: Keizai Koho Center, Institute for Social and Economic Affairs, 1994, pp. 2–5.
Japan Institute of Labor, *Japanese Working Life Profile: Statistical aspects*, Tokyo, 1994.
Japan Institute for Social and Economic Affairs, *Japan 1994: An international comparison, facts and figures*, Tokyo: Keizai Koho Center, Japan Institute for Social and Economic Affairs.
Lehner, U.C. and A. Murray, Strained Alliance: Will the U.S. find the resolve to meet the Japanese challenge? *The Wall Street Journal*, July 2, 1990, p. E2.
Magaziner, I.C. and T.M. Hout, *Japanese Industrial Policy*, Berkeley, CA: University of California Press, 1980.
March, R.M., *The Japanese Negotiator: Subtlety and strategy beyond Western logic*, Tokyo, Kodansha International, 1988.
Mitsubishi Corporation, *Tatemae and Honne: Distinguishing between good form and real intention in Japanese business culture*, New York: The Free Press, 1988.
Morikawa, H., *Zaibatsu: The rise and fall of family enterprise groups in Japan*, Tokyo: University of Tokyo Press, 1992.
Ozawa, T.L., *Role of General Trading Firms in Trade and Development: Some experiences*, Tokyo: Asia Productivity Organization, 1987.
Prestowitz, C.V., *How America Allowed Japan to Take the Lead*, Tokyo: Charles E. Tuttle Company, 1988.
Sethi, S.P., N. Namaiki, and C.L. Swanson, *The False Promise of the Japanese Miracle: Illusions and realities of the Japanese management system*, Boston, MA: Pitman, 1984.

Takahashi, E., Direct Investment: Asians pour cash and confidence into Japan, *Japan Update*, Vol. 42, 1994, pp. 12–13.

US Department of Labor, Bureau of International Labor Affairs, *Foreign Labor Trends: Japan*, FLT 94–26, 1994.

van Wolferen, K., *The Enigma of Japanese Power*, New York: Alfred A. Knopf, 1989.

World of Information: Asia and Pacific review 1993/1994, 13th ed., The Economic and Business Report, London: Kogan Page and Walden Publishing.

CASE ONE

TOYOTA MOTOR CORPORATION IN 1994*

One of the dreams I have is to see our automobiles being driven in every corner of the world, allowing people to lead fuller lives. I intend to undertake every effort so that Toyota will be able to meet whatever challenges may emerge and continue to build attractive products.

Shoichiro Toyoda, Chairman,
Toyota Motor Corporation

Toyota Motor Corporation, the third largest automaker in the world, was acknowledged by both industry observers and its competitors as the "best car maker in the world." Headquartered in Toyota City, approximately 150 miles west of Tokyo in central Japan, Toyota was the largest industrial enterprise in Japan and the fifth largest in the world, according to *Fortune's* Global 500. In fiscal 1993, Toyota had sales of US$95.4 billion, a net profit of US$1.6 billion, and about US$15.6 billion in cash, earning it the nickname, the "Bank of Toyota." Overseas revenues were 26 per cent of the company's total revenues in 1993. Under the leadership of current President Tatsuro Toyoda, Toyota Motor's most significant accomplishments include:

- Developing a fundamentally new approach to manufacturing, admired and emulated by competitors, that was predicted to eventually transform the way things were made in virtually every industry.
- Maintaining its status as the most efficient automaker in the world, having achieved this feat in 1965.
- Being the undisputed quality leader in automotive manufacturing, making three of the four cars with the fewest defects sold in the US in 1990.
- Introducing one of the most successful luxury automobiles, the Lexus, which was consistently ranked No. 1 in quality in the US.
- Having outstanding labor relations.

---

* This case was prepared by Jana F. Kuzmicki of Indiana University Southeast for class discussion and for no other purpose.

Toyota had plants in more than 20 countries, including the United States and the United Kingdom. In 1992, Toyota held 35.5 per cent of the Japanese car market, about 9.5 per cent of the global market, and 8 per cent of the US vehicle market. Toyota's sales of autos and trucks in the US had consistently exceeded 1 million since 1990. Toyota's goals included producing 6 million vehicles and securing 10 per cent of the global vehicle market (the "Global 10" strategy) by the turn of the century. Articulated as early as 1969 by then President Taizo Ishida, Toyota's long-term ambition was to become worldwide what it was in Japan—*Ichiban* or No. 1—thus guaranteeing a battle with GM, the current global leader, for the world's top spot by the turn of the century.

As the mid-1990s approached, changes in the domestic and global competitive markets presented unique challenges to Toyota's management: declining domestic demand, continuing appreciation of the yen, increasing government pressure to reduce annual work hours of employees (combined with a declining labor force), persisting trade frictions with both the US and Europe, and intensifying competition from a revitalized US auto industry. Exhibit 1 presents the global market shares of the companies vying for world leadership of the auto industry. Exhibit 2 provides summary financial information in respect of Toyota.

Exhibit 1 Global Market Shares of the Top Twelve Motor Vehicle Producers, 1987–92* (%)

Company	1992	1991	1990	1989	1988	1987
General Motors	14.5	14.8	14.8	16.5	17.0	16.7
Ford	11.7	11.3	11.7	13.3	13.7	13.2
Toyota	9.5	9.9	9.7	9.3	8.1	7.9
Volkswagen	7.1	6.6	6.1	6.1	5.9	5.9
Nissan	6.0	6.5	6.1	6.3	5.7	4.9
Fiat Group	4.5	5.2	5.4	5.1	4.5	4.2
Chrysler Corp.	4.4	3.1	3.3	5.0	5.4	4.8
Peugeot-Citroen	4.1	4.3	4.4	4.6	4.4	4.2
Renault SA	4.1	3.8	3.5	4.3	4.1	3.9
Honda	3.7	4.2	3.9	3.9	3.7	3.4
Mitsubishi	3.7	4.0	3.6	2.3	2.7	2.7
Mazda	3.0	3.3	3.2	3.1	2.6	2.6

* Based on total production of all vehicles, including cars, trucks, buses, tractors, and commercial vehicles.

Source: *Automotive News*, Market Data Book Issue, 1993, p. 3; 1990, pp. 3 and 6; 1989, p. 6.

COMPANY HISTORY AND BACKGROUND

Toyota's beginnings could be traced to Sakichi Toyoda, an inveterate tinkerer, who eventually received a total of 84 patents for his inventions. The automatic loom, his most famous

Case One

Exhibit 2 Summary Financial Information, Toyota Motor Corporation, 1989–93 (US$ '000)—Year Ending June 30

	1993	1992	1991	1990	1989
Sales	95,368,396	80,798,839	71,548,258	60,488,874	55,826,452
Net income	1,648,174	1,890,828	3,132,327	2,903,767	2,409,984
Market capital	52,835,246	42,599,881	44,510,677	52,070,549	50,310,907
Common equity	43,771,975	37,300,899	33,168,907	27,872,018	25,818,656
Total assets	87,220,451	75,968,284	65,186,974	55,476,605	49,784,087

invention, resulted in the establishment of Toyoda Automatic Loom Works in 1926. Early in his career in 1910, Sakichi Toyoda became discouraged with his work and decided to visit the US, where he spent six months inspecting factories. Several years after his return, Sakichi Toyoda stated to a group of engineers:[1]

> *To tell you the truth, I felt that my eyes had been opened. As I viewed the plants in cities all across the United States, and felt the tremendous energy of the Americans, I got angry at myself for being so blind. I was ashamed for having been ready to throw everything away after only a few failures.*

Kiichiro Toyoda, son of Sakichi Toyoda, inherited his father's inquisitive nature, but his interest lay in the fledgling auto industry. Like his father, Kiichiro Toyoda visited the US in 1930 to study the art of automaking. Armed with US$500,000 from the sale of the automatic loom patent to a British company in 1929, Kiichiro Toyoda pursued the development of a small passenger car. Initially, he concentrated on learning the techniques of mass production. For inspiration, Kiichiro Toyoda often turned to Henry Ford's book, *My Life and Work*, urging others in the company to read it. By the middle 1920s, both Ford and GM had built assembly plants in Japan, turning out 18,000 vehicles a year. The auto quickly caught on in Japan, resulting in early dominance of the Japanese auto market by American automakers.

Kiichiro Toyoda was handicapped in his endeavors by the underdeveloped Japanese parts and machinery industries. Typically, these firms were family enterprises, and their products were either unreliable or high-priced. Undaunted, Kiichiro Toyoda focused on the kind and number of automobiles to build to develop a successful enterprise. He decided it was essential to mass produce a passenger car of the size most in demand in Japan. According to Kiichiro Toyoda:[2]

> *Instead of avoiding competition with Ford and Chevrolet, we will develop and mass produce a car that incorporates the strong points of both and that can rival foreign cars in performance and price. Although we will base our method of production on the American mass-production system, it will not be an exact imitation but will reflect the particular conditions in Japan.*

Kiichiro Toyoda's persistent efforts culminated in the production of Toyota's first passenger car prototype in 1935.

Meanwhile, the government took steps to stimulate domestic auto production. In 1936, the Law Concerning the Manufacture of Motor Vehicles was passed to promote the establishment of the Japanese auto industry and to curb vehicle imports from abroad. The law required that companies manufacturing more than 3,000 units annually within Japan be licensed by the government, that a majority of the stockholders in such companies be Japanese, and that 100 per cent domestic production of all vehicle parts be a goal. Ford and GM were never granted a license, resulting in the eventual end of their Japanese auto operations.

Toyoda Automatic Loom Works was granted a license, officially designating it as a company eligible to make motor vehicles. Aware of the importance of a brand name, Kiichiro Toyoda held a public contest, which drew 27,000 entries, for a new Toyoda logo. "Toyota" was the winning entry. As a design, the Japanese symbol imparted a sense of speed, was considered aesthetically superior, and required eight (8 is considered a lucky number in Japan) strokes to write it. The automotive department was separated as a new company in August 1937, resulting in the formation of the Toyota Motor Company. The Toyoda precepts, embodying the philosophy and convictions of Sakichi Toyoda, were to serve as guidelines for the operations of the companies in the Toyota group (see Exhibit 3). In the following year, Toyota completed construction of its first major plant located in Koromo (today's Toyota City).

Exhibit 3 The Toyoda Precepts

1. Be contributive to the development and welfare of the country by working together, regardless of position, in faithfully fulfilling your duties.
2. Be at the vanguard of the times through endless creativity, inquisitiveness, and pursuit of improvement.
3. Be practical and avoid frivolity.
4. Be kind and generous; strive to create a warm, homelike atmosphere.
5. Be reverent, and show gratitude for things great and small in thought and deed.

Source: Toyota Motor Corporation, *Toyota: A History of the First 50 Years,* Toyota, 1988, pp. 37–38.

In designing the Koromo plant, Kiichiro Toyoda's ideas provided the foundation for what was to become known as the Toyota production system. Kiichiro Toyoda's approach to vehicle manufacturing, codified into a manual four inches thick, described in meticulous detail the flow-production system, or "just-in-time" concept. By this he meant, "Just make what is needed in time, but don't make too much." The manufacturing system Kiichiro Toyoda designed was predicated on four principles:[3]

- Have the 30 or more factory buildings of various sizes laid out so that their proximities to one another will be conducive to the smooth production of complete automobiles.

- Locate machinery in the plant so the layout will facilitate work flow from one machine to the other.
- Build machines that will be flexible enough in function to meet any requirement, bearing in mind that they are to be used for 20 or 30 years.
- Forget the commonly held notion that warehouses are essential in a plant.

"Creating product quality within the process" was another idea of Kiichiro Toyoda. The goal was not to just differentiate between good and bad products, but to find a way to correct whatever needed fixing, be it machinery, equipment, or tools, to prevent defects from happening in the first place. Implementing the system involved thorough training of the employees and getting them to abandon their old ways of doing things.

World War II disrupted Kiichiro Toyoda's vision of producing passenger cars. Automakers were obliged to concentrate on producing trucks for the military due to governmental limitations on the building of small vehicles. Scarce raw materials, such as iron and steel, were a major problem, and Toyota spent more energy scavenging for materials than on building vehicles. Wartime production of trucks and buses peaked in 1941 with 42,813 units built by all Japanese automakers; in that same year, Toyota produced only 208 passenger cars. In 1945, Toyota produced 3,275 trucks and buses and no passenger cars.

POST-WORLD WAR II OPERATIONS

Following World War II, the Japanese auto industry had to start afresh. Determined to enter car and truck production on a full-scale basis, Toyota executives faced several obstacles: producing a variety of vehicles appropriate for a small domestic market; coping with obsolete production equipment and facilities in disrepair; dealing with a native Japanese work force no longer content to be treated as an expandable factor of production; being unable to purchase the latest US and European technology because of lack of capital; and growing interest of expansion-minded foreign motor vehicle producers in building plants in Japan or, at least, serving the Japanese market with vehicles exported from their own domestic plants.

Kiichiro Toyoda firmly believed the era of the small passenger car had arrived. Research on a small car became Toyota's top priority:[4]

> *The passenger car that will be appropriate for Japan will be not an American-style large car, but rather a small car. In Japan, there is some experience accumulated in the area of small cars, yet when it comes to development on the basis of the functions which are peculiar to a small car, the record is quite short. As a result, existing small cars suffer from many problems, such as cramped interiors, excessive weight, low horsepower, and excessive vibration. If these problems could be solved, then naturally people would come to evaluate the utility of small cars on the same level as that of large ones. And undoubtedly, along with such advantageous characteristics would come the possibility of exporting small cars.*

When permission was received to produce a limited number of small vehicles in mid-1947, Toyota launched a small passenger car, named the Toyopet.

Adverse economic conditions in 1949 resulted in a financial crisis at Toyota. A consortium of banks agreed to provide aid to Toyota if the sales department was incorporated as an independent company (Toyota Motor Sales) and substantial personnel cuts were made. In 1950, Eiji Toyoda, Kiichiro Toyoda's cousin, visited the Ford facilities in the US to study the US approach to automaking. Upon his return, when asked how long it would take to catch up to Ford, Eiji Toyoda responded: "Ford's not doing anything we don't already know." If a difference existed, it was due to a large gap in production scale, not in technological know-how.

Eiji Toyoda's reports provided the basis for a five-year modernization plan, affecting all aspects of Toyota's operations. The ultimate goal was to increase production capacity to 3,000 units per month. The Toyota creative ideas and suggestions system, based on the suggestion system used by Ford, was implemented to support company-wide improvements in production methods and efficiency. One outcome of this program was the company slogan, "Good thinking, good products." After 13 years in business, Toyota had produced 2,685 automobiles, compared with the 7,000 that Ford's Rouge plant was producing in a single day. By the early 1950s Toyota's financial situation had improved, enabling it to direct profits into research and development and to expand its capital base.

ROLE OF THE GOVERNMENT

Rapid growth in the development of the Japanese auto industry was aided by government policies. Targeted as one of the high-priority industries after World War II in the government's economic reconstruction program, the government pursued two major initiatives to promote automobile self-sufficiency in the quasi-closed economy. First, the Ministry of International Trade and Industry (MITI) limited imports to about 1 per cent of the Japanese market. Second, a plan was proposed to "rationalize" the auto industry through mergers and specialization. Although the plan never materialized, it resulted in heavy investment by the auto companies, enabling them to become more competitive.

Additional government measures to strengthen and protect the ability of the industry to compete included protective tariffs, restrictions on foreign capital participation and loans, accelerated depreciation, special import arrangements for machinery and technology, and long-term, low-interest loans for the auto parts industry. Unprecedented economic growth (average annual rate of 15 per cent) in Japan in the 1960s, combined with the spread of private car ownership, caused the Japanese auto industry to boom.

The Crown line of Toyota cars, with a top speed of 65 mph, made their debut on January 1, 1955 to an enthusiastic reception by the Japanese public. Barely able to keep up with orders due to brisk demand for the Crown, Toyota decided to construct the Motomachi Plant, which would produce 5,000 units per month. According to Eiji Toyoda, the plant was viewed as a big gamble, but enabled Toyota to

> [rise] head and shoulders above its domestic competitors ... So we gained a decisive edge right from the start. Ever since then, we've continually pressed on for fear of

being overtaken, rapidly putting up one new factory after another ... to keep pace with the wave of motorization that hit Japan in the 1960s. By that time, we had won the confidence of the banks and no longer had difficulty raising capital or securing loans for new construction.[5]

THE TOYOTA PRODUCTION SYSTEM

In the late 1940s, top Toyota executives determined that traditional mass production systems used in the US and Europe were inappropriate for building autos suitable for the Japanese market. That decision, followed by four decades of experimenting with and improving on Kiichiro Toyoda's flow-production system, steered Toyota on a course that resulted in the Toyota production system (TPS). The TPS was a customer-focused, lean production approach to motor vehicle manufacturing—a system so novel and efficient that it represented a reinvention of modern manufacturing techniques. The system began with and was totally geared to the needs of customers and dealers. In contrast, with the mass production approach, the needs of the factory came first and dealers and customers were expected to make any necessary accommodations.

The TPS combined the best features of both craft and mass production, while avoiding the high cost of the former and the rigidity of the latter. Emphasis on teamwork, communication, efficient use of resources, elimination of waste, and continuous improvement guided the development of the TPS. The system focused on excellence—continually declining costs, zero defects, zero inventories, and growing ability to expand product variety. The TPS melded the activities of everyone from top management to line workers, suppliers, and dealers into a tightly integrated process, capable of responding almost instantly to customer demand. The TPS had six components:

- A motivated and extremely productive workforce.
- Low-cost, high-quality factory operations guided by just-in-time deliveries of parts and flow-production techniques.
- Long-term partnerships with suppliers.
- Careful market research and short design-to-showroom cycles to keep models closely aligned with market demand.
- Custom-order production and superior customer service.
- A management approach focused on continuous improvement, teamwork, and decentralized decision-making.

The following sections describe each of these in more detail.[6]

WORKFORCE PRACTICES

Prodded by the Japanese government, Toyota (and many other Japanese companies) agreed to guarantee lifetime employment for employees. Toyota provided a pay scale based on seniority, not job classification, with bonus payments tied to company profitability. In return, employees agreed to be flexible in their work assignments and to commit to initiating improvements rather than merely responding to problems.

A major implication was that the workforce was a significant long-term fixed cost much like the company's plants and machinery. Toyota needed to get the most out of its human resources over their working lifetime. Thus, it was only logical to continuously enhance employees' skills and to gain the benefit of their knowledge and experience as well as their physical strength.

Mutual trust, communication, and continuous training characterized the employment relationship. A labor-management declaration, signed in 1962, symbolized the mutual trust relationship. Eiji Toyoda believed that maintaining a relationship of mutual trust with the employees was largely responsible for improvements in labor-management relations.[7]

> *Mutual trust is the basis of labor relations. Labor relations at Toyota were initially marked by doubts and disbelief, but with time differences were ironed out. The labor-management declaration we signed was simply a written statement of this rapprochement. The purpose of this document was to uphold and sustain the trust that had been built up between management and labor, and to prevent backsliding by either side from this position. It also was intended as a reminder to those who came after to guard the fruits won through the sacrifices made by both sides. The spirit of this declaration still lives on at Toyota.*

Management consistently worked hard at maintaining good relations. Establishing quality circles was integral to the overall relationship. The goal of these employee groups was not just to look for ways to improve product quality, but to improve all facets of production—unit costs, speed of assembly, and delivery schedules. Additionally, management initiated elaborate orientation programs and actively promoted informal contact between employees at all levels of the company. The result was enthusiastic, devoted, conscientious employees who often hung around the assembly line after hours offering suggestions on improvements in work methods. During a recent year, Toyota received 860,000 employee suggestions for improvement; approximately 94 per cent of the ideas were adopted, resulting in estimated savings in excess of US$30 million per year.

FACTORY OPERATIONS

Toyota management regarded final assembly of a vehicle in a typical mass production plant as extremely inefficient. Mass production involved wasted materials, effort, and time. For example, during the late 1940s and early 1950s, an assembly plant might operate normally for only 10 days while remaining idle for 20 days due to a lack of parts. Toyota's goal was to manufacture only what was needed, when it was needed, and of the quantity needed.

Technologically advanced machinery, teams of workers, a high level of work standardization, and small inventories and repair areas typified the factory system. Toyota implemented several innovations to improve production efficiency:

- *Multiskilled assembly workers*: Organizing workers into teams, each team was responsible for determining the necessary operations associated with building a vehicle. Each employee was responsible for operating an average of five machines (multimachine handling). As productivity continued to increase, the teams assumed additional responsibilities, such as housekeeping, minor tool repair, and quality checking, thus reducing the need for engineering and production specialists to perform these functions.
- *Andon boards (electrical signs)*: These were installed at strategic locations in a plant to track daily production, signal overtime requirements, and identify trouble-spots along the line. Individual workers had smaller versions to tell them, for example, whether a bolt was tight enough.
- *Just-in-time or "flow" production*: The objective here was to smooth the flow between the processes supervised by various employees and to drastically reduce the inventories of parts and components. The *kanban* system, using the exchange of various-sized cards, was developed to transfer information between processes. Each card showed the number of parts and parts numbers of items needing replacement. This system was called the "supermarket method," since it imitated the practice in US supermarkets where customers went to stores to buy what they wanted when they wanted it (rather than to store goods) while the supermarket restocked items as they were sold. Thus, a "pull" system evolved—each employee went back to the previous station on the assembly line to retrieve work-in-process, just at the necessary time, getting only the amount needed for immediate processing.
- *Zero defects or built-in quality*: Implementation of a problem-solving system, "the five why's," involved a worker being trained to systematically trace every error back to its initial cause (by asking "why" as each layer of the problem was uncovered) and then devising a method so it would not occur again. Cords were installed above the production line to be pulled by any employee at any time to stop the line if complications arose. Each employee served as the customer for the process just before his and in essence became a quality-control inspector.

Implementation proceeded gradually as employees learned the system. Adjusting production speed, improving production layouts, and gaining experience in error detection and correction resulted in fewer errors occurring.

SUPPLIER RELATIONSHIPS

Auto assembly plants accounted for approximately 15 per cent of Toyota's total manufacturing process, with the rest attributed to the production of the 10,000 or so discrete parts going into a single car. Toyota's suppliers were divided into two tiers, each having different responsibilities. Toyota dealt only with its primary suppliers, numbering approximately 175, on a development project. These suppliers were each assigned a whole component, such as car seats or the electrical system. These suppliers would then contract with secondary suppliers to provide individual parts or sub-system components.

First-tier suppliers were treated as an integral part of Toyota's product development team and were given performance rather than engineering specifications for their assigned component parts. For example, a supplier was told to design a set of brakes that would stop a 2,200-pound car going 60 miles per hour in the space of 200 feet, and do it 10 times in succession without fading. Both the space within which the brakes had to fit and the price were specified. A prototype had to be delivered to Toyota for testing, and if it worked, a production order was awarded. When production of the new model began, suppliers delivered the component parts directly to Toyota's assembly lines, typically several times per day (occasionally every hour or two), with no inspection of incoming deliveries.

Other aspects of Toyota's approach to supplier relationships included:

- Becoming completely familiar with every supplier's operations, including having Toyota design engineers stationed at supplier plants.
- Making equity investments in suppliers' businesses (often, Toyota and its suppliers had substantial holdings of each other's stock).
- Establishing supplier associations that met regularly to share new findings on better ways of making parts.
- Reaching agreements with suppliers that allowed Toyota representatives access to the supplier's costs and profit margins and that provided these representatives opportunities to suggest to the supplier how cost savings might be achieved.
- Providing loans to suppliers, if needed, to purchase cost-saving or quality-enhancing equipment.
- Fostering cooperative, stable, long-term business relationships with suppliers.

PRODUCT DESIGN AND DEVELOPMENT

Leadership, teamwork, communication, and simultaneous development formed the basis of Toyota's approach to designing and engineering a new model. Customer needs and attitudes were carefully analyzed and teams of functional specialists, under the guidance of a *shusa* (chief engineer), were responsible for all activities related to the development of a new product—design, engineering, selection of all suppliers, and marketing strategies. Although they maintained ties with their functional departments, the specialists were committed to the project until their phase of the project was completed. At the inception of the project, team members signed formal pledges to do exactly what everyone agreed upon as a group. If conflicts about resources and priorities occurred, it was at the beginning rather than the end of the process. At the outset of a project, all relevant functional specialties were represented, resulting in the most people being involved at the initial stages. The job of the *shusa* was to force the group to face all the difficult trade-offs they would have to make to reach consensus.

Simultaneous development involved product and manufacturing engineers working closely together under the *shusa* so factory machinery was developed in tandem with prototype testing. Typically, prototype testing led to changes in the car that required alterations in the assembly line; since design and production processes proceeded simultaneously, last minute changes infrequently stalled production plans.

Fewer tools, lower inventories, a higher production of projects going into production on time, no productivity penalty, higher quality, and less human effort resulted in short development times per new car when compared with non-Japanese automakers—less than 40 months for Toyota versus about four years for US automakers and seven years for many European producers. According to one study, Toyota employed slightly more than half as many engineers in designing a new model compared to US companies. As a consequence, Toyota offered a wider variety of models, introducing them to the marketplace more quickly and cheaply than traditional mass producers. By the early 1990s, Toyota produced 26 separate lines of cars, more than most other auto manufacturers.

CUSTOMER AND DEALER RELATIONS

Cooperative links between Toyota, its dealers, and customers were seen as integral to long-term success. In Japan, Toyota had five nationwide dealer "channels" (Toyota, Toyopet, Auto, Vista, and Corolla), each of which marketed a portion of the Toyota line. For example, one channel sold less expensive models while another sold sportier models. The five dealer channels had different labels and model names for their cars, but the main distinction among them was their focus on different types of customers. The major purpose of the channel was to develop a direct link between the manufacturing system and the vehicle owners.

A description of the Corolla channel illustrates how Toyota's distribution system in Japan functioned. Established in 1961, the channel sold the Corolla, Camry, Supra, Celica, and several truck models. The channel consisted of 78 dealer firms, operating from approximately 17 different sites. Corolla owned 20 per cent of the dealerships outright and had partial ownership in others, but most dealerships were financially independent. Corolla provided training to the approximately 30,000 people who made up the sales staff at the 78 dealerships and also offered a full range of services and sales assistance to the dealerships it did not own. In 1989, the Corolla dealer channel, with a staff of some 30,400 people, sold about 635,000 cars and trucks (an average of just over 21 vehicles per staff member). With the exception of the showroom, few similarities existed between a Japanese and a US dealership. A typical Corolla channel dealership in Japan had only three or four demonstrator models and no parking lots of unsold vehicles for prospective buyers to look at. Nor was there a battle over the walk-in customer by the sales staff since the sales team was paid on a group commission, rather than on an individual commission basis.

The sales staff at each Corolla dealership were multiskilled, having been trained in all aspects of sales—product information, order taking, financing, insurance, and data collection—and were divided into teams of seven or eight members. A team meeting began and ended each work day. After developing a profile of all households in the dealership's geographic area and calling for an appointment, members of the sales team made door-to-door sales calls. Updating the household profile was one objective; if the family was ready to purchase a car, a custom order—every Toyota sold in japan was tailor-made to customer specifications—was placed with the factory via an on-line computer. Haggling over price was almost nonexistent, and the deal was not concluded until arrangements regarding financing, trade-in of the old car, and insurance were made. The sales representative delivered the new car directly to the owner's house.

Additional services provided were registration, arrangements for regular maintenance, taking care of rigorous government inspections, fixing any problems encountered by the owner even after the formal warranty expired, providing a car while the car was being repaired, sending birthday cards, and sending condolence cards in the event of a death in the family. The principal objective was not just a one-time sale; rather it was to make the customer feel a part of the Toyota "family," to establish a long-term relationship with the customer, and to build strong brand loyalty. The success of the sales system employed by Toyota (and other Japanese automakers) was reflected by the fact that brand switching was much less common in Japan than in other countries.

The door-to-door sales system was gradually being phased out. Younger buyers, more interested in shopping around than older buyers, wanted to purchase their cars directly from a dealership. Toyota, along with other Japanese automakers, was also having difficulty recruiting salespeople willing to sell cars door-to-door.

Toyota was exploring the use of information technology to cut the high costs associated with the sales system. This involved installing an extensive computer system in the dealerships. A current Corolla owner entering a Corolla dealership inserted his membership card in the system, which displayed all the pertinent information of the owner's household. The owner made relevant changes in the information, and the system then suggested the most appropriate models for the owner's needs, with prices included. The owner also had access to databases dealing with such things as financing, car insurance, and parking permits. If seriously interested in buying, the owner approached the sales team to discuss specific details. The number of cars sold in this way was steadily increasing in Japan, and Toyota hoped to deal with most existing owners using this method. The sales force could then concentrate on "conquest" sales—those to owners currently purchasing other brands.

CUSTOMER RELATIONS OUTSIDE JAPAN. Toyota's sales approach to customers in the US and Europe currently resembled the dealer networks used by American and European producers. Customized orders were not accepted due to the distance involved in supply. Instead, Toyota sold through a network of franchised dealers; to make sure its models were equipped to buyer preferences, Toyota focused on adding a variety of options as standard equipment on their exports, resulting in the customers having more choices. As Toyota established independent production facilities in countries outside Japan, the company planned to investigate the feasibility of building cars to customers' orders and delivering them almost immediately, imitating the approach used in Japan.

TOYOTA'S APPROACH TO MANAGING ITS PRODUCTION SYSTEM

Management of Toyota's production system required different career paths when compared with mass production. In mass production, career progression was virtually nonexistent for production employees, and specialists in engineering, marketing, and finance were promoted on the basis of technical expertise while general managers progressed through the numerous layers in the corporate hierarchy.

At Toyota, however, union members had an opportunity to move into the company's management structure. Each employee's first assignment at Toyota entailed working on the production line. Decentralized decision making was reflected in the career opportunities of all employees, regardless of their career paths. For employees remaining in the factory, the reward system consisted of performance bonuses and pay increases based on seniority. Since fewer layers of management existed, resulting in less opportunity for promotions, the ability to solve increasingly difficult problems was emphasized as the most important aspect of any job, even if job titles did not change. Technical specialists and engineers were assigned to product-development teams; often they had to learn new skills as they progressed through their careers. The goal was to expose these specialists to the day-to-day activities of the company and have them study intensively the changing moods, tastes, and driving habits of vehicle buyers. Responsibilities of general managers consisted of tying supplier organizations to the assembly operations and tying geographically dispersed units of the company together. Often, managers were rotated among the company's various operations, including foreign operations, or they might be assigned to management positions in the supplier organizations.

Overall, the TPS was an exercise in trying to achieve perfection—it focused each employee on anticipating problems and finding preventive solutions. Implementation of the TPS had been a long, gradual process. Begun in the early 1950s, and only after much trial and error, it was in place in all Toyota plants by 1963; subsequently, the TPS was introduced to parts and materials suppliers. By the 1970s, the entire system was firmly ingrained in Toyota's operations and was formally named the "Toyota Production System."

Guided by the philosophy of *kaizen* ("continuous improvement"), Toyota's management constantly pushed for improvements to the TPS and for better and better execution. In the 1980s, Toyota launched bold efforts to make the TPS work more efficiently, responsively, and flexibly to the increased proliferation in car models and to changes in the kinds of cars that consumers wanted. After years of leaving technological innovation to Nissan and Honda, Toyota tripled its R&D spending from US$750 million in 1984 to US$2.2 billion in 1989. Enhancements to the TPS included construction of new integrated facilities, incorporating the most advanced production technology; increased emphasis on maintenance of machinery and equipment; and expansion of automation. Automation involved the introduction of on-line computers for production control; increased use of robots to perform such jobs as spot welding, painting, arc welding, and attaching nuts; and computerization of Toyota's entire operation through the installation of the CAD/CAM (computer-aided design/computer-aided manufacturing) system.

Toyota's overriding objective was to produce only the products demanded in the volumes required. To avoid extreme fluctuations in production volumes associated with changes in customer preferences, Toyota produced the same model simultaneously at more than one plant and produced a number of different models at each plant. Toyota gradually introduced "flexible body lines" (assembly of a number of distinct models on the same product line without decreasing productivity or quality) at its plants, beginning in 1985. Since each line handled mixed production, the time needed to switch to new models was considerably shortened.

As the mid-1990s approached, increasing costs (labor, capital, depreciation, raw materials, and marketing) associated with auto manufacturing in Japan, combined with a plateau in productivity and a labor shortage, spurred Toyota to focus on "modernizing the original idea." Toyota reorganized its product-development activities and embarked on the biggest automation drive in its history. The number of *shusas* had reached about three dozen, which resulted in excessively cumbersome product-development operations. Under the new system, three chief engineers were accountable for the following categories of vehicles: front-wheel drive, rear-wheel drive, and trucks. Each chief engineer was responsible for encouraging cooperation among the *shusas* to achieve the goal of reducing the number of unique vehicle parts by 30 per cent. Although employees were to remain at the hub of the production process, use of computers and robots was expected to increase. One plan involved increasing the amount of mechanized work in Toyota's engine assembly plants from 73 per cent to 85 per cent by 1993. Expanded use of automated design and manufacturing processes was estimated to decrease the design-to-production time from 24 to 22 months. Additional improvements to the TPS included implementing three-crew scheduling systems, which achieved six-day-a-week production at a factory (without overtime), and gradual reduction of the variety of models.

Results of Toyota's most recent enhancements to the TPS were clearly evident at the Tahara manufacturing plant where two luxury models—the Crown Majesta and Aristo (Lexus GS300)—were assembled:[8]

> [The] No. 4 [line at Tahara] is immaculately maintained, remarkably clean, and surprisingly quiet. Since electric vehicle carriers have replaced clangy chain-driven conveyors, people can converse normally. The strains of Beethoven's "Fur Elise" waft through the air over the public address system.
>
> At Tahara workers are hard to find; machines are everywhere. Large motorized platforms called automatic guided vehicles carry steel body panels to the giant stamping presses. Two video cameras help robots perfectly align hoods with engine compartments. Engines, transmissions, and front and rear suspensions rise from the floor, the body descends from above, and the two mate automatically. Machines wielding wrenches attach the bolts. A light board shows when they have achieved proper tightness.

According to the general manager of the plant, the goal of automation was "to make a comfortable working environment for employees and to reduce costly turnover of expensively trained workers."[9] Manufacturing experts indicated that although Tahara's No. 4 line was less automated than some European auto factories, its productivity was unmatched. In the final assembly area, a single shift of 197 employees turned out 192 cars per day. When welding and painting were added in, 16 employee hours were involved in assembling a fully equipped luxury car. Although the time was analogous to producing the Ford Taurus, it was less than half the time necessary for comparable luxury cars: 34 hours for a Lincoln Town Car, 40 hours for a Cadillac Seville, and in excess of 100 hours for a large Mercedes-Benz or BMW.

According to an MIT study conducted in the 1980s, the TPS used less of everything—

"half the human effort in the factory, half the manufacturing space, half the investment in tools, half the engineering hours to develop a new product"—when compared with the traditional mass production methods relied on by American and European manufacturers.[10] Toyota's reinvention of the manufacturing process resulted in a high-quality car or truck built to customer specifications and delivered within 10 days to three weeks.

DOMESTIC OPERATIONS

Nagoya, Japan, home of Toyota City, was the hub of Toyota's worldwide operations network. Toyota City had all the trappings of a "company" town—12 manufacturing plants (4 were dedicated to assembly), factories of nearly 140 of its parts suppliers, company housing (dormitories, apartments, and houses), a huge Toyota sports center (Olympic-size pool, two football fields, four baseball diamonds, two gymnasiums), a Toyota Hospital (free medical care was provided), and clubs of all kinds. Top executives worked out of a flat-roofed three-story structure smaller than a typical US high school.

In 1969, Toyota became the fifth largest automaker in the world, surpassing Fiat. In 1970, Toyota passed Chrysler, advancing to fourth place; in 1971, it jumped ahead of Volkswagen to become the third largest. In 1985, Toyota was producing 40 per cent as many cars as GM with a workforce slightly more than one-tenth the size of GM (part—but only part—of the difference was due to Toyota's greater use of subcontractors). In 1993, Toyota had 108,000 employees, producing nearly 5 million vehicles worldwide. Toyota's share of the passenger car market in Japan was 35.5 per cent in 1991; Toyota's closest rival, Nissan, had a 20.5 per cent share (see Exhibit 4).

The competitive environment of the 1980s and 1990s introduced several factors (some unique to Japanese automakers) that affected the ability to compete both domestically and internationally:

- Slowing economic growth both globally and in Japan (from an inflation-adjusted average annual rate of nearly 5 per cent in the late 1980s, the Japanese economy was expected to grow at an average rate of about 3 per cent during the decade of the 1990s).
- Continuing trade frictions due to trade imbalances between Japan and other countries and the lack of openness of the Japanese market to imports.
- Declining exports to the US and Europe due to import restrictions and strict domestic content laws in other countries.
- Continuing appreciation of the yen (whereas it took 260 yen to equal a dollar in early 1985, by late 1993 it took only 107 yen to equal a dollar).
- Escalating competition in the low-priced car market marked by the entrance of several newly industrialized countries (abundant low-cost labor and rising levels of technology placed them on the heels of the Japanese auto industry).
- Increasing over capacity in the mature, global auto industry.
- Declining sales and profits, combined with increasing costs, in the Japanese auto market.

Exhibit 4 Domestic Market Share of the Five Largest Japanese Automakers, 1970–91* (%)

Year	Toyota	Nissan	Honda	Mazda	Mitsubishi	All Others
1970	29.8	24.7	10.6	6.6	8.9	19.4
1975	39.2	31.3	5.9	6.5	6.2	10.9
1978	37.9	29.2	6.0	6.0	9.1	11.8
1980	37.3	29.0	5.9	6.9	8.8	12.1
1981	38.3	28.1	6.5	7.7	8.2	11.2
1982	38.6	27.1	7.9	8.1	7.4	10.9
1983	39.8	26.6	7.8	7.8	6.0	12.0
1984	41.2	26.0	7.9	6.9	6.4	11.6
1985	42.6	25.2	9.6	6.1	5.4	11.1
1986	43.9	24.3	9.7	6.2	4.6	11.3
1987	44.4	23.4	10.3	6.1	4.8	11.0
1988	43.9	23.2	10.8	5.9	4.9	11.3
1989	40.0	22.6	10.4	6.7	5.3	15.0
1990	37.1	20.7	10.1	7.8	6.2	18.1
1991	35.5	20.5	10.6	7.4	6.9	19.1

* Total new passenger car registrations.

Source: Motor Vehicle Manufacturers' Association of USA, *World Motor Vehicle Data Book*, Detroit, 1993 edition, pp. 69–71, and 1989 edition, pp. 69–71.

To strengthen its position in the highly competitive, global auto market, Toyota focused on enhancing several aspects of its corporate operations. Toyota Motor Company and Toyota Motor Sales were combined in 1982. According to a joint statement by Eiji Toyoda, the new chairman, and Shoichiro Toyoda, the new president of Toyota Motor, the major reasons for the merger were to develop Toyota's international operations and to achieve greater efficiencies in management operations:[11]

> To cope with the turbulent 1980s and to progress further along the path we have taken thus far, a need has emerged to integrate our production and sales functions, which are in fact two sides of the same coin, so that they can augment each other more comprehensively and organically.

Toyota launched the "T-50 Operation" in June 1986 to commemorate the 50th anniversary of its first passenger car. Competitors interpreted the intent of the "operation" as meaning that Toyota aspired to a 50 per cent share of the Japanese passenger car market. According to a manager of a mid-level automaker, "It is a shame for the auto industry to permit Toyota to grab a share of 50 per cent. Toyota, as the leader of Japan's auto industry, should behave in a more adultlike manner."[12] Redoubled sales efforts by the other automakers succeeded in keeping Toyota's share at 49.2 per cent (its highest in history) of all new cars registered in June. This compared with the respective shares of Nissan at 22.8 per cent, Honda at

11 per cent, and Mazda at 5.6 per cent. Typical comments by rival automakers and dealers, who requested anonymity, regarding Toyota's performance included:[13]

> "Toyota is formidable. There is a qualitative difference in its sales system."
> "To be honest, we have received a tremendous jolt. We cannot but ask Toyota to relent a little more."
> "Dealers down to the periphery are exhorted to adhere to orderly sales practices. But such developments may inevitably lead to drastic price-cutting tactics."
> "To be frank, we have no other course but defense. We cannot understand why Toyota cars sell so well. Our parent company (Nissan) insists on fair play and discipline, but we can no longer stick to all our scruples. It is a miracle that Toyota has not adopted the incentive system."

According to rivals, Toyota's strength lay in technical development, enabling it to supply cars exactly matched to customer needs; a powerful distribution system; and near-perfect user services.

By the latter 1980s Toyota's success was, according to industry observers, beginning to breed complacency due to *dai-kigyo-byo* (big company disease) and lagging corporate morale. Former President Shoichiro Toyoda commented: "... things have changed. The days when every employee committed himself completely—and with utter satisfaction—to his job and his company are gone. People are much more varied in their expectations today."[14] Shoichiro Toyoda implemented a "put the customer first" campaign aimed at challenging the company's total approach to making cars and recertifying that customer satisfaction was the first priority. The committee responsible for this customer satisfaction drive was given three years—one thousand days—to get Toyota on the move again and institute *kaizen* on a corporate scale. Additional actions by Shoichiro Toyoda included eliminating two layers of middle management, stripping 1,000 executives of their staffs, and reorganizing product development, putting himself in charge. Toyota's top management stated it was willing to restrain its growth; according to Shoichiro Toyoda:[15]

> We manufacturers realize that we must reexamine and redefine Japan's role in the world, provide positive support, and, taking into account the necessity of contributing to the economies of our trade partners, never forget "coexistence and coprosperity" [the need for kyozon-kyoei or both competition and cooperation].
> The time has come for the industry, taken as a global unit, to learn to live together. In the past, competition was the rule, and some firms went to the wall as a consequence. We cannot have a repeat of this today. The new goal of the car industry must be collective prosperity, not cutthroat competition.

The competitive environment in Japan in the early 1990s found the Japanese automakers mired in their worst slump in 40 years. Appreciation of the yen had converted a Japanese price advantage of about US$1,000 per car in 1985 into a US$2,000 price disadvantage by late 1993; effects of the global recession had resulted in declining vehicle production to 11.5 million vehicles, nearly 2 million less than in 1990; consequences of the "market-share paradox" had resulted in the halving of profit margins although Japanese automakers had tripled sales during the past two decades (losses by at least 4 of the 11 automakers were expected in 1993); and capacity utilization was estimated to be only 80 per cent.

As the dominant Japanese automaker, Toyota faced intensifying pressures from the government, rival competitors, and labor unions to take a leadership role in restructuring its strategies. Known as *risutora* (when translated into English, it meant pruning people, products, and plants), Toyota was urged to lengthen product cycles, raise prices, and call off its drive for market share overseas. Toyota responded by instituting the following changes:

- Implementing changes in the TPS.
- Commencing a companywide cost-cutting campaign, beginning in 1992 (administrative costs were slashed by 30 per cent, which involved cutting expense account budgets for entertainment and business dinners in half, eliminating white-collar overtime, and restricting travel; as part of the "business revolution," 20 per cent of Toyota's 4,000 white-collar administrative employees were shifted from regular jobs to 70 business-reform teams, ostensibly set up to look for corporate inefficiencies).
- Adopting a new corporate slogan—"Making quality cars and friends around the world" (Toyota's actual corporate slogan, printed in a production-methods handbook, was "Taking our destiny into our own hands").
- Slicing the average employee's annual work hours by 50 to 2,050 in 1992 while aiming for additional cuts to 1,900 hours in 1993 (this was slightly less than the average of 1,920 annual hours for US autoworkers).
- Adopting US human resource methods (this included using specific job descriptions, implementing merit pay, cutting managers' bonuses, and creating a new category of temporary professional employees; for example, newly hired automotive designers were hired on one-year contracts, with an annual salary of $89,800 based on individual merit, not seniority).
- Reducing capital spending from an average of $500 billion yen to around $350 billion yen, beginning in April 1993.
- Increasing prices of its vehicles in the US market.
- Announcing an International Cooperation Program, a three-pronged plan aimed at increasing imports, boosting local purchasing by its overseas operations, and furthering cooperation with foreign automakers.
- Building or expanding six assembly plants worldwide with a total capacity of one million vehicles (five were in export markets outside Japan—Britain, Pakistan, Thailand, Turkey, and the US—while a new factory was being built on the southern island of Kyushu).

FINANCIAL OPERATIONS

Toyota Motor Corporation was the largest entity in an affiliation of 13 interlocking companies known as the Toyota Group (see Exhibit 5). The Toyota group was affiliated with the Mitsui

Exhibit 5 The Toyota Group Companies, 1993 (all amounts in US$)

Toyota Motor Corporation
Sales: $10,163.4 billion (06/93)
Tatsuro Toyoda, President
Shoichiro Toyoda, Chairman

Toyota Auto Body
Sales: $605.3 billion (03/92)
Saburo Bito, President
Toyota Motor owns 43.0%

Aisin Seiki Co., Ltd. (Auto Parts)
Sales: $838.5 billion (03/93)
Shigeo Aiki, President
Toyota Motor owns 21.9%

Toyoda Spinning & Weaving (Textiles, Auto Parts)
Sales: N/A
Toyota Motor owns 8%

Hino Motor, Ltd. (Heavy Trucks)
Sales: $632.4 billion (03/93)
Tomio Futami, President
Toyota Motor owns 11.2%

Daihatsu Motor Co., Ltd. (Automaker)
Sales: $875.4 billion (03/93)
Takashi Toyozumi, President
Toyota Motor owns 48.7%

Aichi Steel Works, Ltd.
Sales: $164.0 billion (12/92)
Masaaki Ohhashi, President
Toyota Motor owns 21.8%

Toyoda Gosei Co., Ltd. (Auto Parts)
Sales: $269.5 billion (04/93)
Sheji Ban, President
Toyota Motor owns 40.9%

Toyoda Machine Works, Ltd. (Machine Tools)
Sales: $202.8 billion (03/92)
Toyo Kato, President
Toyota Motor owns 21.1%

Nippondenso Co., Ltd. (Electronic Auto Parts)
Sales: $1,523.8 billion (12/92)
Tsuneo Ishimaro, President
Toyota Motor owns 23.6%

Toyoda Automatic Loom Works, Ltd.
Sales: $583.4 billion (03/92)
Yoshitoshi Toyoda, President
Toyota Motor owns 23.4%

Toyota Central Research & Development Laboratories
Sales: N/A
Toyota Motor owns 54%

Kanto Auto Works, Ltd. (Auto Parts)
Sales: $421.9 billion (03/93)
Fumio Agetsuma, President
Toyota Motor owns 48.7%

Sources: 1. *Business Week*, November 4, 1985, p. 45.
2. *International Directory of Corporate Affiliations*, Wilmette, Illinois: National Register Publishing, 1989, p. 475.

keiretsu. A Japanese *keiretsu*, a form of business alliance, typically consisted of about 20 major companies, one in each major industrial sector, but there was no holding company at the top of the organization. Key companies in a *keiretsu* were banks, insurance companies, and trading companies. The companies were not legally part of a common corporate structure but were held together by cross-locking equity structures—each company owning a portion of every other company's equity—and a sense of reciprocal obligation. Although a key purpose was to help each other raise investment funds, members were also provided protection against hostile takeovers. Another advantage was the ability of group members to obtain low-cost financing from banks in their *keiretsu*.

Toyota was regarded as ultraconservative, a trait which was especially reflected in its cash hoard and strong balance sheet. Successful utilization of *zaiteku* (financial management of surplus cash) resulted in Toyota earning more profits on its financial investments than it did from selling cars. Toyota allocated its investment funds to financial institutions offering the best interest rates, regardless of the type of product, via its competitive bidding system. Thus, Toyota commanded the highest possible interest rates on its cash balances, referred to as the "Toyota rate" in Japanese financial circles, and its interest income had risen over the last several years. Toyota was considered one of Japan's most powerful financial institutions. Toyota's cash-management system closely resembled its *kanban* production system and was typical of its efforts to reduce cost inefficiencies to a minimum. According to one account, Toyota limited employees to one pencil at a time and a sign over the towel dispenser in the restroom at headquarters read: "Visitors Only."

In 1988, Toyota established the Toyota Finance Corporation to provide financing for installment sales and facility leasing for Toyota dealers and affiliated companies. Beginning in 1992, credit brokering and guaranteeing services were furnished to Toyota dealers. Projected services included extending automobile loans to its retail customers, extending housing loans, issuing credit cards, and installing automated teller machines in dealerships. One of Toyota's long-term objectives was to manage its own pension fund.

Toyota's potential plans for its excess cash included building new factories around the world, diversifying through acquisitions in electronics, telecommunications, factory automation, financial, and aerospace, and creating joint ventures with other automakers. According to one high-ranking Toyota executive:[16]

> *If an acquisition looks right, we'll look at the candidates positively. We wouldn't like to refuse some food without even tasting it. Such an acquisition would be for the purpose of winning the survival race in the world automotive business, which is getting more and more heated. It's not that we want to beat General Motors, it's that we want to make sure they won't beat us.*

Exhibit 6 presents the financial statistics of Toyota Motor Corporation.

PRODUCT STRATEGY

By the latter half of the 1960s, Toyota's strategy resembled General Motors'—blanketing

Exhibit 6 Selected Financial Data, Toyota Motor Corporation, 1984–93 (yen, thousands)

	Fiscal Year Ending				
	1993	1992	1991	1990	1989
Net sales	10,210,749,000	10,163,376,000	9,855,132,000	9,192,838,000	8,021,042,000
Cost of goods sold[1]	8,462,160,000	8,352,360,000	8,226,964,000	7,139,641,000	6,409,881,000
Gross income	1,264,487,000	1,339,003,000	1,595,377,000	1,713,784,000	1,316,118,000
Depreciation and amortization[2]	484,102,000	472,013,000	32,791,000	339,413,000	295,043,000
Selling, general and administrative expenses[3]	1,082,589,000	1,120,490,000	1,095,516,000	1,070,789,000	848,178,000
Total operating expenses	10,028,851,000	9,944,863,000	9,355,271,000	8,549,843,000	7,553,102,000
Operating income	181,897,000	218,511,000	499,859,000	642,995,000	467,940,000
Nonoperating interest income	139,709,000	203,070,000	226,709,000	NA	NA
Other income/expenses—net	53,991,000	55,622,000	34,129,000	313,496,000	241,845,000
Interest expense	53,389,000	49,348,000	51,153,000	119,162,000	84,130,000
Pretax income	322,208,000	427,855,000	709,544,000	837,329,000	625,655,000
Income taxes	161,437,000	212,542,000	301,000,000	415,213,000	297,479,000
Minority interest	2,737,000	1,640,000	2,811,000	1,461,000	620,000
Equity in earnings	18,341,000	24,314,000	25,716,000	20,647,000	18,706,000
Net income	176,464,000	237,840,000	431,450,000	441,301,000	346,262,000
Cash and equivalents	1,438,508,000	1,944,163,000	1,753,698,000	2,204,580,000	1,935,887,000
Net receivables[4]	2,222,715,000	2,419,839,000	2,384,198,000	2,624,625,000	933,979,000
Inventories	391,185,000	421,867,000	404,662,000	337,985,000	334,226,000
Total current assets	4,529,754,000	5,180,390,000	4,849,393,000	5,167,190,000	4,343,971,000
Property, plant, equipment—gross	5,745,093,000	5,351,231,000	4,529,224,000	3,860,399,000	3,437,261,000
Accumulated depreciation	3,181,346,000	2,875,127,000	2,543,871,000	2,307,155,000	2,062,606,000
Other assets	90,265,000	71,737,000	40,464,000	360,656,000	1,434,260,000
Total assets[5]	9,338,378,000	9,555,759,000	8,978,922,000	8,431,095,000	7,152,886,000
Total current liabilities	2,592,596,000	2,980,864,000	2,625,877,000	2,691,260,000	1,958,583,000
Long-term debt	1,738,514,000	1,575,359,000	1,481,580,000	1,221,274,000	1,219,463,000
Other liabilities	294,264,000	283,837,000	283,102,000	265,557,000	249,832,000
Total liabilities	4,625,374,000	4,840,060,000	4,390,559,000	4,178,091,000	3,427,878,000
Minority interest	26,496,000	23,762,000	19,643,000	17,135,000	15,431,000
Capital surplus	276,894,000	276,542,000	272,359,000	263,177,000	NA
Retained earnings	4,160,013,000	4,117,147,000	3,986,018,000	3,676,352,000	NA
Common shareholders' equity[6]	4,686,507,000	4,691,937,000	4,568,720,000	4,235,869,000	3,709,577,000
Total liabilities and equity	9,338,378,000	9,555,759,000	8,978,922,000	8,431,095,000	7,152,886,000

[1] 1991—Includes depreciation.
[2] 1991—Excludes depreciation included in cost of goods sold.
[3] 1990—Includes some nonoperating expense (income).
[4] 1993, 1992, 1991, 1990—Includes other current nontrade receivables and/or other current assets.
[5] 1992, 1991—Adjusted to exclude foreign currency translation gains/losses.
[6] 1993, 1992, 1991—Adjusted to include foreign currency translation gains/losses.

Toyota Motor Corporation in 1994

June 30				
1988	*1887*	*1986*	*1985*	*1984*
7,215,798,000	6,675,411,000	6,646,243,000	6,770,250,000	5,908,973,000
5,730,922,000	5,355,276,000	5,172,934,000	5,095,031,000	4,551,097,000
1,226,498,000	1,074,693,000	1,254,226,000	1,484,299,000	1,172,521,000
258,378,000	245,442,000	219,083,000	190,920,000	185,355,000
758,772,000	708,014,000	753,196,000	783,522,000	678,834,000
6,748,072,000	6,308,732,000	5,777,915,000	6,069,473,000	5,415,286,000
467,726,000	366,679,000	868,328,000	700,777,000	493,687,000
NA	NA	NA	NA	NA
164,825,000	170,542,000	−183,650,000	167,166,000	138,489,000
22,296,000	19,041,000	17,442,000	18,542,000	22,503,000
610,255,000	518,180,000	667,236,000	849,401,000	609,673,000
315,027,000	258,526,000	320,636,000	441,912,000	307,646,000
1,477,000	−1,050,000	1,066,000	1,683,000	2,219,000
17,658,000	NA	NA	NA	NA
310,952,000	260,704,000	345,534,000	405,806,000	294,808,000
1,387,721,000	1,262,158,000	1,070,941,000	1,225,561,000	1,055,449,000
803,540,000	698,624,000	654,872,000	642,584,000	602,973,000
261,719,000	259,047,000	268,143,000	307,084,000	265,174,000
2,807,201,000	2,530,168,000	2,248,320,000	2,429,816,000	2,137,375,000
3,086,031,000	2,865,971,000	2,588,990,000	2,318,172,000	2,158,278,000
1,872,704,000	1,724,380,000	1,549,106,000	1,430,078,000	1,319,509,000
1,429,848,000	337,614,000	294,525,000	242,150,000	53,906,000
5,450,376,000	4,870,832,000	4,348,104,000	4,279,218,000	3,686,269,000
1,596,290,000	1,380,921,000	1,277,396,000	1,439,787,000	1,258,488,000
330,493,000	220,996,000	5,306,000	8,135,000	10,235,000
225,259,000	208,389,000	191,340,000	176,069,000	158,995,000
2,152,042,000	1,810,306,000	1,474,042,000	1,623,991,000	1,427,718,000
13,074,000	15,439,000	16,764,000	16,772,000	15,979,000
NA	NA	NA	NA	NA
NA	NA	NA	NA	NA
3,285,260,000	3,045,087,000	2,857,295,000	2,638,455,000	2,242,572,000
5,450,376,000	4,870,832,000	4,348,104,000	4,279,218,000	3,686,269,000

the market with a variety of nameplates, each one a step above the other in size and cost. Initial emphasis was on cars for the family market, rather than specialized models. The Publica, the least-expensive model, was intended for buyers moving up from motorcycles or minicars. Next, in ascending order, was the Corolla (similar in size and price to the VW Beetle), the best-selling Corona, the Corona Mark II (Cressida), and the six-cylinder Crown (about the size of an American compact). Additional limited-production prestige models built, but not exported, were the eight-cylinder luxurious Century and the 2000GT, a two-seater similar to the Jaguar XKE. A limited range of trucks complemented Toyota's autos.

Although new, sportier models (Celica) aimed at the youth market were subsequently introduced, Toyota had lagged behind other Japanese automakers in introducing new models because of its concentrated efforts to meet the emission control standards of the 1970s. Additionally, the oil crises of the 1970s dictated a new approach to developing passenger cars appropriate to the international market—small, fuel efficient, front-wheel drive passenger cars. Toyota's first products in this area were the Tercel and Camry. When the Camry made its debut in 1982, it was hailed by auto enthusiasts as the first in a new generation of front-wheel drive cars; however, some critics thought it lacked elegance owing to its functional styling and plain interior. Toyota entered the high-performance, specialty car market with the MR2 and Supa, introduced in the 1980s. New models were regularly introduced, and by the 1990s, Toyota had vehicles in virtually all market segments. Toyota was beginning to be viewed as a fashion leader, putting to rest its reputation for fuddy-duddy design, evidenced by the introduction of the following vehicles: the Sera (a glass-topped minicoupe with gull-wing doors) and the Mark II (a mid-size car), sold only in Japan; the jellybean shaped Previa, designed in California and a hit with US buyers; and the Lexus, sold in Japan and several overseas markets. One impartial indicator of the attractiveness of Toyota's cars was their price in the used-car market. According to one study, Toyota's vehicles retained more than 70 per cent of their value five years after being purchased. Only three other brands were in this category. Exhibit 7 displays Toyota's overall motor vehicle production.

EXPORT ACTIVITIES

Toyota established an export department in 1950 to explore the feasibility of overseas exports. Toyota's early export efforts were characterized by trial and error since the company was generally unfamiliar with the competitive conditions and import restrictions in foreign countries. Toyota targeted Southeast Asia, Latin America, and the Caribbean as its first export channels because of their proximity and interest. With an increase in local content laws prohibiting the export of completely built autos to several countries, such as Brazil and Mexico, Toyota experimented with a knockdown (KD) system, beginning in the late 1950s. A KD set was one whose shipment price was less than 60 per cent of the total cost of component parts making up a whole car. Problems, such as unavailability of local parts or assembly with incorrect or missing parts, hampered the early exports of KD sets. Toyota revamped the KD system and resumed knockdown exports to several countries beginning in 1962. Toyota continued to export KD sets to several countries, including Africa and Southeast Asia, as part of its export strategy. Toyota's total vehicle exports are displayed in Exhibit 8.

Exhibit 7 Motor Vehicle Production, Toyota Motor Corporation, 1935–92

Year	Cars	Trucks and Buses	Total
1935	0	20	20
1940	268	14,519	14,787
1945	0	3,275	3,275
1950	463	11,243	11,706
1955	7,403	15,383	22,786
1960	42,118	112,652	154,770
1965	236,151	241,492	477,643
1970	1,068,321	540,869	1,609,190
1975	1,714,836	621,217	2,336,053
1980	2,303,284	990,060	3,293,344
1981	2,248,171	972,247	3,220,418
1982	2,258,253	886,304	3,144,557
1983	2,380,753	891,582	3,272,335
1984	2,413,133	1,061,116	3,429,249
1985	2,569,284	1,096,338	3,665,622
1986	2,684,024	976,143	3,660,167
1987	2,708,069	930,210	3,638,279
1988	2,982,922	985,775	3,968,697
1989	3,055,101	920,801	3,975,902
1990	3,345,885	866,488	4,212,373
1991	3,180,054	905,027	4,085,081
1992	3,171,311	760,030	3,931,341

Sources: 1. *Ward's Automotive Yearbook*, Southfield, Michigan: Ward's Communications, Inc., 1993, p. 66; 1991, p. 78; 1990, p. 285.
2. Toyota Motor Corporation, *Toyota: A History of the First 50 Years*, Toyota, 1988, p. 461.

UNITED STATES

Toyota's top management initially opposed exporting to the United States. Numerous doubts existed regarding the suitability of the Toyota car in terms of performance, reliability, and price. Several factors influenced Toyota to begin exporting to the US: growth of the small car market (European competitors, primarily Volkswagen, had captured almost 10 per cent of this market by the late 1950s), US automakers not building small cars, and the probability the US would adopt import restrictions. According to a Toyota executive, "If the US goes ahead and restricts imports, Toyota will be cut out of the American market for good. We've got to get in there now or never."

Toyota shipped two Crown Toyopets to the US in 1957. The Crown was a flop. Lacking power to travel on high-speed roads, it vibrated badly at speeds over 100 kph and overheated when driven over mountains and on desert roads. It was unable to traverse a California hill to the dealer showroom where it was to debut. Shoichiro Toyoda labeled it a "junk" car, unsuitable for American roads.

Exhibit 8 Motor Vehicle Exports, Toyota Motor Corporation, 1965–91

Year	Passenger Cars	Trucks	Buses	Total
1965	33,297	29,855	368	63,520
1966	70,545	33,993	607	105,145
1967	111,461	45,308	1,113	157,882
1968	203,169	73,287	2,631	279,087
1969	287,369	104,376	3,357	395,102
1970	346,462	130,932	4,498	481,892
1971	604,923	176,880	4,484	786,287
1972	555,430	165,037	4,085	724,552
1973	525,056	191,273	4,311	720,640
1974	605,433	242,299	8,533	856,265
1975	612,744	247,788	7,820	868,352
1976	835,817	330,998	10,499	1,177,314
1977	968,270	433,138	11,827	1,413,235
1978	900,366	465,407	16,401	1,382,174
1979	905,392	458,120	20,136	1,383,648
1980	1,149,420	604,673	31,352	1,785,445
1981	1,063,385	615,711	37,390	1,716,486
1982	1,062,841	581,532	21,420	1,665,793
1983	1,069,053	580,368	14,940	1,664,361
1984	1,100,353	672,082	28,488	1,800,923
1985	1,198,982	746,532	34,441	1,979,955
1986	1,210,200	650,677	14,886	1,875,763
1987	1,192,146	560,490	18,301	1,770,937
1988	1,231,906	557,719	26,096	1,815,721
1989	1,139,680	512,461	16,989	1,669,130
1990	1,215,519	440,916	20,692	1,677,127
1991	1,223,917	450,186	29,486	1,703,589

Source: Motor Vehicle Manufacturer's Association, *World Motor Vehicle Data Book*, Detroit, Michigan, 1993 edition, p. 63.

In late 1960, Toyota halted passenger car exports to the US. Determined to make a comeback, it vigorously set about designing and building the right cars for the US market. When Toyota introduced the Corona to the US in 1965, it was a hit with the American consumer. Toyota's strategy involved offering a comparatively luxurious, well-built small car with acceleration superior to other economy imports. Outfitted with a 90-horsepower engine, it was nearly twice as powerful as a VW Beetle. With a larger engine, it was possible to offer options such as automatic transmission and air-conditioning. Toyota also strengthened its dealer network, after-sales service, and advertising promotions, and concentrated its initial sales efforts in Los Angeles. In 1968, Toyota introduced the smaller Corolla which conformed to its policy at that time of avoiding direct competition with the US automakers. Toyota sold 6,388 vehicles in the US in 1965. By 1969, volume exceeded 100,000 and by 1975, the US was Toyota's largest export market, and Toyota had usurped the position of the best selling foreign import from Volkswagen. Aided by the growth in the small-car market (from 43 per cent in 1973 to about 60 per cent in 1980), Toyota's exports climbed rapidly until the early 1980s, when the combination of several events conspired to contain the invasion of Japanese vehicle imports.

Allegations of dumping surfaced when a Volkswagen executive stated that Volkswagen was selling its models in the US at losses ranging from US$250 to US$600 each. A dumping investigation, directed at automakers in eight countries, was conducted. Although Toyota was included in this investigation, it was officially cleared of these charges. However, suspicions that dumping was a common practice among certain automakers persisted. In 1980, based on a change in "definition," the US increased its customs duty on trucks from 4 per cent to 25 per cent. In the same year, the UAW and Ford argued that Japanese vehicle imports had resulted in increasing unemployment among US auto workers and was harming the domestic auto industry. They petitioned the ITC to require Japanese automakers to build plants in the US and to apply volume restrictions on their exports. Although the ITC ruled that there was no direct causal relation between the increase in auto imports and the difficulties experienced by the US auto industry, voluntary restraints on exports were established by the Japanese government, beginning on May 1, 1981. Under the voluntary restraint agreement (VRA), the nine Japanese automakers were limited to a US market share equal to their level of imports during 1974–75. Initially slated to last three years, the voluntary restraints were extended:

1981–83:	1,680,000 vehicles
1984:	1,850,000 vehicles
1985–91:	2,300,000 vehicles
1992:	1,650,000 vehicles

Initially, the quotas actually benefited Toyota. Forced to limit exports, Toyota not only increased prices, it also began to replace its small, inexpensive export cars with larger, more expensive ones loaded with options. Toyota was able to sell all of its allotted quota and often found itself without enough vehicles to sell. Plans for US production of its most popular models, the Camry and Corolla, were implemented, resulting in new and redesigned models being consistently introduced. By the 1990s, vehicles including big trucks and luxury cars were available in all major market segments.

T100. The T100 was Toyota's first foray into the big truck market, which experienced a 12 per cent growth rate in 1992, making it the fastest-growing US vehicle segment (four of the top six vehicles sold in the US in 1993 were in this market, which included pickups, minivans, and sport-utility vehicles). Designed expressly for the US market and built in Japan, the T100 was launched in November 1992. Overpriced (an import fee of as much as US$2,500 was tacked on) and underpowered, it met with a less-than-enthusiastic reception by the American consumer, with sales progressing at a rate much less than the planned 50,000 annual units. The design of the T100 was a compromise since Toyota hoped to avoid a Detroit backlash. It was intermediate-sized, falling midway between three-quarter-sized and full-sized trucks offered by the Big Three, and was powered by a standard V-6 engine.

Future enhancements, including a V-8 engine option and an extended cab version, were planned. Talks had taken place between Toyota and GM about Toyota using one of GM's idle US plants to build the T100, but it was unlikely that an agreement would be reached in the immediate future.

LEXUS. Having mastered the formula for producing and selling low- and mid-priced cars, Toyota hoped to repeat this success in the luxury car market. A dream of chairman Eiji Toyoda, who felt that Toyota did not get the respect it deserved, was to "develop the best car in the world". In 1983, he challenged the Toyota engineers, using Mercedes and BMW as the benchmarks, to pursue this dream and to do what no other automaker had achieved: design a sedan that would travel 150 mph while carrying four passengers in relative quiet, comfort, and safety—without incurring the American gas-guzzler tax. The overall strategy involved marketing a high-performance car equal in quality to Mercedes and BMW, but priced below them and above the US luxury models, Cadillac and Lincoln.

The first step involved purchase of the competitors' cars—four Mercedes, a Jaguar XJ6, and two BMWs—which were subjected to grueling test drives and then taken apart for further study. Next, 11 performance goals, relating to such things as aerodynamics, weight, noise levels, and fuel efficiency, were established. Overall, the extensive development process involved six years, an investment of over US$500 million, creation of a flexible organizational structure to oversee the project, development of a new engine, and establishment of separate marketing and advertising entities, involving a separate dealership organization to sell the car. In contrast to European automakers, which utilized extensive manual labor to achieve quality, Toyota installed the most elaborate automation that was feasible, believing that only mechanized processes could meet Lexus's stringent assembly standards.

Incorporating such advanced features as hydraulic active suspension, a two-stroke engine, and traction control, the Lexus was faster, more fuel efficient, and less expensive than its German competitors:

Acceleration speed (0–60 mph)
Lexus	–	8.6 seconds
BMW	–	10.3 seconds
Mercedes	–	9.3 seconds

Official highway gas mileage
Lexus	–	23.5 mpg
BMW	–	19.0 mpg
Mercedes	–	18.0 mpg

Price
Lexus	–	$35,000
BMW	–	$54,000
Mercedes	–	$61,210

The Lexus 400 was analyzed by the engineers of all of Toyota's rivals; reputedly, no evidence of technical shortcuts was found. Some industry observers suggested that Toyota had lowballed the prices of its Lexus models; Toyota claimed it was earning its usual profit on the car.

According to Shoichiro Toyota, the success of the Lexus depend on how well it was made. "Our biggest challenge will be to have no defects and to build a reliable car that won't break down."[17] The size of the luxury segment (1 million units annually in the latter 1980s) was projected to grow annually by about 10 per cent, reaching about 1.5 million units by the mid-1990s. Growth, combined with gross margins of 20 per cent (versus 12 per cent to 16 per cent on less-expensive models), were additional incentives for Toyota to enter this market.

The LS400 was launched in the US in September 1989; three months after its introduction, three minor glitches, including one that could cause the cruise-control system to remain on after the driver attempted to turn it off, were found in the LS400s, resulting in Toyota's recalling about 8,500 units. Toyota responded by personally calling each owner with two options:[18]

> *Bring the car in yourself to be fixed on the spot, or have Lexus pick it up at night and return it ready-to-go the next morning. Either way, Lexus not only fixed the defect but also washed the car, cleaned the inside and filled it with gasoline. Some dealers even placed a small gift, such as an ice scraper, on the front seat. Owners were mollified, and many were impressed.*

After-sales service was also a top priority:[19]

> *A customer who had just purchased an LS400 rushed back to the dealer, saying he was furious that a new car should break down so fast. When we looked for the problem, we found that the emergency brake was on. When the "faulty car" was replaced at no cost, the customer was so thrilled with the unexpected service that he bought another car.*

According to one industry analyst, "When the Lexus LS400 first came out, people said it was a better value than a comparable Mercedes or BMW. Now they are saying flat out that it is a better car than a Mercedes or MBW."[20] By late 1993, Toyota offered three models—the ES300, priced at US$30,600; the SC300, priced at US$38,000; and the LS400, priced at US$49,900. The Lexus had consistently been ranked No. 1 in the JD Power's Initial Quality Survey of new cars since its introduction. With an estimated market share of almost 10 per cent in the luxury segment projected for 1993, Lexus ranked third behind Cadillac and Lincoln.

Endaka (the rising yen), a desire to reduce trade friction, and declining profits prompted Toyota to increase prices on virtually all of its models several times during 1992 and 1993. Exhibit 9 provides price comparisons of US and Japanese cars as of March 1993. Industry

Exhibit 9 Price Comparisons of Similarly Equipped American and Japanese Cars, March 1993 (US$)

Compact Cars	
Toyota Corolla	14,458
Chevrolet Geo Prism	13,030
Sport Coupes	
Mazda MX-6	21,375
Ford Probe GT	18,886
Mid-Size Cars	
Toyota Camry LE	21,433
Ford Taurus GL	18,902
Honda Accord LX anniversary edition	18,780
Dodge Intrepid	18,729
Oldsmobile Cutlass Supreme	16,445

Source: *The Wall Street Journal*, March 4, 1993, p. A1.

analysts estimated that Japanese cars were priced US$2,500 more than comparable US cars, on average, with Toyota's models being pricier than most other Japanese automakers. Toyota's predicament was partly attributed to its shifting cars dramatically upscale in terms of size and quality. One source indicated that Toyota's new and redesigned models were over-engineered, offering too much quality for the money. According to one US dealer, "They've built too much quality into the cars, and the public's not willing to pay for it." A second price hike in 1993 involved increases ranging from a low of 2.5 per cent on its least-expensive models to a high of 12.7 per cent on its pricier models, and a third increase added about 3 per cent more to all models. Toyota was also using American-style incentives to secure sales, including a leasing program for its vehicles and rebates to dealers or buyers. Exhibit 10 shows the US market share of the major automakers.

EXPORT ACTIVITIES OUTSIDE THE US

Strict import restrictions, idiosyncratic tastes of European consumers in their choice of autos, intense competition in countries having their own automakers, and the great diversity among the European countries hindered Toyota's ability to penetrate the western European auto market. By the late 1970s, several countries had established import restrictions. Toyota's maximum share of the British market was set at 2 per cent (later increased to 11 per cent) of the total market, and France set the maximum share for all Japanese vehicles at 3 per cent of the total market. Quotas in Italy and Spain limited Japan's share to less than 1 per cent. In 1981, the EEC placed passenger cars on the list of import items from Japan to be monitored.

The main attraction of early Toyota vehicles to Europeans was their novelty and simplicity of mechanical structure, making them relatively trouble-free. By the early 1980s, virtually all new European cars were front-wheel drive models. They displayed excellent driving performance, had luxury-class specifications, and offered numerous options. European

Exhibit 10 US Market Share of the Major Automakers, 1973–92* (%)

Year	General Motors	Ford	Chrysler	Toyota	Honda	Nissan	All Imports
1973	44.9	24.4	13.7	2.5	.4	2.0	15.2
1974	42.4	25.9	14.1	2.7	.5	2.1	15.7
1975	43.8	23.6	12.3	3.3	1.2	3.0	18.2
1976	47.6	22.6	13.7	3.4	1.5	2.7	14.8
1977	46.3	23.4	12.0	4.4	2.0	3.5	18.3
1978	47.8	23.5	11.1	3.9	2.4	3.0	17.8
1979	46.3	20.8	10.1	4.8	3.3	4.4	22.7
1980	45.9	17.2	8.8	6.5	4.2	5.8	28.2
1981	44.6	16.6	9.9	6.7	4.4	5.5	28.8
1982	44.2	16.9	10.0	6.6	4.6	5.9	29.6
1983	44.3	17.2	10.4	5.9	4.4	5.7	27.5
1984	44.6	19.2	10.4	5.0	4.9	4.7	24.9
1985	42.7	18.9	11.3	5.3	5.0	5.2	25.9
1986	41.2	18.2	11.5	5.3	6.1	4.8	28.2
1987	36.6	20.2	10.8	6.0	7.2	5.2	32.2
1988	36.3	21.7	11.3	6.2	7.3	4.5	31.2
1989	35.2	22.3	10.4	6.9	8.0	5.2	31.8
1990	35.6	20.8	9.3	8.4	9.2	4.9	26.4
1991	35.6	20.0	8.6	9.1	9.8	5.1	25.7
1992	34.6	21.6	8.2	9.3	9.4	5.1	24.3

*US passenger car sales.

Sources: 1. Ward's Communications, Inc., *Ward's Automotive Yearbook*, Southfield, Michigan, 1993, p. 205; 1990, p. 208; 1984, p. 101.
2. *Automotive News*, Market Data Book Issue, 1993, p. 19.

automakers were discounting their prices in bold competitive moves, and Toyota's exports to Europe were negatively affected. Shoichiro Toyoda outlined Toyota's market strategy at a European dealers meeting in late 1982:[21]

> *The European market holds much potential for Toyota, and it demands only the finest products ... We feel strongly that Toyota must be a leader with vision in Europe and elsewhere, and the first step in becoming a leader is to regain the number one position among Japanese automakers as early as possible, and after that to widen the gap between ourselves and others.... In short, Toyota's success in Europe becomes possible only when your thinking and our thinking are the same, when we share the same goal.*

In 1986, western Europe overtook the US as the largest market for new car sales in the world. With the emergence of the European Community (EC 1992), the region was expected to be a competitive battlefield. Although sales plunged in the early 1990s, they were projected to reach 14.4 million passenger cars by 1995 and 15.2 million by 2000. If potential sales in eastern Europe were factored in, some industry insiders were suggesting that European sales (excluding the former Soviet Union) could approach 20 million by 2000. A 1991 agreement between Japan and the EC limited imports of Japanese vehicles to about 11 per cent until 1998; however, in 1993 the Japanese agreed to reduce their exports even further in response to the declining market.

Meanwhile, Toyota was battling Nissan for the role of the No. 1 Japanese importer. Toyota was the top-selling Japanese automaker in Belgium, Finland, Denmark, Ireland, Norway, and Sweden, and had obtained 9.7 per cent of the market in Greece, 3.1 per cent in Germany, and 2.1 per cent in the United Kingdom. In Italy, France, and Spain, Toyota had minimal presence, holding less than 1 per cent of the market in each country. Beginning in spring 1992, Toyota began exporting its US built Camry wagons to Europe.

To combat the Japanese, European carmakers were exploring possible new relationships with each other to become more competitive. However, with the European carmakers experiencing some of the same problems (inefficiency, quality problems, and slowness of bringing new cars to market) as the US automakers, the Japanese threat was viewed as formidable by European automakers. Toyota had recently begun exporting its luxury and sports cars to Europe, such as the Lexus, and European production of a mass-market model had recently begun. Exhibit 11 shows the European market share of the major automakers.

Exhibit 11 European Market Share of the Major Automakers, 1982–92* (%)

Company	1992	1991	1990	1989	1988	1987	1986	1984	1982
Volkswagen Group	17.5	16.4	15.6	15.2	14.9	15.0	14.7	12.0	12.0
Fiat Group	11.9	12.8	14.2	14.8	14.8	14.2	14.0	12.7	12.3
Peugeot Group	12.2	12.1	12.9	12.6	12.9	12.1	11.4	11.5	12.3
General Motors	12.4	12.1	11.8	11.4	11.0	11.2	11.0	11.1	9.6
Ford	11.3	11.9	11.6	11.7	11.4	12.1	11.7	12.8	12.3
Renault	10.6	10.0	9.9	10.3	10.1	10.6	10.6	10.9	14.4
Mercedes	3.1	3.4	3.3	3.2	3.4	3.5	3.7	3.2	3.2
Austin Rover	2.5	2.6	2.9	3.0	3.4	3.4	3.5	3.9	3.9
Nissan	3.2	3.2	2.8	2.9	2.9	2.9	3.0	2.8	2.9
BMW	3.3	3.1	2.8	2.8	2.7	2.4	2.6	3.0	2.7
Toyota	2.5	2.7	2.7	2.6	2.7	2.8	2.9	2.2	2.3
Mazda	1.9	2.1	2.1	1.8	1.9	1.9	2.0	2.0	—
Volvo	1.5	1.5	1.8	2.0	2.1	2.2	2.3	2.3	2.0
Mitsubishi	1.2	1.4	1.3	1.2	1.2	1.2	1.2	—	—
Honda	1.3	1.2	1.2	1.0	1.1	1.0	1.2	—	—

*Total new passenger car registrations.

Source: Ward's Communications, Inc., *Ward's Automotive Yearbook,* Southfield, Michigan, 1993, p. 82; 1990, p. 269; 1986, p. 65; 1984, p. 54.

Toyota gradually expanded its exports to other countries during the 1960s and 1970s. Distinctive factors associated with some of these countries, including worsening economic conditions, political interests, high foreign debt, and stringent domestic content laws, resulted in declining exports to several countries by the 1990s. However, Toyota had been able to lay solid foundations in several countries, including Australia, Malaysia, India, Taiwan, Brazil, and Columbia, through joint-venture partnerships or companies in which it held an equity interest. By the 1990s, Toyota's major thrust toward global expansion appeared to be focused on establishing production capacity in overseas markets.

OVERSEAS PRODUCTION OPERATIONS

The necessity for establishing local production bases outside Japan became evident to Toyota in the early 1980s. Prior to 1982, Toyota had not engaged in any major strategic alliances or independent overseas production, but the rapidly changing competitive situation prompted the company to reevaluate its posture. Prominent concerns of Toyota executives included the nature of labor-relations practices, the degree to which various components of the TPS could be transferred to facilities in other countries, and the ability to manage an operation on another continent.

UNITED STATES

Lagging behind the other leading Japanese automakers, Honda and Nissan, in establishing production facilities in the US, it was inevitable that Toyota would establish an alliance with a US automaker. Talks of a tie-up with Ford had occurred on four occasions, beginning in 1939, with the last discussion of building a plant together (this time in the US and not Japan) to develop and produce small cars occurring in 1980. According to Eiji Toyoda, the roles were reversed.[22]

> As before, Toyota did the proposing, but the nature of the proposal was different. In 1960, we had asked Ford to teach us everything they could about small cars, but in 1980 the situation had changed. This time, we were offering to jointly produce our vehicle at Ford. The student had traded places with the teacher. This only goes to show how much the world can change in the short space of 20 years.

Like prior discussions, this one did not culminate in an agreement.

Toyota linked up with GM in 1984 to establish NUMMI, its first base of operations in the US. The 50-50 joint venture initially produced Chevy Novas and Toyota Corollas at a shuttered GM plant in Fremont, California. In the late 1980s, the Nova was replaced by the GEO Prism model line, and in 1990 approximately 205,000 Geo Prisms and Corollas were produced and production of a Toyota compact pickup truck was slated to begin in the early 1990s. GM contributed the manufacturing plant and was responsible for marketing and selling the GEO. Toyota managed NUMMI, and former UAW workers were rehired for the production jobs. From Toyota's perspective, the venture would enable it to reduce its risk, allowing it to gain valuable experience associated with local production. Specifically, Toyota wanted to evaluate the competency of US suppliers, the adequacy of the transportation systems, and options for dealing with unionized labor in the US.

To implement certain components of the TPS, Toyota's top priority was to establish stable labor relations with the UAW. Mutual trust and respect between management and labor was emphasized in the negotiated contract, which provided affirmative action before laying off any employee, allowed any employee to stop the production line to fix a problem, eliminated multiple-job classifications to encourage flexible workers, and arranged workers into teams. Team leaders were carefully selected, with on-site training provided in Toyota City. Indoctrination included courses on Toyota's history, corporate policies, production philosophy, quality control circle activities, and the concept of teamwork. Hands-on training involved exposure to production activities and worksite management at the Takaoka Plant for two weeks. Nine groups of 257 trainees participated in this training. American production employees were not typically promoted to management level jobs. In contrast, NUMMI established a contract with the UAW to introduce a foreman-promotion system. As of 1990, 110 employees had been promoted.

The Fremont facility was extensively remodeled with simplicity guiding the process. Renovation entailed (1) replacing old equipment; (2) restructuring the body, painting, and assembly lines into a series of short parallel lines that were less complex and less robotic-intensive than the long, complex, and highly automated assembly lines typical of most GM plants; (3) installing line-stop switches; and (4) establishing the *kanban* system of production control.

The philosophy in selecting suppliers was to abandon the traditional adversarial nature of supplier-buyer relationships. NUMMI established a practice of almost never switching vendors and used only one or two suppliers for each component. Vendors were carefully selected, were expected to utilize the practices of *kanban* or just-in-time inventory control, and had little chance of losing their contracts if they fulfilled the agreed-upon terms. There was no competitive bidding in awarding contracts, and suppliers were expected to meet rigid standards in return for security. At the opening ceremony in April 1985, NUMMI's president commented:[23]

> *Principally as a result of the efforts of the team members of NUMMI and the people in so many related companies who have cooperated in this project, we have built here in Fremont a first-class assembly plant. Thanks to our cooperative parts suppliers and our 1,200 employees, we are now producing cars of world-class quality. Our slogan at NUMMI this year is "Quality assurance through teamwork." People working together means teamwork, and I believe it is teamwork that will be the key to our success.*

The following practices were implemented at NUMMI—an "open office" floor plan, a single cafeteria, common parking facilities, announcement of managerial decisions to the union before implementation, personal announcements of company policy by the president, and a suggestion system focusing on work improvements for use by all employees. Employee attendance reached 97 per cent during the first year of operation. By 1989, productivity levels were 40 per cent higher than typical GM plants, and NUMMI had the highest quality levels GM had ever known.

At about the time NUMMI was launched, Toyota announced plans to begin independent production in North America with the construction of plants in the US and Canada. Toyota's decision to locate the Toyota Motor Manufacturing (TMM) plant in Georgetown, Kentucky, was based on several factors: parts procurement, transportation convenience, land prices, electricity supplies, labor resources, and tax and other preferential treatment (a US$125 million financial incentive package was offered by Kentucky officials). Commenting on the selection decision in late 1985, Shoichiro Toyoda stated:[24]

> *We view today's official announcement of our plant site selection as one of the highlights in our company's history.... In fact, choosing the site for our American plant was one of the most difficult decisions we've ever had to make at Toyota. After considering all of the factors involved, however, we decided that Kentucky is the best location for our American plant. At the same time, we wish to thank all the other states that presented site proposals. More than 25 years have passed since we started our exports to the United States, and since then we have moved steadily forward toward realizing our dream of building a perfect partnership with our American friends. As we continue to move into the future, we intend not only to contribute toward creating more job opportunities and promoting economic growth, but also to try and build a new relationship that will serve everyone's needs.*

Opened in 1988, TMM represented an investment of US$1.1 billion to construct an assembly plant and related facilities to build 240,000 Camrys annually, in addition to engines, axles, and steering components. By 1990, the 4-door Camry was being built at a rate of one every 75 seconds or about 170 per day on a single shift. Domestic content of the vehicle was at 60 per cent but was projected to reach about 75 per cent when the powertrain plant under construction reached full production in 1991.

While quality was high at Georgetown, productivity was initially about 10 per cent below Toyota's plants in Japan. According to a Toyota executive, US suppliers were the problem. Although Toyota preferred to purchase major parts from the 250 Japanese suppliers who had established plants in the US, political concerns, the improving quality of US parts, and the rising yen prompted Toyota to increase its purchases of American-made parts. For example, during the start-up year of operations at Georgetown, Toyota bought US$1.1 billion of US made parts; in 1994, it expected to purchase about US$5.3 billion worth of parts and materials from US suppliers.

Flooded with over 50,000 applicants for the 3,000 factory jobs, Toyota devised an extensive selection system, which focused on employee potential, rather than on education and work experience. The process consumed about 18 hours per applicant and involved tests and simulations that assessed technical, interpersonal, and leadership skills. One new employee (a former hairdresser) likened getting a job at Toyota to winning a lottery. "The odds were tremendous, but I would have swept floors."

In 1990, TMM received the Gold Plant Award from JD Power & Associates and announced expansion plans. A second assembly plant was to be built at Georgetown, increasing production capacity by 200,000 vehicles and increasing jobs to more than 5,000. When completed in early 1994, the Georgetown complex was expected to assemble the Avalon, a new top-of-the-line sedan, in addition to the Camry. TMM achieved another first in August 1992, when it began exporting the first US-built vehicle, the Scepter (a new right-hand drive version of the Camry station wagon), for sale in Japan. According to TMM's president, Toyota's commitment to Georgetown was "a tribute to all team members at Toyota ... Being able to expand operations here is especially rewarding to us."

As the mid-1990s approached, Toyota was on its way to becoming an almost stand-alone US producer able to research and engineer, as well as to design and assemble, its cars in the US. Toyota had established the Calty Design Center in California in the early 1970s. Several models, including the Celica and the new Previa minivan, were developed at the Center, specifically to suit the tastes of US consumers. In 1991, Toyota embarked on a US$220 million program to significantly expand its US-based design and research activities. The program included opening the Toyota Technical Center USA Inc. (Toyota's US R&D arm), a US$46 million prototype-vehicle evaluation facility in Torrence, California; beginning construction of a US$110 million vehicle proving facility near Phoenix, Arizona; opening a US$19 million expansion of the Calty Design Center; and opening a US$41 million evaluation laboratory at its technical center in Ann Arbor, Michigan. Thus, Toyota maintained separate US subsidiaries for sales, manufacturing, engineering, and R&D, each reporting individually to Toyota City.

Toyota was gaining the ability to execute its lean distribution approach of built-to-order cars, but this critical component of the TPS had yet to be achieved. Toyota had expanded its distribution network during the 1980s in the US—in 1983, it had 1,093 new car franchises, and by 1990, the number had increased to 1,248. In contrast, the total number of US car dealerships had steadily declined—from 30,800 in 1970, the number had fallen to 25,100 by 1989. Implementing the lean approach to distribution appeared to be part of the plan.

According to one Japanese auto executive, "The system makes no sense unless cars are built to order and delivered almost immediately. We can do this only as we develop a complete top-to-bottom manufacturing system in North America and Europe by the end of the 1990s."[25] According to one authority, Toyota had not reached its full potential in the US since the TPS worked best when "the entire complement of car production activities are performed as close as possible to the point of final production."[26]

OVERSEAS OPERATIONS OUTSIDE THE US

Calls for protectionism echoed loudest on the European continent. Strict import restrictions had limited the Japanese share to a consistent 11 per cent of the market. By the early 1990s, Honda, Nissan, and Toyota had each opened production facilities in the United Kingdom, using proven formulas from Japan and the US in areas such as site selection and employee training, with most of the output to be exported to mainland Europe. By 1995, the Japanese were expected to be producing 775,000 cars annually in Europe; it was estimated the Japanese automakers could secure about 20 per cent of the European market by 2000. In early 1993, Toyota rolled off its first cars, the mid-size Carina E (its first car designed specifically for the European market), at its new Burnaston plant in Great Britain. Plans called for eventual employment of 3,000 employees and production of 200,000 cars annually by 1997. Toyota had ambitious plans to establish additional production capacity in Europe through equity investment, joint ventures, or independent production; countries being targeted included Germany and Spain.

Toyota's emphasis on establishing overseas production facilities was not restricted to the US and Europe. Restricted by rigorous domestic content laws in several Asian countries, Toyota (along with other Japanese automakers) had a virtual monopoly in the region where the presence of US and European automakers was almost unknown. Auto sales in Asia were projected to grow from 4.7 per cent of global sales in 1987 to 8.7 per cent by 1995. Millions of dollars of investment, combined with long-term thinking, persistence, and flexibility, had aided in Toyota's securing a leadership role.

In countries that banned auto imports, such as South Korea, Toyota had taken minority stakes in Korean auto companies and provided technology or parts supplies. In countries affected by political instability or uncertain economic prospects, such as the Philippines, Toyota had signed on with local partners, cautiously expanding its presence. Toyota had also assisted in building local auto industries in some east Asian countries to alleviate concerns over Japanese domination. Overall, the Japanese automakers had been successful in establishing a regional auto production base. Although major profits had not yet been achieved from the Asian strategy, the pieces were in place, and the region was poised for sustained economic growth. Exhibit 12 displays the location of selected Toyota overseas production facilities.

Toyota's Future

Toyota surpassed Ford in the production of cars in the global market in 1990. By 1995, Toyota anticipated selling 1.5 million vehicles in the US, 50 per cent of them built in the US; Toyota planned on selling 2 million vehicles in the US by 2000, hoping to surpass Ford. According to one industry analyst's projection, Toyota would be producing 6.3 million vehicles annually by 2000. Toyota had recently introduced the newly remodeled Mark II, Chaser, and Cresta luxury cars to the Japanese market while a redesigned Celica coupe, a new mid-size Lexus, and a 300-horsepower Supra sports car were slated for the US market. Toyota's future plans were clearly focused on global expansion, with production facilities located at the center of large overseas markets, including North America, Europe, Southeast Asia, and Oceania, with products being exported to neighboring countries.

However, intensified competition in the global auto industry presented Toyota with significantly different challenges as the mid-1990s approached. The company's ability to achieve its objectives was jeopardized by several factors—declining profits and exports, deteriorating market share in both Japan and the US (declining to less than 8 per cent by the end of 1993), and decelerating growth in numerous industrialized country markets. During the 1980s, the Detroit auto manufacturers had drastically overhauled their operations, enabling them to significantly narrow the gap in the areas of product quality and customer satisfaction compared to the Japanese automakers. Chrysler had become a world leader in

Exhibit 12 Overseas Production Companies, Toyota Motor Corporation, 1994

Geographic Region	Location of Facilities	Local Name of Toyota's Subsidiary
North America	USA	Toyota Motor Manufacturing, USA, Inc.
		New United Motor Manufacturing, Inc. (50-50 joint venture with GM)
	Canada	Toyota Motor Manufacturing Canada Inc.
South America and the Caribbean	Brazil	Toyota do Brasil SA, Industria e Comercio
	Peru	Toyota del Peru SA
	Colombia	SOFASA-Renault SA (Toyota owned 17.5%)
	Venezuela	Servicios de Ensamblaje, CA
	Trinidad and Tobago	Amar Assembly Plant '85 Ltd.
	Uruguay	Ayax SA
	Ecuador	MARE SA
Europe	United Kingdom	Toyota Motor Manufacturing (UK) Ltd.
	Portugal	Salvador Caetano IMVT, SA
Southeast Asia and Oceania	Australia	Toyota Motor Corporation Australia Ltd.
		United Australian Automotive Industries Ltd. (50-50 joint venture with GM)
	New Zealand	Toyota New Zealand (Thames) Ltd.
		Toyota New Zealand (Christchurch) Ltd.
	Indonesia	PT Toyota Astra Motor
	Thailand	Toyota Motor Co. Thailand, Ltd.
	Malaysia	UMW Toyota Motor Sdn. Bhd. (Toyota owned 28%)
	Taiwan	Kuozui Motors, Ltd.
		Fung Yong Co., Ltd.
	Philippines	Toyota Motor Philippines Corporation
Middle East	India	DCM Toyota Ltd.
	Turkey	Haci Omer Sabanci Holding AS (Toyota owned 40%)
	Pakistan	Indus Motor Co. Ltd. (Toyota owned 12.5%)
Africa	South Africa	Toyota South Africa Manufacturing Ltd.
	Kenya	Associated Vehicle Assemblers Ltd.
	Zambia	Rover (Zambia) Ltd.
	Zimbabwe	Willowvale Motor Industries (Pvt.) Ltd.

Sources: 1. Toyota Motor Corporation, *Toyota: A History of the First 50 Years*, Toyota, 1988, pp. 464–65.
2. Various other sources.

product development, while Ford had established the pace in manufacturing productivity; although GM was still grappling with transition problems, it remained the leader in the global marketplace. In addition, the US automakers had returned to profitability, reaping US$9.6 billion in operating profits in 1993 while the Japanese and European automakers lost billions of yen and deutsche marks. However, Donald N. Smith of the University of

Michigan (a long-term Toyota observer) commented, "The worst mistake any competitor can make is to not assume that Toyota will be markedly better five years from now."[27]

ENDNOTES

1. Moskowitz, Milton, *The Global Marketplace: And 101 other global corporate players,* New York: Macmillan, 1987, p. 601.
2. Toyota Motor Corporation, *Toyota: A history of the first 50 years,* Toyota, 1988, p. 45.
3. *Ibid.*, p. 70.
4. *Ibid.*, p. 101.
5. Toyoda, Eiji, *Toyota: Fifty Years in Motion,* New York: Harper & Row, 1985, p. 127.
6. Womack, James P., Daniel T. Jones, and Daniel Roos, *The Machine That Changed the World,* New York: Macmillan, 1990.
7. Toyoda, Eiji, *op. cit.,* p. 128.
8. Taylor III, Alex, How Toyota Copes with Hard Times, *Fortune,* Vol. 127, January 25, 1993, pp. 80–81.
9. *Ibid.*, p. 81.
10. Womack, James P., Daniel T. Jones, and Daniel Roos, *op. cit.*, p. 13.
11. Toyota Motor Corporation, *op. cit.,* p. 314.
12. Rollback by Nissan, Honda and Others, Toyota Nearly Reaches 50% of Domestic Auto Share in Japan, *Business Japan,* Vol. 31, October 1986, pp. 44–45.
13. *Ibid.*, pp. 44–45.
14. Shimizu, Yoshihiko and David Williams, Rusty Guns Threaten Toyota's Grip on Top Slot, *Tokyo Business Today,* August 1989, pp. 14–19.
15. Mino, Hokaji, A View from the Top: Shoichiro Toyoda, President of Toyota Motor Corporation remarks on world and domestic economy, auto market and stronger ties with distributors, *Business Japan,* September 1985, p. 18.
16. Rapoport, Carla, How Japan will Spend Its Cash, *Fortune,* Vol. 118, November 21, 1988, pp. 195–201.
17. Taylor III, Alex, Here Come Japan's New Luxury Cars, *Fortune,* Vol. 120, August 14, 1989, pp. 62–66.
18. Graven, Kathryn and Bradley Stertz, Handling a Recall with Style, *Wall Street Journal,* July 20, 1990, p. A8.
19. Inaba, Yu, The Final Battle: Japan takes on the U.S. luxury car market, *Tokyo Business Today,* Vol. 58, February 1990, pp. 26–31.
20. Taylor III, Alex, Here Come the Hot New Luxury Cars, *Fortune,* Vol. 122, July 2, 1990, pp. 60 and 64.
21. Toyota Motor Corporation, *op. cit.*, p. 351.
22. Toyoda, Eiji, *op. cit.*, p. 130.
23. Toyota Motor Corporation, *op. cit.*, p. 336.
24. *Ibid.*, p. 338.
25. Womack, James P., Daniel T. Jones, and Daniel Roos, *op. cit.*, p. 188.
26. Taylor III, Alex, Japan's New U.S. Car Strategy, *Fortune,* Vol. 122, September 10, 1990, pp. 65–80.
27. Taylor III, Alex, How Toyota Copes with Hard Times, *Fortune,* Vol. 127, January 25, 1993, p. 81.

CASE TWO

Sony Corporation*

Introduction

The fiscal year ending March 31, 1994 was the second year of sharp decline in earnings per American Depository Receipt (ADR), each of which equals one share of common stock, according to Sony's annual report. It was the fourth year of declining overall return-on-investment (ROI), the last two years being especially hard-hit by a combination of appreciation of the yen and the recession that had engulfed Japan and many other leading industrial nations (only the US had begun to emerge from recession). During fiscal year 1994, Sony's electronic business had done somewhat better than its entertainment business although two years earlier the situation had been the reverse (see Appendix for financials).

This case presents, first, a history of the company up to 1980 and then proceeds by time periods, charting not only the company's extraordinary success but also the setbacks and difficulties that occurred along the way.

History till 1980

Eight young engineers began repairing radios in a bombed-out department store in Tokyo in 1946; they were launching what became the Sony Corporation. They were led by Masaru

---

* The case study has been developed mainly from published materials, listed herein, by Robert B. Buchele, College of Business Administration, University of Hawaii. The author gratefully acknowledges help gained from an interview with Mr. Akio Morita in 1986 and correspondence with an aide of his in 1989. This case is intended for instructional purposes only, and not as an example of correct or incorrect administrative action.

Sony Corporation

Ibuka (then 37) and his eventual successor as CEO, Akio Morita (then 25), whose family financed the new small business. The group early displayed strength in research and development of technologically advanced electronic products—this would in time become the company's basic competitive strategy, its competitive advantage.

Sony had developed and was manufacturing tape recorders at a time (the 1950s) when few Japanese knew what a tape recorder was or how one could be used. It was also one of the first producers of transistor radios, and in 1968 gave the world a new standard for color television, the ultra-sharp Trinitron system. In the late 1970s came its most successful product, the Walkman personal tape player as well as the ill-fated pioneering Betamax videotape recorders.

In the course of bringing forth these products, Sony dwarfed the competing products of such American companies as Zenith and RCA. Even among its Japanese rivals, only Matsushita (the Panasonic brand) was bigger in consumer electronics. This is not to say that Matsushita was the only competition in the 1970s. In fact, Sony's sales growth dropped from 166 per cent between 1970 and 1974 to 35 per cent between 1974 and 1978—still strong growth. Not only were a number of Japanese companies learning to give Sony and Matsushita competition but some American companies had also come back, at least temporarily, with successful TV improvements.

INTERNATIONAL ACTIVITIES

Morita made his first visit to the US in 1953 to secure a license to use Western Electronic's transistors. A few years later Sony was selling transistor radios in the US. So strong was Sony's foreign sales effort in the US, England, and Europe that by 1980 only 32 per cent of Sony's sales were in Japan. Establishment of a European plant in 1974 and two US plants (San Diego, California and Dothan, Alabama) at about the same time made Sony one of the first Japanese companies to manufacture abroad. Concurrent with the build-up of foreign sales and manufacture was the build-up of Akio Morita as an international figure, first as a tireless marketer and later as "industrial statesman" speaking and writing on management and international trade issues.

PROBLEMS EMERGE. Sony's 1979 sales were US$2.7 billion, about two-thirds of which were abroad. Profit had grown steadily except for a slight drop in 1978 and a sharp decline in 1979. Sales rebounded 59 per cent and profits reached a new high in 1980. Among Japanese consumer electronics manufacturers, Sony was the leader in new product development and one of the leaders in selling and manufacturing abroad.

Some problems were developing, nevertheless. These were discussed in a February 11, 1980 *Business Week* article, "Sony: An Incongruous Search for Greener Pastures." It pointed out that the company's rate of growth in electronics had slowed, margins had narrowed, and an extensive diversification had taken place over the last two years.

What was "incongruous" was the polyglot nature of the acquisitions which brought Sony's non-electronics sales to 12 per cent of its total sales. Acquisitions ranged from a chain of spaghetti restaurants to the *Sensitive Lady* line of cosmetics, from importing sporting goods, whiskey, and corporate jets to selling life insurance in a joint venture with Prudential.

Most significant, in view of later developments, was a joint venture with CBS Inc. to market phonograph records in Japan.

Also somewhat "incongruous" was Morita's explanation of why the program was undertaken: not only for diversification but also as a sort of personnel development tool that would enable the company to get around the Japanese tradition of lifetime employment by providing positions for persons the company wanted to move out of its electronics businesses.

That explanation and the nature of the acquisitions led *Business Week* to charge that Sony's strategy was "vague." Also, it was suggested that Sony's key executives, almost all scientists or engineers, were not the right people to oversee such a conglomeration of enterprises. The most serious charge in the article was that recently a number of firms, American and Japanese, had beaten Sony to the market with some new hi-tech products.

1980–87: A BASIC PROBLEM IDENTIFIED

A *Forbes* article (October 24, 1983) entitled "Sony's Profitless Prosperity" pointed out that since the 1981 fiscal year, sales had hardly grown and profits had dropped from 8 cents on the sales dollar to 2 cents. Sales of about US$5 billion brought profit of only US$100 million.

The problem, according to *Forbes*, had by now become more serious than merely being beaten to the market on some new products. It was that competitors were regularly and quickly coming out with "me too" products at lower prices. Thus, Sony did not have time to recover its huge R&D investment in its new products. Or, put another way, Sony was producing premium products for a market where it could no longer charge premium prices. So, its basic competitive strategy of high quality innovative products was no longer working. For example, in October 1982, Sony introduced its laser-based compact audio disc player, capping a six-year and US$25 million quest for "perfect sound." Within ten months, Matsushita and Hitachi were selling comparable players at prices which were 35 per cent lower. To add to the misery, it became clear at about this time that Sony's Betamax video recorder was losing out to Matsushita's system.

The article also mentioned the beginning of severe price competition from Korea and Taiwan—the beginning of what came to be known as the "Four Tigers." In some respects Sony was suffering at the hands of other Japanese firms and Asian firms, the kind of competition Sony and others had earlier launched against American firms. As a result of this set of problems, there was a modest reduction of earnings in 1981, but substantial reductions followed in 1982 (recession in the US) and 1983.

FIGHTING BACK

Fully aware of the threat to its competitive advantage, Sony had been busy adjusting its strategy well before the article appeared. This meant putting more emphasis on industrial and governmental uses of its new products—where it could not so readily be copied and underpriced. Sony could lock such customers into longer-term contracts for new components and parts and complete new products. In the past, Sony had neglected to exploit components and parts arising from its development of complete new products. Now, however, it began to sell a lot of 3.5" disk drives from its PC although the computer itself did not sell well. The model for this shift in strategy was Motorola, which had rebuilt and stabilized its business after losing out to "me too" copies of its new products.

Selling to industrial customers meant, however, that Sony would have to focus on cost reduction, especially automation, as much as it had always done on innovation and quality. This drive became the province of Norio Ohga, who became president in 1982 when his predecessor died. Nine years younger than Morita and a stern disciplinarian, Ohga seemed destined to play a larger and larger role. Whereas innovation had been Morita's strength, Ohga's has been more efficient production (curiously, Ohga was a leading opera star when he first consulted with Morita in pursuit of the "perfect sound").

Automation was difficult for Sony because the company improves product technology so often and cost reduction proved difficult in Japan because of adherence to the lifelong employment tradition. It proved difficult outside Japan too, because (to avoid trade restrictions) Sony located its plants in countries that were its main markets while competitors have located plants in countries with cheap labor. This has led, for example, to Sony having a plant in high-cost San Diego, while Matsushita has a plant not far away in low-cost Mexico.

Despite all of these efforts at change, Sony's main strategy continued to be to develop quality innovative consumer electronic products, and its R&D expense as a percentage of sales undoubtedly continued about twice that of Matsushita.

Sony's Lone Battle

An article in *The Oriental Economist* of September 1985, discusses two additions to what Ohga described as the company's long history of "sensationally sophisticated" products. In January the 8 mm videotape recorder (VTR) was introduced in an effort to recapture the share of the big VCR market lost in the decline of the Betamax system. Its outstanding characteristics were its ultra smallness and the usual Sony high quality. It was not compatible with VHS, the system that beat Betamax. In mid-year a new product, the compact disc player, was introduced in the hope that it would usher in the era of compact discs. If it did so, Sony's compact disc and recorded disc businesses would probably boom. The article's title, which may have lost something in the translation, would seem to refer to Sony's persistence in the strategy of R&D excellence, advanced technology, and new products.

By September the 8 mm VTR was selling well enough, but not booming. Some observers thought it would be necessary to lower the price to get it to boom. It was too early to tell how well the compact disc player would sell.

In any case, earnings rebounded in 1984 and it seemed likely that 1985 would surpass 1980 level earnings. The article rendered the following evaluation of Sony's status at the time:

> *Undoubtedly Sony is a blue chip company as far as technical level, product planning ability and brand power are concerned. However, the company lacks overall balance. Its production capacity and marketing capability lag behind its other capabilities. For a trillion-yen company, its corporate organization is immature. These were the*

major factors which caused Sony's earnings to decrease sharply (in '82 and '83, the former a US recession year).

The article went on to say that while Sony was making progress, not only Matsushita but also Sanyo and Sharp were making greater progress.

SUMMARY AS OF LATE 1987

A combination of competition among the Japanese companies and with the "Four Tigers" plus a strong yen hurt all the Japanese competitors' earnings in 1986; however, Sony, with 70 per cent foreign sales, was hurt more than Matsushita and suffered a drop of 75 per cent in earnings at the operating income level, as compared to the latter's 44 per cent. Sony's R&D expenditures as a percentage of sales were still double those of its arch-rival.

In order to cope with these pressures, Sony was building more factories abroad (its stock was listed on 23 exchanges around the world, and foreign ownership was 23 per cent). Another offensive was the launching of twenty new products and increased drive in introducing many new models of established products. While the DAT (digital audio tape) player was not being sold in the US, Walkman, in a lower-price model designed especially for the American market, was selling well, as was the latest model TV, the Profeel. The compact disc player had captured one-third of a small but growing market. The 8 mm VTR was struggling. A reversal in traditional Sony policy was evident with the pricing below cost of the compact disc player—Sony was clearly going for share of market strategy. Sony Corporation of America alone was investing in twenty new businesses including full feature telephones, in which it is the early leader, 3.5" computer discs, and other products for the office of the future.

"Sony's Challenge" (a June 1, 1987 *Business Week* cover story) asserted that Sony was being forced into new markets because it had decided to make a major effort in industrial electronics. An engineering workstation type computer was part of this drive. So, also, was the new direction given to the 8 mm VTR. It was hoped that the latter product could do better in industrial applications than it was doing in the consumer market. To this end, Sony had agreed with 127 manufacturers on 8 mm standards, and it was making 8 mm equipment sold by Pioneer, Fuji, and others.

While the jury was still out on both of these efforts, it was clear that the drive to achieve 50 per cent industrial (or non-consumer) sales overall by 1990, a commitment made by Ohga in 1982 when it was 15 per cent, was behind schedule.

In the article Morita, then 66, stated that he was now spending only about one-third of his time "at Sony" and that while Ohga, as CEO, was running the company day-to-day, he (Morita) as Chairman was still in charge of basic policy. Also, there was mention of Morita's recently published book, *Made in Japan*, which had more to do with international trade relations and plans to stabilize currency relationships than with the management of Sony.

AN EVALUATION PROVED WRONG

Clearly, Sony was struggling hard on many fronts both to build competitive advantages in new fields and to maintain the old competitive advantages. This involved a mix of old (high quality, innovative consumer electronics products) and new (industrial electronics) strategies. In the 1987 article, Morita had predicted a strong recovery for the company and indeed, the poor financial results of 1986 were followed by the start of recovery in the calendar year 1987 (fiscal year 1987 was only five months long due to a shift in fiscal year). Nevertheless, it was hard for an analyst to overlook the indications that Sony was in deep trouble. The weak earnings had gone on so long. The great leader was getting old, and his interests were shifting away from the Company.

BIG, DRAMATIC CHANGE. Late in calendar year 1987 (third quarter, fiscal year 1988) Sony announced a blockbuster acquisition: CBS records for a little over US$2 billion. Thus, Sony became owner of the world's largest record company with which it had long been associated in a venture to distribute records in Japan, and significant diversification beyond consumer and industrial electronics was achieved.

Fiscal year 1988 brought the strong recovery in electronics that Morita had predicted, and fiscal year 1989, was also good for Sony. In consumer electronics, many old products were maintained and progress continued in new products such as compact discs and recorded compact discs (through CBS Records). Sony was a leader in DAT (digital audio tape) recorders (which were not distributed in the US until 1990 because of the controversy over re-recording).

In industrial electronics, workstations were booming, there was progress on the 8 mm videotape recorder, and Sony was a leading supplier of components in which Sony's technology was superior (e.g., superfast processor chips, various factory automation devices, and the display and digital audio systems for Steve Job's advanced computer, NEXT). Also, the filmless Mavica camera was being adapted for use by journalists to make possible rapid transmission of their pictures over telephone lines.

ANOTHER BLOCKBUSTER. The CBS Records acquisition was topped in September–October 1989 (mid-fiscal year 1990) by the US$3.4 billion acquisition of Columbia Pictures, a major American movie studio. Speculation was that Sony saw numerous possible synergies as more and more electronic equipment was going digital and multimedia. Sony would be able to use both CBS Records and Columbia Pictures to supply the software needed by Sony's and others' digital products, especially HDTV (high definition TV), on which Sony had already invested US$200 million in R&D (incidentally, Sony shocked some observers by bidding for a part of a US Department of Defense research project on HDTV. Obviously, Sony was asserting its "multinational-ness"). There could be a huge market for Columbia films, old and new, put onto Sony's tiny cassettes for the 8 mm VCRs. In fact, there were endless software possibilities; some observers felt that in the coming decade there would be far more money made in various kinds of software, some highly innovative, than in electronic hardware.

GRAND STRATEGY. The big move toward multimedia at once potentially created: huge new markets for the equipment divisions—entirely new combinations of equipment working together; and new categories of software developed jointly by the record and movie companies and the electronics companies. While most observers agreed that this was a brilliant and bold strategy, some suggested that a less risky execution of it—one not involving outright purchase of "normally chaotic" movie-making companies—might have been used.

Organizationally with both consumer and industrial electronics going well and the two big entertainment acquisitions made, strategy planning was being "localized" (decentralized) to the major product centers. Also, while Morita would undoubtedly, one way or another, make his influence felt on all company activities, he would be directly involved in only the major deals, according to an announcement from his office. The business press was beginning to write of "Ohga's new programs" instead of attributing all changes to Morita's initiative.

THE POST-FISCAL 1990 STORY

The story of this period is most succinctly told by overall ROI figures for Sony Corporation: FY 1991, 7.92; FY 1992, 7.82; FY 1993, 2.54; and FY 1994, 1.15 per cent.

The FY 1990 results showed a major impact from the Columbia Pictures acquisition and the follow-on investments required by it: revenue was up substantially, dollar profits were up a bit, ROI down from 7.9 to 7.2 per cent, and ROA down (from 3.02 to 2.35 per cent). Columbia Pictures had an operating loss of about US$100 million and a negative cash flow of from US$250 to 350 million. Only exceptionally strong performance by the electronics businesses kept overall figures looking as good as they did.

The fiscal year 1991 results showed the same pattern, but with the Columbia Pictures loss moderating somewhat. Total revenues were US$25.849 billion, including almost US$5 billion from the entertainment businesses. Sony appeared to have solved its problems in consumer electronics and achieved success in industrial electronics with the many new products already mentioned. Also, a number of R&D joint ventures with leading electronics firms around the world were underway.

However, Sony was facing several years of turmoil and heavy expenditures at Columbia before it could expect a return. Sony said it was fully prepared for the financial hit and still viewed Columbia as a key strategic purchase to meld its hardware and software businesses. That it was finding the US entertainment business quite different from anything it had previously experienced was quite clear. In a number of cases it had paid multimillion dollar signing bonuses to movie or record executives who stayed around only a very short time.

Just as the troubles at Columbia were making headlines and many observers were questioning the wisdom of the Columbia acquisition, Matsushita appeared to validate it by acquiring MCA, parent company of Universal Studios and other entertainment units in late 1990. However, most observers agreed that Matsushita had paid relatively less than Sony had paid for RCA. Also, Matsushita had dealt with and retained perhaps the most respected executives in the industry, whereas Sony dealt with and hired notably less-than-respected industry personalities.

THE RISE OF MICKEY SCHULHOF

The chaos in the executive ranks of Sony's entertainment industry was being gradually brought under control by Michael Schulhof, who rose first to the top of Sony's music business, then the entertainment businesses (in 1992) and, finally, to all Sony businessness in the US (in 1993). He stated his intention of moving the Sony entertainment businesses "beyond simply exporting movies, TV shows and records." He aims at creating new types of businesses.

Schulhof, a PhD in physics, came to Sony via the records business, where he had started in 1974 in a semi-technical capacity. He first handled the introduction of DAT, then the marketing of compact discs, and the search for acquisitions in the entertainment field that culminated in the purchases of CBS Records, Columbia Pictures, and Tri-Star (a movie production company purchased to get the services of Peter Guber, now head of Columbia, and an associate who was soon gone with considerable Sony cash in his pocket).

FISCAL YEAR 1992

While income rose slightly in this period, as noted earlier, ROI fell. Sony Music did well (though a spin-off of it—to raise capital—late in the year was not well received by the market). Columbia had some hit pictures late in the year but the electronics businesses in Japan were hurt by the strong yen and by the recession in the US.

FISCAL YEAR 1993

Overall sales were flat and income went down sharply. The electronics businesses were hurt badly by the strong yen and recession in Japan and other countries. Only the US economy was starting to recover. Overall results would have been worse but for some successful currency hedging.

The entertainment businesses were somewhat stronger than the electronics businesses, and they now accounted for 20.8 per cent of total sales. Nevertheless a financial writer in the *New York Times* of November 26, 1993, in "How Japan Got Mugged in Hollywood," ventured the opinion that neither Sony nor Matsushita is likely to see decent profit from its movie company purchase in the twentieth century. In an earlier (October 15, 1993) article entitled "Synergy: The unspoken word," the same newspaper had discussed the problem of securing synergy in the form of new kinds of products from interaction between electronics and movie companies. The writer suggested that the companies that were at the time seeking to acquire Paramount Pictures should review the experience of Sony, indicating that Sony had achieved little, if any, synergy. To the present casewriter this was reminiscent of the experiences of Litton Industries many years ago when it was on a long conglomerating binge. Litton talked glowingly of the synergy possibilities between its shipyards and its electronics companies and between its frozen food company and its microwave manufacturer but nothing every materialized. The highly aggressive Litton division managers, intent on securing huge bonuses for high division performance each year, gave little attention to working with other divisions. No one had synergy as his/her sole assignment.

Throughout the year Sony was aggressively negotiating strategic alliances with various firms or groups of firms: with record companies to launch an MTV channel, with Qualcom, Inc. to make computerized wireless telephones, with Nintendo to develop games, with a group to go into cable television and telephone, with Blockbusters to develop amphitheatres in Europe and elsewhere, etc.

In late November 1993, Akio Morita suffered a cerebral hemorrhage that seemed certain to keep him away from his usual activities for a long time.

FISCAL YEAR 1994

The high yen, recession in Japan, and a run of disappointing movies at Columbia combined to produce a 54.3 per cent year-over-year drop in income although sales were off by only 6.5 per cent.

Toward the end of this fiscal year, in January 1994, before the US stock market dropped, Sony's ADRs went to $61^{3}/_{4}$ although they hadn't been above $50^{1}/_{4}$ since 1991. One analyst speculated that Wall Street was so impressed with the company's plans for a multimedia future that it overlooked weak financial results for the fiscal year. Although the DJIA declined almost 10 per cent over the next few months, Sony stock held at 60 or better through mid-June.

Appendix

Exhibit 1 Consolidated Results for the Fiscal Year Ended March 31, 1994

Yen (millions), US dollars (thousands), except per share amounts

	1993	1994	Change (%)	1994
Total sales	¥3,992,918	¥3,733,721	− 6.5	$36,249,718
Operating income	126,460	99,668	− 21.2	967,650
Income before income taxes	92,561	102,162	+ 10.4	991,864
Net income	36,260	15,298	− 57.8	148,524
Net income per depository share	¥92.2	¥42.1	− 54.3	$0.41

Consolidated Sales Performance by Area

Sales and Operating Revenue	1993	1994	Change (%)	1994
Japan	¥1,028,207	¥1,023,692	− 0.4	$9,938,757
United States	1,215,954	1,154,454	− 5.1	11,208,291
Europe	1,039,802	832,751	− 19.9	8,084,961
Other areas	708,955	722,824	+ 2.0	7,017,709
Total	¥3,992,918	¥3,733,721	− 6.5	$36,249,718

Consolidated Sales Performance by Business Group

(a) Electronics Business

Sales and Operating Revenue	1993	1994	Change (%)	1994
Video equipment	¥828,366	¥668,537	− 19.3	$6,490,651
Audio equipment	928,010	840,723	− 9.4	8,162,359
Television	633,723	617,901	− 2.5	5,999,039
Others	771,779	817,060	+ 5.9	7,932,621
Total	¥3,161,878	¥2,944,221	− 6.9	$28,584,670

(b) Entertainment Business

Sales and Operating Revenue	1993	1994	Change (%)	1994
Music group	¥446,506	¥461,752	+ 3.4	$4,483,029
Pictures group	384,534	327,748	− 14.8	3,182,019
Total	¥831,040	¥789,500	− 5.0	$7,665,048

Case Two

Exhibit 2A Five-Year Summary of Selected Financial Data

Yen (millions), US dollars (thousands), except per share amounts

	\multicolumn{5}{c	}{Year Ended March 31}	Year Ended March 31, 1994
	1989	1990	1991	1992	1993	1994
For the Year						
Sales and operating revenue	¥2,203,601	¥2,947,597	¥3,695,508	¥3,928,667	¥3,992,918	$34,421,707
Operating income	162,628	297,546	302,181	179,549	126,460	1,090,172
Income before income taxes	168,901	232,945	270,697	216,139	92,561	797,940
Income taxes	95,176	126,976	152,398	90,327	49,794	429,259
Net income	72,469	102,808	116,925	120,121	36,260	312,586
Net income per depository share	¥219.7	¥279.0	¥285.9	¥293.1	¥92.2	$0.79
Depreciation and amortization	¥125,790	¥164,751	¥214,116	¥265,208	¥274,477	$2,366,181
Capital investments (additions to fixed assets)	215,613	323,750	411,652	453,115	251,117	2,164,802
R&D expenditures	142,077	165,227	205,787	240,591	232,150	2,001,293
At Year-End						
Net working capital	¥348,476	¥205,642	¥129,904	¥306,553	¥367,009	$3,163,871
Stockholders' equity	911,816	1,430,058	1,476,414	1,536,795	1,428,219	12,312,233
Stockholders' equity per depository share	¥2,933.17	¥3,916.66	¥3,964.04	¥4,119.23	¥3,827.39	$32.99
Total assets	¥2,364,775	¥4,370,085	¥4,602,495	¥4,911,129	¥4,529,830	$39,050,259
Average number of shares outstanding during the year (thousands)	334,336	371,450	417,202	417,599	417,687	
Number of shares issued at year-end (thousands)	282,603	331,929	338,593	373,078	373,158	

Notes:
1. US dollar amounts have been translated from yen, for convenience only, at the rate of ¥116 = US$1, the approximate Tokyo foreign exchange market rate as of March 31, 1993, as described in Note 2 of Notes to Consolidated Financial Statements.
2. Net income per depository share is computed based on the average number of common shares outstanding during each period after consideration of the dilutive effect of common stock equivalents which include warrants and certain convertible bonds. Net income per depository share is appropriately adjusted for the free distribution of common stock.

Sony Corporation

3. During the first quarter ended June 30, 1992, it became apparent that certain undistributed earnings from the Company's foreign subsidiaries on which income taxes had been accrued would not be remitted. As a result, the Company reversed accrued taxes on April 1, 1992 of ¥9,696 million ($83,586 thousand), corresponding to a portion of undistributed earnings which is considered permanently reinvested, as a credit to income taxes for the first quarter ended June 30, 1992.

4. In Japan, no accounting entry is required for a free distribution of common stock of 33,908,621 shares made on November 20, 1991. Had the distribution been accounted for in the manner adopted by companies in the United States, ¥201,708 million ($1,733,431 thousand) would have been transferred from retained earnings to the appropriate capital accounts.

5. On November 22, 1991, Sony Music Entertainment (Japan) Inc., a consolidated subsidiary, issued shares of common stock in a public offering to third parties at a price which was in excess of the Company's average per share carrying value. The issuance was regarded as a sale of a part of the Company's interest in the subsidiary and resulted in a ¥61,544 million gain on subsidiary sale of stock. No taxes were provided for on the gain as the Company has no present intention of disposing of its remaining investment.

6. On November 1, and November 7, 1989, Sony acquired Sony Picture Entertainment (formerly Columbia Pictures Entertainment, Inc.) and The Guber-Peters Entertainment Company, which are operating primarily in the pictures businesses. Sony's consolidated financial statements include the operating results of acquired companies for the period from the dates of acquisition.

7. Certain amounts in the Consolidated Statements of Income and Retained Earnings for the years ended March 31, 1989 through 1992 have been reclassified to conform to the presentation for the year ended March 31, 1993.

Source: Annual Report of Sony Corporation and its Consolidated Subsidiaries, Fiscal Year 1993, ending March 31, 1994.

Exhibit 2B Composition of Sales and Operating Revenue by Area and Product Group—Sony Corporation and Consolidated Subsidiaries

	Yen (millions)					US dollars (thousands)
	Year Ended March 31					Year Ended March 31, 1993
	1989	1990	1991	1992	1993	1993
Sales and Operating Revenue by Area						
Japan	¥786,413	¥934,189	¥1,024,484	¥1,057,648	¥1,028,207	$8,863,854
	35.7%	31.7%	27.7%	26.9%	25.8%	
United States	586,288	857,812	1,055,448	1,119,174	1,215,954	10,482,362
	26.6	29.1	28.6	28.5	30.4	
Europe	498,037	715,652	1,017,804	1,080,005	1,039,802	8,963,810
	22.6	24.3	27.5	27.5	26.0	
Other areas	332,863	439,944	597,772	671,840	708,955	6,111,681
	15.1	14.9	16.2	17.1	17.8	
Sales and operating revenue	¥2,203,601	¥2,947,597	¥3,695,508	¥3,928,667	¥3,992,918	$34,421,707
Sales and Operating Revenue by Product Group						
Video equipment	¥573,493	¥743,709	¥908,399	¥896,379	¥828,366	$7,141,086
	26.0%	25.2%	24.6%	22.8%	20.8%	
Audio equipment	560,772	722,211	881,777	947,770	928,010	8,000,086
	25.5	24.5	23.9	24.1	23.2	
Televisions	341,800	446,436	552,464	592,616	633,723	5,463,129
	15.5	15.1	14.9	15.1	15.9	
Others	387,329	487,529	619,269	713,082	771,779	6,653,268
	17.6	16.6	16.7	18.2	19.3	
Total electronics business	1,863,394	2,399,885	2,961,909	3,149,847	3,161,878	27,257,569
	84.6	81.4	80.1	80.2	79.2	
Music group	340,207	455,203	476,057	449,601	446,506	3,849,190
	15.4	15.5	12.9	11.4	11.2	
Pictures group		92,509	257,542	329,219	384,534	3,314,948
		3.1	7.0	8.4	9.6	
Total entertainment business	340,207	547,712	733,599	778,820	831,040	7,164,138
	15.4	18.6	19.9	19.8	20.8	
Sales and operating revenue	¥2,203,601	¥2,947,597	¥3,695,508	¥3,928,667	¥3,992,918	$34,421,707

Notes:
1. US dollar amounts have been translated from yen, for convenience only, at the rate of ¥116 = US$1, the approximate Tokyo foreign exchange market rate as of March 31, 1993, as described in Note 2 of Notes to Consolidated Financial Statements.
2. The above sales classification shows sales and operating revenue recognized by geographic location of the buyer and product group and does not include intersegment transactions. Therefore, it is different from the business segment information in Exhibit 2C.

Sony Corporation

Exhibit 2C   Financial Information by Business Segment

Business Segment Information

The company operates on a worldwide basis, principally within two industry segments; Electronics and Entertainment. Electronics segment designs, develops, manufactures, and distributes video equipment, audio equipment, televisions, and other products. Entertainment segment manufactures, markets, and distributes music and pictures entertainment products.

Exhibits 2C and 2D present certain information regarding the company's industry segments and operations by geographic areas at March 31, 1991, 1992, and 1993 and for the years then ended.

Industry Segments	Yen (millions) Year Ended March 31 1991	1992	1993	US dollars (thousands) Year Ended March 31, 1993
Sales and Operating Revenue				
Electronics				
Customers	¥2,961,909	¥3,149,847	¥3,161,878	$27,257,569
Intersegment	12,077	9,491	11,537	99,457
Total	2,973,986	3,159,338	3,173,415	27,357,026
Entertainment				
Customers	733,599	778,820	831,040	7,164,138
Intersegment	4,428	4,552	3,990	34,396
Total	738,027	783,372	835,030	7,198,534
Elimination	(16,505)	(14,043)	(15,527)	(133,853)
Consolidated	¥3,695,508	¥3,928,667	¥3,992,918	$34,421,707
Operating Income				
Electronics	¥262,910	¥127,328	¥80,140	$690,862
Entertainment	49,407	65,632	60,027	517,474
Corporate and elimination	(10,136)	(13,411)	(13,707)	(118,164)
Consolidated	¥302,181	¥179,549	¥126,460	$1,090,172
Identifiable Assets				
Electronics	¥2,667,232	¥2,940,331	¥2,673,625	$23,048,491
Entertainment	1,568,881	1,635,271	1,539,974	13,275,638
Corporate assets and elimination	366,382	335,527	316,231	2,726,130
Consolidated	¥4,602,495	¥4,911,129	¥4,529,830	$39,050,259
Depreciation and Amortization				
Electronics	¥168,407	¥219,403	¥227,683	$1,962,784
Entertainment	44,128	44,567	44,857	386,699
Corporate	1,581	1,238	1,937	16,698
Consolidated	¥214,116	¥265,208	¥274,477	$2,366,181

Exhibit 2C Financial Information by Business Segment (cont.)

	Year Ended March 31			Year Ended March 31, 1993
	1991	1992	1993	1993
Capital Expenditure				
Electronics	¥373,888	¥398,296	¥194,920	$1,680,345
Entertainment	34,191	44,757	51,922	447,604
Corporate	3,573	10,062	4,275	36,853
Consolidated	¥411,652	¥453,115	¥251,117	$2,164,802

Exhibit 2D Financial Information by Geographic Area

Geographic Areas	Yen (millions)			US dollars (thousands)
	Year Ended March 31			Year Ended March 31, 1993
	1991	1992	1993	1993
Sales and Operating Revenue				
Japan				
Customers	¥1,447,075	¥1,505,747	¥1,453,215	$12,527,716
Intersegment	887,489	1,002,447	984,496	8,487,034
Total	2,334,564	2,508,194	2,437,711	21,014,750
USA				
Customers	943,059	997,081	1,058,788	9,127,483
Intersegment	32,246	32,035	33,743	290,888
Total	975,305	1,029,116	1,092,531	9,418,371
Europe				
Customers	980,059	1,028,294	1,006,859	8,679,819
Intersegment	5,892	5,324	6,196	53,414
Total	985,951	1,033,618	1,013,055	8,733,233
Other				
Customers	325,315	397,545	474,056	4,086,690
Intersegment	169,971	248,014	291,858	2,516,017
Total	495,286	645,559	765,914	6,602,707
Elimination	(1,095,598)	(1,287,820)	(1,316,293)	(11,347,354)
Consolidated	¥3,695,508	¥3,928,667	¥3,992,918	$34,421,707

Sony Corporation

Exhibit 2D Financial Information by Geographic Area (cont.)

	Year Ended March 31			Year Ended March 31, 1993
	1991	*1992*	*1993*	*1993*
Operating Income				
Japan	¥161,283	¥47,974	¥55,243	$476,233
USA	40,882	43,905	35,098	302,569
Europe	98,927	86,738	60,129	518,353
Other	31,345	38,874	26,185	225,733
Corporate and elimination	(30,256)	(37,942)	(50,195)	(432,716)
Consolidated	¥302,181	¥179,549	¥126,460	$1,090,172
Identifiable Assets				
Japan	¥1,948,043	¥2,188,326	¥2,114,956	$18,232,380
USA	1,613,286	1,659,205	1,481,193	12,768,905
Europe	585,551	600,155	464,852	4,007,345
Other	213,343	290,392	301,694	2,600,810
Corporate assets and elimination	242,272	173,051	167,135	1,440,819
Consolidated	¥4,602,495	¥4,911,129	¥4,529,830	$39,050,259
Export Sales and Operating Revenue				
To USA	¥86,614	¥96,775	¥113,336	$977,035
To Europe	62,993	74,984	73,085	630,043
To other countries	278,092	281,566	243,423	2,098,474
Total	¥427,699	¥453,325	¥429,844	$3,705,552

Transfers between industry or geographic segments are made at arms-length prices. Operating income is sales and operating revenue less costs and operating expenses. Corporate expenses of the geographic segments include certain research and development expenses used in the operations of each industry or geographic segment. Unallocated corporate assets consist primarily of cash and cash equivalents and marketable securities maintained for general corporate purposes.

ENDNOTES

1. Why Stars Like Sony Have Lost Their Glow, *Business Week*, March 15, 1982, p. 145.
2. Even Sony Sometimes Stumbles, *Business Week*, April 18, 1983, p. 49.
3. Supreme Surprise: A decision on state taxation, *Fortune*, July 25, 1983, p. 7.
4. Sony's Slippage: Tone-deaf in the marketplace, *Fortune*, July 25, 1983.
5. Sagging Sony Turns Quiet, *Fortune*, October 31, 1983, p. 98.
6. Max Troubles for Betamax, *Time*, January 16, 1984, p. 60.
7. Japanese Companies Start to Flee the Unitary Tax, *Business Week*, August 27, 1984, p. 30.
8. Thomas, Joe, The Sony Corporation, in Robert Justis, Richard Judd and David Stephens (Eds.), *Strategic Management and Policy: Concepts and Cases*, Englewood Cliffs, NJ: Prentice-Hall, 1985, pp. 589–601.
9. Sony Battles Back, *Fortune*, April 15, 1985, pp. 26–38.

10. Sony's Risky Giant Step into Mini Video, *Business Week*, June 10, 1985, p. 56.
11. Sony's Tiny Video Cameras, *Fortune*, June 24, 1985, p. 9.
12. U.S. Chip Makers Join Forces with Japanese, *Computerworld*, February 24, 1986, p. 100.
13. When Sony was an Up-and-Comer, *Forbes*, October 6, 1986, pp. 98–102.
14. Mr. Walkman Talks, *Fortune*, October 27, 1986, p. 143.
15. Browing, E.S., Sony's Perseverance Helped it Win Market for Mini-CD Players, *Wall Street Journal*, February 27, 1986, p. 1.
16. The "Four Tigers" Are Pouncing on Japan's Markets, *Business Week*, March 24, 1986, pp. 48ff.
17. Video Wars: Sony could get another bloody nose, *Business Week*, May 12, 1986, p. 88.
18. Morita, Akio, Edwin Reingold, and Mitsuko Shimomura, *Made in Japan: Akio Morita and Sony*, London: Collins, 1987.
19. Born in the USA, Sold to Japan, *Time*, November 30, 1987, p. 66.
20. Whiteside, David, Otis Port, and Larry Armstrong, Sony isn't Mourning the Death of Betamax, *Business Week*, No. 35, January 25, 1988, p. 37.
21. Sony's Back in Computers, *Business Week*, February 8, 1988, p. 32.
22. Armstrong, Larry and Sayaka Shinoda, So You'd Like to Watch a Movie on the Subway, *Business Week*, No. 72, October 3, 1988, pp. 135–138.
23. Competitive Does Not Mean Cheap, *World Press Review*, October 1988, pp. 31–32.
24. Cohen, Jeffrey, Whatever Happened to Betamax, *Consumer's Research*, May 1989, pp. 28–29.
25. Japan Goes to Hollywood, *Newsweek*, October 9, 1989, pp. 62–67.
26. Gross, Neil and William Holstein, Why Sony Is Plugging into Columbia, *Business Week*, No. 128, October 16, 1989, pp. 56–58.
27. Lieberman, David, Even for Walter Yetnikoff, This Will be a Stretch, *Business Week*, No. 131, October 30, 1989, pp. 144–145.
28. Landro, Laura, At Columbia, Comeback is the Big Production, *Wall Street Journal*, August 20, 1990, p. B1.
29. Lopez, Julie Amparano, BellSouth, Sony Join up to Test Wireless Phones, *Wall Street Journal*, October 10, 1990, p. B4.
30. Turner, Richard, Laura Landro, and Yumiko Ono, Matsushita Purchase of MCA Could Help Buyer Break Old Mold, *Wall Street Journal*, November 26, 1990, p. A1.
31. Hughes, Kathleen, Japan's Past Ventures in Hollywood Mostly are Less than Stellar, *Wall Street Journal*, November 27, 1990, p. A1.
32. Turner, Richard, Backed by Matsushita's Deep Pockets, MCA Plans to Seek Major Acquisitions, *Wall Street Journal*, November 28, 1990, p. A3.
33. Grover, Ronald and Judith Dobrzynski, Lights, Camera, Action, *Business Week*, No. 191, December 10, 1990, pp. 27–28.
34. Grover, Ronald, The World is Hollywood's Oyster, *Business Week*, No. 195, January 14, 1991, p. 97.
35. Rothman, Andrea, Ronald Grover, and Robert Neff, Media Colossus, *Business Week*, No. 205, March 25, 1991, pp. 64–74.
36. Mahar, Maggie, Adventures in Wonderland, *Barron's*, October 7, 1991, p. 8.
37. Sweet Smell of Excess, *Newsweek*, October 14, 1991, pp. 46–47.
38. Part 3: Ratings & Reports, *The Value Line Investment Survey*, New York, NY: Value Line Publishing Inc., November 22, 1991.
39. Why Sony Music Hit Sour Notes in Tokyo, *Business Week*, December 23, 1991.
40. Ellis, James, Sony's "Gallery" Has Retailers Hearing Footsteps, *Business Week*, No. 245, December 23, 1991, p. 29.
41. Schlesinger, Jacob, Sony is Turning More Cautious After Reverses, *Wall Street Journal*, January 7, 1992, p. B1.
42. Sony Stalks Next Big Hit in Electronics, *Honolulu Star-Bulletin*, New York Times Bureau, February 25, 1992.

43. Grover, Ronald and Robert Neff, Is Sony Finally Getting the Hang of Hollywood? *Business Week,* No. 282, September 7, 1992, pp. 76–77.
44. Reilly, Patrick, Sony to Reorganize U.S. Consumer Unit in Bid to Spur Sales, *Wall Street Journal,* March 31, 1993, p. A8.
45. Roberts, Johnnie, Missing Links: Synergy benefits have so far eluded the entertainment giants, *Wall Street Journal,* March 26, 1993, p. R9.
46. Reilly, Patrick, Sony Combines US Operations under Schulhof, *Wall Street Journal,* May 25, 1993, p. B1.
47. Yoder, Stephen Kreider and G. Pascal Zachary, Digital Media Business Takes Form as a Battle of Complex Alliances, *Wall Street Journal,* July 14, 1993, p. A1.
48. Hamilton, David, Sony Posts 31% Rise in Pretax Profit, Aided by Hedging Against Yen's Rise, *Wall Street Journal,* August 20, 1993, p. A8.
49. Moody's May Lower Sony's Debt Ratings, *Wall Street Journal,* August 25, 1993, p. B6.
50. Landro, Laura, Sony Music Creates Office of Chairman under Schulhof, *Wall Street Journal,* September 28, 1993, p. B8.
51. Sims, Calvin, Synergy: The unspoken word, *New York Times,* October 5, 1993, p. 1.
52. Landro, Laura, Long-term Contracts Go to Sony Aides in Film, Music, Electronic Publishing, *Wall Street Journal,* November 19, 1993, p. B9.
53. Hamilton, David, Pretax Profit at Sony Rises; Nintendo's Falls, *Wall Street Journal,* November 19, 1993, p. B4E.
54. Hamilton, David and Laura Landro, Blurred Picture: Sony loses services of visionary founder at a critical juncture, *Wall Street Journal,* December 3, 1993, p. A1.
55. Hamilton, David, Sony President Brushes off Criticism of Strategy for a Multimedia Future, *Wall Street Journal,* December 6, 1993, p. B3.
56. Hamilton, David, Big Japanese Electronics Firms Begin to See Turnaround after Long Slide, *Wall Street Journal,* February 23, 1994, p. A15.
57. Trachtenberg, Jeffrey, Sony Plans to Unleash Minidisc Offensive, *Asian Wall Street Journal,* March 21, 1994, p. 12.

CASE THREE

ACCORDING TO HONDA, AN AMERICAN LEGEND FACES THE 1990s*

Events have a way of breaking in favor of the Japanese. When the second oil crunch and double-digit inflation hit in the late 1970s, they had cheap, economical cars to sell. When the yen burst through the roof, they had U.S. factories ready to go. But success, as we all know, goes to those who make their own luck.[1]

Honda has been a success story. In the 40 years since Honda Motor Company was incorporated under the laws of Japan to manufacture engines for motorized bicycles, Honda has grown to become the third largest auto manufacturer in Japan, the fourth largest in the United States, and the tenth largest in the world. In the 1960s Japan's Ministry of International Trade and Industry (MITI) tried to discourage Honda's founder from expanding beyond its original business of motorcycles to restrict competition for Japan's existing automakers.[2] Nevertheless, the firm forged ahead. The trigger for Honda's later success in automobiles came in 1972 when its president, Mr. Tadashi Kume, developed the low-pollution, fuel efficient CVCC (compound vortex controlled combustion) engine. Honda, simultaneously introduced the Civic automobile using this engine. Since then the firm's automobile sales, in both units and yen, have increased every year.

---

* This case was prepared by Lynda L. Goulet of the University of Northern Iowa as the basis for class discussion rather than to illustrate the effective or ineffective handling of a managerial situation. Submitted to and accepted by the refereed Midwest Society for Case Research. All rights reserved to the author and the MSCR. © by Lynda L. Goulet, 1990.

WORLD AUTO INDUSTRY

By 1990 approximately 175 manufacturers will be producing nearly 50 million automobiles, trucks, and buses worldwide, generating sales of about US$450 billion.[3] The 12 largest of these producers are listed in Exhibit 1. Although two US based firms, General Motors and Ford, lead the industry with a combined world share of about 30 per cent, the list also includes Chrysler, the four largest European firms, and five Japanese companies. Although the United States is currently the largest market for automotive vehicles, western Europe will shortly take over this spot. Western Europe already leads in vehicle production, followed

Exhibit 1 1988 World Automotive Vehicle Production and Sales (millions of units)

	Productions		Sales	
	Cars	Trucks/Buses	Cars	Trucks/Buses
United States	7.137	4.080	10.545	5.244
Canada	1.027	0.950	1.053	0.509
Western Europe	13.032	1.662	12.682	1.849
Japan	8.198	4.501	3.717	2.715 (estimated)
All others	5.803	2.247	3.755	2.049
Total	35.197	13.440	31.752	12.366

Firms Producing More Than 1 million Vehicles

Firm	Home Country	Production (All Vehicles), 1988
General Motors	United States	7.8
Ford	United States	6.4
Toyota	Japan	4.0
Volkswagen	West Germany	2.9
Fiat	Italy	2.4
Chrysler	United States	2.4
Nissan	Japan	2.2
Peugeot	France	2.1
Renault	France	1.9
Honda	Japan	1.7
Mitsubishi	Japan	1.3
Mazda	Japan	1.2
Total		36.3

Sources: 1. Autos-Auto Parts, *Standard and Poor's Industry Reports*, November 30, 1989, p. A88.
2. Ford Motor Company, *Annual Report*, 1989.
3. *Automotive News*, November 29, 1989, p. 128.

by Japan (which exports 50 per cent of its production). In contrast, the United States is the only major market in the world which is a net importer of vehicles. As more automakers begin to establish facilities in Europe in the 1990s, worldwide overcapacity and overproduction can be expected to increase beyond the 4.5-million level of the late 1980s. As competition intensifies, the consumer may become the big winner of the auto wars.

EUROPEAN MARKET

Western Europe is the largest car market in the world. This market is growing as a result of increasing income levels and relatively low existing levels of car ownership (380 cars per 1,000 people, versus 580/1,000 in the United States). Europe's six major automakers and their share of the European market are summarized below:[4]

Automobile Firm	Share (%)	Automobile Firm	Share (%)
Fiat	14.9	Ford	11.9
Volkswagen	14.8	General Motors	11.0
Peugeot	12.9	Renault	10.4

Japan's automakers have only an 11 per cent combined market share in Europe, primarily as a result of restrictions on imports. France restricts Japanese cars to 3 per cent of sales; Italy and Spain both limit Japan's share to below 1 per cent; Great Britain has a limit of 11 per cent. Only Germany permits free access to Japanese automakers. Even though the European Community (EC) is committed to removing all auto quotas eventually, such a free-entry market is unlikely to happen before the turn of the century. In addition to restrictive import barriers, resolving other regulatory differences among the 12-member nations of the EC will require time. Relevant regulatory barriers include price and margin controls, differences in exhaust emission standards and safety feature requirements, and value-added taxes ranging from 12 per cent in Luxembourg to 200 per cent in Denmark and Greece.[5]

Detroit and the Japanese are turning more of their attention to Europe's lucrative market. Europe already contributes to the majority of GM's and Ford's profits. Ford has the strongest dealer network in Europe with 8,000 dealers. Their strength is in small cars and their lack of a luxury nameplate was remedied with their US$2.5 billion purchase of Jaguar (Britain). GM owns Lotus and recently acquired a 50 per cent interest in Saab-Scania's automotive operations. Chrysler has Lamborghini and a small interest in Maserati. Chrysler, however, lacks overseas operations, although it ranks as the number one exporter of vehicles to Europe (mostly minivans and Jeeps). Chrysler will begin making minivans in Europe with Renault in the early 1990s. In 1986 Nissan opened an assembly plant in England and plans to triple capacity to 200,000 by 1993. Toyota expects to manufacture 200,000 cars in England by 1997, while Honda will make 100,000 there by 1994. Meanwhile, Toyota will begin exporting its Lexus to Europe and Honda will export its US-made Accords by 1991. Honda also owns 20 per cent of the Rover Group with whom the firm now produces the Sterling and already sells about 150,000 cars in Europe, imported from Japan.[6] Toyota is planning to build light trucks with VW in West Germany. Mitsubishi and Daimler-Benz are working on an agreement to jointly produce small trucks, giving Mitsubishi its first vehicle facility in Europe.[6a]

The European automakers will have to work a lot harder to prepare themselves for the Japanese invasion.[7] European car manufacturers are the least efficient in the world and have much to fear if Nissan's plant is any indication that Japanese methods can be successfully transplanted to Europe. Volkswagen's main weakness is the high cost of labor. To partially overcome this problem it plans to move its small-car production to Spain where labor is cheaper. VW, however, ranks first in sales in West Germany, Belgium, Austria, and Switzerland. Peugeot is the only European manufacturer with two full lines of cars—Peugeot and Citroen. However, neither line has a broad European appeal; over 40 per cent of all Peugeot's sales are in France. Fiat similarly has a narrow appeal with two-thirds of its sales in Italy. Renault is the weakest of the major European producers, lacks a luxury nameplate, sells 90 per cent of its cars in France, and is heavily subsidized by the French government. Renault and Volvo are discussing an alliance to develop new cars jointly as 1992 approaches. Volvo is attempting to increase its efficiency by experimenting with the abandonment of the traditional assembly line concept. Teams of 7 to 10 workers will assemble four cars per shift. Workers will be trained to do all assembly jobs and the teams will largely manage themselves. Volvo hopes to substantially reduce its 20 per cent absenteeism rate and its 30 per cent annual turnover rate by improving morale and personal satisfaction.[7a]

JAPANESE MARKET

The Japanese auto market is dominated by five home producers: Toyota, Nissan, Honda, Mazda, and Mitsubishi. Per capita car ownership in Japan is about half the level experienced in the United States. Imports currently enjoy less than a 5 per cent share of the Japanese home market, though this proportion is expected to increase to about 15 per cent by the end of the century.[8] In general, the Japanese feel that most imports lack the quality required to penetrate their market. The best-selling imports in Japan currently are produced by BMW, Volkswagen, and Mercedes-Benz. Luxury cars are currently increasing in popularity in Japan, helping to increase import penetration.

There are 11 automotive vehicle firms in Japan. Toyota leads in the car market with about a 40 per cent share, followed by Nissan with slightly less than 25 per cent share, and Honda with slightly above a 10 per cent share. Mazda and Mitsubishi together account for a slightly above 10 per cent share, as well. Toyota also leads in truck sales, followed by Mitsubishi, Suzuki, Daihatsu, Nissan, Honda, Fuji, and Mazda. Mitsubishi sells more trucks than cars, as do all the other smaller Japanese firms except Mazda. Many of Japan's smaller automakers are struggling and cutting their budgets for capital spending.[9] Daihatsu, 14 per cent owned by Toyota, wants Toyota to increase its ownership to 20 per cent and to assist in product development. This is partially the result of the Japanese government's reduced taxation on large cars, which hurts sales of smaller cars, the main auto products of these small firms. Cooperative arrangements between these smaller companies, or consolidations, may be necessary if they are to survive.[9a]

Honda suffers from several disadvantages in Japan. The firm is still regarded by many consumers as a manufacturer of motorcycles and smaller cars, though the younger Japanese consumers seem to be attracted to Honda's styling and engineering. Honda's dealerships number only half as many as Toyota's. The luxury-car market, defined in Japan as cars having engine capacities of over 2,000 cc, is the fastest growing segment, but Honda is weakest in this segment. In fact, until the introduction of the Acura Legend in 1985, the firm had no entry in this car category. In spite of these weaknesses, Honda is planning to add a third assembly line to one of its Japanese plants.

US MARKET

The automobile market is affected by a variety of factors. These include:

- General economic prospects
- Consumer preferences toward auto size, styling, and fuel economy
- Availability and prices of raw materials, parts, and components
- Exchange rates
- Import restrictions and trade protection attitudes
- Health, environment, and safety regulations
- The trend toward increased local participation in the ownership of enterprises (such as encountered in various countries such as France)[10]

In spite of inroads by the Japanese, automotive vehicle sales in the United States are dominated by the Big Three domestic manufacturers. Financial and sales data for these firms are presented in Exhibits 2A and 2B. Overall automobile sales trends in the market are illustrated in Exhibit 3. Although the Big Three's share of the US market has been declining since the early 1980s, their share of the truck market is rising. Light trucks (10,000 pounds and under) have been the strongest segment for these firms and sales are expected to grow into the 1990s. Sales of compact pickup trucks and vans will come at the expense of car sales and full-size trucks and vans. The highest margins for the Big Three are on light trucks and sporty utility vehicles because these vehicles cost less to make and a 25 per cent import duty on these trucks limits foreign competition.[11]

Although light trucks provide US producers with the prospect of growth, the picture for traditional cars is not nearly as bright. Exhibit 4 illustrates recent growth patterns in each of the major auto market segments. In addition to changes in the growth patterns of the various segments, there have also been corresponding changes in the leading car brands. At the beginning of 1990 Honda's car sales surpassed those of Chrysler, making Honda number three in US car sales. Further, Honda's Accord became the largest-selling nameplate in the United States and four of the top ten car models sold in 1989 were Japanese[12] as shown below:

1. Honda Accord (compact)
2. Ford Taurus (intermediate)
3. Ford Escort (subcompact)
4. Chevrolet Corsica (compact)
5. Chevrolet Cavalier (compact)

6. Toyota Camry (compact)
7. Ford Tempo (compact)
8. Nissan Sentra (subcompact)
9. Pontiac Grand Am (compact)
10. Toyota Corolla (subcompact)

Exhibit 2A Big Three Performance Summary (US$, millions)

	1986	*1987*	*1988*	*1989*
General Motors				
Auto sales	90,863.6	89,890.6	97,777.1	99,440.9
Auto operating income	2,014.3	3,379.9	5,614.5	5,131.1
Total auto assets	46,708.0	60,159.5	60,420.4	64,598.0
Auto capital expenditures	10,257.3	6,127.9	4,524.6	6,287.6
Total corporate sales	115,609.9	114,870.4	123,641.6	126,931.9
Total net income	2,944.7	3,550.9	4,856.3	4,224.3
Total assets	150,157.1	162,343.2	164,063.1	173,297.1
Total equity	30,678.0	33,25.1	35,671.7	34,982.5
Ford Motor Company				
Total auto sales	62,868.3	71,797.2	82,193.0	82,897.4
US auto sales	50,135.0	55,412.0	61,814.0	61,452.0
Auto operating income	4,142.2	6,255.9	6,611.9	4,251.6
Total auto assets	34,020.6	39,734.4	43,127.7	45,819.2
Auto capital expenditures	3,409.4	3,674.0	4,711.5	6,695.4
Total corporate sales	69,694.6	79,893.0	92,445.6	97,145.9
Total net income	3,285.1	4,625.2	5,300.2	3,835.0
Total assets	93,231.9	115,994.4	143,366.5	160,893.3
Total equity	14,859.5	18,492.7	21,529.0	22,727.8
Chrysler				
Auto sales	22,269.5	25,489.0	30,804.0	30,987.0
Auto operating income	2,006.0	2,092.0	1,662.0	594.0
Total auto assets	11,885.7	17,472.0	19,718.0	21,670.0
Auto capital expenditures	2,031.7	1,915.0	1,622.0	1,550.0
Total corporate sales	25,220.2	28,308.0	34,148.0	34,922.0
Total net income	1,389.2	1,289.7	1,050.2	359.0
Total assets	33,090.4	42,478.0	48,210.0	51,038.0
Total equity	5,281.2	6,502.9	7,582.3	7,233.0

Note: Total sales and assets figures include assets and results from financial subsidiaries.
Source: General Motors, Ford and Chrysler, *Annual Reports*, 1986–89.

Only two groups of automakers experienced growth in unit sales in the subcompact category: North America-based Japanese firms and other imports, from South Korea especially. The Korean entry Hyundai is the fourth largest import seller in the US market. In 1991 Hyundai will open a 100,000-unit assembly plant in Ontario, its first in North America. This firm has appealed especially well to the under-24 age group which traditionally

Exhibit 2B Worldwide and US Vehicle Factory Sales ('000 units)

	1986	1987	1988	1989
Total worldwide sales				
Cars	30,342	29,862	31,752	32,281
Trucks	11,029	11,457	12,366	12,310
Total all firms	41,371	41,319	44,118	44,591
Worldwide sales, cars and trucks, US firms				
General Motors	8,576	7,765	8,108	7,946
Ford Motor Company	5,916	6,051	6,441	6,336
Chrysler	2,198	2,260	2,567	2,382
Total worldwide sales, Big Three	16,690	16,076	17,116	16,664
US sales, cars				
General Motors	4,302	3,592	3,516	3,238
Ford Motor Company	2,094	2,171	2,377	2,186
Chrysler	1,298	1,129	1,128	977
	7,694	6,892	7,021	6,401
Total US car sales	11,405	10,192	10,845	9,779
US sales, trucks				
General Motors	1,520	1,520	1,661	1,599
Ford Motor Company	1,404	1,481	1,541	1,523
Chrysler	614	829	1,006	991
	3,538	3,830	4,208	4,113
Total US truck sales	4,921	5,001	5,244	5,067
Total US vehicle sales				
Big Three	11,232	10,722	11,229	10,514
All firms	16,326	15,193	15,789	14,846

Source: As Exhibit 2A.

purchases a significant number of used cars for economic reasons. The steady rise in the yen-dollar exchange rate in the mid-1980s coupled with quotas which encouraged the Japanese to concentrate on well-equipped, expensive models in the US market have helped support the Korean entry. The Korean automakers face no quota restrictions in the United States and are not hurt by the decline of the dollar because the value of their currency is tied to the dollar.[13]

As the US moves into the 1990s intermediate cars are expected to be the only car category with increased sales. This is not unexpected as the population is aging and becoming more affluent, gasoline price increases have moderated, and technological advances have made larger cars cheaper to operate. Further, an older population typically desires larger cars with more interior room. Evidence of this trend can be seen in the fact that seven of the ten top-

According to Honda, An American Legend Faces the 1990s

Exhibit 3 US Retail Auto Sales

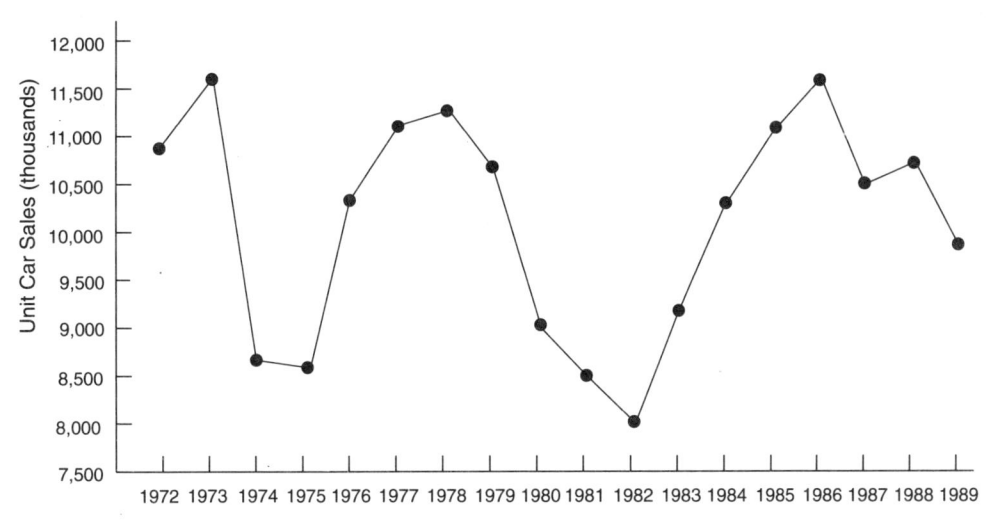

Source: US Department of Commerce, Washington, DC.

selling cars were compacts or intermediates in 1989. This trend does not greatly disturb the Big Three because Detroit sells almost one-half of its cars at a loss, the subcompact models especially. Ford expects to lose money on every one of its redesigned Escorts for 1990. However, even as the larger cars become more popular, the Big Three cannot abandon its small cars because their high fuel efficiency is needed to satisfy federal regulations for fleet mileage and the firms need to have entry-level cars for first-time buyers.[14] The trend toward larger cars is more of a threat to the Japanese who have only recently begun to enter the upscale segments.

These factors above, coupled with increasing competition, have encouraged American carmakers not only to increase car size, but also to make them more luxurious as luxury cars have margins of up to 20 per cent. Luxury cars have traditionally been considered to be those priced above US$20,000. However, this is no longer true. A Range Rover four-wheel drive vehicle now costs over US$35,000, compared to a Lincoln Town Car or Cadillac which are priced at US$25,000 to US$30,000. Most European luxury models are now well above US$40,000 as a result of the weak US dollar. The gap in the US$30,000 to US$40,000 price range is now being filled by the Japanese: Toyota's Lexus, Nissan's Infiniti, and Honda's Acura. The top-selling Cadillac and Lincoln models have been and will continue to target the over-60 age group. The Japanese and Europeans are seeking younger, affluent professionals. Honda's Acura is appealing to the 45-year-old with an average income of US$88,000. The Japanese luxury models are intended not only to improve profits, but to broaden product lines and appeal to their own customers who wish to trade up.[15]

To combat shrinking margins from increased competition. US carmakers have also raised prices. In response to pressure on the Japanese firms caused by the strengthening yen, the Japanese carmakers have been forced to raise prices and the Big Three have followed

Case Three

Exhibit 4 US Automotive Vehicle Retail Sales by Category ('000 units)

	1986	1987	1988	1994 est.
Subcompact cars				
North America	1,325	1,066	960	1,100
Captives	254	280	388	355
Japanese imports	1,142	961	922	600
European imports	66	73	50	25
Other imports	169	325	343	300
Total	2,956	2,705	2,663	2,380
Compact cars				
North America	2,436	2,433	2,799	2,935
Japanese imports	754	741	716	575
European imports	125	93	79	55
Other imports				50
Total	3,315	3,267	3,594	3,615
Intermediate cars				
North America	2,615	2,215	2,169	2,245
Japanese imports	113	100	74	300
European imports	106	139	119	65
Total	2,834	2,454	2,362	2,610
Luxury cars				
North America	1,866	1,554	1,556	1,345
Japanese imports	67	84	111	300
European imports	382	301	254	195
Total	2,315	1,939	1,921	1,840
Grand total cars	11,420	10,365	10,540	10,445
Light trucks	4,603	4,631	4,824	4,880
US Market Shares*				
General Motors	40.9%	36.3%	35.9%	
Ford	18.2	20.1	21.5	
Chrysler	12.0	10.7	11.2	
Honda	6.1	7.2	7.2	
Toyota	5.6	6.1	6.5	
Nissan	4.8	5.6	4.8	
Others	12.4	14.0	12.9	

*Based on dealer sales, new auto units.

Sources: *U.S. Industrial Outlook, 1988, 1989, 1990*, Washington, DC: US Department of Commerce, various years; Autos-Auto Parts, *Standard & Poor's Industry Reports*, November 30, 1989, p. A77.

their lead. As a result, the average new car price has increased faster than the Consumer Price Index (CPI). In addition, the 1986 Tax Reform Act phased out deductions on auto loans. The result is that buyers don't trade as often and seek greater value when they do buy.

	1980	1988
Average car age	6.6 years	7.6 years
Average maturity new car loans	45 months	56 months
Average new car price	US$7,590	US$14,570
Consumer Price Index (1982–1983 = 100)	82.4	118.3
Average autoworker wage	US$10.80/hr	US$16.10/hr

A critical element of the auto distribution channel is the dealer network. This network is under increasing stress. Increased competition and the need to control the rising prices of entry-level vehicles, especially, has resulted in lower margins. Aggressive marketing to fill unused capacity resulting from increased competition and rising productivity has led to costly incentive programs that put additional stress on dealers. Such incentives include accessory packages, improved warranties, rebates, and subsidized interest rates. These promotions have become so common that car sales slow significantly between the periodic incentive programs. These trends, in turn, have resulted in a shrinkage in the number of dealerships and a rise in the ownership of multiple dealerships. Between 1979 and 1989 the number of US Big-Three dealers declined from 23,000 to 20,000. In 1989 GM had 9,450 dealers, Ford 5,430, and Chrysler 5,300. In contrast, all other manufacturers with sales in the United States had a combined total of only 4,900 dealers.[16] Dealers have also attempted to combat their lower margins and slowing sales by increasing the sales of used cars, which now account for 20 per cent of the dealers' total sales.

Although the number of Big-Three dealers has declined, the three major Japanese producers are expanding their dealer networks. All have established separate dealerships to sell their upscale luxury models.[17] When Honda's Acura was introduced in 1986, there were only 60 US dealers, each selling only two basic models, the US$11,000 Integra and the US$20,000 Legend. By the end of 1988, Honda had almost 300 Acura dealers who together sold 128,000 cars during the year.[17a] Half of these upscale Japanese dealerships in the United States are unprofitable as a result of high dealer startup costs and a lack of service business.

AUTO PRODUCTION IN THE UNITED STATES

Although auto production in the United States is still dominated by the Big Three, the Japanese are expected to have the capacity to produce 2 million units annually in North America by the early 1990s (see Exhibit 5). Further, in addition to the outright ownership of a plant by a single company there are a number of production strategies which have begun to blur the distinctions among firms. Captives, transplants, and imports have all clogged the market and have possibly set the stage for the world car.

THE BIG THREE

Ford's Escort, which had held the number one spot in the United States in both 1987 and 1988, and has been the largest-selling car in the world in much of the late 1980s, has lost its market appeal because of an aging design. Ford will be introducing a redesigned Escort

Exhibit 5 North American Automotive Assembly Facilities of Foreign Firms

Company	Location	Date of Opening	Unit Capacity	Comments
Mitsubishi	Illinois	1988	120,000*	Diamond-Star Motors is a joint venture with Chrysler (which owns 12 per cent of Mitsubishi)
		1991	240,000*	Planned expansion of Diamond-Star
Mazda	Michigan	1987	200,000*	Joint venture with Ford (which owns 24 per cent of Mazda)
		1992	360,000*	Planned expansion of joint venture
Toyota	California	1984	200,000*	NUMMI plant is a joint venture with General Motors
		1991	300,000*	Planned expansion of joint venture
	Kentucky	1988	200,000	
	Ontario	1988	50,000	
Nissan	Tennessee	1983	220,000	
		1992	440,000	Planned expansion of above
	Mexico	1966	120,000	
		1993	200,000	Planned expansion of above
	Ohio	1992	100,000*	Joint venture with Ford to build minivans
Honda	Ohio	1982	360,000	
	Ontario	1986	50,000	
		1990	80,000	Planned expansion of above
	Ohio	1989	150,000	
Suzuki	Ontario	1989	200,000*	Joint venture with GM (which owns 5 per cent of Suzuki)
Fuji-Isuzu	Indiana	1989	120,000*	Joint venture of Fuji and Isuzu
		1993	240,000*	Planned expansion of joint venture
Hyundai	Quebec	1991	100,000	

*All joint venture facilities split 50-50 with partners noted.

Note: Planned expansion capacity figures represent *total* capacity after expansion.

Sources: 1. Chappel, L., Big 3, Transplant 7, *Automotive News*, November 29, 1989, pp. 190–192.
2. Autos-Auto Parts, *Standard & Poor's Industry Surveys,* May 12, 1988, p. A62, and November 30, 1989, pp. A87–89.
3. Treece, J. and J. Hoerr, Shaking up Detroit, *Business Week*, August 14, 1989, pp. 74–80.

in early 1990 at cost of more than US$2 billion. However, Ford's limited production capacity will make it difficult for the firm to increase its overall market share. Beginning in 1984, Ford put its workers on overtime rather than increase plant capacity to meet the rising demand for the Escort. As a result of this approach, Ford leads its competition in plant utilization and has the highest productivity and profit per car among the Big Three. Ford's share of the US truck market of just under 30 per cent exceeds its auto market share.

Although Chrysler has steadily recovered from its near bankruptcy in the late 1970s and raised its market share from a low of 7 per cent in 1980, the company still faces numerous difficulties. It lacks the diversification into non-auto businesses and penetration into European markets needed to counter the US auto cycle. Chrysler's acquisition of American Motors in 1987 removed the last remaining domestic firm, gave Chrysler added strength in the utility vehicle market with the Jeep line, and increased the firm's dealer network. However, although chrysler has six different lines of cars, only one fewer than GM, it still lacks a strong mid-sized entry and a full-sized pickup truck. Further, many of its cars lack a distinct image and the cost of differentiating and updating them puts a good deal of strain on Chrysler's limited resources. Chrysler's strength is in its highly profitable Jeep vehicles and minivans. Although the firm now commands over 50 per cent of the minivan market, which has grown to 800,000 units per year, competition is intensifying. This rising competition, coupled with aging capacity and the need to support its broad product line, has dramatically reduced Chrysler's profit per unit in recent years.[18]

General Motors' market share continues to decline, although truck sales are relatively stable at about 30 per cent. By the end of the 1980s GM's auto share was 10 points below that in 1980. In a 1989 survey by J.D. Power and Associates, GM owners were the least likely to recommend their cars to others.[19] Criticisms include a lack of competitive designs and features, such as sophisticated engines and transmissions, a tendency to load many of its models with too many options, raising prices above those of rivals, and a lack of distinctive styling. GM's performance difficulties may have their source in a number of differences between the firm and its rivals. GM has the broadest product line and is the most integrated of the Big Three, making 70 per cent of its own parts. This gives the firm an enormous investment in parts production facilities which is difficult to reduce. Once a source of competitive advantage, this high level of integration has limited GM's flexibility in the increasingly dynamic auto environment. It has also reduced profits by exposing the firm to higher labor costs than those experienced by Ford, Chrysler, and the Japanese who can more easily control costs through outside purchase agreements. GM's huge bureaucracy may also contribute to its difficulties; the firm has 22 layers of management between the CEO and the production worker, compared with 7 of Toyota.[20]

However, GM has set major goals to overcome its difficulties. Its primary goals are to raise its market share and profitability, to become the low-cost domestic producer, and to increase factory utilization to 100 per cent by 1992 (now 75 to 80 per cent). During the 1980s GM has spent US$70 billion worldwide to improve its facilities. Nine new assembly plants have been built and 31 other plants modernized. During the last two model years of the 1980s GM introduced more new or restyled products than in any other two-year period in the firm's history (17 new and 14 redesigned vehicles). In the 1990 model year GM introduced as many new model cars as Ford, Chrysler, Toyota, and Honda combined.[21]

GM's Saturn project is expected to begin production in mid-1990, eight years after conception. At that time Saturn was envisioned as the future model for automotive vehicle production and sales using the most modern robotic technology available to produce 500,000 subcompact cars per year. It has since been scaled down to produce 240,000 compact cars and will incorporate a blend of new technology and a team approach to production. The cars will compete with the Honda Civic and the Toyota Corolla models in both size and price.[22]

To improve their competitive positions, insulate themselves from the US autocycle, create synergies to improve auto productivity, and to provide growth opportunities, all of the Big Three firms have made numerous acquisitions. Chrysler purchased Electrospace Systems in 1987 to add to its existing Gulfstream Aerospace Division, but then reconsidered and sold the entire aerospace division in 1989 to concentrate on its auto and related financial services businesses. Ford's non-auto businesses include Ford Aerospace and tractors and implements. GM has made several significant acquisitions in recent years including Hughes Aircrafts, Electronic Data Systems, significant interests in the home-mortgage market to augment its financial services division, and a joint venture to become the largest manufacturer of industrial robots in the United States.

JAPANESE FIRMS

Perhaps the two most critical factors affecting all Japanese auto producers wishing to supply the US market are the voluntary import restrictions and the strength of the yen relative to the US dollar. In 1981, the Japanese government voluntarily imposed quotas on the export of Japanese-made cars to the United States in an effort to avoid potentially more restrictive trade barriers being established by the US government. These voluntary quotas, now set at 2.3 million units annually, have been responsible for several changes in strategy by Japanese firms.

Imports of light trucks are not subject to the quota, although they are subject to a duty of 25 per cent, and this has been responsible for the development of the minitruck market. Japanese firms have also entered joint ventures and built plants in the United States to avoid the quotas and deal with the changing value of the yen. The primary factors which led to the establishment of the import quota were the rising trade deficit with Japan because of the strong dollar in 1980, and the increasing market share of the imports. The trend toward a rise in onshore production in the United States has been increasingly supported, however, by other economic factors including weakness in the dollar and the rising cost of labor in Japan. By 1988 the average manufacturing wage in Japan was the equivalent of US$12.06 per hour, compared to US$10 in the United States.[23]

Perhaps the single most important factor affecting the behavior of Japanese auto firms since 1985 has been the changing relationship between the yen and the dollar. (See Exhibit 6 for the trend in the dollar-yen exchange rate.) At the beginning of fiscal 1986 (March) one dollar would buy 250 yen. By the end of Honda's fiscal 1988, one dollar would buy only 25 yen. Thus, a car costing the equivalent of US$5,000 to manufacture in Japan in 1985, would have had an equivalent cost of ¥1,250,000 ($5,000 × 250). By 1988, assuming the yen cost of the car in Japan did not change, the US equivalent cost would have risen to $10,000 (¥1,250,000 ÷ 125). It may be noted that at 125 yen to the dollar, it is estimated that it is now less costly to manufacture a typical car in the United States than it is to build a similar car in Japan.[24] Thus, to cover their equivalent costs, the Japanese manufacturers should have raised prices on their exports as much as 100 per cent. Instead,

Exhibit 6 Dollar-Yen Exchange Rates

	Number of Yen Purchased by US$1	
	Fiscal Year End	Average
1989	132.7	129.1
1988	124.7	137.7
1987	153.3	161.3
1986	180.6	223.5
1985	259.5	242.7
1984	233.5	237.1
1983	237.5	250.7

Source: Honda Motor Company, *Annual Reports,* 1983–89.

they only raised their prices about 30 per cent. This should have caused US cars to be more competitive. However, Detroit used this opportunity to raise its own prices about 12 per cent during the 1985 to 1987 period, thus reducing their potential gain in relative prices.[25]

Because competitive pressure did not permit Japanese exporters to raise prices as much as they would have liked, their profits eroded. However, the Japanese have employed several strategies to improve the situation. First, they have found ways to further reduce production costs. The US dealers of these exporters have absorbed some of the price differences through reduced margins. In addition, by building US facilities and reducing dependence on imported parts (Honda cars built in the United States will have 75 per cent domestic parts in 1991) Japanese producers have reduced effective cost increases to the domestic inflation rate. Further, by convention, plastics and oil imported by Japan are priced in US dollars, thus lowering the yen equivalent cost of these inputs.

CAPTIVES, TRANSPLANTS, AND IMPORTS

The definitions of an American car and an American carmaker are not as clear as they one were. Japanese car companies operate in the United States, building cars with US parts and labor. US companies have cars with their nameplates built for them in foreign plants, with foreign parts and labor. These latter cars are called **captives.** Examples of some of these captives are listed in the table below:[26]

Car Model	Manufacturer
Geo Metro (formerly Chevy Sprint)	Suzuki (Japan)
Geo Spectrum (formerly Chevy Spectrum)	Isuzu (Japan)
Geo Tracker	Suzuki
Pontiac LeMans	Daewoo (Korea)
Ford Festiva	Kia (Korea)
Dodge/Plymouth Colt and Vista	Mitsubishi (Japan)
Chrysler Conquest/Eagle Summit	Mitsubishi
Eagle Medallion	Renault (France)

In contrast, **captive transplants** are the Big Three cars made in the United States through joint venture arrangements. Examples include Geo Prizm (formerly Chevy Nova) made in the NUMMI plant, a joint venture with GM and Toyota; Ford Probe, produced in the Mazda-Ford joint venture plant in Michigan; and the Plymouth Laser made in Illinois in Chrysler's joint venture plant with Mitsubishi. By the end of the 1980s the Big Three had slightly less than 300,000 units of captive transplant capacity. This will grow to 500,000 in the early 1990s. However, when the GM-Toyota joint venture ends in 1996, GM may lose its NUMMI capacity as Toyota has an option on the plant.[27]

Agreements between the Big Three and other firms are not limited to manufacturing, however; design and engineering is more frequently a joint arrangement as well, as are the development and production of parts. Ford's hope of the 1990s, the redesigned Escort, was for example, largely designed by Mazda. Corvette's transmission is built by ZF, a West German firm; the engine of the Taurus SHO was designed and is produced by Yamaha. Nor are all joint ventures of the Big Three aimed at US cars: Chrysler will make minivans in France with Renault, for example; Ford will expand one of its US plants to make Jeep-type utility vehicles for Mazda and minivans for Nissan; Chrysler markets the Mitsubishi Eclipse and Fiat's Alfa Romeo through its dealers and Mazda dealers in Japan are marketing Ford's Taurus and Probe models. As of 1990, there were 300 joint relationships among automotive firms throughout the world.[28]

Transplants also include vehicles manufactured by foreign firms for their own nameplates in the United States. In 1989 the Japanese had 1.3 million units of capacity in the United States. By the early 1990s this is expected to rise to nearly 2 million units as shown in Exhibit 5. While the Japanese opened five new plants in the United States from 1987 to 1989, the Big Three closed five. Three more assembly plants are expected to be closed by the Big Three in 1990. Altogether, Japanese transplants and imports accounted for about 25 per cent of all US auto sales in the late 1980s.

QUALITY AND PRODUCTIVITY

A critical factor which enabled the Japanese to penetrate the US auto market in the late 1970s and 1980s was the quality gap between US and Japanese manufacturers. As may be seen below, this gap has narrowed significantly in the last decade.[29]

Defects per Car Produced

	1980	1989
Chrysler	8.1	1.8
General Motors	7.4	1.7
Ford	6.7	1.5
Japanese	2.0	1.2

In spite of tremendous quality improvements, however, the gap between the Big Three and the Japanese big three remains significant. Of the 31 best-rated 1989 car models according to *Consumer Reports* (April 1990), 28 were Japanese; of the 33 worst-rated, 32 were US

Big Three models. *The Wall Street Journal* converted the *Consumer Reports* ratings into a grade point average with the report card shown below.[30]

	\multicolumn{5}{c}{Grade for Each Model}	
	A	B	C	D	F	Gradepoint
Honda	5	1	0	0	0	3.83
Toyota	6	4	2	0	0	3.33
Nissan	1	2	2	0	0	2.80
Chrysler	0	2	13	7	8	1.30
Ford	0	1	10	7	8	1.15
General Motors	0	1	9	9	21	0.75

The trend in productivity is much the same as the quality trend. The Japanese are the most productive automakers in the world, although the Big Three are improving.[31] The Japanese require an average of 19 man-hours to assemble a car, compared to 36 man-hours for the average European carmaker. Of the Big Three, Ford is the most efficient. To build a car, GM requires 5 workers, per day. Chrysler requires 4.4; Ford 3.4; and the Japanese 3.0. The table below compares productivity levels for 12 major car producers.[31a]

Manufacturer	1988 Cars/Worker
Suzuki	70.4
Toyota	61.0
Honda	56.2
Mitsubishi	50.4
Mazda	42.0
Nissan	39.5
Ford	20.0
Chrysler	18.0
Peugeot	13.3
General Motors	12.5
VW	11.2
Fiat	10.1

PARTS PRODUCTION

The output of auto parts and accessories manufacturers peaked in 1978 and was 15 per cent below that level in constant dollars in 1988. This drop in output is explained largely by the drop in US production and the fact that most imports do not contain many US parts.[31b] Even the Japanese transplants still import a large proportion of their parts from Japan. Future prospects for the parts industry are not bright even though the percentage of US parts in Japanese cars is increasing. The average domestic (US) content for transplants is 38 per cent, versus 88 per cent for the Big Three. Many Japanese firms claim a higher percentage content, but this is the result of a content formula which includes advertising and overhead, not just parts.[32] Nevertheless Japanese firms are increasing the plant capacity of their own parts firms in the United States. Honda, for example, intends to produce 500,000 engines in the United States by 1990 (see Exhibit 7). It is also estimated that by 1990, the Japanese will operate 300 parts firms in the United States, up from less than 100 in 1987.

Exhibit 7 Honda Production Capacity Utilization in Japan (rated capacity, '000 units)

	1985	1987	1988	1989
Motorcycles				
Capacity	3,559	2,909	2,269	1,176
Utilization (%)	70	80	70	114
Power products				
Capacity	2,304	1,952	1,964	1,968
Utilization (%)	93	72	70	74
Automobiles				
Capacity	1,079	1,123	1,240	1,308
Utilization (%)	88	96	106	104

Source: Honda Motor Company, *Annual Reports*, 1985–89.

One factor that may further hurt the US auto parts industry is the enforcement of the CAFE (Corporate Average Fuel Economy) requirements. Separate CAFE calculations must be made for each of two car categories and both must meet the 27.5 miles-per-gallon requirement in 1990. The distinction between categories is whether a car has above or below 75 per cent US parts content. The problem facing both GM and Ford is that many of their fuel efficient small cars fall into the below-75-per-cent category. Ford has announced it will import a greater percentage of the parts for many of its large cars to reclassify them as below 75 per cent. GM's response is more pro-US content as it will increase the percentage of US parts in its small-car production in its NUMMI plant.[33]

HONDA IN THE UNITED STATES

Honda is far more at home abroad.[34] Honda was the first Japanese firm to open an auto manufacturing facility in the United States and at the end of the 1980s had the largest US auto capacity of any foreign firm. Before opening its Ohio facility, Honda flew 200 US workers to its Sayana factory in Japan for up to three months where the American workers joined the Japanese assembly lines. Upon their return the workers were then able to instruct co-workers on Japanese assembly methods.[35] Honda's employees, who must go through three interviews before being hired, are called **associates**. The Ohio workers are given the responsibility for such tasks as inspecting their own work. The plant is essentially democratic, as managers wear the same uniforms as the workers, are on a first-name basis, and share parking and lunchroom facilities. There are no enclosed offices. Honda encourages its workers to form ad hoc groups of five to ten workers (called **New Honda Circles**) who voluntarily work together on an area of common concern such as safety, quality, or production efficiency improvements. Such efforts can earn the workers free cars or trips to Japan for their ideas. Approximately 25 per cent of the Ohio workers belong to such groups.

As Honda's methods have met with success in Ohio, the company has increased wages and the number of paid holidays. Attendance bonuses and profit sharing have also been added. The environment encourages management and labor to work together, pursuing a common goal of making quality products economically. Throughout the world, Honda employs more than 71,000 employees, including 19,000 Japanese working abroad. about 90 percent of all nonmanagement employees are members of the Federation of All Honda Workers Union (AHWA), affiliated with the Japanese Council of the International Metalworkers Federation. Basic wages are negotiated annually with the union. Wage increases in fiscal years 1985 to 1989 were 5.9 per cent, 5.1 per cent, 3.6 per cent, 4.6 per cent, and 5.4 per cent, respectively. Each employee is paid a semiannual bonus, a Japanese custom, which is negotiated separately from wages. Every two years the firm negotiates working conditions with the union.

Only three of the seven Japanese assembly plants in the United States are unionized (United Auto Workers), those which are joint ventures with the Big Three: Toyota's NUMMI plant, Mazda's Michigan plant, and Mitsubishi Illinois plant. Nissan workers in its solely-owned Tennessee facility defeated the union (70 per cent against) in mid-1989 and Toyota's new Kentucky plant is also nonunion. However, the nonunion plants pay almost the same wages and benefits as UAW-organized facilities in the United States. While the UAW seems to be establishing wage standards, the Japanese transplants which are unionized have negotiated less restrictive work rules and greater employee involvement in decision making. Many of the Japanese labor practices have been transplanted to the United States: no layoff policies, continual training programs for workers, participation in decision making, team-based production, and profit sharing. As a result of the desire to apply similar work methods in the United States, the Japanese have utilized different hiring criteria. They have mostly hired young, inexperienced workers who have expressed a willingness to work in a team-oriented environment. Their choice of plant locations, in most cases, has also resulted in their hiring a lower percentage of racial minorities than their Big-Three counterparts have. Such practices have provided the transplants with lower health care costs and lower pension liabilities.[36]

HONDA OPERATIONS

Honda's business consists of four operating segments, as shown in Exhibit 8: automotive vehicles, motorcycles, power products, and parts/other. In addition to its four major sources of revenue-generating activities, Honda manufactures many of the main components and parts used in its products, including engines, frames, and transmissions.[37] Raw materials and other components are purchased from numerous suppliers. Steel plate accounts for about 50 per cent of Honda's raw material purchases; other materials include aluminum, glass, plastic, zinc, paint, and special steels. No single source accounts for more than 5 per cent of these outside purchases. Neither is Honda dependent on any one source for an essential components with the exception of ignition switches and clutches.

Exhibit 8 Honda Sales by Business Segment ('000 units, revenue in ¥ billions)

	Fiscal Year*				
	1985	1986	1987	1988	1989
Automotive Segment					
Total unit sales	1,252	1,368	1,558	1,871	1,903
Japanese unit sales	387	474	518	617	628
Total sales revenue	1,620	1,842	2,011	2,394	2,459
Japanese sales revenue	N/A	500	557	736	780
Motorcycle Segment					
Total unit sales	2,954	3,078	2,615	3,053	3,032
Japanese unit sales	1,006	987	803	943	924
Total sales revenue	423	413	330	379	353
Japanese sales revenue	N/A	129	131	160	157
Power Products Segment					
Total unit sales	1,722	1,815	1,625	1,708	1,543
Japanese unit sales	163	172	207	156	116
Total sales revenue	235	250	164	154	103
Japanese sales revenue	N/A	12	14	12	11
Parts and Other Segments					
Total sales revenue	374	405	454	572	571
Japanese sales revenue	N/A	204	258	346	346
Total company revenue by region					
Japan	704	845	960	1,254	1,294
North America	1,485	1,604	1,522	1,646	1,585
Europe	247	263	310	403	372
Other	216	198	169	196	238
Total	2,652	2,910	2,961	3,499	3,489
Operating income	299	306	170	177	177
Net income	129	147	84	108	97

*Fiscal years 1985 to 1987 ended on February 28, and 1988 to 1989 ended on March 31; 1988 results include 13 months of activity.

Source: Honda Motor Company, *Annual Reports*, various years.

Honda has two wholly owned, consolidated subsidiaries specializing in R&D and in the design and manufacture of production machinery. Honda R&D employs approximately 7,600 people and is provided with funds amounting to about 5 per cent of annual sales targets. Honda Engineering Company employs 2,400 people. Overall, Honda employs 50 per cent more engineers per car produced than does GM.[38] The firm is increasing the amount of product design and factory engineering done in its US plants and has restructured its R&D unit to incorporate both its US and European R&D operations.

Though Honda's cars are not always perfect when introduced, the firm is very quick to respond to dealer and customer feedback. For example, in 1982 the first Prelude model had so little power that many consumers referred to it as the "Quaalude."[39] However, by 1983 the car had been redesigned. Honda continually makes technical improvements in its cars, whether or not consumers can actually notice the difference.[39a] The Japanese firms, on average, require about three years to develop, design, engineer, and manufacture a new model vehicle. In comparison, the Big Three require five years and the Europeans over five years. Honda, the fastest of all auto-makers, is attempting to reduce this time to two years. Honda has recently developed a small, 4-cylinder engine that produces 10 to 15 per cent more power than the 6-cylinder engines made by the Big Three: Now fitted in cars sold in Japan, the engine will soon be available in the United States and should help boost Honda's average fuel economy in the future.[40]

AUTOMOTIVE SEGMENT. Honda produces a fairly broad range of automobile models for both its domestic and overseas markets. Honda's current auto models are described in Exhibit 9. These products are produced in two locations in Japan, the United States, the United Kingdom (with Rover by 1989), Ontario, Canada, and New Zealand. Their vehicles are distributed in Japan through three dealer networks consisting of 2,400 total dealerships. In Europe, wholly owned subsidiaries distribute autos through Honda's 1,500 dealers (down from 2,200 in 1985). The United States has 1,200 Honda dealers (up from 850 in 1985). A separate network of nearly 300 dealerships distributes the Acura in the United States. Some Honda Civic and Accord models are shipped unassembled to various parts of southern Asia and the Pacific Rim for assembly and sale in various smaller markets.

Exhibit 9 1989 Honda Vehicle Models

Model Name	Type of Car	Engine Size (cc)
Civic	Subcompact	1300, 1500, 1600
Accord (Vigor)	Compact	1800, 2000
Prelude	Subcompact sports car	2000
City (Japan only)	Subcompact	1300
Acura Legend	Intermediate	2000, 2700
Acura Integra (Quint)	Subcompact	1600, 1800
Concerto (Japan only)	Subcompact	1500, 1600
Acty (Japan only)	Minitruck	NA
	Minivan	NA
Today (Japan only)	Minicar	550

Note: Names in parentheses are comparable Japanese models.
Source: Honda Motor Company, *Annual Reports, 1989*.

In 1989, the Accord was the top-selling US car. It accounts for nearly half of Honda's sales in the United States and has had a record of seven straight years of sales growth since its introduction in 1982. Scott Whitlock, executive vice-president of Honda of America Mfg., Inc., believes "This is the car that's going to support us and satisfy our customers for the next four years."[41] What Mr. Whitlock was referring to was the *new* Accord. With the

1990 model year, Accord entered the mid-sized market to compete with such entries as Ford's Taurus and Sable, Toyota's Camry, and Nissan's Stanza. The new Accord will also be available in a station wagon by fall 1990. Although Honda is developing an NSX model for its Acura line, with a planned price range of US$50,000 plus, Honda's product line lacks trucks, minivans, and a 4-wheel drive sports vehicle.[42]

MOTORCYCLES. Based on unit production, Honda is the world's largest manufacturer of motorcycles. Honda currently manufactures over 100 different models for the Japanese market and over 140 models for markets outside Japan. These range from 50 cc motorbikes and scooters to 1,500 cc, 4-cylinder motorcycles. The Ohio facility produces the Gold Wing motorcycle, a luxury model selling for around US$10,000, which is exported to 15 countries, including Japan. Honda's motorcycles are also produced in three different locations in Japan, as well as in Belgium, Italy, Brazil, and Mexico. In the United States, the largest market for the firm's motorcycles, Honda has 1,400 independent dealers (down from 1,750 in 1985). In Europe the sales network includes 3,200 dealers (down from 4,300 in 1985). Many Honda dealers in the United States also carry Honda's power products, while in Europe many motorcycle dealers also carry both the power products and the firm's automobiles.

Demand for motorcycles in Japan plummeted during 1986 and 1987 when a new law requiring helmets to be worn resulted in negative consumer response. Sales have since rebounded somewhat. The number of motorcycles registered in the United States has dropped steadily since 1981, though sales of new motorcycles peaked in 1984 at 1.3 million units (all manufacturers). Several factors have contributed to this decline. Gasoline prices declined in the early 1980s after the 1979 oil crisis; the health and fitness trend favors walking or bicycling for short-distance travel needs; motorcycle insurance rates have increased as a result of safety concerns (several insurance firms will no longer insure "superbikes"); and almost all states now require helmets. Honda, Kawasaki, and Harley-Davidson are the major US motorcycle manufacturers. Of these three, Harley-Davidson, a US-owned firm, is the only one to have increased sales since 1984. Honda's share in the US market is now around 30 per cent, well below its one-time high of 58 per cent.[43]

POWER PRODUCTS AND OTHER PRODUCTS. Honda produces a variety of power products including portable generators, small agricultural machines, general-purpose engines, outdoor motors, water pumps, snow throwers, lawn and riding movers, and all-terrain vehicles (ATVs). Production facilities for these products are located in Japan, the United States (North Carolina), the United Kingdom, and France. These products are distributed through 4,000 dealers in Japan, 2,600 in the United States (down from 2,800 in 1985), and 3,000 in Europe (down from 4,300 in 1985). ATV sales plummeted in the late 1980s as a result of major safety concerns. Three-wheel vehicles have been demonstrated to be unstable when making rapid turns. Young riders (under 16 years of age), often users of these ATVs, are by and large untrained in their safe use. These concerns have resulted in litigation, legislation, and mutual agreements with manufacturers to provide free training courses and to cease production of the three-wheel vehicles. Manufacturers may also be required to refund the purchase price to all such vehicle owners.

Parts sales are derived primarily from sales of Honda Motor Parts Service Company and Honda International Sales Corporation which trades in used automobiles acquired from Honda dealers. Parts sales have been increasing recently due mainly to a favorable used car market in Japan.

Honda Strategy

In 1985, Honda's stated direction for its motorcycle and auto segments was to move toward the development of unique products that are of high quality, have high performance, and are fuel efficient. In addition, Honda stated a desire to improve the design and operation of its factories and reduce costs to improve their competitiveness. Honda's automotive vehicle strategy has historically been to offer products with more and better features than those of competitors with similar models. The firm now desires to redirect its automotive product emphasis to more expensive product lines where price is less important to the consumer; to move away from the low-price, entry-level, subcompact car segment; and to expand overseas (outside Japan) production facilities.

In a speech on September 17, 1987, Mr. Tetsuo Chino, Head of North American Operations for Honda, announced a five-part strategy for Honda in America.[44]

One: Expansion of US parts sourcing
Two: Expansion of research and development in the United States
Three: Expansion of production engineering in the United States
Four: A major commitment to export US-made Honda products
Five: Further expansion of US manufacturing facilities

On the same day, Mr. Kume announced that by December 1987, a new model of the Accord, to be produced only in the United States, would be exported to Japan. The first shipment of 540 cars arrived in Japan in March 1988. By 1991 Honda intends to export 70,000 of the new, redesigned Accord all over the world. Honda also plans to export US-made cars to South Korea to circumvent South Korean import barriers with the Japanese. The expected exports of 2,000 Accord sedans by 1991 will be sold through South Korea's largest motorcycle manufacturer.[45]

Honda's joint venture with another automaker, Rover, may also help ease their entry into Europe. The car produced by this venture, the Sterling, is also exported to the United States where it competes in the low-end luxury category. In late 1989 Honda announced its sales goals for the first half of the next decade. The firm intends to increase car sales in the United States to 1 million units a year and worldwide sales to 2.5 million units annually.[46] Honda also intends to expand its dealer networks in the United States and has established experimental consumer finance operations in California and Florida so that it can compete with other US manufacturers offering financial incentives.

Case Three

MINOR STRESS AT HONDA

With the rapid growth and success that Honda has enjoyed during the 1980s comes the inevitable strain on human and financial resources. In support of its objectives and strategic directions Honda expended nearly 1 trillion yen in new capital expenditures from fiscal 1986 through fiscal 1989. A breakdown of these expenditures appears in Exhibit 10. As a result of heavy capital expenditures and reduced net income, Honda's 1989 fiscal year internal cash flow fell short of capital expenditures by a substantial margin and the firm's

Exhibit 10 Honda Capital Expenditures (¥ billions)

	\multicolumn{5}{c}{Fiscal Year*}
	1985	1986	1987	1988	1989
Total capital expenditures	137.0	267.0	224.0	187.0	279.0
Percentage allocation					
Automotive (%)	44.9	56.4	61.0	56.5	67.9
Motorcycle	11.4	9.5	6.1	5.3	5.5
Power products	3.9	1.0	0.9	1.5	0.9
Sales, other	39.8	32.9	32.0	36.7	25.7
Resources supplied by operations	223.0	268.0	219.0	244.0	195.0

*Fiscal years 1985 to 1987 ended on February 28, and 1988 to 1989 ended on March 31.
Source: Honda Motor Company, *Annual Reports*, 1985–89.

long-term debt increased to the highest levels ever. The firm's net income has declined dramatically since fiscal 1986, when the dollar began weakening, in spite of increased sales revenue (refer to Exhibit 11). With continued growth in its asset base and equity, the lower net income results in considerably lower return measures for the firm's financial investors (see Exhibit 12).

Growth has also slowed down the speed of decision making. Honda has been working to solve this difficulty by decentralizing its traditional Japan-based R&D unit to increase flexibility. The firm may have made a few errors in marketing, as well. Honda's strategy of emphasizing numerous features and high-margin cars may have resulted in a 1989 model, the Prelude which included many expensive features that customers didn't particularly want; features that the lower-priced Accord also had, but at thousands of dollars less! In April 1989 Honda was forced to offer dealer incentives on Accords for the first time ever. As a result, their advertising budget has been increased by 25 per cent for 1990.

Though Honda installed brand new machinery in the Marysville plant for the redesigned Accord without shutting down for a single day, not everything has gone smoothly. The manager of the new East Liberty, Ohio assembly plant had to borrow workers from the Marysville plant to meet the deadline for its Civic production. Some Civic transmission production had to be transferred to the North Carolina lawnmower plant. Finally, when the Marysville plant began getting ready for the introduction of the redesigned Accord, the workers at East Liberty had to return to Marysville.[47]

Exhibit 11 Consolidated Income Statements Honda Motor Company
(¥ billions except per-share amounts)

	\multicolumn{5}{c}{Fiscal Year*}
	1985	1986	1987	1988	1989
Net sales	2,652.2	2,909.6	2,961.0	3,498.5	3,489.3
Cost of sales	1,736.3	1,917.4	2,110.6	2,547.4	2,544.2
Gross profit	915.9	992.2	850.4	951.1	945.1
Operating expenses					
R&D	109.9	131.8	149.6	177.9	183.7
Advertising	73.0	84.2	86.3	85.7	81.8
Depreciation	94.3	121.5	120.7	142.7	130.9
Other, selling, general, and administrative expenses	339.9	349.2	316.4	368.2	371.6
Operating income	298.8	305.5	177.4	176.6	177.1
Interest expenses, net	22.0	9.2	15.6	10.9	11.7
Other expenses/(income), net	4.1	(5.8)	(8.4)	(28.9)	(6.7)
Earnings before tax	272.7	302.1	170.2	194.6	172.1
Income tax	142.9	158.9	89.1	91.0	80.6
Income before EINSA**	129.8	143.2	81.1	103.6	91.5
Plus: EINSA	(1.3)	3.3	2.6	3.9	5.8
Net income	128.5	146.5	83.7	107.5	97.3
Dividends	9.7	10.7	10.8	12.0	11.3
EPS	138.71	149.14	85.47	106.75	98.48

* Fiscal years 1985 to 1987 ended on February 28, and 1988 to 1989 ended on March 31; 1988 includes 13 months of activity.

** EINSA is equity in income of nonconsolidated subsidiaries and affiliates. It should be noted that Honda is the only Japanese automaker whose stock is listed on the NYSE. Each American share, as evidenced by American Depository Receipts (ADRs), represents 10 shares of the actual Japanese-issued stock. As of March 31, 1989, total issued common shares were 947,994,295, of which 14,318,082 were in the form of ADRs.

Source: Honda Motor Company, *Annual Reports*, 1985–89.

As Honda attempts to broaden their product offerings, increase their dealer networks, and expand capacity on three continents, they will be competing head-to-head with larger automakers. Will their strengths, which were the basis for their phenomenal success in the 1980s, be able to carry them forward to even greater heights of achievement in the 1990s?

Case Three

Exhibit 12 Consolidated Balance Sheets Honda Motor Company (¥ billions)

	Fiscal Year*				
	1985	1986	1987	1988	1989
Assets					
Cash and equivalents	140.0	118.9	214.5	246.4	247.3
Accounts receivable	132.1	126.5	255.5	330.2	402.1
Inventory	412.4	441.0	428.0	416.9	475.2
Other current assets	133.9	155.3	117.5	138.3	144.6
Total current assets	818.4	841.7	1,015.5	1,131.8	1,269.2
Investments and other assets	211.0	194.0	126.6	114.4	149.1
Fixed assets					
Land	147.4	158.4	169.5	181.4	198.0
Buildings	227.6	298.3	342.7	358.9	411.9
Equipment	515.9	619.4	768.8	816.7	935.6
Construction	51.6	45.4	28.2	44.5	91.9
Less accumulated depreciation	(422.0)	(481.8)	(585.7)	(671.1)	(771.3)
Net fixed assets	520.5	639.7	723.5	730.4	866.1
Total assets	1,549.9	1,675.4	1,865.6	1,976.6	2,284.4
Liabilities and Equity					
Notes payable	122.4	92.4	246.1	265.1	356.1
Accounts payable	324.4	406.9	386.1	436.9	389.1
Accured expenses	148.4	155.2	172.7	222.8	272.2
Taxes payable	23.6	15.1	39.0	37.4	30.0
Total current liabilities	618.8	669.6	843.9	962.2	1,047.4
Long-term debt	181.9	213.1	240.0	205.3	301.6
Other long-term liabilities	21.1	31.2	28.7	29.4	34.0
Total liabilities	821.8	913.9	1,112.6	1,196.9	1,383.0
Equity					
Common stock	54.6	55.8	57.8	63.3	68.9
Capital surplus	110.8	116.8	127.7	132.7	155.8
Retained earnings	545.1	679.8	751.7	851.8	936.5
Legal reserve**	11.6	12.7	13.7	15.2	16.5
Adjustments**	6.0	(103.6)	(197.9)	(283.3)	(276.3)
Total equity	728.1	761.5	753.0	779.7	901.4
Total liabilities and equity	1,549.9	1,675.4	1,865.6	1,976.6	2,284.4

* Fiscal years 1985 to 1987 ended on February 28, and 1988 to 1989 ended on March 31.
** Japanese legal reserve is related to divided payments. Currency translation adjustments for the balance sheet are accumulated in shareholders' equity.

Source: Honda Motor Company, *Annual Reports*, 1985–89.

ENDNOTES

1. Taylor III, A., Japan's Carmakers Take on the World, *Fortune*, Vol. 17, No. 13, June 1988, pp. 50–55.
2. Toy, S., N. Gross, and J. Treece, The Americanization of Honda, *Business Week*, No. 3045, April 25, 1988, pp. 32–35.
3. Taylor III, A., Who's Ahead in the World Auto War? *Fortune*, Vol. 116, No. 23, November 9, 1987, pp. 22–32.
4. Tully, S., Now Japan's Autos Push into Europe, *Fortune*, Vol. 121, No. 3, January 29, 1990, p. 96.
5. Keller, M., Facing a United European Automotive Front, *Automotive Industries,* August 1988, p. 8.
6. Lublin, J., Honda Rules out Full Acquisition of UK Carmaker, *The Wall Street Journal*, October 5, 1989.
6a. Tully, S., Now Japan's Autos Push into Europe, *Fortune,* Vol. 121, No. 3, January 29, 1990, pp. 16–20.
7. *Ibid.*, p. 100.
7a. Kapstein, J. and J. Hoerr, Volvo's Radical New Plant, *Business Week*, No. 415, August 28, 1989, pp. 92–93.
8. Taylor III, A., *op cit.*, 1988, pp. 72–73.
9. Borrus, J., J. Treece, and L. Armstrong, Not All Japanese Carmakers are Powerhouses, *Business Week*, No. 3140, February 19, 1990, pp. 26–27.
9a. Ingrassia, P. and K. Graven, Squeeze Ahead, *The Wall Street Journal*, April 24, 1990, pp. A1–A11.
10. Honda Motor Company Ltd., *Annual Report*, 1987.
11. Taylor III, A., Can American Cars Come Back? *Fortune*, February 26, 1990, pp. 34–37.
12. Annetta Miller, Yuriko Hoshias, Harry Hunt III, The Top Ten: Now and then, *Newsweek*, Vol. CXV, No. 4, January 22, 1990, p. 38.
13. Weiner, S., The Road Most Travelled, *Forbes*, Vol. 140, No. 8, October 19, 1987, pp. 60–64.
14. Taylor III, A., *op. cit.,* 1990, p. 64.
15. Taylor III, A., Luxury Cars, *Fortune*, Vol. 119, No. 8, April 10, 1989, pp. 52–53, 58–60.
16. Autos-Auto Parts, *Standard & Poor's Industry Surveys*, November 30, 1989, p. 80.
17. Taylor III, A., *op. cit.,* 1989, pp. 64–74.
17a. White, J., Honda, Trying to Outpace Its Rivals, Unveils New Acura Luxury Cars Today, *The Wall Street Journal*, May 4, 1989, p. 85.
18. Guiles, M., Bumpy Road, *The Wall Street Journal*, November 29, 1989, pp. A1, A6.
19. Ingrassia, P. and J. White, Losing the Race, *The Wall Street Journal*, December 14, 1989, p. A10.
20. Treece, J., Will GM Learn from Its Own Role Models? *Business Week*, No. 3147, April 9, 1990, p. 62.
21. General Motors Corporation, *Annual Reports,* 1988, 1989.
22. Treece, J., Here Comes GM's Saturn, *Business Week*, No. 3147, April 9, 1990, pp. 56–62.
23. Buell, B., Why Japanese Workers Got Underwhelming Raises, *Business Week*, No. 3045, April 25, 1988, p. 82.
24. US Department of Commerce, *1989 US Industrial US Outlook,* Washington, DC, 1989, p. 34.
25. Taylor III, A., *op. cit.,* 1988, p. 67.
26. Guiles, M., GM Puts Captive Imports to New Test, *The Wall Street Journal*, September 16, 1988, p. B1.
27. Hof, R. and J. Treece, This Team Has It All—Except sales, *Business Week*, No. 3113, August 14, 1989, p. 35.

28. Washington, F. and D. Pauly, Driving Toward a World Car, *Newsweek*, Vol. CXIII, No. 18, May 1, 1989, pp. 48–49.
29. Miller, Annetta, Japanese Cars: Born in the USA, *Newsweek*, Vol. CXV, No. 15, April 9, 1990, pp. 32–33.
30. Stertz, B., Big Three Boost Car Quality but Still Lag, *The Wall Street Journal*, March 27, 1990, p. B1.
31. Tully, S., *op. cit.,* 1990, p. 97.
31a. Washington, Frank and J. McElroy, Worldwide Productivity Comparison, *Automotive Industries,* April 1989, p. 62.
31b. Ingrassia, P., Losing Control, *The Wall Street Journal,* February 16, 1990, p. A6.
32. Treece, J. and J. Hoerr, Shaking up Detroit, *Business Week,* No. 3113, August 14, 1989, pp. 30–32.
33. Autos-Auto Parts, *op. cit.,* 1989, p. A85.
34. Toy et al., Americanization of Honda, p. 93.
35. Rice, F., America's New No. 4 Automaker—Honda, *Fortune,* Vol. 112, No. 9, October 28, 1985, pp. 26–32.
36. Treece, J. and J. Hoerr, *op. cit.,* 1989, pp. 74–80.
37. Autos-Auto Parts, *op. cit.,* 1989, p. A84.
38. Taylor III, A., *op. cit.,* 1988, p. 88.
39. Rice, F., *op. cit.,* 1985, p. 32.
39a. Taylor III, A., *op. cit.,* 1989, p. 63.
40. Ingrassia, P., *op. cit.,* 1990, p. A6.
41. White J., Honda Takes Aim at Detroit's Heart, *The Wall Street Journal*, September 18, 1989, p. B1.
42. Taylor III, A., *op. cit.,* 1989, p. 74.
43. US Department of Commerce, *US Industrial Outlook,* Washington, DC, various years.
44. Chino, Tetsuo and Tadashi Kume, speeches delivered at Columbus, Ohio, September 17, 1987.
45. Kanabayashi, M., Honda's US Unit to Export Cars to South Korea, *The Wall Street Journal*, June 15, 1988.
46. White, J. and K. Graven, Driving Ambition, *The Wall Street Journal*, October 9, 1989, p. A8.
47. *Ibid.*, pp. A1, A8.

CASE FOUR

MATSUSHITA ELECTRIC INDUSTRIAL COMPANY*

In the mid-1980s Matsushita Electric Industrial Co. was often cited as one of the premier examples of the management practices and style that had made Japan into an industrial power, with a GNP second only to the United States. Matsushita's own brand names. Quasar, National, Panasonic, Victor (JVC), and Technic, were known around the world. Matsushita was Japan's largest producer of electric and electronic products and one of the world's largest firms in these fields. Why did its management practices work so well? To what extent were they applicable to other companies? What could be adopted outside Japan?

EARLY HISTORY

Matsushita (generally pronounced MatSOOSH'ta) was started in 1918 by Mr. Konosuke Matsushita, one of Japan's now legendary entrepreneurs. In 1911, Mr. Matsushita had joined the Osaka Electric Light Company (at age 15), convinced that electricity had a great future in Japan. Seven years later, then the youngest inspector on Osaka's payroll, he resigned to form his own company.

At that time the few wired Japanese homes typically had only one circuit, and that

---

* Case copyright © 1985 by James Brion Quinn. Research assistants—Penny C. Paquette and Allie J. Quinn. Major sources: (1) Company interviews; (2) Company published records; (3) T. Kono, *Strategy and Structure of Japanese Enterprises* (M.E. Sharpe, Armonk, N.Y., 1985); (4) J. Cruikshonk, "Matsushita," *Harvard Business School Bulletin*, February 1983; and (5) R. Pascale and A. Athos, *The Art of Japanese Management* (Simon and Schuster, New York, 1981). The generous cooperation of Matsushita Electric is gratefully acknowledged.

usually emerged inconveniently from the center of the ceiling in one room. To light another room or to use electricity meant using an awkward extension cord, dangling from the ceiling fixture. And the resident still had only one lighted room. Mr. Matsushita, a tinkerer from his early days in his father's bicycle shop, conceived of a double-ended attachment for the outlet that permitted the main room to be lighted while a swivel socket allowed an extension cord to be guided elsewhere without tangling. When he offered his idea to Osaka Electric, the company was not interested. Consequently, Mr. Matsushita took about US$50 in savings and severance pay and—with his wife and brother-in-law—began manufacturing and selling his unique multiple socket from his home. By using recycled light bulb bases, Matsushita was soon able to cut his already low costs (and prices) by some 30 per cent, discouraging larger competitors from entering his market.

His next product was a bicycle lamp to replace the unreliable battery lamps (or in many cases small metal boxes with candles) then used by the Japanese for cycling at night. Matsushita developed an improved battery, mounted his lamps in well-styled wooden casings, and left samples burning in Osaka's shop windows over weekends to prove that his lights would burn 10 times longer than his competitors'. From these humble beginnings, a great consumer electric products line was born. Matsushita became a public company in 1935. The National brand was registered in 1925; the first National radios were produced in 1930; washing machines, refrigerators, and televisions appeared in the post-World War II era; and a full range of high-fidelity electronics products in the 1960s through the 1980s. In the 1960s and 1970s Matsushita added industrial equipment, communications devices, and measuring systems. Matsushita began producing television receivers in 1952, exported its first TVs to Thailand in 1956, and completed its 75 millionth set in 1985. An analysis of its 1985 product line and summary financials is given in Exhibits 1A to 1D.

A 250-Year Strategy

In 1932 Konosuke Matsushita noticed a tramp drinking water from a water tap on the street. He later said: "I began to think about abundance. And I decided that the task of an industrialist was to make his products widely available at the lowest possible cost to bring a better living to the people of the world" (Cruikshank, 1983: 63). This became his exhortation to his employees on the company's 14th anniversary in 1932—and the cornerstone of the company's "250-year corporate strategy." Exemplifying this philosophy was an incident in the early 1930s. There was a Japanese inventor/investor who then controlled most of the patents for radio circuitry, which was moving from the crystal set era toward the speaker radio. Mr. Matsushita approached this man—who intended to monopolize the new industry—and after lengthy negotiations bought out his patents for a huge price. He then opened the patents to the entire industry "so that everyone could manufacture in a more efficient way."

Mr. Matsushita's 250 Year Plan to eliminate poverty is divided into ten 25-year segments. In May 1982, the Matsushita company began the third 25 Year Plan which was to include "the true internationalization of the Matsushita Industrial Electric Company" (Cruikshank, 1983: 75). Shortly before Mr. Matsushita had noted in this book, *Japan at the brink*, that "the Japanese miracle itself was on the verge of capsizing, politically, economically, and spiritually." He outlined problems of inflation, disaffected youth, what he called ineffective

Matsushita Electric Industrial Company

Exhibit 1A Matsushita's Major Products (1983)—An Overview

The Company is engaged in production and sales of electric and electronic products. For revenue reporting purposes, the Company has classified its products into several categories. Details of these are tabulated in Exhibits 5 through 8.

VIDEO EQUIPMENT

Matsushita produces videotape recorders and related products (cameras, tapes, etc.) for home and professional use. For the year ended November 20, 1983, sales of video-tape recorder products increased rapidly and accounted for ¥1,045 billion or 26 per cent of total Company sales.

The Company manufactures a broad range of color and black-and-white television receivers designed to meet the demands of all segments of the Japanese and overseas markets. The company manufactures color and black-and-white television receivers with screens ranging from 1$1/2$ to 25 inches and 1$1/2$ to 19 inches, respectively, measured diagonally. The Company also manufactures large screen color projection TV systems. For the year ended November 20, 1983, sales of television receivers accounted for ¥399 billion or 10 per cent of total sales of the Company for that period.

AUDIO EQUIPMENT

The Company produces a large variety of audio equipment, ranging from radio receivers, tape recorders and radio cassette combination models to stereo radio phonographs, hi-fi components and digital audio equipment. It also produces electronic organs. For the fiscal year 1983, total audio equipment sales represented ¥481 billion or 12 per cent of the Company total.

HOME APPLIANCES

The major products in this category include: refrigerators and freezers; home laundry equipment such as washing machines and dryers; cooking equipment such as microwave and other ovens, blenders, juicers, food processors and rice cookers; airconditioners and electric fans; electric and kerosene heaters; vacuum cleaners and electric irons. For fiscal 1983, total home appliance sales amounted to ¥596 billion or 15 per cent of total sales of the Company.

COMMUNICATION AND INDUSTRIAL EQUIPMENT

This category covers two-way communication equipment, including push-button telephones, community telephone systems and mobile communication equipment; broadcasting equipment, including radio and television broadcasting installations, broadcast television cameras and CATV systems; measuring instruments, including oscilloscopes and ultrasonic diagnostic systems; automotive accessories, including car radios and stereos; business equipment, including facsimile equipment personal computers, word processors and plain paper copiers; and other products, including hearing aids, electronic calculators, traffic control systems, electronic education systems, point-of-sale systems and professional audio equipment. It also includes electric motors, micro motors, welding equipment, industrial robots, power distribution equipment, power transformers and capacitors, anti-pollution equipment, TLD irradiation measuring systems, vending machines and other electric and electronic industrial devices.

Sales of this product category were ¥581 billion, representing 15 per cent of the Company total in 1983.

Exhibit 1A Matsushita's Major Products (1983)—An Overview (cont.)

ENERGY AND KITCHEN-RELATED PRODUCTS

This category includes many types of batteries; among them, manganese, nickel-cadmium, mercury, alkaline, silver oxide, lithium and air wet cells, storage batteries for automotive use, fuel cell batteries primarily for marine use, and solar cells. It also encompasses various battery appliances, gas appliances, kitchen sinks and cabinets, and solar energy equipment. Sales of these products as a whole reached ¥187 billion or 5 per cent of the Company's 1983 total.

ELECTRONIC COMPONENTS

This category includes a wide variety of transistors, diodes, ICs (integrated circuits) and LSIC (large scale integrated circuits), as well as television picture tubes, other cathode ray tubes, image pickup tubes and magnetrons, for use by the Company and other manufacturers. The Company also manufactures a comprehensive line of incandescent, fluorescent, mercury and sodium lamps, speakers, audio accessories, TV tuners, resistors, capacitors, ceramic components, printed circuits sensing devices and other parts. Total electronic components sales amounted to ¥386 billion or 9 per cent of the Company total for 1983.

OTHERS

This category includes phonograph records, pre-recorded tapes, electric pencil sharpeners, bicycles, and photographic products, including cameras and flash units. Total sales of these miscellaneous products totaled ¥307 billion and accounted for 8 per cent of total 1983 sales of the Company.

Consumer Electronics
TV receivers
   color
   monochrone
   industrial
Transistor radios
   portables
   clock radios
Headphones
Radio cassette recorders
Cassette recorders
Car audios
Transceivers
Music centers
Hi-fi components
   turntables
   tape decks
   amplifiers
   receivers
   tuners
   speaker systems
Videotape recorders
Video cameras
Video projection systems
Videotape printers

Video editing machines
Video mixing apparatus
Electronic organs
Hearing aids

Industrial Equipment
Welding machines
   light beam
   electron beam
   arc
   automatic CO_2
Component insertion machines
   (PANASERT*)
Automatic riveting machines
Automatic screw feeding and
   driving machines
High voltage transformers
Power capacitors
Power distribution equipment
Circuit breakers
TLD (Thermoluminescent
   dosimeter)
Medical equipment
   (PANAVISTA*)
Vending machines

Refrigerated showcases
Card readers
Measuring equipment
Elevators
Escalators
Anti-pollution equipment

Business Machines
Small business computers
Facsimile equipment
Plain paper copiers
Word processors
Electronic cash registers
Electronic calculators
Key telephones
Intercom systems
Automatic slide processors
Pencil sharpeners
Staplers
Letter openers

Home Appliances
Refrigerators
Microwave ovens
Gas and electric ovens
Rice cookers

Exhibit 1A Matsushita's Major Products (1983)—An Overview (cont.)

Toasters
Blenders
Food processors
Coffeemakers
Tempura-fondue cookers
Joy Cook (Induction heating cooker)
Kitchen units
Water heaters
Dishwashers
Disposers
Pumps
Washing machines
Dryers
Vacuum cleaners
Polishers
Electric fans
Ventilating fans
Air and water purifiers
Water coolers
Electric irons
Electric blankets
Air-conditioners
Heating and cooling systems
  electric
  gas
  kerosene
Dehumidifiers and humidifiers
Hair setters
Bicycles
Flash units
Clocks

Lighting Equipment
Incandescent lamps
Fluorescent lamps
Mercury discharge lamps
Metal halide lamps
Sodium lamps
Infrared ray lamps
Halogen lamps
Lighting fixtures

System Products
LL (Learning laboratory) systems

Broadcasting systems
Sound systems
Traffic control systems
Tunnel systems
Disaster alert systems
Hotel service systems
Dam control systems
Meteorological robot buoy systems
CATV systems
POS (Point of sale) systems
POSTA (Post office service total automation) systems
Lighting systems
Surveillance systems
Public address systems
Mobile telephone systems

Electronic Components
Transistors
Diodes
ICs
LSIs
Thyristors
Cathode ray tubes
Image pickup tubes (NEWVICON*)
Receiving and transmitting tubes
Indicator tubes
Magnetrons
Hybrid microcircuits (Hi-MIC*)
Capacitors
Resistors
Ceramics (PCM*, ZNR*)
Printed circuit boards
Transformers
Coils
Switches
Connectors
Sensors
Display and graphic devices
System modules
Tuners
Speakers

Tape heads (HPF*)
Microphones
Antennas

Motors
DC motors
Micro motors
Transistor motors
Stepping motors
Servo motors
Coreless motors
Flat motors
Fan motors
Blower motors
Capacitor motors
Hermetically-sealed motors
Clutch motors
Needle positioning motors
Shaded pole motors
Synchronous motors
Geared motors
General-purpose motors
Universal motors

Batteries
Manganese dioxide batteries
Alkaline management batteries
Lithium batteries
Mercury batteries
Silver oxide batteries
Air batteries
Paper-thin batteries
Lead-acid batteries
  car batteries
  storage batteries
  PANALLOID* batteries
Nickel-cadmium batteries
Battery charges
Solar batteries
Fuel cells
Carbon electrodes
Battery-operated golf carts and other appliances

*Trademark of Matsushita Electric.
Source: Matsushita Electric, SEC Form 20-F, November 20, 1983; and Annual Report, 1983.

Exhibit 1B Sales Breakdown by Products and Geographic Areas (billions of yen)

	\multicolumn{6}{c}{Year Ended November 20}
	1981		1982		1983	
Products						
Video equipment	1,109	(32)	1,329	(36)	1,444	(36)
Audio equipment	543	(16)	485	(13)	481	(12)
Home appliances	591	(17)	590	(16)	596	(15)
Communication and industrial equipment	429	(12)	464	(13)	588	(15)
Energy and kitchen-related products	166	(5)	181	(5)	187	(5)
Electronic components	313	(9)	310	(9)	386	(9)
Others	300	(9)	291	(8)	307	(8)
Total	3,451	(100)	3,650	(100)	3,989	(100)
Geographic Areas						
Japan	1,872	(54)	1,965	(54)	2,128	(53)
North America (United States and Canada)	640	(19)	670	(18)	842	(21)
Others	939	(27)	1,015	(28)	1,019	(26)
Total	3,451	(100)	3,650	(100)	3,989	(100)

Note: All the figures given within brackets are in percentage.

Source: Matsushita Electric, *SEC Form 20-F*, November 20, 1983; *Annual Report, 1983*.

government, and a national lack of philosophical bearings. Among his many starting recommendations was the suggestion that Japan should abolish half of its universities. He felt much of the education was not worthwhile and that Japan's needs could be better met by other institutions. Selling off the assets of Tokyo University (the nation's most prestigious university) alone would save the country some US$500 million per year.

These incidents suggest the creative quality which Mr. Matsushita has lent to his company. When General MacArthur's advisors decided to eliminate the *zaibatsu* (or "financial clique") which had controlled Japanese industry prior to World War II, they removed Mr. Matsushita as head of his company. Numerous delegations of workers approached the authorities, saying Matsushita represented the very entrepreneurial spirit which the Americans were professing. While tolerated by the *zaibatsu*, they said Matsushita was distinctly not a part of it. He had welcomed a union in the post war era, reiterating his conviction that labor and management must work together for a greater good. But the American authorities refused to listen to these supplications, and for four years during Mr. Matsushita's enforced exile, his company shrank from 20,000 to 3,800 employees, with many divisions closing permanently. Only when he was reinstated in 1951 did the company begin to return to its former strength.

Exhibit 1C Selected Financial Data (billions of yen, except per share amounts and yen exchange rates)

	Year Ended November 20				
	1979	1980	1981	1982	1983
Net sales	2,363	2,916	3,451	3,650	3,989
Net income	98	125	157	157	183
Per common share					
Net income	69.54	87.13	101.48	100.79	116.29
Dividends	8.26	8.26	9.09	10.00	12.50
	($0.036)	($0.038)	($0.038)	($0.041)	($0.053)
Net working capital	495	548	615	676	768
Total assets	2,139	2,478	2,946	3,174	3,451
Long-term indebtedness	68	59	35	49	40
Minority interests	200	242	302	339	377
Stockholders' equity	922	1,092	1,272	1,435	1,602
Yen exchange rates per US dollar					
Year-end	246.20	213.70	218.65	257.85	235.95
Average	213.94	231.79	220.74	245.55	239.58
High	193.95	206.50	199.05	214.20	226.75
Low	247.00	261.40	246.10	277.65	257.05

Notes: 1. Per share amounts have been appropriately adjusted for free distributions of shares.
2. Dividends per share are those declared with respect to the income for each fiscal year and dividends charged to retained earnings are those actually paid.

Source: Matsushita Electric, *SEC Form 20-F*, November 20, 1983.

JAPAN'S INDUSTRIAL STRUCTURE

In this period, Japan was a nation still emerging from feudalism and a military system gone berserk. Its industrial infrastructure had been destroyed, its youth decimated, and its illusions of military conquest dashed. The nation had no significant energy resources, few natural resources, a small land mass relative to its population, and a very poorly paid labor force. Many ordinary amenities had disappeared and its social system verged on breakdown or revolution. But for 300 years, its dominant feudal and religious (Confucion and Shinto) groups had emphasized devotion to one's family and organization. Personal courtesy had been ingrained in numerous rituals and was a necessity for a large population living on a small land mass. But respect for laborers had not been a widely held value, nor had wealth been widely distributed.

In the disillusioned and labor-deficient post-war era, more democratic values began to appear. There began a concerted national effort to improve the ordinary Japanese' standard of living. Through its Ministry for International Trade and Industry (MITI) the government targeted certain industries for expansion and assisted them in developing their own technologies

Exhibit 1D Matsushita Electric Industrial Co., Ltd. and Consolidated Subsidiaries—Consolidated Balance Sheet, November 20, 1983 and 1982

Assets	1983 (Yen millions)	1982 (Yen millions)
Current assets		
Cash	553,988	492,509
Marketable securities, at cost, which approximate market	212,762	120,028
Trade receivables		
Related companies	75,321	78,044
Notes	118,386	112,186
Accounts	365,761	343,061
Allowance for doubtful receivables	(14,582)	(15,040)
Net trade receivables	544,886	518,251
Inventories	528,529	556,953
Other current assets	179,179	158,577
Total current assets	2,019,344	1,846,318
Investments and advances		
Nonconsolidated subsidiaries	164,281	169,235
Associated companies	76,054	71,762
Other investments and advances	590,942	508,061
Total investments and advances	831,277	749,058
Property, plant and equipment		
Land	73,584	66,926
Buildings	330,193	308,874
Machinery and equipment	642,789	568,098
Construction in progress	22,168	17,540
	1,068,734	961,438
Less accumulated depreciation	603,709	508,942
Net property, plant and equipment	405,025	452,496
Other assets	134,947	125,848

Liabilities and Stockholders' Equity	1983 (Yen millions)	1982 (Yen millions)
Current liabilities		
Short-term bank loans	195,011	245,929
Current portion of long-term debt	1,200	1,413
Trade payables		
Related companies	36,959	32,991
Notes	82,325	75,101
Accounts	243,263	213,401
Total trade payables	362,547	321,493
Accrued income taxes	161,253	113,187
Accrued payroll	114,892	104,918
Other accrued expenses	198,375	173,324
Deposits and advances from customers	76,956	75,536
Employees' deposits	83,107	76,374
Other current liabilities	58,453	57,725
Total current liabilities	1,251,794	1,169,899
Long-term debt	40,405	49,158
Retirement and severance benefits	179,247	180,340
Minority interests:		
Capital stock	39,273	38,082
Surplus	337,800	300,928
Total minority interests	377,073	339,010
Stockholders' equity		
Common stock of ¥50 par value: Authorized—2,700,000,000 shares; issued—1,589,239,462 shares (1982—1,576,298,513 shares)	79,462	78,815
Capital surplus	216,719	205,797
Legal reserve	30,011	27,831
Retained earnings	1,282,536	1,117,689
Cumulative translation adjustments	(3,820)	12,237
	1,606,908	1,442,369
Less cost of 7,005,397 shares (1982—16,641,324 shares) of common stock held by consolidated subsidiaries	2,834	7,056
Total stockholders' equity	1,602,074	1,435,313
Commitments and contingent liabilities	3,450,593	3,173,720

and in importing foreign technologies. To stabilize society, large Japanese companies began to emphasize lifetime employment (to age 55) and to take over many of the social roles other institutions provide in Western countries. Companies often provided employee housing, recreation facilities, and a focal point for sports activities. Even today the Japanese government provides few unemployment or retirement benefits to workers. Instead, it attempts to stabilize price levels, manages the economy to maintain employment and offers supplementary employment opportunities only when necessary—through the national railroad system, public works, and public service (sanitary, groundskeeping, etc.) activities. Income and social security taxes are low. In most large companies employees are considered partners in the enterprise, not interchangeable parts of production; and in times of recession, employment is continued at the cost of profits or dividends. Japanese executives often say that since maintaining sales and profit levels is the management's responsibility—not that of factory workers—management (not workers) should bear the brunt of any layoffs which are unavoidable.

Another unique features of Japanese industry has been its financial structures. Large Japanese companies are heavy users of loan capital, with an equity ratio of only 20 per cent being average. The largest equity shareholders, however, are also banks and insurance companies, which are forbidden individually to own more than 10 per cent of a given company. They hold stock to secure a long-term relationship more than to reap current profits. Other shareholders tend to be important suppliers or buyers from the companies. Only some 30 per cent of all stock is held by individuals. Some typical financial data are illustrated in Exhibits 2 through 5.

Exhibit 2 Corporate Profits in Four Countries—Average Return on Profits for Manufacturing Firms in the United States, the United Kingdom, West Germany, and Japan

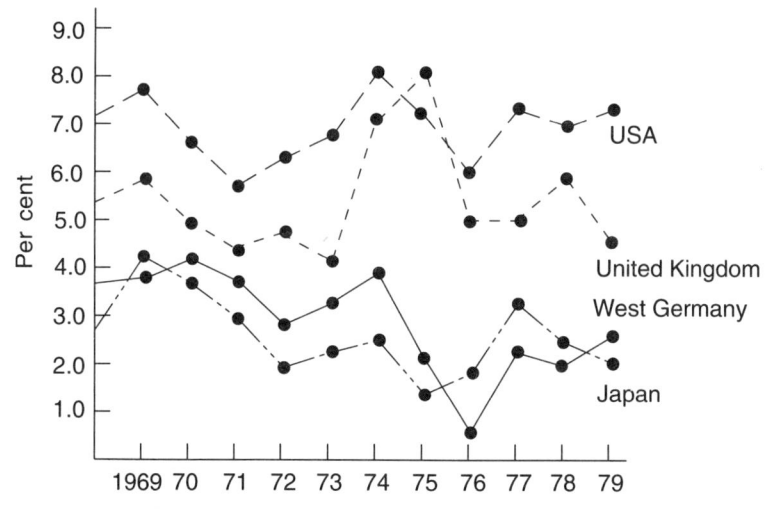

Source: Industrial Policy Bureau, MITI, Japan, *Sekai no Kigyo no keiei Bunseki*, in William H. Davidson (Ed.), The *Amazing Race,* Tokyo, 1980, p. 20. Copyright © 1984 John Wiley & Sons. Reprinted by permission of John Wiley & Sons.

Exhibit 3 Financial Ratios for Selected US and Japanese Firms (1978)

Company	Debt-Equity Ratio	Profit/Sales	Inventory Turn Ratio
Burroughs	0.538	10.46%	4.24
IBM	0.538	14.76	6.24
NCR	0.923	12.18	4.23
Control Data	0.786	4.65	4.38
DEC	0.639	9.90	3.58
Hitachi	2.99	2.56	5.45
Toshiba	5.08	1.52	3.56
Fujitsu	2.68	2.37	4.77
NEC	5.18	1.09	4.10
Oki	17.05	0.57	3.8
Mitsubishi Electric	5.67	1.71	3.78
Matsushita	1.01	3.34	16.47
Sanyo	2.02	1.93	21.32
Ricoh	1.43	4.15	12.10
Casio	1.60	3.54	7.82
Sony	0.923	4.35	5.65
Sharp	2.125	2.76	9.64

Source: Industrial Policy Bureau, MITI, Japan, *Sekai no Kigyo no Keiei Bunseki,* in William H. Davidson (Ed.), *The Amazing Race,* Tokyo, 1980, p. 29. Copyright © 1984 John Wiley & Sons. Reprinted by permission of John Wiley & Sons.

COMPANY PHILOSOPHY

Within this general framework, Matsushita company has developed its own unique and extraordinarily powerful philosophy. Matsushita's stated mission is "to contribute to the well-being of mankind by providing reasonably priced products and services in sufficient quantities to achieve peace, happiness, and prosperity for all." This is supported by "5 Principles":

1. Growth through mutual benefit between the company and the consumer
2. Profit as a result of contributions to society
3. Fair competition in the marketplace
4. Mutual benefit between the company, its suppliers, dealers, and shareholders
5. Participation by all employees

"Seven Spirits" then provide the code of behavior for employees to follow in making decisions (Kono, 1985: 50). These are:

1. Spirit of Service through Industry
2. Spirit of Fairness and Faithfulness

Exhibit 4 A Comparison of Productivity Adjusted Labor Costs in the United States and Japan (1970–80)

Year	Average Annual Japanese Wages in Manufacturing* ÷	Japanese Output per Labor Hour Divided by US Output per Labor Hour** =	Adjusted Japanese Labor Cost	US Labor Cost[†]
1970	$ 1,787	0.508	$ 3,517	$ 7,439
1972	2,693	0.580	4,643	8,719
1974	4,224	0.649	6,508	9,947
1976	5,633	0.701	8,036	11,780
1978	10,009	0.782	12,799	14,063
1980	10,724	0.918	11,682	15,008

*These data cover the contracted cash payments to workers in manufacturing firms with 29 or more employees. From *Economic Statistics Annual*, Research and Statistics Department, Bank of Japan, 1981, pp. 293 and 294.

**This variable is created by dividing the average output per labor hour for Japanese industries by the average output in US industries. Data are taken from the US Department of Labor, Bureau of Labor Statistics.

[†]From Bureau of Labor Statistics, *Monthly Labor Review*, for manufacturing only.

Source: William H. Davidson (Ed.), *The Amazing Race*. Copyright © 1984 John Wiley & Sons. Reprinted by permission of John Wiley & Sons.

Exhibit 5 Leading World Semiconductor Companies Sales (Discrete and Integrated Devices, 1982)

Company	Total ($, millions)	Company	Total ($, millions)
Motorola	1310	Signetics (Philips)	384
Texas Instruments	1227	Mitsubishi	380
Nippon Electric	1220	Mostek	335
Hitachi	1000	Advanced Microdevices (Siemens)	282
Toshiba	810	Sanyo	260
National Semiconductor	690	AEG	196
Intel	610	Thomson-CSF	190
Philips*	558	Sharp	155
Fujitsu	475	SGS-ATES	150
Siemens*	420	Oki	125
Matsushita	340		

*Not including US affiliates.

Source: Hambrecht and Quist, The Japanese Semiconductor Industry, in William H. Davidson (Ed.), *The Amazing Race*. Copyright © 1984 John Wiley & Sons. Reprinted by permission of John Wiley & Sons.

3. Spirit of Harmony and Cooperation
4. Spirit of Struggle for Betterment
5. Spirit of Courtesy and Humility
6. Spirit of Adaptation and Assimilation
7. Spirit of Gratitude

Exercises and Discussions

Every morning at Matsushita's plants in Japan (and in most areas throughout the world) every employee attends a "morning meeting," at which the Matsushita creed, principles, and/or spirits are recited aloud. Only a skeleton force of telephone operators, guards, process controllers, etc. is not present. In Japan the meeting begins with prearranged exercises learned in early grade school. Then in "relaxation exercises" each person massages and pounds the back of another person, and then both turn around to give or receive similar benefits. Following the Company Song and these recitations, a discussion leader—a task rotated daily—poses a question for the group to discuss and try to resolve. This can be an operating problem, a new opportunity, or an important philosophical issue designed to provoke interest. After 15 minutes or so, everyone goes off to work. At work stations the exercise routine is repeated for 5 minutes at the end of each hour and for 10–15 minutes at mid-morning and afternoon.

In the company's early years, Mr. Matsushita used to interview all employees himself. this is no longer possible. But annually he and his wife host a gathering of newlywed employees. There are announcements and awards on "Adults Day" every January 15th to celebrate trainees becoming full employees. And there are constant company messages in each employee's paycheck to personalize the company-individual relationship. Mr. Niwa, chairman of Matsushita Electric Works, says, "We try to develop the supportive idea that 'we are always with you' psychologically" (Cruikshank, 1983: 65). Within most plants is a "trophy area" where individual and plant awards for outstanding performance are displayed. Much emphasis is given to company awards and to the performance of company sports teams competing with those of other companies.

Mr. Kosaka, head of Matsushita's Overseas Training Center says: "We feel you must create a spirit in which everyone can share.... It's not a theory, formulated after reading other people's books, but something based on *experience*. Once the philosophy is clear, it talks to every individual, and all communication in the company can be based on it" (Cruikshank, 1983: 63). In Matsushita's Japan operations virtually all employees wear company-provided blue uniforms with white tennis shoes. Overseas the company provides the uniforms, but the choice is up to individuals.

An Organized Maverick

Despite what appears to be conformity and regimentation in its philosophy, Matsushita has consistently been a maverick in Japanese industry. From the first, Matsushita violated the usual rules used by Japanese and American companies of the era. Rather than attempting to recoup investments as rapidly as possible, Matsushita has consistently cut its prices quickly and sought profits in the long run. While other companies used manufacturers representatives to reach established retail channels, Matsushita set up its own distribution networks and went directly to retailers. Instead of an arms length transaction with retailers, Matsushita offered innovative trade financing for them and pioneered the use of installment sales and point-of-purchase advertising in Japan. Rather than using the Matsushita name, the company promoted its National, Victor, and Panasonic brands.

A Decentralization Pioneer

In the mid-1930s, paralleling DuPont's pioneering efforts with a decentralized divisional structure Matsushita and his talented controller, Takahashi developed a similar concept with only 1,600 employees at the time. Matsushita was attracted not only to the organizational clarity and control the system offered, but to its motivational advantages as well. He wanted to keep things small, entrepreneurial, and market-oriented in the rapidly emerging ratio and small consumer appliance fields the company was in.

This decentralized divisional concept still dominates today's organization. But, recognising the inherent disadvantages of this system, Matsushita also centralized four key functions which remain so to the present. first, he created a cadre of controllers reporting directly to headquarters and a centralized accounting system across the company. Second, he institutionalized a company "bank" into which 60 per cent of all divisional profit flowed and from which divisions have to seek funds for capital improvements. Divisions have no bank accounts except for day-to-day transactions. Divisions' "float" must be cleared monthly, and borrowings beyond this are charged out at prime plus 2 per cent. Third, Matsushita centralized the personnel function; no employee is hired without a central prescreening, and all management promotions are reviewed and monitored by headquarters. Fourth, he centralized the company's training system with its heavy emphasis on the values described above. Each university-level employee goes through an approximately eight-month training cycle to inspire him with the company's goals and philosophies, as well as to provide him with essential technical skill.

A Product Group Matrix

This basic organization has since oscillated back and forth with more (or less) autonomy given to the divisions depending on external economic or competitive conditions. In 1953 Matsushita introduced Product Groups with division heads reporting, vertically to the President and horizontally to group vice-presidents, who serve as specialists with detailed knowledge of a whole family of similar products (Pascale and Athos, 1981: 33). This innovation was some 10 years ahead of the widespread use of matrix organizations in the US. Matsushita tried not to take its formal organization charts too seriously and to "humanize" some of the inherent conflicts in the matrix structure. Controllers were called "coordinators" and houses directly in the factories they served (*Ibid.*: 35). To relieve some of the resistance to this matrix concept, Matsushita constantly reminded executives that everyone grew up with two bosses (a mother and a father), a situation that generally seemed quite tolerable. Even at the top level Matsushita established a three-person executive council to handle major decisions.

He then slowly withdrew himself into a strategic role as chairman, although he reserved the right to reemerge to assume direct control in times of crises.

COMPETITION AND COOPERATION

Japanese corporations compete intensively with companies in the same line of business, but often cooperate extensively with other companies in a complementary relationship. For example, Matsushita has 120 "fully controlled" wholesalers selling only its products. It has 20 per cent or more equity interest in all these distributors and serves them and other retailers through 100 sales offices which provide management assistance, showroom facilities, and other services to Matsushita's Japanese distribution network. Retailers include 25,000 National shops, where Matsushita products accounts for 80 per cent of sales and another 25,000 National stores where its products exceed 50 per cent of sales.

Matsushita does not hold shares in these retailers, but controls them by long-term contracts and the special services it provides: management training, classes on new technologies, shared advertising, and some special rebates. Typically, products are sold at list in these channels, but they may have to meet the prices of the discount stores now becoming more common in Japan. Other separate channels exist for: industrial and non-industrial construction products, and commercial, industrial, and government customers. Marketing for Matsushita is controlled from headquarters. Each product division can sell directly to its wholesalers or large customers like the government, but under rules established at headquarters. Export sales are handled by an independent subsidiary, Matsushita Trading Co., which has worldwide sales branches for all products.

TECHNOLOGY AND MANUFACTURING

Matsushita is heavily integrated on the components side. It produces its own batteries, vacuum tubes, integrated circuits, circuit boards, condensors, transformers, speakers, tuners, magnetic heads etc. But it buys standard raw materials (wire, steel, aluminium sheet, etc.) outside. Purchases from subsidiaries amount to about 80 per cent of the value of all purchased materials. The company also sells components to outside groups. It only consumes about 50 per cent of its component production and is the largest single component manufacturer in Japan, with ¥386 billion sales in 1983. These manufacturing divisions are all profit enters, able to buy components outside if they so choose. These manufacturing divisions sell through the marketing channels described above. Products are sold by divisional salesmen, shipped directly to distributors or retailers, and transferred to Marketing at internal transfer prices. The Central Marketing group handles sales planning, marketing coordination, and promotional functions.

Although Matsushita started with two innovative products, it has rarely pioneered entirely new technologies (Pascale and Athos, 1981: 30). Instead, it emphasizes quality and price. Its experience with videotape recorders (VTRs) is perhaps typical. Sony was generally acknowledged as the real pioneer of VTR technology with its Umatic and Betamax formats. While Matsushita had also done excellent early work on the technology, it took a license under Sony's early VHS-like format and turned its several divisions loose on improving the device for the marketplace. Discovering that customers wanted a 2–4 hour recording capacity (as opposed to Sony's 1 hour format), Matsushita designed this into a more compact VTR that was highly reliable and could be priced 10–15 per cent below Sony. When Sony came up with its superior quality Beta format, Matsushita stayed with its well-developed VHS concept, got other major Japanese and US firms to adopt its preferred format, and by the late 1970s manufactured 2.3 of all VTRs sold.

"Figure Out How to Do the Job Better"

Matsushita consistently invested some 4 per cent of sales in R&D, much of which went into production engineering. The company had some 20 production engineering laboratories equipped with the latest available technology. Most of these were attached to individual product divisions, but Matsushita's Central Production Engineering Laboratory at corporate level was one of the world's outstanding units. The company also had a Central (basic) Research Laboratory, Wireless Research Laboratory, and Research Institute Tokyo (which operated on an independent basis and conducted research for both company and outside groups). In addition, there were a Corporate Product Development Division, Corporate Quality Assurance Division, and corporate patent and Legal Division under the Central Engineering structure.

The company's focus in R&D was said to be "to analyze competing products and figure out how to do the job better" (Pascale and Athos, 1981: 31). Its Engineering and Research Laboratories were backed by one of the world's most awesome production line suggestion systems. Matsushita processed some 460,000 employee-generated suggestions or improvements per year. The company's motto was "Matsushita produces capable people before it produces products." Thus Matsushita's eight-month training for all university graduates involved three weeks of headquarters training classes, three months in retail stores, one month in the factory, one month in cost accounting, and two months in marketing lectures and activities. Lesser time, but equal attention went into training rank and file workers. Job rotation was common throughout all ranks; 5 per cent of all employees (comprised 1/3 managers, 1/3 supervisors, and 1/3 workers) rotated from one division to another each year, and some 80 per cent of all employees participated in quality circle activities. About 15 per cent of all suggestions were accepted and formally implemented, others were simply implemented by informal agreement among supervisors and employees (Kono, 1985: 304). Of these about 35 "super suggestions" occurred each year. These won coveted awards, and sponsors of patentable suggestions could receive patents and monetary awards in their own names (Cruikshank, 1983: 71).

"Manage from Goodwill"

Not only could workers suggest improvements, they could stop the production line if they were not satisfied with quality. Production plants tended to be spotlessly clean. Cleanliness standards were dictated from headquarters and were not subject to interpretation anywhere in the world. Work stations were typically separated by 8–10 feet, aisles were extremely wide (15–30 feet), noise levels were relatively low around work stations, and the production line itself moved more slowly than was typical in western plants. A substantial amount of small scale automation was generally visible at individual work stations. Individual workers were directly responsible for quality results at their own stations, but heavily automated quality control and test facilities were in evidence all along the electronics and consumer products lines. Employee turnover in Japan was of course extremely low, but even overseas plants tended to have 1/4 the turnover of comparable plants in their host countries—and often they rejected local unions.

Matsushita managers attributed this to the attempt to "manage from goodwill" and to "foster a homey, family atmosphere. We are first interested in nurturing a relationship of trust between management and labor. Once we achieve that goal, we can develop other things like suggestion systems, quality circles, and so on." North American employees responded, "You're not under a lot of pressure here; it's a comfortable place to work. You do the best you can. Everyone understands we're all here to help each other, and to put out the best product we can" (Cruikshank, 1983: 86). In 1974 Matsushita Electric Company of American (MECA) had bought a 25-year-old Westinghouse heavy equipment plant near Toronto. Although 7 of the 12 competitors in the market then had left by 1983, MECA had the highest growth rate in its industry in Canada over the decade.

PLANNING AND CONTROL SYSTEMS

Matsushita had derived its planning system from Phillips (NV), the Dutch electronics giant. On New Year's day some 7,000 managers assembled to hear the chairman and president declare the basic policy for the year. This contained some key dimensions and figures, but more broadly, it presented the important elements to be emphasized in the company during the year. These strategic directions were later conveyed to all employees through the company magazine.

Every six months each division manager presented three plans. The first was a long-term (five-year) plan, updated as new technologies and environmental events occurred. The second was a two year (mid-term) plan which stated how the division would translate its long-term plan into such things as plant capacity or specific new products. Neither was extensively reviewed by topline management, but each was scrutinized closely by the product group side of the organization matrix (Pascale and Athos, 1981: 36).

Most attention was given to the Six Month Operating Plan. Here the division stated its monthly forecasts of sales, market share, profits, inventories, accounts receivable, capital expenditures, head count, quality targets etc. When variances occurred, the division manager and his controller had to be prepared to explain them. Particular attention was given to market share, return on sales, asset turnover, and actual versus budgeted costs, since these were considered to be under the division managers' control. Matsushita had rigorous standards for collections from its customers and payments to its suppliers—normally both less than 30 days—but the corporation could extend long-term credit to build sales channels, develop new markets, or meet special competitive needs.

Everyone understood that key variables would be tracked monthly and reviewed scrupulously. Figures were available within a few days after the end of each month and were widely shared in Matsushita's "open information system" (Pascale and Athos, 1981: 39). Performance was judged and rewards made on the basis of actual versus planned results. Reviews were performed by three groups: corporate line officers, corporate staff, and "peer review" by the heads of other divisions. Matsushita expected every division to be completely self-sustaining within five years and strongly resisted subsidizing losing divisions.

The 60 per cent of each division's profits paid to headquarters covered Product Group Management, R&D, Production Engineering, and an equity return. The remaining 40 per cent belonged to the divisions for facilities updating, production engineering, and new product development. But the funds were held at corporated and earned interest for the division. Matsushita expected each division to make sure its current and future product lines were healthy and did not use "portfolio" concepts favored in US companies.

Performance Reviews

Corporate headquarters was kept deliberately lean, with only 1.5 per cent of the company's total personnel there (excluding the Engineering Research Laboratories). However, each month the division manager spent several days at headquarters, going over each performance item and variance in detail with the Finance Office and with senior management. Key criteria were: the ability to stay on plan, and whether the division's management was "doing its best" and "as well as anyone in the market." If not, poor performers might be quickly transferred to other areas, "where their talents better fit circumstances" (Pascale and Athos, 1981: 37). In the quarterly, "peer review" process summary operating results were shared before all divisions. Divisions were grouped A, B, C, or D; the A (outstanding) groups made their presentations first, the D's last. Though individuals or divisions were not singled out for embarrassment, each group's relative performance was clear to all.

Matsushita's sales force and executives were monitored through exacting prospect lists and yield statistics, and the salesforce was backed by the largest advertising budget in Japan. Senior sales executives were expected to visit retail outlets regularly and to seek group level help when they needed it. To support its strong sales channels, Matsushita also operated an elaborate network of "customer clubs" to keep itself informed about its users' needs and to solicit ideas for improvement of products or services. Even top executives, like Mr. Matsushita and Mr. Yamashita (president), were expected to spend most of their time out of their offices and with customers. At various times both had gone into the field to solve specific crisis situations themselves. And in a 1970 recession, even assembly-line workers were shifted to door-to-door selling to cut inventories and to bring costs into line.

Overseas Operations

Overseas, Matsushita operated 46 production facilities in 27 countries and 34 sales companies in 28 countries. In addition to marketing through its own affiliates, Matsushita also produced for private label distribution of OEM's abroad. In addition, it had a series of licensing arrangements with foreign companies, notably RCA (nonexclusive) and Phillips (exclusive) with the latter owning a minority position in Matsushita Electric Company. Matsushita had a variety of ownership arrangements in various host countries from full ownership to joint ventures, but never had less than a 50 per cent board position.

Overseas units were almost always headed by a Japanese, and many middle managers were Japanese. Almost all managerial people—whether Japanese or not—were put through Matsushita's Overseas Training Center in Osaka, which offered specialized training in English, in overseas operations, in company policy, and in the company's value system. Because of scales of operation, tariff barriers, distances from Japan (etc.), the specific organization of each subsidiary might be quite different. For example, the Malaysian subsidiary had a small local market, was close to Japan, was heavily protected by tariffs, and had to deal with significant "local content" rules. The UK and Canadian plants were bound by few such rules, but served huge domestic markets. Because of the company's size, its stock was traded on several of the world's stock markets (including the US) and it often raised funds locally.

A Pragmatic Approach

Matsushita had a pragmatic approach to all problems. The heart of its style was "to get to the problem and fix it" (Pascale and Athos, 1981: 43). There was much latent conflict between its competing division, its matrix units, and in its "Venture Capital Funds," administered from the corporation's 60 per cent of profits. Divisions made proposals asking the Fund's managers to support new products or concepts which did not fit normal capital allocation processes well. Yet Matsushita executives expressed surprise when asked if there was much interdivisional fighting. They said, "We conflict without conflicting. Our underlying premise is that in life we make adjustments.... We presuppose that parties will fundamentally strive to pull together rather than push apart" (*ibid.*).

Employees were not viewed as "participating in management" but their opinions were sought. The company's books were open to the union, and the union was consulted directly as each division prepared its long-term and six-month plans. Matsushita encouraged long-term managerial continuity in its divisions with 5–7 years in key spots being common, but the Central Personnel group also tracked the top several performers in each division and consciously moved these people to openings as they occurred. Matsushita's maxim was "extraordinary results from ordinary people" (*ibid.*: 47). It did not make particular efforts to hire from the elite schools, and was willing to jump younger people over dozens of their seniors if their performance so warranted. Another maxim was, "If you make an honest mistake, the company will be very forgiving. Treat it as a training experience and learn from it. You will be severely criticized [a euphemism for dismissed] however if you deviate from the company's basic principles" (*ibid.*: 51).

COUNTRY PROFILE

HONG KONG*

HISTORY

The island of Hong Kong came under British rule as a result of the First Opium War (1839–40), and its status as a British colony was officially confirmed at the Treaty of Nanjing in 1842. In 1860, the Kowloon Peninsula was ceded, and in 1898, Britain was granted a rent-free 99-year lease on the more sizable New Territories and Outlying Islands. This lease will expire on July 1, 1997. Turmoil once again touched Hong Kong in 1941 when the Japanese occupied it during the Second World War. In 1949, the Communist Revolution spilled many refugees into Hong Kong.

In 1984, the Sino-British Joint Declaration was signed between Britain and the People's Republic of China. Its basic principle called for a "one country, two systems" approach. For the next 50 years, Hong Kong would retain the same political, economic, legal and social systems. However, there is some uncertainty whether China will honor its commitments, especially after the tragedy that occurred in Beijing in 1989. This uncertainty has caused for some of its citizens to leave to other countries and for some companies to move their home offices out of Hong Kong. The following figures are evidence of the "brain drain" that has occurred in Hong Kong:

Year	Emigration from Hong Kong
1980	22,000
1987	30,000

---

* This country profile was prepared by Pamela Schrader, Ann Young, Robert Yamamoto, and Wende Yamamoto of the University of Hawaii.

1988	45,800
1989	42,000
1990	62,000
1993	53,000

Of the 53,000 people that emigrated in 1993, 23,000 were in professional, technical and managerial positions. It is also estimated that 10 per cent of Hong Kong's 1.6 million families have documents enabling them to emigrate. Surveys in 1989 and 1990 indicated that at least half of Hong Kong's doctors were planning to emigrate and as a result were charging more for their services in order to save money for the move.

In 1990, the "mini-constitution" was promulgated by China after five years of deliberation. The Basic Law document established the political and legal structure after 1997. The Chinese have stated that the Basic Law could not be amended before 1997 to allow for more directly elected seats at the time of conversion. However, Hong Kong's governor, Chris Patten, called for an electoral reform in 1992. Patten's plan to give the people more influence on electing officials was strongly opposed by China. Following eight months of Sino-British negotiations which ended without agreement in November 1993, the Hong Kong government proceeded to adopt and implement the governor's proposals.

GEOGRAPHY

The territory of Hong Kong covers 415 square miles and some 235 islands. The primary islands include Hong Kong Island, Lantau Island, Lamma Island, and the New Territories, which have border with China. The territory consists of low-lying hills of which only 8 per cent suitable for crop production and roughly 15 per cent for development. This makes real estate expensive especially on Hong Kong Island and Kowloon where most of the population reside.

The country has few natural resources. Water is scarce and about 70 per cent of it is piped in from China. The rest is supplied from rainwater and reservoirs. The only agricultural products Hong Kong produces are vegetables, flowers and dairy products. It is less than 20 per cent self-sufficient with shortages of rice and wheat.

DEMOGRAPHICS/POPULATION

Hong Kong's population has increased by 13 per cent over the past decade. In 1993, the population was 6 million. It has one of the highest population densities in the world—about 14,400 persons per square mile. It is estimated that 98 per cent of the population is Chinese who have family origins in Guangdong in China. Roughly 60,000 are Europeans and Americans. About the same are Filipinos and 30,000 are Indians and Pakistanis.

LANGUAGE

Hong Kong has two official languages—Cantonese and English. Government and law documents are available in both languages. The most commonly spoken language is Cantonese. Mandarin should increase in importance as Hong Kong is integrated with China.

RELIGION

Taoism and Buddhism are the primary religions in Hong Kong, making up roughly 90 per cent of the practiced religions. About 10 per cent of the people practice Christianity. The philosophy of Confucianism is also prominent in Hong Kong.

THE ECONOMY

Since Hong Kong has few natural resources, it is dependent on imports for raw materials, food and fuel. As a result, Hong Kong is known as a trading center. Hong Kong offers many advantages such as its strategic location at the center of Asia and at the doorstep of China, its natural harbor, its excellent communication network and efficient transportation system, as well as its position as a financial center. Due to all the advantages that Hong Kong offers, it has developed into a hub for trade, finance, and business services in the Asian region.

The Hong Kong government does not have a specific industrial policy. The government has adopted a policy of non-intervention. This means keeping taxes low and not spending government revenues on anything that might interfere with industry and commerce. In other words, the Hong Kong government keeps to its *laissez-faire* traditions. The government's role is to provide a stable framework in order that commerce and industry can function efficiently and effectively with a minimum amount of interference. As a result, the government restricts itself mainly to providing essential support services, such as housing and education. But today, there are signs that this type of government policy is eroding—increasing amount of dollars are being allocated to major infrastructure programs such as Port and Airport Development Strategy (PADS).

In Hong Kong there is very little state ownership except for the postal system, water supply, harbor, airport, Mass Transport Railway, Kowloon-Canton Railroad, and Radio Television Hong Kong. The bulk of Hong Kong's economy is privately controlled. Many of the companies publicly listed on the stock exchange are not widely held. Only 25 per cent of the issued shares are required to be offered to the public. The remaining 75 per cent are usually retained by the original shareholders. Hong Kong's government policy is to allow private enterprise to play the dominant role in Hong Kong's development. As a result, Hong Kong is a free enterprise and free-trade economy.

The Hong Kong government welcomes foreign investment and does not discriminate between domestic and foreign businesses. In fact, Hong Kong considers itself a favorable place to do business due to its low taxes, hands-off policy, highly developed transport and telecommunications infrastructure, industrious workforce, and financial stability. In 1994, Hong Kong was ranked one of the top ten cities in the world for business. Hong Kong offers unique access to the fastest-growing economy and the biggest potential market—China. It is also has the most pro-business government in the region, corporate profit tax of 17.5 per cent, personal income tax rate of 15 per cent, no import tariffs except on tobacco, cosmetics, alcoholic drinks, methyl alcohol and some hydrocarbon oils, no capital gains tax, no withholding tax, and its close proximity to China. In addition, the businesspeople are very resourceful and can open doors in China through a network of contacts and distant relatives.

The annual GDP growth averaged 7.7 per cent between 1980–1988. A downturn occurred in 1989–1990 due to the Beijing massacre. From 1991–1994, the GDP has grown steadily, but 1995 and 1996 are forecasted to ease down to 4.5 per cent and 3.5 per cent, respectively. Since Hong Kong is becoming a more service oriented economy, in 1995, the government will also publish GNP figures. The GNP figure is projected to be greater than the GDP figures.

In 1994, Hong Kong experienced the largest trade deficit in history of US$10.4 billion and this is forecast to increase to US$12.7 billion in 1995, and to US$14.0 billion in 1996. Although Hong Kong has experienced a strong growth in total exports, it has not been able to accumulate a trade surplus. Hong Kong's main trading partner for exports is China followed by the US and then Germany. As for imports, China is still at the top of the list followed by Japan and Taiwan. China is a growing trading partner with Hong Kong. For re-exports, China is the main country of origin and the main destination point. The main commodity traded for exports was clothing and textiles, accounting for 39.4 per cent of the total in 1993. The second largest item was electronic components, which is still growing.

The garment industry remains the most important export industry for Hong Kong. The garment industry is the most active in shifting operations across the border to such places as Guangdong, a province in southern China. This move is to take advantage of lower operating costs such as lower land costs and greater supply of relatively cheap labor. China is Hong Kong's largest market for both re-exports, domestic exports and imports.

Hong Kong has become integrated with China, especially with southern China's coastal region and has become dependent on southern China's growing trade, especially since many manufacturing facilities were moved to places such as Guangdong. It is estimated that in 1993, Hong Kong employed approximately 3 million workers in Guangdong. In addition, Hong Kong has become a business and financial center indispensable to the economic development in mainland China and its neighbors to the south.

The Hong Kong government has no direct powers through which it can control prices, rates of inflation, money supply or other components of the economy. Since 1983, the Hong Kong dollar has been linked the US dollar at a fixed rate of HK$7.8:US$1, but has been allowed to trade closer to HK$7.75:US$1. As a result, it is safe to say that Hong Kong's monetary policy is effectively set in Washington because the local currency is pegged with the US dollar.

MANAGEMENT AND ORGANIZATIONAL BEHAVIOR PRACTICES

REGULATION OF BUSINESS

The Hong Kong government has traditionally adopted a policy of non-intervention toward regulation of the territory's business and industry, and this policy has contributed to

Hong Kong's attractiveness to foreign investors. While the degree of regulation in Hong Kong remains lower than that of many developed economies, the trend in recent years has been toward more regulation, particularly in the financial sector.

ORGANIZATIONAL STRUCTURE AND LEADERSHIP STYLES

Small business plays an important role in Hong Kong. In 1990, more than 80 per cent of companies employed fewer than ten people. The typical business organization in Hong Kong is family-owned and family-run. This is similar to the organization of a family dynasty. Influenced by Confucian thinking, the managerial style is described as hierarchical, paternalistic and autocratic. Business is typically run by the sole proprietor where control is centralized. The employees are expected to adhere to the authority of their supervisor and they remain relatively passive in the relationship.

Organizational charts generally depict sections, departments and division, except for one or two positions. The responsibilities and reporting relationships are described in collective terms. There are basically three different kinds of organization in Hong Kong:

1. Typical Chinese family businesses (which account for the majority of the organizations)
2. Locally based firms with a high profile
3. Multinational corporations

The large Chinese-owned organizations, called *hongs*, are loosely linked, diversified conglomerates controlled through a central holding company. The *hongs*, such as Jardine Matheson, are foreign-owned corporations, and have their own distinctive organizational structures.

SOCIALIZATION AND HUMAN RESOURCE DEVELOPMENT

The majority of Chinese companies in Hong Kong are family-owned corporations with strong centralized control. The goal of a traditional Chinese corporation is to secure the long-term financial stability of the family. Chinese business draws on the family for its capital and human resources and is concerned less with profit than with establishing and securing family assets, which in turn are passed on from one generation to the next. Family unity and prosperity, under the direction of the patriarch (and in some cases the matriarch), is the backbone of the Chinese entrepreneurial system.

In recruitment decisions, it is likely that a family member would be hired over a more qualified outsider. Loyalty and trustworthiness are critical traits sought by Hong Kong employers. Since the typical organization is built around the family structure, it is not surprising that it is difficult for a foreigner, or *gweilo* to enter. It is best to be introduced by a family member to the organization or the outsider would be very thoroughly scrutinized. In addition to a tendency toward nepotism, Chinese companies gather a cadre of loyal employees who function as honorary family members. Through their behavior, these employees demonstrate fidelity to the company, and the leaders in turn develop a paternal obligation to them. Business in general, is based on mutually supportive relationships with suppliers of goods and services.

There is some indication that the younger generation entrepreneurs are moving toward a more contemporary management model, which encourages growth and openness to outsiders to expand the business. However, most Chinese companies still have the incentives to remain small, familial organizations. The problem of staff turnover is a matter of serious concern to many companies in Hong Kong. Unlike other Asian countries where lifetime employment is valued, Hong Kong employees continue to be on the lookout for better opportunities. Therefore, every business must focus on recruiting the best staff and developing reward systems to keep them.

Training and development are given high regard in Hong Kong. This is what helps Hong Kong employees obtain the skills that set them apart from employees of other areas of southeast Asia. In 1960, the Hong Kong Management Association was established with the goal of improving the effectiveness and efficiency of management in Hong Kong. The organization has been successful in numerous activities such as setting up management training courses, providing consulting services and producing a bi-monthly journal.

PLANNING AND DECISION MAKING

As a collectivist culture, Hong Kong organizations look at emphasizing group harmony and loyalty. In business negotiations, decision making is much more consultative than in Western cultures. A final decision may not be made until discussions with all persons concerned have been evaluated. A study conducted on the decision making behavior of Hong Kong managers reflected that they are required to accommodate social expectations as they have a high external locus of control. In comparison, managers from the United States make decisions much more quickly and are willing to take on more risks.

Additionally, status and rank is important in Hong Kong's highly structured society. Executives use "top down" communication style where suggestion is understood as direction. Deference is always expected when dealing with the leadership of these companies; informal behavior is inappropriate. Decisions must be addressed to the proper authority or a higher level manager may be offended. In comparison with other Asian collectivist cultures, however, decision making is more rapid due to the highly volatile market in Hong Kong. Therefore, the cultural value of group participation may be outweighed by the demands of the business environment.

OFFICE RELATIONSHIPS

Hong Kong's educational system has a strong impact on office behavior. Education generally follows the traditional Chinese style which relies heavily on memorization and repetition. This teaching style limits students' creativity and affects interpersonal relationships. In the classroom, the teacher-student relationship is one of great respect for the teacher. Teachers are not openly questioned or challenged. Since information is accepted uncritically, creativity is not valued and students are dependent on the teachers as their major source of information.

Transposed into the work environment, these qualities result in a workplace that can be characterized as an uncritical abdication of responsibility to higher authorities. Lower ranking employees and low-level managers demand clear directives and specific instructions from their supervisors. Subordinates do not question their supervisors, much less confront them.

Chinese exposed to Western education, however, tend to be inclined to take initiative, assume responsibility, and be more direct. There is, and always has been, a strong work ethic among the Chinese. Partly because of their cultural heritage and partly because of the needs of a predominantly refugee community, the Hong Kong Cantonese are a strong and hardworking people. Absenteeism is negligible, and there is no tradition of unionism which would polarize industrial disputes and create strikes.

Women managers are probably more readily accepted in the business environment in Hong Kong than elsewhere in Asia because of Hong Kong's long exposure to more egalitarian Western views, and also because of the presence of large numbers of well-educated women. While women may not be accepted as equals because of the overriding Confucian ethic which accords men a superior position, Hong Kong women are professional equals and are judged according to their skills and expertise.

Working Conditions/Wages and Salaries

Fairly stringent employment-rights laws protect nonmanagerial staff in Hong Kong, guaranteeing statutory holidays with pay, sick leave, sickness allowance, paid maternity leave, rest days, and seven days' annual leave. There is no statutory minimum wage in Hong Kong; supply and demand determine wage levels. The lone exception is the minimum wage paid to foreign domestic help, which is set by the Hong Kong government.

Women and young children are protected by many regulations. Benefits may also include free medical treatment, subsidized meals, a good-attendance bonus, and transportation to and from work. In many cases, a Lunar New Year bonus, which is equal to a month's wages, is included in a benefits package.

Most semi-skilled and unskilled workers in the manufacturing industries are piece-rated, although daily rates of pay are also common. Monthly-rated industrial workers are usually employed in skilled trades or in technical, supervisory, clerical, and secretarial capacities. However, monthly rates of pay are most common for workers in the nonmanufacturing sectors. Men and women receive the same rates for piecework, but women are generally paid less when working on a time basis. Wages are customarily paid weekly or monthly. In September 1990, 75 per cent of manual workers engaged in manufacturing industries received daily wage rates (including fringe benefits) of HK$142 or more, and 25 per cent received HK$216 or more.

Executive and professional pay scales vary widely, and it is not possible to give a meaningful average. However, salaries at this level are at least as high as those attainable in the major capitals of the world. In addition, it is normal for companies to provide their executive-level staff with generous fringe benefits. Total salary packages paid to expatriate and local staff continue to differ significantly. However, the main difference now lies in the noncash fringe benefits such as housing. There is very little difference in actual cash salary levels.

Motivation, Discipline and Enforcement

Hong Kong employees are highly motivated and upwardly mobile. In low uncertainty-avoidance countries, high job mobility is typical. Money and salary are key motivators in employment. Employees have a strong belief in working hard and sacrificing to get ahead. There is a belief in Chinese culture that working hard is for the good of the family, again inspired by Confucian thinking. However, there is a surprising difference between the mainland and the Hong Kong Chinese, which is the Hong Kong employee's strong proclivity to spend. The strong "work" ethic is matched by a very strong "play" ethic. The Hong Kong Chinese enjoy the fine things of life and work hard to be able to afford them. This attitude may be attributable to the underlying lack of confidence in the future of the country beyond 1997.

LABOR RELATIONS

EMPLOYER-EMPLOYEE RELATIONS. Since the 1920s Hong Kong has had a workplace inspection policy as well as laws to maintain safety standards, health, and workers' compensation. Its reputation for implementing and enforcing the International Labor Organization Conventions is also outstanding. The Commissioner for Labor is the principal adviser to the government on labor matters. Labor legislation is initiated in the Labor Department, which also ensures that Hong Kong's obligations under international labor conventions are observed. The Labor Tribunal, which is part of the judiciary, provides a quick, simple and inexpensive method of settling claims arising from contracts of employment and the provisions of the Employment Ordinance, which is applicable to all employees of Hong Kong.

UNIONS. There is no strong trade union movement in Hong Kong. The unions that have been set up are more like "self-help" groups and not at all militant. Trade unions in Hong Kong have the legal status of corporate bodies through a system of registration with the Registrar of Trade Unions under the Trade Unions Ordinance. Once registered, unions enjoy immunity from certain civil suits. At the end of 1990, 452 employees' unions were registered. About one-third of these are either affiliated or associated with one of the two local federations that support opposing political groups. Divergent loyalties have prevented the unions from merging into effective organizations.

Industrial disputes are not a major problem in Hong Kong, and production is seldom interrupted. Membership in a trade union is not obligatory, however, every employee has the right to become a member of a trade union. At end-1990 union membership stood at 439,500, which represents only about 15 per cent of the total labor force. Overall, there has been little labor conflict. Thus, although trade unions are active in Hong Kong, they have not gained the same power as they have in most Western countries. The unions and employers do not enter into binding contracts and settlements as in some other developing countries, and no sanctions can be brought against the unions.

BUSINESS HOURS

The business offices of most Western enterprises, as well as the larger Chinese business offices, banks and government departments, are typically open from 9:00 a.m. to 5:00 p.m. on weekdays, with a break for lunch between 1:00 p.m. and 2:00 p.m. On Saturdays, the hours are from 9:00 a.m. to 12:30 p.m. Retail stores are generally open every day of the year, with the exception of the first two days of the Chinese New Year. Typical store hours are from 10:00 a.m. to 8:00 p.m.

Public Holidays

Sundays are observed as holidays by the government and by nearly all business offices. Also observed, are seventeen public holidays, eleven of which are statutory, requiring employers to give the day off with pay.

Socio-Cultural Values

Traditional Values and Beliefs

Confucian thought has been a pervasive influence on the Chinese for over 2,000 years, and despite the radically different political and economic make-up between mainland China and Hong Kong, the basic values of mainland Chinese living under Communist rule are very similar to those of the Chinese living in Hong Kong. There are four key cultural tenets attributable to Confucianism and manifested by the Chinese in a wide variety of contexts, including business, social and family relationships. Underlying each of these tenets is the Confucian imperative of working to achieve harmony. The first tenet is respect for hierarchy and age. For centuries, the Chinese have been socialized to respect authority. A hierarchical system is omnipresent in Chinese cultures, where officials typically desire to maintain a "power distance" between themselves and subordinates. Officials have no problem with making distinctions between themselves and the rank and file.

The second major tenet is group orientation. In Hong Kong, group needs are satisfied ahead of individual needs. The Chinese see themselves as part of family, school, work and government units.

The third tenet is commonly known as the preservation of face, and is based on the idea that harmony lies in the maintenance of an individual's "face" or one's dignity, self-respect, and prestige. Social and business interactions are conducted in a manner conducive to the preservation of face.

The fourth Confucian tenet is *guanxi*. The term refers to a special relationship, or trust between two persons (not groups) and can best be understood as friendship wherein there exists an unspoken agreement that favors will be performed by either side without question.

Social Life

The people of Hong Kong have traditionally had little leisure time, given that many work a six-day week. The trend today, however, is toward a shorter work week, which has increased the amount of leisure time available. Since the majority of people live in a dense, high-rise environment, outdoor activities are popular. Given the population density, Hong Kong's parks and beaches are extremely crowded on weekends and holidays. There is great enthusiasm for horse racing, soccer, rugby, golf, tennis, basketball, and watersports, as well as for indoor sports such as squash and bowling.

Most expatriates in Hong Kong belong to one or more of the social and sporting clubs in the territory. Many of the more popular clubs have waiting lists for membership, creating a waiting period from a few months to several years from the time of application to acceptance. Membership alone may cost over US$100,000 plus monthly dues. Such social and sporting clubs are considered good settings for business meetings. Dining out is very popular, as Hong Kong boasts a large number of restaurants offering many types of cuisine. Given the relatively small living accommodations, most entertaining is done outside the home in private clubs or restaurants.

SUPERSTITIONS, RITUALS AND CEREMONIES

Among the hallmarks of Chinese life is the Chinese tendency toward superstitious belief. Belief in superstition pervades even the highly educated and Christian segments of the Hong Kong population, and may be attributed to an inner belief in natural harmony, based on the polar forces of *yin* and *yang*, as well as the energy forces of nature called *fung shui* (literally "wind and water").

Fung shui is the practice of geomancy, which is based on the belief that luck is related to the balancing of the forces of heaven and earth, with the forces within individuals and families. It is the belief that there is a continual and ever-present relationship between the earth and the cosmos, and that every spot on earth houses either a positive or negative spirit. That spirit has power to influence and control whatever exists or lives at that location. *Fung shui* affects every aspect of life—from the location of offices and placement of furnishings, to the choice of a license plate number. People consult *fung shui* experts for all types of decisions, including the location of doors to a building, and the selection of opening dates for new businesses. The consequence of poor *fung shui* is bad luck, and Hong Kong is replete with stories about the influence of *fung shui*. Thus, even those who don't fully believe in the superstition will often follow it anyway, just to be safe.

During the year, there are many Chinese festivals celebrated, such as the Chinese New Year, and the Mid-Autumn Festival. Hong Kong shuts down almost completely for three days, particularly for the Chinese New Year. Besides these festivals, Christmas, Easter, and other Western holidays are also celebrated in Hong Kong.

PROTOCOL

In the business world, appointments need to be arranged in advance. Hong Kong businessmen, like their Chinese counterparts, traditionally use an intermediary to introduce possible new venture partners and work as a go-between where parties are unfamiliar with each other. Intermediaries are used primarily because the Chinese prefer to deal directly with someone they know, have a long-standing relationship with, and can trust. When dealing with an unfamiliar person or organization, the Chinese will often project an attitude of disinterest. The Chinese consider a negative response impolite and would rather ignore a request or invitation from an unfamiliar party than respond negatively.

Business discussions are often held during meals, mostly at lunch, and are usually paid for by the host. Punctuality is important and preparations for meetings are critical. Business cards are exchanged at the first meeting, thus, as a practical and polite gesture, it is important for foreigners to have business cards printed in Chinese on one side.

Names and proper decorum in addressing people are critical in Hong Kong, as they are in Chinese society. Formal introductions by titles are important. People address each other by last name and by Mr., Dr., Mrs. or Miss. A slight bow is customary, although hand shaking is common for men and women in business settings.

Dress is important to the Hong Kong Chinese as a statement of respect, and strong impressions are made based on the style and appropriateness of one's attire at a business meeting. People tend to dress conservatively and formally. Dark suits with subtle patterns and conventional ties are recommended for men, and blouses and dresses for women.

Gift giving is widely used by the Chinese to fulfill a variety of social obligations, like showing appreciation, and as payouts, or souvenirs. Gifts associated with the individual's business organization or country are proper. Flowers, however, are not considered appropriate as they are associated with funerals. Foreigners should recall that Hong Kong citizens are big importers of consumer goods and have sophisticated tastes. Blue and white colors in packaging, promotional materials, and gift wrapping are associated with mourning. Red, gold, and green are popular colors.

When conversing with Hong Kong citizens, popular topics of conversation are business, shopping, and the cost of living, especially in comparison with the individual's country. Personal and direct questions (e.g., about salary and marital status), which are often asked by the Chinese, are considered appropriate in Hong Kong, and are intended as a sign of genuine and friendly interest.

EDUCATION

The Hong Kong community places a very high value on education, both as a key to personal advancement and as a major factor in social stability and economic development. This is reflected not only in the public resources allocated to education (no other program takes a larger share of the government budget), but is evident in the contributions made by individuals to schools, advisory boards, executive authorities and governing bodies of educational institutions.

In the 1970s, universal primary education (i.e., three years of compulsory secondary education) was introduced. The Hong Kong Department of Education thus offers free schooling for all children up to age fifteen—from grades 1 through 6 and junior secondary education from grades 7 through 9 (or as they are referred to in Hong Kong, Forms I through III). Students at the end of their Form III year are assessed to qualify for places, most of which are subsidized, in senior secondary classes. The government is attempting to offer subsidized places for senior secondary education to about 85 per cent of the 15-year-olds. Today, men and women are considerably better educated than their parents. Approximately one-fourth of Hong Kong's population is enrolled in schools, colleges or other educational institutions.

Elementary and secondary education for English-speaking children is provided by a number of private schools and by the English Schools Foundation, which runs several schools in the territory. The English Schools Foundation curriculum is structured according to the English system. Other private schools cater to children of American, Canadian, Japanese, French, and German families and offer teaching streams that follow the curriculum set in those countries. The tuition fees charged by these private schools vary considerably. Hong Kong schools are overcrowded. "Bi-sessionalism," by which students work in shifts and where two schools essentially occupy one building, is a common practice. To overcome the problem and to meet its target, the government has had to purchase places in private schools.

Vocational and industrial training, as well as technical education are very popular in Hong Kong. Most people attend different kinds of classes in order to enrich their knowledge for job promotion opportunities since competition among colleagues is extremely high. College-level education is not free but is heavily subsidized by the government and student financing is made available to means-tested applicants. Most degrees awarded by Hong Kong universities and polytechnics are recognized internationally. There are three universities, and two polytechnics in Hong Kong with limited places. Each year, thousands of high school graduates must fight for these. Most of them must look for universities abroad, such as in the United States, Canada, Britain and Australia.

THE FUTURE OF HONG KONG

As 1997 approaches, many theories have been formulated regarding the future of Hong Kong. The following are the three most widely held theories:

(i) **DE FACTO INDEPENDENCE.** Basically, the people of Hong Kong will ignore China and try to carry on business as usual. The approach of "one country, two systems" would be taken to the extreme. Hong Kong would continue to be the best point of entry to the Chinese market. Those who fled before 1997 would return.

(ii) **HONG KONG AND CHINA WOULD CONVERGE IN A VERY RATIONAL WAY.** China will not scare off potential investments. China will remain on its path of economic reforms and will learn from Hong Kong the best ways to live in the international market economy.

(iii) **HONG KONG WILL SLOW TO CHINA'S PACE.** Investments will slow as people continue to emigrate from Hong Kong because of uncertainty of the future. China is not overly concerned with this scenario because it considers it the price that must be paid for the stability of China.

These theories may be the extreme scenarios. A more likely scenario would be a combination of several factors. Regardless of the theories proposed, there are several key variables that will shape the future of Hong Kong and China:

(i) **LEVEL OF EMIGRATION.** The problem is not so much the number, but the quality of those that leave. As a result, inflation would be a natural result of people demanding more wages to stay on or to come in to replace those who have left.

(ii) **RATE OF INVESTMENTS FROM INSIDE AND OUTSIDE HONG KONG.** As confidence fades, so does the willingness to pump money into the country. If this happens, slowed economic growth would be the result.

(iii) **CHANGES TO THE LEGAL SYSTEM.** Hong Kong is governed by English law, modified to suit local conditions. Any abrupt changes to the British-style legal system would drastically disrupt Hong Kong's earnings and investment climate.

(iv) **RELIGION.** In Hong Kong there is total freedom of religion. China has a history of trying to control religion by imprisoning or expelling religious leaders who become too outspoken, especially missionaries.

(v) **CULTURAL DIFFERENCES.** Hong Kong is known for its free intellectual atmosphere and casual social attitudes. Some of these are bound to spill over to mainland China, especially in Guangdong and the Fujian provinces, which lie closest to Hong Kong.

(vi) **PERSONAL FREEDOMS.** The Hong Kong people fear for their loss of personal freedoms such as speech, the press, foreign travel and personal belief and morality. However, Peking has promised not to tamper with Hong Kong's "way of life". As the people of mainland China become exposed to these freedoms, they may strengthen their demands for them.

(vii) **CHINESE ECONOMIC REFORMS.** The degree of commitment that China has to its economic reforms will influence the pace of the economies for both China and Hong Kong.

(viii) **CORRUPTION.** If the widespread problem of corruption in China is allowed to spread into Hong Kong, the inefficiencies caused by corruption could greatly slow down the Hong Kong economy.

The Chinese government has promised that the "way of life" of the people of Hong Kong will not be changed after 1997, but the fact remains that no present-day government of China can foretell or guarantee what its successors will do. However, the economic relationship between the two is so significant that China's leaders, present and future, would be foolish to jeopardize it.

SUGGESTED FURTHER READINGS

Chen, Min and Winston Pan, *Understanding the Process of Doing Business in China, Taiwan and Hong Kong,* Lewiston, NY: Edwin Mellen Press, 1993.
Cheng, Leonard K., Strategies for Rapid Economic Development: The case of Hong Kong, *Contemporary Economic Policy*, January 1995, pp. 28–36.
Economist Intelligence Unit (UK), *Country Profile—Hong Kong, Macau, 1994–95*, 1995.
―――――, *Country Report—Hong Kong, Macau, 1st Quarter 1995*, 1995.
Emerging Market Indicators, *Economist*, Vol. 334, February 11, 1995, p. 100.
Japan Times Weekly, National Edition, February 6–12, 1995, p. 17.

Lanier, Alison R., *Update Hong Kong,* Yarmouth, ME: Intercultural Press, 1992.

Lethbridge, David G., *The Business Environment in Hong Kong,* Hong Kong: Oxford University Press, 1993.

Levin, Mike, Business before Politics, *Asian Business,* November 1993, pp. 30–41.

Price Waterhouse, *Doing Business in Hong Kong*, New York, 1992.

Prospering in Sea of Change, *Asian Business,* November 1994, pp. 28–41.

Ralston, David A., David J. Gustafson, Priscilla M. Elsass, Fanny Cheung, and Robert H. Terpstra, Eastern Values: A comparison of managers in the United States, Hong Kong, and the People's Republic of China, *Journal of Applied Psychology*, October 1992, pp. 664–671.

Ralston, David A., Robert A. Giacalone, Robert H. Terpstra, Ethical Perceptions of Organizational Politics: A comparative evaluation of American and Hong Kong managers, *Journal of Business Ethics,* December 1994, pp. 989–999.

Segal, Gerald, *The Fate of Hong Kong,* New York: St. Martin's Press, 1993.

The World's Best Cities for Business, *Fortune,* November 14, 1994, pp. 114–124.

US Department of State, *Background Notes: Hong Kong*, Washington, DC, September 1994.

Whitley, Richard D., The Social Construction of Business Systems in East Asia, *Organization Studies,* December 1, 1991, pp. 1–28.

Will, Huge, *Hong Kong 1993,* Hong Kong: H. Myers, 1993.

CASE FIVE

JARDINE MATHESON HOLDINGS LIMITED[*]

Jardine Matheson Holdings Limited ("Jardines") is one of the giant *hongs* of Hong Kong, with a market capitalization of some US$6 billion. In fact, in terms of venerability, it could be thought of as *the* Hong Kong *hong*. It was founded in Canton as a partnership in 1832 to engage in import and export trading and distribution and servicing operations. It came to Hong Kong in 1841, the year that Britain took possession of the colony.

Note that the "Hong" in Hong Kong is the Chinese character which means fragrant: Hong Kong means "fragrant harbor."

The "hong" that describes Jardines is the one that means business firm.

The two hongs sound alike, mean different things, but go together like, well, rice and chopsticks.

The Jardine hong is one of several hongs in Hong Kong. These hongs are companies that might also be called "conglomerates" if that word had not achieved such a generally negative connotation in the US in the recent past: a firm gobbling up this, gobbling up that, trying to digest the indigestible and frequently failing; and then selling off non-core pieces at a loss to return to its own basic nature.

By contrast, the hongs of Hong Kong, beginning usually as trading companies, have pieces that generally fit together well (and if not, they sell pieces to each other), enabling each hong to reach out for international opportunities (rather than seeing itself limited by the small (6 million), but profitable Hong Kong market) while enjoying the fruits of being

---

[*] This case was prepared by Neil Holbert, then Senior Lecturer in the Department of Marketing, Chinese University of Hong Kong. Currently, he is the Assistant Professor of Marketing, The American College in London.

Case Five

rooted in a British colony which is the epitome of free-enterprise capitalism: the government goes beyond laissez-faire all the way to positive non-intervention.

In the following section, we will set forth the structure of Jardines (banking, retailing, auto sales, securities, hotels, etc.), but to know the background, it would suffice to look briefly at three *other* leading Hong Kong hongs: Hutchison Whampoa, Swire Pacific, and Wharf Holdings. Looking at these three we will see that Hutchison controls (among other things) Park'N Shop Supermarkets and Hong Kong International Terminals. Wharf has in its portfolio the Star Ferry, Hong Kong Tramways, the Cross-Harbour Tunnel Company, the Hong Kong School of Motoring, and Modern Terminals. Swire has interests in Cathay Pacific Airways; Dragonair Hong Kong; Modern Terminals (same as Wharf, as already noted); Pacific Place Mall; Marathon Sports; the Hong Kong franchise rights for Reebok, Ellesse, Coca Cola, Kentucky Fried Chicken; and much more. So what of *our* hong, Jardines? Its cross-holdings have always been a matter of interest and fascination, and as recently as 1986, Jardines unveiled a major reorganization centering on Jardine Strategic Holdings, while not diluting the overall control of the Keswick family. The structure of Jardines is outlined in Exhibits 1, 2, and 3.

As might be guessed, Jardines has an eventful history. It was founded in Canton in 1832

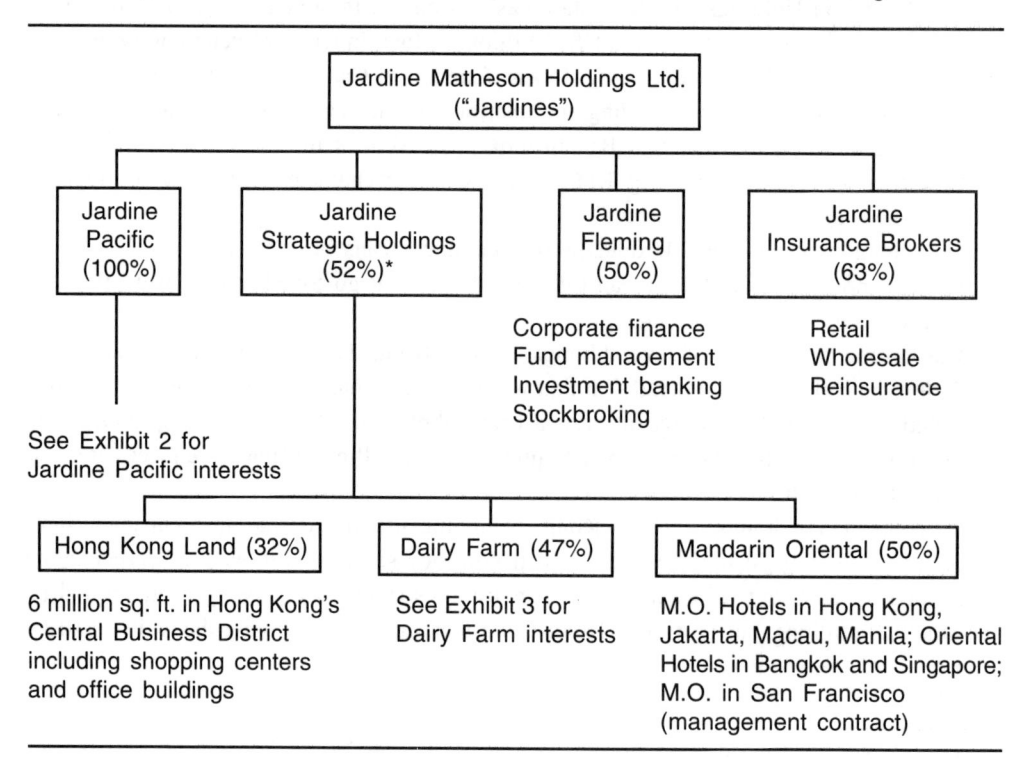

Exhibit 1 Jardines: A Skeleton of the Structure of the Hong

```
                    Jardine Matheson Holdings Ltd.
                              ("Jardines")
    ┌──────────────┬──────────────────┬──────────────┬──────────────┐
  Jardine        Jardine            Jardine        Jardine
  Pacific        Strategic Holdings Fleming        Insurance Brokers
  (100%)         (52%)*             (50%)          (63%)

                                    Corporate finance   Retail
                                    Fund management    Wholesale
                                    Investment banking Reinsurance
                                    Stockbroking
See Exhibit 2 for
Jardine Pacific interests

    ┌──────────────────┬──────────────────┬──────────────────┐
  Hong Kong Land (32%)  Dairy Farm (47%)   Mandarin Oriental (50%)

  6 million sq. ft. in Hong Kong's   See Exhibit 3 for    M.O. Hotels in Hong Kong,
  Central Business District         Dairy Farm interests Jakarta, Macau, Manila; Oriental
  including shopping centers                             Hotels in Bangkok and Singapore;
  and office buildings                                   M.O. in San Francisco
                                                         (management contract)
```

Note: Jardine Strategic Holdings also holds 35 per cent of Jardine Matheson Holdings Ltd.

Exhibit 2 Selected Interests of Jardine Pacific

Caterpillar (Heavy construction and earth-moving equipment)
Chubb Hong Kong (Insurance)
Gammon Construction
Hong Kong Air Cargo Terminals
Hong Kong Air Terminal Services
IKEA (Hong Kong franchisee)
Jardine Airport Services
Jardine Engineering
Jardine International Motor Holdings (Sole Mercedes-Benz distribution in Hong Kong)
Jardine Marketing Services
Jardine Office Systems
Jardine Securicor (Armored cars)
The Optical Shop
Pizza Hut (Hong Kong and Taiwan franchisee)
Schindler (Elevators)
Sizzler (Australia)
Taco Bell (Mexican-style fast-food, Hawaii franchisee)

Exhibit 3 Selected Interests of Dairy Farm

Franklins (Australia)
Kwik Save (United Kingdom)
Mannings (Drug stores)
Maxim's (Restaurants, cake shops)
7-Eleven (Hong Kong franchisee)
Simago (Retail, Spain)
Wellcome Supermarkets (Hong Kong, Taiwan)
Woolworths (New Zealand)

and moved its headquarters to Hong Kong in 1841. The hong—now employing 140,000 people on five continents—became listed in 1961, and four other units joined in subsequent years: Jardine Fleming in 1970, Jardine Insurance Brokers in 1973, Jardine Strategic Holdings in 1986, and Jardine Pacific in 1989. More is said about the various constituent parts in the following paragraphs.

In Asia, relationships with governments are typically as important as anything else in understanding the course of a company, for governments—except Hong Kong, of course—either control, exhort, or set the agenda for business ... or try to. Such is the story of Jardines and China.

In 1984, the United Kingdom and China were winding up their long negotiations about the return of Hong Kong to China in 1997. Months before the signing of the Joint Declaration, establishing Hong Kong's right to maintain capitalism till 2047 as a Special Administrative Region under a "one country, two systems" formula Jardines redomiciled to Bermuda— the first hong to do so, changing its name from Jardine, Matheson & Company, Limited, to Jardine Matheson Holdings Limited, a new holding company.

Whatever words and whatever construction one could put on this, it was clear to China (and probably correctly so), that this was a vote of worry (at least) about the promised post-1997 Hong Kong. Jardines could say (as the Hong Kong and Shanghai Banking Corporation would say almost ten years later) that the action wasn't a vote of "no confidence," but rather a prudent move to best promote stockholders' interests.

Yet one can see that China wouldn't necessarily see it that way. China further reacted in 1992 by bringing up once again what one would have thought had been long since buried: Jardines' origins as one of the traders of opium, bringing this curse (as China saw it) to China for 30 pieces (or more) of silver. Nonetheless, as far back as 1987, Jardines (through Jardine Fleming) unveiled a plan for an investment company (with capital of US$23 million) to seek out commercial opportunities in, or associated with, China. And today, China, with its legendary potential, plays a large role in the doings of the hong.

In 1992 too, after much wrangling, Jardines' primary listing was transferred to the London Stock Exchange, and a secondary listing was granted on the Hong Kong Stock Exchange.

The webs—political, international, and familial—continue to be spun. The Keswick family has tightened its hold, the hong has continued to seek haven in its Bermuda domicile if the 1997 handover becomes soured, and while it remains very much a Hong Kong entity, it also is looking to London while remembering that Beijing is coming.

> *Minority shareholders of the Jardine group of companies will now find it difficult to benefit from a takeover bid after new statutory provisions became law earlier this month within the Bermuda Takeover Code.*
>
> *Jardine, which shifted its corporate domicile to Bermuda in 1984, has managed to graft the British Code on Takeovers and Mergers into Bermuda Law. This code is far more strict than Hong Kong's takeover and merger rules.*
>
> *As a result, the Keswick family, which controls the Jardine group despite owning only an estimated nine per cent of Jardine Matheson, has firmer control over the business empire.*
>
> *While Jardine will remain bound by the Hong Kong takeover code, it now has the ability to break away from the territory's regulatory authorities in the future and still have a regime in place to protect the interests of shareholders.*
>
> *The Bermuda Jardine Matheson Holdings Ltd Consolidation and Amendment Act 1988 was amended to incorporate the Bermuda Takeover Code, which will come into force on July 1, 1994.*
>
> *In a circular sent to shareholders recently, Jardine chairman Simon Keswick diplomatically described the Bermuda Takeover Code as "a natural progression: of the process begun in the 1980s in conforming to the rules to which the company is subject.*
>
> *"Your board does not believe that the implementation of the Bermuda Takeover Code will have any significant effect on the business of the company, but will instead provide statutory protection for the company's shareholders in takeover and related situations," he said.*

Jardine Matheson Holdings Limited

However, Jardine's strategic moves over the past decade to shift its primary listing to London and position itself in Bermuda to fall under the auspices of the UK code are all part of a concerted effort to remove all legal ties with Hong Kong.

It also applies not-so-subtle pressure on Hong Kong's regulatory authorities to move closer to the adoption of British rules when it comes to dealing with companies whose primary listing is in London....

Looking briefly at the four major constituents of the hong, we may begin with the biggest (half of Jardines' profits in 1992): *Jardine Pacific* (see Exhibits 1, 2, and 4).

Exhibit 4 Segmental Analysis: Profits after Taxes and Outside Interests

	Profits in US$ billions					Percentage				
	1988	1989	1990	1991	1992	1988	1989	1990	1991	1992
By Business										
Jardine Pacific	70	86	93	130	159	51	44	40	48	50
Jardine Strategic	40	60	84	82	91	29	31	36	30	29
H.K. Land	23	33	47	50	50	17	17	20	18	16
Dairy Farm	18	31	37	35	43	13	16	16	13	14
Mandarin Oriental	8	12	17	10	10	6	6	7	4	3
Jardine Fleming	22	33	37	42	38	16	17	16	16	12
Jardine Insurance Brokers	12	16	20	22	12	9	8	9	8	4
Total	138	195	230	271	317	100	100	100	100	100
By Geographic Area										
Hong Kong and China	91	105	133	169	216	66	54	58	62	68
North America	17	16	12	26	30	12	8	5	10	9
Europe and Middle East		16	9	1	24		8	4		8
Southeast Asia	8	18	13	26	22	6	9	5	10	7
Australasia	4	10	12	9	14	3	5	5	3	5
Northwest Asia (including Japan)	18	31	52	40	11	13	16	23	15	3
Total	138	195	230	271	317	100	100	100	100	100

Notes:
1. Under the Business rubric, the sum of the four underlined components does not add to total due to balancing item "Data for Head Office and Other Interests" not being shown.
2. The sum of the three listed components of Jardine Strategic Holdings does not add up to total due to balancing item "Term Loans and Finance Charges" not being shown.
3. Under the Geographic rubric, sums may not always add to total due to rounding off.

Jardine Pacific is 100 per cent owned by Jardine Matheson Holdings, and it was formed in 1989 to hold the hong's Asia-Pacific trading and service operations. Its turnover is about

US$2 billion, and its employees number about 55,000. It operates throughout Asia, Australia, New Zealand, the US, and the UK. Hong Kong is still the largest contributor to Jardine Pacific's turnover and profit.

There is seemingly no end to the possibilities for expansion in Asia-Pacific, long *the* growth region of the world. For example, in May 1993, Jardine Pacific announced plans to set up jointly with Pepsico (Pizza Hut's name owner) a chain of Pizza Hut restaurants in China in the provinces of Guangdong, just north of Hong Kong and one of the great recent economic engines of the world, and its much less developed western neighbor, Guangxi.

The largest single contributor to Jardine Pacific profits is its auto subsidiary, *Jardine International Motor Holdings,* which sells Mercedes-Benz cars. Unlikely as it frequently seems to many, Mercedes sells very well in China. In 1992, 1200 Mercedes cars were sold there, up from just a handful only a few years ago. However, car sales in China are always subject to political as well as economic considerations, and the recent government-engineered cooldown there (to seek to contain inflation) may produce sluggish results in the short term.

The trading arm of Jardine Pacific was negatively affected in 1992 by the recession in Japan, with the drop in sales of wines and spirits. This same glum Japan picture continued into 1993.

> *Jardine Pacific, the main profit contributor to the Jardine Group, is still being affected by the Japanese recession and will not match last year's earnings growth, says Jardine managing director Anthony Nightingale.*
>
> *Commenting on this year's performance, Nightingale said: "It will be a significantly less strong year."*
>
> *"There will be continued negative effect on earnings from Japan."*
>
> *He said this would lead to significant job losses in the Japan consumer goods division and increased pressure on margins.*
>
> *"I don't think Japan will pull out of its recession for at least another year," and, therefore, Jardine Pacific is "anticipating another tough year in 1994".*
>
> *Nightingale declined to put a figure on the slowed earnings growth, but said continued sluggish performance in Japan meant the company would initiate a major restructuring of its consumer goods division in that country.*
>
> *"There will be some downsizing and margin improvement. This will have a significant impact," he said.*[2]

Delays in building projects in Thailand and Malaysia have caused problems for Jardine Pacific's engineering arm, Schindler (elevators); and Hawaii's downturn has hurt Jardine Pacific's Caterpillar (heavy construction and earth-moving equipment) businesses. But its building arm, Gammon Construction, has been building the 32-storey tower addition to Hong Kong's Peninsula Hotel.

Jardine Pacific's presence is also visible in personal computers, a huge business in technomanic Hong Kong. In early 1992, Jardine Pacific's Jardine Office Systems division purchased Hong Kong's top personal computer distributor ABA Office Automation Company, raising Jardine Pacific's share of this market to 50 per cent. Among the names it will handle are IBM and Apple. Jardine Pacific believes that, while computer products are per se, becoming more and more similar to each other, service facilities will be an important plus for the new operation, and that the brand names they market will become even more affordable.

In its expansion drive, Jardine Pacific's philosophy is to acquire only healthy, well established companies; develop business through joint ventures; and transplant successful business concepts from one country to another.

Nonetheless, the company is aware of the dangers of becoming over-stretched.

"Specialisation is the name of the game—you can't do everything," says Jardine Pacific's deputy managing director Rodney Michell. "We're aiming for bigger business units and fewer profit centres, to provide coherence and maximise our expertise."[3]

Jardine Strategic Holdings is the second largest profit-maker of the hong's four major constituents, contributing 29 per cent of profits in 1992. It is a basket of Jardine group companies selling at a discount to its underlying holding. It emerged in 1986, having been incorporated in Bermuda two years after the hong's redomiciling there. It was formed to hold stakes in various Jardine units as a step towards restructuring its strategic investments (see also Exhibits 1, 3, and 4).

In 1992, it acquired a minority interest in the Singapore-based conglomerate Cycle & Carriage, a major auto distributor with interests in property, food, retailing, and hotels.

Jardine Fleming is a merchant bank, the first such in Hong Kong. It was established in 1970, and provides a full range of merchant banking services in the Far East, including investment management, deposit-taking, foreign exchange, and corporate financing. It is equally owned by the London-based merchant bank Robert Fleming and the Jardine hong. When last assessed in 1991, Capital Information Service gave it an AA rating, the best of any financial institution at the time.

Jardine Fleming—with 1500 staff and representation in 26 countries worldwide—does a large business in mutual funds (unit trusts), and offers many such funds covering Asia-Pacific countries. There are 39 such funds in all with more than 30,000 clients around the world. (See also Exhibit 5.) There are single-country funds (e.g., Malaysia, Thailand, New Zealand, Japan OTC, India Pacific, etc.), as well as broader ones, e.g., Pacific Smaller Companies, which attracted much attention on its first day of offer in May, 1993.

Questions about performance arise all the time, and it is sometimes said that Jardine Fleming is best on upswings, moving into the right investments at the right time. Jardine Fleming does not especially agree with this somewhat narrowed perception. Its head of corporate communications recently said that Jardine Fleming's USP was more how deep Jardine Fleming's roots lay in each country: there are 83 researchers in 15 countries. In 1993, a *Business Post* survey rated Jardine Fleming best for blue-chip research; and fifth for second-line, third-line, and China securities.

For more than 11 years, Jardine Fleming had sought a full banking license in Hong Kong. In April 1993, they got it, and immediately said that they intended to use that new status

Exhibit 5 The Jardine Fleming Unit Trust Family

Asia-Pacific Regional Funds
JF ASEAN Trust
JF Eastern Trust
JF Eastern Smaller Companies Trust
JF Far Eastern Warrants Trust
JF Pacific Income Trust
JF Pacific Securities Trust
JF Pacific Smaller Companies Trust

Asia-Pacific Single Country Funds
JF Australia Trust
JF China Trust
JF Hong Kong Trust
JF India Pacific Trust
JF Korea Trust
JF Malaysia Trust
JF New Zealand Trust
JF Philippine Trust
JF Thailand Trust

Japan Funds
JF Japan Trust
JF Japan Ninja Leveraged Trust
JF Japan OTC Trust
JF Japan Smaller Company Trust
JF Japan Technology Trust
JF Japan Warrants Trust

International Funds
JF American Growth Trust
JF Continental European Trust
JF Germany Trust
JF Global Bond Fund
JF Global Convertibles Trust
JF Global Securities Trust
JF Managed Currency Fund

Money Funds
JF Money Fund—US$
JF Money Fund—HK$
JF Money Fund—Yen
JF Money Fund—DM
JF Money Fund—£
JF Money Fund—SFr
JF Money Fund—ECU
JF Money Fund—C$
JF Money Fund—A$

to enhance services already offered to private clients, rather than enter the retail sector. As a broker recently noted: "Lending money in Hong Kong is like printing money." (The rates for deposits are around $3^1/_2$ per cent and for lending about $7^1/_2$ per cent.)

Jardine Insurance Brokers is a leading international insurance broking company (the eighth largest in the world) with over 3500 employees. The ambit of this Jardine arm is ever-seeking. One of its latest moves, for example, was a joint venture with Shun Tak Holdings Ltd., a company involved in shipping, property, restaurants, air transport, and hotel operations in the Asia-Pacific region. This new venture will operate mainly in Macau (a Portuguese enclave across the South China Sea from Hong Kong that will revert to China in 1999, two years after Hong Kong), where Jardine Insurance Brokers will act as professional consultants.

The December 1992 attack on Jardines by China sent Hong Kong's Hang Seng Index down 3 per cent in one day, and Jardines' stock down by 6 per cent. It is believed that China perceives Jardines as the most visible symbol of British business interests in Hong Kong. The Jardines in the UK were advisors to Margaret Thatcher and John Major. The Keswicks may not have been mending fences with China enough to please China (although the hong's interest in doing business in China has never flagged), and their support for the democratization moves in Hong Kong may also have offended China. In the opinion (and hope) of many, China's views on politics and economics should be separated out in their dealings with Hong Kong, but like sports and politics in the Olympics, has it ever been so, and *can* it ever be?

In September, 1993, Nigel Rich left as Jardines' managing director, after a 19-year career with the hong. His successor was Alastair Morrison, a 20-year Jardines veteran, who was the head of Hong Kong Land. There is speculation that Hong Kong Land might become one of the hong's major investment vehicles. Indeed, Nigel Rich will become chief executive of UK property company Trafalgar House, which is effectively controlled (a 25 per cent stake acquired in 1992 and 1993) by Jardines' Land unit. Jardine's Land unit's ideas for the troubled Trafalgar House seem to be to nurse Trafalgar's assets—through writedowns, provisions, and nationalizations in a bid to boost the Company's poor balance sheet before selling things, and also to use Trafalgar's construction and engineering expertise in Asia.

Yet, the Trafalgar House move has also been seen "by some analysts as a possible 'bolt

Exhibit 6 Jardine Financials

A. Consolidated Balance Sheet: Selected Items (US$, billions)

	1988	1989	1990	1991	1992
Fixed assets	0.8	0.8	1.8	1.8	1.9
Properties	0.5	0.5	1.3	1.3	1.3
Plant and Machinery	0.1	0.1	0.2	0.2	0.2
Leasehold Improvement, etc.	0.2	0.2	0.3	0.3	0.4
Investments	2.1	2.1	2.1	2.2	2.6
Current assets	1.9	2.3	2.7	3.1	3.5
Current liabilities	1.8	2.1	2.8	3.2	3.3
Deferred liabilities	1.9	2.0	2.4	2.4	2.7
Net tangible assets	1.1	1.2	1.4	1.6	2.0

B. Consolidated Profit and Loss Items (US$, billions)

	1988	1989	1990	1991	1992
Turnover	4,278	4,638	5,992	7,190	7,900
Pre-tax profits	363	470	562	613	687
Profits after taxes	280	358	433	460	557
Profits after taxes and outside interests	138	195	230	271	317
Profits attributable to shareholders	138	239	226	381	348
Earnings per share, fully diluted (US cents)	25.13	36.15	42.13	48.15	54.59
Dividends per share (US cents)	8.33	12.18	14.25	16.40	18.70

C. Selected Ratios

	1988	1989	1990	1991	1992
Current ratio	1.10	1.10	0.94	0.98	1.07
Long term debt/equity	0.61	0.52	0.62	0.51	0.34
Return on assets (%)	2.89	3.73	3.49	3.74	3.97
Return on turnover (%)	3.22	4.21	3.84	3.77	4.01
Return on equity (%)	12.79	16.63	16.76	16.51	15.78

hole' if conditions get too hot in Hong Kong (for the Jardine hong)."[4] Land has been both buying into and selling properties in Hong Kong, as if to signal its intention to remain in Hong Kong in spite of its tenuous relations with China (reference to which has been made earlier). In the article just cited, the political element of the Jardines story that won't go away is mentioned yet again:

> *The deteriorating relations between Britain and China over Hong Kong's political future have undermined Jardine's position in Hong Kong, as it is regarded by many as the embodiment of British colonial business interests in the territory.*[5]

The six-month results for Jardines show 1993 profits up by 14 per cent over 1992, with turnover up 6 per cent. Among the units, Jardine Pacific's profits were up 9 per cent (held back by continuing decline in sale of wines, spirits, and luxury goods in Japan, while its Jardine International Motors arm showed profits up by 21 per cent thanks to strong Mercedes-Benz sales in China); Jardine Fleming's profit rose by 81 per cent because stockbroking was good, especially in Japan, where such activity was strong, and Jardine Fleming's fund management also did well); Hong Kong Land's profits were up by 9 per cent; and Dairy Farms' by 11 per cent. These, taken with a turnover of US$8 billion with a workforce of 140,000 are impressive numbers indeed.

The Keswick family (who control Jardines) interests have managed, through cash-flow-oriented businesses and international diversification, to maintain a steady, if unspectacular, growth pattern; and its involved corporate structure has kept it out of the hands of local interests, unlike other old hongs.

But what will the Keswicks' and Jardines' future relations with China be after Hong Kong reverts to China in 1997? Can one evade that question? Will Jardines' off-again on-again relations with China be more "on" or "off"? And what of global diversification that shows 68 per cent of the hong's profits still arising from Hong Kong-China (higher than in 1988)?

ENDNOTES

1. *South China Morning Post*, December 30, 1993, p. 84.
2. *The Hong Kong Standard*, December 3, 1993, p. 21.
3. *Asian Business*, May 1992, p. 10.
4. *International Herald Tribune*, January 5, 1994, p. 13.
5. *Ibid.*

CASE SIX

Chinese Entrepreneurs—The New Hong: Cheung Kong (Holdings) Limited*

Introduction

Listed as a "merchant" in the "Who's Who of Hong Kong," Li Ka-shing is the wealthiest man in Hong Kong. His personal net worth is approaching US$4 billion.[1] He is popularly known as "Superman" in the Chinese press. His rags-to-riches story is a typical tale among the territory's top tycoons.[2] Born on June 13, 1928 in Chuozhau, China, Li came to Hong Kong at the age of 11. His father died three years later. As a teenager, he was the sole support of his family. He started his career as a toy salesman for a factory in Western District, eventually obtaining his high school diploma and being appointed general manager of the factory. In 1950 he started a small business manufacturing wigs and plastic flowers. By his shrewdness and savings, Li built up the Cheung Kong construction empire. Li, in an unexpected move, bought up the British Hutchison *hong* (business enterprise) when it got into financial difficulties in 1979. Hutchison Whampoa has since become a substantial global power. Now in his 60s, Li oversees an empire that includes container terminals, supermarkets, power plants and property. Li's empire today includes everything from Calgary Oil and huge Vancouver and Hong Kong real estate to Hong Kong Electric, Park'N Shop, the Sheraton and Hilton hotels in Hong Kong, Cavendish International, and the Canadian Imperial Bank of Commerce. Cheung Kong's associates are now representing a market value of US$22.2 billion, about 15 per cent of the total capitalization of the territory's stock exchange. The billionaire is using his global alliance to shop for bargains in the West.

---

* This case was prepared by Irene H. Chow, Senior Lecturer of the Department of Management, The Chinese University of Hong Kong, for the purpose of class discussion rather than to illustrate the effective or ineffective handling of an administrative problem.

Cheung Kong (Holdings) Limited, a blue chip property developer in Hong Kong, has faced ups and downs in the property market during the last two decades, rising to its present prominent status in the Hong Kong economy. The major strategic issue is how the company may stride into the uncertain future.

HONG KONG, THE CITY BUILT ON THE ROCK

Hong Kong consists of Hong Kong Island, Kowloon Peninsula and the New Territories (see Exhibit 1). Hong Kong Island was ceded to Great Britain in perpetuity by China under the Treaty of Nanking in 1842. Kowloon Peninsula and Stonecutter's Island were ceded in 1869. In 1898, the New Territories were leased to Great Britain for 99 years.

The current (Communist) Chinese government regards these treaties as "unequal treaties," and has always insisted that the entire territory must be returned to the People's Republic of China upon the expiration of the 99 years' lease in 1997, and indeed in 1997 Hong Kong will become a Special Administrative Region of China with a high degree of autonomy. In 1984, an agreement was signed between the government of the United Kingdom and Northern Ireland and the government of the People's Republic of China on the future of Hong Kong (also known as the Sino-British Agreement or Joint Declaration). The provisions of the Agreement guarantee there will be no change in the existing systems, i.e., capitalistic economic and political system, for 50 years beyond 1997. Efforts will be made to guarantee its stability and prosperity.

Hong Kong, Britain's last major colony, has been under British rule since 1841. The population has grown from 1.6 million in 1940, to 5.7 million in 1990, while the usable land remained very limited. This growth in population has been accompanied by overall economic growth as measured by GDP per capita. Hong Kong ranks second only to Japan in Asia in disposable income per capita.

THE IMPORTANCE OF THE PROPERTY AND CONSTRUCTION INDUSTRY IN THE HONG KONG ECONOMY

Land is a particularly valuable and scarce resource in Hong Kong. Property is more important to the state of the economy than in many major cities of the world because land is so limited, and everything is so crowded. The population of 5.7 million people lives on usable land which represents less than 15 per cent of the total area of 1068 square kilometers (400 square miles), a mere 14.8 sq. km (55 square miles) in the urban area. Here are some key numbers:

(i) EMPLOYMENT. In the fourth quarter of 1991, 228,200 or 8.2 per cent of the labor force, were employed in the construction industry.

(ii) CONTRIBUTION TO GDP. The contribution of building, construction and property development to GDP has averaged over 24 per cent since 1980, compared with 12 per cent and 7 per cent in 1980 and 1970 respectively. The relationship between GDP and property construction output is given in Exhibit 2.

Exhibit 1 Cheung Kong's Major Developments

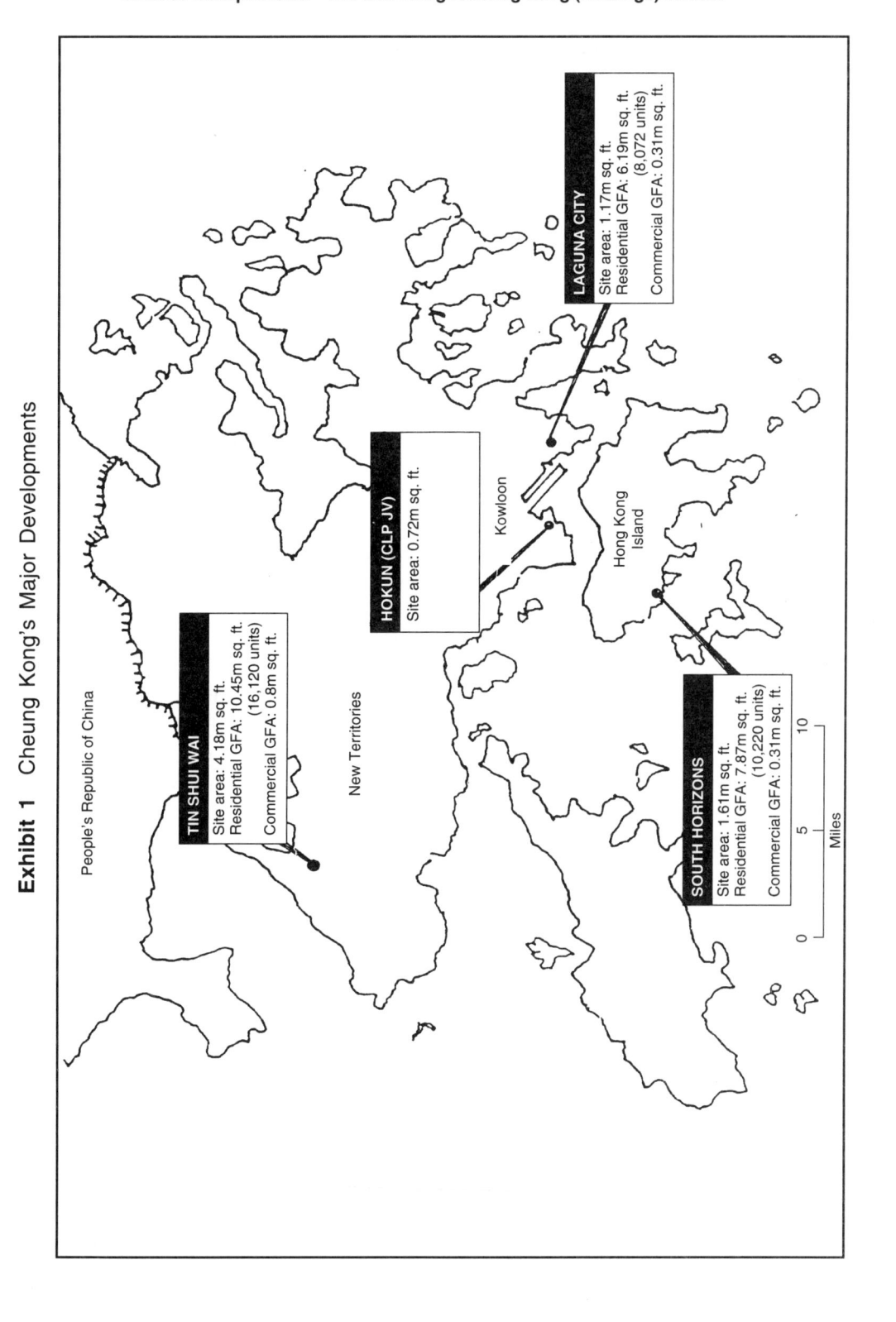

Chinese Entrepreneurs—The New Hong: Cheung Kong (Holdings) Limited

TIN SHUI WAI
Site area: 4.18m sq. ft.
Residential GFA: 10.45m sq. ft.
(16,120 units)
Commercial GFA: 0.8m sq. ft.

HOKUN (CLP JV)
Site area: 0.72m sq. ft.

LAGUNA CITY
Site area: 1.17m sq. ft.
Residential GFA: 6.19m sq. ft.
(8,072 units)
Commercial GFA: 0.31m sq. ft.

SOUTH HORIZONS
Site area: 1.61m sq. ft.
Residential GFA: 7.87m sq. ft.
(10,220 units)
Commercial GFA: 0.31m sq. ft.

People's Republic of China

New Territories

Kowloon

Hong Kong Island

Exhibit 2 Output of the Property and Construction Industry and the Economy

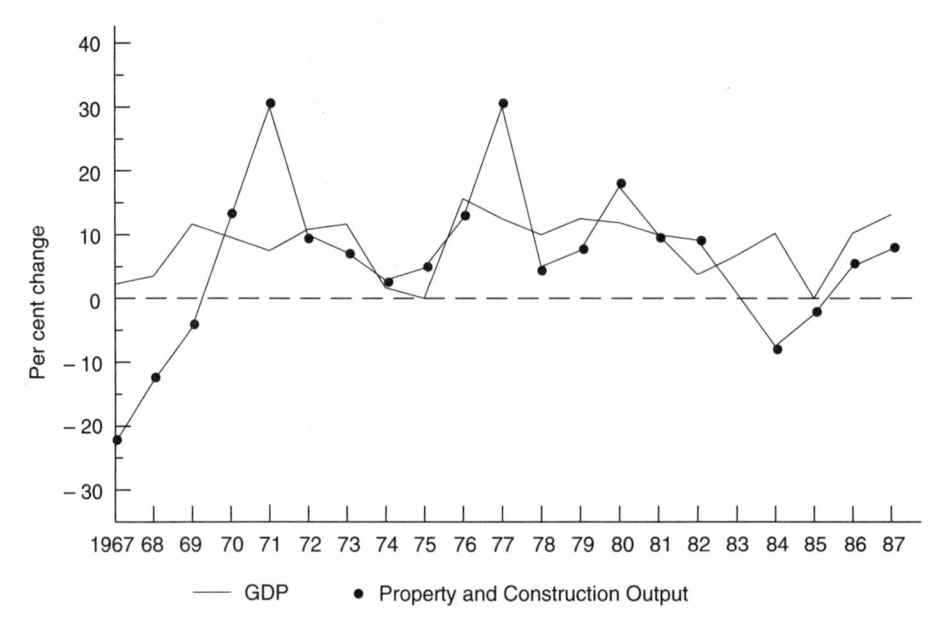

[Graph showing Per cent change from 1967 to 1987, with GDP line and Property and Construction Output points, ranging from about -22 to +30 per cent]

— GDP   • Property and Construction Output

Source: Walker, A., et al., Hong Kong: Property, construction and the economy, London: The Royal Institute of Chartered Surveyors, 1990, p. 19.

(iii) VALUE OF PROPERTY STOCK. Property development accounted for 26 per cent of the total value of the stock exchange of HK$650,409 million in 1990 (HK$7.80 = US$1.0).

(iv) LOANS FOR PROPERTY. A large portion of loans made by banks (32 per cent) and deposit-taking companies (40 per cent) in Hong Kong were related to development or sale and purchase of real property.[3]

(v) GOVERNMENT REVENUE. About one third of the sources of revenue of the Hong Kong government were derived from property and related business, mostly through auction sales of crown land. In 1973–74, property rates and land sales accounted for less than 11 per cent of the revenue. This figure increased to over 25 per cent in 1978–79, and further increased to 36 per cent in 1981–82. The Hong Kong Government has been accused as being a partner in a conspiracy with banks and property developers in maintaining an artificially high level of property prices.[4]

THE BUSINESS CYCLE AND THE PROPERTY INDUSTRY

During the last two decades, the property industry experienced its phenomenal growth and decline for two complete cycles. The movements of the Hang Seng Index vs. prime office rents for the last two decades are given in Exhibit 3. Along with the property boom, Hong Kong's stock market prospered. The Hang Seng Index reached a new high of over 6000, up

Exhibit 3 Hang Seng Index vs. Prime Office Rents

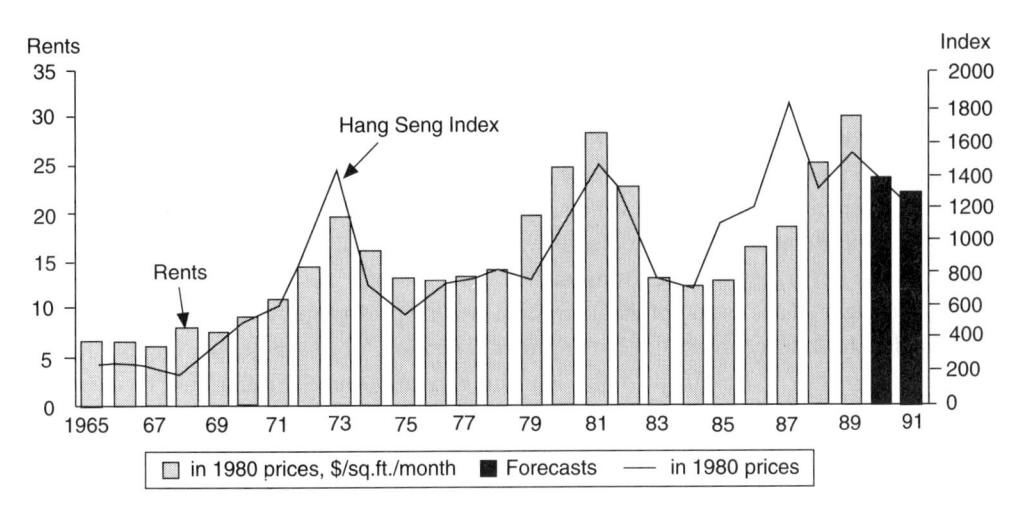

Source: *Asian Property*, April 1990, p. 12.

from 3700 a year ago, with turnover of over HK$6.4 billion. The Hong Kong stock market is dominated by property shares. Their market capitalization ranged from 25 per cent to 28 per cent of the total value from 1984 to 1989. The sectoral sub-indices on properties have outperformed the Hang Seng Index. The index of share price for properties increased 426 per cent from 1984 to 1989, as compared with 276 per cent for the Hang Seng Index as a whole. The index reached a record high of 9980 in June 19, 1992 compared with 5990 a year ago, a 67 per cent increase within one year. The index reached a record high of 9980 on June 19, 1992, compared with 5970 a year ago, a 67 per cent increase within one year. There has been criticism that the stock market serves as a means of secondary speculation in real estate.

The business cycle of the property industry is between five to seven years. Residential prices rose by around 440 per cent during the first cycle 1967–74 and dropped by 10 per cent in 1975. Hong Kong's second property boom peaked in 1980–81. The overheated property market was attributed to high economic growth, expanding business with China, and speculative forces. In the second cycle, prices increased by 310 per cent in the up-phase (1975–81).[5] The property market showed signs of weakening in the late 1981 and began to fall when negotiation started between Britain and the People's Republic of China on Hong Kong returning to China's sovereignty, and eventually crashed in 1982–83. Property prices plunged by about one-third. The property slump bottomed out in 1984 after the signing of the Sino-British Agreement. The recent cycle began in 1984. After a series of disturbances, i.e., the worldwide stock market crash in 1987, the June 4 event in Beijing in 1989, and the Gulf War in 1991, the property market has regained its momentum and has moved to an historical high record in 1992.

SUPPLY AND DEMAND OF PROPERTY

In 1991, 2.66 million people comprising 45 per cent of the population lived in private housing. About the same percentage of the low income population are now living in permanent public housing, at rental rates of approximately 7 to 15 per cent of their income. They are also encouraged to purchase their own flats through the government-sponsored Home Ownership Scheme. The Home Ownership Scheme constructs 12,500 flats annually for purchase by better-off public housing tenants to encourage them to vacate their heavily subsidized rental flats, and by those now living in rented private flats who could not otherwise afford to own a flat. As for the higher income group and expatriates, they can generally afford to live in luxury housing, perhaps as part of the total compensation package provided by their employers. The middle class suffers most under the present situation. They are neither eligible for low rent public housing nor entitled to any housing benefits from their employers.

Despite the rapid pace of construction, the supply of residential, commercial, and industrial buildings in Hong Kong was far below demand. The supply and vacancy rates of various kinds of properties for the last decade are given in Exhibit 4.

Exhibit 4 Supply and Vacancy*

Year	Residential Small Units (< 100 m^2)		Residential Large Units (> 100 m^2)		Office ('000 m^2)		Commercial ('000 m^2)		Flatted Factories ('000 m^2)	
1981	33500	5.9%	2500	7.3%	319	11.0%	315	8.9%	1122	7.5%
1982	23100	6.0	2500	9.1	546	17.6	386	10.7	1041	10.5
1983	21600	4.5	2600	9.9	519	20.6	270	10.1	629	8.9
1984	22300	4.0	1400	6.4	219	13.6	255	9.9	429	5.2
1985	22900	3.7	1950	5.8	308	11.1	249	9.0	456	5.5
1986	31550	3.7	2550	6.6	46	6.0	174	7.8	611	3.8
1987	32350	3.3	2000	4.5	247	5.5	284	5.4	541	1.7
1988	31300	2.6	3150	6.3	247	2.7	238	5.5	1105	4.5
1989	33800	4.1	2700	5.4	269	5.3	197	5.6	864	5.1
1990	27400	3.2	2000	6.2	200	6.1	239	5.2	586	5.3

*Vacancy at the end of the year, expressed as a per cent of total stock.

Source: Rating and Valuation Department, Hong Kong Government, *Property Review*, various years.

Under the Joint Declaration, the Hong Kong government can release only a 50-hectares limit of crown land for sale each year. Half of the price of land that the government sells at auctions for private development is set aside in a fund for use by the government of the future Special Administrative Region. Because of the limited supply, developers bid high prices at land auctions and records are broken one after another. Despite the shortage of supply, the vacancy rate is high. The number of empty residential flats rose to 30,000 units by the end of 1991. This number represents a substantial portion of the available units in

Hong Kong, more than the annual average new construction between 1981–90. Ironically, most estimates indicate that additional units are needed to meet Hong Kong's requirement because the local Chinese prefer to own something solid and they are rushing in to buy property.

The 1991 census statistics showed that 61.6 per cent of domestic households were nuclear families, an increase from 54.4 per cent a decade ago. There is a genuine demand, especially for small to medium size residential flats. The population growth trend has slowed down to 0.6 per cent in 1991. The growth of new families was 1.7 per cent. The rate of household formation has slowed to 26,000 annually in 1990, from 41,000 in the early 1980s. The demand for residential units will ease in 1994. By 1993, demand for luxury accommodation will be strong as expatriates arrive to work on infrastructure and airport projects.

Hong Kong is not only physically close to China, but also maintains close relations with it. It is an ideal place for setting up a base for stepping into the China market. The potential of economic activity in the People's Republic of China has increased the attractiveness of Hong Kong as a base of operations. Eighty-nine per cent of the AmCham (American Chamber of Commerce) members responded favorably to Hong Kong's investment climate for the next five years.[6] The influx of overseas operations in Hong Kong has created a great demand for office space and luxurious residential flats.

Since the early 1980s, the Hong Kong manufacturing base has gradually shifted to China. The demand for manufacturing factories is low. Many manufacturing firms reallocated their resources towards property development because property trading and dealing promised quick cash turnover. The price of residential property varies depending on the size, location, facilities, convenience and infrastructure. Small to medium units (500–700 sq. ft.) are in great demand, and are now priced above HK$3000 per sq. ft. The price of property in selected districts is given in Exhibit 5 for reference. A small one-bedroom apartment in a new development costs HK$2.25 million.

Exhibit 5 Hong Kong Property Prices

District	Name	Size	Capital Value (HK$/sq. ft.) (Dec. 1990–91)	Increase (%) (Dec. 1990–91)
Tuen Mun	Tuen Mun Town Plaza	MS	2144	96.6
Tai Po	Tai Po Centre	MS	2440	73.8
Shatin	City One	MS	2764	70.4
Aberdeen	Aberdeen Centre	MS	2598	64.4
North Point	City Garden	M	3044	62.0
Mid Levels	Parkway Court	L	2837	57.9
Quarry Bay	Tai Koo Shing	L	3032	57.5

Note: MS = 431–752 sq. ft., M = 753–1075 sq. ft., L = over 1076 sq. ft.

Source: Brooke Hillier Parker Research.

Prices for small to medium-sized residential units increased 20 to 30 per cent during the first quarter of 1991 and 60 per cent for the whole year. The housing price spiral is linked to inflation, a double-digit inflation rate, the very low interest rate, (2 per cent in May 1992, negative interest rate if inflation rate is taken into account), and limited supply of land. The double-digit inflation and low interest rate resulted from the Hong Kong dollar being pegged to the US dollar at the exchange rate of US$1 to HK$7.8 in 1983 to safeguard confidence in the Hong Kong dollar.

The influx of overseas companies interested in doing business in China since 1980 has driven up the price of offices. Prime office (Grade A) prices are likely to reach over HK$6000 per square foot in the face of strong demand and shortage of space. At the present stage, the market is consolidating because the prices are too high. However, most property developers plan to slow down some of their projects rather than ease the price of current projects. They would rather control the gap between supply and demand.

AFFORDABILITY. The relationship between household income and mortgage payments is shown in Exhibit 6. Residential property prices were out of the average income-earner's reach and end-users during the boom period in the early 1980s. The majority of potential buyers found property prices far from affordable. The Affordability Ratio measures the relationship between the amount of mortgage payments and the monthly income. The median monthly household income was HK$9964 in 1991,[7] up from HK$2213 in 1979, with 50 per cent falling between the HK$2000 to HK$6000. Housing in the mid-1980s was more affordable than it has been since 1980. Most families would be willing to use 50 to 60 per cent of their

Exhibit 6 Mortgage Costs for Small to Medium Size Flat 1979–1991

Year	Mortgage Rate	Monthly Payment	Median Household Income	Affordability Ratio
1979	13.7500%	$3797	$2213	171.6%
1980	15.0000	5211	2645	197.0
1981	18.7500	7044	3084	228.4
1982	15.5000	4789	3694	129.6
1983	13.5000	3549	4194	84.6
1984	13.7500	3098	4508	68.7
1985	9.5000	2939	4930	59.6
1986	8.2500	2969	5410	54.9
1987	8.0000	3586	6096	58.8
1988	9.2500	4782	6891	69.4
1989	11.2500	7369	8558	86.1
1990/5	12.2500	8166	9175	89.0
1991/4	9.5000	9497	11069	85.8
1991/12	9.7500	12771	12730	100.3

Note: Monthly payment based on 20% downpayment and 15-year mortgage instalments for a 500-square-feet flat.

income to pay for mortgages. As the rise in property prices has been far more rapid than of household income in 1991–92, about 85 per cent of the first-time buyers cannot afford to buy a flat in the territory.[8]

SPECULATION. Speculation in the property market is always active during boom periods, especially in the early 1980s and early 1990s. Some property speculators made 60 per cent profits within a few months. Unlike the property market in the early 1980s where the interest rate on mortgages was very high, around 20 per cent, the property market in the 1990s is still being fuelled, at least in the residential sector, by negative bank deposit yield in real terms, and continued prices escalation and speculation. The prices have increased at a much greater rate than inflation. People view property purchase as a hedge against inflation. In April 1991, Sceneway Garden—developed by Cheung Kong—came into the market and was virtually sold out within a few hours. Sources in the industry indicated that 60–70 per cent of the buyers were speculators.

Despite the sharp rise in price, the rental yield for flats has come down from 9 per cent in early 1991 to around 5 per cent. Since a high percentage of the recently completed flats were still unoccupied, it is clear that buyers are not end-users. On the whole, 33,000 private residential units were left vacant at the end of 1991, representing 4.2 per cent of the total stock. These speculators expect to gain substantial profits if they can hold on to the empty premises for several months.

A rush for residential units has driven prices to the point where Hong Kong banks have tightened mortgage policies in an attempt to stabilize the market and thwart rampant speculation. The decision in November 1991 by major banks to cut down loans to 70 per cent of the mortgage value helped to eliminate many speculators. Speculation is not restricted only to the boundaries of Hong Kong, but extends to Shenzhen. Shenzhen, the largest Special Economic Zone across the border experienced an 80 per cent rise in residential property price in 1991–92. The average price of HK$950 a sq. ft. is still lower than the nearby Sheung Shui price of HK$2650 per sq. ft. in the northern New Territories. Most of the property buyers in Shenzhen are from Hong Kong.

CHEUNG KONG'S PERFORMANCE

Cheung Kong was incorporated in 1971 as a private limited company under the name of "Cheung Kong Real Estate Co., Ltd.". The name "Cheung Kong" means continuous flowing long river in Chinese, one with many tributaries. On July 31, 1972 the company changed its name to Cheung Kong (Holdings) Ltd. In October 1972, it became a public listed company in the Stock Exchanges. Its issued and fully paid capital amounted to HK$84,000,000.

Since its establishment, Cheung Kong has focused its efforts on property development. Property development involves acquisition of land, followed by planning, design, construction and finally the sale of completed units for a capital gain, whereas property investment is the acquisition of completed property for a recurrent rental income. Its primary business is concentrated in property and related business, i.e., properties, property development, and real estate. Cheung Kong engages in all high class, middle class and low class residential, industrial and commercial buildings. Ninety per cent of Cheung Kong's 21 million sq. ft.

land bank is geared to the mass residential sector, the most promising in the property market (see Exhibit 1 for location). Cheung Kong's investment in these large scale residential projects in Laguna City, South Horizons and Tin Shui Wai are the best bet in property market. Cheung Kong has a land bank that is one of the largest in the territory, comprising 65 per cent residential, 6 per cent commercial and 29 per cent industrial properties. This land bank is largely concentrated in four large residential complexes at Kwun Tong, Lam Tin, Ap Lei Chau and Tin Shui Wai which are projected to be ready for occupation by 1995. The investment involved in these four developments is set at HK$17.5 billion.[9]

The group's turnover by activities and their respective contribution to group profit (in million HK$) for the year 1991 are given as follows:

	Turnover	Contribution
Sales of properties	8282	3064
Cement and quarry operation	1455	264
Property investment	77	41
Real estate agency and management	176	159
Investments and finance		734
Others		16
Total	9990	4278

Source: Cheung Kong (Holdings) Ltd., *Annual Report*, Hong Kong, 1991.

Based on the Hong Kong Business Research report, Cheung Kong (Holdings) Limited was ranked No. 7 among the top 100 companies in terms of net profit in 1990. It was rated as one of the top performers by Baring Securities. Like most of the major Chinese property companies, Cheung Kong experienced a period of rapid growth during the 1970s, mainly due to the booming property market, together with prosperity of the economy. During the past two decades, the after-tax profits of Cheung Kong showed a high growth rate (see Exhibit 7). The good financial performance was partly due to the rocketing property prices in Hong Kong during the last two decades.

In 1992, the price range of Cheung Kong stock was of the order of HK$20 to 27.60; the number of issued shares was 2197.5 million. Cheung Kong's market capitalization was estimated to be HK$27,909 million by the end of 1990. It accounted for 4.29 per cent of the total market and was ranked fourth among the top 20 leading companies, just after Hong Kong Telecommunications, Hutchison Whampoa and Hong Kong Bank.

The company achieved record profits in 1991. The Group's audited consolidated net profits after tax for the fiscal year 1991 amounted to HK$8,889,000,000 (US$1,139,615,000), 50 per cent higher than the previous year. The earnings per share were HK$2.22. Cheung Kong's profit leap came from its all time high sales of residential properties during the year. The income statement and balance sheets for the years 1987–1991 are summarized in Exhibit 8. Dividends per share showed a sharp decrease in 1987 only because of the share split, a private share placement and the rights issue.

Exhibit 7 Cheung Kong (Holdings) Ltd. Group Profit after Tax

HK$, million (thousands)

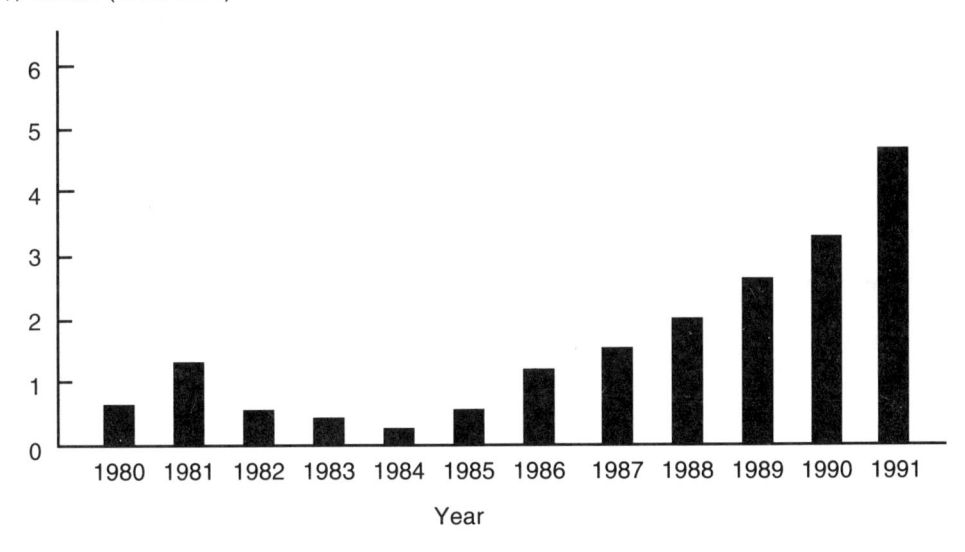

Source: Annual Report.

CORPORATE CULTURE AND PHILOSOPHY

The company has faced challenges and critical stages during the last two decades. The directors and department heads are all very experienced and some of them have been working since the establishment of the company. As the company expanded rapidly, more young and energetic people were recruited. The philosophy of the company is to provide high quality buildings and good living environment to the public. The goodwill of the company is highly valued and emphasized. The company has created the image of great potential and flexibility, which has the ability to cope with the challenges of the future.

THE ENTREPRENEUR'S MANAGEMENT STYLE AND HUMAN RESOURCES STRATEGY

Like many other typical Chinese businesses in Hong Kong and Southeast Asia, Cheung Kong is headed by the entrepreneur who founded the company. Li Ka-shing is the chairman and managing director of Cheung Kong. He holds 35 per cent of the company's outstanding shares. Cheung Kong is considered to be Li's personal investment vehicle. Li retains overall control of the major operation decisions. He uses a very autocratic, top-down type decision making style. He secures consent and compliance by authority rather than by voting or by general consensus. Considering the nature of its business, the number of critical decisions is relatively small, but the amount involved in each transaction is very substantial, and significant delegation of power and authority is limited.

Exhibit 8 Cheung Hong (Holdings) Ltd.: Group Financial Summary ($, millions)

	1987	1988	1989	1990	1991
Profit and Loss Account					
Turnover	2,323	2,258	5,044	4,413	9,990
Profit before extraordinary items	1,581	2,090	2,775	3,251	4,886
Extraordinary items	281	567	1,238	349	403
Profit attributable to shareholders	1,862	2,657	4,013	3,600	5,289
Dividends	472	637	835	1,055	1,494
Profit for the year retained	1,390	2,020	3,178	2,545	3,795
Balance Sheet					
Fixed assets	17	1,413	1,778	1,751	1,944
Investments	9,455	11,413	14,243	15,233	17,102
Net current assets	3,099	1,618	2,683	5,234	6,395
	12,571	14,444	18,704	22,218	25,441
Deduct:					
Long-term bank loans	216	216	1,300	2,210	1,628
Bills and notes payable	1,222	950	700	800	
Deferred items	8	191	158	126	936
Minority interests	69	160	214	177	129
Total net assets	11,056	12,927	16,332	18,905	22,748
Representing					
Share capital	1,099	1,099	1,099	1,099	1,099
Share premium	2,752	2,752	2,752	2,752	2,752
Reserves and retained profits	7,205	9,076	12,481	15,054	18,897
Total shareholders' funds	11,056	12,927	16,332	18,905	22,748
Earnings per Share	0.77	0.95	1.26	1.48	2.22
Dividend per Share	0.22	0.29	0.38	0.48	0.68
Net Asset Value per Share	5.03	5.88	7.43	8.60	10.35

Source: Annual Report.

A good project management team is of vital importance in the property development business. Such a specialized department calls for skilled workers, experienced architects and consultants for designing its projects and building a good reputation for the company. The brain drain and the labor shortage problem will be major obstacles for the industry in the 1990s. The number of reported vacancies in the construction business was 560 in December 1991, representing a vacancy rate of 0.9 per cent, dropping from 1.9 per cent a year ago. The government has approved the importation of foreign labor for construction of the port facilities and airport. It is estimated that over 10,000 construction workers would be required. Importing workers may be an alternative in the short-term to solve the labor problem. For longer-term solutions, it will be necessary to attract more new entrants to work on the construction sites, and to gain increased labor efficiency through the use of advanced construction equipment and through better training of construction workers.

High turnover and emigration are serious problems in human resource management. Government data suggests that about 62,000 people emigrated from Hong Kong in 1990. The most popular destinations are Canada, Australia and the United States. It is estimated that 55,000–60,000 people would leave Hong Kong in the next few years. Most of the emigrants are young, well-educated, professional and experienced managerial staff. Eighty-five per cent of local chartered surveyors intended to emigrate before 1997. By September 1989, over 50 per cent of them had already had passport applications approved or submitted.[10]

Like most Chinese business organizations, Cheung Kong is relatively weak in providing staff training. There is usually only on-the-job training, a typical Chinese style of grooming staff. Evaluation is based on performance. However, Li tries to fully utilize the talent of individual staff. Part of his strength is derived from the core group of trusted top executives who helped direct his empire. Li has a network of powerful allies. A team of Chinese and Western managers give him access to information and ideas for business decisions. He put together a group of expatriates to manage his global conglomerate. Simon Murray, 52, managing director of the group, is Li's ambassador to Western business. The list of directors of both Cheung Kong (Holdings) and Hutchison Whampoa is given in Exhibit 9.

Exhibit 9   List of Directors

Cheung Kong (Holdings) Ltd.
  Li Ka-shing, Chairman and Managing Director
  George C. Magnus, Deputy Chairman
  Chow Chin Wo, Deputy Managing Director
  Chow Nin Mow, Albert, Deputy managing Director
  Fok Kin-ning, Canning, Deputy Managing Director
  Charles Yet Kwong Lee
  Leung Siu Hon
  Hung Siu-lin, Katherine
  Li Tzar Kuoi, Victor
  Kwok Tun-li, Stanley
  Frank J. Sixt

Hutchison Whampoa Ltd.
  Li Ka-shing, Chairman
  George C. Magnus, Deputy Chairman
  Simon Murray, Group Managing Director
  C.Y.K. Lee, Executive Director
  W. Shurniak, Executive Director
  A.N.M. Chow, Executive Director
  C.K.N. Fok, Executive Director
  Frank J. Sixt, Executive Director
  S. Robert Blair, Director
  Sir Horace Kadoorie, Director
  Li Fook-wo, Director
  P.E. Selway-Swift, Director
  P.A.L. Vine, Director
  C.H. Wong, Director

COMPETITION

The property development industry in Hong Kong is highly centralized, with a small number of developers dominating the market. Cheung Kong and its associate, Hutchison Whampoa, make up more than one-third of the market share. Other competitors include major local Chinese property companies, such as Sun Hung Kai Properties Limited, Hopewell Property Limited, and New World Development Company Limited. The profiles of the two major competitors are given in Exhibit 10. New World Development's strengths came mainly from real estate investment and development plus its hotel holdings. These two combined account for close to 85 per cent of the revenues. Its land bank consists of 7 million sq. ft. New World is the third largest property developer after Cheung Kong and Sun Hung Kai. The two prime sites are New World Centre in Tsim Sha Tsui and the huge convention complex in Wan Chai. These two properties accounted for close to 45 per cent of New World's net asset value.

During the property recession in the early 1980s, many of the property developers were forced out of the market. Some survived the slump at the expense of substantial write-offs. Generally speaking, a strong balance sheet, abundant cash flow and banker's support are vital for survival. In order to regain responsiveness and to exert complete control over the projects, Cheung Kong bought out its partners in a number of joint ventures during the slump when they faced financial difficulties.

Cheung Kong, among those who survived the property market collapse in the early 1980s, reassessed its development strategy. Realizing that the real demand in the local market was for small residential flats, Cheung Kong learned from the experience and focused on the mass residential units. Its competitive advantage comes from gearing to this market niche, and obtaining the economies of scale involved in three large scale residential developments.

The product of property development, in a sense, is somewhat unique. The value-added features of the flat, such as improved material finishes, additional household items provided and improved management and maintenance provision create a good quality image. These features can be easily emulated and matched by other competitors.

MARKETING STRATEGIES

The skyrocketing price of private property makes cost leadership very important. The successful strategy to capture the low-end market is low cost. Land cost often constitutes over half of the total development cost. The ability to acquire cheap land is of ultimate importance. Cheung Kong obtained its Tin Shui Wai (a newly developed mass residential area) construction site at a relatively low cost of HK$198 per sq. ft., in a remote area to help construct a new town for middle income families. Construction costs were carefully monitored and controlled, using standardized and simplified design with provision of basic minimum facilities. The finishing was left to the end-users themselves.

The price of property varies according to size, layout, location, quality, view and floor level of a particular unit, travel convenience, infrastructure, supply in the neighborhood, etc. The property developer can charge a price as high as the customers are willing to pay. Another strategy is incremental pricing. Incremental pricing strategy makes potential customers

Exhibit 10 The Profiles of the Competitors

Sun Hung Kai Property Ltd.—1991 Financial Summary

Turnover (HK$, million)	8755
Profit before extraordinary item (HK$, million)	3430
Earnings per share	2.4
Dividends and special cash bonus per share	1.11
Shareholders' funds per share	14.97
Property sales (HK$, millions)	7730
Cross rental income (HK$, millions)	1345
Land bank (million sq. ft.)	34.1

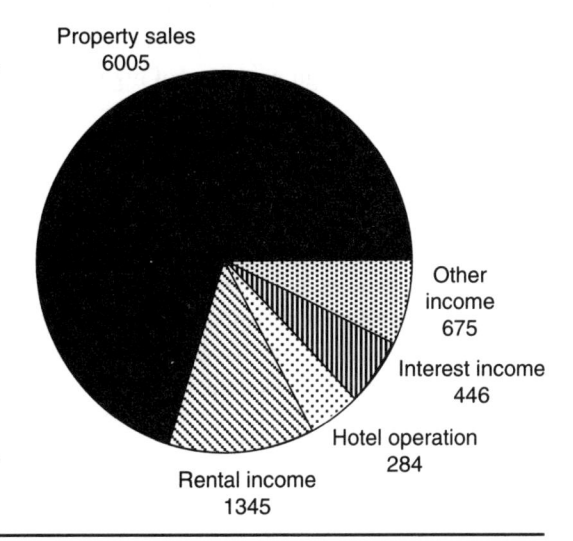

Pie chart:
- Property sales 6005
- Other income 675
- Interest income 446
- Hotel operation 284
- Rental income 1345

New World Development Co. Ltd.—1991 Financial Summary

Turnover (HK$, million)	9677
Profit before extraordinary item (HK$, million)	1168
Earnings per share	0.87
Dividends per share	0.50
Geographic location	
Hong Kong	8,042,564
S.E. Asia & P.R. China	75,209
North America	525,230
Europe	927,242
Australia	83,179
Others	23,999
Total	9,677,423

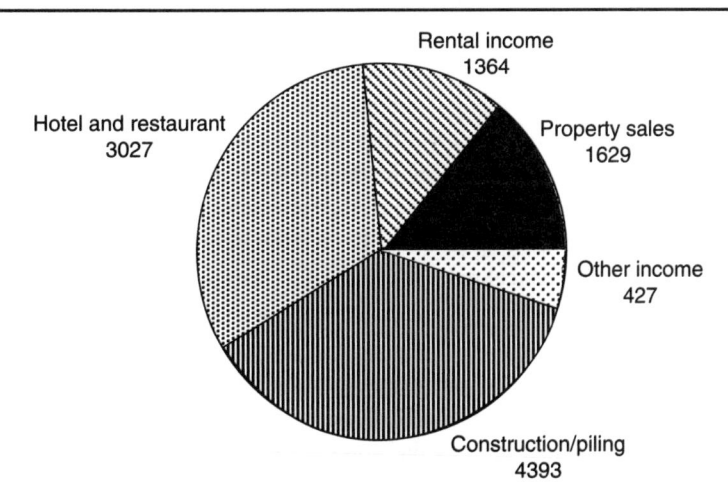

Pie chart:
- Rental income 1364
- Property sales 1629
- Other income 427
- Construction/piling 4393
- Hotel and restaurant 3027

Source: Annual Reports.

feel "it will be more expensive in later phases" and the customers are persuaded to make their commitment early. Customers are willing to pay more when developers differentiate their products. Cheung Kong's product differentiation strategy focuses on providing good value to buyers through provision of high quality finishes to make the units more attractive with well-maintained public areas, e.g., corridors, lifts, lobbies; maximizing the amount of open space and recreational facilities; adequate amenity facilities, good external appearance; well-organized commercial complexes and proper management and maintenance service. Security and maintenance of the property is a salient feature. Cheung Kong's large scale residential areas are self-sustained. These residential blocks are promoted to be higher profile developments.

Cheung Kong tries to respond quickly to the needs of the end-users. In order to test consumer needs, a model flat was built in advance of sales to study the response of end-users. A sales office was set up at the head office in Central and on site to better serve the customers. During the property sales period, the company extended its office hours beyond 5 p.m. on weekdays and kept its office open on Sundays. Free transportation was provided to carry potential customers to these remote sites for viewing. The promotional activities were well-coordinated. Newspaper advertisements and posters were scheduled throughout the year. TV advertisements were screened during the period of sales. Other promotion campaigns included mailed pamphlets. Occasional press releases were used to create word-of-mouth publicity and good public relations.

FINANCING

A property developer invests a huge amount of money in land and construction costs. It usually takes one to two years to complete the construction before cash from sales proceeds flows in. The need to control budget, schedule, and projects is important. The funds come mainly from debt and equity financing. Li is developing the property mostly with other people's money. He usually forms a joint venture with the land-owner, promising a higher return than the owner would have received in an outright sale. Such arrangement releases the advance payment of land, which in Hong Kong amounts to about 60 per cent of real estate developments.[11] Much of the remaining capital can be obtained through pre-sale arrangements, a unique way of raising operating funds in Hong Kong. After obtaining a building permit, a developer may sell the flats before completion (actually it is a contract to sell) getting 10 to 20 per cent down payment. As the developer passes each of the successive phases of construction, he calls in further payments from these prospective owners. The contract to sell will be trading actively like a future contract on a commodity market before the completion and physical delivery of the flat. Response to pre-completion sales of flats was generally favorable. Crowds of thousands queued up several days and nights to lodge purchase applications.

The property industry maintains a very close relationship with the banking sector. Li was also Deputy Chairman of the Hong Kong Bank before he resigned in April 1992. According to government statistics, 34 per cent of the domestic credit extended by the bank is in the form of property-related loans. Among these extended credits, 69 per cent are loans and advances for construction and development, the other 31 per cent being personal mortgages.

Due to keen competition among banks and financial institutions, some banks lent up to 90 per cent of the appraised value of the property as collateral. The payment period was extended to over 20 years. These liberal and aggressive lending policies make property more affordable.

GROWTH STRATEGY

Cheung Kong's growth strategy has focused on acquisition, joint ventures, direct investments, and others. Acquisition provides a cheap source of land, and joint ventures are one way to pool resources and increase the chance in competitive bidding. The company pursued a policy of backward vertical integration initially in 1978 with the acquisition of 22 per cent stake in Green Island Cement Co. Ltd. to ensure its supply of cement—a major material for construction. The stake since then was raised, and finally the cement manufacturer was taken over and incorporated into Cheung Kong in 1989. Further investment in the construction material business took place in 1989 with the acquisition of Anderson Asia from Hutchison. Cheung Kong also invested HK$1 billion in China Cement (H.K.) Ltd. These interests provide synergy with the Group's property activities in ensuring a steady supply of construction materials. Another strategic move was the acquisition of 22.4 per cent of the British-dominated Hutchison Whampoa Limited in 1979 because of its cheap sources of land. Since then the stake was further increased to 40.3 per cent. Hutchison Whampoa is a Hong Kong-based, highly diversified international corporation. Its core business includes container terminal operation, retailing, telecommunications and media, energy, finance, and investment with over 100 principal subsidiaries and associated companies. The consolidated financial statements of Hutchison Whampoa are given in Exhibit 11. Li's strategy was to buy into large British Corporations in order to form a global alliance. Cheung Kong, Hutchison Whampoa and its associates now accounted for 15 per cent of the capitalization of the Hong Kong Stock Exchange. The simplified structure of the group is given in Exhibit 12.

PROPERTY. The Group's involvement in large scale private housing development began with Whampoa Garden, undertaken by its associate, Hutchison. The property market showed a strong demand for small- to medium-sized residential units. Laguna City in East Kowloon and South Horizons on Hong Kong Island will provide a total of 16,000 units when completed. All the units offered for pre-sale were sold.

HONG KONG INTERNATIONAL TERMINALS (HIT). HIT is located in Kwai Chung, one of the world's busiest container ports, which handled 2.5 million TEUs (20-foot equivalent units), that is half of the throughput of the Hong Kong container port capacity. Further expansion is planned and it is estimated that in 1994, the combined capacity will total over 4 million TEUs.

RETAILING. The retail business is mainly carried out through its A. S. Watson (pharmacies and drug store) and its Park'N Shop supermarket chain. There are 112 Watson's Personal Care stores spreading all over Hong Kong, Singapore, Taiwan, China and Macau. Park'N

Exhibit 11 Hutchison Whampoa Ltd.—Ten-Year Performance Summary

		1982	1983	1984	1985	1986	1987	1988	1989	1990	1991
	Turnover	3,717	4,361	5,215	5,466	7,529	10,524	12,875	17,685	15,975	19,212
Consolidated Profit and Loss Account HK$, millions	Profit before extraordinary items	952	1,171	1,029	1,194	1,630	1,864	2,340	3,031	3,519	3,328
	Extraordinary items	52	123	269	369	563	764	1,283	3,049	851	1,012
	Profit attributable to shareholders	1,004	1,294	1,298	1,563	2,193	2,628	3,623	6,080	4,370	4,340
	Preference dividends	40	42	134	51	44	37				
	Profit attributable to ordinary shareholders	964	1,252	1,164	1,512	2,149	2,591	3,623	6,080	4,370	4,340
	Transfer from reserves		811								
	Ordinary dividends	964	2,063	1,164	1,512	2,149	2,591	3,623	6,080	4,370	4,340
	Special dividends	199	280	437	553	690	1,022	1,308	1,644	1,980	2,073
			1,779								
	Profit for the year retained	765	4	727	959	1,459	1,569	2,315	4,436	2,390	2,267
Consolidated Balanced Sheet HK$, millions	Fixed assets	3,216	3,337	3,989	4,977	4,847	7,066	13,040	18,856	20,781	27,381
	Deferred expenditures									168	894
	Long-term investments	352	475	463	3,276	5,179	11,600	13,869	14,773	15,150	17,097
	Property under development for sale					923	904				
	Net current assets	1,877	743	1,475	327	300	3,116	1,822	6,012	5,575	491
	Employment of capital	5,445	4,555	5,927	8,580	11,249	22,686	28,731	39,641	41,674	45,863
Performance Data	Share capital	846	846	922	850	771	755	757	761	762	762
	Reserves	3,541	2,624	4,179	5,656	9,050	13,641	15,094	21,752	23,834	26,893
	Shareholders' funds	4,387	3,470	5,101	6,506	9,821	14,396	15,851	22,513	24,596	27,655
	Minority interests	450	480	472	341	335	4,298	4,055	4,764	5,092	6,023
	Loan stock	595	594	167	166	165	161				
	Long-term liabilities	13	11	17	1,468	831	2,313	7,794	11,469	11,925	12,074
	Deferred items			170	99	97	1,518	1,031	895	61	111
	Capital employed	5,445	4,555	5,927	8,580	11,249	22,686	28,731	39,641	41,674	45,863

Earnings per ordinary share (cents)	40	49	35	42	57	65	77	100	116	109
Dividend per ordinary share (cents)	8.7	12.2	16.3	20.3	25.1	34.6	43	54	65	68
Ordinary dividend cover	4.6	4	2	2.1	2.3	1.8	1.8	1.8	1.8	1.6
Return on ordinary shareholders' funds (%)	22.9	36.9	19	18.4	16.5	12.6	14.8	13.5	14.3	12
Current ratio	3.3	1.3	2.1	1.2	1.1	1.5	1.3	1.9	1.7	1
Gearing (%)*	NA	NA	NA	17.8	20.5	8.3	32.8	22.2	7.5	12
Net assets per ordinary share: book value (HK$)	1.8	1.4	1.8	2.3	3.6	4.7	5.2	7.4	8.1	9.1

*Gearing represents the ratio of net borrowings to shareholders' funds and minority interests. NA (not applicable) indicates cash balances exceed borrowings. Net borrowings is defined as total borrowings net of bank balance and other liquid funds, long-term cash deposits and managed funds.

Source: *Annual Report.*

Exhibit 12 Group Structure of Cheung Hong (Holdings) Ltd.

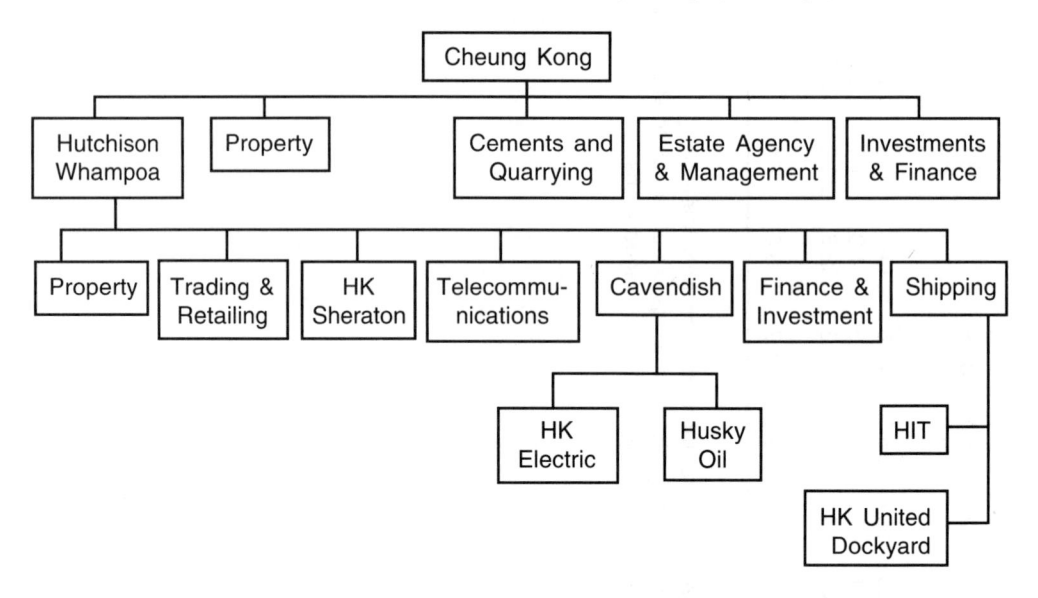

```
                          Cheung Kong
    ┌───────────┬─────────────┬──────────────┬────────────┐
Hutchison    Property    Cements and   Estate Agency   Investments
Whampoa                   Quarrying    & Management    & Finance
    │
┌────┬────────┬─────────┬──────────┬──────────┬────────────┬─────────┐
Property  Trading &   HK      Telecommu-  Cavendish   Finance &    Shipping
          Retailing   Sheraton  nications              Investment
                                            │                        │
                                      ┌─────┴─────┐                 │
                                      HK        Husky              HIT
                                      Electric  Oil                 │
                                                              HK United
                                                              Dockyard
```

Shop has a total of 163 stores in Hong Kong, Taiwan, and China. Hutchison China Trade has formed a joint venture with Procter and Gamble in Guangzhou to distribute toiletry products. The rapid growth in overseas markets and the expansion in Hong Kong and within Southeast Asia continues to broaden the retail operations.

HUTCHISON TELECOMMUNICATIONS. Hutchison Telecom operates paging businesses in Hong Kong, UK, Australia and Thailand. It has become one of the UK's largest cellular communications companies through a series of acquisitions.

HUTCHVISION. Hutchvision has established a five-channel (Sport channel, Music channel, Chinese-language program channel, News and Informational channel and Star Plus) with Star TV satellite television service reaching most of the Asian countries (38). More than 1.8 million homes (2.7 billion people) are able to view Star TV. Its chief executive officer is Li Ka-shing's son, Richard. Metro Broadcast is Hong Kong's second commercial radio station. On July 26, 1993, the Li family sold 63.6 per cent stake in HutchVision Limited, the supplier of programs to the Star TV Service, to the News Corporation led by Mr. Rupert Murdoch. The agreed price of US$525 million represents approximately six times the initial investment in the satellite television business.

HONG KONG ELECTRIC HOLDINGS. Hong Kong Electric has been supplying electricity to Hong Kong Island and Lamma Island for over a century. It continues to benefit from rising demand for electricity on Hong Kong Island.

HUSKY OIL OF CANADA. Husky Oil is one of Canada's largest privately owned, independent fully integrated gas companies. It is involved in the exploration, production, refining and marketing of crude oil, natural gas liquids and sulphur.

DIVERSIFICATION

Cheung Kong (Holdings) continues to diversify its businesses, especially its non-property activities. Security investment is also part of the diversification program. It subscribed to a HK$100 million convertible note issued by Asia Financial Holdings. Other plans included expanding property investments in both China and Hong Kong. Cheung Kong has gone into partnership with the Land Development Corporation to build a one-million-square-foot office and retail development in Central by 1996.

Hutchison Whampoa took the opportunity of the strong share market to raise funds to finance the privatization of Cavendish International. The privatization was intended to simplify management and eliminate the overlapping of businesses.

After the westward adventures, the superman has shifted focus. His sights are set firmly on China. Cheung Kong is actively looking at a number of property projects in Guangzhou and other cities. It spent HK$500 million to lift its stake in Pacific Concord which offers good potential to expand into China. Besides property development, Cheung Kong would also consider a subway network and other infrastructure projects in southern China. Cheung Kong entered into a joint venture with Shenzhen Investment and Management Company, which belongs to the Shenzhen municipal government. This movement adds financial and political strengths to Cheung Kong, and at the same time provides it opportunities to enter into industry, commerce, real estate, telecommunications, finance and energy through its vast portfolio of billions of yuen. The joint venture allows Cheung Kong vital access to the Shenzhen market which foreigners find difficult to penetrate.

The potential of Hong Kong's property business is good. A ten-year forecast carried out by the Shui On Group suggests that the territory will experience a construction boom from 1992 to 1999 based on the construction of airport, port and infrastructure works planned by the government and the private sector.[12] The peak is likely to occur in the year 1994. Business confidence in Hong Kong is further strengthened by Deng Xiaoping's recent call for speeding up of the pace of economic reform in China. In the next few years, Cheung Kong is expected to reach the climax of development completions with huge cash inflow coming from Sceneway Garden, Laguna City and Tin Shui Wai. The cash-rich Cheung Kong probably will continue its acquisition trail. It has already snapped up a HK$68.26 million stake in the floppy disc firm Hanny Magnetics (Holdings), using an interest-bearing convertible note. Local sources hint that Li is showing interest in acquiring individual properties of the troubled Canadian giant Olympia & York.

Hong Kong is small and property prices are probably too high. Diversification outside Hong Kong seems to be an obvious alternative. Mr. Li's offshore holdings have increased markedly over the past few years. He successfully snapped up a sixth of downtown Vancouver. (This project, the Expo lands, was a joint venture with partners Cheung Yu-Tung of New World Development Company and Lee Shau-Kee of Henderson Land.) Li's diversification plans continued in 1990, with emphasis on expansion in the Southeast Asia region.

Uncertainty over the Future of Hong Kong

Hong Kong is running out of time as described by Han Syjin's *A Borrowed Place—a Borrowed Time*. Every successful merchant wants to join for a quick profit in trading. Such short-time orientation is partly due to the expiration of the lease in the New Territories in 1997 and the reversion to China. The 1997 "doomsday" will become a critical issue while top executives formulate their strategic plans.

Jardine, Matheson & Co. Ltd. shocked Hong Kong by transferring its domicile to Burmuda in 1984. Many others followed suit. The Hong Kong Bank has restructured, grouping its overseas operations under a London-based holding company. Every time a big company relocates overseas, confidence in the territory drops by a notch. People just worry that capital flight and fleeing business will diminish local financial resources. About 80 per cent of Li's corporate assets are in Hong Kong, He faces an incalculable political risk. He plans to increase his overseas investment to 40 per cent. His multi-billion dollar Suntec City commercial project in Singapore has earned him permanent resident status in Singapore. This fuelled further speculation about his plans to move some of his "empire" out of Hong Kong. It is logically safe to invest outside the colony, especially given the uncertainties of its impending reversion to Chinese rule in 1997.

Succession Plan

The trinity of Li Ka-shing and his sons Victor (29) and Richard (27) is extremely powerful. At the age of 63, it may be too early for Li to think about retirement. In an open announcement Li confirmed that he would step down from the Cheung Kong empire before 1997.[13] Chinese entrepreneurs would like to groom their sons to succeed to the family business. Both of Li's sons, Victor and Richard, studied at Stanford. Victor started a property development firm in Vancouver, while Richard was the youngest partner in a Canadian investment bank in Toronto. Li's likely successor is his elder son, Victor, currently executive director of Cheung Kong and the family's Canadian investment guru. The second son Richard, at the age of 25, was heading Hutchison, the satellite Star TV, with a potential audience of around 2.7 billion people in Asia, before it was sold to Murdock's News Corporation. Richard became deputy chairman of Hutchison Whampoa. The second generation of the Li dynasty has been groomed for corporate stardom since birth. They sat in on business meeting in babies' chairs and conversations at dinner table revolved around business.

Endnotes

1. Kraar, Louis, A Billionaire's Global Strategy, *Fortune*, Vol. 125, June 29, 1992, p. 20.
2. *Hong Kong Tatler*, January 1992, p. 76.
3. Hong Kong Government, Census and Statistics Department, *Hong Kong Annual Digest of Statistics*, 1992.
4. Davies, Derel, Traveller's Tales, *Far Eastern Economic Review*, Vol. 113, July 1981, p. 25.
5. Hang Seng Bank, *Hang Seng Economic Monthly*, May 1992.
6. Horne, Lucinda, AmCham Survey shows Big Surge in Confidence, *Business Post*, June 10, 1992, p. 3.

7. Hong Kong Government, *Census Statistics,* 1991.
8. Chu, Kennis, Property Faces Uncertainty Year as Prices Slip, *South China Morning Post,* May 15, 1992.
9. Have Cash Will Travel, *Far Eastern Economic Review*, Vol. 155, March 5, 1992, p. 56.
10. Walker, Anthony, *et al.*, *Hong Kong: Property, construction and the economy*, London: The Royal Institute of Chartered Surveyors, 1990, p. 59.
11. Kraar, Louis, A Billionaire's Global Strategy, *Fortune*, Vol. 125, June 29, 1992, p. 22.
12. Source: *Shui On Construction Review*, 1990.
13. Empire of the Son, *Hong Kong Tatler,* January 1992, pp. 76–77.

CASE SEVEN

CATHAY PACIFIC AIRWAYS LIMITED*

INTRODUCTION

Cathay Pacific Airways Limited (Cathay) has been called *"The Airline of Hong Kong,"* and one of its boasts is that *"every flight is an international flight."*

This boastful statement is certainly true. Hong Kong itself is only 400 square miles in area, about twice the size of Singapore (whose own airline, by the way, could well make the same claim). Cathay's "international" slant is further enhanced by its emphasis on having cabin crew stewardesses from ten Asian lands, each speaking English plus at least one Asian language, each providing the natural (rather than forced) warmth that typifies "Asian" service.

"The Airline of Hong Kong" statement is perhaps a bit stretched. Actually, Cathay was founded as a British-registered airline (the Union Jack was on the tail) by an American and an Australian, and only recently has it adopted its current identity.

While it may still be Hong Kong's own, it would appear still to be more *British* rather than *Chinese* (i.e., ethnic Chinese) Hong Kong's. In the list of Directors shown in the 1992 Annual Report, eight of the 23 Directors were ethnic Chinese; and among the 14 Executive Officers (ten of whom are also Directors) there are only two ethnic Chinese.

MANAGEMENT CULTURE

Management orientation is strictly contemporary Western corporate, with all the familiar

---

* This case was prepared by Neil Holbert, then Senior Lecturer in the Department of Marketing, Chinese University of Hong Kong. Currently, he is the Assistant Professor of Marketing, The American College in London.

ideas of opportunity, customer service, and work orientation **upfront**. **Workshops** are offered focusing on the business (strategy and competition and all the rest) and on the manager himself (leading and delegating and self-understanding). Career orientation literature is straightforward and task-oriented:

> *Will you be graduating ... in the future? ... If you are looking for a challenging and rewarding career with one of Hong Kong's most respected companies ... we are interested in you. There is prestige attached to working at Cathay Pacific ... Our achievements so far have resulted from hard work, bold business decisions, the use of ... advanced technology, (and) dedication to people: our customers and our staff.*

And help wanted advertising is of the thoroughly contemporary universal genre.[1]

SUPERVISOR—LOYALTY MARKETING
Database and Relationship Marketing is becoming an increasingly important way to identify and communicate with our customers. As Supervisor-Loyalty Marketing, you will act as an internal consultant to our overseas sales and marketing staff. You will implement database systems, brief and train staff, and, acting as a consultant, assist in the execution of profitable marketing activities from the database. Starting with a sales database project, you will oversee its implementation and support in your assigned region of our network. Later you will move onto CUDOS, Cathay Pacific's customer database, organising training support and assisting in database management. You will also assist and be consulted [with duly] in direct marketing activities.

This challenging and dynamic position will best suit someone [looking at] pursuing a long-term career in Relationship/Direct Marketing.

Requirements:
- *Tertiary qualifications*
- *2–3 years' work experience, preferably in marketing or in direct customer service*
- *Excellent spoken and written English*
- *Hands-on experience with popular PC applications*
- *Experience in sales/marketing database applications an advantage*
- *Availability for regular overseas business travel*
- *Customer orientation and excellent presentation skills*

Salary:
- *Will not be less than 11,137 (Hong Kong Dollars p.m. = about US$17,000 p.a.)*

Our fringe benefits include 12 days annual paid leave, 5-day week, concessional air travel, a profit-sharing scheme, company medical/dental scheme and long service/ retirement gratuity....

It can probably be said that although Cathay is *in* the East, it is not necessarily *of* it in terms of understatement and indirection. Its goals are clear, and its statement is forthright.

With clear goals and contemporary outlook, a major problem in the personnel area nonetheless exists: one shared with many other Hong Kong firms. That is, of course, the reversion of Hong Kong to China on June 30, 1997, at which time it will cease to be a British colony and will become a Special Administrative Region of China. The reversion issue has, in addition to posing questions about what a "Hong Kong" airline really will mean, led to a steady emigration annually of 50,000 or so of Hong Kong's best and brightest. Of 700 key Cathay managers, up to 10 per cent emigrate each year, some (for example) to Austrialia (and its Qantas Airways) where citizenship is the lure.

Over and above this, Cathay has been trying—in response to a strongly competitive environment—to cut costs without affecting service. For flight attendants, this has meant limits to salary increases and attempts to increase productivity. Industrial unrest broke out in January 1993 (during the busy and crucial Chinese New Year holiday), and charges of harassment by management were levelled by the Flight Attendants Union; there was also dissension within the Union's ranks, between its leadership and its members.

LABOR UNREST

It was a strike that seemed to catch Hong Kong by surprise. Hong Kong had had no real Western-style strike in decades, and both the non-confrontational Asian ethos and the absence of strike-focused laws or procedures in laissez-faire Hong Kong added to the trouble. The issues were not unfamiliar in labor relations: assignment of duties not in line with employees' past duties and efforts at cost containment, but the unfamiliar stage made the actors even more sharply focused, and in some ways it was like the "Guns of August" that set the great nations of Europe going around like sleepwalkers (as the historian Barbara Tuchmen said) and starting off a war, World War I, that nobody really wanted.

The chronology was as follows:[2]

> *DECEMBER 18: Three first class pursers are sacked for refusing to work as junior flight attendants, maintaining a work-to-rule campaign initiated by the Flight Attendants' Union (FAU) on December 7 in protest against staff shortages.*
>
> *DECEMBER 19: The union considers boosting its industrial campaign with a strike by cabin crew over Christmas and the New Year holiday period.*
>
> *JANUARY 13: The 3,700-member FAU calls a lightning strike at 10 pm after negotiations over manning levels and a wage increase break down.*
>
> *JANUARY 14: There are chaotic scenes at Kai Tak as the strike starts to bite, with 13 of Cathay Pacific's 41 scheduled flights cancelled, five aircraft chartered from other airlines and only 23 flights out of Hong Kong operating normally.*
>
> *Striking attendants set up picket lines, maintained throughout the strike, outside Cathay pacific offices and 29 staff membes are suspended, facing possible dismissal.*
>
> *JANUARY 15: Labour Department officials set up talks between the FAU and Cathay Pacific management as an estimated 2,100 flight attendants join the strike.*
>
> *JANUARY 16: Early afternoon talks between the union and the airline's management go into the early morning before ending in a deadlock. The union wants the three*

attendants reinstated, staffing levels reviewed, and a three per cent pay rise on top of a cost-of-living increase.

Cathay Pacific is estimated to be losing HK$20 million a day during the strike, and later admits to losses of between HK$10 and HK$15 million a day. Four outgoing flights and 18 incoming are cancelled.

JANUARY 17: Taiwan's China Airlines, which has been carrying most of the passengers Cathay has been unable to fly, warns it will not be able to continue providing extra flights over the Lunar New Year holiday period. Cathay cancels 22 incoming and nine outgoing flights as talks continue.

JANUARY 18: Peace talks founder, with the company rejecting as impractical a union proposal to organise staff for flights on the condition that negotiations continue. Meanwhile, 12 outward flights are cancelled and only 19 of 44 scheduled inward flights arrive.

The FAU describes the management's offer to donate all profits for the next seven days, about HK$35 million, to the Hong Kong Community Chest if the union agrees to suspend negotiations and industrial action as "emotional blackmail".

JANUARY 19: Cathay Pacific Management says it is prepared to reinstate the three attendants and review manning levels but says the pay rise issue was introduced after the strike began. The union is not satisfied by the compromise proposed.

JANUARY 20: Cathay Pacific prints an open letter to shareholders in newspapers, setting out its position and objections to the FAU's actions. Both sides agree to restart negotiations as the airline cancels only two outgoing flights and flies 18 of 38 incoming flights.

JANUARY 21: Thirteen-hour talks fail to resolve the dispute. Agreement is reached on most major issues, but talks fail on the threat of disciplinary action against those "actively" involved in the strike. Only two flights are cancelled.

JANUARY 22: The picket line moves to Government House in the early morning, where about 1,000 striking attendants, and three Legislative Councillors, appeal to the Governor, Mr. Chris Patten, to intervene after 13-hour talks fail.

JANUARY 23: The strikers continue to stake-out Government House after sleeping outside overnight. Negotiations continue, unsuccessfully, but no flights are cancelled.

JANUARY 24: Cathay sets a deadline for striking staff to return to work by midnight, January 27, saying crew not than registered for the February roster will have their contracts frozen and need to apply in writing to be considered for further duties. No flights are cancelled.

A coalition of 34 groups including trade unions, community and religious groups is formed in support and claims the company's intention to discipline striking staff threatens workers' rights.

JANUARY 25: The union claims international support for its strike will result in a boycott by overseas unions and warns it could take its case, particularly concern over infringements of the right of workers to strike, to the International Court of Justice in The Hague.

The vigil by strikers outside Government House moves to the Central Government

Offices as negotiations still fail to reach a settlement. Both the FAU and the company print open letters setting out their positions.

JANUARY 26: Support for the strike slips, with the union admitting some attendants are leaving the picket line to return to work and 23 Legislative Councillors refusing the FAU's call to directly intervene in mediating the dispute.

The International Transport Workers Federation says unions overseas have expressed their support for the strike but no union has given a commitment to support industrial action.

JANUARY 27: Deadline day dawns. About 1,000 workers have signed a pledge not to return to work before the dispute has ended, but by the end of the day a high-profile member of the FAU executive committee, official spokeswoman Miss Rachel Varghese, resigns from the committee to return to work. The company says it is pleased with the numbers responding to the ultimatum.

And the strike was over before the end of the month. But the unpleasant echoes remain: Allegations of sexism and racism amid images of Filipina stewardesses as spokespeople for the Flight Attendants' Union; the unpreparedness and seeming heavy-handedness by management counterpoised with scuffles, disruptions, and general disarray; and the firing of strikers then and later.

HISTORY OF CATHAY PACIFIC

Its initial investment was HK$30,000, and its one Douglas DC-3 was a converted World War II C-47 military transport aircraft. The founders were the American, Ray C. Farrell, and the Australian, Sydney H. de Kantzow, who had met during World War II while flying Douglas C-47 transports "over 'the hump'" from Calcutta, India, to Kunming, China. That DC-3 (called "Betsy") was designed to be a cargo carrier, and her first flight—in 1945—was from New York to Shanghai, carrying morning coats and toothbrushes. Her second was to Sydney via Hong Kong and back to Shanghai with woolen goods.

In 1946, they moved their operations to Hong Kong (from Shanghai), and registered Cathay there. They formed an export-import company and an airline, Cathay Pacific Airways. The former would lease aircraft from the latter, thus avoiding heavy taxes. By 1948, a fleet of eight planes was operating passenger and cargo charter flights on a route that included Hong Kong, Macau, Manila, Bangkok, Rangoon, and Singapore. In the same year, the Hong Kong trading company, Butterfield & Swire (new John Swire & Sons (Hong Kong) Ltd.), took a 45 per cent interest in Cathay. Swire, through its Swire Pacific Limited arm, now owns 52 per cent of Cathay.

Direct local competition emerged from another Hong Kong trading company, Jardine Matheson. Its airline, Hong Kong Airways, was given the northern routes out of Hong Kong in 1949, and Cathay the southern routes. Hong Kong Airways ran into trouble, however, in the aftermath of the Communist victory in China in 1949, and in 1959 Cathay absorbed it, now becoming a truly regional carrier. By 1967, the route network had spread from Calcutta in the west to Tokyo in the east, and from Seoul in the north to Singapore in the south.

Cathay spread beyond Asia in 1970, adding Perth, Australia to its destinations. By the mid-1970s, the Middle East was added too: Bahrain in 1976, and Dubai in 1977. It was the Rolls-Royce-powered B-747 that enabled Cathay to enter the "jumbo" era. In 1980, the airline added a Hong Kong-London route. In the following years, there were added (among other places) Frankfurt, Vancouver, Amsterdam, Beijing, Denpasar (Bali), Paris, Rome, San Francisco, Zurich, Manchester, Paris, Hanoi, and Jakarta. In 1986, Cathay obtained a public listing on the Hong Kong Stock Exchange, and in the following year it was named *Air Transport World* magazine's "Airline of the Year." The popular Marco Polo Business Class cabin was set up in 1988.

Meanwhile, in 1985, a second "Hong Kong airline," *Dragonair* (Hong Kong Dragon Airlines, Ltd.), was formed. Its thrust was to open flights to places in Asia that had not been covered before by major airlines—places like Dacca (Bangladesh), Kathmandu (Nepal), and Xiamen and Guilin in China. This seemed to be a competitive move, but in 1990 the following shares of Dragonair were purchased by these entities: Cathay: 5 per cent Swire Pacific (which owns 52 per cent of Cathay, as noted): 30 per cent and CITIC (the China International Trust & Investment Corporation, which owns 12.5 per cent of Cathay): 38 per cent.

Cathay nominates key management executives to Dragonair, and supplies administrative and technical support to the airline, although Dragonair remains independent and retains a separate identity, concentrating on developing services from Hong Kong to regional points, particularly in China, including the major destinations of Shanghai and Beijing.

The Cathay-Dragonair relationship, which might be called a strategic alliance or an arrangement for complementarity, may be considered a singular kind of Hong Kong happening, where the Government, dominated by business interests, refrains extensively from involvement in approval or disapproval of things like mergers and acquisitions.

Actually, Dragonair has been doing very well of late, having undergone major changes since the Cathay and CITIC buy-ins. It now flies to 14 cities in China, and its timetable and reservations are tied into Cathay's. Says Dragonair of its relationship with Cathay: "Cathay regards us as a separate company, and our relationship is strictly arm's-length."

Performance of Cathay

The Gulf War and the Recession affected Cathay's 1991 performance. Like all airlines, Cathay was faced with a situation in which people did not want to fly frequently while the war was on. Not only was the Middle East itself regarded as unsafe, but the threat of air hijacking anywhere in the world a concern as well. In response to this, Cathay, like its competitors re-routed planes to maximize efficiency. As part of the issue, the price of aviation fuel also went up substantially.

Cathay looked at prospects this way in early 1992:

> *The worldwide economy is forecast by some to be picking up, albeit slowly, but the signs are not very clear. Inflation in Hong Kong is easing, although it is still at a very worrying double-digit level. It would be easy to be pessimistic about 1992's results. However, the airline's capacity increase will be much higher than that in*

> *1991, and with a return of Japanese traffic and a strong performance by the economies of most Asian countries, load factors should increase. Whilst we are, therefore, hopeful of improved revenues, a very major issue will be our ability to control costs. Bearing in mind particularly the high inflation rate in Hong Kong, it will be vital to contain these costs if we are to achieve the results that we want in 1992. We look forward to a more prosperous 1992, albeit with some caution in respect of the progress of the world's major economies.*

But early in 1993, Cathay was a bit more guarded.

> *1992 saw no reduction on the problems confronting the aviation industry. A worldwide excess of capacity ... produced a continuation of the fare wars first seen in 1991 ...*
> *Traffic from Japan, Australia, and Europe was below our expectations. Towards the end of the year there were the first tentative signs of a recovery in the US, but these were not sufficiently convincing to increase the number of passengers travelling ... (o)pportunity is (re)presented by the growing economic links between Hong Kong and China ... and our links with China's aviation and travel industries ... It is likely that 1993 will be a more difficult year than 1992.*

Indeed 1993 interim earnings were well below 1992 levels—down 46 per cent in the first half compared to the previous year, but it should not be overlooked that in 1992 Cathay was still the second most profitable airline in the world, behind only Singapore Airlines. (Incidentally, the top five, in addition to these two included three other Asia-Pacific carriers: China Airways, Thai Airways, and Qantas.)

CATHAY PACIFIC—1997 AND AFTER

As noted already, Hong Kong will revert to China on July 1, 1997; so with 1997 come those issues as yet impossible to sort out. What *will* be the effective positioning for this "Airline of Hong Kong" when there is really no longer any such practical entity as Hong Kong since it will become a Special Administrative Region of China. What *will* be the relationship between Cathay and China's own airline, CAAC, now divided into five regional airlines? To be sure, capitalism is guaranteed in Hong Kong for 50 years after reversion—to the year 2047, but how will the freewheeling nature of Cathay—adding this, seeking that, experimenting with the other—fare in the face of the unpredictable Chinese need for control, particularly in an industry such as airlines, which is in every way visible to all, and one of the symbols of a modern nation? And what will be the consequences of China entities (including CITIC) already owning 24 per cent of Cathay? How "Chinese" will Cathay become, and how Chinese will it want to become?

Many scenarios exist with regard to the 1997 transition. On a purely economic basis, China, with a huge stake of US$20 billion in Hong Kong, obviously wants Hong Kong to continue to prosper. In Hong Kong, many "liberals" and "democrats" have a vision of a Hong

Kong moving virtually independently from China (except for foreign affairs and defense), and creating a continuing example of prosperity-through-freedom. Will there be a clash between China (i.e., Beijing) and the Hong Kong Special Administrative Region (of China)? And what might be the consequences for Cathay? Many feel that open clashes will be avoided, that economic interests will prevail, that high level (elitist) negotiations will be the rule, and that Cathay will be seen as China's "modern and successful" wings to the world, even as (the former) CAAC continues to seek to improve itself within China and to nearby areas.

But, of course, it remains to be seen.

INTERNATIONAL IMAGE-BUILDING

Cathay has gone all out to play up its international image: those air hostesses from ten countries; at one time using Michael Chang, the Chinese American tennis player who won the French Open as spokesman sponsoring the Hong Kong Rugby Sevens (with teams from five continents); and a tagline of a "new world arriving on Cathay." All of this image-building has been in addition to further route enhancements: non-stop flights to Zurich and Johannesburg, daily non-stop flights to London's Heathrow Airport, and service to Ho Chi Minh City (Saigon) and Hanoi.

The epitome of the international flavor, and a strong reinforcement of its image as a global carrier out of Hong Kong was Cathay's "Hong Kong: Super City" advertising campaign. This 1991 effort underscored the global nature of the city of Hong Kong itself, projecting it as a place where the East and West, as well as the ancient and the modern meet, and where culture and entertainment back up the well-known shopping image of the city. The campaign seeks to root Cathay in a dynamic city, at the same time giving it wings to span the world.

All of this excitement was topped off by a further major move that raised more than a few eyebrows.

It was not so much the HK$10.5 million revamping of their First Class service, with the name "Cathay Pacific First," and the following spiel in their advertising:

> ... a contemporary interpretation of a time when the privileged few travelled in extraordinary comfort and style ... crafted from the ground up ... offer(ing) more personal control and more flexible, personalized service than ever before ... an ... oasis of privilege and recognition, sheltered from the inconvenience of ordinary travel ...

(A lot to say indeed to play to Cathay's long-standing slogan: "Arrive in Better Shape." And as it happens, this effort coincided with a reduction in demand for first class seats, so it is clearly pitched to elitist standards.)

> On the question of food ... Cathay ranks one up. Plentiful Royal Oscietre caviar ... on ice garnished with blinis, and washed down with old ... vodka or champagne. Canapes are not normally a thing to get excited about, but those served between London and Paris were exquisite ...[3]

It was not, however, the enhanced service that seemed to be the key issue, even though it included seats that turn into beds, built-in personal television sets, and meals and wines that could be ordered at any time, but the disclosure that 70 per cent of the promotion money for the new service would go, not to conventional (so-called "above-the-line") media advertising, but to "below-the-line" (collateral supplementary efforts such as sales promotion) in the form of *direct mail*.

There were both surprise and skepticism at this announcement. One competitor, the British Airways, seemed to believe that the announcement was a shock tactic more than anything else, since it noted that its own "World's Greatest Offer" promotion had already used "below-the-line" extensively. (This US$90 million effort involved giving away 50,000 free flights on British Airways on April 23, 1991.) All of this in the teeth of the Gulf War. Others believed that while Cathay's move seemed to put marketing objectives ahead of classical advertising campaigns in traditional media, it wasn't clear how Cathay could actually execute it.

Be that as it may, turbulence about seeking an advertising agency that would better focus on Cathay's ideas about integrated marketing communications ("advertising" plus "below-the-line") led the company to change agencies in 1993: from Leo Burnett to McCann-Erickson.

What will that mean in the short and long term? Cathay may well be doing something right. It was voted best carrier in a poll of 34,000 economy class passengers by the Consumer Association of the UK in 1991. A London Business School study put it in tenth place in a list of the thirty most successful companies in the world with US$1 billion plus in sales. No other airline appears in this list.

Asian Business magazine's survey of 9000 top managers in Asia, asking their opinions of the most admired companies in the Continent in terms of quality of goods or services, quality of management, potential for growth, etc. showed Cathay in seventh place overall.

Cathay is in an advantageous and disadvantageous position at the same time. Advantageous because it is in the heart of Asia—the growth spot of the world; specifically, it is centered in Hong Kong, the heart of the ebullient Hong Kong–Guangdong–Pearl River Delta area, surely the hottest growth spot in Asia. Growth in the area has been consistent throughout the 1980s and into the 1990s, and many expect it to march confidently ahead into the next century—the "Pacific Century." But there are problems. Its competitors are among the best in the world. Singapore Airlines, for example, was the *number one company overall* in the *Asian Business* survey just cited; and, as noted already, was the most profitable airline in the world in 1992. Cathay's very location makes its future uncertain after 1997.

FACING THE CHALLENGES

The situation for airlines of Asian countries, overall, may be changing dramatically. As noted, interim 1993 earnings are down for Cathay (46 per cent in the first half); Singapore Airlines' are down too (8 per cent off in the year to March); and Thai is down 67 per cent for the nine months to June.

Recession in key markets overseas (Japan and the West) lingers; overseas rivals have transferred flights to Asia; and airlines of Asian countries which belong to the most dynamic region of the world, are facing inevitable labor cost pressures at home. For Cathay, whose

1992 net profit was HK$3.0 billion, Jardine Fleming estimates net profit as follows: 1993: HK$2.2 billion; 1994: HK$2.7 billion; and 1995: HK$3.0 billion. Said Cathay itself in its interim report of August 25, 1993:

> *The main cause of the drop in profits was the effect of the continuing recession in the Company's major markets, particularly Japan and Europe ... Inflation in our home base in Hong Kong, at a much higher level than our competitors, continued to erode our profit margin. Industrial action by flight attendents in the early part of the year also reduced profits. It is not possible to put a precise figure on the effect of the strike in terms of additional cost and loss of revenue, but our estimate ... is a reduction in profits of ... HK$240 million.*

That HK$240 million is about 40 per cent of the six-month year-over-year drop reported. Not the first strike in Cathay's history (there was a strike in 1975, and another in 1984), this one (as noted) has indeed left a bitter legacy.[4]

> *It was a strike which should never have happened. But the fact it was widely predicted for so long somehow did nothing to stop (it), sparking Hong Kong's costliest conflict in recent years.*
>
> *... why (would) Cathay ... persevere with a strike that could eventually cost hundreds of millions of dollars, jeopardize hard-won business, affect their share price and tarnish their prized image as one of the world's favourite airlines (?).*
>
> *Cathay's explanation is brutally frank:* "We are thinking of the long term. We have made a huge capital commitment for the coming ten years. We are trying to maintain our present successful position in the world airline industry ... to maintain our competitive power...
>
> "It is a long-term capital investment in terms of new aircraft and routes. So in view of the airline industry as a whole, which is basically loss-making, we need to increase our productivity so we can be one of the leaders."

Cathay's dilemma—trying to balance productivity, service, image, and profit—is not unique perhaps, but it would seem not to go away easily. Later it was said that Cathay was

> *... flying planes with fewer emergency exits than planned by the manufacturer, "balancing" safety with commercial concerns, it was claimed yesterday ...*
>
> *A company spokesman said that ...* "pilots would be happier with five doors as opposed to four, but they would also want six instead of five ... Their main concern is with safety. The management of the airline is also faced with commercial decisions and balancing that with safety ... Safety and security are the paramount concerns of Cathay Pacific and if that door was going to have an effect on safety, it would have been kept..."
>
> *(Noted a Pilots' Union spokesman):* "We accept Cathay's commitment to safety and security, but it seems they only come first after they have sorted out the money."[5]

And money is indeed an issue that remains, and was unsurprisingly so. Already Cathay—while constantly seeking to maintain its image as the airline of Hong Kong, and indeed to forge a new "Chinese-tinted" stance—has moved its database headquarters to Sydney, Australia, and its accounting operation to China itself—to Guangzhou (Canton). Both are money-saving moves. Thus, Cathay's relation to Hong Kong remains poised between loyalty to Hong Kong, profit considerations, and the 1997 handback of Hong Kong to China. So while still profitable, Cathay and other carriers are clearly aware of problems with continued profitability, including competition from aggressive Western airlines. Indeed in July 1993, Cathay, Singapore Airlines and Malaysian Airline System (which in December 1993 reported a 95 per cent plunge in half-year earnings) joined together to form their own frequent-fliers program "Passages," which will apply only to First Class and Business passengers. Such programs typically cost the airlines about 3 per cent of total revenue.

New visions and challenges constantly emerge as strategy is formed and reformed both from internal visions and external challenges.

Cathay's *vision* includes a continuing reassessment of its fleet. In December 1993, in the midst of concerns about costs (see above), it became one of the few airlines in the world to make fresh aircraft purchases, buying US$801 million worth of Airbus Industrie's A340–300s. These will be used primarily on Cathay's non-stop European and Australian runs, and are believed to be more suitable than the larger (and higher-breakeven) Boeing planes. The vision was expressed thus by Cathay Chairman Peta Sutch:

> *Although Cathay, and indeed the whole airline industry, is currently facing difficult times, we believe that this is a good time to buy aircraft, given that we foresee a better business environment in the second half of the decade.*[6]

The *challenge* came from Britain's Virgin Atlantic Airlines, and its charismatic head, Richard Bronson. Virgin inaugurated London-Hong Kong and Hong Kong-London service on February 21, 1994. Its point of differentiation was to be computerized gambling on the plane en route via individual seatback television sets. (Later Bronson envisioned expansion to other Asian destinations: Singapore, Kuala Lumpur, Bangkok, China; and a splitting of his airline into a Virgin Atlantic and Virgin Pacific.)

While Cathay responded to the gambling element by announcing it wouldn't follow suit, it has been more upset by Bronson's plan to cut prices on the London-Hong Kong/Hong Kong-London route for First Class and Business Class fliers. Two years into Virgin's debut on the route, Economy fares for Cathay and Virgin were on a par (round-trip per person on Virgin £780, on Cathay £778). But indeed Virgin *has* used its marketing boldness to create new names for its First and Business sections and to price them considerably below Cathay. Cathay's First was £3990, Virgin's equivalent "Upper Class" £2652; and Cathay's Business was £2311, vs. Virgin's equivalent "Premium Economy" of £1202.

So as for many successful world players playing in a new world of increased deregulation, competition, globalization, consolidation, reconfiguration, and strategic alliances, the struggle goes on for Cathay.

And for Cathay in particular, surely time (especially 1997) will tell a lot more.

Cathay Pacific Airways Limited

APPENDIX

Exhibit 1 Cathay Pacific: Balance Sheet 1988–92 (HK$, billions)

	1988	1989	1990	1991	1992
Fixed assets	9.3	11.4	14.8	17.7	20.8
Other long-term assets and investments	0.8	0.7	1.2	1.0	1.3
Net current assets	4.5	4.8	6.7	8.1	11.8
Deferred items	1.5	(0.2)	(0.8)	(0.7)	(2.4)
	16.1	16.8	21.9	26.1	31.7
Financing					
Share capital	0.6	0.6	0.6	0.6	0.6
Reserves	5.5	7.6	9.2	11.0	12.7
Shareholders' funds	6.1	8.2	9.8	11.6	13.3
Long-term liabilities	10.0	8.5	12.1	14.6	18.4
	16.1	16.8	21.9	26.1	31.7

*Note HK$7.80 = US$1.00

Exhibit 2 Cathay Pacific: Key Financial Ratios (1988–92)

	1988	1989	1990	1991	1992
Current ratio	1.63	1.52	1.75	1.78	2.22
Quick ratio	1.58	1.47	1.68	1.72	2.14
Debt/Equity ratio	0.77	0.34	0.43	0.47	0.46
Interest cover	6.80	27.5	22.5	15.3	11.4

Exhibit 3 Cathay Pacific: Key Financial and Operating Measures (1988–92)

	(HK$, billions, except as noted)				
	1988	1989	1990	1991	1992
Passengers (million)	6.2	7.1	7.7	7.4	8.4
Passenger load factor (%)	77	78	76	74	74
Passenger revenues	11.8	13.8	15.7	16.3	18.1
Cargo revenues	2.6	2.7	3.1	3.4	3.7
Total revenues	15.1	17.3	19.8	20.9	23.3
Operating costs	11.4	13.5	16.2	17.2	19.7
Operating profit	3.7	3.8	3.6	3.7	3.6
Taxes	0.4	0.6	0.6	0.6	0.5
Net profit	2.8	3.3	3.0	3.0	3.0
Earnings per share (HK$)	0.99	1.16	1.05	1.03	1.05
Dividends per share (HK$)	0.36	0.42	0.42	0.42	0.42
Number of aircraft	30	36	41	45	49

ENDNOTES

1. *South China Morning Post,* December 11, 1993.
2. *South China Morning Post,* January 29, 1993, p. 13.
3. *Hong Kong Business.*
4. *Window,* January 22, 1993.
5. *South China Morning Post,* November 5, 1993.
6. *South China Morning Post,* December 9, 1993, p. B5.

CASE EIGHT

Splendid Duesseldorf Production Limited*

Introduction

Splendid Duesseldorf Production Limited is engaged in the manufacturing, exporting, and retailing of leather garments. It had its beginnings with a company called Splendid Duesseldorf GmbH, which was founded by Messrs. Hermann Gerlach and Karl Heinz Kuepper in 1982. This was initially an agency business contracting production facilities in the Far East (primarily Korea and Hong Kong) to produce fashionable leather garments for well-known design houses selling to the European market. Their primary objective was to combine their European marketing contacts, fashion knowledge, and sources of supply with local management and production skills and low production costs to produce a high quality European product. With an initial investment of HK$600,000, a joint venture between Splendid Duesseldorf GmbH (51 per cent ownership) and a local Hong Kong entrepreneur resulted in the establishment of a small leather garment manufacturing operation in Hong Kong in 1983.

At that time, Kuepper remained in Duesseldorf, Germany, and assumed responsibility for European marketing and distribution. Gerlach, on the other hand, moved to Hong Kong in order to oversee garment production and to control the sourcing of raw materials. The operation proved to be more difficult to establish than anticipated, and the Hong Kong shareholder, who had other pressing financial concerns, withdrew from Splendid Duesseldorf Production Limited. In late 1985, he sold his share to Gerlach and Kuepper for HK$1.00 per share. Shortly thereafter, Kuepper decided to concentrate solely on European distribution

---

*This case was prepared by Julie H. Yu, Lecturer in the Department of Marketing, The Chinese University of Hong Kong.

and did not wish to continue his involvement in the Hong Kong manufacturing operation. Kuepper and Gerlach purchased shareholdings in the GmbH and the production company, respectively, from each other. Gerlach thus became the sole owner and Managing Director of Splendid Duesseldorf Production Limited in mid-1986. He then invited an expatriate banker and friend, Edward Harris, to join him as financial advisor. In this capacity, Harris was to help in negotiations with Splendid's bankers in order to free Gerlach to devote his efforts to overseeing the business and its operations. In July 1986, Splendid's share capital was increased by a further HK$300,000. Harris acquired a 10 per cent stake in the increased share capital, and replaced Kuepper in jointly (with Gerlach) and severally guaranteeing Splendid's banking obligations.

During the next couple of years, Splendid became quite profitable, and began to pay dividends to its shareholders. By 1989, it had expanded its business to market more aggressively to the US and Japanese markets and undertook a growth strategy. The company leased additional space on another floor of the building which housed its garment factory, and set up a subsidiary in Thailand to augment its production capacity.

Splendid (Thailand) Limited was incorporated in December 1989 with the promotion of the Thailand Board of Investment, and moved into leased factory space early in 1990. Under the direction of Andreas Kirn, a master furrier, the company began to hire and train sewing staff in January 1990 and began production on a small scale a couple of months later. Specific details relating to the production process are discussed in a later section.

Corporate Philosophy

The original founders of Splendid Duesseldorf Production Limited noted that a strategic window was open in the early 1980s. Certain opportunities seemed to exist, and they had the necessary resources to take advantage of such opportunities. They set out to create a market niche by combining their marketing and fashion technology strengths with the competitive advantages of low cost and flexible production facilities in Asia. This original principle has been maintained by Gerlach, and is the key to Splendid's continuing success today.

Leather Garment Industry

In order to gain an understanding of how Splendid has been able to succeed in the competitive garment industry, it is necessary to consider the special characteristics of leather as a raw material. Leather is, in essence, only a material out of which garments are crafted, and in this sense is no different from silk, cotton, wool, or synthetic textiles. It does, however, have two characteristics which make it fundamentally different from textiles as a raw material for garment production. Leather is produced from animal skins which, by nature, are not easily standardized with respect to size, shape, texture, or color, whereas textiles are easily standardized. Also, a given quantity of leather is far more expensive to produce than the same quantity of most other textiles.

These two characteristics force the production and sale of leather garments to be handled somewhat differently from the way in which the manufacture and sale of textile garments is managed. The high cost of leather as a raw material and the wide variety in its quality and appearance make the manufacturing of leather garments a process in which it is difficult to obtain significant economies of scale through high production volumes. The high price of the finished garments makes them less suitable for the type of mass marketing which generates the need for high production volumes in the first place, and makes the style risk in carrying large garment inventories relatively higher than would be the case with textile garments. The variability of the leather skins themselves also works against high volume economies of scale because of the difficulties in producing a standard appearance and quality of garment in large volumes without correspondingly high wastage.

The leather garment industry copes with these difficulties by selling garments in relatively smaller quantities and by minimizing style risk through a process of advance sales through wholesale down to retail levels, by the production and marketing of samples shown and sold largely through trade fairs and the distribution channels of major wholesalers. For instance, Splendid does not produce any garments (other than samples and garments destined for the factory outlet store) except against firm customer orders, which are usually supported by letters of credit.

Traditionally, the most expensive, highest quality leather garments have been produced in Europe (in Italy, France, and Germany), while the lower quality, higher volume production work has generally been done in Turkey, Yugoslavia, and the Far East (primarily Korea and Taiwan). This division of labour between western Europe and eastern Europe and the Far East has developed in part because of the wage differentials between the two key production centres; this has necessitated that the more expensive labour be used to produce the higher quality, more expensive products.

Another factor driving this west/east production split is culture. Garment factories in western Europe are very close to, or in some cases even located within, the fashion centres themselves. It is, therefore, much easier for an Italian factory manager to understand the garments he is asked to produce than it would be for his Korean counterpart, who has very little exposure to western fashion in his daily life.

Fashion houses rarely work only with leather. They design garments in a range of materials, and leather constitutes only one line. Because of the variability of leather and its high cost, a designer seeking to produce high quality, high value garments will want to work closely with the manufacturer to be sure that the final product fits his requirements. This is much easier if the manufacturer has a culturally similar understanding of fashion. For lower quality, higher volume production, the working relationship between the designer and the producer need not be as close, and price becomes the deciding factor in choosing a particular manufacturer. The lowest-cost producer gets the high volume, low value orders.

Since the founding of Splendid, Gerlach has maintained close personal links with leading German fashion wholesalers and has kept himself and his staff updated with respect to developing fashion trends. In addition, Splendid has superior raw material sources built up by Gerlach's extensive travels throughout Europe in search of the best quality tanneries. All skins are inspected at source prior to shipment by a German inspector resident in Europe who also provides Splendid with up-to-date information on sources of supply and new technical developments. Splendid works with over 300 different types of leather sourced primarily from Europe, and can offer a broader understanding of leather as a basic garment material than virtually any other Asian competitor. Over the past eight years, Splendid has developed a flexible manufacturing system which enables it to produce garment orders as small as 50 pieces as cost effectively as orders of 1000 pieces or more. All these factors enable Splendid to position itself as an essentially European manufacturer with a relatively low cost structure.

FINANCE

Splendid reported its first profitable year in 1985, earning HK$398,000. However, it was only with the mid-1986 capital increase and the HK$1.42 million profit of 1986 that its accounts could go into the black. In 1987, the company's growing reputation for quality and reliability allowed it to double its sales and more than double its profits, and with its improved capital base resulting from the retention of all earnings, the company began to expand production capacity to handle increased demand for its products. The factory outlet was moved to separate premises, and the space thus freed was used for additional production.

In 1988, Splendid's sales increased by 60 per cent, and the company earned HK$3.8 million. During that year, the US dollar surged in value against the Deutsche mark, and the Hong Kong dollar, whose value remained pegged at HK$7.80 for one US dollar, also surged against the Deutsche mark. This drastically affected Splendid by making its products relatively expensive in Germany and the rest of Europe. To combat this problem, Splendid diversified its sales and began to sell more aggressively in the US and Japanese markets. This diversification led to a significant increase in sales, which was reflected in the 1989 total sales figure of HK$78.8 million (and HK$5.8 million net profit). All profits since the company's founding had been retained up until 1989, so the company was in a strong capital position and was able to secure larger credit facilities to finance its increasing inventory levels and fund its continuing growth.

Relevant financial information, including the balance sheet and profit and loss account, are provided in the Appendix.

MARKETING

Splendid produces fine leather garments for both men and women by analyzing what the market needs and wants. It serves as part of the design team, and advises its clients on the best raw materials for the products desired, from the standpoint of industrial design. By offering its customers garments which it believes will be most marketable, it serves in the capacity of a sophisticated tailor which customizes its products. The management believes that it should limit output, and thus provide better value for the customers' money.

The products offered by Splendid are diverse, and range from rough motorcycle styles such as the so-called "Bomber Jacket" of antiqued leather lined with lambswool, and the

"Marlboro Man" type of heavy, double-faced sheepskin coat, to very fine printed pig suede ladies' jackets and soft, tailored-looking, full aniline leather skirt-and-jacket ensembles. As a manufacturer, Splendid is generally not concerned with branding. In essence, it makes a generic product, and the brand name is attached by its customers. Splendid's products are sold under a variety of labels in Germany, Sweden, the United Kingdom, Japan, and the United States. Splendid makes garments in more than 200 styles for 59 different customers including such well-known fashion names and houses as Valentino, Ungaro, Robert Comstock, Kenneth Gordon, Gant Sportswear, Quelle Madeleine, Hein Gericke Speedwear, and Rene Lezard. It also has Harvest, its own label.

As already noted, leather as a raw material is relatively more expensive than alternative materials. However, since Splendid has the competitive advantage of lower costs in Asia, it can compete very well against its western European counterparts. Given its solid reputation, buyers now come to Splendid while design concepts are still fluid, seeking guidance on how to convert their ideas into reality with a marketable and competitively-priced garment. With an updated knowledge of available raw material sources and the advance knowledge of fashion developments that this consultative selling process gives Splendid, the company is better positioned to forecast its production schedules, costs, and profits than most other competitors. This, in turn, allows the company to financially outperform its competitors.

Splendid does not engage in any advertising or sales promotions at present. Given its production capacity, it has more customers than it can handle at any given time. Thus, it must be very selective in choosing its customers. In general, Splendid does not deal with those who are price-sensitive, i.e., those who want to buy many units at the lowest price possible. Personal selling is perhaps the most important promotional element used by Splendid. Gerlach's relationships with leading German fashion wholesalers are critical for the organization's continued success, so he may be regarded as the primary salesperson. In addition, ten merchandisers serve to follow up on the work force, and may also be regarded as a sales team which provides post-purchase services.

The management believes that attendance at trade fairs may be important for future growth and development, but no attempt is being made at the present time to attend such fairs, primarily due to production constraints. With respect to distribution decisions, Splendid Duesseldorf Production Limited's production facilities are located in Hong Kong, Thailand, and China. These locations have been chosen in consideration of their cost efficiency. However, Gerlach believes that a global market exists for his leather garments, i.e., he regards the world as his market. Thus, a total systems approach, which takes into account both transportation and storage costs, must be adopted.

MANAGEMENT ISSUES

With production facilities in three locations, it is vital to give close attention to detail. In 1985, when the Hong Kong shareholder withdrew from the organization, Gerlach made several changes in the management systems and key personnel. These changes included:

1. the establishment of a factory outlet to sell garments produced with excess leather during periods of idle capacity
2. implementation of a standard costing system and revised pricing formulae
3. the replacement of staff involved in the purchasing and sourcing of local submaterials (i.e., buttons, zippers, thread, etc.)

Today, Splendid employs 220 workers in Hong Kong and 200 in its Bangkok factory.

PRODUCTION FACILITIES

Splendid Duesseldorf Production Limited has established two production facilities. Splendid-Hong Kong occupies 25,000 square feet and at capacity produces 5,000 garments per month. The factory employs 220 workers and operates six days per week on a single eight-hour shift basis. The factory is in leased premises, but all equipment, furniture, and fixtures are owned by Splendid.

During the past two years, there has been a dramatic reduction in numbers among the traditional low-wage leather garment producing countries. Civil war in Yugoslavia has eliminated that country as a meaningful source of supply. Korea and Taiwan have experienced tremendous inflation in wage rates as well as assets, which has encouraged many manufacturers to close down and divert their energies to real estate and stock market speculation. Even Hong Kong is experiencing shrinkage in its leather garment industry as rising labour costs make it too expensive for producing low value garments and most local manufacturers lack Splendid's ability to attract higher quality, higher value orders.

New countries such as India and China are emerging to take the place of lost production in the traditional low-cost countries, but tremendous infrastructural problems in these countries make supplies uncertain. Splendid has begun to shift its production base to Thailand where it is, thus far, the only leather garment manufacturer producing significant volumes of European-quality garments.

The Splendid-Bangkok factory occupies 1700 square meters, employs 200 workers, and operates six days per week on a single eight-hour shift basis. The factory is in leased premises, but all equipment, furniture, and fixtures are owned by Splendid (Thailand) Limited which, in turn, is owned by Splendid Duesseldorf Production Limited. All raw materials and submaterials are pre-cut and sorted into individual garment packs by Splendid Duesseldorf Production Limited in Hong Kong and then sent by air freight to Splendid (Thailand) in Bangkok for assembly (sewing and finishing) before shipment to buyers overseas. As of now, Splendid (Thailand) Limited is producing approximately 5,000 garments per month from pre-cut and pre-sorted packs prepared in Hong Kong. Using this same pre-cut pack technique to control quality and wastage, Splendid has, since mid-1990, been successfully using a number of small factories in Guangdong province in the People's Republic of China to produce garments on a subcontract basis in order to handle excess production requirements during seasonal peaks.

Rapidly rising wage rates in Korea and Taiwan have forced leather garment buyers and designers who have traditionally used those countries to supply the bulk of their production requirements to look elsewhere for production arrangements. Splendid, with its Hong Kong, Thailand and China operations, has been able to provide some of the capacity needed to meet this demand. Consequently, even though the worldwide market for leather garments contracted during the second half of 1990 and most of 1991, Splendid's business has continued to grow. By the end of 1991, Splendid had shipped 100,000 garments and had achieved record sales levels of approximately HK$115 million.

In making the move to Thailand, Splendid has relied on the most modern technology in order to generate high quality output despite the initially lower skill levels among workers. For example, it uses German Pfaff sewing machines specifically designed for leather work and computer-grading pattern machines. The latter help to standardize procedures, thus improving quality control and resulting in higher quality products.

Results to date have been encouraging, and the quality of production being obtained by Splendid (Thailand) is equal to that obtained by Splendid in Hong Kong. The rates of production are slower, but low factory overheads and low wage rates more than compensate for this, and production rates will rise as the work force gains in skill over time. In the short time that Splendid (Thailand) has been in operation, the company has overcome most of the infrastructural problems which plague new manufacturers setting up in and around Bangkok and is thus far ahead of any competition which may emerge at a later time.

One of the most serious bottlenecks to be overcome is the clearance of raw material imports through customs. This particular problem can either result in inordinate delays or require the provision of costly and often redundant bank guarantees. The problem was solved by establishing a bonded warehouse in part of the factory premises so that Splendid, in effect, cleared its own imports of raw materials against the re-export of finished goods.

FUTURE STRATEGIES

Splendid's plans for the future call for expansion of its Thailand operation to three times its present size. In order to accomplish this, the company will purchase land and build a new factory. The permission to purchase land is not ordinarily granted to foreign-owned companies, but Splendid has obtained this privilege through its Board of Investment promotion. Because of industrial zoning requirements, Splendid will require at least 9000 square metres of land, which will cost approximately US$1 million for a suitable area with adequate road access and water and power supplies. Factory construction will require another US$2 million, and equipment will cost approximately US$500,000.

Production will be moved from Hong Kong to Thailand with subcontractors in China continuing to be used to handle excess production requirements in peak seasons. Hong Kong will become Splendid's centre for design, purchasing, marketing, and overall management. If the return of Hong Kong to Chinese sovereignty in 1997 presents serious difficulties (which are not anticipated), then the Hong Kong management centre can be easily moved to Thailand or elsewhere.

Splendid also plans in the future to develop its marketing and distribution arms for North America, Europe, and Japan to distribute garments under its own labels. The initial investment in this direction will require the hiring and positioning of personnel in the United States,

Germany, and Japan who will travel to trade exhibitions, organize exhibition booths, and step up direct sales to boutiques, large retail outlets, and small wholesalers. The financial cost of this effort will appear primarily as increased management overhead rather than as large capital outlay, but the process will require several years before it can begin to show meaningful results. As a long-term strategy, the Splendid management foresees the firm's entry into other materials such as textiles. This growth strategy may take approximately ten years.

CONCLUSION

Splendid Duesseldorf Production Limited, as a manufacturer of high quality leather garments, has many competitive advantages. By establishing production facilities in several Asian locations, it has been able to minimize its production and labour costs. Hong Kong provides the advantages of easy import, export, access to materials, good infrastructure and no tariffs. Thailand and China, on the other hand, provide even lower labour costs, but at the same time suffer from the drawback of poor infrastructure with respect to transportation and communications.

The management believes that its continued success has been dependent upon several major points. First and foremost, Splendid has the ability to make the appropriate products to suit its customers' needs. In addition, it has good management to follow up on the production process and other details. Quality, as a core element of its products, is always consistently high. Splendid also has a very good reputation of on-time delivery, thus maximizing customer effectiveness. Finally, price is only a secondary concern to its customers, as product quality assumes primary importance.

Given its basic management philosophy and the growth of the Asian market, it appears that Splendid has a very promising future.

APPENDIX

Splendid Duesseldorf Production Ltd.—Balance Sheet as on 30 November 1995

	31 Oct. 1995 HK$	31 Dec. 1994 HK$
Fixed Asset		
Plant and machinery	533,052	762,924
Furniture and fixture	74,492	0
Office equipment	215,421	258,265
Leasehold improvement	402,387	304,241
Motor vehicles	0	121,604
	1,225,353	1,447,034
Current Assets		
Raw material	10,606,802	10,579,471
Provision for obsolete stock	(2,255,860)	(2,255,860)
WIP	3,592,754	2,507,900
Outlet stock	272,284	1,020,789
Provision for obsolete stock-outlet stock	(262,889)	(535,141)
Consumable store	810,023	423,098
Bank accounts	1,920,836	1,195,053
Petty cash	15,000	8,000
Fixed deposit	1,160,552	9,072,210
Account receivable	3,879,614	5,360,946
Bills receivable	4,246,859	5,428,071
Utilities deposits	1,167,485	786,820
Prepayment and temporary payment	1,453,351	255,721
Current A/C—Splendid Thailand	7,637,362	5,905,772
Current A/C—Core Sino Ltd.	0	0
Investment A/C	4,288,570	3,188,570
	38,532,743	42,941,420
Current Liabilities		
Bank loan	4,762,380	4,867,231
Deposit received and temporary received	910,685	2,941,084
Account payable	1,142,193	1,135,790
Bills payable	2,537,117	3,668,917
Accrued expenses	573,533	380,543
Sundry provisions	2,566,225	1,840,725
Deferred taxation	141,668	278,880
	12,633,801	15,113,170
Net current asset/liabilities	25,898,941	27,828,250
Net assets	27,124,295	29,275,284
Capital Employed		
Capital account	900,000	900,000
Retained profit B/F	20,989,920	26,433,138
Profit for the year	5,234,375	1,942,147
	27,124,295	29,275,285

Case Eight

Splendid Duesseldorf Production Ltd.—Turnover
Schedule 1

	Hong Kong	Thailand	China	Total	YTD
Sales					
Leather garment	850,774	1,999,089	693,874	3,543,736	109,492,985
Sample garment	161,929	0	0	161,929	0
Textile garment	420,312	0	0	420,312	0
Sales return	(13,794)	0	0	(13,794)	(411,738)
	1,419,221	1,999,089	693,874	4,112,184	109,081,247

Cost of Sales
Schedule 2

	Hong Kong	Thailand	China	Total	YTD
Raw material	446,421	0	348,960	795,380	15,961,377
Cost of finished goods	284,040	1,298,570	0	1,582,610	52,452,267
Import cartage	21,522	503	0	22,025	235,259
Import insurance	17,933	0	0	17,933	93,813
Import freight	60,382	437	0	60,819	714,831
Processing charges	6,270	0	0	6,270	420,921
	836,569 59%	1,299,510 65%	348,960 50%	2,485,038 60%	69,878,468
Outlet sales	28,474	0	0	28,474	663,671
Cost of outlet stock	0	0	0	0	(631,060)
	28,474	0	0	28,474	32,611
Contribution II	611,127	699,579	344,914	1,655,620	39,235,390

Factory Overheads
Schedule 3

	Hong Kong	Thailand	China	Total	YTD
Factory rent and rates	79,255	0	0	79,255	1,195,902
Factory electricity and water	11,061	0	0	11,061	137,551
Depreciation on plant and machinery	32,368	0	0	32,368	356,044
Indirect wages	306,948	0	0	306,948	3,710,169
Severance pay	0	0	0	0	614,196
New year bonus	39,730	0	0	39,730	436,197
Workers welfare and refreshments	22	0	0	22	4,271
Insurance	6,500	0	0	6,500	78,064
Factory printing and stationery	2,993	0	0	2,993	138,391
Repairs and maintenance	22,000	0	0	22,000	341,304
Tools and spare parts	17,846	0	0	17,846	107,476
Factory cleaning expenses	7,483	0	0	7,483	15,442
Factory general expenses	190	0	0	190	10,763
Packing material	22,395	16,894	0	39,289	340,726
	548,791	16,894	0	565,685	7,486,497

Splendid Duesseldorf Production Ltd.—Selling and Distribution Expenses   Schedule 4

	Hong Kong	Thailand	China	Total	YTD
Commission paid	530,872	0	0	530,872	5,183,390
Certificate and declaration fee	11,192	0	610	11,802	132,427
Export cartage	8,667	1,912	0	10,580	290,990
Export insurance	7,774	0	0	7,774	77,970
Export freight	7,964	80,616	0	88,580	1,159,476
Inspection charges	0	0	0	0	593,305
Product design and development	0	0	0	0	265,318
Sampling charges	13,162	0	0	13,162	186,957
Transportation and storage	17,030	0	1,455	18,485	278,194
Advertising	0	0	0	0	5,040
	596,660	82,528	2,065	681,254	8,173,066

Administration Expenses   Schedule 5

	Hong Kong	Thailand	China	Total	YTD
Office rent and rates	50,164	0	0	50,164	756,008
Office electricity and water	4,740	0	0	4,740	55,748
Performance bonus	0	0	0	0	0
Salaries and allowance	425,551	34,800	0	460,351	5,007,144
Housing allowance	188,579	0	0	188,579	1,823,236
Double pay	33,900	0	0	33,900	398,805
Provident fund	13,471	0	0	13,471	107,209
Staff welfare and refreshments	10,000	0	0	10,000	120,000
Staff recruitment and training	19,227	0	0	19,227	97,304
Insurance	19,464	0	0	19,464	213,878
Office printing and stationery	11,003	0	0	11,003	110,570
Telephone and fax charges	26,252	0	0	26,252	218,362
Office cleaning expenses	3,207	0	0	3,207	7,174
Office general expenses	1,261	0	0	1,261	95,593
Local travelling	1,084	0	0	1,084	11,678
Entertainment	6,265	0	0	6,265	119,869
Overseas travelling	40,000	4,254	396	44,650	667,713
Motor vehicles expenses	21,878	0	0	21,878	117,419
Stamp duty and postage	23,048	792	0	23,840	134,336
Computer expenses	6,880	0	0	6,880	96,811
Discount allowed	234	0	0	234	107,083
Subscription	6,181	0	0	6,181	15,731
Donation	0	0	0	0	0
Audit fee	7,000	0	0	7,000	77,000
Legal and professional	55,959	0	0	55,959	313,750
Disposal of fixed asset	0	0	0	0	(37,081)
Depreciation on F and F	1,520	0	0	1,520	16,723
Depreciation on office equipment	25,587	0	0	25,587	205,378
Depreciation on leasehold improvement	18,454	0	0	18,454	481,266
Depreciation on motor vehicle	0	0	0	0	98,685
	1,020,910	39,846	396	1,061,151	11,437,392

Case Eight

Splendid Duesseldorf Production Ltd.—Financial Charges — Schedule 6

	Hong Kong	Thailand	China	Total	YTD
Bank OD and bill interest	82,233	0	0	82,233	734,505
Bank charges	38,729	0	0	38,729	481,460
Exchange gain/loss	(120,741)	1,160	0	(119,581)	408,778
	221	1,160	0	1,381	1,624,74

Other Income — Schedule 7

	Hong Kong	Thailand	China	Total	YTD
Income—Claim received	0	0	0	0	(39,506)
Income—Discount received	(4,807)	0	0	(4,807)	(52,285)
Income—Interest received	(5,235)	0	0	(5,235)	(141,182)
Income—Sales scarp leather	(10,109)	0	0	(10,109)	(156,345)
Income—Profit/Loss on leather sales	0	0	0	0	11,895
Income—Sundry income	(7,217)	0	0	(7,217)	(150,564)
Income—Profit/Loss sales Thailand	0	9,572	0	9,572	(577,994)
	(27,368)	9,572	0	(17,796)	(1,105,981)

CASE NINE

HONGKONG AND SHANGHAI BANKING CORPORATION LIMITED*

GLOBAL STRATEGY

The Hongkong and Shanghai Banking Corporation Limited (The Hongkong Bank or HSBC Holdings plc) has been described as "the world's fastest growing bank" and as having "the largest market capitalization of all quoted banks in the world."

The Hongkong Bank has begun to diversify its business and is going international in order to reduce the political risk after 1997. Knowing about China's intention for the future of Hong Kong, it accelerated its overseas acquisition and diversification. The global banking approach as stated by the chairman of HSBC would probably be the key development strategy in the near future.[1] With the merger with Marine Midland and other banking groups, HSBC serves both retail and wholesale banking in a global network. HSBC's head office is in London, a center of world banking power. In the last few decades, it has outperformed it competitors, established a special relationship with the Hong Kong government, gained the support from local businessmen, and survived a series of banking crises. It grew as Hong Kong developed into the financial center it is today. Finally, it became a dominant bank in Hong Kong and developed its global financial empire. It also became one of the most powerful foreign banks in China, the first foreign bank to set up a full branch in that country.

---

* This case was prepared by Irene Chow, Senior Lecturer in Department of Management, Chinese University of Hong Kong.

Case Nine

Brief History

The Hongkong and Shanghai Bank was founded in Shanghai in 1865 to finance the development of China trade. The Chinese characters chosen were 匯豐 "Way Foong"—abundance of remittances.[2] It was incorporated with limited liability in Hong Kong in 1866. The Bank started with an original capital of HK$5,000,000. It opened its branches simultaneously in Hong Kong and Shanghai to finance the development of the growing trade between China and the United States and Europe.

Hongkong Bank played an important role in financing Hong Kong's industrialization during the period 1950–1966.[3] When the Communists took over in China and with the outbreak of the Korean War, Hong Kong switched from an entrepot trade to manufacturing industries. It was estimated that Hong Kong's GDP grew at an annual compound rate of about 8.3 per cent in nominal terms, or about 7 per cent in real terms from 1950 to 1966. HSBC was the largest bank responsible for providing Hong Kong's industrialists and entrepreneurs with necessary finance for creating and expanding the territory's manufacturing industries. HSBC provided 48.3 per cent of the total bank finance to the manufacturing sector in June 1966.

From the 1940s to the 1990s, the Hongkong and Shanghai Banking Corporation has developed from a regional bank to a multinational group. The HSBC Group is an international banking and financial services organization. The successful merger with Midland Bank of England in 1993, along with the recovery in earnings of its overseas banks, has made HSBC Holdings one of the world's 10 largest banks. The total number of shares outstanding at the end of 1992 was 1,691,030,535 and their market value was HK$139,868,257,401. Its shares are held by shareholders in over 80 countries.

The Group's long-term strategic objective is to become one of the top **transnational** financial institutions of the world: to diversify internationally to such an extent that Hong Kong will eventually account for an insignificant proportion of the Group's total assets and profits. The acquisition of Midland fulfilled its long-standing strategic goal to establish a major presence in Europe to complement its extensive network in Asia-Pacific and the Americas.

Hongkong Bank's Major Business Lines and Principal Activities

Hongkong Bank is a global financial conglomerate that comprises a wide array of financial institutions. The Bank and its subsidiaries and associated companies provide a comprehensive range of commercial and investment banking, insurance and other financial and related services through a network of more than 3,000 offices in 66 countries in Asia, Europe, the Middle East, Australia and America.[4] It ranks among the top 10 banking groups in the world with a staff of more than 99,000. It provides an array of financial services to individuals, businesses, governments, and financial institutions. Its principal activities and companies include commercial banking, merchant banking and capital markets, investment, transportation, securities services, financial services, insurance retirement benefits, and finance company trustee and nominee companies. Its activities include mortgages, credit cards, personal finance, trade financing and syndicated loans.

Hongkong Bank has a well-established retail banking network. In order to cope with the strong and growing demand for banking services resulting from Hong Kong's rapid industrialization, HSBC has opened more and more branches. It offers the convenience of 239 branches throughout Hong Kong. Aside from Hongkong Bank's commitment to Hong Kong, expansion is being planned for the nearby countries.

THE BANKING INDUSTRY

Hong Kong has emerged as an important financial center. The banking sector employed a total of 76,110 employees. The Hong Kong banking system adopts a three-tier system which is formed by the following three deposit-taking intermediaries:[5]

(i) LICENSED BANKS. Licensed banks are authorized to accept deposits of any amount at any maturity in the normal course of business. Their interest rates are subject to the agreed rate of the Hong Kong Association of Banks. The number of licensed banks rose considerably from 115 in 1980 to 168 in 1990. In 1992, the number of licensed banks in operation was 164, with a total of 1409 branches. Among the 164 licensed banks, 30 were incorporated in Hong Kong, while the other 134 were incorporated outside.

(ii) RESTRICTED LICENSE BANKS. Restricted license banks are allowed to take deposits of any maturity at any rate of interest provided the amount of each deposit is not less than HK$500,000 or its equivalent in any other currency. Only deposit-taking companies having a minimum authorized capital of HK$100 million and paid-up capital of HK$100 million or its equivalent, are eligible to be licensed subject to the permission of the Financial Secretary. Unlike the licensed banks, they are not authorized to provide current account facilities to their customers. In 1992, the number of restricted license banks was 56.

(iii) DEPOSIT-TAKING COMPANIES. Deposit-taking companies are allowed to take deposits only of maturities exceeding three months at any rate of interest provided each deposit is not less than HK$100,000 or its equivalent. The criterion of minimum paid up capital is raised to HK$15 million. The number of deposit-taking companies dropped from 302 in 1980 to 147 in 1992.

LOANS AND DEPOSITS. In 1992, Hongkong Bank had captured 38 per cent of the deposits in the local market; Hang Seng Bank (part of the HSBC group) accounted for 17 per cent— a total of 55 per cent. Bank of China Group, the second largest network, accounted for 23 per cent in 1991. Bank of East Asia had 3 per cent of the market share. In 1992, the total loans to customers were HK$2,470 billion, and deposits from customers were HK$1,503 billion. The share of total loans and deposits for licensed banks were 94 per cent, the rest being equally split between the restricted license banks and deposit-taking companies.

Despite increased competition and activity, the industry is enjoying an increase in its earnings. The profit growth was in the range of 25 to 45 per cent in 1992. Banks in Hong Kong are able to earn a wide spread in interest differential. Total deposits rose by 9 per cent in 1992.[6] However, the deposit growth rate in the Hong Kong market has begun to decline. The reason is that the growth in local currency deposits was slower than that of loans. Exhibit 1 presents total deposits in Hong Kong. The growth rate of Hong Kong currency deposits dropped from 24 per cent in 1991 to around 13 per cent in 1993. The interest rate from savings account is only 1.5 per cent while inflation runs at 9 per cent. The decline in bank deposits appears to stem from customers' desire for higher return on investments, particularly in the stock market and the property market which enjoyed a record bull run after the Gulf War in 1991. There was also a shift towards demand and savings accounts as depositors preferred to stay liquid to take advantage of investment opportunities, particularly in the stock market. The loan to deposit ratio in Hong Kong dollars for the banking system as a whole fell slightly in 1992. The shortage of Hong Kong dollar funds of licensed banks has influenced their operating strategy. They are increasingly focusing on fee-based income instead of their traditional lending business.

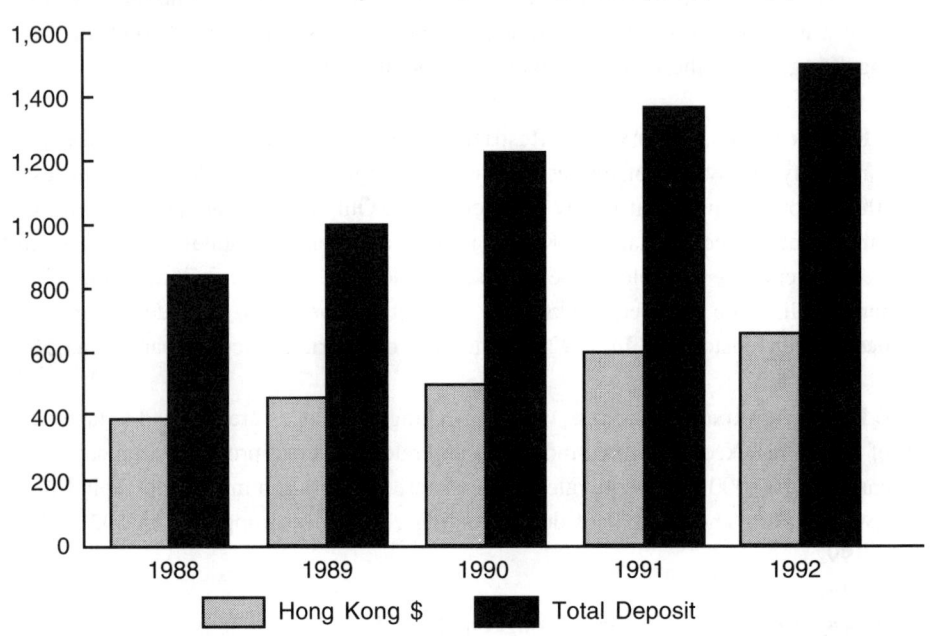

Exhibit 1 Total Deposits from Customers (HK$, billion)

Source: Commissioner of Banking, Hong Kong, *Annual Report*, 1992.

COMPETITION. The banking industry in Hong Kong is operating under fierce competition. To gain insight into the competitive environment, there are 367 authorized financial institutions with 1,485 branches in a small city state with six million people. The Hongkong Bank Group is the market leader in the banking sector.

Despite keen competition, certain specializations exist in the banking sector. The banks tend to group according to their policies. Hongkong Bank concentrates on international and wholesale banking while Hang Seng Bank deals with local retail banking. The Bank of China group is involved mainly in financing the sales of mainland products and investment in China, thereby accommodating foreign exchange reserve for China. Other European, Asian, and American banks specialize in the finance of foreign trade, especially concerned with the finance of trade with their home countries. First Pacific Bank concentrates its effort on mortgage loans while Bank of East Asia has well-established branches in China.

THE HONGKONG BANK AS A QUASI-CENTRAL BANK

There is no central bank in Hong Kong. The Hongkong Bank historically has taken over some of the functions of a central bank in Hong Kong. The Commissioner of Banking exercises supervision and control through the Banking Ordinance. The functions of a central bank are carried out by different private and public companies. Hongkong Bank and Standard Chartered Bank are the banks of the government and serve as financial advisors. They are also the settlement banks of commercial banks. The Office of the Commissioner of Banking monitors the administration of all authorized financial institutions.

HSBC used to play the role of the quasi-central bank in Hong Kong. It also serves as the banker to the Hong Kong government. The majority of the central banking functions have been carried out by HSBC. It runs the clearing house in Hong Kong and issues over 80 per cent of the Hong Kong currency. It is a prominent member of the Hong Kong Association of Banks (HKAB) which acts as a medium of regulation for changes in the deposit interest rate of the licensed banks. The interest rate agreement of the Hong Kong Association of Banks can be used as an instrument of macro-monetary policy.

In view of the special privileges accorded HSBC—such as statutory chairmanship of HKAB; performing the functions of principal banker to the Government; acting as agent of the Government in monetary policy actions; allotment of a permanent seat on the highest policy-making body, the Executive Council; running the Clearing House; and acting as settlement bank—HSBC has access to confidential information about the clearing positions of its main rivals. The special relationship with the government and special power in the Hong Kong banking industry give HSBC some competitive advantages.[7]

It is very unusual that a bank combines the roles of a profit-making commercial bank and a quasi-central bank. There has always been criticism that there may be a conflict of interest between commercial banking and central banking functions—between profit motive and social responsibility. With the setting up of a separate monetary authority, some of these priviliged activities will be taken over by the Hong Kong Monetary Authority. It may help to solve some of the problems and prevent conflict of interest and concentration of power.

CURRENCY ISSUING BANKS

The Hongkong Bank and the Standard Chartered Bank are two major currency-issuing banks in Hong Kong. The Hongkong Bank, the largest currency-issuing bank in Hong Kong, issues about 80 per cent of the currency in Hong Kong. As one of the note-issuing banks, Standard Chartered Bank pursues a defensive strategy to maintain its present market share and position with no further expansion in the local market. In the transitional period, the Bank of China Group will issue notes in Hong Kong starting 1994.

THE NAME AND IDENTITY CHANGE. As Hong Kong had been transformed into a major world banking and commercial center, the Hongkong and Shanghai Bank had grown into a global bank. There was a need for a new head office to meet the expansion requirement of a new era in the Bank's operation. A modernized steel-framed building was built in 1986 by Foster Associates, symbolizing the "high tech" approach in British architecture. The new bank tried to develop a new corporate image with its red and white hexagon logo. The symbol of the lions were kept.

The redevelopment of Queen's Road Head Office showed the Bank's commitment to Hong Kong and confidence in its future as an international financial center. With Hong Kong due to revert to China in 1997, Hongkong Bank was restructured with a new holding company, HSBC Holdings plc, domiciled in Britain and with dual primary listing in London and Hong Kong in 1990. The Chinese authorities in Beijing strongly criticized HSBC's decision to shift its domicile to London. The Bank restructured itself again in 1993 to create a London-based parent, HSBC Holdings plc, and Hongkong Bank became its wholly owned subsidiary. As a leading bank in Hong Kong, HSBC also donated some funds to carry out its social responsibility, e.g., to support socio-cultural activities, education (scholarships and language development), environmental protection (Center of Environmental Technology), and to sponsor charity activities in health and welfare (hostel and day-activity center for the mentally handicapped, Rehabilitation Center and Cancer Fund). Advertising and promotional campaigns were launched.

GROUP ORGANIZATIONAL STRUCTURE

Following the acquisition of Midland bank in 1992, the HSBC Group reorganized its senior management structure. The Group's worldwide activities were restructured under four key lines of business: commercial banking, investment banking, private banking and insurance. The global business was arranged into four regional areas: Asia-Pacific, America, Middle East and Europe. The HSBC Group's Organizational Structure Chart is shown in Exhibit 2.

Exhibit 2 Hongkong and Shanghai Banking Corporation—Organization Structure

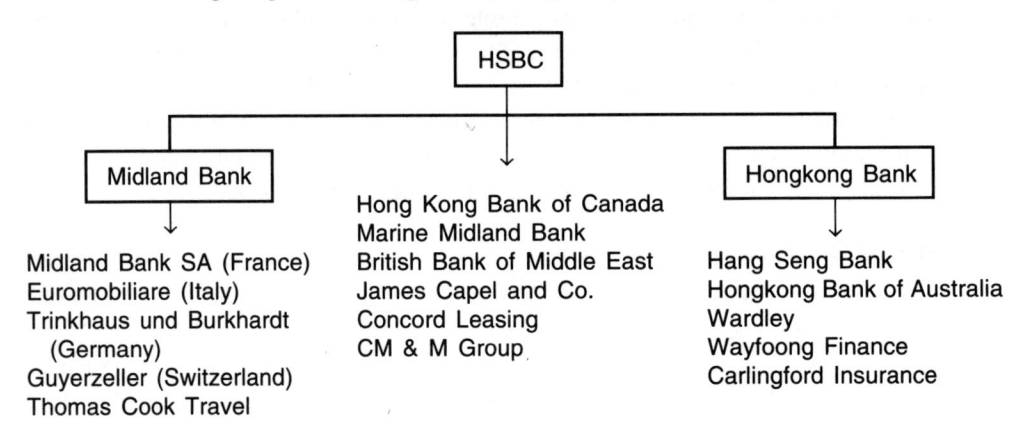

```
                          HSBC
        ┌──────────────────┼──────────────────┐
   Midland Bank                            Hongkong Bank
        │         Hong Kong Bank of Canada         │
        │         Marine Midland Bank              │
Midland Bank SA (France)   British Bank of Middle East   Hang Seng Bank
Euromobiliare (Italy)      James Capel and Co.           Hongkong Bank of Australia
Trinkhaus und Burkhardt    Concord Leasing               Wardley
  (Germany)                CM & M Group                  Wayfoong Finance
Guyerzeller (Switzerland)                                Carlingford Insurance
Thomas Cook Travel
```

For such a large "empire," the reorganization, especially in decentralizing the decision making power, is necessary to put management back to branches which are closer to the customers. It redefines itself as a global federation of well-capitalized autonomous banks and financial houses. HSBC group chairman and chief executive, Sir William Purves, said, "We have a policy of delegating responsibility to individuals depending on experience."

A majority of the members of the Board of Directors are British expatriates. The number of foreign staff sitting on the Board of Directors is 18 out of 20, or 90 per cent. Many of the Group's senior officers joined the company straight out of British schools. Sufficiently well-defined career paths and career planning are used to assure that quality officers will be available to meet the Group's requirements. HSBC has established a regional training center to provide a wide range of training activities for its employees. The chairman of the Group is described as the most powerful man in Hong Kong, next to the governor. He sits on the governor's Executive Council, a high-level advisory body. During the bank failures in the mid-1980s and the stock crash of October 1987 and bank runs in the early 1990s, HSBC helped to stabilize the monetary system in Hong Kong. All the large companies kept the government tuned in to the interest of business.

The HSBC was among the first banks to computerize its banking operations. It now operates a system of Automated Teller Machine (ATM) services jointly with the Hang Seng Bank in Hong Kong. It is also the founder of the Easy Pay System. It offers a technologically developed office automation systems computerized network enhancing cost effectiveness of banking operation, more sophisticated services such as telephone banking service, ATMs, global banking services, and credit card operations through ATMs. It provides customers with access to more than 150,000 ATMs in over 60 countries. Its computerized banking operations help ease the problems of labor shortages and high operating costs due to high inflation. Other coping strategies have included moving the data entry section across the border into China and hiring high-potential graduates from China to fill teller positions.

PERFORMANCE

In 1992, HSBC's pretax profits soared by 94 per cent, to HK$2.6 billion, and Hong Kong provided HK$1.7 billion of the total profits. Loan demand soared by 20 per cent. It dominated consumer and business lending and controlled 40 per cent of Hong Kong's capital-to-assets ratio, among the strongest of any bank in the world. Of the Group's pre-tax profits 51.8 per cent were derived from the Asia-Pacific region.[8] The income statement and balance sheet are shown in Exhibits 3 and 4. The Hongkong Bank and Hang Seng Bank, the most profitable, occupied the top two positions according to their profit after tax. These two banks together accounted for approximately 55 per cent of the total deposits in Hong Kong. Here are some key financial indicators:

From 1960 to 1980, the growth rate of HSBC registered a 37.5-fold increase over the 20 years. There are no other banks and very few other companies with a profit record comparable to that of HSBC. HSBC's ratio of profit to deposits (as a measure of its efficiency) were: 0.75 per cent in the 1960s; 0.8 per cent in the 1970s; 1.0 per cent in 1978; and 0.92 per cent in 1992.

Exhibit 3 HSBC Holdings plc—Income Statement

Consolidated Profit and Loss Account for the year ended December 31, 1992

1991 £m		1992 £m	1992 HK$m	1992 US$m
6,364	Interest income	8,999	105,540	13,633
(4,523)	Interest expense	(5,661)	(66,392)	(8,576)
1,841	Net interest income	3,338	39,148	5,057
1,204	Other operating income	2,626	30,798	3,978
3,045	Operating income	5,964	69,946	9,035
(1,779)	Operating expenses	(3,377)	(39,605)	(5,116)
1,266	Operating profit before charge for bad and doubtful debts	2,587	30,341	3,919
(502)	Charge for bad and doubtful debts	(1,185)	(13,898)	(1,795)
764	Operating profit	1,402	16,443	2,124
25	Share of profits less losses of asociated undertakings	38	446	58
789	Profit before exceptional items and taxation	1,440	16,889	2,182
91	Exceptional items	270	3,167	409
880	Profit before taxation	1,710	20,056	2,591
(173)	Taxation	(283)	(3,319)	(429)
707	Profit after taxation	1,427	16,737	2,162
(121)	Profit attributable to minority interests	(206)	(2,416)	(312)
586	Profit attributable to the shareholders	1,221	14,321	1,850
(207)	Dividends	(472)	(5,536)	(715)
379	Retained profit for the year	749	8,785	1,135

Other Financial Highlights

1991 Pence	Per share	1992 Pence	1992 HK$	1992 US$
36.06	Earnings	62.07	7.28	0.94
12.71	Dividends	19.00	2.23	0.29
295.62	Net asset value	319.55	37.48	4.84

£m	Balance sheet	£m	HK$m	US$m
4,819	Shareholders' funds	8,011	93,952	12,138
85,786	Total assets	170,450	1,999,037	258,232

Comparative figures for 1991 have been amended to conform with the current year's presentation following the disclosure of the Group's inner reserves in 1992.

Source: Annual Report, 1992.

Exhibit 4 HSBC Holdings plc—Consolidated Balance Sheet at December 31, 1992

1991 £m		1992 £m	1992 HK$m	1992 JS$m
	Assets			
23,221	Cash and short-term funds	35,386	415,007	53,610
8,363	Placings with banks maturing between one and 12 months	14,148	165,928	21,434
2,765	Trade bills and certificates of deposit	6,324	74,168	9,581
2,757	Hong Kong government certificates of indebtedness	4,313	50,583	6,534
6,473	Investments	14,576	170,947	22,083
39,385	Advances to customers and other accounts	90,517	1,061,583	137,133
82,964		165,264	1,938,216	250,375
148	Investments in associated undertakings	404	4,738	612
2,674	Premises and equipment	4,782	56,083	7,245
85,786		170,450	1,999,037	258,232
	Liabilities			
2,761	Hong Kong currency notes in circulation	4,318	50,642	6,542
76,089	Current, deposit and other accounts	151,801	1,780,322	229,978
147	Proposed dividend	356	4,175	539
78,997		156,475	1,835,139	237,059
	Capital Resources			
1,274	Loan capital and preference shares	4,665	54,711	7,067
696	Minority interests	1,299	15,235	1,968
1,120	Share capital	2,054	24,089	3,112
3,699	Reserves	5,957	69,863	9,026
4,819	Shareholders' funds	8,011	93,952	12,138
6,789		13,975	163,898	21,173
85,786		170,450	1,999,037	258,232

The ratio of advances to deposits at the end of 1990 was 54.8 per cent. The ratio increased to 59.6 per cent in 1992. Advances to customers and other accounts totalled HK$1.1 billion. The Group has set a target of bringing the advances/deposits ratio down to 50 per cent, making HSBC the most liquid international bank in the world, along with geographic spread with a good profit record. The Group's total capital adequacy ratio was 12.3 for 1991 and 1992.

The assets of the group have continued to increase rapidly. The growth of profits and assets was generated basically from internal resources. During the period 1981 to 1990, the relative shares of its two principal geographical areas, Asia Pacific and Europe, increased from 37.5 per cent to 50.8 per cent and from 14.3 per cent to 20.2 per cent respectively. In 1990 the Hongkong Bank Group's worldwide geographic distribution of assets was 50.8 per cent in Asia-Pacific, 26.3 per cent in America, 2.7 per cent in the Middle East, and 20.2 per cent in Europe, compared to the position a decade ago, 38 per cent in Asia-Pacific, 42 per cent in America, and 18 per cent in Europe. Its assets doubled after the acquisition of Midland Bank. The acquisition of Midland Bank shifted 45.8 per cent of the Group's total assets to Europe. At the end of 1992, the total assets of the Group increased to £170.5 billion, 99 per cent more than the previous year, while shareholders' funds showed an increase of 66 per cent in the same period. The major components of assets consisted of advances (49.7 per cent), fixed assets (3.2 per cent), cash and short-term funds (23.2 per cent), and placings with other banks (14.1 per cent). By any measure, the Hongkong Bank Group performed well.

EXPANSION AND DIVERSIFICATION. In its home-based market, Hong Kong Bank acquired a controlling stake (51 per cent) in the Hang Seng Bank, which had been the target of a bank run in 1965. Wardley Limited was formed in Hong Kong in 1972 and is specialized in corporate finance, investment services and other merchant banking activities. The wholly owned subsidiary Wardley Ltd. and Jardine Fleming Holdings Ltd. were upgraded to licensed banks in March 1993. It has grown in sophistication and expanded its empire. HSBC took the first step in its global ambitions in the 1980s when it racked up billions in losses on a takeover of Buffalo, New York-based Marine Midland Bank Inc. and loans to Canadian real estate developer Olympia & York Development Ltd. The investment in Marine Midland Banks incorporation by HSBC first took 25 per cent of the shares, further reached 41 per cent in March 1980 and 51 per cent in October 1980. The transaction had cost HSBC US$314 million. The purchase of 51 per cent of the shares of Marine Midland Bank Inc. saw a major shift of assets from its Hong Kong base to America. In December 1990, Hongkong Bank announced a proposal to reorganize the group under a new holding company, HSBC Holdings plc. In 1991, HSBC Holdings plc was incorporated in England. Hongkong Bank will be the principal subsidiary of the new group. Hongkong Bank announced a split between its Asia operations and other overseas assets in HSBC Holdings plc, with dual primary listing on the stock exchanges of London and Hong Kong.

HSBC was seeking an entry point into European banking with a merger. The acquisition of Midland Bank and the shift of its registration to London showed that HSBC wanted to expand its business worldwide. The bank's first attempt to acquire 14.9 per cent of Midland Bank's stock took place in November 1987. In 1993, HSBC Holdings successfully took over British Midland Bank, the fourth largest bank in Britain and gained a major European presence. The £3.9 billion bid takeover-battle with Lloyds Banks for Midland Bank involved offering 120 HSBC Holdings shares plus £65 cash or bonds for every 100 Midland shares. The transaction created a bank-holding company with assets of HK$1.9 trillion (US$246 billion) and 3,200 branches and offices throughout the world.

OVERSEAS OPERATIONS. HSBC's overseas operations were not as successful as its performance in the Asia-Pacific region. After the acquisition of Marine Midland and Hongkong Bank of Australia, the Group suffered heavy losses from its overseas subsidiaries. The value of commercial property in many parts of New York State had fallen by 40 per cent. Marine made losses of almost US$500 million because of massive bad-debt provisions on its property and a highly leveraged transaction lending book. Billions of dollars were made to cover its huge overseas losses. Charges for bad and doubtful debts amounted to £1,185 million in 1992.

With the acquisition of Midland Bank, HSBC pursues a global operating strategy in Asia, America and Europe. The merged group has formed one of the top 10 largest banks in the world, with total assets of £164 billion, and 100,000 staff in more than 3,200 branches in 66 countries with assets spread over five continents—in North America, Europe, and Asia Pacific.

THE BANK AND THE FUTURE

The financial services market will become more complex and turbulent. The HSBC Group envisions establishing and sustaining a competitive advantage in terms of market position across business lines and diverse geographic markets. Diversification and expansion present significant opportunities, but also uncertainty. Given HSBC's strategic role in Hong Kong's financial system, its future moves, especially after the transfer of sovereignty in 1997, will be of great concern to Hongkong. Will Hongkong Bank gradually leave Hong Kong? The withdrawal of the Group will have catastrophic effects on Hong Kong's financial system. Will its competitor, the Bank of China Group, being the second largest banking group in Hong Kong (its affiliates already have 300 branches in Hong Kong), replace HSBC after 1997?

Over half of HSBC's profits were derived from the Hong Kong-based operations, with Hongkong Bank and Hang Seng Bank the main contributors to the profit of the Group. The Bank will remain a strong presence in Hong Kong. China's vigorous economic growth has contributed to the momentum of Hong Kong's economy. Hong Kong would be able to participate in the economic expansion in southern China. The Group will continue to benefit from its strong position in the Asia-Pacific region. The Asia-Pacific region comprises 37 per cent of the Group's total assets but contributes about half of the group's profit. It will still play an important role in Hong Kong in the transitional period. Beijing needs the bank's capital and know-how to maintain prosperity and stability of the Hong Kong economy. HSBC will not move its base from Hong Kong because it is the most profitable place to be, maybe anywhere in the world. HSBC's image is associated with it being a Far East-based bank, and it remains essentially a Hong Kong-based company. It will continue to serve the needs of the people of Hong Kong. Sir William Purves' strategy is to make the bank appear to be a local bank, having an international presence at the same time. The Bank is well-prepared for the future. Maintaining a good relationship and cultivating a tie with China's elite are good strategies to ensure its position in the post-1997 era.

Top management is clearly optimistic and views 1997 as an opportunity. China offers great potential for financial development. Hongkong Bank is trying to re-establish its preeminence in China. The Bank has adopted an expansionary policy as seen from its presence in many major ports on the China coast. Now it has 13 offices scattered around the country. The HSBC aspires to continue to maintain its leadership position to and beyond 1997.

APPENDIX

Top 10 Financial Institutions in Hong Kong (profit after tax)

Rank 1991	Rank 1992	Name of Institution	HK$ (millions)
1	1	Hongkong and Shanghai Banking Corp.	11,810
2	2	Hang Seng Bank	5,698
3	3	Bank of East Asia	685
5	4	Nanyang Commercial Bank	589
6	5	Po Sang Bank	569
4	6	Shanghai Commercial Bank	501
8	7	Wing Lung Bank	391
7	8	Security Pacific Asian Bank	367
9	9	Wayfoong Finance	356
10	10	Overseas Trust Bank	353

ENDNOTES

1. Global Banker: Willie Purves is racing to remake Hong Kong's big bank, *Business Week*, No. 3307–3637, May 24, 1993, pp. 42–46.
2. Collis, Maurice, *Way Foong: The Hongkong and Shanghai Banking Corporation,* London: Faber and Faber, 1965.
3. Jao, Y.C., Financial Hong Kong's Early Postwar Industrialization: The role of the Hongkong and Shanghai Banking Corporation, in Frank H.H. King (Ed.), *Eastern Banking: Essays in the history of the Hongkong and Shanghai Banking Corporation,* London: Athlone Press, 1983, pp. 545–574.
4. The HSBC Holdings plc, *Annual Report*, 1992.
5. Commissioner of Banking, *Annual Report*, Monetary Affairs Branch, Government Secretariat, Hong Kong Government, 1992, pp. 40–43.
6. *Ibid.*
7. Jao, Y.C., The Role of the Hongkong Bank, in R.Y.K. Ho, R.H. Scott, and K.A. Wong (Eds.), *The Hong Kong Financial System,* Hong Kong: Oxford University Press, 1991.
8. HSBC Holdings plc, *Annual Report*, 1992.

COUNTRY PROFILE

CHINA: THE EVOLVING ECONOMIC FORCE*

OVERVIEW

POPULATION AND GEOGRAPHY

China's unique characteristics include its vast land size of 3.7 million square miles populated with 1.2 billion people. Two-thirds of China's vast territory is mountainous or desert and only one-tenth of its lands is cultivated. Its eastern half is one of the best watered lands in the world with three river systems providing water for its farmlands. The official language is Mandarin and the main religions and philosophies are Confucianism, Buddhism and Taoism.

GOVERNMENT

China's government structure can be described as centralized because all of China falls under one government. Its government structure basically has two levels, the central government and the regional/local governments. At the highest level in government is the National People's Congress (NPC) which is a body of elected officials and defined by the constitution as the highest body of power in the state. China's governing system basically has three branches, all of which fall under the NPC. The three branches are the legislative/executive, judicial and arms branch.

---

* This country profile was prepared by Laurence Marsh, Hayeley Miyagi, Janis Kawano, and Carol Wilhelman, University of Hawaii.

HISTORY

The history of China can be traced back 5,000 years when the first signs of Chinese culture existed in the form of a primitive communal system which comprised clans, collective ownership and sharing. This primitive communal system evolved through various transitions into higher and more unified forms of society as can be seen through China's imperial period.

THE IMPERIAL PERIOD

The socio-economic development of China during the imperial period includes the **Shang Dynasty** (16th to 11th century BC) during which time the Chinese began using a written script and a calendar to keep historical records. Following the Shang Dynasty was the **Zhou Dynasty** (11th century to 221 BC) during which time Chinese philosophers such as Confucius, Mo Zi and Lao Zi lived. It was during this time that the "One Hundred Schools of Thought" developed which included Confucianism, Legalism, Mohism and Taoism. All these schools of thought have influenced Chinese managerial and administrative behavior even up to the present time. However, of all the schools of thought, Confucianism had the greatest impact on China. Confucius' ideas have continued to affect Chinese thinking long after his death and thrive even today. Confucius believed that all men were equal. He also believed in the appointment of "good and capable" people to official posts. Despite his beliefs, however, he never opposed the existing hereditary system. He also regarded benevolence as the highest type of morality. He believed that in order to bring order and peace, we all need to recognize our place in the world. By this, he meant that sons obey their fathers, subjects follow the rulers, etc. This resulted in the presence of hierarchical pyramids in many aspects of the Chinese society. Also of importance during the Zhou Dynasty was the Legalist school. One of the most important contributions that Legalism is noted for is the establishment of the civil service system. This consisted of an education system for training civil servants, a public examination system for recruitment, a merit system for promotion, and minute regulations on classification, salary and rotation (Laaksonen, 1988, p. 40).

The list of ruling dynasties continued down to include the **Qin, Han, Tang, Song, Yuan, Ming and Qing Dynasties**. One element which played a significant role in Chinese history is the famous **Hanlin Academy**. This academy was formally developed during the Ming Dynasty but has roots in the Tang Dynasty. The Hanlin Academy was a government institution with close ties with the emperor and was responsible for training management personnel to fill the future high governmental positions. However, it perished in 1906 during the Qing Dynasty and when it died, the training of civil servants and the entrance examinations died with it. The presence of the civil servants training and entrance exams provided public management with quality, strength and respect. When it disappeared, the Chinese government became corrupt and weak.

In sum, Chinese philosophical thinking developed during a time when China's political system was very unstable and the country was experiencing constant internal turmoil amongst its states. Therefore, Chinese philosophical thinking in all its various forms addressed and influenced Chinese politics, administration and warfare. The basic structure of the imperial government consisted of two parts, the **central government** and the **local government**. The central government was located in the capital city with the responsibility of governing the entire country. The local government consisted of many bodies each with limited responsibilities for particular areas. Imperial China was governed through two primary methods, the **feudal** and the **provincial**. Under the feudal system, rights and responsibilities were granted and usually given to imperial family members who reported directly to the Emperor. Under the provincial system, people were appointed by the central government to salaried positions to administer defined areas. The imperial government tried its best to hold the large country together but it suffered from three significant problems. The first great problem was the problem of centralization or decentralization of decision making power. The central government did not know how much power to give to the local governments. The second problem was the lack of competent and capable persons to serve the state. And the third problem was the strong conservatism of the government which prohibited innovative measures which were needed to keep pace with the changing environment.

CHINA AS A REPUBLIC (1912–49)

The revolution of 1911 destroyed the Qing dynasty and brought an end to China's imperial period which had lasted for more than 2,000 years. The revolutionary group was called the **Chinese Revolutionary League** and it was led by Sun Yat-sen. The revolutionary group succeeded in overthrowing the Qing monarch. On February 12, 1912, an edict was issued by which the monarchy renounced its throne and declared the republic to be the constitutional form of the government. With the overthrow of the dynasty, China found itself in a very unstable state and began to look for anything that could bring it stability. It realized that the October Revolution in Russia was successful so it began studying Marxist ideas and Russia's process of revolution and leaning towards them.

MAO ZEDONG AND THE COMMUNIST PARTY

The Chinese Communist Party (CCP) which still plays a very influential role in Chinese politics and economics was established in Shanghai in July 1921. From the time it was first formed, it had two wings, each with a different ideology. The two wings eventually split into two independent bodies. One was called the **People's Party** and represented **capitalism** under the leadership of **Chiang Kai-shek**. The other group kept the name **Communist Party** and represented communism under the leadership of **Mao Zedong**. Both parties battled each other for control. During this civil war, Japan decided to go to war with China in 1937 and take advantage of its vulnerability. The war with Japan ended in 1945, the civil war continued for another four years. Finally in 1949, the civil war ended with the Communist Party as the victors. On October 1, 1949 at Tiananmen Square in Beijing, Mao Zedong proclaimed the establishment of the People's Republic of China with himself as the Head of State. This marked the beginning of the rule of the Communist Party in China. Today, the CCP is a political organization that represents the will of society and the interests of the people. It comprises only a small percentage of the Chinese population yet it is very influential in China.

China's Situation in 1949

Prior to 1949, China was involved in many external and internal wars which cancelled whatever industrialization China had achieved. Therefore, in 1949 under Communist rule, China was an enormous country sick with economic problems. It was unfortunately a country that was unquestionably underdeveloped but lacked a literate labor force and as a result it was impossible for China to decentralize its industries since decentralization requires a lot of written communication. The wars, and the epidemics and famines that accompanied them, reduced considerably the quality of life in China and the life expectancy to a mere 27 years. The wars also damaged agricultural land significantly reducing agricultural productivity and output. Also, what China had in terms of a transportation system was badly damaged during the wars. Transportation had always been a big problem in China, a large country with lots of mountainous terrain in its main areas. Other problems that plagued China in 1949 were the lack of a developed legal system as China had very few written laws to protect businesses and industries; also, the communication network had been damaged during the wars. Therefore, having poor transportation and communication systems, important messages either took a long time to reach or were lost on the way.

Five Year Plans

The Chinese government has been setting Five Year Plans (FYPs) to accomplish its goals of industrialization and modernization. Its first FYP (1953–1957) was geared for building up heavy industry and moving its agriculture, industry and trade towards the system of "collectives." The second FYP (1958–1962) was aimed at further increasing industrialization and was also known as the "Great Leap Forward." This was followed by the third and fourth FYPs (1966–1970 and 1971–1975). During the third FYP, the Cultural Revolution somewhat slowed down the economic growth and foreign trade, but the fourth FYP was claimed to have been successful. The next plan was a ten-year plan (1976–1985) designed to modernize China's agriculture, industry, defense and technology. During this period, China implemented the "open door" policy which opened up China to foreign investment. China's seventh FYP (1986–1990) continued to promote foreign investment, called for modernization of its infrastructure, and encouraged increased development of housing and manufacture of consumer goods. The most recent FYP (1991–1995) emphasizes economic growth through modernization of China's agriculture, power, transportation, telecommunications and electronics industries as well as increasing its technological knowledge.

Economic Sectors

State-Owned Enterprises

The Chinese Communist Party's central planning of the economy depended on government control of industry and agriculture. The key to the modernization of China, in the judgement of communist leaders, was the development of a strong industrial sector under government control. This led to the establishment of state-owned enterprises. All aspects of the production process were controlled by the government bureaucracy and the communist party. The distribution of investment funds, securing of inputs, the level and type of output, and most decision making was dictated by the Central Planning Committee. For managers in these enterprises, political connections and good relationships with higher government officials took precedence over performance. The emphasis of the state-owned enterprises was on output, not efficiency. Responsiveness to market demand was not a consideration and any new ventures had to receive approval from the central planning committee.

Since the late seventies, Deng Xiaoping has undertaken economic reforms to move from a centrally planned economy to a socialist market economy. Central economic planning was relaxed and eventually eliminated, even though the government still controls certain key industrial inputs. The reforms included increasing the powers of enterprise managers and making them responsible for making their enterprises more effective financially. A contract responsibility system has been instituted under which the managers are held responsible for maintaining the output and for effective management of the firm. Under the system, the firm must produce a fixed minimum output to be purchased at state-determined prices and any output above the quota can be sold at market prices. The system requires the posting of performance bonds by senior level managers which are forfeited if performance is not up to the mark. The managers, however, are allowed to be more responsive to market demand.

State-owned enterprises constitute approximately half the industrial output of the People's Republic of China and dominate the larger industrial sectors such as chemicals, petroleum, coal, iron, steel, and automobiles. State-owned firms are also present in most medium and small industry sectors. Although the market reforms have been continuing, state-owned enterprises are plagued by severe problems. It is estimated that most enterprises are overstaffed by at least one-third. Employment in a state-owned enterprise is linked to housing, medical care, and education and thus taken with the policy of full employment for the populace creates a situation where few employees are terminated, even if they are not needed. Productivity and efficiency of state-owned enterprises remains low and their return on investment is poor compared to non-state enterprises. Nearly two-thirds of the state-owned enterprises are losing money. Because state-owned enterprises are given preferential treatment in funds from the Central Bank of China, enterprise managers tend to fund investment via debt rather than equity. This has led to a debt crisis for the state-owned enterprises. Many have defaulted on loans from state banks and foreign lenders.

The current round of reforms for state-owned enterprises centers on allowing foreign investors to invest in state enterprises to help bail them out. Because the government and banking system are currently cash-poor, foreign investment is needed to bring the firms back to profitability. An increasing number of state-owned enterprises have been allowed to enter joint ventures and have been listed on foreign stock exchanges. Other suggested reforms include allowing the state-owned firms to file for bankruptcy. China has had a bankruptcy law since 1986, however, state-owned firms had not been allowed to go bankrupt. It has been suggested that the least profitable state-owned enterprises be allowed to go bankrupt and have the assets sold to private investors. The pricing system must also be revised. Part of the problem for state-owned enterprises is that the prices of production inputs have been rising while the government purchasing prices have remained static making the firms unprofitable. Analysts feel that many state-owned enterprises would become profitable if the pricing system was revised or eliminated.

AGRICULTURAL SECTOR

In the Maoist communist ideal, the agricultural sector provided the support via food production for the industrial sector. The rural areas were confined to agriculture and small-level industries were allowed to support food production. Following the communist victory in 1949, land reform redistributed land to the peasants for farming. In 1952, mutual-aid teams were formed to increase government control of agricultural production which were followed in 1953 by government-owned cooperatives. In 1958, the People's Communes were formed. These communes were organized as the main producers of agricultural products in the centrally planned economy. The communes provided support to peasants and combined small plots into large expanses for food production. The results of the central planning were not always successful and food shortages occurred regularly. Food and grain prices were kept artificially low for the benefit of urban residents and to keep inflation down, but this policy resulted in widespread poverty in the rural areas.

After Deng Xiaoping rose to power, he instituted reforms to decentralize agricultural production while guaranteeing food production. The communes were broken up and a contract responsibility system was established which assigned production quotas to households. The two types of contracts, the *baochan daohu* and the *baogan daohu*, differed in access to agricultural inputs but allowed any production over the quota to be sold at market prices. The government grain purchasing price was also increased to encourage peasant farmers to produce. Huge grain surpluses in the early 1980s caused the government to reduce the grain purchasing price, however, an additional reform allowed rural households to engage in light industries to supplement income. Incentives were given to household-run enterprises.

A major goal of the agricultural policy of China was to provide work for the surplus labor pool generated by advances in agricultural production. The rural sector has benefited from the diversification of agriculture and growth of rural industries. The producers of agricultural products, including the state-run farm system, have been allowed to become more responsive to market demand for more varied and nutritional foodstuffs. The result has been an improvement in the diet of the Chinese and more efficient use of land. Rural industries are growing at a record pace and the economic policy has encouraged joint ventures with rural industries via tax incentives and access to raw materials. The reforms have also produced a new economic form in China called the town and village enterprise (TVE) which will be discussed later. Rural incomes are rising, but, incomes from agricultural activity are falling reflecting the diversification of the rural sector.

RURAL SECTOR VS. URBAN SECTOR

The economic policy of the government has clearly favored the urban sector over the rural sector. The policy created a disparity in the standards of living for the Chinese population. The disparity has been a source of tension between Beijing and the provincial governments. While the central government has been very willing to ensure employment in the urban areas via state-owned enterprises, it did nothing to curb poverty in the rural areas, poverty caused in part by artificially low food prices forced by the government. The reforms instituted by Deng Xiaoping have allowed the rural areas to prosper mainly because government policies authorized economic activity but gave no real financial support while unprofitable state-owned business have had continued access to loans and investment funds. The investment in infrastructure continues to vary between the urban and rural areas but the Beijing government has promised to remedy the situation. The rural sector is enjoying increasing prosperity, however, very little can be attributed to direct government investment.

The effects of this policy have been felt in Chinese society and are resulting in social problems. While rural incomes are increasing, everybody is not benefiting. Poverty is increasing in western rural areas, primarily in provinces where the population is more dependent on agriculture. Also, an increasing number of peasants are out of work because the rural industrial sector has not been able to absorb the surplus labor pool generated by advances in production methods and diversification of products. Many peasants have abandoned their land and migrated to growing coastal and urban areas placing a burden on social service organisations and resources. The immigrants compete with urban residents for jobs and opportunities and this is causing some tension in the Chinese economy. Guaranteed employment is becoming less and less prevalent as state-owned enterprises attempt to become profitable. The immigrants also tend to be less educated which limits their employment potential. A mobile population is something new to Chinese society where migration was limited in the past.

INFRASTRUCTURE

China is currently plagued with infrastructure problems that it must address and solve if it wants to sustain or improve its economic development. China's inadequate power, transportation and telecommunication systems need to be modernized. In terms of power, China experiences frequent electricity breakdowns and lacks adequate supply of power. China currently cannot meet its power needs, yet it wants to grow industrially and economically which will require even more power in the future. In terms of transportation, China needs to improve and expand its ports and waterways, railroads, roads and airports. China's most severe transportation problems occur inland because of its poor roads and air cargo facilities, which prevent goods from getting to the markets. In terms of telecommunications, China has an alarmingly low 2 per cent telephone coverage. Effective communication is vital for any country's economic development. China is currently trying to address all these infrastructure problems by giving them priority, setting goals and setting time frames to accomplish these goals.

FOREIGN INVESTMENT

In the past 10 years China has established over 200 laws and provisions aimed at attracting and securing foreign investment. For the convenience of the foreign investors, China has adopted an Open Door policy and the Chinese government has set up five special economic zones in Shenzhen, Zhuhai, Shantou, Xiamen and Hainan Province and further opened 14 coastal cities and several coastal open economic areas including over 200 counties and cities. The Chinese government has also put large amounts of domestic funds and loans from the World Bank and foreign governments on improving the infrastructure and communications of these areas. As of 1991, the Chinese had approved the establishment of 42,027 foreign-funded enterprises. There are five main forms of foreign investment in China:

EQUITY JOINT VENTURES. These are enterprises jointly established by foreign individuals or organizations and Chinese organizations investing within the territory of China. They are set up as limited-liability companies under the Sino-Foreign Joint Venture Law. Each partner can invest in cash, equipment, knowledge, land-use rights, or materials and these joint ventures are set up as separate legal entities and are protected by Chinese laws. In these enterprises, the supreme power comes from a board of directors appointed by the parties involved. These directors choose a manager who is responsible for the day-to-day operations. The time limit for this EJV is decided after negotiations between the parties. Some of them have no time limit. By the end of 1991, China had approved 24,684 joint ventures which involved a contractual amount of US$21.328 billion in foreign capital.

COOPERATIVE VENTURES (ALSO CALLED CONTRACTUAL JOINT VENTURES). In this form of venture, "each partner's responsibility, rights, and obligations are ascertained on the principle of equality and mutual benefit after negotiations between the relevant parties. Chinese and foreign partners may invest in cash, objects, land-use rights, industrial property rights, non-patented technology and other property rights. Generally, Chinese partners offer land, factory premises, existing machinery (and equipments), labor, resources and a part of cash while foreign partners offer capital in foreign exchange, technology, equipment and raw materials." These are also protected by Chinese laws and the management is similar to the EJV. However, when the contract expires, the whole permanent assets will be owned by the Chinese partner. By the end of 1991, China had approved 11,089 cooperative ventures with a contractual value of US$18.306 billion.

WHOLLY FOREIGN-OWNED ENTERPRISES. According to Chinese laws, wholly foreign-owned enterprises are permitted only if they are beneficial to the development of the Chinese economy, able to gain remarkable economic results and meet at least one of the following requirements: adopting advanced technology or equipment or exporting all or majority of product. At the time of application, the foreign company must set up an account book in China and conduct separate accounting and state its term of operation. By the end of 1991, China had authorized 6,180 wholly foreign-owned enterprises with contractual value of US$9.288 billion.

CONTRACTUAL EXPLORATION AND EXPLOITATION OF OFFSHORE OIL. Under this form of foreign investments, foreign companies and groups (usually after competitive bidding) sign contracts for offshore oil prospecting and drilling with Chinese companies. The main feature of this arrangement is that the two sides do not need to form corporate entity and a joint management council acts as the supreme power. "During the exploration stage, the foreign side undertakes the whole investment and can terminate the contract if no commercial oil or gas field is found within the approved areas indicated in the contract. The Chinese company bears no compensational economic risks. If both sides recognize unanimously the commercial finding after their joint evaluation, the Chinese partner is entitled to make a maximum investment of 51 per cent at the exploratory stage the exploitation is taken over gradually by the Chinese partner in the ripe condition." By the end of 1991, 74 projects had been approved with contractual value of US$3.416 billion in foreign capital.

COMPENSATION TRADE. This means that the Chinese enterprises import machinery (and equipment), technology and other materials on the basis of credits, and will pay in instalments and interest as stated in their contracts. Direct compensation is usually the method of repayment but indirect compensation can also be chosen with the approval of the Chinese Ministry of Foreign Economic Relations and Trade. By the end of 1989, China had approved the import of equipment valued at US$2.771 billion.

China has enacted some preferential policies aimed at attracting investment by foreign firms. Some of the tactics used by the Chinese government are:

FORMS OF INVESTMENT. China allows firms to invest in a variety of ways including money, machinery and equipment, raw materials, transportation, patent, trademark, and technical know-how.

IMPORT OF MATERIALS. Foreign investors in China do not have to pay customs duty and consolidated industrial and commercial tax on equipment.

SCOPE OF INVESTMENT. The Chinese government offers a wide range of investment to foreign investors. This range is expected to continue to expand according to the readjustment of the national economy.

PROPORTION OF SHARES. China places no limit on the shares to be owned by foreign investors in a joint venture.

LEGAL REPRESENTATIVESHIP. China allows foreign shareholders to be the legal representative of a joint venture, namely the chairman of the board of directors.

DURATION OF JOINT VENTURES. China generally places no limit on the duration of joint ventures. Even in some industries in which limited foreign investments are allowed, duration of joint ventures in such industries is usually quite long, and they can apply for an extension upon expiry of the first duration.

PURCHASE OF RAW MATERIALS AND SALES OF PRODUCTS. In China, enterprises with foreign investment are allowed to purchase raw materials directly from the world market and sell their products in the domestic market, but they are encouraged to export their products.

EMPLOYMENT OF STAFF AND WORKERS. The Chinese government encourages foreign-funded enterprises to employ Chinese staff and workers, but they are also allowed to introduce foreign technical experts and senior management personnel.

LOW TAX RATE AND LONG PERIOD OF TAX REDUCTION OR EXEMPTION. Normally, foreign-funded enterprises located in China are required to pay 30 per cent of their taxable income, plus 3 per cent of local income as tax. However, China also stipulates fairly long periods of tax reduction and tax exemption in the new tax law (China Business Guide Book, 1993).

WHAT CHINA CAN OFFER THE FOREIGN INVESTOR

China can offer "mind boggling" profits to a foreign company. Many foreign investors are drawn by China's vast pool of low-cost labor as well as its huge market potential. China's market contains one-fifth of the world's population (Kraar, 1994).

PROBLEMS ENCOUNTERED BY THE FOREIGN INVESTOR

Foreign investors have come across some obstacles to doing business with the Chinese. One problem is that since the economy is changing so rapidly the government regulations in China are changing just as rapidly. Some foreign investors find it difficult to keep pace with the varying policies of the government. Also, simply getting government approval is difficult because of the abundance of red tape.

For a foreign firm, the start up costs are quite high in China because the country is so poor and the Chinese do not have the capital needed to begin a business. Quite often, the foreign investor becomes solely responsible for raising the needed capital while the Chinese partners are content with limiting their outlay to finding the land or providing the labor. Hiring workers can be difficult since due to the low level of literacy, most workers lack technical and management skills.

Corruption, as previously mentioned, plays a part in establishing a joint venture because the politician in charge may have a different political agenda than the foreign company. Many foreign investors are not used to dealing with this kind of government. Poor infrastructure is a problem in China and it is difficult to transport goods to port or supplies to the plant. The government, in trying to lure a joint vesture to China may at times promise infrastructure that fails to appear. There have been some extreme cases where plants run "phantom night shifts" to produce batches of products that the foreign partner never sees (*The Economist*, August 16, 1994, p. 57). A further problem with doing business in China (and the reason Levi-Strauss and Co. decided not to continue doing business there) is the frequent and pervasive human rights violations (Kaltenheuser, 1995).

TOWN AND VILLAGE ENTERPRISES (TVEs)

Town and village enterprises have rapidly emerged as a growing industrial force in China. These include rural, non-agricultural, non-State enterprises, usually collectively owned enterprises which account for almost a third of the country's industrial output and nearly half of the total industrial employment. Long-time community residents and former agricultural collectives establish these forms of income sharing (Naughton, 1994). TVEs are controlled by local township and village governments where the town leaders control the residual income, the right to dispose of assets, and the right to appoint and dismiss managers. The community gains by added employment, social services provided and paid for by the success of the TVEs, and the low marginal tax break granted. There are about 19 million TVEs currently in existence most of which are small, service businesses, although many export-oriented and joint-venture TVEs are also coming up. TVEs first came about as China's answer to a rapidly changing economy and developing market, most of them are publicly owned which makes them unique in the world (Naughton, 1994).

In 1991 TVEs accounted for around US$18 billion dollars or 25 per cent of China's total export earnings. The products range from textiles to complex electronics. These TVEs are popular because they are allowed more flexibility than the State enterprises in responding to the demands of the global marketplace (Zweig, 1992). TVEs view a joint venture as a means of improving their export performance by gaining direct access to foreign importers. Two advantages to TVEs consist of their ability to attract skilled workers and managers and their ability to keep labor costs down because of their size. Another advantage is that the Chinese government gives special incentives to rural industrial enterprises including tax concessions, tax holidays, and favorable fund allocations.

CHINA'S RELATIONS WITH HONG KONG

Hong Kong is actively involved in helping China because of the market potential and money to be made, and also as a form of political insurance. Since their imminent future partnership, Hong Kong has been working closely with China to help develop the latter's economy. Hong Kong has taken on several roles for China including that of a financier, trading partner, middleman and facilitator. Hong Kong is helping to finance China's economic expansion by listing 12 of the state-owned companies on the Hong Kong Stock Exchange (Weinberger, 1995). From 1979–1989 Hong Kong accounted for close to 60 per cent of foreign investment in China (Sung and Tam, 1994) and has also become involved in joint ventures with China. Hong Kong is assisting with the infrastructural improvements in China by helping with the Chinese Superhighway while at the same time importing labor from China and China is helping with the container terminal (Larocque, 1994).

It has been surmised that if China is to expand into the world market successfully, it will rely on the expertise of Hong Kong. Hong Kong will have to provide education and training in management and technology for China while China will have to be willing to learn from their future partner. China will also need to develop economic ties and markets outside its borders and Hong Kong is the best avenue for the expansion (Chan, 1994).

CORRUPTION

Given the one party system, bureaucratic control, excessive regulation, and lax enforcement, it is little wonder that corruption is rampant in the Chinese economic system. Foreign investors have complained about the corruption of business and government officials. Because there is little supervision, bribery to gain approval of products and favorable treatment is rampant and Beijing has been able to do little about controlling it. Widespread corruption has been cited by leaders of the democracy movement as a major issue and they have called for increased accountability of government officials.

DEFINITION

The Chinese cultural system of *guanxi* and face involves the exchange of gifts between government officials, business partners, and potential clients. While this practice may seem somewhat questionable to Westerners, it is generally accepted in Chinese society and should not be considered as corruption. The type and size of the gifts are dictated by cultural norms and can be differentiated from truly illegal behavior. Corruption is not defined only in terms of personal gain, it also includes illegal activity which benefits a firm. There are many cases of managers of state-owned enterprises engaging in illegal activities which benefited their firm and resulted in no personal gain for themselves.

The historical problem with identifying corruption is differentiating between true anti-corruption activities and the use of anti-corruption laws to eliminate political enemies. In the past, anti-corruption campaigns have been used for enforcement of political ideology and protection against Western influence. Crimes such as living lavishly or acquiring too much wealth were punished. Also, only those corrupt officials who were politically vulnerable were targeted. Corrupt officials with strong political ties with the right people were rarely prosecuted. The political aspect obstructed the true elimination of illegal economic activity.

REGULATORY ENVIRONMENT

Efforts to curb corruption are hampered by lax enforcement or the absence of proper regulation. Local officials are notorious for tolerating illegal activity and hesitating to enforce regulations on other members of the local community. Although China is a signatory to the Berne Convention which protects American patents and copyrights, enforcement is almost non-existent. Although the Beijing government has improved environmental regulations, enforcement is sporadic, especially in rural areas. Vice Premier Zhu Ronji instituted banking reform in 1993, however, there were not enough regulations in place to prevent activity which allowed corruption to enter the system. To his credit, several corrupt bankers were executed when caught abusing the system. As China attempts to create a financial market, holes in securities regulation become apparent. Last month, bond trading was suspended due to the lack of regulatory control on the fledgling market. The regulatory environment needs to be strengthened to combat the widespread corruption. To encourage foreign investment, which China needs, corruption has to be curbed. The regulatory environment needs to be strengthened to protect copyrights and financial transactions. Corrupt government officials and businessmen need to be eliminated because they act as a barrier to business development. Foreign firms are under pressure from their own governments to avoid corruption in overseas business transactions. True corruption must be dealt with effectively. As part of improving the business environment, human rights abuses need to be eliminated. The use of child and prison labor must be stopped along with illegal detention without due process. These measures will contribute to the stability needed to attract more investment.

EDUCATION IN CHINA

The present education system in China includes five major branches—preschool programs, primary schools, middle schools (which encompass junior and senior levels as well as vocational and technical schools), institutions of higher education, and various television, part-time, and spare-time schools that overlap in level with the more standardized full-time schools (Townsend, 1986, p. 217).

During the mid-1970s and thereafter, China's public education system changed drastically. Prior to this latest reform, the major emphasis has been on propagating revolutionary values, such as the dignity of manual labor and the importance of the collectives to students. Since then, academic study has moved to the forefront of the educational system with the teaching of political values being regulated to second place. Chinese leaders feel that this way, students are both "red" (politically advanced) and "expert" (having technical and academic expertise) (Townsend and Womack, 1986, p. 216). Other notable changes within the education system included restructuring the educational system whereby studies in the area of management and social sciences have been expanded. Moreover, mid-level occupations such as technicians, teachers and other skilled occupations necessary for modernization to be successful in China have been expanded. Another change worth mentioning is the new enrollment and admission standards where entry to higher level schools is based on test results from national education examinations versus recommendations from other workers and Party officials (Kaplan, 1981, p. 277).

With this new emphasis and broader reach to the masses, education has improved in China but still lags behind other countries. As of 1988, studies have shown that the average person in China has less than six years of schooling and middle school enrollment is at 44 per cent, which is 8 per cent below the world average. Also, university and college student enrollment were at 1.8 per cent, much lower than the average developing countries' 8.3 per cent (Jin, 1993). The problem of literacy in China exemplifies even more the need for better education as the literacy rate fluctuates in different parts of China from 30 per cent in Tibet to 86 per cent in Liaoning (Hook, 1991, p. 113).

WAGES IN CHINA

STATE-OWNED ENTERPRISES

In China's state-owned enterprises, the wage system is sometimes referred to as a system that is too difficult or complicated to describe. It is a complex system and we shall go over the main components of this system here. Established in 1956, the wage system is really a relatively compatible collection of tables of wage scales (Korzec, 1992, p. 56). The scales vary between different occupations with the high wage levels being in heavy industry and mining and the lower wages being in light industry and services. This is due to price differences and hardship compensations (Korzec, 1992, p. 57). In 1978, two new reforms in the area of piece wages and bonuses were introduced to provide incentives for better work effort and productivity. Piece wage systems are used in labor-intensive or technologically deficient areas in China to reward those individuals whose output is above a given level. Bonuses were also used as incentives to employees whereby employees received a smaller base wage but received larger bonuses dependent upon how the company was doing (Korzec, 1992, p. 58). Wage reform continues to be an ongoing issue in China.

JOINT VENTURES

Wages in China's joint ventures follow very stringent rules that are spelled out in a contract before the business goes on stream. Any agreement drawn up for compensating managerial staff must have the approval of the supervisory agency and must comply with the Law and Regulations of Labor Management in China. The wages are determined by the workload, qualifications, and contributions the employee makes to the joint venture. Usually, basic pay for the general manager, deputy general manager, section heads, staff members and workers is specified in Chinese currency. For example, an employee will receive 120–150 per cent of the real wages of workers of a state-owned enterprise of the same trade in the locality. An extra 30 per cent of the base pay is included for pension and insurance. Another 30 per cent is included for fringe benefits. Annual wage increases are given to provide incentive for better performance and the increases follow the schedule of the Chinese public enterprises in related industries (Ho, 1990, p. 27).

HUMAN RESOURCE MANAGEMENT IN CHINA'S STATE-OWNED ENTERPRISES

As most businesses in China are state-owned enterprises, human resource management issues for each company are not as prevalent as they would be in the United States. The government is the authority that makes the decisions regarding recruitment, employment, benefits, etc. The most recent major changes have come in the area of labor and how this has affected employment in China. Prior to 1986 when sweeping reforms were introduced regarding employment, China lived by the rules of the "3-irons," the iron rice bowl, the iron chair, and the iron wage. The iron rice bowl is described as lifelong employment for an individual and his/her family, such that even if the individual were to pass on, his/her family member could replace the individual in his/her position. The iron chair describes employment security for state cadres—those individuals with higher education working for the state. These individuals would never be terminated from their positions once they were in (Korzec, 1992, p. 26). The iron wage refers to how every individual in China is entitled to a wage (whether it be fair or not) for the work that they do.

The state labor system is one that is filled with too many employees and low morale. This gives way to low productivity and complacency. Thus, in 1986 reforms were enacted to try to help revive the state-run enterprises. Individuals were hired for contracts of a limited duration instead of being offered lifetime employment, qualified individuals were recruited instead of through administration allocation or internal recruitment, enterprises were given the power to dismiss workers for violating policy, and a system of social security and old age pensions was established. This "labor contract system" was to be a key factor in the reform of the Chinese state-socialist economy (Korzec, 1992, p. 27). However, due to rising unemployment rates and pressure from the majority of people who were unhappy with the set-up, in 1989 the labor contract system was dissolved. This system did show the state the possibilities of what could happen when reforms such as the ones implemented went into effect. How they plan to correct labor issues in the future may involve some components of the system that was used here (Korzec, 1992, p. 51). China needs to deal with HR issues such as work productivity, compensation, and employee relations. This is difficult to do, considering the history of how management was previously conducted and the influence of the socialist government in the workplace. To the present day, we can see the effect of history, as children of top Communist officials, known as "princelings," have been able to advance to high positions in China through patronage and nepotism. Although this type of advancement is not as blatant as in the past, it is still very much a part of China's employment practices (Engardio et al., 1995). We do not see this changing in the near future.

SOCIO-CULTURAL VALUES IN CHINA AND ITS BUSINESS RELATIONS

With China's history dating back some 4,000 years, it is easy to understand how its culture influences the business practices and style. Discussed below are just a few of the many aspects of Chinese culture that can be seen in the business setting. This will give an indication of how deeply ingrained China's culture is in its people and how sometimes it may cause difficulties for the country to move forward and change. Confucianism runs deep in the minds of the people of China and with it are family values that are in evidence in their business practices. These values consist of harmony and collectivism, respect for age and hierarchy, face preservation, and the importance of relationships (Lockett, 1988). In that Confucian philosophy stresses the importance of the group rather than the individual, one can see in business organizations that there is a tendency to avoid conflict and to instead compromise to obtain the group's goals. Age and hierarchial structures are also very important as the older an individual, the higher is his/her status with whoever they are conducting business. This should be kept in mind when sending representatives for conducting business as sending over an assistant will not make a good impression with the Chinese counterpart as they view having to deal with someone of lower standing as a waste of time and also feel offended. Hierarchial structures are very prevalent in the business realm and this could lead to problems as decision making is slowed down greatly by questions being referred to the top management level since no one wants to take on the responsibility for the outcome. Saving face is another value that flows naturally into a business setting. The Chinese will avoid at all costs direct confrontation as it is considered shameful and a "loss of face." Instead, they will use indirect methods to get their point across. Finally, the importance of relationships can be seen in the business relationship through concepts such as *rengin* and *pao* which mean favor and reciprocation, respectively. These concepts along with g*uanxi* (connections) help to solidify a personal relationship with a prospective business partner which is very important in China. The exchanging of gifts or favors and also the mutual concessions that are given in a negotiation will further enhance a future professional business relationship. *Guanxi* is most necessary when doing business in China as it will help an individual to gain access to certain businesses that may not have been accessible to them before (Kirkbride, 1991; Zhao, 1993).

Another issue that has roots in China's culture that is reflected in business is their concept of time. As China has such a long history, much of their decision making is based upon what happened in the past. Therefore, new ideas, innovations, and change do not come easily to the Chinese as they often perpetuate old practices (Lockett, 1988). Moreover, in business planning, the work is thought to be more task-oriented with little emphasis on how much time it takes to complete the project (Zhao, 1993). Because of this cultural value, work is completed at a much slower pace and there is no basis to speed things up. It is easy to see how this also affects efficiency and productivity in the workplace.

FUTURE PROSPECTS

To become a major global player, China must focus on the following:

INVEST IN INFRASTRUCTURE IMPROVEMENTS. China's current infrastructure cannot support the economic development it is seeking. Energy sources, transportation, and port facilities must be improved. Currently, power outages and transportation difficulties are the norm, especially in the rural areas, where the growth is greatest.

ATTRACT INCREASING LEVELS OF FOREIGN INVESTMENT. Currently, the Beijing government does not have the capital needed for economic development, primarily, the funds to bring the state-owned enterprises back to profitability. Also, improvements in infrastructure have to be funded by foreign capital.

REDUCE THE GROWTH OF THE GOVERNMENT SECTOR AND INCREASE PRIVATIZATION. The state-owned sector must be allowed to fade slowly in favor of increased private ownership. With this capital and resources which can be and are utilized more efficiently by the private sector will be released and the state sector will not continue to drain the central government's resources. The evolutionary process will be more stable than a radical restructuring which could be potentially destructive.

USE HONG KONG AND SINGAPORE AS EXAMPLES OF ECONOMIC DEVELOPMENT AND MAINTAIN THE HONG KONG SYSTEM AFTER 1997. Singapore provides an example of economic growth under the kind of control Beijing is accustomed to and the Singapore system can be used as a guide for fostering economic development in China. The system in Hong Kong must be examined also to identify the factors for success. The integration of the China system and Hong Kong system must be a gradual process.

REFORM CORRUPTION AND REGULATORY ENVIRONMENT. Corruption and human rights abuses must be eliminated to provide a stable environment for investment and economic development. More stringent regulations regarding business transactions, copyright protection, and the environment must be enforced to prevent corruption from undermining economic development.

REFERENCES

Chan, Kwok Kei, China and Hong Kong's Zig-Zag Path, *Euromoney*, June 6, 1994, pp. 126–128.
China Business Guide Book (English Version), Hong Kong: China Intril Ltd., 1993, pp. 271–278.
Engardio, Pete with Dexter Roberts and Bruce Einhorn, China's New Elite, *Business Week*, June 5, 1995, pp. 48–51.
Ho, Alfred Kuo-Liang, *Joint Ventures in the People's Republic of China: Can capitalism and communism coexist?* New York: Praeger, 1990.
Hook, Brian (Ed.), *The Cambridge Encyclopedia of China*, New York: Cambridge University Press, 1991.
Jin, Ling, China's Comprehensive National Strength, *Beijing Review*, August 16–22, 1993, pp. 22–25.
Joint Ventures in China: Soya coming, *The Economist*, Vol. 332, No. 875, August 6, 1994, pp. 56–57.
Kaltenheuser, Skip, China: Doing business under an immoral government, *Business Ethics*, May–June 1995, pp. 20–23.
Kaplan, Fredric M. and Julian M. Sobin, *Encyclopedia of China Today,* New York: Eurasia Press, 1981.
Kirkbride, P. with S.F.Y. Tang, and R.I. Westwood, Chinese Conflict Preferences and Negotiating Behavior: Cultural and psychological influences, *Organization Studies*, December 3, 1991, pp. 365–386.
Korzec, Michael, *Labour and the Failure of Reform in China,* New York: St. Martin's Press, 1992.
Kraar, Louis, The New Power in Asia, *Fortune*, Vol. 130, No. 9, October 31, 1994, pp. 80–88.
Laaksonen, Olivia, *Management in China during and after Mao in Enterprises, Government, and Party*, Berlin: Walter de Gruyter, 1988.
Larocque, Alain, Piercing Import Barriers, *China Business Review*, Vol. 21, No. 3, May 1994, pp. 41–43.
Lockett, M., Culture and the Problems of Chinese Management, *Organization Studies,* September 4, 1988, pp. 474–495.
Naughton, Barry, Chinese Institutional Innovation and Privatization from Below, *American Economic Review*, Vol. 84, No. 2, May 1994, pp. 266–270.
Sung, Yun-Wing and Mo-Yin S. Tam, The China-Hong Kong Connection: The key to China's open-door, *Economic Development and Cultural Change*, Vol. 42, No. 4, July 1994, pp. 906–909.
Townsend, James R. and Brantly Womack, *Politics in China,* Boston: Little Brown and Company, 1986.
Weinberger, Caspar W., Hong Kong: Two-and-a-half years away from China, *Forbes*, Vol. 155, No. 1, January 1, 1995, p. 33.
Zhao, Duo, Path of Pluralism, *Far Eastern Economic Review,* January 7, 1993, p. 13.
Zweig, David, Reaping Rural Rewards: China's town and village enterprises can make good investment partners, *China Business Review*, Vol. 19, No. 6, November–December 1992, pp. 12–16.

SUGGESTED FURTHER READING

Ash, Robert, Agricultural policy under the impact of reform, in Y.Y. Kueh and Robert Ash (Eds.), *Economic Trends in Chinese Culture*, Oxford: Oxford University Press, 1993.

China Stirs Its Sleeping Giants, *The Economist*, Vol. 332, August 27, 1994, pp. 53–54.

Doing Business in the People's Republic of China, New York: Price Waterhouse, 1993.

Engen, John, China Moves toward Bank Reform, but Corruption is the Pace, *American Banker*, Vol. 159, June 28, 1994, p. 4.

Hill, Kay, China's State Farms Go Corporate, *China Business Review*, Vol. 21, No. 6, November–December 1994, p. 28.

Kalirajan, K.P. and Cao Yong, Can Chinese State Enterprises Perform Like Market Entities: Productive efficiency in the Chinese iron and steel industry, *Applied Economics*, Vol. 25, No. 8, August 1993, p. 1071.

Khan, Mumtaz and Lucy Perkins, Investors Please Apply, *China Business Review*, Vol. 20, No. 3, May–June 1993, p. 27.

Lam, Alexa C., Infrastructure Investment Tips, *China Business Review*, September/October 1994, pp. 44–50.

Lazovsky, George, Global Outlook: Hong Kong, *Best's Review (Property/Casualty)*, Vol. 95, No. 6, October 1994, p. 15.

Oi, Jean, Reform and Urban Bias in China, *Journal of Development Studies*, Vol. 29, No. 4, July 1993, p. 129.

Red Ink: China's bad debts, *The Economist*, Vol. 333, No. 7890, November 19, 1994, p. 88.

RSVP, and Please Bring a Cheque: China, *The Economist*, Vol. 328, No. 7820, July 17, 1993, p. 32.

Smith, Craig, Halt to China Bond Futures Shakes Market Confidence, *Asian Wall Street Journal Weekly*, May 22, 1995, p. 25.

The Commanding Heights, *The Economist,* Vol. 325, No. 7787, November 28, 1992, p. 9.

CASE TEN

NIKE, INC.*

"JUST DO IT"

The Nike advertising slogan, and indeed, its call to the world, reflects exactly the spirit of this company, so American in tone and so filled with all the possibilities of life that epitomize the country itself. And yet, like most major American companies, indeed like most major companies everywhere, Nike has had to seek to reach out beyond its home base and go international, to sell to the world its footwear and its apparel, its technology, its image, and its vision.

Tucked way away in the back of its 1993 Annual Report, Nike says of itself very simply:

> Nike has attained its premier position in the industry through quality production, innovative products, and aggressive marketing.

These are the threads that we will seek to further explore the subject of this case write-up.

NIKE: THE HISTORY

Nike's world headquarters is located at One Bowerman Drive, in the small American town of Beaverton, Oregon. The address honors one of the two founders of Nike, the former University of Oregon track coach Bill Bowerman. The other founder (each contributed US$500 to start the company in 1964) was its present Chairman of the Board and Chief

---

* This case was prepared by Neil Holbert, then Senior Lecturer in the Department of Marketing, Chinese University of Hong Kong. Currently, he is Assistant Professor of Marketing, The American College in London.

Executive Officer, Philip H. Knight, a former middle-distance runner on Bowerman's teams in the late 1950s. A key date in Nike history is 1962, when Knight, now a graduate student at Stanford, wrote a marketing research paper that asserted that a low-priced, high-tech, well-merchandised running shoe made in and exported from Japan could displace the German leaders in the field, primarily Adidas.

After much running back and forth and negotiation with Japan and the Japanese, the Nike name (Nike was the ancient Greek goddess of victory) was born in 1971. The company took the name Nike, Inc. in 1978. The Marathon, a lightweight running shoe, appeared in 1967. In 1972, Nike invented the "Waffle" outsole, and the "Air-Sole" cushioning system appeared in 1978. Further technological advances ensued, as did an unending series of endorsements by Nike sports celebrities in baseball, football, track and field, tennis, and, especially, basketball.

Nike entered the Canadian market (its first foreign foray) in 1972. It opened its first US manufacturing plant in 1974; before that its shoes had been made in Japan. Factories in Taiwan and Korea were opened in 1977, and in that year its shoes were sold for the first time in Asia. In 1980 (just after the Open Door), negotiations began to produce Nike in China and in 1981 Nike joined forces with the Japanese trading company Nissho Iwai (which had worked with Nike on letters of credit ten years earlier) to form Nike-Japan. In the period 1985–1987, Nike went through its "billion-dollar-bump" stage: a stage some companies go through when sales get very big and previous relaxed methods of management seem not to work so well any more.

> *Then in the mid-1980's, Nike lost its footing, and the company was forced to make a subtle but important shift. Instead of putting the product on center stage, it put the consumer in the spotlight and the brand under a microscope—in short, it learned to be marketing oriented (Geraldine E. Willigan, High-Performance Marketing: An interview with Nike's Phil Knight,* Harvard Business Review, *July–August, 1992, p. 91).*

In Knight's own words (*loc. cit.,* p. 92):

> *Nike is a marketing-oriented company, and the product is our most important marketing tool ... marketing knits the whole organization together. The design elements and functional characteristics of the product itself are just part of the overall marketing process. We used to think that everything started in the lab. Now we realize that everything spins off the consumer. And while technology is still important, the consumer has to lead innovation. We have to innovate for a specific reason, and that reason comes from the market. Otherwise, we'll end up making museum pieces.*

In brief, Nike went through a period of consolidation and re-evaluation—watching Reebok prospering in aerobics, and misjudging the market: failing to catch the brass ring on a presumed trend towards casuals—but was led out of difficulty by belt-tightening, by renewed strong leadership by Knight, by the emergence of the now-legendary Michael Jordan (more about him in later sections) and his "Air Jordans", and by the "Just Do It" tag. Indeed it was in 1989, one year after the creation of that tag, that Nike overtook Reebok for first place in the branded athletic shoe market. Currently its US share is 30 per cent, vs. Reebok's 24 per cent, and its worldwide sales are US$4 billion. Nike is a high-profile marketer of athletic footwear (mainly) that was built on a dream, is sustained by a vision, is underpinned (at least in concept) by technology, is energized by advertising, and is seeking worlds beyond its small-town US origins.

Over the years, the Nike story has been told in articles, in television specials, and elsewhere, featuring its "waffle" bottom, and its "air cushion" (later, with its secret gas, made visible in the sole). Much particularly has been written about Knight, prototypically American in his boyishness, enthusiasm, and explicit modesty. Expressions of the inspirational and mythopoeic nature of the Nike saga—attuned to the protoamerican "little guy" becoming a success due to hard work and ability—are not hard to find. One such can be found right at the beginning of the 1993 Annual Report, by the side of a picture of Nike endorser Gail Devers on her way to victory in the 100-meter dash at the 1992 Barcelona Olympics. It reads,

> *Take a moment to consider a world record. It is a paradox . Unapproachable yet inevitable. The key to its attainment is strength, not just of muscle but of conviction, a belief in your own mastery of circumstance. This is the nature of power. It is our inspiration.*

That Report—written in a style both lively and revealing—also offers many other insights into the Nike of 1994. Some excerpts:

> *So let's sum up the year of this report thusly: Fiscal 93: Great job. End of discussion.*
> *What people want to know about is (1) Nike's position in the perceived "collapse of consumer brands," and (2) why our earnings for '94 are likely to grow at a slower pace than our own target of 15 percent.*
> *From my view—which is really no more sophisticated than any other consumer's—the reported decline of consumer brands in the '90's was triggered by panic on the part of Philip Morris. It reduced the price on its Marlboro brand 40 per cent to fight the growing market share of house brand cigarettes.*
> *Well, they could reduce their price 100 per cent and it wouldn't affect me.*
> *On the other hand, I drink Coca-Cola, not Coola Select.*
> *But then the Marlboro move was mimicked, although not to the same degree, by others, including Kimberly Clark in diapers and Kellogg in breakfast cereals.*
> *So Wall Street extrapolates that trend to all athletic footwear and apparel, but (are you ready for this?) different consumer products industries are.... different.*
> *Athletic shoes and clothes—especially shoes—are not commodities. Try this: run a marathon, or even a mile, in a pair of $19.95 Wal-Mart specials. That will end that discussion.*

Brands are powerful when they communicate underlying value. In our industry, and probably in other consumer products, consumers will not trade down if there is value and quality in the high end. Ergo, I am glad we sell sports and fitness products, not cigarettes.

I am also glad that we sell sports and fitness products, not fashion products. Grunge fashion is making headlines this year; and with it the casual shoes that are part of that look. Nike has certain shoes in its Outdoor line which compete with some of these items. In those areas where we don't compete, into which the brand does not naturally flow, we will give up that business. We will not stretch the brand beyond its natural limits and will not worry about those lost sales or next year's fashion....

Never before has social energy been so focused on sports. Tearing down all barriers of culture and geography, sports has grown far beyond its existence as a simple diversion. Its unique combination of athletic excellence and egalitarian competition is attracting the world.

As a global brand franchise, we focus on distinct, culturally relevant messages that reflect the mindset of sports and fitness enthusiasts everywhere. This focus has allowed Nike to develop a consistent worldwide brand image. Whether it is the voice of network news or the urban street athlete, Nike is spoken of as the technical and popular leader in sports and fitness. Authentic. Athletic. Innovative....

COMPANY OPERATIONS

The Nike financials (Exhibits 1 and 2) show steady growth in revenue and income, with

Exhibit 1 Income Statement (years ending May 31)

	\multicolumn{5}{c}{In US$, millions}
	1989	1990	1991	1992	1993
Revenues	1711	2235	3004	3405	3931
Gross profit	636	851	1153	1316	1544
Gross profit % (of revenue)	37.2	38.1	38.4	38.7	39.3
Net income	167	243	287	329	365
Net income % (of revenue)	9.8	10.9	8.6	9.7	9.3
Earnings per share (US$)	2.22	3.21	3.77	4.30	4.74
Dividends per share (US$)	0.27	0.38	0.52	0.59	0.75
Cash flow from operations	169	127	11	436	265
Ratios					
Return on equity (%)	34.3	36.1	31.6	27.8	24.5
Return on assets (%)	21.8	25.3	20.5	18.4	18.0
Inventory turns	5.1	5.2	4.1	3.9	4.5
Current ratio	3.0	3.1	2.1	3.3	3.6

Nike, Inc.

Exhibit 2 Balance Sheet (years ending May 31)

	\multicolumn{5}{c}{In US$, millions}
	1989	1990	1991	1992	1993
Cash and equivalents	85	90	120	260	291
Inventories	223	309	587	471	593
Working capital	422	565	666	967	1168
Total assets	825	1095	1708	1873	2187
Long-term debt	34	26	30	69	15
Shareholders' equity	582	784	1033	1332	1646

fiscal 1993 sales approaching US$4 billion. Expansion has put some strain on return on equity and assets, however.

As to 1993 operations specifically, this is how the Annual Report put it:

> Increased revenues and improved gross margins were again a highlight of earnings growth in 1993, as they were in 1992. Despite a sluggish economy in the United States and abroad, the Company has been able to gain market share as a result of strong consumer demand and excellent customer service. The Company has continued to invest in international infrastructure in order to prepare for future growth, and accordingly, selling and administrative expenses have increased as a percentage of revenues. The Company expects to continue the aggressive marketing and infrastructure spending. However, until economies in the US and Europe show sustained improvement, the Company does not expect to show growth rates experienced in previous years.
>
> The 15 per cent growth in 1993 revenues is attributable to growth in both domestic footwear and international footwear and apparel. Domestic footwear revenue growth of 13 per cent, three times the rate of growth in the overall market, is attributable to a 10 per cent increase in pairs shipped and 3 per cent increase in average sales price per pair. International revenues continued to show strong growth with a 24 per cent increase over 1992, composed of a $182 million, or 21 per cent, increase in international footwear revenues and an $86 million, or 32 per cent, increase in international apparel revenues. Increases in international revenues are a result of gains in market share, expansion of the international market for sports and fitness products, and the establishment of Nike owned operations in place of independent distributors in order to control all aspects of the business....
>
> The Company's international operations are subject to the usual risks of doing business abroad, such as the imposition of import quotas or anti-dumping duties. In this regard, most of the countries within the European Community (EC) have for some time maintained quotas restricting the importation of footwear manufactured in the People's Republic of China (PRC). Because some EC markets have remained open to imports from the PRC and because, once entered, such goods may freely be transported within the EC, such quotas have not greatly restricted the Company's

ability to supply its EC markets with goods manufactured in the PRC. However, it is possible that the EC Commission may begin to allow individual Member States to restrict the importation of such footwear from other countries within the EC. As an alternative to national quotas and in consideration of the EC internal market objectives, the EC Commission is proposing the imposition of EC-wide quotas that would restrict the importation into the EC of footwear manufactured in the PRC. Such quotas would be applicable throughout all 12 of the Member States that comprise the EC. As of July 7, the date of this report, the matter was blocked because it is formally linked to a controversial plan by the EC Commission to change the EC voting rules with respect to anti-dumping cases and other trade-related matters. The Company is unable to predict (i) when such EC-wide quotas are likely to go into effect, (ii) to what extent, if any, technical athletic shoes would be covered by such quotas, (iii) the quota volume levels that would be applicable to its products, (iv) the method of quota allocation and (v) to what extent safeguard measures may be granted to individual Member States in the interim. The Company continues to closely monitor this situation and develop contingency plans. The Company believes that it is prepared to deal effectively with any such quotas that may arise and that any adverse impact would be of a short-term nature.

DISTINCTIVE FEATURES

Four things seem to differentiate one sportsgear company from another when it comes to the basis product: footwear. These are:

- Technology
- Philosophy
- Advertising and all the imagery associated therewith
- Segmentation strategy

Of technology we have already spoken a bit, about how the shoes are made and what makes them different? Certainly the Nike air-cushion and "waffle" sole and the Reebok "pump" (for example) are attempts to make the shoe stand out, and surely comfort, durability, and performance (to say nothing of style) are all vital for something so elemental as a shoe. Yet shoes, for all of that, are not a contemporary invention, and it is perhaps audacious to use the same word, *technology*, for a shoe and a space-orbiting navigational satellite. So it may be that, all shoe technology advances notwithstanding, it is more than technology that sets one shoe apart from another.

In the section that follows, we will look briefly at the Nike philosophy. In later sections, we will look at advertising; and throw some light on segmentation strategy.

THE NIKE PHILOSOPHY

The essence of the Nike message—embedded in "Just Do It"—seems to be free-spiritedness, "self-empowerment," a will to do what one wants, and indeed *can* do. But turning from the message to the market (though they are of course always interrelated) we may ask who *is* Nike for: athletes, or who else?

Is it for athletes? Well, the technology, the "waffle" and the Air Max air cushion would seem to suggest that. After all, while Reebok seems frequently to reach for fashion, Nike seems to stick more to notions of authenticity and straightforwardness and to the shoes themselves. (Obviously, Nike *apparel* is also important, at 18 per cent of total revenues—see Exhibit 3—unchanged since 1991.) And what an enduring marketing-driven image there is of the American tennis player Jim Courier wearing not only Nike footwear at the Australian Open, but also a tennis shirt designed by Nike to echo Courier's affection for the Cincinnati Reds baseball team. Still, it is certainly the shoes that are at the heart of the Nike sell. But what *of* the athletes? What *of* those who really play the game of basketball, for example, in the truly violent and all elbows and knees way that its creator, Dr. James Naismith, never envisioned? (He saw it as a non-body-contact sport where sheer height and weight wouldn't matter as much as finesse. So much for founders' visions!) And what of those who play tennis with the unearthly power, anticipation, and endurance of the professionals?

Exhibit 3 Revenues: Domestic vs. International and Footwear vs. Apparel (years ending May 31)

	In US$, millions				
	1989	*1990*	*1991*	*1992*	*1993*
Domestic footwear	1058	1369	1680	1744	1968
Domestic apparel	208	266	327	368	360
Other brands	96	120	135	158	200
Total	1362	1755	2141	2270	2529
International footwear	NA	NA	652	868	1049
International apparel	NA	NA	210	267	353
Total	349	480	862	1134	1402
Grand total	1711	2235	3004	3405	3930
Percentage Breakdowns					
Domestic footwear	62	61	56	51	50
Domestic apparel	12	12	11	11	9
Other brands	6	5	4	5	5
Total	80	79	71	67	64
International footwear	NA	NA	22	25	27
International apparel	NA	NA	7	8	9
Total	20	21	29	33	36
Grand total	100	100	100	100	100

Note: Sum of categories may not always add up to total due to rounding.

It has been observed that no more than, perhaps, 5–10 per cent of those who buy footwear such as Nike are truly such "athletic" athletes. For the rest, it is the image that matters. Whether the shoes are for basketball, tennis, walking, general workouts (cross-training) or whatever, it is the image of Just Do It that is probably the key, always backed by dedicated innovation and quality. However, even as the image generated by the advertising is dynamic and sometimes quite funny (as the dog walking across a tennis court and urinating at its sideline: "Just Do It"), it is also disciplined. Two strains seem to be always there: the strong, uninhibited, even humorously violent side, depicted in (say) the Andre Agassi "Challenge Court" pool, in which the tennis ball is smashed unmercifully; and the disciplined, relaxed, modest, "ah-shucks," side represented by Jim Courier ("Supreme Court"). And, thinking of Courier, has anyone except Tom Cruise looked more like the All-American Boy in recent years?

The two sides of the sought-after Nike appeal, the athlete and the wannabe, the vigorous and the relaxed, the "technical" and the "human," then, seem never far away from the thoughts of those who spin the Nike legend.

SPINNING THE NIKE LEGEND

For all the spokesathletes in its advertising stable, it is, of course, the Phil Knight story (already alluded to) that is the wellspring. The runner, his coach, his roots in environmentally-aware Oregon (away from the difficulties plaguing much of big-city America), his determination to make a better running shoe and to keep making it still better, his cheerful, optimistic, American openness. And if Knight is the wellspring, it is the spokesathletes who constantly fill the cup till it runneth over, creating and re-creating the image, and playing out everlastingly by answers to the spoken and unspoken question of the shoebuyer: "What does the product, this Nike, say about me?"

For Nike, the list of recent spokesathletes includes: from the world of athletics, the triathlete Joanne Ernst; from basketball, Charles Barkley, David Robinson, and Michael Jordan (he of the "Air Jordans"); from boxing, George Foreman; from ice hockey, Wayne Gretzky; from tennis, Andre Agassi, Jim Courier, and John McEnroe; from baseball and football, Deion Sanders; and from baseball, football, and many other sports, Bo Jackson. And from the world of entertainment, the multitalented Spike Lee. It is around such as these that the Nike attack is built. It is an attack that is (in a nice sense) outrageous, and also filled with fun (maybe even serious fun). A recent Charles Barkley pool, for example, shows the Phoenix Suns star engaging the monster Godzilla in a slamdunk contest in Tokyo. When the outclassed monster looks despondent at losing to the aerodynamic Barkley, Barkley looks down at Godzilla's feet and asks: "Say, you ever thought about wearin' shoes?" Memorable and cheeky. Barkley and Godzilla? Why not? Just do it.

PUBLICITY AND ADVERTISING

Nike's principal advertising agency since 1986 has been the Portland, Oregon-based Wieden & Kennedy, which was selected as *Advertising Age*'s Agency of the Year for 1991. Nike was a charter client of Wieden & Kennedy in 1982. In 1983, Nike moved to Chiat/Day in anticipation of the 1984 Los Angeles Olympics. And in 1986 the account moved *back* to

Wieden & Kennedy. Creative freedom and irreverence roamed and roam there, probably topped by the Bo Jackson pool, with the baseball/football player doing everything in sports (with the help of Nike). But with it all, Wieden & Kennedy puts an emphasis not only on "the definitive skills of writing (but also on) how to focus strategically ... to look at people as people.... Too many ads have to be too many things to too many people.... The success of (Wieden & Kennedy) is that people don't take themselves seriously." (*Advertising Age Creativity Magazine Supplement*, January 1990, p. 45.)

While the Nike campaign has featured athletes, it may also be thought of as featuring *ideas*, for it would seem that Nike is as much of an idea, a concept, a vision, as anything else, a philosophy (as we've said already) which is indeed summed up, perhaps, in Just Do It. The Wieden & Kennedy "signature" in print, for example,

> *may be a tone of voice accompanying an image, spoken in the language of the prospective customer. A Nike spread, for example, shows a photo of a freckle-face teenager on the left page, opposite a copy block on the right.*
>
> *"This is a picture of a 40-year-old woman," begins the copy in oversize type. Smaller type follows: "or perhaps just a picture of the way a 40-year-old woman feels.... If you believe your age, you might not climb whatever hills you are supposedly over. If you believe 25 or 30 or 48 or 62, you might believe it is time to stop. When you are really just beginning to go."*
>
> *No picture of a sneaker. No reference to footwear. Just a small Nike logo in the upper right corner* (Advertising Age, *April 13, 1992, p. S-3*).

Says Dan Wieden (of Wieden & Kennedy):

> *In all of Nike's advertising, we try to make honest contact with the consumer, to share something that is very hip and very inside.... (We seek) to be true to the athletes by talking to them in a way that respects their intelligence, time, and knowledge of sports ... a spec sheet approach to marketing won't sell anything. As the world gets more dehumanizing, people want the trust and familiarity of a long-standing relationship. Building that relationship requires a brand with a personality.... To me (advertising) takes the place of the human contact we once had as consumers* (Willigan, Harvard Business Review, *loc. cit., p. 97).*

The care that goes into the making of Nike shoes also extends to the making of their Promotion—not just the TV commercials, but even to brochures. To repeat, it is not that the Reality of shoe design is not important, but rather that the illusion of Promotion is just as important, if not more so.

> *Los Angeles photographer Scott Morgan is well-known for the abstract photograms, multiple images and other striking photographic alternations seen in annual reports*

and a current Kodak print campaign, among other places—but when Nike's in-house promotional unit approached him about a brochure to launch an upcoming new Air line of athletic shoes, the company had something a bit unusual in mind, even by Morgan's freewheeling standards: The assignment, he says, was to illustrate gravity.

"They wanted a more conceptual than technical approach, one that could be subtly manipulated without being visually complicated," explains Morgan, who found a key to the solution in a spec fashion piece in his portfolio that juxtaposed oversized everyday objects with smaller images of people orbiting around them.

The sepia-toned images that resulted are shot from odd angles and set in varying scales against white backgrounds to create an illusion of weightlessness....

... Morgan ... photographed the models seen in the ads as they vaulted and jumped on a trampoline in his studio, and composited the images in the darkroom (Advertising Age, *July 6, 1992, p. 4C*).

Among all US advertisers, Nike ranked 48th in 1992, with total advertising expenditures of US$231 million, up 3 per cent from 1991. (By contrast, archrival Reebok was 81st in 1992, with US$143 million, up 11 per cent from *its* 1991 total.) Nike's spending for its Nike and Cole-Haan (Shoes) brands made it the largest apparel advertiser in 1992, exceeding Levi Strauss' US$212 million. In terms of *brand names* (AT&T, Ford, Sears, etc.), the "Nike" name alone was 30th, just ahead of such familiars as Honda, Pizza Hut, and Tylenol (first half of 1992 data on brand names).

THE SHOE WARS

Even as Nike has its gallery of spokesathletes, so has Reebok too, including perhaps the most spectacular of all today's active basketball players, the Orlando Magic's Shaquille O'Neal. Adidas (a once-powerful European-centered force which had fallen upon difficult times) and Converse (an older brand whose cry was real simplicity and down-to-earthness) have their basketball players too: John Starks for Adidas, and Larry Johnson for Converse.

And so if one looks at the shoe wars, it is apparent that they are to a large extent "star" wars: star performers as spokespeople: image battles that loom large besides battles to unscramble (or maybe scramble) categories and reaching out for globalization. Of course there are problems in this, as in any category that relies heavily on endorsers, endorsers whom we seek to invest with credibility through apposite reputations and accomplishments.

Problems like moving back and forth from company to company. Like, for example, five-time US Open Tennis champion Jimmy Connors, former "bad boy" of tennis (a spot later to be filled by John McEnroe), and later a darling of the crowds moving to Reebok from Converse in 1993, after ten years with Converse. (Who really cares? Can't we always get anybody to talk for us in the "star" wars? Sure we can. It's all fun and games isn't it, and doesn't everybody know it?)

Problems with personal lives perhaps, as with Nike spokesman Michael Jordan. In the summer and fall of 1993, Jordan successively became enmeshed in allegations of excessive gambling (his father was murdered under circumstances at first thought suspicious) and then he announced his retirement at 30—the finest basketball player of his time who had led his Chicago Bulls to three successive NBA championships.

> *Michael Jordan's retirement from the National Basketball Association last month hasn't deflated sales of Nike's Air Jordan basketball shoes—at least for now.*
>
> *Air Jordan remains the best-selling basketball shoe in the US, racking up an estimated $200 million in sales last year, according to Sporting Goods Intelligence, an industry newsletter.*
>
> *And athletic shoe retailers say Air Jordan shoe sales have remained strong since the retirement of their superstar namesake.*
>
> *"When we have them, they sell out fast," said Chris Chanly, manager at Ike's Fantastic Feet in New York. "They're still the fastest-selling shoe on the market."*
>
> *Mr. Chanly said the Chicago Bull's change in professional status hasn't affected the brand's standing as the most comfortable and stylish basketball shoe on the market—even if they are red and black and cost $140 a pair.*
>
> *A manager for a Foot Locker store in Los Angeles noted sales stay strong each year because the shoes have a collectible value, as Nike markets a different generation of the shoe every year. So far, he said, Mr. Jordan's retirement has only increased the shoes' value (Advertising Age, November 1, 1993, p. 3).*

And "star" war hero problems that have an even darker side perhaps.

One school of thought sees a rise too of the *anti*-hero. Charles Barkley ("Sir Charles," the sullen leader of the Phoenix Sun basketball team) has already declared in a shattering Nike spot: "*I am not a role model.*" Barkley made his point very solemnly. He noted that young people should look up to their parents, teachers, and other more traditional figures for role referencing. Nike clearly had heard the echoes of the Magic Johnson AIDS revelation and the potential problems (since cleared up) with Michael Jordan. (And the controversy surrounding singer Michael Jackson, a former L.A. Gear spokesman.) What Nike seemed to be saying (through Barkley) was that athletes should be admired for their performance on court (perhaps preferably wearing the sponsor's shoes or whatever), but that their outside lives were not being held out and held up necessarily to be emulated in all regards. In a serious time like the 1990s, this playing-down seems much in line with America's problems of crime, drugs, unwanted pregnancies, and dubious education. These won't be helped, the message seems to be, by idolizing sports stars unqualifiedly or by seeing sports as the only way up and out, especially for minority youngsters. Indeed who could hope to keep the glare of publicity out of their stars' private lives anyway in a media-run world in which everyone is famous (or infamous) for 15 minutes?

Nike's recent "Unplugged" campaign speaks to this issue.

> *The "Unplugged" ads feature basketball superstar Michael Jordan and other National*

> Basketball Association players, including (Charles) Barkley, ruminating on the cost of celebrity and what it takes to play the game.
>
> "Those Nike spots express exactly the way kids feel today—that athletes are not infallible, and they respect them only for how they perform on the court," (said Richard Leonard, a marketing consultant).
>
> The campaign is a departure for Nike, whose previous efforts featuring Mr. Jordan and baseball player Bo Jackson displayed a more traditional style depicting the athlete as modern hero.
>
> Nike said the "Unplugged" ads are not a repudiation of previous advertising but part of a continuing effort to capture the essence of sports.
>
> "The idea was to strip away the hype and get down to the basics of not just who they are, but more importantly, the sport itself," a Nike spokeswoman said (Advertising Age, September 27, 1993, p. 10).

And what do kids say about these "star" wars and flaps?

Predictably that they're not one bit influenced by who is the spokesathlete for which shoe.

> Nope, the characteristic most important to these discriminating consumers is quality. Or at least, that's what young people said when Advertising Age spent a recent Saturday roaming malls and shoe stores in several US cities, asking high school-age footwear shoppers their views on the athletic shoe category.
>
> A cool-looking sneaker has long been a crucial part of the pre-adult wardrobe, but teens said they are not such slaves to fashion that they would sacrifice comfort, support and durability.
>
> Today's young people, skeptical and media-savvy, tend to discount advertising's persuasive power and seem to regard it more as entertainment, examining Nike and Reebok International commercials like film critics debating the merits of a recent release.
>
> As for (Michael) Jordan, who uttered the "It's gotta be the shoes" line in one of his ads, and the rest of his high-price athlete-endorser ilk, young people steadfastly refuse to admit even their favorite stars have any impact on their shoe purchases.
>
> Yet for a factor seemingly so irrelevant, very few didn't know which athlete pitched for which company (Advertising Age, November 29, 1993, p. 3).

SEGMENT STRATEGY

And what of segment strategy? As suggested already, there seems to be a leitmotif running through the category that suggests that Nike concentrates on performance perhaps, while Reebok stresses style. Perhaps performance is more enduring. Yet Reebok has also stressed workout (especially among women) with its Step Reebok aerobics program, while Nike has emphasized a less serious dimension with a relaunch of its Side 1 shoes (and apparel) for fashion-conscious young women (a market it would like to get more of) who may be less earnest in their sports involvement.

Historically, Nike seems to have had limited luck in appealing to women. Its down and dirty sports advertising with mostly male figures may not have said enough to women. Just do what?

> *That's why Nike struck a chord with women when Ms. (Deb) Johnsen's marketing team decided to take a reflective approach in the company's first TV campaign dedicated to the women's market. This approach involved softening Nike's image for women without compromising its athletic roots.*
>
> *In three spots that broke in February, Nike encourages women to use exercise as a way to take time for themselves and to achieve a balance in life.*
>
> *To make its marketing efforts as multidimensional as the women they speak to, Ms. Johnsen plans to step up Nike's involvement in programs appealing specifically to teenage women and to the 18-to-80-year-old participants in the popular Jazzercise dance exercise program.*
>
> *"Our charge is to make people understand that we do spend a lot of time and research on (products for) the women's fitness market," says Ms. Johnsen. "Without messengers like Charles Barkley, you have to work harder and longer to make that known," she says* (Advertising Age, *July 5, 1993, p. S-10*).

And in 1993 Nike was No. 2 in the women's sports, health, and fitness business, with US$400 million in sales in the US, an 18 per cent share of course, objectives can be multi-faceted, complex, even confusing, and, surely, ever-evolving.

The notion of segments here can surely be elusive. The casual segment is conceptually somewhere between serious athletic shoes and conventional footwear, and everybody's after it.

The *women's* market (workout and less serious) has been mentioned. Targeted shoes for *basketball; tennis; golf; soccer; children* (as in the delightfully named Weeboks from Reebok, and in which area Nike had US$306 million in sales in the US in 1993 and a half billion dollars around the world); *work* (as in L.A. Gear's Kombat work boots and Converse's Doc Martens-like Lug boots); *walking shoes* (as in Reebok's Rockport's Rocksports: comfortable but not definably "athletic"); *outdoors; cross-training* (who knows what we'll do, but I only want to buy one kind of athletic shoes); *hardscrabble city basketball courts* (as in Reebok's tough and reasonably-priced Blacktops); *"Generation X"* (the 1990s offspring, physically and emotionally, of the Yuppies of the 1970s and 1980s), as is Reebok's Boks; *environmentally friendly shoes; sports sandals;* and so on.

Can one still believe that once there were just "sneakers"?

THE INTERNATIONAL SPHERE

The international sphere is a vital one for Nike. In 1993, of the total Nike revenues, 36 per cent were outside the US (28 per cent being Europe); of operating income 33 per cent was outside the US (30 per cent being Europe); and of assets, 38 per cent were outside the US (20 per cent being Europe). The growth in this international arena is further evidenced by the fact that while 36 per cent of 1993 revenues came from overseas (as just noted) the figure was only 20 per cent in 1989. (See also Exhibits 3, 4, and 5.)

Exhibit 4 Revenues by Geographic Area (years ending May 31)

	In US$, millions				
	1989	1990	1991	1992	1993
US	1362	1755	2141	2270	2529
Europe	241	334	665	920	1086
Asia/Pacific	32	29	56	76	178
Canada, South America, and other countries	75	116	141	139	138
Total	1711	2235	3004	3405	3931
Percentage Breakdown					
US	80	79	71	67	64
Europe	14	15	22	27	28
Asia/Pacific	2	1	2	2	5
Canada, South America, and other countries	4	5	5	4	4
Total	100	100	100	100	100

Note: Sum of areas may not always add to total due to rounding.

Exhibit 5 Per cent Changes in Revenues

	1992–1993	1989–1993
Domestic footwear	13	86
Domestic apparel	(2)	73
Other brands	26	108
Total	11	86
International footwear	21	na
International apparel	32	na
Total	24	302
Total Nike	15	130

Like any international marketing effort, Nike has gone through changes over time. Usually, in line with standard practice, a local partner has been found (such as the Inchcape group in Hong Kong), who typically handles advertising, distribution, and other functions. Later on, Nike itself has taken over sometimes, as in Hong Kong, and now runs the Hong Kong operation directly; in fact, Hong Kong is Nike's Asian headquarters. (It should be noted that Procter & Gamble, for example, also took over *its* Hong Kong operation directly from *its* local partner.)

Not only are international sales and profits obviously vital to Nike's business planning and its future, but the international slant fits in perfectly with the nature of the essential Nike message of the universality of sport and what it represents, the universality of the triumph of the human spirit, of "Just Do It." Nike explicitly expresses its pride (if that is the word) in being the shoe people for such diverse aggregations as the Kenyan cross-country running team and the Brazilian soccer team (which played in World Cup '94).

Noted Nike in its 1993 Annual Report, speaking of its foreign and US spokesathletes:

The link ...? People around the globe have a passion for these athletes, and these athletes wear Nike. That's global branding. Thanks to them ... all ... who give flesh and emotion to earnings per share.... No other company in the world can tie these powerful human assets to superior products, public relations, advertising, design, retail presentation, distribution and selling talent like Nike can....

As a global brand franchise, we focus on distinct, culturally relevant messages that reflect the mindset of sports and fitness enthusiasts everywhere. This focus has allowed Nike to develop a consistent worldwide brand image....

In all, Nike products are being designed, developed, manufactured, transported, marketed, and sold in more than 80 countries on six continents. We are a strong, aggressive, and successful global company, and we make no apologies for it. We see a world of opportunity. So does everyone else. The difference is, at Nike we have the power and determination to turn the opportunity into new world records.

Manufacturing overseas of course, has become common for US-based companies. Whatever the reason or reasons—lower labor costs, lower land costs, less union involvement, fewer government regulations, proximity to markets, desire to get in early in emerging economies—companies have been doing it for a long time. But if you are Nike—so high-profile, so ebullient, so—well—so *American* after all—you may face a lot of flak about it. This is how *Advertising Age* reported it (October 26, 1992, p. 1):

The "Made in the USA" Foundation is launching, a nasty ad campaign (see ad in Exhibit 6) against major US companies that manufacture products overseas—and Nike is the first target.

The foundation has scrapped its original plan for a $50 million-plus "buy American" campaign and instead will try to shame major marketers, such as Nike, into bringing some of their manufacturing back home.

The non-profit lobbying group has $1 million set aside for the Nike effort and plans to break the ads in 20 major market daily newspapers within the next two weeks, as well as in union publications. Several papers have been approached, but the media buy hasn't been made.

Exhibit 6 Ad from "Made in the U.S.A." Foundation

FRIENDS, RUNNERS AND COUNTRYMEN:
SEND PHIL YOUR SHOES

Phil is Philip Knight, Chairman of the Nike Corporation. We are asking you to send Nike a message: Come Back Home to the United States and start making shoes here once again. All three presidential candidates agree on one thing: we need to be an economic superpower as well as a political one. George Bush wants us to be an export superpower. We can't do that if our companies do not manufacture in the United States. Bill Clinton wants American companies, like Nike, to be more American. And Ross Perot wants our children to have jobs in the future manufacturing products, not just flipping burgers.

Send Phil a message. Tell him not to make excuses. Tell him that other companies, like New Balance and Saucony make high-quality athletic shoes in the United States and that he can do it too.

JUST DO IT, PHIL.
Send your old, dirty, smelly, worn-out Nikes to:
Philip Knight, Chairman
Nike
1 Bowerman Drive
Beaverton, OR 97005

Tell Phil that you will not buy another pair of Nikes until he commits to building a manufacturing plant in the United States. It's the right thing to do. Tell Phil to JUST DO IT!

Source: *Advertising Age,* October 26, 1992, p. 1.

Made in the USA has been encountering "some resistance" from newspapers in running the ad, said Chairman Joel D. Joseph. However, he declined to name the newspapers.

"We assume they are refusing because Nike is a big advertiser," he said.

The ads urge consumers to send their "old, dirty, smelly, worn-out Nikes" to Chairman Philip Knight to "send Nike a message" to "come back home to the United States and start making shoes here once again." Nike, based in Beaverton, Ore., both sources and manufactures components of its shoes in the US, but final assembly is generally done in the Far East by contractors.

The ad, which was created in-house, urges consumers to tell Mr. Knight they won't buy another pair of Nikes until the company commits to building a US manufacturing plant.

The anti-Nike ad follows an October 1 letter to Mr. Knight from Mr. Joseph, who asked Nike to manufacture its top-of-the-line shoes in this country, since Mr. Joseph contends they can be made here profitably. Nike said it has no apologies for its manufacturing practices.

"We're the No.1 company in the business so we're willing to take the shot," said Dusty Kidd, public relations manager at Nike. "We would hope that those who criticize us would be better informed."

Mr. Kidd said 1,200 of Nike's US work force are involved in manufacturing.

> "We have more manufacturing workers in the US than any other athletic footwear company," he said.
>
> "We're proud of our work in the US and our contribution to the American economy," he added.
>
> Nike said it doesn't directly employ any workers in the Far East but employs contractors there that then undertake the manufacturing.
>
> "Any factory we use is required to meet their government's standards for minimum wage," Mr. Kidd said.
>
> It's unlikely Nike will start any counter advertising, he said.
>
> This "take your gloves off" approach was adopted by Made in USA instead of a general buy-American effort because "I think we can get more results and more (news) coverage," Mr. Joseph said. "We're going for impact."
>
> Mr. Joseph refused to name other marketers the group plans to target.
>
> "We are promoting buy American, but we also are taking our gloves off and going after companies that we think are responsible for the trade deficit," he said.
>
> In a news release, Made in the USA also noted that in the 1980s, more than 65,000 US footwear workers lost their jobs as Nike and other shoe manufacturers began importing from the Pacific Rim. Made in the USA alleges that Nike now manufactures some shoes in Indonesia where the workers are paid 14¢ an hour. It cites a press report that said it costs Nike $5.95 to make a pair of Nike Crosstrainers in Indonesia, while these shoes retail from $44.99 to $124.99 in the US.
>
> "We go where we can make the best product at the best price. If we made Air Jordans in the US, they would (sell for) $300. We are not price gouging," Nike's Mr. Kidd said.

It is probably true that this sort of brouhaha goes with the territory. And Nike (with its 6,200 employees in the US and 8,000 more overseas, and sourcing and manufacturing in 20 countries) has written about such matters in its literature (spring 1993). It is worthwhile to quote extensively from this, including the Indonesian part, which has also been featured in a television documentary.

> *Manufacturing jobs in the Third World are among the best paying jobs in those economies. The 2,800 rupiah average minimum wage—it varies slightly by region—gives the entry-level worker in Indonesia five times as much as the typical farmer. The assistant line supervisor on a footwear line in China earns more than a surgeon with 20 years' experience. The entry-level worker receives a minimum wage, plus subsidies for housing, food and health care, and bonuses for attendance and skill levels, as well as transportation allowances for housing off the premises. Paid holidays and pregnancy and menstrual leave are mandated by law. These living benefits, when added to the basic wage, often double the daily equivalent income. And there is the added assurance that benefits such as free housing or food cannot be converted to cash. That mitigates the tendency of workers all over Asia to send virtually all of*

their wages home to a family in need, while accepting a very low standard of living for themselves.

These jobs also produce broad benefits locally, both in terms of income for workers moving from subsistence levels to fixed wages that generate savings potential, and in terms of building a local manufacturing base that spawns wider income growth. One need only look to the growth of economies in Japan, Korea, Taiwan, Thailand and now China to see the impact of light manufacturing on economic growth. Indonesia is on the first step of that ladder, and is likely to move up. Athletic footwear manufacturing will generate more than $1.5 billion in export sales this year alone—375 times what it generated in 1988 ($4 million).

The Indonesian footwear industry has taken enormous strides even in its first five years. And the Indonesian factories Nike is associated with are among the most modern footwear facilities in the world. Nike believes Indonesian factories like Pao Chen and HASI are model manufacturing facilities. In Pao Chen's case, benefits include an on-site clinic staffed by physicians; a mosque for worker prayers; clean, free housing; three free meals a day (four for overtime days); and clean, well-lit, well-ventilated workspaces. HASI was cited by the Far Eastern Economic Review as a "model" of how managers can help a rural workforce make the transition to light manufacturing, noting "Its factory is, as footwear factories go, superb." HASI was also cited recently for special distinction by the Indonesian government for its enlightened policies and advancement of women.

The typical consumer product—whether it is an athletic shoe, a sweater, a bicycle or a stereo system—is usually priced on the 1-2-4 proportion. Nike, for example, buys the product for $10, adds development, marketing, shipping and other costs, plus profits, and sells to the retailer at $20, which in turn adds similar costs and profits and sells to the consumer at $40. The labor input on an Indonesian footwear product is at least several dollars, depending on the model, and in proportion not markedly different from other consumer products made almost entirely by hand, such as apparel. The typical athletic shoe and or a children's shoe produced for Nike in Indonesia is a middle-price point model ($45–$80). As workers become more skilled and factories more efficient, the mix will include more complicated and expensive models. If the history of Korea, Taiwan and Japan is any guide, wages and benefits will rise further as Indonesia moves up the manufacturing ladder.

There are 2.5 million new workers coming into the Indonesian labor market each year, which numbers 78 million people and suffering from 40 per cent underemployment. Almost half the workforce is engaged in agriculture, and earns about one-fifth the income found in the factory. Footwear manufacturing jobs are much sought after, not only for the wages and benefits offered now, but for the potential those entry-level jobs hold for the future.

Nike profits are roughly in line with the sporting goods industry average—9.6 per cent after tax. Most of those profits are used to fuel company growth and product development, a strategy of success. Though it is generally true that new subcontractor bases such as Indonesia have lower wage rates than more established manufacturing *bases like Taiwan and Korea, it does not necessarily follow that Nike shoes made in Indonesia generate higher profits. First, because development costs are higher working with new sources. Second, because the new factories produce at far lower levels of efficiency. The typical stockfitting line in Korea uses about 60 per cent of the labor needed in Indonesia to produce the same number of shoes. Third, because the models produced in Indonesia are moderately-priced to begin with.*

Indonesia is just one of 20 countries in which Nike products and components are sourced and manufactured, and one of more than 70 where Nike products are sold. Indeed, Nike is the largest single employer of American manufacturing workers of any athletic footwear company. More than 1,200 people are directly employed by Nike in eight US manufacturing operations in five states. That does not count thousands of other workers employed by Nike subcontractors throughout the United States.

With 6,200 corporate employees in the United States—a number that has grown steadily for six years—and with more than 8,000 employees worldwide, Nike is an example of an American company generating jobs throughout the global economy: professional, technical, design and managerial jobs as well as manufacturing jobs in the United States, and manufacturing, marketing, managerial, technical and sales jobs abroad, including managerial and technical jobs in Indonesia.

In Asia, the "Just Do It" story is conveyed through that very slogan in the many markets on that continent. Since Nike's US advertising agency, Wieden & Kennedy, (as mentioned above) does not have a strong international web, Nike uses various agencies, principally Grey, in Asia. There is close cooperation between Asia and Nike's US headquarters, and while creative is centralized in the US, there is high priority placed on communication between Asia and the US, to make sure that the Nike story plays well in Asia. After all, Asia has so many different markets, different in history and government and language, but yet similar in their adherence to values still widely held, centering on family and diligence, rather than, perhaps, on the individual and impulsiveness.

Yet marketers *have* often found one voice for Asia.

Satellite television (noted Richard Li Tzar-kai, son of Hong Kong tycoon Li Ka-shing, and an executive involved with the Asiawide Star-TV satellite system) will create new markets by linking advertisers and newly affluent consumers. In fact, the ability to span many nations and cultures will permit the creation of increasingly unified and regionally oriented promotion strategies. Multinational companies can now design a single, pan-Asian advertising campaign—as opposed to the traditional country-by-country approach. Sony, Matsushita, Coca-Cola and Nike have all designed effective regional messages (Asia, Inc., August 1993, p. 96).

Still, regional marketing can pose problems for an advertiser like Nike when it comes to its agency assignments. Leo Burnett, for example, was the Nike agency in Singapore, but, in 1993, after three years, Nike and Burnett parted ways because Reebok named Burnett to be *its* Asia regional agency.

As suggested, advertising has played a major part indeed in the Nike story, and Nike's tribute to Burnett (in an ad prepared by Grey Nike's agency in Hong Kong) was, to put it mildly, extraordinary (*Media*, February 19, 1993, p. 6).

THREE WORDS A GOOD AGENCY SHOULD NEVER TAKE FROM ITS CLIENT

A good agency should have a mind of its own.

It isn't there to answer to a client's call. To pander to the client's whims. To listen, and simply obey.

Full credit to Leo Burnett Singapore then. For 3 years, we were their client.

JUST DO IT.

For 3 years, we worked together, through thick and thin. For better, or for worse. (Mostly for better we might add.)

For 3 years, we formed a partnership that resulted in some very successful campaigns.

They were always what an agency should be. Professional, creative and strong-minded.

For that, we would like to say thank you.

We never told them to "just do" anything. And if we had, we doubt if they would have done it anyway.

Commented *Media (loc. cit.)*:

What is a fact is that Nike has gone out of its way to express appreciation.

Usually the split between client and agency results in a bitterness that most broken marriages could never hope to achieve.

The vitriol comes spewing out after being bottled up for years.

"After the fact" is usually the only time the agency really speaks its mind. Sadly, they feel this is the only time they can.

Yet here we have a client plainly saying that agencies are not there to pander to the client's whims and stating that agencies should actually be strong minded.

Thoughts such as these are pretty radical stuff in the modern economic climate where agencies are setting new records for gutlessness as they cling on to their clients.

No wonder that so much of today's advertising appears to lack a point.

The Nike ad is encouraging.

If the thought gets around that clients may actually be pleased if agencies treat them as equals, rather than trying to pre-emotively "yes" them every waking moment, the quality of advertising is likely to take on much needed freshness and purpose.

And still further, reacted Burnett in this rather poignant and telling matter (*Media*, March 19, 1993, p. 6):

> *Obviously, we were very pleased with the ad (i.e. the "THREE WORDS" as cited above).*
>
> *With Nike, we achieved very good sales results and helped move the brand from No. 4 to No. 1 in just 18 months in Singapore.*
>
> *Not bad by any standards.*
>
> *In addition, awards were won on the account across the world (again killing the lie that award-winning work doesn't produce sales).*
>
> *The Nike account was a joy to work on and the client was a delight to work with. They were always challenging, intelligent, witty and adventurous.*
>
> *They were everything a creative person could have wanted from a client. And more.*
>
> *But they didn't do it because they were nice people or because they had 15 MBAs.*
>
> *Nike quite simply understood that if you nurture, excite, challenge and encourage the team that works on your account, you get better ads, you sell more shoes and you make more money.*
>
> *It's really very simple....*

Finally, Nike's sensitivity to advertising and agencies—and to Asians for that matter—is still further underscored by the fact that it employs in the US in addition to Wieden & Kennedy, another agency, Muse Cordero Chen Inc., whose very forte is cultural sensitivity.

> *China-born David Chen, managing partner of the multi-ethnic Los Angeles advertising agency, Muse Cordero Chen Inc., says language is only one of the many pitfalls companies face when trying to reach the US Asian market. "People don't know the language, the cultural nuances, the size or location of the market, or even whether or not the target audience likes the product," he says....*
>
> *Chen understood what many US ad agencies are only beginning to realize: Asians comprise many different markets. "What is appropriate for one group can be wrong for another," says Greg Sullivan, president of Asian Television stations. Chen recalls how a telephone company ran a print ad aimed at Taiwanese in the US that pictured a smiling Chinese farm woman along with the Chinese message: "If you miss your mother's* jiao tse *(dumplings), why don't you phone home." But the company missed its mark. Most mothers of the affluent immigrants are not farmers, and Taiwanese farm women would not typically make* jiao tse, *a northern Chinese delicacy* (Asia, Inc., *February, 1993, p. 75).*

MARKETING IN ASIA. Asia is on the mind of every international marketer today: the 1.2 billion in China; the 880 million in India; the 125 million in Japan; to say nothing of little dragons Hong Kong, South Korea, Singapore and Taiwan; and a host of other economies (including Vietnam) exploding or waiting to explode. And Asia is becoming more and more important for Nike.

Asia-Pacific, running at 1–2 per cent of total Nike sales in the period 1989–1992, jumped to 5 per cent in 1993. (See also Exhibit 4.) But can "Just Do It" really "do it" in Asia? Is the spirit that it represents one that can be translated into a normative Asian ethos of groupism (rather than individualism) and modesty (rather than hype)?

It can be argued that it can *not* be so translated, that it is a case where a slogan born in the West came over to the East, that the very call to "Just Do It" is, if nothing else a call to the kind of hedonism (immature at that) that typified the times of the now-legendary Yuppies. ("Yuppies have no parents/yuppies have no kids/yuppies just have egos/yuppies just have ids.") It can also be argued that it *can* be translated, literally "carried over" to the East. It can be argued that "Just Do It" means more than the kind of triviality alluded to above. It can be argued that sports (which is Nike's emotional framework) is, in fact, an expression of life and the life-force itself, a call to modernity and to accomplishment. And it can be argued that "Just Do It," if anything, is the very heart and soul of an emerging and constantly unfolding Asia. For "Just Do It" can also mean accepting the challenge of taking economies that had been shackled by decades of colonialism, war, warlordism, ignorance, and misery, and building them into world powerhouses. Which Asians have done.

So, why *not* "Just Do It"? They've *done* it, haven't they? Yes, but what about that most enigmatic and often most mysterious of all Asian prizes? What about *Japan*? Even with Nike's historic connections with Japan, can "Just Do It" do it *there*?

Japan, spiteful talk notwithstanding, does truly love Western products and that are not forced upon it: Italian sweaters, French perfumes, German cars, American cigarettes and fast food. But what of Nike, whose name is so associated with basketball (not a major sport with the somewhat smaller Japanese) or tennis (not yet quite golf in Japan, even though its top female tennis player, Kimiko Date, has entered the top international ranks)? Nike seems hopeful, even in the face of a Japanese culture which is still quite brittle and formalistic, and where in any sense (literally or figuratively) hardly anyone "just does it" without "it" being a thing done and done in a uniquely appropriate way, in Japanese eyes. Indeed, on January 12, 1994, Phil Knight came to Hong Kong, and, in a conference that beamed in Michael Jordan (of "Air Jordan" fame) live from Tokyo, kicked off Nike's "Just Do It" campaign in Japan.

MARKETING IN CHINA

> *The mix of merchandise is firmly weighed in favour of imports and joint venture produce at the upmarket Shanghai Orient Shopping Centre on the outskirts of the downtown district. Profits will be slim this year, admits Liu Lihe, General Manager of the Sino-Hong Kong joint venture, which opened last January. Overheads are high, compared with those of home-grown competitors. He notes, for example, that the rent per square metre on his premises is about 10 times what (Shanghai Department Store) No. 1 pays.*
>
> *Nevertheless, Mr. Liu, who was the No. 1's Party Secretary until last year and had the honour of guiding Deng Xiaoping through the department store during the senior leader's southern tour in early 1992, believes a large number of Shanghai consumers are prepared to pay top dollar for high quality.*

"Our central government says that some people should become rich before the others. Some people have money, they have cash, like artists, entrepreneurs, self-employed people.... They want better goods," he said.

It is that reading of the market which has lured practically everybody who is anybody to Shanghai over the past few months. At one end of the fashionable Huaihai Road, a new shopping plaza is just starting up with names like Cerruti 1881, Dunhill, Yves Saint Laurent and Liz Claiborne. Further down the road are the likes of Puma, Nike, and Giordano, with the crowning touch being the Japanese Isetan department store.

Getting the product right is often just a matter of experience. "So far it's just so-so," said Innoxa Kwong, retail manager of the Burberrys boutique at the Hilton Hotel, where a woman's coat can set one back about US$1,000 (HK$7,800). "They have money to spend, but not everyone. On average they can't spend so much money," said Ms. Kwong. She reckons it could be two or three more years before the boutique breaks even.

The small Nike shop, on the other hand, has been profitable from day one, according to Ms. Shanberge. At times the doors have to be closed temporarily to control numbers. But a video display keeps customers entertained while they wait. Once inside, they are free to handle the produce and try it on. In contrast, many state-owned shops keep merchandise under glass cases or behind counters, and there are no change rooms to try on clothing.

These sorts of services, taken for granted in a place like Hong Kong, are still relatively new to the mainland. But competition is becoming so fierce in Shanghai that retailers are offering all sorts of new services and gimmicks to draw in customers (South China Morning Post, *January 16, 1993, p. 25*).

And then let us note what Nike today is thinking corporately about China (from the *South China Morning Post,* January 14, 1994, p. B2).

Nike Inc. is devoting more effort to expand its business in Asia, with China playing a stronger role in production.

Co-founder chairman and chief executive Philip Knight said the company considered Asia the fastest-growing area for business in the world.

"We are very bullish on the whole economy in Asia," he said.

Demand for Nike products in Asian markets was rising and the company would work to expand its presence, Mr. Knight said.

He pointed to Nike's recent acquisition of distribution rights in Japan.

Mr. Knight expected sales in Asia to increase by more than 10 per cent for the year to May 31.

He said China's role as a major production base for Nike was growing, as existing factory facilities in China accounted for about 35 per cent of the company's total production.

Five years ago, China factories represented only about five per cent of Nike's output.

Mr. Knight said the footwear market in China was of huge potential for growth, but it was difficult to gauge and project its growth.

Nike products made in all factory facilities contracted by Nike in China were virtually all for export.

These mainland factories are located in Fujian and Guangdong provinces and are funded by Taiwanese companies.

In China, Nike concentrates on marketing its products mainly in three major cities—Guangzhou, Shanghai and Beijing.

To summarize the China story, then, for Nike, we see a picture of a market where manufacturing is done (as it is done for other footwear companies) and has been done for a while (Nike finally found its way through the Chinese maze after much difficulty, typical of the early days for many international marketers); where most is made for export (taking advantage of the relatively low costs of land and labor in China); and where the domestic sales potential is, in principle, vast (even with prices of US$100 or so per pair), but is always pawn to changes in government policies (combating inflation, better or worse relations with the West and especially the US), currency fluctuations, and many other imponderables.

NIKE VS. REEBOK—A REVIEW

If one of the key elements in strategic thinking is inaugurating and responding to competitive actions, then the Nike vs. Reebok battlefield must particularly be reviewed briefly. In 1989, as already mentioned, Nike overtook Reebok as the leader in the US athletic footwear market: Nike now has 30 per cent, Reebok 24 per cent.

The rivalry is global, including Asia and China. Nike's Shanghai shop has already been mentioned. It needs a turnover of about RMB 20,000 a day (about US$2,300) just to break even. Nike's China marketing director, Erica Kerner, notes that such showcase stores, in addition to impress customers, are also

meant to educate Nike's domestic retailers about store design and operation. "It's a chance to show them what Western standard merchandising is," she says.

Based on remarks by company officials, it appears the two sport shoe giants (Nike and Reebok) will wage the same covert war in China as elsewhere, with Nike trying to show it represents "pure athletics", as opposed to its "fashion" rivals, while Reebok presents itself as "the human face of sport", less "self-indulgent" than others.

To prove their points, Nike has lined the shelves of its Shanghai store with shoes autographed by big-name sports stars, while Reebok is busy organizing tennis tournaments for children in Beijing and Guangzhou.

But despite the fanfare of showcase stores, Nike's Kerner says the company is devoting more time to setting up corners in major department stores, where the company builds a display and hires and trains specialized staff. "Store corners are fairly new to China retail," she says. "But if you just leave it to the department store, your product will get no customer service." Only a few of the 100-odd department stores selling Nike products in China have specialized corners (Asian Advertising and Marketing, *June 18, 1993, p. 5*).

Wherever the war goes, Reebok seems to fire back at Nike, and vice versa. And indeed Reebok *has* replied with heavy salvoes over time to Nike's never-ending barrages. It has—as noted—enlisted Shaquille O'Neal for its worldwide campaign, and its Planet Reebok campaign features unbridled imagination and vivid imagery. If imagery is what the market is about, then Reebok is not short of it either: it *does* fire back: after all, as Reebok proclaims, Life Is Not A Spectator Sport.

Nonetheless, imagery or not, Reebok has had its problems on the advertising and globalization fronts. It recently fired its US agency Chiat/Day (once a *Nike* agency), who created Reebok's campaign, and has signed on global powerhouse Leo Burnett. (Nike has said that it intends to keep Wieden & Kennedy, although Wieden & Kennedy does not have a major international presence, as noted already.)

As *Advertising Age* (September 20, 1993, p. 3 ff.) reported:

Last week, Reebok consolidated its $140 million worldwide account at Leo Burnett Co., Chicago, dropping Chiat from the $80 million US account and Euro RSCG, Paris, from the $60 million pan-European business.

In Reebok's eyes, Chiat's creative boutique image and its focus on the US instead of international expansion made the agency a less than ideal marketing partner at a time when Reebok was looking overseas for growth.

Enter Burnett, an agency already handling Reebok's Latin American and Far Eastern business with US and international marketing capabilities that go well beyond advertising.

Reebok's goal is to become the No. 1 sports and fitness brand in the $12 billion global athletic shoe market by 1995 and achieve a 30 per cent share of the business around the world.

To reach its objectives, Reebok has singled out five strategic footwear priorities: outdoor; pre-season cleated; soccer; women's sports and fitness; and basketball.

The company will also concentrate on overall Reebok brand shoe technology and refocus its efforts in apparel, a small business with less than $500,000 in sales, on technology-driven sports clothing.

But Reebok has a long way to go to reach its lofty goals.

Currently, its global share is about 17 per cent based on $2.2 billion in worldwide athletic footwear sales. Its US market share is higher at 24.4 per cent for 1992, but down for the first six months of 1993.

Sporting Goods Intelligence, an industry newsletter, reported that Reebok's U.S. sales were off 3.4 per cent through June to $683 million from the year-earlier period.

This comes as the overall US industry is running about 3 to 4 per cent ahead and Nike is even further out front, posting a sales increase of 18 per cent to $995.5 million in the first six months of 1993.

And as much as Reebok needs to expand internationally, it also needs to shore up the US business to realize its potential value as a global brand.

To reach its global goals, "we came to the realization that what we seriously want is a partner," said David Ropes, VP-marketing services worldwide for Reebok, which went through its own internal global reorganization last year.

"Chiat did not have the global resources and we made the decision three weeks ago that it was an opportunity to take another look at the kind of resources we needed," Mr. Ropes said. "We had wired together a global network using Chiat as the lead agency and Burnett and Euro RSCG overseas, but there was no partnership between those three.

"So, we asked Burnett to come in...."

In assessing Burnett's capabilities, Mr. Ropes cited an example in Asia where Burnett helped organize and orchestrate the Chang Challenge, a junior tennis tournament last year based on Reebok's association with tennis player Michael Chang, a Reebok endorser.

"They came up with the promotional event and ran the whole thing for us," Mr. Ropes said....

What of the future and its strategic dimensions? Nike still seems bent on speaking in a bold and brash way with deliberate and delightful overstatement, to keep up the level of excitement that appears to be a key determinant for success in the loud world of athletic footwear (and its offshoots). Their latest TV pool carries on the tradition.

The "crazed ref" character Dennis Hopper plays in Nike commercials might be incoherent, but the actor has no trouble making his own thoughts perfectly clear.

"I find this really absurd. It's silly and stupid," Mr. Hopper said of the controversy surrounding the gungy, psychotic National Football League follower he plays in five spots for Nike's $110 Air Veer football shoes.

"It's obviously a comedy," he said of the commercials. The fifth and final spot of the campaign, featuring Mr. Hopper and players from teams competing in the NFL playoffs, broke January 8.

In his first-ever turn as TV ad spokesman ... Mr. Hopper plays a schizo fan so enamoured of the game that, in one spot, he sneaks into the Buffalo Bills locker room to sniff Bruce Smith's Nike shoe.

Still, Mr. Hopper insisted, "Nobody's making fun of crazy people...." The National Stigma Association, an advocacy group for the mentally ill, received wide publicity when it voiced displeasure about the spots (Advertising Age, *January 2, 1994, p. 2).*

Nonetheless, will other factors, such as the proliferation of categories, and the inevitable continuing march towards globalization become even greater factors than the imagism that seems to drive Nike? Reebok may give us a clue (*Advertising Age, loc. cit.*):

> *As Reebok International restructures its senior marketing management, its new agency, Leo Burnett USA, Chicago, appears on the verge of unveiling a new campaign themed "Reebok. Believe." Angel Martinez, formerly president of the Reebok fitness division, becomes exec VP-global marketing. Dave Ropes remains VP-marketing services but will now report to Mr. Martinez instead of Reebok Chairman-CEO Paul Fireman. Mr. Fireman said the changes address Reebok's effort "to develop a unified global structure." A Reebok spokesman would not comment on the new campaign.*

Can the industry keep running, as it were, but still keep its feet planted in reality too, the reality of a world that is getting both smaller and bigger at the same time?

CASE ELEVEN

THE CAISHIKOU BARBERSHOP*

Inside the Caishikou Barbershop, Li Xing Yin (pronounced Lee Shing Yin) sat in his third floor office pondering several important decisions he needed to make soon about worker salaries, benefits, and the acquisition of new equipment. On the two floors below, workers were busy giving haircuts, shampoos, and permanents. Outside, on busy Guangaumennei Dajie, bicycle bells could be heard from a steady stream of riders headed home from work in the late afternoon sun. Some paused to buy copies of *Renmin Rebao* (People's Daily), vegetables, and summer fruit from the small market stands that lined the street. Another warm evening was ahead for the Xuanwu District located southwest of Beijing's Tiananmen Square.

Several weeks earlier in August, 1986, Li Xing Yin and his fellow workers took advantage of a major change in the way business is done in China. Since 1983 the authorities in Beijing had allowed private citizens, collectives, and families to lease certain small size enterprises in the service trades in return for monthly lease payments. Officially the new policy on leasing was known as "separating ownership and management." Leasing was intended to stimulate business activity while not changing the economy's socialist nature since ultimate ownership remained with the state. By the summer of 1986 about one-third of the 3,300 barber, catering, repair, and non-staple food shops in Beijing's eight suburban districts were leased from the state.

---

* This case was prepared by Steven M. Dawson, University of Hawaii and Visiting Professor, University of International Business and Economics, Beijing, as a basis for class discussion and not to illustrate either effective or ineffective handling of an administrative situation. © 1988. All rights reserved to the contributors and the North American Case Research Association. Permission to publish the case should be obtained from the author and the North American Case Research Association. Published in *Case Research Journal*, Spring 1990.

Rather than the state controlling virtually all enterprises, leasing was said to make it possible for individuals to have management control and to retain profits. In leased enterprises the managers enjoy independence in business and labor decisions, and in the use of funds. Formerly their decisions were subject to many restrictions on matters of manpower, finances, materials acquisition, production, and marketing. A lease makes the enterprise, not the state, responsible for both profits and losses. This works both ways: if business is good, profits can be kept by the enterprise instead of going to the state as before, but if losses are incurred the state does not simply provide the funds to make them up. How far the new economic reforms would be allowed to go, and how fast, was by no means certain, and Li Xing Yin felt a sense of relief and accomplishment that he had the two-year contract signed.

After 16 years of working under government ownership and management at the Caishikou Barbershop, Li, as the signer of the lease, felt considerable motivation to be a good manager both for himself and for the 70 other employees. "Before we were the masters, but we did not have a sense of responsibility. Now we really feel we are the masters of the enterprise," said Li, "because the performance of each worker is directly linked to the honor and future of the shop."

One of Li's first actions after signing the lease was to ask his fellow workers for suggestions on how to improve the barbershop's operations. His objective was two-fold: to learn from their experience and to build a sense of identification with the enterprise. The response to the request was overwhelming and encouraging: 210 suggestions were received in the first week. Li felt that the workers were really excited by the opportunity to have a say in management. Another 20 suggestions came in later. This was quite a change. Before the lease was signed, the workers, including Li, felt little responsibility for the success of the enterprise. There was little incentive to do well since salaries were fixed, they often did not reflect a worker's contribution, workers couldn't be fired, and bankruptcy did not exist in China for state-managed enterprises. Absenteeism was high among the barbershop workers and there were many complaints from customers about the bad quality of service provided.

After reviewing his fellow workers' suggestions, Li selected for early consideration three areas with a direct and significant financial impact. First were proposals to change the payment of wages from the former fixed salaries to a basic wage plus a bonus. This would recognize the workers' contribution to the enterprise's success. Second was to initiate or continue several worker-related benefit programs including a nursery, personal and health insurance, lunches, and housing for some single workers. Third was a proposal to buy new equipment not included with the leased premises and to expand the services provided by the barbershop.

THE BUSINESS ENVIRONMENT

In China's socialist economy as of the early 1980s, virtually all medium and large size enterprises were owned by the state as the representative of the people. Each enterprise reported to a specific state supervisory unit that was their "department in charge." The Caishikou Barbershop came under the Beijing Xuanwu District Service Corporation. An enterprise's fixed assets and regular "circulation fund" (net working capital) were provided free of charge by the state. In return, the enterprise turned all its profit over to the state, its products were purchased at a fixed price by state commercial departments, and its labor force was provided by state labor departments. Each year the enterprise needed to apply to the department in charge for funds for working capital, equipment replacements, and any new ventures. Acceptance, revision, or rejection was more likely to be based on how the request related to the state's five year plan rather than to its financial feasibility. With little power or responsibility, enterprises often did not emphasize profitability or efficiency and merely tried to meet state output plans. It was to the enterprises' advantage to keep their output target as low as possible so that it could be met or exceeded, and to increase financial and material allocation from the state. There were penalties for not meeting production targets, but not for having excess funds and materials.

In service enterprises prices were set by the state and the services were provided to the public on a more or less take-it-or-leave-it basis. Whether customers patronized the enterprise or not did not affect the interests of the staff one way or the other. This led to inertia and inefficiency associated with the "iron rice bowl" of guaranteed employment and the "big pot" of state enterprise employment in which wages were not determined by results of the individual enterprises.

The difficulties encountered with state management and ownership of enterprises did not escape notice. The problems were particularly noticeable and disturbing in service industries. A consensus gradually evolved that these enterprises should be responsible for the efficient use of state funds and that service to customers might improve if enterprises were given the right to retain part of their profits. Part of the extra profit earned through improved management could be used for the workers' collective welfare or distributed as bonuses among these workers who made greater contributions. As the economist, Xue Muqiao, noted, "The superiority of the socialist system cannot be brought into full play unless the interests of the state, the workers, and staff, including the factory leaders, are integrated and all are interested in increasing production and practicing economy."

The first enterprise lease agreement was made in January, 1982, when Wu Jilong signed a contract with an electroplating copper factory in Taiyuan, Shanxi Province, to manage its industrial silicon production workshop which had lost almost 2 million yuan the previous year. Under the contract all the workshop's equipment was still owned by the factory and the lessee bought the raw material, produced the product, and sold it to the factory. After five years of losses before the lease, a profit was made. By the end of 1985 the cumulative profit was 4.18 million yuan. Reports about the workshop lease reached Hu Yaobang, General Secretary of the Communist Party of China's Central Committee who suggested that what Wu Julang had done be tried in other smaller state enterprises. In Beijing, leasing was experimented with in small service-related enterprises like green groceries, restaurants, bicycle repair shops, and barbershops. The authorities were especially interested in leasing those enterprises which were operating at a loss and thus creating a drain on available state financial resources.

Leasing of state-owned enterprises to individuals marked a major reversal of official policy—especially after the ten years of the Cultural Revolution from 1966 to 1976 when an often fierce campaign was waged against all capitalist tendencies. Previously it was firmly believed that having all businesses owned and managed by the state was the best choice for China's socialistic economy. The need to justify the new economic policy was noted in the 1984 "Decision of the Central Committee of the Communist Party of China on Reform of the Economic Structure" which pointed out that "As market theory and the practice of socialism have shown, ownership can be duly separated from the power of operation by the state institution." Commenting on this policy statement, the *Beijing Review* said:

> *When the state leases the enterprises to the lessee, the ownership remains in the hands of the state. Feudal society was based on landlords leasing land to the peasants; in capitalist society, what is leased is companies or factories from one capitalist to another. In socialist China, the nature of leasing is different. The lessor is the state, the lessees are laborers identified as masters of the state and the enterprise. Ownership remains with the state, the enterprise is still publicly owned. The only thing that has changed is the method of operation. The form of ownership of the means of production and of distribution is an important criterion for judging the nature of a social system. Therefore, the leasing business of China remains socialistic in nature.*

THE LEASE

A two-year lease was signed by Li Xing Yin, representing his fellow workers, and the Xuanwu District Service Corporation. The monthly lease payment to the state was set at 6,000 yuan plus an additional 1.5 per cent of sales revenues, to be paid to the state's worker education fund. Since this was a collective lease in which Li signed for all the barbershop workers, rather than a lease to individuals, no deposit was needed. One of the other six barbershops in the district was leased to an individual and he had to put 10 per cent of the profit target down as deposit. The Caishikou lease set targets of 450,000 yuan per year (37,500 per month) for sales and 82,000 yuan (6,833 per month) for profits before bonus and tax. If sales were below 450,000, the percentage of pretax income available for bonuses could be lowered by the service corporation, but the amount of reduction was not known now and would depend upon the results of the other six barbershops in the district. Alternatively, the bonus percentage would be raised if the sales target was exceeded. If the agreed profit target was no met, no bonuses would be paid and the base salaries would be cut by an amount equivalent to the profit target deficit. If the financial shortcomings were serious enough, the lease could be terminated by the state. All the workers would retain their jobs, but the barbershop would again be under state management. If profits were made after tax and other required payments, the lease provided that they could be retained by the barbershop. Initially it was agreed with the District Service Corporation that 50 per cent would go to the enterprise development fund and 50 per cent to the worker benefit fund. The development fund could be used for working capital, to buy new assets, and to repay loans used to finance assets. The workers benefit fund was for bonuses above those which are tax deductible and for other outlays that would benefit the workers.

Two years is a fairly short period since many of the decisions to be made have long-term implications and Li already anticipated applying for renewal. Also under discussion with the District Service Corporation was an extension of the existing lease. Since it is a collective lease and all the workers were part of the leasing unit, when it came time to renew the lease they could vote for Li Xing Yin to represent them again, or if they wanted someone else they could change managers. Li Xing Yin could also be replaced prior to the lease expiration if the workers so wished. The District Service Corporation was on record as saying they did not care who signed the lease or represented the workers as long as they were confident the person had the ability to run the barbershop.

As its part of the lease, the state provided the existing equipment and premises occupied by the barbershop. Also included was the circulation fund, the equivalent of net working capital, owned by the state but available for use by the barbershop. The circulation fund remained at 93,600 yuan, the same as before the lease was signed. It, the building, and the equipment provided by the state should be maintained and returned in equal condition, given reasonable wear and tear, at the conclusion of the lease. Offsetting credit or a refund could be provided by improvements or new assets paid for by the barbershop. The Xuanwu District Service Corporation also made available the services of Liu Young Ming, secretary of the party branch for all seven barbershops in the District. His main responsibility was to see that the barbershop was operated according to the lease contract. He could also "give ideas on management," but the barbershop can still make its own decisions, do ideological work, get market information, and help locate needed materials.

THE POST-LEASE PERIOD

Initial results were very encouraging. Not only did the workers respond positively to the request for ideas on how to improve management by preparing the 210 suggestions, but also the first month's financial results showed a big jump in revenues, a smaller jump in expenses, a healthy reported profit, and a balance sheet that was in good shape. Sales revenues rose to 44,731 yuan from 36,000 a year earlier and profit after tax as shown in the income statement in Exhibit 1 was 2,942 yuan. In theory, the profit could have been even larger but Li had found that although some expenses were fixed and remained constant with the rise in revenues, other expenses, specifically fuel, water and electricity, materials, repairs, incidental expenses, the lease payment to the worker education fund, and the turnover tax, went up in line with the revenue increase.

The distribution of profit before tax in the income statement was fairly structured. Of profit before tax, 48 per cent goes to income tax, 10 per cent is paid to the District Service Corporation as a location tax (the amount is based upon the enterprise's location with those in the city center paying more and those in the outer districts less than 10 per cent), 15 per cent goes to the Ministry of Commerce, and 15 per cent of profit after income tax and after the payment to the Ministry of Commerce goes to the State Energy Fund.

Li suspected that the large revenue increase in September might have occurred because many customers wanted to see whether better service was now being provided following the publicity the barber shop received when it was leased. Expenses were also lower than they

Exhibit 1 Caishikou Barbershop: Revenue for September, 1986 (in yuan)

Income	44,731
Less Expenses:	
Fuel	268
Water and electricity	626
Materials used	2,102
Base salaries	5,254
Welfare	956
Repairs	403
Depreciation*	849
Incidental expenses	492
Lease: state	6,000
Lease: worker education fund	671
Pension for retired workers	2,545
Other expenses	369
Turnover tax	1,476
Operating profit before bonus	22,719
Bonus	9,088
Profit before tax	13,632
Income tax	6,543
Location tax	1,363
Ministry of Commerce	2,045
Energy fund	757
Net profit after tax	2,924
Enterprise development fund	1,462
Worker benefit fund	1,462

* Paid to state for state-owned assets.

would probably be in the future if the additional financial incentives he was now considering were implemented.

Regarding the revenues, Li recognized that there were enough barbershops in south Beijing, plus the individual barbers who set up shop in the outdoor markets, for the shop's revenues to fluctuate widely. In the past, the state-run barbershop did not provide high quality and satisfactory service. Li realized that if he could gain a reputation for providing quality service at a fair price with well-trained and courteous staff, he would have a decided market advantage. Given the population in the area and the existence of other barbershops, 60,000 yuan per month was Li's best estimate of the high end of the possible revenue scale while the worst outcome short of an outright reputation disaster was 25,000.

The balance sheet as of September 30, 1986, is presented in Exhibit 2. Because it is against state policy in China for the actual balance sheet of an enterprise to be made public, the balance sheet in Exhibit 2 shows reasonable relationships among the individual entries for an enterprise like the Caishikou Barbershop but the figures for each outlay are not accurate.

Exhibit 2 Caishikou Barbershop: Representative Balance Sheet*
September 30, 1986

	(in yuan)	
Sources of Funds (Liabilities and Net Worth)		
State-owned circulating fund**	10,000	
Enterprise development fund†	5,000	
Accounts payable	500	
Pre-deductions††	1,000	
		16,500
Renewal (Equipment)**	1,000	
Worker benefit fund†	1,000	
Bonus payable	1,000	
Pension	500	
Welfare fund†††	1,000	
		4,500
State-owned net fixed assets	10,000	
Depreciation	3,000	
		13,000
Total		34,000
Uses of Funds (Assets)		
Materials	5,000	
Furniture and utensils	10,000	
Cash	1,000	
Accounts receivable	500	
		16,500
Specialized deposits		4,500
Fixed assets		13,000
Total		34,000

   * Yuan figures do not equal actual figures, but the relationships between accounts are believed to represent relationships between the real figures.
  ** Provided by the state.
   † From profit after tax.
  †† Expensed in advance: included items like provisions for repairs.
 ††† From income statement.

VISITS WITH WORKERS

As a first step toward building a new attitude among his fellow workers Li Xing Yin decided to visit each of the 70 employees in their homes to learn about their problems and to identify ways in which the enterprise could assist them. The visits to the workers' homes went well and a number of people commented to him that this was the first time anyone from the barbershop had indicated an interest in their problems of daily living. In thinking back over his visits, Li put together a list of problems. These problems, which were frequently raised were, among others:

- Inadequate access to a place to bathe
- No lunches provided at work nor was there a place to eat
- No kindergarten at work for small children
- Problems getting to work by public transportation, especially in bad weather when bicycles could not be ridden
- No health insurance
- No personal insurance
- No place for a midday rest

Although Li sensed that creating a new and more positive attitude among the workers toward the barbershop was important, he could not just seek to improve their welfare without regard to their attitude and ability. Those workers who wanted to work hard could have morale problems if workers who were not suitable were kept. Thus Li fired one of the workers in the first month because he did not do the work well. This was the first worker fired in many years. Finding new workers was not a problem since they could be hired by the barbershop directly. As long as the present policy toward leased service enterprises continued, it would not be necessary to work with the state labor office.

The visits to the workers' homes, the 210 suggestions he received, and his review of the initial income statement led Li Xing Yin to consider three principal modifications in the way the shop was managed that would have an early and potentially significant impact on the financial results.

THE POLICY CHOICES

One reason for the poor quality of service was clear: salaries were too low. There also was little relationship between the workers' salaries, the amount of work done, and the profit made by the barbershop. This needed to be changed if there was to be hope of improving worker attitudes, the quality of service provided, and the reputation of the barbershop.

The existing base salary range was from 60 to a little over 100 yuan per month and the average was just 74 yuan for the 71 workers. No bonuses of any significance were paid before the lease was signed: each worker merely received his or her base salary. Now that the barbershop was leased, bonuses could be paid either as tax deductible salary expenses or out of the worker benefit fund after taxes were paid. The Xuanwu District Service Corporation required that the deductible bonuses be equal to a minimum of 36 to a maximum of 50 per cent of the reported profit before taxes and bonuses. The actual percentage for each month was set by the Service Corporation using a method which was not clear to the barbershop. In September profits before tax and bonus were 22,719 yuan of which 40 per cent or 9,088 was paid out to workers as a bonus. As the elected manager, Li's salary was equal to 65 yuan plus 15 yuan as manager. His bonus each month would be equal to the average bonus paid to each of the barbershop's other workers who received bonuses.

The September bonus reflected the substantial improvement in the barbershop's profitability during the first month. It was clear that the system of base salary plus bonus could be a powerful factor in improving worker attitudes. There were two primary alternatives proposed for consideration. First, the September experiment with the existing base salary averaging 74 yuan plus bonus could be retained. Second, some workers thought that all employees could receive an increase in their base salary, perhaps to around 150 yuan on average, with accordingly smaller bonuses available. A base salary of just 74 yuan, these workers said, did not recognize the skills, dedication, and experience of the workers in a leased enterprise rather than a state enterprise. The higher base would also take into consideration the workers' risk of a wage cut if the sales and profit targets were not met.

The method for determining the size of each worker's bonus was to award one point for every 30 yuan of revenues the worker generated above their base task. At the end of each quarter the total bonus available was divided among the workers based upon the points they accumulated. Workers who did not generate revenue directly received a bonus equal to the average bonus paid to all the barbershop workers. The only exception was the accountant whose bonus was 2.3 per cent of total bonuses. So as to avoid too much emphasis on the quantity rather than the quality of work, workers whose work quality was not good or who quarreled with customers only received one half point for each 30 yuan of revenue generated. When there were serious problems, no point would be given. If each worker merely met his or her basic task, Li estimated that monthly revenues would be about 25,000 yuan.

The second policy issue involved expenditures for worker welfare. After making the home visits and identifying a number of problems that his fellow workers faced in their daily life, especially as it involved the barbershop, Li continued some worker welfare programs made available by the barbershop when it was a state enterprise and identified others that might be added. None of the costs identified below were included in the September revenue and expense statement in Exhibit 1 since existing benefits like the kindergarten were paid for by the workers. The costs per month at current employment levels would be as follows:

- Shower room: 135 yuan per month for supplies
- Lunch and a lunchroom: 250 yuan
- A kindergarten for workers' children: 180 yuan
- Rent rooms: 100 yuan
- Personal insurance: 71 yuan
- Health insurance: 350 yuan
- Place for mid-day rest: no charge, use an existing room
- Recuperation trips: 167 yuan

A tough problem to solve involved transportation. Although there were six million bicycles in Beijing, not all workers had one, and bicycles were a problem in bad weather. The Beijing bus service was often crowded and difficult to use. As a way to solve transportation problems, some workers thought that a van should be purchased but that would create too many problems Li thought. An alternative to the van was to rent rooms from individuals near the barbershop where 8 to 10 workers could stay when going home was inconvenient. Perhaps these rooms could also be used for housing for single workers who had problems getting access to an apartment because of the priority given to married couples. Another partial solution to the transportation problem was flexibility in the starting or finishing times for workers with commuting difficulties.

Although there was some feeling that the barbershop should start its own kindergarten for young, preschool age children of workers, this seemed to be much more expensive and difficult than sending the children to the kindergarten run by the District Service Corporation. The total cost was only 180 yuan per month and this is what was done before the lease.

The workers also identified concerns about insurance. Li investigated and found that personal insurance, which would make a payment of 1,000 yuan to the worker's family in case the worker died, could be purchased for just 1 yuan per worker per month. Health insurance could be purchased for 4 yuan per worker per month. In addition the barbershop paid 95 per cent of health costs not covered by the insurance if the worker had worked at the barbershop for 20 years, and 90 per cent if they had worked there for less than 20 years. All hospital costs were paid by the barbershop. The total cost of the health insurance and other health benefits was about 350 yuan per month.

The last worker benefit under consideration was intended to make the barbershop a prestige place to work. Each year 10 workers can go to a nice place, such as the ocean beach resort at Beidaihe, or another scenic spot, for rest and relaxation with all expenses paid by the barbershop. Workers would be selected each year based upon their contributions to the success of the barbershop.

The expenditures for worker benefits, both the existing outlays of 956 yuan for welfare in September and the added expenses identified here, required a substantial outlay and Li viewed them as desirable in theory but they would mean less profit would be available. Two alternatives to the fixed monthly payments were suggested. The first suggestion was to allocate a portion of revenues to these purposes. That way, if the barbershop did well, the funds would be available. If revenues were larger than needed, extra services could be added. Of course, if revenues dropped, some services would need to be curtailed. If this was the choice, Li tentatively decided to set the percentage of revenue allocated to employee benefits to be equal to the amount needed to finance these outlays using September's revenue level. Existing benefits would thus be allocated at 2.14 per cent of revenues. The new benefits, assuming all were funded, would be covered by 2.8 per cent of revenues. The second alternative was to eliminate all worker benefits from tax deductible expenses and to pay for them from the worker benefit fund consisting of 50 per cent of after-tax profits.

The third policy issue involved the purchase of new equipment for the barbershop. Although the total demand in the Xuanwu District for hair cuts and related personal services remained reasonably constant over time, individual shops were vulnerable to considerable competition and instability of revenues. This was especially true in the lower end of the market, the simple haircut. To upgrade the appearance of the barbershop and to provide services that would be relatively free from competition with other barbershops and the individual barber with scissors and a chair who set up shop in an outdoor market, Li decided to substantially improve his equipment to provide diversified and upgraded services. Included were the following outlays:

1. Ironing machine (6,000 yuan): The barbershop already had a washing machine. The ironing machine would be used for workers' uniforms. The appearance of the staff was an important part of the new image of the barbershop.
2. Air conditioner (35,150 yuan): This could be a real competitive advantage during the summer months.
3. New barber chairs (35,400 yuan): The present ones had been in the shop for a long time and new chairs were needed for improving the barbershop' appearance and providing better service.
4. Work tables (8,800 yuan): These would be in front of each chair and would hold the workers' equipment.
5. Equipment (6,000 yuan): This was required for use by the workers.
6. New boiler (4,635 yuan): The present one was not adequate for supplying enough hot water.
7. Face lift for barbershop (13,400 yuan): Many years had passed since the walls had been repainted. The entrance way and waiting room also needed attention and many new pictures could be placed on the walls showing the latest styles. New working rooms were also needed for new services.
8. Laser medical machines (13,000 yuan): This would be a major expansion of services. Many customers had facial skin problems, especially acne, and these machines could be used to treat them.

Monthly depreciation for the eight listed expenditures itemwise would approximately be as follows:

1. 24 yuan
2. 141 yuan
3. 142 yuan
4. 35 yuan
5. no depreciation
6. no depreciation
7. 54 yuan
8. 52 yuan

Items which individually cost less than 5,000 yuan are not subject to the regular depreciable. Instead 50 per cent of the purchase price goes into the income statement as an expense when the assets are purchased using accelerated depreciation and another 50 per cent is expensed when the asset is disposed of. Normally, state enterprises in China pay the state an amount in cash equal to depreciation, but as a leased enterprise the barbershop would not need to do this if it purchased the equipment with its own funds.

Payment for these purchases should not be a problem. Although the enterprise development fund did not have nearly enough in it to pay for everything, the Beijing Service Corporation, the Government of Xuanwu District, and the Xuanwu District Service Corporation were prepared to provide funds. No interest would be charged and repayment would be in two equal payments at the end of 1988 and 1989. If the lease was terminated, the loan would be payable at that time. The first payment was still 28 months away. There was the possibility that the Beijing Service Corporation would provide up to 100,000 yuan of the full loan with no need to repay, but that had not yet been fully decided upon. Li decided to assume the full purchase price would be borrowed and repayment would have to be made for the entire loan. If the non-repayment part of the total loan was used, the barbershop would have the use of those funds and assets, but not the ownership, and would need to pay the related depreciation expense to the state each month. The new assets would also not count toward the "maintenance of the value of leased assets as of the time the lease ends" clause in the lease. Manager Li needed to decide whether to take the repayable loan and thus get ownership of the assets, decide not to go ahead with these expenditures (a course of action with negative implications for the success of the barbershop), or to hold out for the no repayment loan.

The operating procedures of the Caishikou Barbershop specified that Li's financial plans must be presented to the workers' council for approval before he could proceed. This was a group of 24 workers who were selected by their fellow workers and it had a voice in management policies and workers' benefits. Now that the information had been obtained, it was time to begin making decisions about the way worker salaries would be paid, the worker benefits that would be financed, how they would be paid for, and about the acquisition of new assets. Adding to Li's desire to do a good job of managing the barbershop was an item in the day's paper. "After some delay for revisions, China's new Law on Bankruptcy has been submitted for approval to the Standing Committee of the Sixth National People's Congress. In the past the state had held that bankruptcy is a capitalist concept and incompatible with socialism. According to the new draft law state enterprises with serious deficits due to poor management will be declared bankrupt upon application by creditors. The draft law stipulates that those responsible for the failure will be disciplined."

CASE TWELVE

GOLDLION HOLDINGS GROUP: A HONG KONG COMPANY ENTERS CHINA*

INTRODUCTION

Goldlion—written as one word and pronounced, perhaps for its French-soundingness, "gold-lee-*ON*"—is a Hong Kong firm that saw opportunities in Hong Kong and began small there, and has since sought further opportunities in the People's Republic of China (PRC). It is principally engaged in the marketing and distribution of men's apparel and accessories which are sold primarily under the Goldlion brand name. The Group's range comprises ties and related products, garments, leather goods and menswear accessories. Among these products, garments and ties represent the major part. The Group manufactures ties and leather goods in Hong Kong and China. Other garments and accessories are contracted out.

It has established an extensive regional distribution network for its products in the PRC, Hong Kong, and Singapore, and in a number of other Asian countries like Malaysia, Indonesia, Thailand, and Taiwan. It has about 600 distributors in the PRC, 130 in Hong Kong, and 90 in Singapore. The Group also markets its products under the brand names of Silverlion and VanGarie.

THE BEGINNINGS

In 1968, in Hong Kong, one might have wondered how to get into the menswear business. Well, what about an area where excess cloth from other goods could be used; where size

---

* This case is adapted from material orginally prepared by Chan Cheuk-tung, Chan Wai-man, Lin Wa, and Ng Lui. Our appreciation is extended to them.

was not a problem; and where there was a vision of producing a product with a foreign-sounding name, but made locally to compete with European brands, and sold at a fraction of the price?

What about *ties*?

So, displaying exemplary Hong Kong entrepreneurship, Mr. and Mrs. Tsang Hin-chi started a small home-based operation for manufacturing ties. Mr. Tsang—who got to know ties when working in the 1960s with his brother, a businessman in Thailand—sold the ties to shops in central Hong Kong and Tsim Sha Tsui (the busy commercial areas) with a target of 60 ties per day. In 1969, the Goldlion trademark (the name suggests good fortune in Chinese) was registered with the design of a lion. In 1970, Mr. Tsang established a trading relationship with major Hong Kong department stores like Wing On and Daimaru. In the same year, Mr. Tsang set out to promote his ties on Father's Day, through advertising in newspapers. In 1971, a newly designed trademark was registered in Hong Kong, and he incorporated it as Goldlion Far East Ltd.

The promotion efforts for Goldlion became more aggressive. It sponsored the performance of China's national table tennis team in Hong Kong in 1971, and the television program of the 1972 visit to China of the American President, Richard Nixon. In 1973, Goldlion Far East commenced its own counter sales in local department stores. From 1974 to 1980, Goldlion Far East expanded its product range to men's leather goods and accessories. It purchased advanced machinery from Germany to manufacture its products. Its production site was in Tsuen Wan, an industrial area in Hong Kong.

Goldlion Singapore was incorporated in 1981 to undertake the sale of the Group's products in Singapore and Malaysia. It launched a new brand, VanGarie, for men's ties and belts. Goldlion Far East started to promote the brand Goldlion and its products in the PRC in 1984. In the same year, San Raphael was incorporated to manufacture leather goods, and Silverlion (China) was incorporated to manufacture ties in China. In 1984 and 1985, Goldlion Far East purchased more advanced machinery from Germany to enhance its productivity. In 1986, Silverlion started to manufacture ties under its own brand, Silverlion, for the PRC market. In 1987, Goldlion Far East further expanded its product lines to menswear. In 1990, Goldlion China was established to manufacture leather belts.

As part of a corporate reorganization prior to its floatation on the Hong Kong Stock Exchange in 1992, Goldlion Holdings Group became the holding company for all the other companies comprising the Group.

The Goldlion structure is shown in Exhibit 1.

THE MANAGEMENT STRUCTURE

The founder, Tsang Hin-chi, who is a graduate of Zhongshan University in the PRC, is the managing director of the Group and has overall responsibility for the Group's policy and management. He is a member of the Hong Kong Advisory Group of the PRC, the honorary treasurer of the Chinese General Chamber of Commerce in Hong Kong, a deputy to the National People's Congress of the PRC, and a committee member of a number of other trade associations in both the PRC and Hong Kong. He is in charge of key decision making

Case Twelve

Exhibit 1 The Goldlion Structure

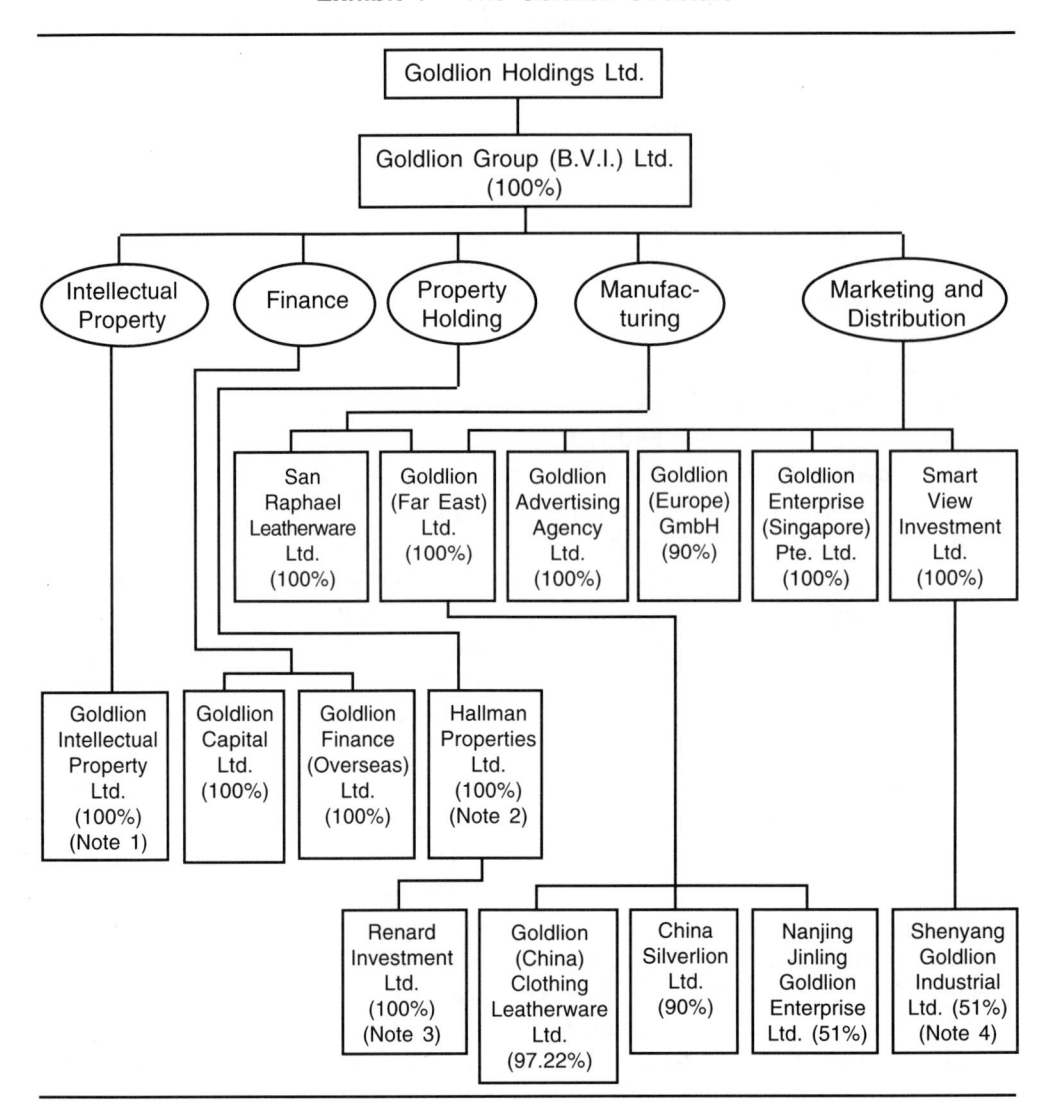

```
                          Goldlion Holdings Ltd.
                                   |
                        Goldlion Group (B.V.I.) Ltd.
                                  (100%)
                                   |
   ┌──────────────┬─────────────┬──────────────┬──────────────┐
Intellectual   Finance      Property       Manufac-      Marketing and
 Property                   Holding         turing        Distribution
```

Subsidiaries:
- San Raphael Leatherware Ltd. (100%)
- Goldlion (Far East) Ltd. (100%)
- Goldlion Advertising Agency Ltd. (100%)
- Goldlion (Europe) GmbH (90%)
- Goldlion Enterprise (Singapore) Pte. Ltd. (100%)
- Smart View Investment Ltd. (100%)

- Goldlion Intellectual Property Ltd. (100%) (Note 1)
- Goldlion Capital Ltd. (100%)
- Goldlion Finance (Overseas) Ltd. (100%)
- Hallman Properties Ltd. (100%) (Note 2)

- Renard Investment Ltd. (100%) (Note 3)
- Goldlion (China) Clothing Leatherware Ltd. (97.22%)
- China Silverlion Ltd. (90%)
- Nanjing Jinling Goldlion Enterprise Ltd. (51%)
- Shenyang Goldlion Industrial Ltd. (51%) (Note 4)

Notes:

1. The Group intends to transfer the intellectual property rights of the Goldlion brand name in Hong Kong and the PRC from Goldlion Intellectual Property Limited to a new wholly owned subsidiary of the Guarantor to be incorporated in Hong Kong.
2. Holds the property of the Group's European office in Dusseldorf, Germany.
3. Holds the property of the Group's corporate headquarters in Shatin, Hong Kong.
4. In May 1993, Smart View Investment Limited, a wholly owned subsidiary of the Guarantor, entered into an agreement with two PRC partners to form a joint venture company, Shenyang Goldlion Industrial Ltd., of which Smart View Investment Limited has a 51% equity interest, to operate a department store of approximately 200,000 square feet located in the central business district of Shenyang.

Source: Adapted from Goldlion's Annual Report, 1993.

for the Group's PRC business. Only a few of the senior management people have degrees in the fields of their responsibility. However, all of them have substantial business experience. For example, the general manager of the Group has over 24 years' experience in fashion retailing with several major department store chains in Hong Kong and Taiwan, and the assistant general manager of Goldlion Far East has been with the Group since 1970. Mr. Tsang has three sons. One is a manager responsible for the computer department and property management, and had worked as a general manager in a number of trading companies for seven years before joining the Group. Another is a manager responsible for business development, and had over eight years' experience in leatherware manufacturing before joining the Group. The youngest is a manager responsible for sales and marketing in the PRC.

Price Waterhouse, London, has valued the trademarks owned and used by the Group at HK$300 million. The Group's head office is located in Shatin, a satellite town near central Hong Kong. The Group has substantial property interests in Hong Kong, the PRC, and Singapore. The properties are mainly for operation or production; some are for rental use.

PROFITABILITY

The Group has shown steady profit growth over the past few years.

Year Ended March 31, 1992 (HK$, millions)

	1989	1990	1991	1992	1993
Profit before tax	33	42	80	107	173
Profit after tax	27	35	67	88	143

Sales in 1993 were HK$668 million, as compared with HK$462 million in 1992. This gain of 45 per cent corresponds with a gain of 62 per cent in after-tax profits (see above).

In 1993, on a geographic basis, sales and profits were:

	HK$, millions		Per cent	
	Sales	Profits before tax	Sales	Profits before tax
PRC	351	81	53	47
Hong Kong	212	69	32	40
Singapore	56	10	8	6
Others	49	13	7	7
Total	668	173	100	100

The PRC remains the biggest contributor to the Group's sales and profits. Other buoyant markets have been Macau, Thailand, and Taiwan. Garments now account for 38 per cent of the Group's sales, versus 30 per cent for ties, 22 per cent for leather products, and 10 per cent for menswear accessories.

The Group was the proud recipient of the 1992 Hong Kong Governor's Award for Industry in Export Marketing. Export marketing is a new category of award designed to recognize the growing importance of export skills to Hong Kong's overall trade performance. In the PRC, the Group won more than 15 citations from leading department stores in various major cities for outstanding sales performance achieved during 1992.

SALES STRATEGY AND TACTICS

Goldlion's advertising budget in the PRC in 1993 was HK$36 million—about 10 per cent of its sales there. "It's a Man's World" has become a well-known slogan used in Goldlion advertising in the PRC, Hong Kong, Singapore, and other Asian countries. The advertising media used by the Group include television, radio, newspapers, magazines, billboards, and promotional brochures. Television is the medium that is most heavily employed by the Group, as the Directors believe that the Group's brand name promotional campaign can be most effectively implemented through this medium. For example, the Group advertises in the PRC on over 25 television channels on a regular basis. In addition, the Group has also sponsored major sports events such as the Goldlion Cup series of soccer tournaments in 1986, the Ladies Soccer World Cup in 1991 in the PRC, and the 1987–88 Football Association Cup in Hong Kong. In 1991, the Group started organizing an annual exhibition of its products in the PRC to which both existing and potential customers from all over the PRC were invited. Around 400 participants attended the exhibition held in Shenzhen (a Special Economic Zone just north of Hong Kong) in June 1992.

The success of Goldlion is closely related to the "China concept" of its founder, Mr. Tsang. As already mentioned, one year before President Nixon's historic visit to China in 1971, the Chinese national table tennis team visited Hong Kong as part of its "Table Tennis Diplomacy." Television Broadcasts Limited (TVB), the largest television broadcast company in Hong Kong, looked for sponsorship and found Mr. Tsang. As HK$30,000 was rather expensive, TVB allowed Mr. Tsang to pay in several instalments and made television ads for him. They became the first TV ads for Goldlion. In 1971 and 1972, sales of Goldlion grew rapidly. In 1973, Goldlion was able to sell in large department stores and chain stores via specialty counters and Mr. Tsang's business took off.

From that turning point, Mr. Tsang was very impressed by the magic power of TV ads. When he decided to expand Goldlion to China, he launched an intensive advertising bombardment first. In 1986, Mr. Tsang established a joint venture company, "Silverlion," in Guangdong, as the base of his market penetration into China. Since 1989, advertisements for Goldlion and Silverlion have appeared on national and regional television channels and newspapers every day. In 1993, the advertising budget for Goldlion of Southeast Asia, Hong Kong, and Europe exceeded HK$40 million, of which China accounted for the largest share. Now, Goldlion advertisements are shown on nearly 40 TV channels to support the establishment of specialty shops in China. TV advertising accounted for 30 per cent of operating costs, one of the highest among branded products.

High recognition of Goldlion as high-class ties and shirts in China is attributed to the "first mover" effect. When Goldlion first entered, there were no branded ties or shirts in

China. As the advertising was impressive compared with the "primitive" local efforts, Goldlion drew much attention. Advertisements on TV and newspapers educated Chinese consumers to the concept of "brand." Wearing branded products became a status symbol. However, considering the consumption power of Chinese consumers, Mr. Tsang set the price carefully. His strategy was *high-class image, middle-class price.* To keep a consistent image, standardized pricing was adopted. Goldlion never initiates discounts. Besides TV, newspapers are another effective medium. Students and blue- and white-collar workers all read newspapers and nearly 90 per cent of newspaper readers read newspaper advertisements carefully. It may be said that they often cannot separate propaganda from fact.

The second strategy of Goldlion is a public relations effort: charity. When Mr. Tsang established Silverlion to manufacture and market ties in China, China had not yet opened its domestic market. Mr. Tsang then donated all the profits of Silverlion to education in exchange for domestic distribution rights. These charity efforts brought many benefits such as better taxation terms, latitude in cost allocation, reduction of the psychological resistance to "capitalistic goods" by conservative consumers, and a furthering of the reputation of Mr. Tsang. Mr. Tsang was appointed a Hong Kong representative to the Chinese National Political Consulting Committee. China even named a satellite after him. In China, the fame of a person is an important asset for the promotion of goods. Mr. Tsang successfully linked Goldlion with himself and used this creatively.

In 1993, Hong Kong movie stars and singers held a large-scale movement to help alleviate disasters and poverty in China by nationwide charity performances. Mr. Tsang announced that he would donate the entire 1992 profit of Silverlion to the movement. As Mr. Tsang focused marketing on Goldlion, which is the major source of profit, the actual expenditure was limited. In 1992, the net profit of Silverlion was about RMB 40 million. However, it made a great impression on consumers. The effect was much greater than would have been the case had the same money been spent on TV ads.

Another victory in promotion was in April 1993 when Mr. Tsang, as one of the Hong Kong Affairs Advisors, was going to attend a meeting in Beijing. Mr. Tsang published a full-page advertisement for the "Tsang Hin Chee Education Fund" in the *People's Daily Overseas*. At the same time, Mr. Tsang held a meeting with a number of companies to support China's bid for the Olympic Games in 2000, and invited Hong Kong and Macau representatives of the National People's Congress. Mr. Tsang also handed out Goldlion ties and shirts at the 14th Meeting of the National People's Congress. The creative use of news exposure successfully strengthened the "authority" image of both Mr. Tsang and Goldlion.

The Goldlion logo—proudly sewn on its ties—is another effective publicity tactic, especially in China. For a consumer, wearing a tie with a brand name and logo projects the image that he is wearing a quality product; and so by extension, it announces that he is a special person. When lots of people do the same thing, the impact is significant. "Consumers as advertisers" augments the producer's or seller's ability to charge a higher price, due to an increase in brand value. To hedge against inflation in China, Goldlion raises prices when the market does so, and sales performance is not affected.

Besides aggressive advertising campaigns, large-scale sales promotion is also done in

China. Lucky draws are regularly held to boost sales. Moreover, the sales force is highly motivated by bonuses. Typically, Goldlion sales are on a cash basis rather than on credit, thus generating a lot of cash for its development and hence, Goldlion rarely relies on debt financing. To reduce forex risk, sales are all in Hong Kong dollars. Silverlion is a wholly owned subsidiary of Goldlion in China. It is responsible for all the sales in China in RMB (the Chinese currency), which it then reinvests to explore the China market, establish distribution networks, etc. Goldlion sells its products to import and export agents who buy in Hong Kong dollars and sell the goods to Silverlion in RMB at an agreed rate. If RMB depreciates, Silverlion transfers the cost to consumers.

A high-class image must be backed by good product design and quality. Therefore, product design emphasizes uniqueness to satisfy consumer demand. There were 1,000 tie styles in 1993, and the company employed 200 German designers. Though the Group is strong on promotion, there is no infrastructure for marketing research. For the Hong Kong market, consumer taste information is mainly gathered through the salesgirls in the outlets. For China, it follows the basic trends in Hong Kong outlets and makes some minor adjustments. Management personnel also visit retail outlets to gather information. However, the Group concedes that its method of gathering information on consumer trends is not reliable.

THE RETAIL ARRANGEMENT

There are over 600 retail outlets in the PRC that sell Goldlion products. These include department stores, franchised shops, leather goods shops, and specialty stores. Goldlion has franchised the selling rights of its products free of charge since November 1993, for the purpose of rapid expansion. In the first half of 1993, ten specialty stores which sell Goldlion products exclusively were opened in the PRC. Another 16 specialty stores are currently being planned for operation by licensees. Product display is standardized. Goldlion maintains tight control over an outlet's display in China. Whenever a new outlet is to be opened, the Goldlion people train the local staff on display techniques, store layout, etc., to ensure service quality.

Certain retailers have independent counters that adopt a design and layout similar to Goldlion counters to display the Group's products. The Group's retail manager usually provides assistance in the setting up of these independent counters. Positioning Goldlion products at good outlets is a key to customer appeal. For certain other counters that sell the Group's products as well as other products, the Group provides signboards, lightboxes, and/or posters. Goldlion counters located within department stores in Hong Kong and Singapore have a standard design and layout in accordance with the Group's specifications. All Goldlion counters are managed by the Group's uniformed sales staff under the Sales Manager. For the sake of rapid expansion and to try to fend off the increasing presence of foreign (especially European) brands in China, the Group does not charge licensing fees. To increase the distribution network, the Group has held annual sales conferences in the PRC for both existing and potential customers since 1991. Approximately 650 participants attended the conference held in Guangzhou, China, in June 1993.

INVENTORY AND QUALITY CONTROL

Goldlion maintains a high finished goods inventory, mainly ties and leather goods, to meet the dynamic demand in China. It constituted 25 and 36 per cent of sales in 1992 and 1993, respectively. Outlets and department stores in China do not have a system of merchandise re-ordering. They order whenever their stocks are almost sold out. Thus goods must be delivered to them within 2–3 days after they order, and a quantity of inventory must exist to meet consumers' flexible demands. For instance, for one style of tie, an outlet may order 100 pieces so Goldlion has an inventory of at least 6,000 to avoid lost sales.

Production capacity is expanding to serve increasing demand. Goldlion has invested HK$100 million in a new 80,000-square-meter factory which will be completed in 1994 in Meizhou, China. In addition, it has invested HK$490 million in a 300,000-square-foot industrial building in Shatin, Hong Kong, to boost its manufacturing, packaging, and wholesaling capacity. It produces only its core products, ties and leather goods, in its own factories.

Garment manufacturing is subcontracted out with the same quality control process as for inhouse production. Supply sourcing is diversified, and good relations with suppliers are maintained. No single supplier can supply more than 13 per cent of raw materials to Goldlion. The total supply by its five biggest suppliers amounts to only 33 per cent. Moreover, Goldlion builds up an interdependent relationship with key suppliers. Almost all (98%) the tie-cloth manufacturers in Germany appoint Goldlion as their sole agent for the China, Hong Kong, and Macau markets.

Goldlion integrates horizontally to transfer capability. It is now buying many new brands from Europe in response to competition in China. Furthermore, the product line is being diversified to include women's clothing and accessories, cosmetics, etc., to make good use of the established Goldlion brand name. Investment is diversified into property and raw materials. It purchases mainly office premises, warehouses, and production plants to reduce its long-term rental costs. On June 10, 1993, Goldlion signed a joint venture of US$200 million with the Meizhou municipality to build a factory.

Though the Group believes that strict quality control is one of its secrets of success, there is no system of overall standards for quality control. At present, quality control is done through the following groups of people, each performing quality checks using his or her own criteria:

- Quality control people in production plants
- Sampling checkers when handing over goods
- Supervisors when selecting goods
- Salesgirls when selling goods

DIVERSIFICATION

As China is becoming increasingly attractive to investors, more and more brands are striving to enter the market. For casual wear, there are Hong Kong brands like Giordano, Apple, and

Bossini. For middle-class brands, there is Theme. For European brands, Montagut has also set up two specialty shops in Beijing and Shanghai. Pierre Cardin is a pioneer in the China market. It entered China in the 1980s. Now it is expanding to Guangzhou, Beijing, and Wuhan. Diskson Concepts International is a company representing many famous brands in clothes and accessories, like Polo, Ralph Lauren, Charles Jourdan, Guy Laroche watches, and ST Dupont lighters and writing instruments. Dickson switched its business focus to China in the early 1990s. It held exhibitions and set up joint-venture specialty shops and department stores in large cities like Beijing, Shanghai, and Guangzhou in 1992. Its business includes clothing, watches, and jewellery. Though some products like shirts are specially designed and manufactured in China, their products range from the middle to the high end and have a European image. The group has said that it will teach Chinese consumers what a REAL brand is. In addition, there are various brands from Japan and Korea that want to get a piece of the pie in this booming market.

China's domestic manufacturers are not sitting idle either: they are establishing their brand names to keep a competitive edge. As some of them are OEM (original equipment manufacturers) for some famous brands like Pierre Cardin, the products and designs are almost as good as those foreign brands. The difference is the price. Their prices are usually half those of the foreign brands; domestic brands like Qiao Shi shirts are very attractive to the common people. To face the coming competition in China, the Goldlion line "It's a Man's World" is delicately shifting to "Gentlemen are in Goldlion." Advertising, especially on television, is critical for such image building.

In order to meet the increasing competition from both domestic and foreign, especially European, brands in China, Goldlion is seeking to diversify. As the market for ties is limited, the Group is trying to shift more to promoting shirts. Product diversification includes introduction of men's accessories, writing instruments, lighters, shoes, and watches. Another important move is to enter the women's clothes market. This new series of products succeeded in test marketing in Hong Kong. The target will be the China market. However, such a move may be hindered by the male image of Goldlion. To deal with this the Group has introduced other products for the female market, such as shoes and handbags. However, the management admit that the risk of brand image dilution is a problem. The female image also needs investment in promotion in the future.

The preference of Mr. Tsang to hold real estate has also led to diversification into the real estate market as the property market in China booms. Goldlion is involved in shopping malls, office buildings, factory buildings, warehouses, and even residences. Mr. Tsang now owns 40,000 square meters of land in Harbin in northern China, which is to be jointly developed into a business building with some Hong Kong developers. A wholesale center is planned too. The Group, however, focuses on Shanghai, which is the leading city in fashion and is a "hot" shopping place. The Group purchased an eight-storey building as its regional headquarters and wholesale center. Diversifying into the real estate market helps the Group in expanding its national distribution network. On the other hand, the retail business helps the Group to avoid some legal restrictions in the real estate market.

Though the Group is trying to diversify, such diversification efforts may lead it into head-on competition with competitors like Dickson. Goldlion has succeeded in transforming the Group from a family business to a large company. In the scenario now developing, the Group will need to keep adjusting itself to meet further challenges in the future.

COUNTERING COUNTERFEITERS

Despite the success of Goldlion's products in China—or because of it—the emergence of counterfeit goods can be traced back to 1984, when Mr. Tsang first introduced his famous brand name into the Chinese market. The problem has become more severe over the years. According to Mr. Tsang, despite efforts to stop the counterfeiting activities, it is estimated that there are at present 5,000 manufacturers imitating Goldlion products illegally. It is not uncommon to see counterfeit goods imitating high quality products of famous brands anywhere, and it is especially so in a burgeoning economy such as China. Certainly, the environment in China is ripe for the emergence of counterfeit goods. When a country is at the stage of economic take-off or is moving rapidly towards industrialization, the appearance of counterfeit goods in large quantities is only to be expected. That is exactly the case with China. With the development of a "commodity economy," consumer goods have rapidly become plentiful, resulting in its transition from a sellers' market to a buyers' market. One of the causes of the emergence of counterfeit goods in large quantities is that it is simply beyond the capability of some emerging local enterprises to market their own goods through fundamental technical innovations.

In addition, in the past nearly all the products of various enterprises in China were sold exclusively by the State and as there was no competition, it was naturally difficult for many Chinese people to distinguish between fair and unfair competition. As a matter of fact, culturally many Chinese enterprises still do not see anything wrong in imitating or counterfeiting the products of others. What is more, the consumers' craze for brand names has also helped to build a market of "demand." Many people are either unaware of the difference between genuine goods and fakes, or are willing to buy the fakes, or even deliberately seek out counterfeit "famous brand products" so that they may own them in spite of their limited ability to afford the genuine articles. The latter phenomenon has become quite common among the younger generation of consumers in recent years.

China's retrenchment policy of a few years ago has also influenced counterfeiting of brands. Owing to an overheated economy, China has had to enforce a policy of retrenchment. The consumption craze cooled down suddenly and dramatically, even for one of the major segments of consumers, namely China's officials. It has thus become even harder for goods lacking competitive power in the first place (i.e., before the retrenchment policy) to find buyers. As a result, counterfeiting of Goldlion's products is seen as a quick and easy way for these uncompetitive enterprises to find a market in order to survive.

In order to create an environment of fair competition, it could be argued that not only should a proper sense of business ethics be fostered in people, but that it is also essential to establish a set of compulsory mechanisms of prevention, restitution, and punishment. From the early 1980s to the present, China has successfully formulated a fairly complete set of laws and regulations regarding intellectual property, but loopholes remain. For example, links between the various laws are not close enough, and there is no law for the repression of unfair competition. Moreover, protection of intellectual property is quite a new concept in China. Law enforcers in that sense are not experienced enough, even though policy makers are eager to stamp out counterfeiting.

In dealing with cases of intellectual property infringement, the courts, procurators, and administrative authorities need to establish a more scientific and complete set of procedures and rules; manpower needs to be increased and the quality of the personnel improved; the duties of organizations related to the stopping of counterfeiting activities such as the customs, commodity inspection agencies and the police need to be clearly defined in legislation, so that they may actively involve themselves in anti-counterfeiting activities. At present, the Bureau of Industry and Commerce, the official government organization fighting counterfeiting activities, has no power to arrest suspects or check company records. It needs assistance from the police, who typically believe that they don't have any obligations in such matters. As a result, counterfeiters are not duly punished, nor are their activities effectively dealt with.

After the counterfeiting of goods or other infringements are discovered, they should receive the utmost attention and be stopped promptly. This is a real problem for Goldlion. Today, the amount of counterfeit goods is about 60 per cent of the actual sales of real goods, or even greater in some coastal cities such as Shanghai and Guangzhou. In the past, Mr. Tsang used to talk to a friend who is also a senior government official in Beijing. His friend then delivered the message to the Bureau of Industry and Commerce. Feeling the pressure from above, the Bureau would send people out onto the streets to check for counterfeit goods. However, the operations have never been thorough enough to bring any significant changes. Since there is no legal relationship between Mr. Tsang and the Bureau, the latter often regards such an instruction from a senior government official as a single event. There has never been any careful follow-up and after the anti-counterfeiting operation is completed, they close the file and forget the matter. The Bureau of Industry and Commerce also is not knowledgeable enough to tell the difference between genuine and fakes goods. Therefore, no matter how large the size of the anti-counterfeiting operation, there is no significant reduction in the number of fakes.

Are there still any further possible countermeasures that Goldlion can try? Unfortunately, the answer is perhaps "No." Counterfeiting will not be stopped until the consumption patterns of Chinese consumers change and they no longer find counterfeit products attractive in terms of price, quality, and image. A method that helps reduce the damage is the establishment of specialty shops and counters. These authorized dealers give confidence to consumers. Those who want to buy real Goldlion products will buy there. Specialty shops are becoming popular for foreign brands.

THE PROSPECTS

Goldlion has the corporate culture of a family, with Mr. Tsang as a father figure. Employees treat Goldlion products as their own goods. As Mr. Tsang is very knowledgeable about Chinese business, he exercises strict control over the strategies in China. However, there is probably less power conflict among family members in Goldlion than in other family business enterprises, according to Goldlion's Public Relations Manager. To form and re-form the management team, the Group uses two methods:

- Head-hunting for new department heads. It reduces training costs and it means that it can start production quickly. However, this entails very high costs in the short run.
- Recruitment on the management level is based largely on "sincerity," which is judged by the managing director, besides obvious basic requirements of intelligence and experience.

Thus, the turnover rate is said to be low at the management level. The Chinese market presents a mighty challenge. Goldlion got in early but must now face the front-runners among multinational, regional, and local competitors. It must keep abreast of the Chinese culture while also making sure that its own corporate culture is in tune with the times.

CASE THIRTEEN (A)

THE NUGENT COMPANY: STRATEGIC OPTIONS FOR MARKETING A HIGH-TECH PRODUCT IN CHINA*

The Nugent Company** had to make decisions in 1981 about its marketing efforts in the People's Republic of China (PRC). They had, in particular, to decide whether to invest capital in a joint venture. They had avoided doing this when the Chinese government was trying hard to persuade all high-tech firms to undertake joint manufacturing ventures. What alternatives presented themselves; and could a bridgehead be found through co-production or in other ways?

THE NUGENT COMPANY IN CHINA

The name is a pseudonym for a well-known Western conglomerate which employs more than 30,000 people in manufacturing and selling a wide variety of electronic, high-tech devices. The range includes radar, navigation aids, data communication systems, civil and military radios, cellular radio and security devices. Most items are for professional, defence, business, and government use; only a small proportion is for consumer use. The products are high-tech in worldwide terms, not only in Chinese terms, and are subject to national and multilateral export licensing rules.

The company's production facilities are mainly in the West, but it already had significant experience in overseas production in the Third World when it decided to take a detailed look at the PRC to seek ways of entering that market. Nugent had a strong reputation in other

---

* This case was prepared by Sally Stewart.
** The names of the Western company, its staff, and the Chinese factory, have been changed.

parts of the world but had not achieved any major penetrations of the PRC market when it started to think seriously about it in 1981.

The management considered that although its success overseas in the Third World had some relevance in terms of expertise and organization, the potential China market was sufficiently large to justify a dedicated market research and support effort, and that this effort could not be provided by existing sections. It therefore created a China unit specifically to handle the exercise.

Establishment of a Special Unit

The China Marketing Unit (CMU) was based on the concept of a Western director, to ensure easy communication between the Unit and the divisions of the group, with Chinese staff to promote the best possible relations with Chinese counterparts and provide expert linguistic support.

The first move in setting up the Unit was the recruitment of a seasoned Western director with good overall knowledge of the China scene, a solid Chinese language background, and some knowledge of the group's areas of activity. While the ideal candidate for the post would have been technically trained, commercially experienced, linguistically expert, and thoroughly versed in the PRC market as well as familiar with the hierarchies in the company, it was not possible to find such a paragon. Webster, who was recruited for the job, however, knew both Mandarin and Cantonese, and had long experience of China and the Chinese. His team now consists of ten people based partly at headquarters in the West and partly in Hong Kong.

The existence of the CMU enabled the company to provide from the very beginning both language support and a cultural bridge during negotiations. As the team grew, it also helped in the implementation of contracts.

Initial Steps

The company started its focused approach to the China market with few preconceived notions. Webster had a four-word brief from the CEO: "Get us into China."

The preliminary work of the China Unit developed along the following lines:

1. A general survey of the growing body of literature on Chinese developments, both political and economic, which provided the backdrop to all the company's work in China
2. A study of Chinese priorities and Chinese requirements as they related to the company's products, strengths and skills
3. Personal contact with relevant ministries, corporations and, at the second stage, with selected potential partners in factories and institutes
4. Operational support for the company's personnel as they visited China
5. Building contacts with Chinese officials in the West

It very soon became clear that serious players in the Chinese technical market must always keep offers of long-term partnerships, assistance in 'the four modernizations', and technological transfer at the centre of their planning.

Bearing this in mind, various options were identified. These are described now.

STRATEGIES FOR MARKETING IN CHINA

A thorough study of the possibilities showed that there was a wide variety of vehicles available for electronics technology transfer to China. In practice, they were not a series of discrete structures, but a spectrum of overlapping forms of business. The four major forms of cooperation then open to the company and major options still open in 1991 were:

THE MANUFACTURING EQUITY JOINT VENTURE (MEJV). The EJV in all its forms was in 1980 [and still is] clearly the Chinese favourite, and much effort already went into developing a legal and taxation framework. These ventures take the form of a separate limited liability company, created under Chinese law, in which shares are held by one or more Chinese enterprises and one or more foreign concerns. The foreign investment usually amounts to 25 to 50 per cent of the total; in the MEJV it often takes the form of technology or production equipment instead of, or as well as, cash. It is almost always the case that the Chinese side contributes its investment in the form of existing buildings, labour force, and land-use rights.

Since the foreign partner shares the responsibility for managing the EJV and shares the risks of the project, if the foreign partner is to recover his investment a successful transfer of management techniques is essential in addition to a successful transfer of technology. This is, of course, easier said than done in all newly formed partnerships, particularly in developing countries. A further formidable difficulty in many developing countries is converting profit from local currency into foreign exchange. This is certainly a problem in China.

LICENSING. Faced with the complexities of the EJV, potential transferors of technology often look at licensing as an alternative. Licensing focuses on the core of technology transfer—that is, on the intellectual property rights (IPR)—but often includes associated services.

Webster was aware that in the aircraft industry, leases of aircraft are divided into 'wet' and 'dry' types with a 'dry lease' being one that covers the aircraft alone, while a 'wet lease' includes associated services, such as training or hiring of pilots and, possibly, cabin crews, overhauls and so on. He borrowed this terminology and the company examined the possibilities of both 'dry' and 'wet' licences in China, dividing them according to the degree of associated services included in the package. Webster also realised that, in view of the gap between the two countries in technological development, a US-China technology transfer will probably work only as a 'wet' licence, whereas a US-German technology transfer, for example, would likely be a 'dry' licence since both parties are, broadly speaking, at the same level of development.

Webster advocates 'wet' licensing because it allows the risks to be divided: if the Chinese side does not absorb the technology, they have to negotiate for the provision of extra associated services. The Chinese, however, feel that the 'wet' licence does not legally commit the foreign partner to unlimited, open-ended support to achieve the success of the project.

In practice, of course, the relationship between the foreign exporter and the Chinese customer is much more complex than 'mere selling' and, if the foreign partner is committed to the concept of a long-term relationship, solutions will be found on the basis of 'mutual benefit' rather than on a strict interpretation of the letter of the contract.

CO-PRODUCTION. Co-production relies on a middle course between 'wet licensing' and the EJV. It is a flexible form of business that divides the risks between the partners but makes the transferor responsible, within reasonable limits, for the absorption of the technology by the recipient. The foreign partner is assured that he will be paid for his efforts and the Chinese partner is assured of the former's commitment to the success of the project. The foreign partner does not contribute equity capital, nor does he share responsibility for the management of the factory.

Webster found that there were a number of high-technology transfer projects running in China on a co-production basis and, as the name implies, they were all concerned with manufacturing. Co-production in some cases included buy-back of product and advice and assistance in export marketing. The co-production approach, like the licensing approach, has also been described dismissively by the Chinese as 'mere selling' and is not publicly favoured by the authorities.

WHOLLY FOREIGN-OWNED ENTERPRISES (WFOEs). WFOEs can be regarded as a special form of foreign investment. Originally, they were referred to by the semantically unsatisfactory title of 'Wholly Owned Joint Ventures'. The foreigner has complete control of the business, but loses the advantage of a local counterpart to help him through the Chinese bureaucracy and, of course, risks hostility from antiforeign elements of the local society.

EXPERIENCE OF MEJVs

At the time that the Nugent Company was first considering manufacturing in China, a survey of joint ventures already operating in the PRC revealed the following common problems encountered by foreign investors in MEJVs:

1. Unsatisfactory telecommunications
2. Low quality and uncertain availability of raw materials
3. Poor transportation facilities
4. Problems relating to foreign exchange
5. Insufficient autonomy (for example, the ability to hire and fire workers freely)
6. Insufficient working capital and borrowing difficulties
7. Unsatisfactory electric power and water supplies

Many of these problems were acknowledged at the highest level, but they have not been solved in practice; they perturbed Webster, who was also conscious of the difficulty in selecting a satisfactory Chinese partner. But, even with the right partner, although many of these problems can be solved locally, there is uncertainty about most of them, unless the project is so important and the partner so powerful that total priority can be assured.

NUGENT'S FIRST MANUFACTURING VENTURE IN CHINA

Nugent was not initially convinced of the wisdom of setting up an equity joint venture, and a less complicated form of cooperation was sought for their initial venture. Talks on this started with the Xin Hua factory in 1982, after an initial contact had been made the previous year. The contract, which was formally signed in 1984, was to last for five years.

The original discussions with Xin Hua started on the basis of a mutual understanding that the product was one where Nugent had an international reputation and which was already well-tested operationally. It was a significant help that there was an international requirement that this type of instrument should be used and the Chinese needed to find a domestic answer to this international requirement.

A major issue facing Nugent was how to turn the co-production venture to its long-term advantage. It should be noted that, while the essential demand on the Chinese side was for the transfer of the technology required to produce the equipment, from Nugent's point of view, the venture was regarded as a first step in a long-term commitment to the Chinese market and it was, therefore, vital that the whole arrangement be a success.

For this reason among others, the contract in the case was developed on the basis that the transfer of technology was *not* to be a mere licensing agreement: a 'dry' license where, in theory, the supplier, having transferred documentation, the prints and intellectual property rights, could walk away, leaving the customer to struggle as best he could to replicate the processes of the original equipment manufacturer.

Nugent made a conscious decision to design a co-production package which would give every possible support service to ensure successful production, and guarantee that the transfer of technology would be 'wet', not 'dry'. It was recognized that, since effective technology transfer required the comprehension of the recipient, transmission of information, whether by documentation or training, would not be sufficient to ensure absorption and that long-term support in the Chinese factory would be essential. Training of Chinese engineers in the West alone would not suffice.

TRANSFERRING TECHNOLOGY TO THE DEVELOPING WORLD

The Nugent philosophy considered the fact that in a technology transfer there are often two kinds of technology to be transferred: the production technology used to manufacture the product, and the development technology used to invent it. The former, which is crucial to the short-term economic success of the project, can be absorbed relatively easily through repeated use. The latter is superficially more attractive, especially to senior engineers but, if no opportunity exists for the recipient to practise it under the transferor's guidance, the development technology is often only transferred in theoretical form and is frequently not successfully absorbed.

A further problem concerned the design, since Nugent, like most Western electronics companies, aims in new products, to reduce costs and increase reliability by reducing the direct man-hour content. This can be achieved in a number of ways, including an increase in the number of assembly operations carried out by automatic equipment. This tendency to reduce the labour content makes it difficult for countries like China to compete in the world market. Not only is the basic economic advantage of lower labour costs reduced to near insignificance, but also more money has to be invested in equipment and training. Successful exporting may then require that the new producer (or, more likely, his government) subsidize sales, which may then bring forth cries of 'dumping' from established producers and thus lead to the imposition of tariff barriers.

The growing sophistication of production methods brings another difficulty for the PRC producer. Learning by doing repeatedly is most likely to achieve success, but the process will probably be a slow one and costly in terms of foreign manpower.

There are signs that these special problems are beginning to be appreciated in China. Zhang Zhidong, assistant general manager of China Electronic Import and Export Corporation (CEIEC), has been reported as seeking cooperation with European firms in 'low automation' electronics products, such as radar, transformers and loudspeakers. He is quoted as saying: "Cooperation is meaningless in highly automated industries because low cost labour cannot display its advantage."

A problem of a different sort is caused by the pace of technological change, which will also often hamper a developing country's efforts to break into overseas markets. Product life-cycles in electronics are now likely to be shorter than the time required to negotiate a contract, set up the overseas production line, fully train the production workers, and so on. Since both sides often wait, for good reason, until the goods are in production in the transferor's factory (the transferor wishes to be sure of the technology to be transferred, and the recipient wishes to assess the value of the technology by reference to the finished article), the product is almost by definition obsolescent by the time the recipient is in a position to export it. This is particularly so in the case of recipients like China, whose bureaucratic procedures are such that negotiations take a long time.

CHOICE OF A PARTNER

Having decided that it was premature to enter into a MEJV, the problem of the selection of an original a partner became less difficult. In the end, the Xin Hua factory was chosen for the first venture in consultation with the electronics ministry, after visits to several factories working in the relevant field. It was finally agreed to work with a factory that is under the supervision of the Ministry and conveniently situated in central China, and has close links to the target industry. While the partner has turned out to be able to produce satisfactorily, it has shown no marketing ability and has not demonstrated the necessary dynamic qualities likely to be required to deal with the problems of any future EJV.

THE NEGOTIATIONS

About one year elapsed between the initial contact between Nugent and the Chinese in 1981 and the start of serious negotiations on this topic in 1982. During this initial year, considerable resources were put into briefings and demonstrations for the Chinese side at the Western home base. These sessions included entertainment and discussions at exhibitions in the Nugent division concerned. Technical talks continued in China leading to technical negotiations and finally to commercial negotiations also held mostly in the PRC. The amount of paper generated during this exercise was, of course, considerable, with much detail spelled out.

The core of the Nugent negotiating team was made up of three people: a senior director with technical, marketing and production experience, a CMU representative to deal with linguistic and cultural problems, and a Nugent lawyer acting as secretary and legal advisor.

The Chinese team varied between five and ten in number and consisted of a constant leader from the local chapter of the China Electronic Import and Export Corporation (CEIEC) and a team of representatives from the Xin Hua factory, including members of its administrative, technical and production staff. They were supported by Beijing representatives of the electronics ministry, who frequently appeared outside the negotiating room as well.

When considering the length of time taken to negotiate this contract, the following points must be borne in mind:

1. Both sides were experimenting in an unfamiliar culture.
2. The use of interpreters more than doubled the time required for negotiating.
3. The 'open door' had not been long in operation.

Nevertheless, the negotiating time was dangerously long from the point of view of the Nugent team, whose expenditure of senior officer time, as well as back-up resources at home, began to look very large, at a time when the company's knowledge of Chinese procedures was limited and confidence in the outcome was more a matter of faith than experience.

Later negotiations by Nugent have taken much less time, the improved performance being attributable to increased experience on both sides, the existence of Nugent precedents in China, and the general flowering of the 'open door' policy.

The main points that slowed down the negotiations were:

(i) ARGUMENTS ABOUT THE VALUE OF THE INTELLECTUAL PROPERTY RIGHTS. The Chinese side required a lot of persuading that it was reasonable that they should contribute to the initial costs of research and development, as well as pay for documentation and training.

(ii) THE NEED FOR JUSTIFICATION FOR PRICES OF COMPONENTS AND SUB-ASSEMBLIES. The main problem here was costing overheads. Many hours were spent describing the concept of overheads, which was alien to a factory which had been run by the state and saw cost basically in terms of raw material and labour.

(iii) THE FINAL PRICE. On the seventieth day of the face-to-face negotiations, the Chinese side cheerfully announced that they were satisfied in general with the package and could sign quickly if Nugent dropped its price by 30 per cent! This suggestion was not well received by the company, who had not padded their prices with a special 30 per cent China mark-up.

The price point was, of course, always there. Probably no discussion in China takes place without a Chinese claim that the price is too high and competitors are much cheaper. In this case, the price eventually agreed upon was within 5 per cent of the original offer.

THE FINAL TERMS OF THE ORIGINAL CONTRACT

The contract provided that Nugent would transfer the technology to the Xin Hua factory, and payment was scheduled in stages as the transfer took place. The first payment was to be for initial training in Nugent's own factory, documentation, and overall support and transfer fees. The second was to be for purchase and delivery of complete built-up units (CBUs) manufactured in Nugent's factory by the Chinese trainees under supervision; the third for the first batch of semi-knocked-down (SKD) kits and the fourth for completely knocked-down (CKD) kits. Thereafter, the contract was open to extension as more kits were required, taking into account any variations caused by the introduction of Chinese components.

THE NUGENT CO-PRODUCTION PACKAGE

The final form of the agreement achieved in 1984, after 21 months of negotiations, was a co-production and marketing package which basically provided the following:

1. Transfer of technology—
   - documentation
   - explanation
   - intellectual property rights (IPR)
2. Establishment of a production line—
   - supply of production equipment
   - supply of test equipment
3. Supply of—
   - complete built-up units (CBU)
   - semi-knocked-down units (SKD)
   - completely knocked-down units (CKD)
4. Training in Nugent home factory and Chinese factory—
   - assembly
   - production
   - quality control and assurance

- management
- marketing
5. Continuing support—
    - updating of technology
    - visits to factory
    - overseas marketing and domestic marketing
6. Import substitution

IMPLEMENTATION AND EXTENSION OF THE CONTRACT

The successful implementation of a co-production contract had always led, in Nugent's experience, to extensions. The Chinese proved no exception and, although on each occasion there was a price negotiation, the introduction of new products proved easy to arrange and took place in both 1986 and 1987.

The biggest problems encountered in implementation of all the contracts were:

1. Transfer of staff by the factory, resulting in a loss of trained personnel
2. The Chinese factory environment and managerial procedures, which were initially barriers to carrying out the lesson learned on the ground in Nugent's home factory
3. The establishment of a new store handling system
4. The introduction of an effective quality control system

All these difficulties were resolved after some time, but they presented significant obstacles initially.

It will be observed that these problems all stemmed from the fact that the Nugent production line was being established in an existing Chinese-managed factory. A green field site providing a new environment and an opportunity to create a fresh system would clearly have been advantageous, but the intricacies involved in any joint equity and joint management arrangement were thought to be too high a price to pay at this early stage.

EPILOGUE

The contract proved to be effective in general; Nugent made a reasonable profit as it worked with Xin Hua to develop the transfer of technology. There were some specific disappointments for Nugent. The hope that the Xin Hua team would actively develop a China market for the product was illusory. Xin Hua's marketing was not dynamic. A second disappointment, allied to this marketing point, was the fact that the Chinese national bureaucracy showed itself to be totally incapable of, or perhaps disinterested in, turning the Nugent–Xin Hua venture into a national point of excellence for the product by protecting the new product line against unbridled imports of similar goods produced overseas. These twin failures meant that the venture remained valid but limited in scope.

CASE THIRTEEN (B)

THE NUGENT COMPANY: DEVELOPING A BRIDGEHEAD FOR MARKETING A HIGH-TECH PRODUCT IN CHINA*

The Nugent Company** had to make decisions in 1989 about the future of its marketing efforts in the People's Republic of China (PRC). They had, in particular, to decide whether or not to invest capital in a joint venture. They had avoided doing this when the Chinese government was trying hard to persuade all high-tech firms to undertake manufacturing joint ventures, but are beginning to feel that the time may have come to commit themselves.

THE NUGENT COMPANY IN CHINA

The name is a pseudonym for a well-known Western conglomerate which employs more than 30,000 people in manufacturing and selling a wide variety of electronic, high-tech devices. The range includes radar, navigation aids, data communication-systems, civil and military radios and cellular radio and security devices. Most items are for professional, defence, business, and government use; only a small proportion is for consumer use. The products are high-tech in worldwide terms, not only in Chinese terms, and are subject to national and multilateral export licensing rules.

The company's production facilities are mainly in the West, but it already had significant experience in overseas production in the Third World when it decided to take a detailed look at the PRC to seek ways of approaching that market. Nugent had a strong reputation in other parts of the world but had not achieved any major penetrations of the China market when it started to think seriously about it in 1981.

---

* This case study was prepared by Sally Stewart.
** The names of the Western company, its staff, and the Chinese factory, have been changed.

The management considered that, although its success overseas in the Third World had some relevance in terms of expertise and organization, the potential China market was sufficiently large to justify a dedicated market research and support effort, and that this effort could not be provided by existing sections. It therefore created a China Unit specifically for the task and this has been headed since the beginning by Webster, a Chinese-speaking executive with wide Asia experience.

As a first step toward long-term development and commitment in the market, the Nugent Company chose to offer a co-production deal—a mixture of 'wet' licensing, technological transfer, production training, and engineering support—to their PRC partners.

This decision was taken on the basis of general experience, as well as on the basis of points specific to China. The Equity Joint Venture (EJV) for manufacture was not regarded as a viable option at the initial stage since, in Nugent's view, much time was required for familiarisation with the PRC and thorough investigation of the market.

The Chinese partner in the co-production arrangement, the Xin Hua Corporation, was keen to develop a new production line; a new high-tech product, and new technical skills. Xin Hua's 'mother-in-law' (the nickname for the various bodies with rights to interfere such as ministries, foreign trading corporations, and bureaux), although preferring the EJV, which they saw as guaranteeing greater commitment as well as providing foreign currency, accepted the co-production option as a second best which went part of the way to meet their need for technological advance.

NUGENT'S MANUFACTURING EXPERIENCE IN THE PRC

Nugent's major experience of manufacturing in the PRC has, therefore, been in partnership with the Xin Hua Corporation's factory, in a co-production contract signed in 1984. This agreement proved to be generally successful for both sides and, although there were initial disappointments, the partnership settled down effectively as such side gained more experience and adjusted its expectations.

The contract included a promise to offer updated equipment to Xin Hua as it was developed by Nugent. The agreement was carried out by Nugent in both spirit and in letter and new products, and modifications to old, were offered to Xin Hua as they became available to Nugent's own factories. This process caused no difficulty and led to further contracts for other equipment of the same family but with a later specification. However, the limited foreign exchange available to Xin Hua prevented major expansion of the programme.

THE FUTURE

A central issue facing Nugent, as it renegotiated its original agreement in 1989, was the question of how best to exploit the goodwill provided by its initial venture with Xin Hua.

Webster wanted to use the opportunity to penetrate the domestic market and emphasized economies of scale, savings of foreign exchange through import substitution and the like, but the Chinese authorities pressed for exports from the project.

Webster also hoped to broaden the range of products being produced in the PRC, as well as to increase domestic market share and introduce designs specifically tailored for the Chinese requirements for export and foreign exchange earnings. In this latter connection he has made great efforts to find Chinese products that might be suitable for countertrade deals, particularly buy-back, but so far without success.

One current issue worries Nugent's headquarter's staff: that, as Chinese components are being introduced into the product, quality is suffering. The progress toward sourcing of components in China followed the following pattern:

Stage 1. First assembly of product in semi-knocked-down (SKD) form in the West by Chinese engineers; end product shipped to China.
Stage 2. Second assembly of product in SKD (further modules removed) in the West as before.
Stage 3. First assembly in China of SKD.
Stage 4. Second assembly in China of SKD (further modules and components removed).
Stage 5. Third assembly in China of product in SKD/CKD (completely-knocked-down) form.
Stage 6. Introduction of Chinese content.

At the end of each stage, full testing and inspection of the assembled product and quality assurance procedures are carried out, but there are still doubts at the Nugent home factory about whether the products manufactured in China are up to the standard of those made in the West.

The quality point has two aspects: on the one hand, Nugent does not wish to be associated with any lowering of standards; but on the other, if Xin Hua does not use Nugent's name and sticks to the domestic market, the question of standard becomes academic to Nugent.

EXPORTS

The Chinese Government has consistently taken the line that ventures involving foreigners should earn their own individual foreign exchange requirements—needed, for instance, to pay for the use of patents and certain components—and have not usually accepted the argument that 'import substitution' is as valid an activity as exporting. Nugent has, therefore, had to pay a lot of attention to trying to export the products made in China.

Webster has stressed to the authorities that the profile of any potentially successful co-production project with a significant capacity to export from China is likely to look as follows:

- Volume of product   High to minimize cost per unit
- Labour content   High to maximize advantage of low labour cost

- Raw material or Chinese component supply   Adequate sources in China at low cost
- Technology   High to fight off local competition

In the case under discussion, the profile does not fit, and successful exporting would require an element of subsidy. Volume is small, allowing no economies of scale; standard Chinese components, or sub-assemblies of the appropriate quality, are not readily available to substitute for foreign, imported, components and the product is not labour-intensive.

As an aide memoire for the staff involved in the 1989 decision making process, a Strengths, Weaknesses, Opportunities and Threats (SWOT) matrix (Exhibit 1) has been drawn up by Webster to show possible strategies for exporting from China:

Exhibit 1   Exporting from a Chinese Factory

Internal Factors / External Factors	Strengths (S) Low labour costs Low raw material cost Enjoys national priority Low overheads	Weaknesses (W) Inexperienced labour Weak labour discipline Low quality control Bureaucratic complexity Power shortages Uncertain materials supply
External Opportunities (O) Price-sensitive markets Major markets Long-term demand	S/O: Maxi - Maxi S O Low price Long-term plan Good marketing network	W/O: Mini - Maxi W O Massive training Specify responsibilities Heavy technical support
External Threats (T) Quota problems Competition from LDCs World economy downturn New unknown producer	S/T: Maxi - Mini S T Flexible production plan Keep overheads down	W/T: Mini - Mini W T Update technology New products Promotion

THE EQUITY JOINT VENTURE OPTION

The biggest decision that now faces the Nugent Company in China is whether to become involved with a manufacturing equity joint venture (MEJV) in the electronics field. Webster says that Nugent's several years of experience in China, which have included the establishment of service joint ventures and investigations into MEJVs, have reinforced his opinion that the MEJV option, while certainly an important one, should be looked at with considerable care and should only be pursued if it is able to be self-financing in foreign exchange. He also points out that, in addition to all the problems listed above, there is one other key question: the problem of finding an effective partner.

While the choice of the right partner is obviously important in the successful development of any business, and certainly for co-production, the danger of a wrong choice of partner for an equity joint venture can be disastrous. In this case, although the co-production project has succeeded within its limited objectives, there is no evidence that a viable EJV can be built with Xin Hua with the items so far produced. The indications are against successful export.

The opposition to Webster is led by Eagle, an export director at headquarters, who has spent a lot of time with Chinese Embassy officials listening to their persuasive comments on MEJVs and is anxious to demonstrate that the Company is fully committed to China. As Eagle says, there is no better way of showing commitment than by 'putting one's money where one's mouth is'.

Eagle is also worried by the growing number of other foreign EJVs and feels that they may squeeze Nugent out in the long term. She sees involvement in an EJV as a necessary part of the process, however painful, of buying membership in 'the China Club'. Indeed, for similar reasons, she is also anxious to see Nugent set up a representative office in Beijing.

Webster, on the other hand, continues to be concerned that Nugent should not become involved in loss makers in China, but should only embark on a MEJV when satisfactory answers have been found to the many potential problems. He is also anxious to avoid the high cost of a presence in Beijing, although pressure is being put on Nugent by its home government, which is anxious to increase the number of its national companies 'showing the flag' in China's capital. In Webster's view, the correct recipe for China business is to plan for the long term but to spend resources only to achieve profitable business, not on goodwill gestures.

CURRENT SCENARIO

The shape of the future relationship with Xin Hua remains unresolved. The three main approaches to the current debate are as follows:

(i) **THE EAGLE APPROACH.** It urgues immediate investment in an MEJV and, if possible, the establishment of an office in Beijing.

(ii) **THE XIN HUA APPROACH.** This carries on with co-production on existing and further products but start re-exporting or having Nugent buy back part of the output.

(iii) **THE WEBSTER APPROACH.** It continues to develop the successful partnership in co-production but expand volume by effective domestic marketing in collaboration with Xin Hua.

There is much common ground between Xin Hua and Webster on the general merits of the co-production system, which has been successfully adopted. The differences and problems which remain to be resolved include:

1. How much further and faster can Chinese components and content be incorporated into the product, while maintaining quality standards? Should a new philosophy be adopted?
2. Will the Chinese authorities fully recognize that co-production deals offer potential savings in foreign exchange, and impose an effective system to discourage the import from foreign suppliers of analogous systems in a fully built-up state?
3. Should emphasis be given to continuing production of the earlier models, which are no longer in production in Nugent's home factory but are not only well-tested but also offer the prospect of reduced costs?
4. What emphasis should be laid on moving on to the latest 'state-of-the-art' products? Although earning plaudits from officials and scientists on the Chinese side, the arrangement would diminish the opportunity for cost reduction through increased volume.
5. How can Xin Hua, which has grown up in the tradition of a state factory accepting a quota rather than seeking a market, build up marketing expertise and a dynamic philosophy so as to increase domestic sales?
6. How can Xin Hua's marketing and sales staff be motivated to learn and practise real marketing and sales skills?
7. Can Xin Hua accept a sufficiently low export price to make its products competitive in the world market and, therefore, saleable through Nugent's own channels?

In one sense the Nugent Company is faced with a central dilemma: whether it is prepared to plunge into an MEJV, having at least learnt a great deal more about its partner and the China scene since 1984, or whether it wishes to continue with variations on the co-production theme. The problem common to both solutions is that of price in relation to the export market; whatever the type of cooperation chosen, so long as the domestic market remains limited there is no economy of scale to reduce unit cost, and it is difficult to see, short of outright subsidy by Xin Hua, or Nugent, how the price can be competitive in the export market. Unlike the tame, tied, domestic market, which has no choice but to accept the Xin Hua product price, the export market will insist not only on competitive pricing but probably on a discount to compensate for the fact that the product is manufactured in a strange factory.

The debate at Nugent continues and the tragic events of June 1989, while not affecting the facts, have created more doubt in the Head Office. The arguments in favour of an MEJV remain weak in Webster's view. The volume of each product is small, the domestic market remains static, and, although Xin Hua has absorbed technical skills, it has not progressed commercially. Eagle is, of course, right: an MEJV would be perceived by the Chinese side as demonstrating greater commitment but, until Eagle can find a viable solution to the problems of export marketing from Xin Hua, the MEJVs will only make profits in the internal Chinese currency (RMB) and Nugent will depend on the generosity of the Chinese authorities for any foreign exchange swaps and remittances.

COMMITMENT. Webster and Eagle agree about the value of an MEJV as a gesture showing commitment to China, but Webster considers that the goodwill may be bought at too high a price unless the venture can not only make a profit but also remit the profit in hard currency. He has a similar reaction to the proposal that representative offices should be set up: goodwill will indeed be generated, but costs will be very high. Webster's view is that long-term commitment can best be demonstrated by viable commercial projects. Expensive experiments are likely to sour the head office and lead to despondency at home and disappointment in the PRC.

MEJV: PROBLEMS IN GENERAL

In looking at the difficulties facing MEJVs in the PRC, it is evident that the core issue—and indeed this is true whatever the form of cooperation—is shortage of foreign exchange, which leads the Chinese to demand that foreign exchange should be procured through exporting.

But this, of course, is something which is endemic throughout the developing world, in which for present purposes the communist states can be included. Indeed, almost all the problems facing Nugent and Xin Hua are not unique to China. Misunderstanding of the

Exhibit 2 Possible Strategies in China

Internal Factors / External Factors	Company's Internal Strengths (S) High technology Overseas experience Financial background International reputation Good management Experienced engineers Strong R&D	Company's Internal Weaknesses (W) Not totally committed Insufficient experience in China Distance from China Language and culture gap Short-term view Type of organization
Opportunities in China (O) Long-term market Expanding market	S/O: Maxi - Maxi S O Use Chinese raw materials and Chinese components Find expert partner	W/O: Mini - Maxi W O Build company specialist team Use Asian forward base Provide linguists Build on beachhead Increase promotion Take long-term view
Threats inside China (T) Weak infrastructure Inexperience Alien cultural climate Political uncertainty Bureaucratic complexity International competition Export licence problems	S/T: Max - Mini S T Carry out market research Choose right place Offer service and technical follow up	W/T: Mini - Mini W T Anticipate competition Involve senior Chinese cadres Accept cultural differences Detailed planning and contracts Train staff both in China and at home base Patience Perseverance

middleman's role; failure to recognise the validity and necessity of his efforts to produce a balance between foreign demand and local supply; and the fact that the factory itself is largely uninterested in exporting its output, are common experiences in socialist countries.

While in some parts of the PRC economy effective ways of exporting have been achieved, as indeed trade figures show, at the state factory level, exporting is not seen as 'fun', as former British Prime Minister Harold Macmillan labelled it, but as hard and unfamiliar work for which there is no personal reward, and which may involve some personal risk. The official PRC line is difficult to translate to factory directors, who can perceive the complications of foreign trade and the additional work but no obvious reward except, perhaps, job satisfaction.

To help the debate, Webster has prepared the SWOT analysis diagrammed in Exhibit 2 with suggestions about some general principles that Nugent possibly should follow. He has also listed some recent publications that may provide useful background material for those involved in plotting Nugent's future strategies for marketing in the People's Republic of China.

SUGGESTED FURTHER READING

Campbell, N., *China Strategies: The inside story,* Manchester: University of Manchester/University of Hong Kong, 1986.

⎯⎯⎯⎯, *A Strategic Guide to Equity Joint Ventures in China,* Oxford, UK: Pergamon Press, 1988.

Cohen, J.A., Equity Joint Ventures: 20 potential pitfalls that every company should know about, *The China Business Review,* Vol. 9, November–December 1982, pp. 23–29.

Daniels, J.D., J. Krug, and D. Nigh, U.S. Joint Ventures in China: Motivation and management of political risks, *California Management Review,* Vol. 28, Summer 1986, pp. 46–58.

Davidson, W.H., Creating and Managing Joint Ventures in China, *California Management Review,* Vol. 24, No. 4, Summer 1987, pp. 77–94.

Hendryx, S.R., The China Trade: Making the deal work, *Harvard Business Review,* Vol. 64, July–August 1986, pp. 75–84.

Killing, P., Technology Acquisition: License agreement or joint ventures, *Columbia Journal of World Business,* Vol. 15, No. 3, 1980, pp. 38–46.

Lockett, M., Culture and the Problem of Chinese Management, *Templeton College Management Research Papers,* 85/88, Oxford, 1985.

Stewart, Sally, One Billion Customers? *Asian Affairs,* Vol. XVI, Part III, October 1985, pp. 265–272.

⎯⎯⎯⎯, Countertrade in China, *Euro-Asian Business Review,* Vol. 5, No. 1, January 1986, pp. 25–27.

⎯⎯⎯⎯, The Transfer of High Technology to China: Problems and options, *International Journal of Technology Management,* Vol. 3, No. 1/2, 1988, pp. 167–179.

Wang, N.T., United States and China: Business beyond trade: An overview, *Columbia Journal of World Business,* Vol. XXI, No. 1, Spring 1986, pp. 3–12.

Warrington, M.B. and J.B. McCall, Negotiating a Foot into the Chinese Door, *Management Development,* Vol. 21, No. 2, 1983, pp. 3–13.

CASE FOURTEEN (A)

KENTUCKY FRIED CHICKEN IN CHINA*

In late September 1986, Tony Wang leaned back in his leather chair in his Singapore office and thought of the long road that lay ahead if Kentucky Fried Chicken (KFC) were ever to establish the first completely Western-style fast food joint venture in the People's Republic of China. Wang, an experienced entrepreneur and 7-year veteran of KFC had only 2 months previously accepted the position of company vice president for Southeast Asia with an option of bringing the world's largest chicken restaurant company into the world's most populous country. Yet, as he began exploring the opportunities facing KFC in Southeast Asia, Wang was beginning to wonder whether the company should attempt to enter the Chinese market at this time.

Without any industry track record, Wang wondered how to evaluate the attractiveness of the Chinese market within the context of KFC's Southeast Asia region. Compounding the challenge was the realization that although China was a huge, high profile market, it would demand precious managerial resources and could offer no real-term prospects for significant hard currency profit repatriation—even in the medium term. Wang also realized that a decision to go into China necessitated selecting a particular investment location in the face of great uncertainty. It was equally clear that while opportunities and risks varied widely from city to city, the criteria for evaluating suitable locations remained unspecified. With

---

* This case was prepared by Professor Allen J. Morrison, with assistance from Professor Paul Beamish, as a basis for classroom discussion rather than to illustrate either an effective or ineffective handling of an administrative situation. Funding was provided by the Federation of Canadian Municipalities' Chinese Open Cities Project through a grant from the Canadian International Development Agency (C.I.D.A.), and by The Centre for International Business Studies of The University of Western Ontario. © 1989 C.I.D.A. and The University of Western Ontario.

limited information to go on, Wang realized that a positive decision on China would be inherently risky—both for the company and for his own reputation. And while Wang was intrigued by the enormous potential of the Chinese market, he also knew that many others had failed in similar ventures.

HISTORY

The origins of Kentucky Fried Chicken can be traced to Harland Sanders, who was born in 1890 in Henryville, Indiana. When Sanders was a boy, he dropped out of the sixth grade and began a stream of odd jobs, concentrating eventually on cooking. In time he opened his own gas station with an adjoining restaurant. In the 1930s, Sanders developed a "Secret" recipe for cooking chicken by first applying a coating containing a mixture of 11 herbs and spices and then frying the chicken under pressure. This "southern fried chicken" eventually became a hit at the gas station and in 1956 Sanders decided to franchise his novel concept. By 1964 he had sold almost 700 franchises. Much of Sanders' success in this pioneer industry lay in his near-obsession with product quality and a commitment to maintaining a focused line of products.

In 1964, at the age of 74, Harland Sanders finally agreed to sell the business in exchange for $2 million and a promise of a lifetime salary. The sale of the business to John Brown, a 29-year-old Kentucky lawyer, and his financial backer Jack Massey, 60, was accompanied by the assurance that Sanders would maintain an active role in both product promotion and quality control of the new venture.

With new, aggressive managers and a rapidly evolving American fast food industry, KFC's growth soared. Over the next 5 years, sales grew by an average of 96 per cent per year, topping $200 million by 1970. This same year, almost 1,000 new stores were built, the vast majority by franchisees.

A key element in this rapid growth was Brown's ability to select a group of hardworking entrepreneurial managers. Brown's philosophy was that every manager had the right to expect to become wealthy in the rapidly growing company. By relying heavily on franchising, the company was able to avoid the high capital costs associated with rapid expansion while maximizing shareholder equity. Rapid sales growth provided promotion and stock opportunities for company managers as well as the opportunity for franchisees to improve margins by spreading administrative costs over a broader base of operations. This was critically important given the high fixed costs associated with each store. Volume, both at the individual store level and within a franchisee's territory, was thus essential in determining profitability. Profitability in turn assured the attractiveness of KFC to potential future franchisees.

In 1971, Brown and Massey sold KFC to Heublein Inc. for $275 million. Heublein, based in Farmington, Connecticut, was a packaged goods company which marketed such products as Smirnoff vodka, Black Velvet Canadian whisky, Grey Poupon mustard, and A1 steak sauce.

CHALLENGES AT HOME AND ABROAD

The establishment of KFC's international operations began just prior to the company's acquisition by Heublein, KFC opened its first store in the Far East in Osaka, Japan in 1970 as part of Expo-70. By 1973, KFC had established 64 stores in Japan, mostly in the Tokyo area. KFC also moved quickly into Hong Kong, establishing 15 outlets there by 1973. Other areas of expansion included Australia, the United Kingdom, and South Africa.

Shortly after the acquisition, KFC's small international staff was merged with Heublein's much larger international group in Connecticut. In spite of Heublein's efforts to impose rigid operational controls, KFC country managers were frustrated by the imposition of US store designs, menus, and marketing methods on culturally divergent host countries. Resistance to corporate control grew and led many stores to develop their own menus: fried fish and smoked chicken in Japan, hamburgers in South Africa, and roast chicken in Australia. In some cases local managers seemed to know what they were doing; in other cases they clearly did not. After heavy losses, KFC pulled out of Hong Kong entirely in 1975. In Japan, operations also began on shaky grounds with losses experienced throughout much of the 1970s.

In addition to poor relations between country managers and corporate staff, the 1970s presented a much more challenging environment for KFC in the United States. The fast food industry was becoming much more competitive with the national emergence of the Church's Fried Chicken franchise and the onset of several strong regional competitors. Important market share gains were also being made by McDonald's hamburgers.

With the Heublein acquisition, many top managers who had been hired by Brown and Massey were either fired or quit, resulting in much turmoil among the franchisees. By 1976, sales were off 8 per cent and profits were decreasing by 26 per cent per year. To make matter worse, rapid expansion had led to inconsistent quality, unclean conditions and a burgeoning group of disenchanted franchisees which represented over 80 per cent of total KFC sales. At one point, even white-haired Harland Sanders was publicly quoted admitting that many outlets lacked adequate cleanliness while providing shoddy customer service and poor product quality.

TURNING OPERATIONS AROUND

In the fall of 1975, with rapidly deteriorating operations both at home and abroad, Heublein tapped Michael Miles to salvage the chain. Miles was initially brought in to head Heublein's international group, which by this point was dominated by KFC. Miles had come to Heublein after managing KFC's advertising account for 10 years with the Leo Burnett agency. At Heublein, he had risen to vice president in-charge of the Grocery Products Division. While he had little international experience, he had developed a strong reputation for strategic planning. His challenge in late 1975 was to install consistency in international operations by increasing both corporate support and control. One of his first decisions was to move KFC-International back to Louisville where it could begin to develop a degree of autonomy within the corporation. Within 18 months, Miles was asked to manage KFC's entire worldwide turnaround, including operations in the United States.

The basic thrust of Miles' strategy was a return to back-to-basics in terms of menu selection and commitment to quality, service, and cleanliness (QSC). The back-to-basics strategy was supported by a new series of staff training programs, random inspections of company-owned and franchisee stores, and a new "we do chicken right" advertising program. The goal was to focus consumer awareness on a sleeker, more customer-oriented KFC which would make one product—chicken—better than any of its competitors.

The results of the turnaround strategy were dramatic. By 1982, KFC had become Heublein's fastest growing division, with real growth of 2.3 per cent. From 1978 to 1982, sales at company-owned stores jumped an average 73 per cent, while franchise unit sales rose by almost 45 per cent. Much of this growth came from KFC's international operations where company units out-numbered even McDonald's outside the United States. While chicken is eaten almost everywhere in the world, the same is not true of beef which has been poorly received in many countries. This provided KFC with a considerable advantage in penetrating foreign markets. Nowhere was this more true than in the Pacific Rim, where by 1982 KFC had nearly 400 stores in Japan. In Singapore alone, KFC had 23 franchised outlets.

ACQUISITION BY R.J. REYNOLDS

Although KFC had made dramatic progress, growth was limited by restricted expansion capital at Heublein. Most of the profits generated by KFC were being used to revive Heublein's spirits operations which were themselves facing flat sales and increased competition. By 1982, KFC was receiving only $50 million per year in expansion funds compared with the $400 million being spent by hamburger giant McDonald's. KFC also had one of the lowest ratios of company-owned to franchisee stores in the industry. Many franchise stores were slow to upgrade facilities and it was understood that major investments would be required to assure the integrity of the overall KFC network.

In the late summer of 1982, R.J. Reynolds of Winston-Salem, N.C., acquired Heublein for $1.4 billion. The acquisition was supported by Heublein directors fearful the company might be taken over and sold in pieces. Reynolds had been seeking expansion possibilities in the consumer products industry where its marketing skills and huge cash flow could best be put to work. Although hugely profitable, Reynolds' tobacco operations were being attacked by soaring taxes and consumers' declining interest in smoking. The acquisition of Heubelin was only part of a group of companies Reynolds acquired during the late 1970s and early 1980s, including Del Monte Corporation in 1979, Canada Dry and Sunkist Soft Drinks in 1984, and Nabisco Brands in 1985.

Soon after the acquisition, Mike Miles left the company to become president of Dart and Kraft. He was succeeded as CEO of KFC by Richard Mayer who had worked with Miles on the turnaround. Mayer had put in a 10-year stint at General Foods where he rose to become head of the Jell-O product group. Mayer characterized the acquisition as "marvelous."

INTERNATIONAL EXPANSION

The heavy financial backing of Reynolds resulted in further growth for KFC. Betting that health-conscious consumers would increasingly shift consumption to chicken, Reynolds designed an ambitious worldwide expansion plan that promise $1 billion in funds over five years. Much of this expansion would come outside the United States where markets remained largely untapped.

As was the case with domestic operations, franchising played a major role in KFC's international growth. Franchising became the mode of choice in many markets where political risk and cultural unfamiliarity encouraged the use of locals. Another advantage with franchising was that KFC could be assured a flow of revenues with little investment, thus leveraging existing equity. This was a particularly attractive option internationally where potential deviations of franchisees from KFC operating procedures could be more easily isolated.

The downside of a reliance on franchisees was that it permitted an erosion of system integrity. Local franchisees typically controlled a portfolio of companies, with KFC sales representing only a portion of revenues. Local franchisees, driven by a desire to maximize profits, often cut corners of "milked" operations. While this type of strategy would generally not compromise short-term profitability, it often led to the deterioration of operations over the longer term. This problem was only exacerbated internationally where control was more difficult to maintain.

SOUTHEAST ASIA OPERATIONS

By 1983, KFC had established 85 franchise stores in Southeast Asia including 20 stores in Indonesia, 27 stores in Malaysia, and 23 stores in Singapore. This area was recognized as the Southeast Asia Region, one of five separate geographic regions within the corporation. Harry Schwab headed the area office, where he served as a company vice president. Schwab had been successful in managing KFC's South African operations where he eventually built a chain of 48 company-owned stores and 95 franchise outlets. After returning to Louisville to assume the position of KFC vice president for international franchising, he was given the added responsibility of supervising the company's Southeast Asia area. Exhibit 1 presents a partial map of Asian Pacific nations.

THE CHINESE MARKET

After a 10-year absence, KFC moved back into Hong Kong in 1985. During KFC's long absence from Hong Kong, McDonald's, the Burger King, Wendy's, and Pizza Hut had entered the market, providing the local population with a taste for Western fast food. After preparing a new Cantonese version of the "we do chicken right" advertising campaign, KFC opened its first of 20 panned stores. During its first week of operation, the store sold more than 41,000 pieces of chicken, the most any start-up ever sold during its first week of operation. With renewed confidence that management had finally learned how to balance the need for corporate control with the demands for local responsiveness, the company began contemplating a much more ambitious move into the Chinese mainland.

The initial discussions over the feasibility of entering the huge Chinese market were held in early January 1985 between Richard Mayer and Ta-Tung (Tony) Wang, a former executive of KFC. Tony Wang was born in Sichuan province in the People's Republic of China in 1944. When Tony was 5 years old the family made its way to Taiwan where in 1968 he graduated from Chong-Yuan University with a degree in engineering. He later moved to the United States and in 1973 completed a master's degree in management science from Stevens Institute of Technology in New Jersey. Wang then attended New York University where in 1975 he earned a post-master's certificate in international business management.

Case Fourteen (A)

Exhibit 1 Partial Map of Pacific Asian Countries

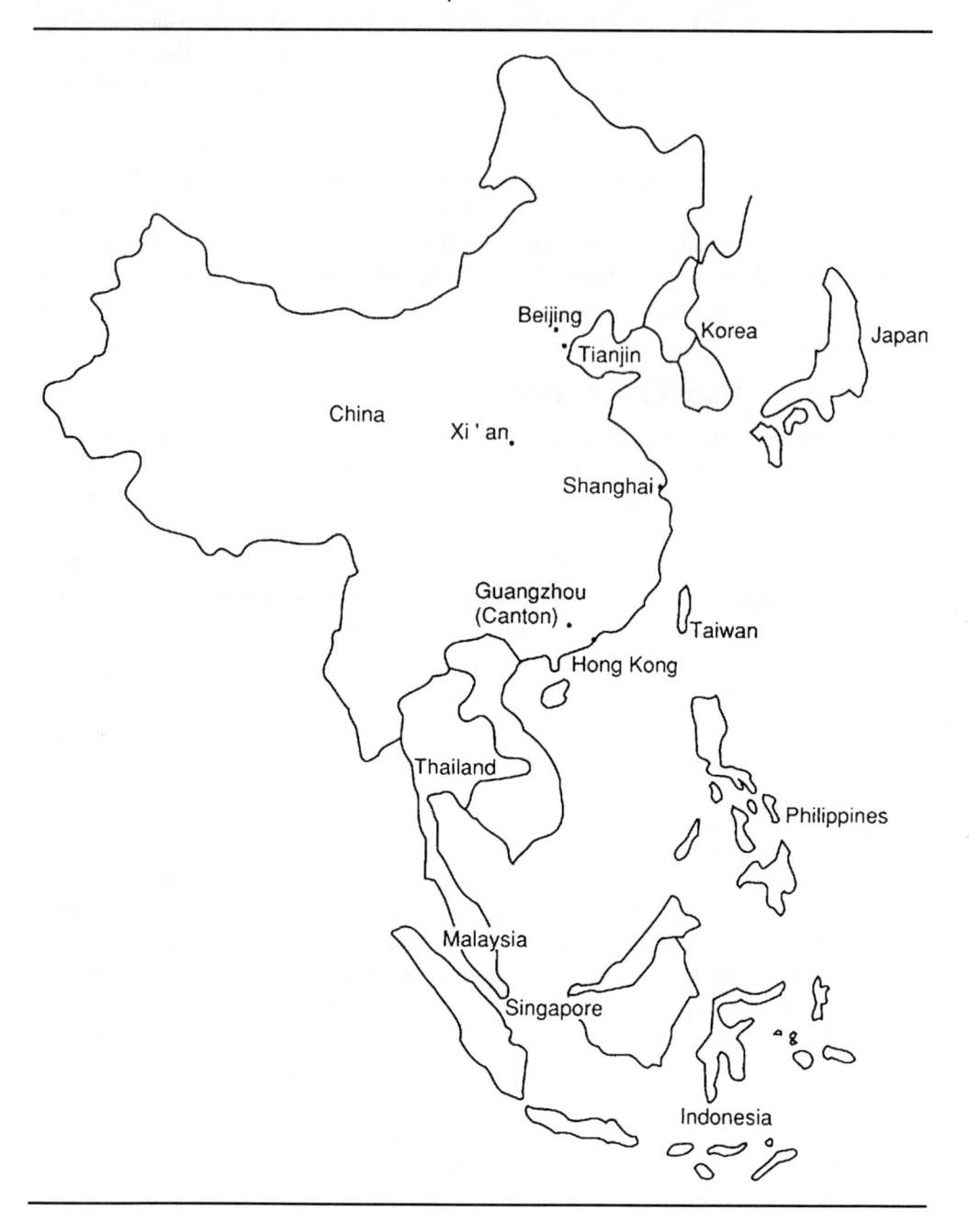

Upon completion of his studies in 1975, Wang accepted a position in Louisville with KFC. A series of promotions culminated with his assuming the position as director of business development for the company. In this position, Wang reported directly to Mayer where the two developed a close personal relationship. Yet, by 1982 Wang was feeling increasingly uneasy at KFC. Although KFC had completed a dramatic turnaround, Wang felt strongly that the company had been too conservative in penetrating international markets. Wang's conviction was that the company was afraid to take real investment risks, particularly in the Far East where American managers were culturally out of touch. In his capacity as director of business development, Wang also saw some of the enormous profits that many of his projects were generating for franchisees. In Wang's view he was merely a bureaucrat, "enriching a conservative, ethnocentric corporation." He plotted his departure. This eventually led to the establishment of QSR Management Company where Wang served as president. QSR was principally engaged in franchisee operations of Wendy's restaurants in northern California. The company also provided management consulting to other franchisees of major fast food companies.

THE TIANJIN EXPERIENCE

In spite of QSR's highly profitable operations in California, Wang remained convinced of the enormous potential for American style fast food in the Far East. In the summer of 1984, the mayor of Tianjin (the third largest city in China with a population of 7 million) visited San Francisco and spoke to a small group of Chinese-Americans about investment opportunities in his city. Wang attended the meeting and was later invited by the mayor to serve as an advisor on improving the food service industry in Tianjin. Wang's counterproposal was to not only serve as an advisor but as an investor in a joint Chinese-American style fast food restaurant. The mayor welcomed the idea. Primary backing for the project came from a group of Chinese-American investors in the San Francisco bay area; additional backing was provided by Don Stephens, the chairman of the Bank of San Francisco. With this support Wang reached a 50-50 joint venture agreement with a local Tianjin partner to establish "Orchid Food," the first ever Chinese-US joint venture in the restaurant industry in China. The 80-seat combination takeout restaurant was hugely successful from its first day of operation with revenues averaging 100 per cent above break-even.

Buoyed by this success, Wang began reflecting on the tremendous potential KFC had in China. Wang's interests were in bringing KFC into China through personally winning the franchise rights for key regions of the country. Barring this, he would try convince his friend Richard Mayer to become a partner in a three-way deal involving Wang, KFC, and a local and as yet undetermined partner. In a letter to Mayer in mid-January 1985, Wang argued that the time was right for KFC to move "aggressively" into China.

> *I am totally convinced that KFC has a definite competitive edge over any other major fast food chain in the United States in developing the China market at the present time. In spite of the fact that McDonald's is trying to establish a relationship there, it will be a long while before beef could become feasibly available. On the*

other hand, the poultry industry is one of the top priority categories in China's agriculture modernization and it is highly encouraged by the government. It is my opinion that KFC can open the door in China and build an undisputable lead by first establishing a firm poultry-supply foundation.

Movement into China was also being encouraged by KFC's parent, R.J. Reynolds, itself interested in penetrating the vast Chinese market for cigarettes. Executives at RJR had long realized that unlike North American demand, the demand for cigarettes was soaring in Third-World and communist countries. American cigarettes in particular enjoyed almost unlimited demand. China seemed like the perfect market for the company.

Mayer approached Wang's offer to bring KFC into China with great interest. Wang had a long and productive history with KFC. Mayer could trust him. He was aggressive and had a proven track record of successfully negotiating with the Chinese. He was also Chinese—he spoke perfect Mandarin and felt at ease in either Beijing or Louisville. If anyone could get KFC into China, it seemed that Tony Wang was the person. However, Mayer also had considerable concerns about turning over such a strategically important market to a franchisee. Experiences in other international markets had shown the perils of relying on franchisees. The granting of franchise rights could also jeopardize KFC's ability to later expanding in other regions of the country. According to Mayer, China was "too important to not be developed as a company operation."

Tony Wang himself was beginning to have serious doubts about his ability to move KFC into China by relying on his own resources. His experience in Tianjin had only reemphasized his conviction that major changes in the attitudes of Chinese employees would almost certainly be required for operation under the KFC banner. These changes could only be achieved through time-consuming training programs, suggesting heavy pre-start-up costs which Wang could not adequately support. Wang was also concerned about the upfront money needed in finding and negotiating a partnership, signing a lease, and gaining operating permits. By late fall 1985, it was becoming increasingly clear to Wang that "China is too big a market for individuals."

CHANGES IN MANAGEMENT

It was in April 1986 that Mayer decided to make his move. He telephoned Tony Wang with several announcements: Steve Fellingham was being promoted to head all of KFC's international operations. Fellingham had over 10 years' experience in KFC International and was widely respected as someone who would move much more aggressively internationally by relying less on franchisees and more on joint ventures with local partners. This observation was confirmed by Mayer. Mayer also announced that KFC was buying up its Singapore franchisee which now operated 29 KFC stores. This would result in considerable new administrative responsibilities for KFC's Southeast Asia regional office. Finally, Mayer was moving Harry Schwab out of Singapore, and restructuring the Southeast Asia region. The job of running the region was Tony's if he wanted it. Mayer also expressed his encouragement that Wang pursue the China option according to his best judgment and efforts.

After some soul-searching, Wang accepted the position and in the summer of 1986 officially became vice president of KFC Southeast Asia with headquarters in Singapore. According to Wang, he accepted the job because of the "personal challenge to develop KFC in China." Wang viewed this opportunity of establishing the first Western-style fast food operation in China as a historic opportunity—both personally and for the company as a whole. He also realized that with this very visible challenge came high personal risks should the venture fail.

With the assumption of responsibility for all KFC operations in Southeast Asia, Wang began to see the decision to invest in China in a different light. A singular objective of getting into China would now have to be balanced with other investment opportunities in the region. KFC had enormous growth potential throughout Southeast Asia. The national markets of the region, while together smaller than the entire Chinese market, had already been exposed to Western-style fast food; patterns of demand for KFC's products were well understood. Compared to China, targeting these markets for growth had certain appeal. Control over partners and employees would be rather simple to maintain, leading to rapid growth and higher returns. Hard currency was also readily available. China, in contrast, would demand a huge amount of scarce managerial resources. The primary constraint was the limited number of Chinese-speaking KFC managers, many of whom were already being pushed to the limits in Hong Kong and Singapore. As a consequence, by the late summer of 1986, Wang was beginning to wonder whether committing these resources to China would be in the best interests of the region for which he was now responsible. Exhibit 2 presents selected national economic and population statistics for the Southeast Asia region as well as KFC location and sales figures.

Exhibit 2 Selected Country Statistics, Southeast Asia and China (1986)

	Population (millions)	Life Expectancy	GNP per Capita (US$)	Annual Real GNP Growth Rate (%)	Kentucky Fried Chicken Number of Units	Kentucky Fried Chicken Sales (US$, millions)
Thailand	52.6	64	790	5.3	4	1.5
Singapore	2.6	73	7,450	7.3	26	15.0
Malaysia	16.1	68	1,830	1.8	53	27.0
Indonesia	166.6	55	500	1.2	25	6.8
Hong Kong	5.4	76	7,030	12.1	4	2.7
People's Republic of China	1,054.0	69	300	7.9	—	—

THE CHINA OPTION: INVESTIGATING ALTERNATIVES

Wang's reaction to the ambiguity surrounding the China option was to investigate the Chinese market more thoroughly. Here, the principal question facing Wang was the intended geographic location of a first Chinese store. The location decision would potentially have a dramatic effect on profitability, future expansion elsewhere in China and managerial resource commitments—all vital considerations in a go/no-go decision.

In considering where to establish a first store, Wang initially thought of Tianjin. Through his earlier experiences, he had developed excellent contacts within the municipal government of Tianjin and he appreciated that Tianjin was one of three municipal governments in China that were administered directly by the central government in Beijing. (The other two were Shanghai and Beijing.) Yet, he also recognized that the city had several shortcomings. First, Tianjin lacked a convenient supply of grain-fed chickens. Experience in Hong Kong—where in 1973 KFC had entered the market using fish-meal fed chickens—suggested that Chinese consumers placed a high value on freshness and taste. This would be particularly important with a product prepared in a way that was unfamiliar to the Chinese. Another problem with Tianjin was that the city was not generally frequented by Western tourists. While Wang anticipated that most sales would be from soft currency *renminbi* (RMB), some hard foreign currency sales would be essential for profit repatriation and/or the purchase of critical supplies such as chicken coating, packaging, and promotion materials.* Finally, and perhaps most important, Tianjin would be unable to provide KFC with the profile necessary to facilitate eventual national market penetration. In fact, Tianjin was generally regarded in China as a gateway to its larger sister, Beijing, only 85 miles to the west.

Other cities presenting viable alternative locations for KFC's entry into China included Shanghai, Guangzhou, and Beijing. The location of these cities is presented in Exhibit 1. Each of these cities will be discussed in more detail.

SHANGHAI. As China's largest city, Shanghai is home to some 11 million people, almost 9,000 factories and is the country's busiest harbor. Metropolitan Shanghai is widely regarded as China's most prosperous business center. The city alone accounts for approximately 11 per cent of China's total industrial output and almost 17 per cent of the country's exports. It is also one of three self-administered municipalities.

Shanghai has a long history of involvement with Westerners. The Treaty of Nanking, thrust upon the Chinese by the British during the middle of the 19th century, set Shanghai aside as one of five Chinese port cities open to foreign trade. Western commerce and cultural influence flourished. Foreign gunboats continued to patrol the river until well into the 20th century. Complete expulsion of foreigners came in 1949 with the communist victory over the Nationalist Chinese army. However, since then the city has maintained an interest in international business and trade. Today, the city contains a large variety of Western hotels and business facilities, and is host to numerous tourists.

Shanghai also had the benefit of providing easy access to a seemingly ample supply of quality chickens. In fact, through joint ventures, a Thailand-based company—the Chia Tai

---

* Like virtually all communist economies, the Chinese economy operates through two separate currencies: renminbi, or the "People's Currency," which is used by local Chinese for the purpose of goods and services; and FEC (Foreign Exchange Certificate) which is used by foreigners to represent the value of hard currency while in China. FEC is required at all hotels, taxis, restaurants and shops which cater to foreigners. A growing black market for FEC exists in most large Chinese cities.

Group—had established 10 feed mills and poultry operations in the region and was the largest poultry supplier in Shanghai. KFC's Southeast Asia office had good relations with Chia Tai and was currently negotiating with one of the company's divisions as a potential franchisee in Bangkok.

While Shanghai remains a major center for business, its noise and pollution have discouraged tourists. For KFC, the sheer population of a host city is important, although less so than the mix of potential customers. And while Shanghai could provide KFC with eagerly sought-after media exposure, the operation would also need to promise an adequate return in KFC before an investment could be justified. Here, the concern was whether or not Western businesspeople would be attracted to KFC or would prefer to frequent more fashionable restaurants. Clearly no one knew.

GUANGZHOU. Another alternative was the city of Guangzhou, located in southeast China only a short distance from Hong Kong. Guangzhou, historically known as Canton, is one of 14 special coastal cities set apart in 1984 as preferential treatment centers for foreign investment. As such, Guangzhou was given greater autonomy in approving foreign investment projects, reducing tax rates, and encouraging technological development. By the end of 1986, about 80 per cent of the almost $6 billion foreign investment in China had been located in these open coastal cities. In addition, Guangzhou is the capital of Guangdong Province, which contains three of the country's four "Special Economic Zones" (SEZs), designed specifically to attract foreign investment. The SEZs were initially set up as part of the broad economic reforms that were launched in China in the late 1970s.

Guangzhou was frequented by Western business people as well as by tourists who visit the city on one-day excursions from Hong Kong. Due to its proximity to Hong Kong—less than 75 miles away and easily accessible by road or train—an operation in Guangzhou could easily be serviced out of the company's Hong Kong office. The Chinese in this region were also more familiar with Western management practices and culture. In fact, the people in Guangzhou speak Cantonese—the language spoken in Hong Kong. Cantonese Chinese is quite different from the Mandarin Chinese spoken elsewhere in China. Preliminary investigations also indicated that little difficulty would be anticipated in locating an adequate supplier of chickens.

BEIJING. Another location that warranted closer inspection was Beijing, China's second most populous city (after Shanghai) with 9 million citizens. Since its establishment as the Chinese capital by the Mongols in the 13th century, Beijing has remained the political and cultural center of China. For example, although China spans a breadth of 3,000 miles, the entire nation runs according to Beijing time—an indication of the power of the central government. As the nation's capital, Beijing also sports a subway and freeway system and an international airport complete with airconditioning and moving sidewalks.

Chinese citizens from all over the country pour into Beijing, eager to attend meetings or represent their factories or districts before the authorities of the central government. The city is also the educational capital in the country with university campuses ringing the city. These factors all contributed to the relatively high levels of affluence and intellectual enlightenment of the population—critically important in generating RMB sales. Beijing was also a tourist center for Western visitors anxious to see the Forbidden City, Summer Palace, and nearby Ming Tombs and the Great Wall. This would mean a ready supply of FEC currency. Finally, without doubt a start-up in Beijing would grab the people's attention and would communicate the tacit approval of the central authorities thus facilitating future expansion outside the city.

Beijing could provide considerable advantages to a company eager to expand throughout China. A preliminary investigation indicated that several poultry producers were operating just outside the city. Yet, politically and operationally, Beijing would be more of a gamble than alternative locations. High-profile operations heightened the possibility of government interference for political purposes.

WEIGHING THE DECISION

In his heart, Tony Wang knew he liked taking risks and clearly China qualified as the risk of a lifetime. However, it was also clear that the location of the first store could mitigate much of the obvious risk of moving into China. Left undetermined was whether the low-risk alternatives were worth pursuing. What was needed was to weigh out the possibility of reducing the risks against the potential benefits that could be achieved through the investment.

Clearly, Wang had staked out a position as the person who could bring KFC into China. However, he now had different responsibilities which also demanded his attention and for which he would surely be evaluated. He was certain that there would be little second guessing by Richard Mayer if he recommended that, after careful consideration, KFC should hold off for the present from China. He also realized that because there were no competitors as of yet in China, the present time could be the most opportune time for making the move. Indeed, even if a Chinese location were selected, it would likely take years of negotiations before operations could start. To delay any further ran the risk of ceding the market to others. The challenge to Wang would be in balancing these possible risks with the possible returns.

CASE FOURTEEN (B)

KENTUCKY FRIED CHICKEN IN CHINA—EXPANSION AND CONSEQUENT PROBLEMS*

In early March 1988, Tony Wang stared out the third-story window of Kentucky Fried Chicken's (KFC) Beijing restaurant at the crowds gathering on the street below. It was barely 10:00 on a Sunday morning and already people were lining up to purchase a meal that for most would cost over one-quarter of their weekly salary. To Wang, vice president for KFC for Southeast Asia and China, the crowds came as no surprise. In fact, in only four short months since opening, the Beijing restaurant had become the highest-selling single KFC store in the world. What was surprising to Tony Wang were his growing reservations about proceeding further in the Chinese market.

Wang was particularly worried about the mounting uncertainty of the entire venture. Although the restaurant had been successful in capturing the interests of Chinese consumers, conflicts with the company's two local partners were frequent and showed no signs of immediate resolution. Most of these disputes revolved around the imposition of KFC's management practices, which Wang regarded as essential to the operation's profitability. KFC's control mechanisms were designed to ensure standard levels of quality, service, and cleanliness (QSC) at all of the restaurant's chain stores around the world. Yet, the strictness with which these standards were enforced angered the local partners, who felt left out of the decision making and believed lower requirements would be equally acceptable to customers.

In spite of these concerns, sales continued to climb to the point where chicken supplies

---

* This case was prepared by Allen J. Morrison, University of Western Ontario, with assistance from Professor Paul W. Beamish. Funding was provided by the Federation of Canadian Municipalities' Open City Project through a grant from the Canadian International Development Agency (C.I.D.A.), and by the University of Western Ontario. © 1989 C.I.D.A. and the University of Western Ontario.

were running out. Adding to the confusion were the requests of both local partners for more rapid expansion into other Beijing locations. Should KFC feel compelled to spearhead further expansion at this point in time? Tony Wang wondered how and when to respond to his partners, his employees, and the burgeoning Chinese market.

Choosing the Tiananmen Square Location

With the partners in place, Beijing KFC (B-KFC) in early 1987 had decided to pursue the location just off Tiananmen Square. The site featured a vacant three-story facility in excellent condition. The location in the heart of the city would provide unsurpassed visibility.

However, with the benefits of visibility came the possibility that the location would be difficult to obtain. Much time could be wasted in negotiations that could be publicly encouraged by government officials eager to seek political gain from the West. The fear was that in the end the site would be silently vetoed by Communist party leaders troubled by the cultural imagery of Colonel Sanders in the shadow of Mao's tomb.

In winning the site, it was becoming ever more apparent that the imagery battle would be critical. According to Wang, their key strategy was "to convince the government that the restaurant would represent a symbol and statement of the People's Republic of China's commitment to an open policy with the West. Just as our image was important, we tried to play on the Chinese concern that they present a positive image with the outside world."

While this strategy was supported in principle by the two local partners, Animal Production and the Tourist Bureau knew they had far more to lose than their American partner by pushing the government too hard. According to Mr. Jue Xia, Chairman of B-KFC and a senior manager for Animal Productions, "We had several disagreements. Our position was that we shouldn't push too much. Government backlash was always possible."

Through sensitive negotiations, a government backlash was avoided and a lease was finally approved in April 1987 for the Tiananmen Square location. The lease represented a 10-year commitment from B-KFC. The store's facilities would represent KFC's largest restaurant in the world, with 1,400 square meters of space allowing for a capacity of 500 seats and considerable office space for B-KFC staff.

Still lacking was a building permit (to make renovations to the site) and hookups for water, gas, and heating. Many times in Beijing applications for service would get "misplaced" or service would be "unavailable" for no apparent reason. Heating was a particular problem—all facilities in the city were heated by common pipes from central Beijing heating plants. In these matters, KFC relied on the local partners for assistance but often found them reluctant to press for timely and adequate service.

KFC's Organization in China

By contractual arrangement, KFC was to provide a general manager responsible for the day-to-day operations of B-KFC. The man who held this position was Sim Kay Soon, a 30-year-old Singaporean. Sim joined the KFC system in 1980, and was selected for this position by Wang in the spring of 1987. In the interim period he had held the area manager and more recently the training officer positions. As general manager, Sim reported to Daniel Lam, KFC's newly appointed area director for China. Lam was based in Hong Kong and spoke fluent English, Mandarin, and Cantonese.

As events in China progressed, Wang began relying more and more on Lam for management support. Wang's attention was increasingly being split with his other duties in Southeast Asia. Estimates were that by the end of 1988 KFC would have 155 units established in the region, an increase of 45 units in the last two years. Exhibit 1 presents a breakdown of sales, by country, for Southeast Asia.

Exhibit 1 KFC Regional Sales Estimates for 1988

	Number of Units	Sales (US$, millions)
Malaysia	66	33.9
Indonesia	34	11.3
Hong Kong	13	12.3
Thailand	7	2.8
Singapore	33	27.0
Total	155	64.1

For Sim, the move to Beijing represented an 18-month appointment out of the booming regional office. It also represented a significant promotion. Nevertheless, the position was somewhat of a hardship posting as few of the conveniences found in Singapore were available in Beijing. Sim expected that a combination of stress and monotony would characterize his stay. His intended residence for 18 months was a Chinese hotel room negotiated by the Tourist Bureau.

HIRING LOCAL WORKERS

When initial announcements were made in the local papers that B-KFC would soon begin hiring, the joint venture was flooded with applicants. The decision to hire any particular applicant was made by Sim as the general manager of B-KFC. From the outset, KFC insisted on a policy that treated all applicants equally. No referrals would be accepted under any circumstance. This was a unique move in China, where family contacts were often used to land highly sought-after jobs. This was also a move that was initially opposed by the two local partners.

Working for a foreign joint venture was an attractive opportunity for many Chinese, because foreign partners often paid considerably above local wage levels. In Beijing, for example, it had been reported the English-speaking doormen at the joint-venture Sheraton Great Wall Hotel could earn up to three times as much as the top brain surgeon in the country. At KFC, the base salary promised to applicants was set at RMB 140 per month. This level was about 40 per cent more than could be received at typical industrial facilities and up to 10 per cent more than the remuneration received by associate professors at the country's universities. As was common among foreign joint ventures, B-KFC also devised an additional incentive scheme to encourage worker productivity. Incentive pay for conscientious employees could amount to another RMB 150 per month. For the Chinese worker it was a bonanza. So attractive was the compensation package that 20 people applied for every opening available.

The example of Mrs. Liu is indicative of the type of employees hired by B-KFC. Before coming to work for B-KFC, Liu was employed as an English teacher at a local Beijing public school. According to Liu:

> As an English teacher I was not well paid. The job was very dull, although most of my students enjoyed learning English. Still, I wasn't getting ahead. I was teaching English, but I wasn't learning English—I had no one to speak to. At KFC you have more chances to use and learn English. We are paid more here but we also work harder.

CONCERN ABOUT EMPLOYEES

While employees were attracted to B-KFC because of the opportunities for high pay and training, KFC was concerned about the abilities of employees to provide the levels of quality, service, and cleanliness demanded by corporate standards. Employees seemed to have little understanding of these principles. The Chinese had limited exposure to quality products, long (and reluctantly) accepting goods of substandard quality as normal. The attitude was one of making do, of lowering expectations. Because employment was guaranteed in Chinese society, hard work was also viewed by some as something to be avoided. Some workers were apathetic toward their jobs and found little incentive to overcome the challenges inherent in most work. This could potentially impact on the Western norms for cleanliness and service.

Control over workers was exercised through three primary mechanisms: hiring, training, and incentive pay. Under Chinese joint-venture law, B-KFC was given the power to hire and fire workers according to its own criteria. Hiring at B-KFC was based on five key qualifications: acceptable applicants must be high school graduates, must speak some English, must be presentable in grooming and dress, must demonstrate a willingness to work hard, and were not to have had previous restaurant work experience. The typical applicant was in his or her early 20s, and had taken some English in school.

With almost 120 of the most promising applicants hired by early August, B-KFC set out on the arduous task of acculturating employees and training them in the fine art of American fast food. Under previous arrangements, all training expenses were borne by the franchiser—KFC. Training began with the extensive playing of a videotape of KFC's operations in both Hong Kong and Singapore. According to Tony Wang, "We customized the training videotape that we had used elsewhere in Southeast Asia to meet particular Chinese needs. Our main objective was to show the employees what fast food was like."

Beyond this, the company imported cooking equipment, blending machinery, heating racks, cash registers, etc., to begin hands-on training of the employees. Concurrent with these efforts, four new assistant managers—all Chinese nationals—were sent to Singapore for intensive training at local restaurants. According to Anthony Leung, a senior manager in KFC's Singapore office who helped supervise the training and who was latter transferred to Beijing as B-KFC General Manager, "These new employees were bright, hardworking, and eager to take in all that there was to learn. It was a very positive experience."

Incentive pay played a major role in improving employee attitudes toward QSC. Every job was assigned an index of 100 points. Unsatisfactory work meant a reduction of points, with a corresponding cut in bonus pay. According to Mrs. Liu:

> *All employees get bonuses, unless they miss work, then they only get a percentage of their bonuses. Each job has standards set; if the standards are not met, we get points taken off. This also means a smaller bonus. The average bonus each month is from 50 to 150 RMB. The best I could ever expect in a factory would be about 120 renminbi per month.... So we work harder, but we get paid more. I like this.*

STARTUP OPERATIONS

To add real-life experiences to the training, B-KFC began experimenting with sales to the public in September. Chicken was purchased from Beijing Animal Production, while potatoes, cabbage, and carrots were all purchased locally. Cases of Pepsi and 7Up were shipped in from southern China. A small dry-goods warehouse was leased in the city and uniforms were ordered. According to Anthony Leung: "We opened on a trial basis in the fall of 1987. We were only open seven hours a day—from 10 A.M. to 2 P.M. and from 5 P.M. to 8 P.M. The times we were closed in the morning and afternoon we spent reviewing and training."

By this time, the store had been connected with electricity and gas, but was lacking heat. As the fall weather approached, the lack of heat was becoming increasingly problematic. With the startup of operations, the restaurant was drawing between 2,000 and 3,000 customers per day and the fear was that with the onset of colder weather many of these customers would be scared off if there was no heat. To make matters worse, a visit by corporate QSC inspectors resulted in the fledgling startup receiving failing grades. Much more work was clearly needed.

After testing various menu options, a decision was made to limit the number of items offered to the bare requirements of KFC. Attempts at producing quality french fries had ended in failure—adequate frying potatoes could not be found in China. Mashed potatoes and gravy were offered instead. Chicken was regular flavor only. The restaurant was decorated with two life-size statues of Colonel Sanders and posters of American cities.

Setting prices for the store was a unique challenge. With no other fast food available in the city, prices were set to meet expectations of operating efficiencies, raw material costs, and "market pressures" for restaurant meals in the city. Prices for a three-piece dinner including potatoes, gravy, and a bun were set at RMB 9.40. FEC (Chinese Foreign Exchange Certificate) prices were set at the same rates. While this seemed high compared to street food in Beijing, it was comparable with prices charged at many city restaurants. When asked about price, one teenaged customer observed: "The prices are really very good. When you consider the food as a treat, it is very affordable. Besides, where in Beijing can you find such a nice atmosphere? This is a perfect place to take a girl on a date."

After months of training and trial meals, operations had reached a point when corporate inspectors could recommend an official opening. A gala affair was planned for November 12, 1987, and included speeches by the US ambassador, the mayor, the chairman of KFC, and other dignitaries. The international and domestic news media were also invited. The opening was covered by local newspapers and the national press and was watched with great interest by tens if not hundreds of millions of Chinese.

From the outset, sales were brisk. The restaurant opened with eight cashiers on duty—seven for local RMB sales, one for FEC sales. The crowds were so large that it was not unusual for local customers to wait up to 45 minutes in line to be served during peak times. Rarely were there more than a few people in line at the FEC counter. A separate window was also opened for take-out orders. Average daily sales during the winter of 1988 were about RMB 25,000 per day, equal to about 750 chickens. However, the trend was upwards, with demand rising on many days in March to well over 1,000 chickens per day.

With sales booming, discussion among the partners centered around the feasibility of adding an additional restaurant in Beijing. Clearly, existing capacity was being overstretched. B-KFC was overwhelmed by customer interest. The operation was also generating huge cash flows. There were early predictions that the initial investment of the three partners would be repaid within the first year of operation. Also, it seemed that the city was pleased with the way the venture was being run. Even the heat had finally been turned on, indicating that patience and tenacity were qualities that eventually would pay off in China.

UNRESOLVED PROBLEMS

Still, many doubts were lingering in Tony Wang's mind and he wondered if the venture should adopt a slower approach. His first concern lay with challenges in imposing Western management practices on the employees. Even though incentive pay had played an important part in improving employee productivity, the employees still required constant supervision. According to Anthony Leung:

> *There are major differences which separate American management practices from the Chinese perspective. In America, managers try to be objective—they assess people's performance. In China, they judge employees by other criteria. What is their personality like? Are they friendly? How well can they talk? Let me give you an example. I recently asked one of our employees to mop the floor. He told me that it had just been mopped. When I pushed him on this he admitted that he really didn't know when it had been mopped. Finally, after some arguing he agreed to mop it "again." However, when I returned later I saw that the job had still not been done. Again, he used the same argument that "it was mopped earlier." What can you do?*

> *In fact, we have a very mixed group of employees here. It is a constant challenge to get employees to follow QSC procedures. Probably the biggest problem is that they feel very insulted when you try to tell them how to do a particular job. They may agree in principle, but this is seldom enough.*

The need to supervise employees placed a particular strain on local management. Most of this team had been imported on term assignment from Singapore or Hong Kong. For these managers, Beijing was regarded as somewhat of a hardship post; most were eager to leave at the earliest possible time. A serious challenge facing Tony Wang was in replacing these managers with competent and motivated KFC managers who spoke Mandarin Chinese and preferably some English. Even in Singapore and Hong Kong these people were hard to find.

Personnel problems were also having an effect on the relationship among the partners. These problems often stemmed from Chinese partners' resentment of the imposition of Western management practices. With offices located within B-KFC's Tiananmen Square store, Chun Fang Gao and Jue Xia both received salaries from the company and selected and employed their own small personal staffs. The restaurant's operations were clearly observable, as were conflicts between the KFC-appointed managers and the local employees. Not infrequently, disagreements erupted over the handling of employee disputes. Furthermore, employees had a tendency to turn to the local partners for support in dealing with the KFC-appointed managers. The frequency of disputes increased the concern among both local partners that perhaps KFC's rigid QSC expectations were unnecessary for Chinese employees or customers. In fact, the belief among employees was the sales would not suffer and morale would improve with a slackening of company standards.

From KFC's perspective, the local partners were overstepping their authority. Tony Wang viewed the primary role of the Tourist Bureau as one of facilitating a smooth relationship with the government. Yet, with operations booming, good public relations were coming more naturally, thus diminishing the importance of the partner. As for Animal Production, its responsibility was to provide a constant supply of quality chickens. However, with skyrocketing sales, Animal Production had reached its capacity and it appeared that a second supplier would be necessary. From KFC's perspective, the partners were becoming more of a bother than a necessity. This became increasingly so as they delved more and more into the day-to-day operations of the company. This perspective was echoed by Anthony Leung: "It seemed that the partners were overly enthusiastic. They wanted to get involved in everything. The KFC people were pushing very hard for them to back off."

Not surprisingly, the partners had different perspectives of their roles. Their belief was that they understood Chinese customers much better than did KFC and so they could and should participate in improving operations. From the Tourist Bureau's perspective, Gao maintained that just as their active involvement had been essential for the project to get off the ground, it would be required to ensure its smooth operation in the future. The only obstacle to expansion was KFC. The position of Animal Production was in many ways similar. According to Xia:

Case Fourteen (B)

I think that we all would agree that our biggest problem is interpersonal. Each partner controls who it will send as its representative. Just as I cannot control who KFC brings in as general manager, KFC cannot control who Animal Production brings in. With Chinese and American partners, we are bound to have conflicts. My personal belief is that profits are helping to diminish the inherent conflict between partners.

Our major concern with KFC doesn't revolve around operating matters, but around their quality standards. They only accept chickens from us that have been raised for seven weeks. Yet, far more money can be made by keeping the chickens for another week when weight gain is most rapid. But KFC refuses to go along with this. We have other places that can provide more money for our chickens than B-KFC. So we thought "this is not a really good deal for us." Yet, we are strong supporters of more rapid growth. Problems with chicken supply can be overcome. We have no problem with using outside suppliers.

Problems with employees and partners and the difficulty of finding an adequate supply of chicken raised important questions in Tony Wang's mind about the long-term desirability of operating in China through B-KFC. Clearly customer demand had been great, suggesting many opportunities outside Beijing. Indeed, letters had begun pouring in from enterprises throughout China eager to explore joint-venture opportunities. Yet, what had been learned from the B-KFC experience? Other than a greater appreciation of the difficulties of working in China, Tony Wang wasn't sure what he would do differently the next time around—if there was to be a next time.

Even though the Tiananmen Square store was generating attractive profits, it remained uncertain what the money could be used for. It appeared that hard currency generated from the operation would amount to about $50,000 per year. This was a respectable sum, but hardly seemed commensurate with the efforts put into setting up and running the venture. Hard currency profits would likely represent an even lower percentage of sales at alternate locations in the country. Expansion costs for a new store would also be high. It was estimated that KFC spent about US$250,000 in training and materials costs for the Tiananmen Square location alone. Tony Wang wondered if this one store would ever be worth it from a hard currency profit perspective. What good was soft currency to KFC, when there were ultimately few things to buy in China?

The challenge of setting up an American-style fast food restaurant in China had met phenomenal success. Tony Wang felt that he had made a significant positive impact on Chinese perceptions of Americans in general and American food in particular. He had appeared on national television and had been quoted in newspapers around China. Yet, the future remained uncertain. Clearly, much more needed to be done to improve existing operations. However, cleaning up disputes was not something that Tony Wang found personally compelling. He was beginning to wonder whether the personal challenge of China was beginning to wane. He had made perhaps too many trips to Beijing as it was. In fact, he suffered regular flare-ups of gout brought on by his constant travels. He wondered if he could assign others to do the job. Furthermore, it was uncertain what sort of time table the expansion plans should follow. To delay would result in more friction among the partners and might foreclose on future expansion possibilities. What was not clear at all was whether the time was right for expansion. Perhaps instead of placating the partners, expansion would exacerbate existing problems. Furthermore, why these partners; why not others, in other cities? Why China at all? Indeed, corporate resources might be better directed at other emerging markets throughout Southeast Asia—Thailand, Malaysia, Indonesia, and the Philippines. Time was running out for some sort of response.

CASE FIFTEEN

EXPORTING POLLUTION TO CHINA[*]

The Nantong Cellulose Fibers Company (NCFC),[1] a US/Chinese joint venture, has to decide what pollution control equipment to install in its expanding plant. NCFC has recently opened a large chemical processing plant in Nantong, China, which produces "tow"—the material from which cigarette filters are made. At the time of this case the company is planning an additional plant to make acetate flake, the major raw material for its "tow" operations.

The parents of NCFC are the US Cellulose Fibers Division of the giant Hoechst/Celanese Corporation and the China National Tobacco Corporation—which in the industry are typically called just Celanese and CNTC. Celanese has 30 per cent and CNTC has 70 per cent of the joint venture's registered capital; and NCFC's dividends are divided in that ratio.

However, regardless of the ratio of financial investment by the partners, the joint venture agreement specifies that top direction of the company shall be on a 50/50 basis. Each partner names four members of the board of directors. So, assuming that the Chinese directors vote as a block and the foreign directors do likewise, concurrence by the two parent corporations is necessary for action by the top board.

Broadly, Celanese provides the technology and specialized equipment; CNTC provides all the services (buildings, power, steam, accounting, etc.) and does the marketing which is confined to China. For the first few years Celanese nominates a US general manager; thereafter the position rotates between a Chinese and a foreigner.

Potential pollution from an operation such as NCFC's has recently taken on a world

---

[*] This case was prepared by W.H. Newman, Center for Chinese Business Studies, Graduate School of Business, Columbia University, New York (1994). For permission to publish, contact the Center for Chinese Business Studies or the author at 725 Uris Hall, Columbia University.

dimension. The issues are complex. For instance, a recent study ("American Interest in China's Environment" by the National Committee on US-China Relations) refers to global warming, ozone depletion, acid rain, resource conservation, pest control and fertilizer, biodiversity, water supply and purity, nuclear safety, and others. And the problems are worldwide; e.g., Mexico's pollution controls are a controversial issue in the North American Free Trade Agreement.

The particular questions confronting NCFC's management deal with air pollution and water pollution.

AIR POLLUTION

The Celanese directors propose the current US anti-air-pollution standards for new plants be followed in constructing NCFC's new acetate flake plant in Nantong. In addition to NCFC and its parents being recognized in China as "non-polluters," such action in China would help Celanese in its US union relations.

Celanese workers in the US local plants are fearful that the China venture will take throughput away from their plants and cut their employment. Part of this argument is that lax pollution requirements in China will lead to lower costs which, in turn, will induce Celanese to shift production from the US to China. So, Celanese wants to be in a position to assure its US workers that its pollution standards in China are just as stiff as those in the US.

On the other hand, the Chinese are unhappy with the Celanese proposal because it imposes unnecessary capital and operating costs on NCFC. In fact, the Chinese government is also deeply concerned about air pollution, and has recently issued a rather stern set of regulations focused on industrial plants. The CNTC directors point out that while the Chinese regulations are not so burdensome as those of the US, they are better suited to the situation in China; and since 70 per cent of the excess cost created by following US standards would be taken out of their dividends, they would be bearing most of the burden for a purely US matter.

In answer to this the Celanese directors say, "Yes, but from a world viewpoint, the US standards are really better and the difference in NCFC's total outlays is not great."

WATER POLLUTION

The situation with respect to water pollution is somewhat different. Chinese government regulations in Nantong are unclear, and CNTC directors agree that some controls beyond local legal requirements should be undertaken. The question is, what?

Again the Celanese directors propose adopting US standards. This involves above-the-ground treatment tanks for discharges from the flake plant, with the purified effluent going directly into the Yangtze river.

The city of Nantong and the CNTC directors point out that the entire city needs an improved treatment and drainage system. So instead of an expensive system at the flake plant alone, which would have no perceptible effect on the water in the Yangtze river, they suggest that the same amount of money be donated to the city for improving its basic system. This would have a much greater effect on discharges into the river than a system confined to the flake plant.

If the Celanese directors accept the suggestion from the city of Nantong, they will be unable to say that Celanese-US practice regarding low-polluting plants is being followed by the Nantong joint venture, i.e., "Our plants in China meet the same standards as those we build in the US."

ENDNOTE

1. For a fuller account of the Nantong Cellulose Fibers Company, refer to W.H. Newman, *Birth of a Successful Joint Venture* (Lanham, Maryland: University Press of America, 1992).

CASE SIXTEEN

EXPORTING US BUSINESS ETHICS TO CHINA*

The managers in this case face an ethical problem. Should they, as business managers, when in Rome do as the Romans do, even though such behavior at home would be considered immoral? Or more specifically here, whose ethical code should prevail in this international joint venture?

THE SETTING

The Nantong Cellulose Fibers Company, an unusually successful Chinese/US joint venture, is confronting this troublesome question. A company director commented, "Our technical problems can be solved by studying the facts, but business ethics are more subtle."

The parents of the Nantong joint venture are the US Cellulose Fibers division of the giant Hoechst/Celanese Corporation, and the China National Tobacco Corporation (CNTC). In the industry, these organizations are typically called just Celanese and CNTC. Celanese has 30 per cent and CNTC has 70 per cent of the joint venture's registered capital; and dividends are divided in that ratio. However, management is a 50-50 arrangement; Celanese and CNTC have equal representation on the board of directors—four directors each.

Broadly, Celanese provides the technology and specialized equipment; CNTC provides all the services (buildings, power, steam, accounting, etc.) and does the marketing which is

---

* This case was prepared by W.H. Newman, Center for Chinese Business Studies, Graduate School of Business, Columbia University, New York (1994). For permission to publish, contact the Center for Chinese Business Studies or the author at 725 Uris Hall, Columbia University.

confined to China. For the first few years Celanese nominates a US general manager; thereafter the position rotates between a Chinese and a foreigner.

The joint venture has recently opened a large chemical processing plant in Nantong, China to produce "tow"—the material from which cigarette filters are made. Careful and thorough planning prior to start-up enabled this venture, during its first year, to produce world quality products in excess of 100 per cent of the plant's estimated capacity. This was a remarkable achievement for the first plant of its kind in China.[1]

Regardless of current achievements, however, a joint venture such as Nantong Cellulose Fibers company may face new problems due to dynamic changes in either of its parents' situations or in its own environment.

The business ethics issue (addressed in this case) arose partly because Celanese in its domestic operations is formalizing its code of acceptable behavior. At the same time, business practice in China is adjusting to "decentralization" and a loosening of constraints on company and individual activities formerly set by the central government. Both of these developments are putting pressure on the Nantong joint venture's board of directors.

PARTICULAR ATTENTION ON BUSINESS ETHICS

In the US during the last few years an increasing number of companies have asked their employees to read and sign a printed code of business conduct. Partly due to exposures of graft and corruption by individuals in public positions, and partly due to the current resort to law suits, control of ethical behavior is becoming formalized and additional records are required.

Celanese, for example, has written out its already existing policies on a variety of issues, and printed these in a booklet that is sent to all employees each year. This Celanese "Business Conduct Policy" has sections on:

- Conflict of interest
- Environment, health and safety
- Equal opportunity
- Antitrust compliance
- Inside information
- Political contributions
- US legal controls on international commerce
- Other laws, e.g. bribery

The section on conflict of interest (which we focus on in this case) states:

> Hoechst Celanese expects all employees to give their undivided business loyalty to the company when conducting their job-related duties. A conflict of interest arises when an employee's loyalty to the company is prejudiced by actual or potential personal benefit from another source.

Each employee is expected to avoid any investment, interest or association which might interfere or seem to interfere with his or her ability to make independent judgements on the company's behalf.

Conflicts of interest generally arise in four situations.

1. *When an employee or a member of an employee's family has a significant direct or indirect financial interest in, or obligation to, an actual or potential competitor, supplier or customer of the company, or any company in which Hoechst Celanese has an ownership interest;*
2. *When an employee conducts business on behalf of Hoechst Celanese with a supplier or customer of which a relative is a principal, officer or representative;*
3. *When gifts worth more than $100 from a current or potential supplier or customer are accepted by an employee, a member of the employee's family, or any person, charity or other entity designated by the employee; or*
4. *When an employee misuses information obtained in the course of his or her employment.*

Until released to the public, material information concerning Hoechst Celanese's plans, successes or failures is considered "inside" information and, therefore, confidential. Inside information is "material" if it is important enough to affect anyone's decision to buy, sell or hold a company's securities.

For any person to use such information for personal benefit or to disclose it to others outside the company violates the company's interests. This includes not only knowledgeable directors and officers, but also non-management employees and persons outside the company (spouses, friends, brokers, etc.) who have acquired the information directly or indirectly through tips.

Bribery is the giving of money or anything else of value in an attempt to influence unlawfully the action of a public official. No employee should pay, offer or authorize any bribe or make other unlawful payment on behalf of Hoechst Celanese. This prohibition extends to payment to consultants, agents or other intermediaries when the employee has reason to believe that some part of the payment or "fee" will be used for a bribe or otherwise to influence government action.

These excerpts from Celanese seventeen-page booklet on its business conduct policy indicate the kind of behavior that senior managers are clearly barring.

In addition to the strongly worded statement, the following steps are being taken to discourage employees from tossing the booklet in a back drawer.

1. A procedure is set up for calling direct the Celanese's General Counsel for an interpretation of how the policy applies to a specific situation.
2. Every year each employee must sign a statement saying that he or she has read and understands the booklet.
3. In the signed statement the employee must affirm that he or she is not aware of any other employee who is violating the policy.

A toll-free telephone hot line is available twenty-four hours a day for employees to report, anonymously if they prefer, on dubious behavior that they may have observed.

Clearly, the senior executives at Celanese are staking their personal reputations on identifying Celanese as an ethical and responsible company.

APPLYING THE POLICY IN THE CHINESE JOINT VENTURE

The earnest righteousness of Celanese's business conduct program, while well suited to the US, does complicate the position of Celanese employees when working abroad. For example, the Celanese-appointed directors of the Nantong joint venture and the general manager—like all Celanese employees—must sign the policy statement. And this applies not only to their direct behavior but also to their knowledge of the behavior in China of all employees of the joint venture.

Aside from this legal interpretation (which could be debated), if the values and practices set forth in the business conduct booklet are sound for US operations, should they not also be applied to the operations in China? Indeed, a vital part of what Celanese is expected to contribute to the Nantong Cellulose Fibers Company is managerial as well as technological know-how.

So, prompted by their parent company program, the board members from Celanese are recommending that a similar business conduct letter, in Chinese, be sent to employees of the joint venture in Nantong. The conflict of interest provisions quoted above, among others, would apply in China as well as in the US. Note that personal conscience, continuing employment by Celanese and its affiliates, and legal liability would all be at stake.

This approach to business ethics is new for the Chinese directors. Broadly speaking, ethical conduct has long been emphasized in China under the Communist government, Honesty, equality, submergence of personal desires in favor of the common good for instance are important parts of the ideology. Daily behavior in China is noticeably more puritanical than in the US.

Also, corruption is widely viewed in China as a serious crime. One of the primary complaints of the students who protested in Tiananmen Square was the corruption that was creeping into the central government. Likewise, one of the recognized serious drawbacks of the growth of independent enterprises in China is that the independence granted to such ventures opens opportunities for corruption.

So, the idea of a code of acceptable conduct is not strange for the Chinese. While the Chinese directors do feel that the procedure specified in the Celanese booklet is legalistic and bureaucratic, they readily accept the desirability of preventing corruption.

However, one of the Chinese directors cautioned,

> Your ideas and Chinese ideas of what unethical behavior is really may differ. For instance, the Celanese statement (quoted above) about "conflict of interest" raises serious questions when we think of the Chinese cultural practice of helping one's

friends. For centuries in China helping a friend has been a virtue.... The practice is somewhat like mutual aid on the American frontier; giving and receiving assistance is considered worthy and expected.

Another Chinese director explained,

When I need raw materials or just the quick issue of a routine permit, I know I can depend on the help of a friend; with a stranger it is much more risky. Especially if the needed help is to come from an organization or maybe in another city where I don't know my way around, I naturally turn to a cousin or other friend for help. Your booklet seems to say that doing that is wrong. It says I will be a suspect if I call on my friends and relatives for help.

In fact, in China an enterprising person may build up a whole network of friendly associations. In this setting, one's friendship with people who really matter is important in getting something done. Such a person has *guanxi*. So when a Chinese reads that "all employees [should] give their undivided business loyalty to the company," they ask, how does one retain friendships which are so important in getting things done?

The directors appointed by Celanese replied, in effect,

Our experience is that only by open competition can Celanese keep its costs down and remain competitive. But quite aside from such economic theory, to hold our jobs at the company, we have to sign the business ethics code, and that code requires us to promote the 'undivided interest' in all branches of Celanese operations. We have no choice; we are required to act that way.

Said a Chinese director,

There is a different angle. Will you please explain to me how the requirement to report unethical behavior by other employees works? I think you sometimes call it "whistle-blowing." As you know, in China we believe in showing respect for other people. We are careful not to insult people or in other ways cause them to lose face. How do you raise a question about the behavior of a co-worker or manager without insulting them? If someone steals money, that is clear enough. But this "divided interest" issue is far from being clear-cut. Do you expect an employee to report, and thus insult, a coworker when the standards are fuzzy?

These comments by the Chinese directors indicate that they are reluctant to adopt the Celanese business conduct policy as completely as they adopted Celanese technology. At the same time, the US directors feel that they are expected to maintain Celanese business conduct standards throughout all of Celanese operations. The stand of each group has a deep cultural base.

ENDNOTE

1. For a full, in-depth account of the launching of Nantong Cellulose Fibers Company, see W.H. Newman, *Birth of a Successful Joint Venture*, Lanham, MD: University Press of America, 1992.

CASE SEVENTEEN

FOSTER'S BREWING GROUP LIMITED*

INTRODUCTION

What's in a name? Contrary to the belief of Shakespeare's Juliet, a great deal. At least for Foster's Brewing Group Limited ("Foster's"), which up until 1990 was known as Elders IXL Limited, and was by heritage an Australian "pastoral" (agribusiness) concern.

Agribusiness would certainly seem to be the very essence of a country of 18 million people whose area is equivalent to that of the continental US, a country which has "lived off the sheep's back," a sun-drenched land of ease where in one state oranges and wheat both grow, and which is one of the few exporters in the world of both meat and wheat.

In its 1989 Annual Report the (then) Elders IXL spoke of its 150 years of growth:

> In the Summer of 1839, Alexander Lang Elder set sail ... for the new colony of South Australia. His ship ... carried a mixed cargo of the materials required by hardy pioneers developing a farming-based economy. On arrival (he) hung up a single shingle: "A.L. Elder, General and Commission Agent".
>
> From this simple basis was built Australia's largest farm service organization, and new one of the world's foremost brewers ...
>
> Elders' objective is to create wealth for its shareholders by achieving above-average performance from its core business groups ... The corporate strategy to achieve this objective is to build the competitive position and financial management

---

* This case was prepared by Neil Holbert, then Senior Lecturer in Department of Marketing, Chinese University of Hong Kong. He is currently Assistant Professor of Marketing, The American College in London.

resources of each operating group as independent businesses (and) develop each operating group into a global business, using the Elders IXL network of offices and contacts ...

While the globalization process continued, the very nature of Elders was changing. Its chairman and chief executive back in 1989 was John Elliott. Elliott, a major figure in Australia's Liberal (conservative) Party, was a man of great ambition. Throughout the 1980s Elliott had gotten Elders into food manufacturing, oil and gas, and forestry. And as far as beer went, that 1989 Annual Report noted that the brewing group was the fourth largest brewer in the world, with its flagship Foster's Lager (marketed in 80 countries around the world), the leader in both Australia's domestic and export markets. Its other two brewing units (outside Australia) were Courage Limited (in the UK and continental Europe) and Molson (in North America). While brewing accounted for 32 per cent of Elders' assets in 1989, it accounted for 69 per cent of its operating profit before income tax.

Jumping ahead to 1993, not only (as noted) had Elders IXL Limited become Foster's Brewing Group Limited, but the company—as the name change indicates—had changed radically. Brewing now accounted for 77 per cent of assets and 162 per cent of operating profit before income tax. For total operating profit before tax was 326 million Australian dollars, vs. brewing's A$527 million. Pastoral and finance (another of Elders' historical arms) had essentially disappeared, John Elliott had left the Company in 1992 (to be replaced by Edward T. ("Ted") Kunkel, a long-time brewing executive), and investments and net interest expense showed large negatives.

Reported 1993 operating revenues after income tax of A$311 million showed a dramatic turnaround from the negative operating revenues of A$949 million the year before, which included massive provisions for losses and writedowns in asset values. It had been decided to do it then all at once, instead of waiting until a more uncertain future time.

FOSTER'S STEPS TOWARDS BECOMING A BEER COMPANY

Foster's was now a brewing company with pastoral interests (5 per cent of assets) and a financial business which the company is continuing to divest itself of and wind down. As noted in the 1993 Annual Report:

> *Apart from the brewing business the other activities currently conducted (by Foster's) are not seen as being part of (its) long-term strategy. The pastoral business, however, is being retained and operated as a growing concern until a suitable long-term ownership structure is determined. The finance division (on the other hand) has continued to be run down through further realization of assets.*

Debt was also accumulating, amounting to A$5.6 billion in 1992, with a resultant high debt/equity ratio of 4.03. Debt was down to A$3.9 million in 1993, with the debt/equity ratio down to 1.55. In the fall of 1992, A$700 million equity was raised by a rights issue to improve the company's credit rating (see Exhibits 1 to 3).

Exhibit 1 Foster's Brewing Group Limited—Consolidated Data, Fiscal Years Ending June 30

Australian $ (millions)

	1989	1990	1991	1992	1993
Total current assets	2,613	3,699	2,545	1,973	1,631
Total non-current assets	6,791	4,206	6,449	6,184	5,740
Total assets	15,284*	10,577*	8,994	8,157	7,370
Total current liabilities	2,118	2,403	2,602	3,856	1,918
Total non-current liabilities	3,880	3,295	3,878	2,914	2,966
Total liabilities	11,374*	7,936*	6,480	6,769	4,884
Shareholders' equity	3,910	2,641	2,514	1,388	2,486
Gross operating revenues	17,647	15,406	10,632	10,366	9,979
Operating profit after income tax	660	105	235	(949)	311
Current ratio	1.23:1	1.54:1	0.98:1	0.51:1	0.85:1
Debt (current)	3,328	2,773	2,162	3,440	1,491
Debt (non-current)	3,125	2,694	2,974	2,153	2,364
Debt (total)	6,453	5,473	5,136	5,593	3,855
Debt/Equity (%)	165	207	204	403	155

*Includes finance subsidiaries' assets/liabilities.
Note: Some totals may not add to sum of parts due to rounding.

Since June 30, 1993, Foster's has sold off non-core (i.e., non-brewing) assets worth A$536 million, including A$311 million in pastoral assets. These proceeds are being used to further reduce the debt. According to Ted Kunkel, "The strong cash inflows from non-core asset sales already this year (1993) augur well for our continuing debt-reduction program." Sales of non-core assets continued well into 1993, as Foster's sold another large chunk of pastoral business to ConAgra. As the *South China Morning Post* (December 3, 1993, p. B9) reported:

> Australian Treasurer John Dawkins says he will make no objections to a ConAgra Inc., plan to increase its stake in Australia Meat Holdings Pty Ltd., to 90.9 per cent from 50 per cent.
> ConAgra is buying the shares from Foster's Brewing Group Ltd., unit Elders Meat Investments Pty Ltd., in a transaction worth about A$100 million (about HK$513 million).
> Fosters said it made a profit of about A$47 million on the deal.
> Mr. Dawkins said: "In reaching this decision that the proposal was not contrary to the national interest, the Treasurer took into account the contributions ConAgra has made to date and proposes to make to Australia's meat processing industry."

Exhibit 2 Foster's Brewing Group Limited—Consolidated Basis, Fiscal Years Ending June 30 (Sectoral: By Business) (in million Australian dollars)

	Assets					Per cent				
	1989	1990	1991	1992	1993	1989	1990	1991	1992	1993
Brewing Total	4,911	4,565	5,579	6,054	5,689	32	43	62	74	77
Carlton	NA	NA	1,242	1,299	1,417	NA	NA	14	16	19
Courage	NA	NA	3,669	4,087	3,700	NA	NA	41	50	50
Molson	NA	NA	668	669	572	NA	NA	7	8	8
Pastoral	NA	NA	647	437	351	NA	NA	7	5	5
Residual finance	NA	NA	1,808	1,099	926	NA	NA	20	13	13
All others	NA	NA	960	567	404	NA	NA	11	7	5
Total	15,284	10,577	8,994	8,157	7,370	100	100	100	100	100

	Operating Profit before Income Tax					Per cent				
	1989	1990	1991	1992	1993	1989	1990	1991	1992	1993
Brewing Total	507	550	488	554	527	69	229	190	NA	162
Carlton	NA	NA	232	191	211	NA	NA	90	NA	65
Courage	NA	NA	168	244	208	NA	NA	66	NA	64
Molson	NA	NA	89	120	107	NA	NA	35	NA	33
Pastoral	NA	NA	—	—	—	NA	NA	—	—	—
Residual finance	NA	NA	—	—	—	NA	NA	—	—	—
All others	NA	NA	(232)	(1,504)	(200)	NA	NA	NA	NA	NA
Total	739	240	256	(949)	326	100	100	100	100	100

Australian investors will raise their stake to 9.1 per cent from five per cent by buying the balance of Foster's 45 per cent stake.

Australia Meat Holdings, a large beef processor and exporter, has annual sales of more than A$900 million.

In 1992, BHP, Australia's largest company (mining, etc.) acquired a 32 per cent interest in Foster's. Its future intentions are the subject of much speculation, but are as yet unknown. Not unknown, however, are the reasons why Foster's has made the transition already discussed—from a pastoral to a beer company. They were stated in the 1990 Annual Report as the company looked out and saw a different world than the world of Elders IXL in days past. That document announced a reconstruction of the company into a single-purpose international brewing company and the divestment of all non-brewing interests. The reasons given were:

- Equity markets were downgrading conglomerates.
- Single-purpose companies with lower gearing were increasingly favored by equity markets.

Exhibit 3 Foster's Brewing Group Limited—Consolidated Basis, Fiscal Years Ending June 30 (Sectoral: By Geographic Area) (in million Australian dollars)

	Assets					Per cent				
	1989	1990	1991	1992	1993	1989	1990	1991	1992	1993
Australia/Pacific/Asia	8,752	6,207	3,799	2,815	2,498	57	57	42	34	34
UK/Continental Europe	3,984	3,196	3,830	4,131	3,756	26	30	43	51	51
Canada/US	2,429	1,082	1,222	1,194	1,101	16	10	14	15	15
Total*	15,284	10,577	8,994	8,157	7,370	100	100	100	100	100

	Operating Profit before Income Tax					Per cent				
	1989	1990	1991	1992	1993	1989	1990	1991	1992	1993
Australia/Pacific/Asia	414	229	182	(623)	165	56	95	71	NA	51
UK/Continental Europe	120	50	23	(371)	47	16	21	9	NA	14
Canada/US	192	(48)	52	45	110	26	NA	20	NA	34
Total*	739	240	256	(949)	326	100	100	100	100	100

*Includes all others, not shown separately.

- The company had significantly low-yielding investments which were already affecting earnings.
- The regulatory, economic, and financial environment was not conducive to the continued operation of Elders Finance.

So beer is where Foster's is.

In 1983 Elders purchased Carlton and United Breweries (CUB) to complement Elders' own Foster's mark. All beer was consolidated in CUB. In the complex world of global markets and strategic alliances, this is what Foster's brewing interests look like at the time of the 1993 Annual Report.

THE AUSTRALIAN ARM. Carlton and United Breweries are the Australian arm of Fosters. The main brands of beer produced by these breweries are Foster's Lager and Victoria Bitter. Australia's beer market declined 3 per cent over the year, but volume and earnings for CUB, Australia's largest brewer, were up. (Wine, it should be noted, has surpassed beer as Australia's favorite beverage.) The Australia-Pacific-Asia area represented only 34 per cent of total company assets and a five-year low of 51 per cent of its operating profits before income tax. But, like much of the rest of the world, CUB was discovering China. A joint venture with

Shanghai's Huaguang Brewery was announced, for Shanghai's Pudong Development Zone. (This zone is said to be the wellspring for major Chinese industrial growth, perhaps in the next decade, perhaps later; nobody knows.) This joint venture is called Shanghai Foster's Brewing Limited, and is owned 60 per cent by CUB, and 40 per cent by Huaguang Brewery. Moreover, a second Chinese joint venture is being developed in Doumen county, just north of the Portuguese enclave of Macau (west across the South China Sea from Hong Kong), in the Zhuhai-Zhongshan Special Economic Zone. In this also, 60 per cent is owned by CUB.

SPREADING OPERATIONS IN CHINA

Foster's outlay on these two joint ventures has been A$40 million already, and will rise to A$220 million over the next four or five years. Further prospects in China are also being explored. Chinese beer consumption has been averaging growth of 17 per cent over the last six years; growth in 1992 was almost equal to the entire Australian beer market.

The allure of beer marketers for other Asian countries is quite evident.

Country	Estimated per Capita Consumption (lt.) (a)	Population (millions) (b)	Total Estimated Consumption (million liters) (a) × (b)
Australia	80	18	1,440
Japan	54	125	6,750
South Korea	35	44	1,540
Philippines	24	64	1,536
India	1	886	886
Taiwan	40	21	840
Vietnam	4	72	288
Thailand	4	59	236
Hong Kong	20	6	120
Indonesia	0.5	189	94
Malaysia	4	19	76
Singapore	22	3	66

Source: San Miguel Corporation, *Asian Business*, November 1992 (for annual per capita consumption of beer, in liters).

While the per capita consumption may be somewhat low now, populations and potentials are both impressive. For example, Lion Nathan (a New Zealand–Australia beer giant) sees its growth opportunities in Asia, and plans no further acquisitions in its home markets. In the potentially important South Korea market (see above), Lion Nathan is exploring a proposal to set up a brewery along with Coors, the American brewer. As to China, Lion Nathan's chief executive Doug Myers said that Lion Nathan had looked at South America and Eastern Europe, but has decided that its future was in Asia and Australasia. According to him:

The market potential (in China) is huge, China is estimated to be the biggest beer market in the world by 2001 so the time to move is sooner rather than later ... We are confident about moving into China. The Chinese like beer, there is no restriction on the point of sale of beer and they are also very receptive to foreign beers.

And what of Foster's in Asia? We have already cited their China joint ventures, and the balance of Asia is in focus too. Just as Lion Nathan is looking at South Korea, so Foster's is looking at *India* (among other places); India's population of 886 million—second in the world only to China's 1.2 billion—has caught the attention of many major players in all fields, and McDonald's, for example, has plans to open there, probably selling veggieburgers and lamburgers rather than hamburgers. As for *Japan*, in the web of strategic alliances around the world, it should be recalled that Japan's Asahi owns 17 per cent of Foster's. What might that mean for Foster's and for Asahi?

THE AUSTRALIA PACIFIC-ASIA-OPERATION

Foster's Australia-Pacific-Asia sphere (and the company itself) is, of course, based in Australia. Back in Australia, CUB continues to expand beyond its Victoria stronghold (and New South Wales and Western Australia) and into booming Queensland in Australia's North. The 1993 Annual Report noted the move of CUB to Yatala in Queensland, 40 kilometers south of Brisbane, where CUB's Queensland production had been. This was because Yatala is the home of Queensland Breweries Pty. Ltd., a joint venture between CUB and Power Brewery Company, but late in 1993, Power said it was pulling out of this joint venture, and indeed out of all brewing activity in Australia, because of poor sales.

As noted in the *South China Morning Post* (September 30, 1993):

Power's exit from brewery was predicted as part of a consolidation in the Australian industry. Beer sales have been flat because of the economic downturn, tighter drunk-driving laws and a switch to wine, which is cheap in Australia. "There is a lot of instability in the industry," (said) Peta Annand, a spokesman for investment bank Schroders Australia, a consultant to Power.

The 1993 Annual Report also noted:

- Another joint venture, in Hobart, Tasmania, with Cascade Brewery, Australia's oldest brewery.
- Productivity-based enterprise agreements made with a focus on expanding skills, responsibilities, and opportunities for all staff.
- New launches included Carlton Cold Filtered Bitter (a product of sub-zero cold-filtration technology); Victoria Bitter on tap; Redback Bitter (in Queensland); and Fremantle Bitter Ale (in Western Australia).

And in Australia, new advertising was being put in place.

> *Maj. Les Hiddins, the high-profile star of Australian TV's "Bush Tucker Man", about surviving in the wild, is leading an ad charge with the help of Mojo Australia. The Vietnam veteran is the focus of a campaign for Foster's Lager beer, popular internationally but sagging locally....*
>
> *Carlton & United Breweries, a subsidiary of Foster's Brewing Group, moved to Mojo (advertising agency) in August, ending 20 years with George Patterson Pty., Melbourne, which still handles Foster's sister brand Victoria Bitter.*
>
> *Foster's share has steadily dropped to 10 per cent this year from 16 per cent in 1987 in the highly competitive $3.5 billion beer market, languishing at No. 2 behind Victoria Bitter's estimated 15 per cent.*
>
> *Carlton & United Breweries will spend $4 million during the Down Under summer months to bolster Foster's, using three commercials that tell Australians, "It doesn't get any better than this." The 60-second spots, which broke December 5, were filmed as the former combat survival instructor explored and fished in the breathtaking Kimberley Ranges in the remote Northwest.*
>
> *The three-month campaign is backed by newspaper, magazine and outdoor ads, plus major merchandizing promotions.*
>
> *The Mojo team spoke with awe of the conditions during the eight-day shoot: temperatures up to 122 degrees in the shade that forced the crew to abandon work one day since the equipment was too hot to touch. Cooling off was tough, and very brief, because of crocodiles.*
>
> *Foster's and Mojo said the actor was chosen after the agency's extensive research showed his universal appeal as an "archetypal Australian" even though 80 per cent of the nation lives in urban areas (Advertising Age, December 13, 1993, p. 14).*

FOSTER IN THE UK AND CONTINENTAL EUROPE

Foster's arm in the UK and Continental Europe, where Foster's has been since 1986 and which merged with Grand Metropolitan in 1991, is Courage. The UK beer market—in which Courage is number two—continued to decline (down 3.3 per cent, while Courage was down 3.7 per cent), due to poor economic conditions and high unemployment. Another problem in that market was the requirement of freeing pubs from ties: Courage freed 1,900 pubs, but 80% of the business was retained.

In the fast-growing premium packaged lager segment, Courage line extensions included flagship Foster's Lager Export Strength in a distinctive bottle, Holsten Bier, and Asahi Super Dry. In Continental Europe, Courage volume was up 12 per cent for the year. Growth was registered across all markets, in both distribution and consumer appeal. The Foster's label did well in Germany, where it is brewed under license by Holsten. It was launched in Finland, Denmark, Holland, Hungary, and Russia.

FOSTERS IN CANADA AND THE US

The third Foster's arm is *Molson Breweries,* in Canada and the US. Molson retained its position as Canada's leading brewer, and also formed a strategic alliance with the Miller Brewery Company. Miller is the number two beer in America, and is a unit of Philip Morris, whose worldwide sales (cigarettes, beer, food, etc.) amount to some US$50 billion vs. Foster's total of about US$6.6 billion. (Molson also handles US' Coors Light.)

Similar to the UK story, beer sales in Canada continued to decline due to economic conditions and high unemployment. Molson's sales were down 6 per cent as compared with the market drop of 3 per cent.

The big product story was Molson Canadian Ice, whose technology as already mentioned is similar to that of Carlton Cold Filtered Bitter in Australia. It surpassed all other beer introductions in Canadian history, and it is planned to export it to the US.

Reflecting the worldwide imperative for cost reduction, Molson sought savings from conversion to a common bottle and a strategic packaging line reconfiguration. In the US, Molson and Foster's continued to be strong in the imported beer segment, and, as stated above, in a further strategic alliance with Miller (see above), Molson USA became a wholly owned subsidiary of Miller.

Foster's has worked hard to promote its name and image in the US, not least by utilizing spokesman Paul Hogan, a "fair dinkum" Aussie who spearheaded Winfield cigarettes to a leadership position with his famous "Any'ow 'av a Winfield 25's." In America, Hogan became legendary as "Crocodile Dundee," and for his Australian tourism line: "Throw another shrimp on the barbie." For Foster's it was: "Foster's is Australian ('A-stry-lyan') for beer, mate ('myte')."

Foster's: Australian—and yet global.

With the tumultuous business of moving from a pastoral company to a beer company largely behind it, and with the tumultuousness of the personality clashes between major stockholders extending to buying of each other's shares and related legal assets in the late 1980s also behind it, what lies ahead for Foster's?

FUTURE CHALLENGES

In the beer business as a major player, it faces a world of major players, some of whom, as noted above, it has made strategic alliances with. But with its (at least) eleven brand names (headed by Molson, Foster's, and Victoria Bitter) in three major areas, it still faces stern competitors. These include such names as the US' Anheuser-Busch (Budweiser), Germany's Lowenbrau, Holland's Heineken, and the Philippines' San Miguel, to name just a few—all global players too.

As a company, Foster's not only understands the need for a global spirit combined with local involvement, and the avoidance of the "imperial country" syndrome, whereby Australia seeks to call the tune everywhere. Indeed, it understands that it must be a multilocal company too: in the words of its 1992 Annual Report, "business does not operate in a vacuum, but is a vital and integral part of the community." In this spirit, it gets involved with educational, health, arts, and other causes in many of its markets.

As a global company too, it has, as noted, formed strategic alliances with major players in many places. These will work only when the strategic aims of the allies not only jell together now, but up ahead too, and where the future is permanently seen as unfolding rather than fixed. Globalization of technologies, such as in the cold-brew process for Carlton Cold Filter Bitter and for Molson Canadian Ice, is also part of the process of being a successful world-girdler, and future opportunities will surely be watched for.

Most of all, what of its position as the (essentially) one-product company that Foster's has become? What if the total market for beer around the world continues to erode? Can Asia "save" it? Having become a one-product company should it seek re-diversification, and, if so, into what? What if still more problems here and there continue to becloud the industry: World differences in taste perception, drinking-age issues, narrowing of promotion possibilities, etc.?

CONCLUSION

Finally, Asia again.

Will this Australian company, whose citizens and government still seem to have ambivalent attitudes towards Asia and Asians, be able to make its presence felt in Asia in constructive and profitable ways? Will the Australian breeziness and cheekiness about "face" (as in the Australian Prime Minister's calling the Malaysian Prime Minister "recalcitrant" for not attending a big international meeting and the latter threatening to break ties for the perceived gratuitous insult) be restraints to growth in an Asia where face and form still matter mightily? Will it remember the warning of Australian Sir Roderick Carnegie in the 1980s that Australia had better look out and look up, or else it could become the poor white trash of Asia?

Foster's has been dramatically restructuring itself, and so it is fully accustomed to change, but how will it fare as we move towards the Pacific Century; will its "Pacific" orientation by geography be a positive factor in a race which, for everybody, far transcends anybody's home base?

CASE EIGHTEEN

THE CHINA STRATEGY: A TALE OF TWO FIRMS*

Political patronage created the Taibao venture; but not only was it unable to ensure the ultimate success of the project, it appears to have contributed significantly to its failure. Our guanxi *with the central leadership in China didn't automatically lead to cooperation at the local level and we paid heavy prices for that.*
          —*Ray Schon, Chairman, Western Energy, Inc.*

The heart of our success lies at our willingness to work with local suppliers, ensure quality standards, and support a nationwide dealer network in China.
  — *John White, Vice President, International Operations, American Copier Co.*

"I am very sorry to hear about the tragedy of Mr. Arnold Tanner. We have been friends for years." In September 1990 on a plane to China, John White, vice president of international operations of American Copier Co. (ACC), happened to sit next to Ray Schon, chairman of Western Energy, Inc. (WEI), and they compared notes on their firms' experiences in China.

White was a good friend of Arnold Tanner, then chairman of WEI, who suddenly passed away at the age of 85. Schon was Tanner's successor. One of his first priorities was to terminate a deal—the Taibao coal mine—that Tanner struck with the Chinese. The $700 million joint venture was plagued by a host of problems almost from the time the contract was signed in 1982. But the personal commitment of Tanner and China's supreme leader

---

* This case was prepared by Mike W. Peng of the University of Washington as a basis for class discussion rather than to illustrate either effective or ineffective management practice. Copyright © 1994 by Mike W. Peng. First published in C. Hill and G. Jones, *Strategic Management: An integrated approach,* 3rd ed., Boston, MA: Houghton Mifflin, 1995.

Deng Xiaoping, which elevated the venture into a symbol of China's "open door" policy, kept the project going while Tanner was still alive. Schon clearly lacked this political commitment and intended to withdraw from this unprofitable deal as part of the new restructuring program at WEL.

White was surprized to hear Schon talk about WEI's intended withdrawal from China. He himself was flying to China to visit with ACC Shanghai, to celebrate its third anniversary and to review ACC's China strategy with the joint venture's resident managers. Formed in late 1987, the $30 million ACC Shanghai joint venture already was number one in China's expanding copier market and planned to capture an even greater market share. Recalling his first trip to China in 1983, which was encouraged by his friend Tanner, White began to think why ACC successfully stayed in China while WEI had to pull out.

ARNOLD TANNER, WESTERN ENERGY, INC., AND CHINA

BACKGROUND

Primarily an oil company, Western Energy, Inc., conducted business in more than 100 countries and employed more than 78,000 people worldwide. With annual sales of around $10 billion in the 1980s and the early 1990s WEI was among the top ten major energy firms in the United States. WEI consisted of one of the world's largest petroleum (oil and gas) operations, a growing chemical business, a coal exploration business, and a nationwide retailing operation in the United States. Its strategy emphasized foreign production, and the firm had production facilities in Argentina, Bolivia, Canada, Ecuador, Malaysia, Pakistan, the Philippines, Syria, and the UK, North Sea as well as the United States when it entered China in 1980. (See Table 1 for a five-year summary of selected financial data for WEI.)

From 1962 to 1990, Arnold Tanner was first the CEO and then chairman of the San

Table 1 Western Energy Inc., Five-Year Summary of Selected Financial Data

	1991	1990	1989	1988	1987
Operations ($, millions)					
Revenues	10,096	11,509	10,939	10,351	9,415
Operational income (loss)	379	(1,715)	247	295	102
Net income (loss)	460	(1,697)	293	316	220
Financial Position ($, millions)					
Total assets	16,115	18,619	19,557	19,533	16,861
Total debt	5,546	7,425	7,738	7,227	5,925
Stockholders' equity	4,340	4,114	5,901	6,218	5,144
Per Share Data					
Earnings (loss) per share from operations ($)	1.25	(5.89)	0.89	1.19	0.39
Earnings (loss) per share ($)	1.52	(5.82)	1.06	1.27	0.96

Francisco-based firm. Before becoming the CEO in 1962, he worked for WEI for 25 years in various capacities. His long years of service at WEI and his leadership role made an enormous impact on WEI. Tanner was well respected as a dynamic and charismatic leader in the industry. Moreover, Tanner's foresight on business opportunities led his firm actively to seek opportunities in the Eastern Bloc. His legendary achievements included striking one of the first deals between a Western businessman and the Soviets in the 1930s, supplying the Soviets during World War II, and trading with Eastern Europe since the détente in the 1970s. As a result, his name was well recognized in many quarters of the Eastern Bloc. When China started its open door policy in 1979, China's political leaders naturally looked to Tanner for his initiatives.

Tanner responded to the Chinese inquiry with enthusiasm. His first visit to China was in 1979 and he later became a frequent flyer to Beijing. As always, he took a high-profile approach and befriended China's supreme leader Deng Xiaoping. In the early 1980s China desperately needed to prove to a suspicious West that its open door policy was credible and that direct investment from abroad was genuinely welcome. Well respected both in the West and in the Eastern Bloc, Tanner became an ideal candidate to bridge the gap between China and the outside world. Of course, Tanner did not respond to the Chinese interest with goodwill only. Earnings of WEI were flat in the late 1970s and Tanner was exploring new avenues in foreign exploration and production for growth of sales and earnings. Tanner sensed that if WEI penetrated China early, it might be able to capitalize on some first mover advantages[1] like preempting rival Western firms in the acquisition of China's energy resources.

In short, China's new open door policy, its drive for modernization, Tanner's long-time interest in doing business with the Eastern Bloc, and WEI's desire to expand its global operations into a new market made WEI a pioneering American firm in entering China.

POLITICS AND THE TAIBAO COAL MINE

Since the initiation of the open door policy in the late 1970s, developing the energy sector to support industrial development has become a priority goal of the Chinese government. Among various energy resources, coal is the most important to China as three-quarters of the country's energy demand is met by coal. China's proven coal reserves exceed 900 billion tons, behind only the Soviet Union and the United States. Total estimated reserves, however, are in the neighborhood of 2 trillion tons; at current production levels it would take 2,000 years to exhaust the total supply.[2]

Despite the abundance of coal supply, the lack of capital and technology to effectively exploit the coal in sufficient amount to meet energy needs led to a national crisis in the 1980s. In many parts of China, factories had to shut down for one or two days a month due to energy shortages; at one time Shanghai had only two days' worth of coal reserves on hand for power generation. It is evident that without the development of its energy sector, China's goal of modernization will not be realized. Therefore, seeking foreign partners to help develop China's energy resources became an important part of its policy.

In 1980 China opened its premier coal mine—the Taibao coal mine in Shanxi Province of northern China—to international bidding and sought a foreign partner. One of the largest open-pit coal mines in the world, the Taibao mine became the largest energy project in

China ever opened to foreign firms at that time. Eight Western firms participated in the bidding, including three from the United States, two from Germany, and one each from France, Japan, and the United Kingdom. Not surprisingly, Tanner's WEI beat all the competitors.

Politics was instrumental in this process and China's central leadership was heavily involved in this "pet project." Politically, China preferred having a major US company as its partner as an unambiguous signal to American investors that the open door policy was for real. Unlike European and Japanese companies which had been doing business with China for years, the United States had virtually no business with China until 1979, when the two countries normalized their diplomatic relations. Decades of hostility between the two countries made American investors especially suspicious at that time. However, China sensed that the United States possessed more advanced technologies and more abundant capital and that courting American investment would be of strategic importance to its policy.[3] Among the three American firms that entered the bidding, WEI was better respected and financially stronger. Moreover, Tanner's assiduous cultivation of developing *guanxi* (connections)* with Chinese leaders, especially Deng Xiaoping, and previous contacts throughout the Eastern Bloc played an important role in China's selection of WEI as its sole foreign partner.

THE ECONOMICS OF THE TAIBAO JOINT VENTURE

Upon winning the bid, Western Energy, Inc., became the foreign partner in this 50–50 equity joint venture, which was incorporated as the Taibao Mine Group in China in 1982** A 30-year, renewable joint-venture contract was signed. The Chinese partners included a consortium of Chinese organizations led by China National Coal Corp., the country's leading coal producer. The venture called for $700 million in capital endowment, with each side contributing $200 million and the remaining $300 million syndicated by 39 international banks (see Table 2). At full capacity, the mine should produce 12 million tons a year and employ 3,000 workers, 20–30 of whom would be WEI expatriates.

Table 2 Equity Participation and Financing of Taibao Mine Venture

United States (10 per cent share)	China (50 per cent share)
Western Energy, Inc. (responsible for $200 million initial capital)	China National Coal Corp. China Coal Import/Export Corp. China International Trust & Investment Corp. Province of Shanxi (Chinese partners responsible for $200 million of initial capital)
$300 million loan syndicated by 39 international banks (each side guarantees 50 per cent of the loan)	

---

* See Appendix 2 for a description of *guanxi* in China.
** See Appendix 1 at the end of this case for a summary of China's joint venture law.

In the initial courtship during 1980–1982, WEI responded to Chinese interest with a number of extravagant promises, ranging from the scale of the mine to Chinese workers' salaries to the amount of coal it could export. It agreed to export 75 per cent of total output and to assume complete responsibilities of marketing the coal in the export market. Noted for their preference for "general principles" in the negotiations, the Chinese were serious about those promises and treated them as a foundation upon which details could be worked out later with WEI.

However, by the time the joint venture contract was signed and the feasibility study began, the economics of the project were already shaky in the light of falling world coal prices. WEI was forced to hedge its earlier promises and began to pressure the Chinese side to grant it various concessions. For instance, WEI tried to make China Coal Import/Export Corp., one of the Chinese partners, buy WEI's share of the export coal at prevailing international prices, thus completely retreating from its earlier promise to sell the coal itself in the international market. The Chinese negotiators were surprised, and intense arguments between the two sides ensued. On several occasions during the negotiations, disputes at the working level came close to derailing the project. But Tanner and the Chinese political leadership always intervened to enforce a solution. Numerous public ceremonies throughout the negotiation phase bound the prestige of Tanner and the Chinese leadership even more tightly to the consummation of the project. Eventually, WEI won several concessions from the Chinese side in 1985, including shifting the responsibilities of export marketing to China Coal Import/Export Corp.

OPERATIONAL PROBLEMS: CENTRAL VS. LOCAL *GUANXI*

The operational phase of the Taibao venture since 1986 proved to be even more problematic than the negotiation phase. Although getting the mine up and running was undeniably a major achievement, the project, as of September 1990, still was not certified as "complete," despite having been operational for four years. In 1990, its best year in terms of production, it produced only three-quarters of its 12-million-ton capacity and suffered a $31 million loss. Exports were probably less than half of the 8–9 million tons WEI had originally anticipated.

Four sources of problems contributed to the venture's lackluster performance. First, continuing low world coal prices prevented the venture from earning the foreign exchange necessary to break even. Second, lower-than-expected coal quality, with high sulphur content in one seam and high ash content in another, further depressed the marketability of the coal produced at Taibao. Technical problems like defective equipment and the workers' lack of training were the third source of problems. The largest source of problems came from the lack of cooperation between WEI and its local partners, despite its influential *guanxi* with the central leadership.

Tanner was very skillful in cultivating *guanxi* with the central leadership in Beijing and was able to use his central *guanxi* influence to make his Chinese partners grant him concessions. However, WEI failed to develop close *guanxi* relations with local partners, which caused many problems. Many WEI managers reported that disputes over production and marketing strategies were common among partners. For instance, the Americans wanted to decrease the production of high sulphur coal, which could be sold only on the domestic market for local currency, and to increase the production of low-sulphur coal for the export market. The Chinese insisted that due to the depressed export market, producing a large amount of low-sulphur coal would result in large inventories, thus further worsening the venture's already bad cash flow situation.

Instead of working together, both sides seemed to develop an appetite for blaming the other for whatever problems occurred. On another occasion, WEI accused the China Coal Import/Export Corp. of failing to market the coal aggressively in the export market. In response, the Chinese managers pointed out the insincerity on WEI's part by retreating from its earlier promises and relinquishing the entire responsibility of international marketing. Due to political pressure from China's central leadership, China Coal Import/Export Corp. reluctantly assumed the exporting functions for the Taibao venture in 1985. Now a depressed world market and the less-than-expected coal quality gave the reluctant Chinese partner an excuse for not living up to its promises. Many WEI officials believed that their Chinese partners deliberately exacerbated these problems in spite of the political pressures that forced them to make concessions to WEI in the first place.

STILL MORE POLITICS

In June 1989 the Tiananmen incident in Beijing shocked the world. Foreign businesspeople were pulling out of China immediately following the incident, and international investors led by the World Bank became hesitant to commit further funds to China. The Chinese leadership desperately needed to prove to the world that despite all the tragedies, China's ten-year-old open door policy would continue. As the government's credibility declined to a record low, it needed a live example to convince the West it was sincere about its policy. Once again, the Taibao venture played into the hands of the Chinese leadership. In spite of internal disagreement at WEI, in late 1989 Arnold Tanner went back to China in a "business as usual" fashion to meet with the Chinese leaders, who promptly used this visit by an "old friend" as a photo opportunity to appease the West.

Inside WEI, as the company's financial situation worsened in the late 1980s with increasing debts, discussions of withdrawing from the Taibao venture became more frequent and intense. In a manner similar to the way Deng Xiaoping ruled China, Tanner dismissed such ideas and urged for a "long-term" perspective. The Chinese leadership, on the other hand, had the strong desire to save its political face and to avoid the failure of a flagship project. Therefore, despite huge financial losses which depleted WEI's cash flow, the Taibao venture continued until Tanner's sudden death in August 1990.

EXIT?

Within weeks of becoming WEI's new chairman, Ray Schon reassessed the company's overall strategic position and concluded that "the business climate of the 1990s is vastly different from that of the 1980s." To him, the 1990s seemed to be defined by lack of liquidity in financial markets, recessionary pressure on global economies, increasing volatility in energy prices, and chronic instability in world markets. The year 1990 left the company with a net loss of $1.7 billion (see Table 1). In response, Schon started a major restructuring and divestiture program aimed at "building on proven strengths and having the operational and financial flexibility to responded in a timely manner to unpredictable markets." Specifically, this program would sell off unprofitable lines of business to reduce debt, which stood at $74 billion in 1990, and would focus WEI's resources on those businesses in which it already excelled—oil, natural gas, and chemicals.

The changes in corporate strategy decided the fate of the Taibao venture. In his announcement to start the restructuring program, Schon publicly announced his intention to withdraw WEI from the unprofitable project, which was Tanner's favorite project but never part of WEI's core business. To do that, WEI would have to write off $200 million in unprofitable investment but would be relieved of $150 million in loan guarantees. WEI would have two options: to sell its share to its Chinese partners or to sell to another foreign investor. One way or the other, Ray Schon understood that his trip to China would be a stormy one

Schon told White on the plane:

> *Political patronage created the Taibao, but not only was it unable to ensure the ultimate success of the project, it appears to have contributed significantly to its failure. Contrary to our expectations, our guanxi connections with the central leadership didn't automatically lead to cooperation at the local level and we paid heavy prices for that. The business in the 1990s simply won't be the same as when Tanner was around; we can no longer afford to support such an unprofitable business.*

AMERICAN COPIER CO. IN SHANGHAI

Unlike Western Energy, Inc.'s approach in China, characterized by early entry, high profile, and central *guanxi*-developing, American Copier Co.'s (ACC) China strategy was markedly different: it was cautious, low profile, and aimed at building cooperative relations with local partners. It took about four years (1983–1987) of long negotiations for ACC to set up its Shanghai joint venture, but the project was apparently worth waiting for. For ACC, China proved a good choice, offering both low-cost design and labor and a growing market for copier machines and products. Formed in late 1987, the $30 million ACC Shanghai became Number One in China's growing copier market by 1989 and planned to capture an even greater market share.

CHOOSING JOINT VENTURING IN SHANGHAI

With annual sales in the neighborhood of $10 billion throughout the 1980s, ACC is a global company serving the worldwide document processing markets. (See Table 3 for a five-year summary of ACC's selected financial data.) Its activities encompassed developing, manufacturing, marketing, servicing, and financing a wide range of document processing product and service offerings. Its copiers, duplicators, production publishers, electronic printers, facsimile products, scanners, and computer products were marketed in over 130 countries. In addition to a worldwide network of dealers and distributors, ACC

Table 3 American Copier Company, Five-Year Summary of Selected Financial Data

	1991	1990	1989	1988	1987
Operations ($, millions)					
Revenues	12,869	12,692	11,720	11,152	10,438
Operational income	454	605	653	347	542
Net income	454	243	704	388	578
Financial Position ($, millions)					
Total assets	31,658	31,635	30,088	26,441	22,450
Total debt	9,886	10,579	10,754	7,874	5,722
Stockholders' equity	5,140	5,051	5,035	5,371	5,105
Per Share Data					
Earnings per share from operations ($)	3.91	5.51	6.05	3.09	4.94
Earning per share ($)	3.91	1.66	6.56	3.49	5.30

maintained research and development (R&D) facilities in Canada, Great Britain, Japan, and the United States. Moreover, before joint venturing with the Chinese, ACC already had substantial experience from its joint venture operations in Australia, Brazil, Germany, Great Britain, India, and Japan.

When ACC entered China in the early 1980s through exporting, the copier market in China was dominated by Japanese makers, including Canon, Minolta, Ricoh, and Toshiba. Many of these companies had a longer history of serving the China market, but ACC was the only copier producer thus far to establish a joint venture in the country. Though it would take ACC significantly longer than its competitors (some of which signed technology transfer agreements with Chinese firms) to show a return on its $15 million investment, the company's dominant position in a restricted-size market undoubtedly reflected greater official support for the joint venture than for its competitors.

ACC's initial exports to China in the early 1980s were considered moderately successful. In order to capture a larger share of the growing market, ACC initially considered a technology transfer agreement in 1983. But it soon decided to pursue a joint venture instead due to considerations of China's underdeveloped intellectual property protection regime. Numerous sites were considered for the venture, and all the local authorities that learned of ACC's interest courted ACC for its investments. ACC avoided being too involved with local Chinese politics and did not provide vague promises or agree on "general principles" which the Chinese wanted to hear. Eventually, ACC settled on Shanghai due to the large concentration of components suppliers and the number of skilled labor in the area.

The capital constitution of the Shanghai venture is shown in Table 4.

ACC's Shanghai venture partners included Bank of China, which held 5 per cent of the venture and provided for $10 million of investment, and the Shanghai Photo Industry Co., which held 44 per cent of the share and contributed existing plants, equipment, and some personnel assessed at $5 million. ACC held the remaining 51 per cent of the venture and invested $15 million (see Table 4). Signed in 1987, ACC Shanghai has a 30-year, renewable joint venture contract and a 10-year renewable technology license for production of desktop

Table 4 Equity Participation and Financing of Shanghai Venture

United States (51 per cent share)	China (49 per cent share)
American Copier Co. (responsible for $15 million initial investment)	Shanghai Photo Industry Co. (holding 44 per cent share and contributing plants and labor, assessed at $5 million) Bank of China (holding 5 per cent share and responsible for $10 million investment)

copiers and accessories and other copier products. The license gave ACC Shanghai the right to use ACC's desktop office copier technology. ACC Shanghai was designed to produce low-end and mid-range copiers suitable for the China market and was capable of switching to produce more advanced designs. At full capacity, which should be reached in 1994, ACC Shanghai will be capable of producing 40,000 units anually and will employ 900 workers. In September 1990 ACC Shanghai employed more than 600 people, six of whom were expatriates.

LOCALIZING PRODUCTION

Despite the Chinese preference for having a high percentage of the venture's output exported, the ACC negotiation team, led by John White, managed to persuade the Chinese that the models ACC would introduce to China would be mid-range to low-end ones suitable for China and the focus should be on the domestic market. In return, ACC accepted a stipulation insisted on by the Chinese that 70 per cent of the venture's components would be sourced locally by the end of 1992. To date, ACC managers claim that the ventures is on track to achive this goal, though the process is difficult since none of the local suppliers initially had the technical expertise or equipment necessary to produce the quality components needed by ACC Shanghai.

To overcome these obstacles, ACC heavily engaged in "vendor development" in the United States. ACC, through its Shanghai venture, either transferred technology or provided technical support to approximately 60 suppliers, mostly in Shanghai. Aside from training the suppliers on how to use the technology or equipment transferred, ACC coached them in materials management and handling, as well as in accounting. Moreover, ACC Shanghai developed close working relations with the Shanghai Foreign Investment Commission, which provided funding to local companies to enable them to upgrade their plants and purchase the new technology.

ACC estimated that it spent several million dollars in training, support, and monitoring of Chinese suppliers to ensure consistent quality and delivery. Some of these development costs were charged to the suppliers, and the rest was absorbed by ACC Shanghai. While the training did pay off in improved quality of local supplied components over the past few years, Chinese components still tended to be produced at above world market prices, thus forcing up the final cost of ACC Shanghai copiers. By company estimates, locally sourced components cost an average 10–20 per cent more than imported ones.

Ensuring Quality

ACC was renowned throughout the world for its quality products. All components used by ACC Shanghai were subject to quality standards established by ACC. The parent company also instituted its corporate quality control culture in the venture to ensure that ACC Shanghai's output was on par with ACC products manufactured in other countries. ACC attempted to reinforce the concept of quality at all levels, not just in interaction with the end user. The company's LUTI system—learn, use, teach, and inspect—was ongoing, with each management level teaching it to the level below, as well as to new employees.

A Customer Satisfaction Review Board, which met on a monthly basis, was established by ACC Shanghai to ensure the reputation of its products. The board, composed of representatives from the venture's marketing, service, distribution, management, engineering, and quality control departments, examined complaints and conducted customer surveys to determine where improvement was needed. The results from the first survey, conducted in 1989, one year after the first copier rolled off the production line, indicated 90 per cent customer satisfaction with the venture's products. Further proof of ACC Shanghai's success in attaining high quality came from the Shanghai municipal government, which awarded the venture the Shanghai Quality Award in 1989 and 1990, and from the parent company, which awarded the venture an in-house quality award in 1990.

Capturing the Market

The first ACC Shanghai 2020 copier was produced in October 1988, little more than a year after the joint-venture contract was signed. A mid-range model, the 2020 did not incorporate the latest technology, but its reliable, sturdy operation was very suitable for China.

In order to meet demand outside the Shanghai area, ACC Shanghai—with help from its partner Shanghai Photo Industry Co.—established a nationwide distribution, sales, and service network in China. The network included over 100 dealers throughout China, all of whom were trained by ACC Shanghai. Three ACC representative offices—in Beijing, Guangzhou, and Shanghai—provided additional dealer support in such areas as training, inventory, and advertising.

In 1987, a vigorous advertising campaign was launched through television and newspaper media in China to increase the publicity of ACC Shanghai. Competing against Japanese brands like Canon, Minolta, Ricoh, and Toshiba, ACC Shanghai skillfully named its products "Shang Am" ("Hu Mei" in Mandarin Chinese pronunciation), which stands for "Shanghai Beauty."* American name brands usually carry a premium among Chinese customers, and products from Shanghai are renowned for their high quality in China. Thus the eye-catching name "Shanghai Beauty," which highlighted the combination of American technology and Shanghai production, created an attractive and trustworthy image among Chinese users. Moreover, despite the high components costs, ACC Shanghai competitively priced its copiers to be within the range of Japanese offerings.

---

* "America" ("Mei Guo"), when pronounced in Mandarin Chinese, China's official language, stands for "beautiful country."

Vigorous quality standards, extensive dealer networks, and an aggressive and skillfully executed advertising campaign coupled with reasonable prices led ACC Shanghai to become the number one copier seller in China. In 1989, ACC Shanghai gained 32 per cent of the Chinese desktop copier market which went up to about 45 per cent by late 1990.

PROBLEMS

As expected, the China market was full of problems, some of which were anticipated and some which were not. The original feasibility study proved to be overly optimistic in its assumptions of production costs and size of the copier market in China. "These miscalculations were perhaps unavoidable," John White said to a frustrated Schon on the plane, "given the unforeseen nature of some of the factors that have affected ACC Shanghai's performance."

Besides high costs of locally sourced components produced in China, the devaluation of the Chinese yuan against the US dollar in the mid-1980s resulted in higher costs of imported components. Perhaps more important, the introduction of government purchase controls as part of the government's austerity policy begun in 1988 led to a far smaller market than ACC had originally envisioned. In order to purchase a copier, a prospective buyer first had to obtain permission from several government agencies. This market-restricting policy was further strengthened in the post-Tiananmen implementation of the government's austerity program. This system seriously inhibited market forces; ACC estimated the real market in China to be five times its present size.

Despite the government's austerity program, the general open door policy was to continue, and the policy to support joint venture companies was unchanged. In this difficult situation, ACC's joint venture strategy paid off since government agencies were more likely to approve the purchase of a domestically produced, reasonably priced copier like *Shang Am* than to buy an imported model, even when the two models were of the same performance and price. Thus ACC Shanghai was able to receive greater official support though it did not deliberately cultivate *guanxi* with the government.

Problems unrelated to the macroeconomic environment also confronted ACC Shanghai. For instance, the paper feeders initially produced by the venture malfunctioned due to the poor quality of Chinese paper. The feeders were redesigned by ACC Shanghai to handle the low-grade paper used in most Chinese offices and were reportedly functioning well.

FUTURE PROSPECTS

In September 1990 ACC Shanghai was approaching its third year of operations and John White was going to review the parent company's China strategy with the joint venture's resident managers. He envisioned that in the immediate future, ACC Shanghai would focus on designing two new products—a low-end model for developing segments in the China market and a more sophisticated, high-end model for the upper-stream segments. ACC Shanghai engineers initially worked in conjunction with ACC corporate engineers to develop the prototypes for the two models, but total design responsibility was recently turned over to ACC Shanghai. The first model of the low-end copier, which was expected to become a major product line in China, was scheduled to enter the China market in 1992. According to a similar plan, small volumes of the high-end model would hit the market in 1993.

Looking several years ahead, with the existing 2020 mid-range model, ACC Shanghai will have three models each concentrating on the low-end, mid-range, and high-end segments of the China market. Whether other new product lines will be manufactured by ACC Shanghai is undetermined as of now. White explains:

> *My inclination is to continue the three-model operations with ACC Shanghai for a few more years. We have built up a vendor base there and have spent a long time training people in quality control and other areas. But starting a new product line is very taxing—I wouldn't let our joint ventures in India and Brazil, for example, even contemplate it. While there are advantages to keep everything in one organization, it could be too much for a young venture like the one we have in Shanghai. I want to make sure that ACC Shanghai continues to operate on a sound financial footing. This venture is already ahead of where our first venture in Japan was at the equivalent time. Eventually, I'd like to see it become like ACC Japan or ACC UK, a stand-alone operation with its own product lines.*

White noted that whether ACC Shanghai could meet such lofty aspirations would depend on two factors. First, the market would have to expand, which would require the abolition or liberalization of the government purchase-control system. However, the Chinese government did not seem to be willing to liberalize its stringent purchase-control policy, and ACC found it had little influence on the government. To expand customer bases (and to project a good corporate image), ACC Shanghai recently started a school program to give selected high schools in China a gift package consisting of copiers and accessories. Second, costs would have to come down, which would require further improvements in the local supplier network. Given existing good *guanxi* with the local suppliers built up on years of cooperative working relations, ACC Shanghai felt confident it could overcome the components cost problems and could bring the cost of locally sourced components at par with international levels in a few years.

EPILOGUE

As the plane landed in Shanghai, John White shook hands with Ray Schon, wished Schon "good luck," and then stepped out of the plane. Though the future was still daunting, he was delighted with ACC Shanghai's past three years and had strong hope that the Shanghai venture would turn out to be a successful one for his company.

After a two-hour stop, the plane continued its journey to Beijing. Schon, already exhausted, decided not to stop in Beijing to meet Tanner's "old friends" in the Chinese leadership; instead, he made up his mind to go directly to Shanxi to terminate the Taibao venture as soon as possible.

Appendix 1

Summary of the Law of the People's Republic of China on Joint Ventures Using Chinese and Foreign Investment (Adopted in 1979 at the Second Session of the Fifth National People's Congress)

1. Foreign companies and individuals within the territory of the People's Republic of China (PRC) may incorporate themselves into joint ventures with Chinese companies or other Chinese entities with the objective of expanding international economic cooperation and technology exchange.
2. The Foreign Investment Commission must authorize joint ventures, and if approved, ventures are required to register with the General Administration for Industry and Commerce of the PRC, which will then issue a license within three months.
3. Joint ventures shall have limited liability and the foreign parties will contribute not less than 25 per cent of the registered capital.
4. The participants will share profits, risks, and losses of the joint venture in proportion to their capital contributions.
5. The equity of each party may be capital goods, industrial property rights, cash, and so on, in the ventures.
6. The contributors of technology or equipment run the risk of forfeiture or damages if the technology or equipment contributed is not truly advanced and appropriate for Chinese needs. If losses are caused by deception through the intentional provision of outdated equipment or technology, compensation must be paid for the losses.
7. Investments by the Chinese participants may include the right of use of a site but it shall not constitute a part of the investment as the joint venture shall pay the Chinese government for its use.
8. A joint venture will have a board of directors and the chairman of the board is to be appointed by the Chinese participants. The foreign parties may appoint two vice presidents. They do not necessarily have to be Chinese but must be approved by the partners of the joint venture.
9. A joint venture agreement must stipulate procedures for the employment and discharge of the workers and staff members and comply with Chinese laws.
10. The net profit of a joint venture shall be distributed in proportion to the parties' respective investment shares after deductions for reserve funds. Bonuses and welfare funds for the workers, the expansion funds of the venture, and the profits or losses shall be in accordance

with the capital investment of the parties involved and be subject to the tax laws of PRC and expatriation.
11. Joint ventures must maintain open accounts in a bank approved by the Bank of China.
12. All foreign exchange transactions shall be in accordance with the foreign exchange regulations of the PRC.
13. Joint ventures may borrow funds directly from foreign banks. Appropriate insurance will be provided by Chinese insurance companies. A joint venture equipped with up-to-date technology by world standards may apply for a reduction of or an exemption from income tax for the first two or three profit-making years.
14. A joint venture is encouraged to market its products outside China through direct channels, its associated agencies, or Chinese foreign trade establishments. Its products also may be distributed in the Chinese market.
15. The contract period of a joint venture must be agreed upon by both parties and may be extended subject to authorization by the Foreign Investment Commission.
16. Disputes that cannot be settled through consultation between partners may be settled through consultation or arbitration by a Chinese arbitral body or an arbitral body agreed upon by the parties involved.

APPENDIX 2

THE IMPORTANCE OF GUANXI (CONNECTIONS) IN CHINA

Guanxi is the word that describes the intricate, pervasive network of personal relations which every Chinese cultivates with energy, subtlety, and imagination. It is a relationship between two people or organizations containing implicit mutual obligation, assurances, and understanding and governs Chinese attitudes toward long-term social and business relationships. If a *guanxi* relationship of trust and mutual benefits is established, an excellent foundation will be built to develop the future relationship. *Guanxi* ties also may be helpful in dealing with the Chinese bureaucracy as personal interpretations are often used in lieu of legal interpretations.

Though the use of *guanxi* networks has mushroomed during the reform in China since 1979,[4] *guanxi* has much stronger and deeper roots embedded in Chinese society. Traditionally, the strong value of family ties has placed an emphasis on getting things done through those you know. One of the most important aspects of the *guanxi* network is that it is neither officially acknowledge nor written down. Members of *guanxi* networks highly value reciprocity, trust, and the implicit understanding between the two parties involved (i.e., "I give you a favor now and I believe that you will return a favor to me in the future whenever I need it"), thus reducing the need to write everything down.

Due to cultural differences and language barriers, the visitors to China are not in a position to cultivate *guanxi* with the depth possible between two Chinese. Nevertheless, *guanxi* is an important aspect of social life in China and deserves attention so that good relations may be developed and things can get done. If a foreigner seeks to develop *guanxi* with the Chinese, he or she should be pleased when called an "old friend" by the Chinese. Among American dignitaries, Richard Nixon, Henry Kissinger, and Jimmy Carter who brought about diplomatic relationships with China in the 1970s enjoy the "old friend" status.

ENDNOTES

1. Lieberman, M.B. and D.B. Montgomery, First Mover Advantage: A survey, *Strategic Management Journal*, Vol. 9, Summer Special Issue, 1988, pp. 41–58.
2. Huang, J.P., Fuelling the Economy, *The China Business Review*, March–April 1991, p. 22.
3. Chen, B.S., Economic Development Strategy for China's Coastal Areas and US Investment in China, *Meiguo Yanjiu* (Journal of American Studies, Beijing, China), Vol. 2, No. 3, 1988, pp. 7–25.
4. Peng, M.W., Organizational Changes in Planned Economies in Transition: An eclectic model, *Advances in International Comparative Management*, Vol. 9, 1994, pp. 223–251.

CASE NINETEEN

ACER INCORPORATED[*]

INTRODUCTION

Stan Shih founded Multitech in 1976 with an initial investment of US$25,000, five co-founders, 11 employees, and a steadfast belief in the potential of microprocessor technology. Multitech started by importing electronic components and publishing trade journals, and later went on to design its own video games and IBM clones. In 1988, the firm's name was changed to Acer for a couple of reasons. First, the name Multitech was already being used by a small US company. Second, Shih wanted to globalize, and felt that the name Multitech was too long and too common for a brand name. The Latin meaning of "acer" is sharp, penetrating, energetic, and spirited, so it was favored by Shih because it "is short, easy to remember, and its various meanings epitomize our strengths and beliefs" ("Multitech Goes Global with Its Computer Clout," 1988).

As chairman and CEO, Shih has built this company into a world player during the 20 years of its existence. Its present worldwide organization covers 80 offices in 38 countries servicing a network of more than 200 distributors in over 100 countries.

Shih is regarded as one of the best-known and most admired businessmen in Taiwan. He is truly an "MIT" (Made in Taiwan) product! Born into a middle class family and educated locally, Shih's career has paralleled his country's development. Prior to founding Acer in 1976, Shih worked for Unitron and Qualitron, where he developed the first penwatch and Taiwan's first calculator.

---

[*] This case was prepared by Julie H. Yu, Lecturer in the Department of Marketing, The Chinese University of Hong Kong.

Shih and Acer have given Taiwan self-respect, removing its stigma as an island of unscrupulous fakers and influencing the government to move decisively to protect intellectual property. They have also contributed to developing its electronics industry to become mature and vertically integrated.

Original equipment manufacture (OEM) still accounts for 40 per cent of Acer's turnover, with companies like Fujitsu, NEC, Unisys, Bull, ICL, Siemens, and AEG as customers, and gives it the necessary financial and technological cushion. But Shih's battle all along has been to establish his own brand name. He has not relied upon copying others or on cheaper prices, but has instead emphasized product innovations, quality of design and functioning, and after-sale servicing (Roy, 1989).

PERSONAL COMPUTER INDUSTRY

The PC industry has undergone a number of rapid changes during the past few years, due in part to the high technology aspect of this industry. In the US market, sales by new no-name vendors has increased quite markedly. Dataquest believes that "this reflects a significant increase in (South) Korean and Taiwanese penetration into the US market" (Johnstone, 1989). Acer America Corporation's President and COO, Ronald Chwang, believes that several factors are critical for survival in this industry. First, a competitor must have critical mass, in the neighborhood of US$1 billion. Secondly, it must be diversified for stability, with respect to regional sales and types of sales. Acer gets 33 per cent of its sales from the US, 16 per cent from Europe, and the rest from other parts of the world. With respect to types of sales, 50 per cent of Acer's sales are from original equipment manufacturers (OEMs). Finally, it must have manufacturing capability. Acer is the sixth largest color monitor producer in the world. In its joint venture with Texas Instruments, it is producing 6 million 4-megabit DRAMs a month (Willett, 1993).

South Korea's huge conglomerates initially misjudged the PC business as being too small for their consideration. By the time the *chaebols* changed their minds, the market was crowded, and entry was costly. Lacking marketing skills and sales channels, South Korean firms were forced to rely on OEM contracts. Unfortunately, large OEM customers define the products, and profit margins are very thin. Competition on the basis of price alone cannot be sustained indefinitely. The Taiwanese, with lower costs and a better developed infrastructure, can undercut the South Koreans by 10–15 per cent. Even lower cost competitors are also fighting for market share. If the *chaebols* want to stay in the PC business, they must move upmarket with more powerful machines and establish a name for themselves, particularly in Europe, which they have so far largely neglected in favor of the US.

Workstations have emerged as an important segment of the desktop market, and they differ from PCs in a number of ways. They are bigger, with high resolution screens. They have more powerful processors and memory capacity, and can thus run several applications at once. Workstations are connected into networks which share the same resources. They run on a more powerful operating system, Unix, which can juggle several programs simultaneously. They are also more expensive.

Despite the potential of the workstation sector, Acer has delayed its decision to produce clones of Sun Microsystems' workstations. The size of the market is somewhat uncertain (200,000 workstations were sold in 1988 compared with 19 million PCs). There is also some reservation about the ability of clone makers to compete against Sun, which is a very powerful rival. However, there is no question that Sun needs high-volume clone makers to establish a standard.

There seem to be some inevitable trends for PCs of the future. They will be easier to use, more powerful, and smaller. Organized into networks, they will be based on universally accepted technical standards (Johnstone, 1989).

SITUATION IN TAIWAN

Taiwan is now the third largest supplier of PCs, after the US and Japan. Taiwan's computer makers are playing a critical behind-the-scenes role as designers and manufacturers of the world's PCs and peripherals. Many foreign companies now sell Taiwanese equipment under their own brand names. Robert Lo, Intel's former country manager in Taipei, believes that "Taiwan has become the arms dealer of the computer wars."

Taiwan is also proving itself as a source of innovative design. "The Taiwanese are no longer relying on reverse engineering," says Daniel A. Heyler, a Dataquest analyst in Taipei. "They are becoming the pacesetters in cost-performance" (Engardio, 1993). Reverse engineering is a process whereby a marketer takes a competitor's product apart and steals the design. Thus, the emphasis is on imitation, a strategy which has proven to be very important for late industrializing countries.

Industry growth in the first half of the 1980s was due largely to foreign-owned firms; foreign multinationals were responsible for the majority of the industry's exports until 1986. In 1984, offshore manufacturing accounted for almost 60 per cent of total exports, but fell to 35 per cent by 1989. Despite rising costs, OEM business has accounted for a steady proportion of the industry's total production during the same period. In the long term, OEM is likely to become less important. While some firms still rely heavily on OEM business, others such as Acer and Mitac are seeking to convert from OEM to own brand manufacturing (OBM). By developing OBM, Taiwan's information companies are pursuing stability and simultaneously moving to higher value-added products with better profit margins (McDermott, 1991).

Taiwan's PC industry is polarized at the present time. There are a number of competitors at the low end competing on price (e.g., Datatech). Competitors at the other end of the spectrum, however, compete by offering the highest performance (e.g., Acer, Mitac). The industry is characterized by a large number of small firms; the top 20 companies account for only 54 per cent of production (Johnstone, 1989). In 1989, Taiwan's production of information products totalled US$5.5 billion, of which exports accounted for 96 per cent. The information industry was responsible for 2.7 per cent of Taiwan's GNP; and information products ranked as the country's third largest export earner. Five thousand firms and a labor force of 80,000 are engaged in this industry.

Although the US has been the largest export market for Taiwan's information products in the past, exports to other markets are increasing at a faster rate. Taiwan's strongest export companies in the electronics industry have been targeting Europe in preference to the US in their marketing strategies since 1986, and have succeeded in making it Taiwan's fastest growing export market. The formation of the European Union (EU) in 1992 and fears of "Fortress Europe" have resulted in a wave of Taiwanese investments in the European community (McDermott, 1991).

ACER'S PRESENT POSITION

Acer and Mitac are Taiwan's leading producers of information products (i.e., computers and peripherals). There are, however, several differences between Acer and its local competition. Shih invests heavily in engineering and is diversifying Acer's product line of computers and peripherals to an extent which is unusual among Asian computer makers. Acer is also beefing up marketing. Says Shih: "We want to be a multinational company from Taiwan. We want to use Taiwanese cost structure but [offer] international, first-class products, services, and image." By taking advantage of an abundant supply of local engineers, the company can differentiate its products through engineering effort instead of competing on price alone (Shao, 1987).

MISSION AND BASIC STRATEGIC DIRECTION

Shih's goal is to make Acer one of the world's top five computer companies. In its global operations, Shih wants to emulate Philips, Sony, and Honda, but in character and drive he intends to become an IBM or Hewlett-Packard. As Taiwan's largest maker of computers and semiconductors, Acer is among the world's top three producers of color monitors and keyboards. Within a few years, Acer's wafer fabrication venture with Texas Instruments, now devoted to memory chips, will hopefully expand into microprocessors.

In 1993, it posted US$89 million in profit on sales of US$1.88 billion, as compared to a loss of US$25 million two years before. By 1995, revenues were up to US$5.8 billion with earnings topping US$413 million. This recovery was due to a number of factors: a streamlined assembly process, brisk sales of inexpensive PCs through chains such as Best Buy and CompUSA, and a rush of orders from big-name PC companies which buy from Acer in preference to building their own. Several years ago, Shih's dream had started to fade, due to acquisitions and two years of heavy losses in the US PC market. In response, Acer defined a new route to its goal (Engardio, 1993). This route takes into account the following factors:

1. Rather than focus only on its brand name products in the US market, the company is content with 40 per cent of its output going to other manufacturers (OEM). For example, Acer built some of Apple Computer's PowerBook 145 notebook PCs, a deal which was estimated to be worth US$100 million for Acer in 1993. Like many other Taiwanese firms, it is revamping to provide one-stop shopping for computer makers—everything from design work, to building complete systems, to creating chip sets.
2. Acer will spread out geographically, e.g., Japan, where PC price wars are starting to

force computer companies to use low-cost Taiwanese manufacturers. China is also a promising market for the future. Acer is an expert in Chinese-language computing. Present problems such as the ban by Taiwanese authorities on direct trade with China, the fact that Chinese consumers do not yet have the spending power to be a large PC market, and Acer's inability to provide service back-up must first be overcome ("A Well-Worn Road to Dominance," 1988).
3. The company is redefining manufacturing trends. Acer's just-in-time manufacturing system has boosted output and reduced its workforce.
4. Acer has converted all 39 worldwide assembly sites to modular assembly so that Acer retail outlets can in the future assemble customized PCs on their own, using parts supplied by regional distribution centers or directly from Asia-based factories.

ORGANIZATIONAL STRUCTURE

Acer's growth from a local Taiwanese operation to a multibillion, multi-product multinational company with subsidiaries and operations around the world has created a number of challenges. Shih has had to address the issues of how to adjust Acer's corporate culture as a global company, how to bring different sides of operations in different countries together into one integrated management whole, and how to uplift it to a higher level of sophistication.

In its effort to globalize and enter the US market, Acer has made several overseas acquisitions. It acquired startup Counterpoint Computers for US$6 million in 1987, Service Intelligent for US$500,000 in 1989, and microcomputer pioneer Altos Computer Systems Inc. for US$94 million in 1990. In its US ventures, however, it has not assigned enough senior management personnel to the task. The top man was always an American, and only junior, inexperienced Chinese managers were sent to keep an eye on things. Thus, they never took real charge of the US operations (Montagu-Pollock, 1992).

Many Asian companies are using cross-border strategic alliances to secure their positions in world markets. Shorter product life-cycles, tighter profit margins, and soaring R&D costs are prompting companies to seek partnerships with foreign groups in a wide variety of sectors. While the Asian partner gains new technology and western markets, the western partner gets access to low-cost engineering skills, closer knowledge of Asian markets, and a large manufacturing capacity. Taiwanese PC manufacturers have been under increased pressure to integrate design and manufacturing, and cut the number of suppliers. By teaming up with established western semiconductor firms, they can keep costs down and get new products on the market faster. The role of matchmaker in these courtships is played by the Taiwan government (Flannery, 1990).

In 1989 Acer entered into a joint venture with Texas Instruments (TI) to build a wafer fabrication plant in Taiwan's Hsinchu science-based Industrial Park. Production of 4-megabit DRAMs began in May 1991. Co-owned by each company, this joint venture has its own identity and management structure. One of the primary reasons for this partnership was the sharing of R&D costs. In semiconductors, for example, each new generation of DRAM chip requires a doubling of investment. Since Acer did not have the resources to develop DRAMs on its own, the alliance with TI made sense. Bridging the cultural divide has helped this partnership to succeed. Acer managers are sent on 6–9 month trips to TI's facilities in the US and Japan, while a team of 25–35 senior TI managers rotate through Taiwan. Acer's executives are very familiar with US management practices; many of them have studied in the US and/or worked in Silicon Valley. Acer has also hedged its bets by forming an alliance with National Semiconductor, one of TI's competitors (Selwyn and Valigra, 1991).

MANAGEMENT

In 1989, Acer underwent a drastic corporate reorganization. Decision making became decentralized, and departments became independent business units. Dr. Leonard Liu, a veteran from IBM, was brought in to recast the group's management into the multinational environment (Roy, 1989).

Stan Shih's management philosophy has enabled the company to solicit commitment from its employees through incentives such as promotions and employee stock ownership. He has made creative use of the local talent, and employs a large number of staff in the R&D department (Moore, 1988). Shih's mature managerial mentality includes emphasis on (King, 1986):

1. Educating and providing an environment whereby the staff can spend more time trying to contribute to the company; Shih encourages employees to take risks and innovate, not only with respect to products, but in management and decision making, so that they learn by themselves (encourages creativity).
2. Persuading employees to view working for the group as a long-term career.
3. Fostering a sense of participation.

FINANCE

Acer's financial position has fluctuated somewhat during the past decade. Selected financial data are provided in the following tables and figures (Acer Incorporated, 1992; Goldstein, 1990). When the company went public in November 1988, its initial public offering (IPO) was oversubscribed 118 times. Acer has shown tremendous growth in recent years, despite the slowdown in world PC markets. Net revenues of the Acer Group were more than US$5.8 billion in 1995, an increase of 80 per cent over revenue of the previous year. During the same period, profits rose to US$413 million from US$205 million in 1994. Although these figures are impressive, they do not compare to its average growth of 100 per cent a year during the first ten years of its existence. After years of putting growth before profits, Shih has only recently reversed his strategy.

MARKETING

Stan Shih has adopted an aggressive international marketing strategy in attempting to make Acer one of the top five computer companies in the world. Shih likens marketing to a Go board, on which the player attempts to surround his opponent without himself being surrounded: "We went from the countryside to the city, from the periphery to the core" (i.e., the US, where Acer found itself surrounded by more recognizable names) (Tanzer, 1991).

Acer has used a market concentration strategy to enhance its own brand sales by starting with developing countries and moving to more competitive markets once it achieved a market position within the top five. It is now the market leader in many less developed countries (McDermott, 1991).

Acer developed one of the world's first Chinese language computer terminals and input systems, and then went into the clone business. It has an unusual strategy. Unlike other clone makers who manufacture goods that are sold under foreign brands, Shih insists on selling under his own brand name and investing in global distribution. While most clonemakers are content to assemble off-the-shelf components, Acer invests heavily in research and development (2 per cent of total revenue) and vertical integration (Tanzer, 1991).

Unlike many competitors in late industrializing countries, Acer does not compete on price alone. The firm operates instead on the high end of the spectrum, along with its close competitor Mitac, by offering high performance. Thus, its primary competitive advantage is product differentiation through engineering effort. Acer chooses its distributors carefully, and gives them better incentives to offer better service. It is also considering entering the direct sales channel as an increment to its business. However, it must first build up the infrastructure (e.g., shipping, service structure) and engage in heavy advertising (Willett, 1993).

As noted earlier, Acer was known as Multitech prior to 1988, but it dropped that name because it lacked distinctiveness. In 1990, its marketing slogan was changed from "Your Computing Friend Cares Everywhere" to "Global Partner in Computing." Approximately 6–7 per cent of group revenues are spent on worldwide promotion and advertising. Acer's tactics are comparable to those used in Go, the Chinese chess game, in which the objective is to make territorial gains rather than capture the opponent's pieces. For Acer's international marketing development process for its own brand products, refer McDermott (1991).

APPENDIX

Acer Incorporated and Subsidiaries: Consolidated Balance Sheets, as at December 31, 1994 and 1995 (in thousands of New Taiwan dollars and US dollars)

	1994	1995	
Assets	NT$	NT$	US$
Current assets:			
Cash and cash equivalents	2,445,695	6,271,645	229,899
Pledged time deposits and trust funds	3,671,555	3,652,349	133,884
Short-term investments	42,758	25,793	945
Notes receivable	83,750	131,852	4,833
Accounts receivable	7,463,683	13,291,379	487,220
Less: Allowance for doubtful accounts	(351,913)	(407,833)	(14,950)
Net accounts receivable	7,111,770	12,883,546	472,270
Receivables from related parties	679,236	2,329,618	85,397
Inventories	10,276,834	19,907,022	729,730
Prepaid expenses and other current assets	670,107	1,815,919	66,566
Total current assets	24,981,705	47,017,744	1,723,524
Long-term equity investments	6,407,754	10,051,023	368,439
Property, plant and equipment:			
Land	279,132	289,690	10,619
Buildings and improvements	1,394,128	1,437,637	52,699
Machinery and equipment	865,716	1,246,901	45,708
Mold equipment	170,451	259,232	9,503
Research and development equipment	224,494	274,960	10,079
Transportation equipment	53,307	60,837	2,230
Furniture and fixtures	287,794	278,309	10,202
Other equipment	125,491	221,696	8,127
Leased equipment and leasehold improvements	93,252	49,546	1,816
Construction in progress and advance payments for purchases of machinery and equipment	677,278	651,220	23,872
Less: Accumulated depreciation	(1,073,454)	(1,186,045)	(43,477)
Net property, plant and equipment	3,097,589	3,583,983	131,378
Advance payment for purchases of land and land held for development	2,815,277	2,977,470	109,145
Deferred charges and other assets	1,093,947	846,250	31,021
Total assets	38,396,272	64,476,470	2,363,507

Acer Incorporated and Subsidiaries: Consolidated Balance Sheets, as at December 31, 1994 and 1995 (in thousands of New Taiwan dollars and US dollars) (cont.)

	1994	1995	
Liabilities and Stockholders' Equity	NT$	NT$	US$
Current liabilities:			
Short-term borrowings	8,261,848	9,812,031	359,678
Current instalments of long-term debts	702,501	411,209	15,074
Notes payable	1,765,140	3,464,092	126,983
Accounts payable	6,206,517	10,975,580	402,331
Payables to related parties	949,287	2,070,670	75,904
Deferred intercompany profits	71,160	149,925	5,496
Advance collection from sale of land	418,672	418,672	15,347
Accrued expenses and other current liabilities	3,459,693	5,466,039	200,368
Total current liabilities	21,834,818	32,768,218	1,201,181
Bonds payable	1,373,376	1,929,070	70,714
Long-term debts, excluding current instalments	1,197,263	991,618	36,350
Long-term payables to related parties	779,262	–	–
Other liabilities	320,587	831,206	30,469
Total liabilities	25,505,306	36,520,112	1,338,714
Stockholders' equity and minority interest:			
Common stock	4,770,328	9,450,565	346,428
Stock dividends to be distributed	715,549	–	–
Legal reserve	45,038	354,075	12,979
Capital surplus	4,078,322	10,207,749	374,185
Unappropriated earnings	3,097,263	6,658,424	244,077
Translation adjustment	(111,870)	(48,691)	(1,785)
Total stockholders' equity	12,594,630	26,622,122	975,884
Minority interest	296,336	1,334,236	48,909
Total stockholders' equity and minority interest	12,890,966	27,956,358	1,024,793
Commitments and contingencies			
Total liabilities and stockholders' equity	38,396,272	64,476,470	2,363,507

Acer Incorporated

Acer Incorporated and Subsidiaries: Consolidated Statements of Income, for the Years Ended December 31, 1994 and 1995 (in thousands of New Taiwan dollars and US dollars)

	1994	1995	
	NT$	NT$	US$
Operating revenue	63,017,022	107,063,298	3,924,608
Cost of operations	(53,360,238)	(93,569,719)	(3,429,975)
Gross profit	9,656,784	13,493,579	494,633
Operating expenses:			
Selling expenses	(4,613,567)	(7,506,266)	(275,156)
General and administrative expenses	(2,136,031)	(2,051,170)	(75,190)
Research and development expenses	(1,070,860)	(1,703,135)	(62,432)
Total operating expenses	(7,820,458)	(11,260,571)	(412,778)
Operating income	1,836,326	2,233,008	81,855
Non-operating income and gains:			
Interest income	392,507	457,500	16,771
Foreign exchange gain, net	53,788	–	–
Investment income, net	1,785,715	3,644,140	133,583
Gain on disposal of property and equipment	61,819	1,022	37
Gain on disposal of net investment, net	3,837	11,584	425
Other income	132,373	476,992	17,485
	2,430,039	4,591,238	168,301
Non-operating expenses and loss:			
Interest expense, net of capitalized interest of $299,825 and $309,904 for 1994 and 1995, respectively	(710,279)	(731,105)	(26,800)
Foreign exchange loss, net	–	(168,809)	(6,188)
Loss on disposal of property and other assets	(106,198)	(6,596)	(242)
Loss on inventory devaluation	(109,296)	(240,523)	(8,817)
Other loss	(83,344)	(52,585)	(1,927)
	(1,009,117)	(1,199,618)	(43,974)
Income before income tax, minority interest and pre-acquisition loss	3,257,248	5,624,628	206,182
Expected income tax benefit (expense)	(87,583)	45,213	1,657
Income before minority interest and pre-acquisition loss	3,169,665	5,669,841	207,839
Minority interest in net income	(69,725)	(138,843)	(5,090)
Pre-acquisition loss	–	5,008	184
Net income	3,099,940	5,536,006	202,933
Net income per common share (in NT$ and US$)	3.88	6.45	0.24

REFERENCES

A Well-Worn Road to Dominance, *Economist,* Vol. 308, No. 7568, September 17, 1988, p. 76.

Acer Incorporated, *Acer Incorporated Annual Report,* Taipei, 1992, pp. 22–26.

Bedi, Hari, Stan Shih's Dragon Dream, *Asian Business,* Vol. 29, No. 9, September 1993, pp. 50–51.

Engardio, Pete, Taiwan: The arms dealer of the computer wars, *Business Week,* No. 3325, June 28, 1993, pp. 36–37.

Flannery, Russell, Taiwanese Majors Learn Mating Game, *Asian Business,* Vol. 26, No. 5, May 1990, pp. 58–60.

Goldstein, Carl, Acer in the Hole, *Far Eastern Economic Review,* Vol. 150, No. 50, December 13, 1990, pp. 62–63.

Johnstone, Bob, Asia: Technology—Into the next generation, *Far Eastern Economic Review,* Vol. 145, No. 35, August 31, 1989, pp. 48–54.

King, Robert, Can This Dragon from Taiwan Slay the West? *International Management,* Vol. 41, No. 2, February 1986, pp. 30–31.

McDermott, Michael, Taiwan's Electronic Companies are Targeting Europe, *European Management Journal,* Vol. 9, No. 4, December 1991, pp. 466–474.

Montagu-Pollock, Matthew, Hard School of Takeovers, *Asian Business,* Vol. 28, No. 3, March 1992, pp. 46–52.

Moore, Jonathan, Apple of Taiwan's Eye, *Far Eastern Economic Review,* Vol. 141, No. 28, July 14, 1988, p. 62.

Multitech Goes Global with Its Computer Clout, *Asian Finance,* Vol. 14, No. 2, February 15, 1988, pp. 54–56.

Roy, Barun, Acer's Stan Shih: Against all odds, *Asian Finance,* Vol. 15, No. 11, November 15, 1989, pp. 17–23.

Selwyn, Michael and Lori Valigra, Making Marriages of Convenience, *Asian Business,* Vol. 27, No. 1, January 1991, pp. 26–28.

Shao, Maria, Stan Shih Wants 'Made in Taiwan' to Mean First-Rate, *Business Week,* No. 3002, June 8, 1987, pp. 109, 112.

Tanzer, Andrew, Computers/Communications: The great leap forward, *Forbes,* Vol. 147, No. 8, April 15, 1991, pp. 108–110.

Willett, Shawn, Chwang Says Acer Has the Critical Mass to Survive, *Infoworld,* Vol. 15, No. 3, January 18, 1993, p. 98.

COUNTRY PROFILE

South Korea*

Background

The Land and the People

South Korea is located in the southern part of the Korean peninsula. Officially, it is called the Republic of Korea. At 38,330 square miles, the country is relatively small in land area, but not in population. South Korea's population totalled 43.9 million people in 1993. Seventy-two per cent of the population is now classified as urban. Most of the population live in the south and southwestern regions. The major cities of South Korea include Seoul, Pusan, Taegu, Inchon, and Kwangju. The country has one of the highest population densities in the world. In 1993, the density was estimated at 1,146 people per square mile. The ethnic composition of South Korea is highly homogeneous. Only a small percentage of the population is non-Korean. Korean culture dates back several thousand years. The official language is Korean. The major religions are Buddhism, Confucianism, and Christianity. South Korea boasts of a high rate of literacy. In 1993, 97 per cent of the population was literate. The unit of currency is the won (W).

History

The anti-Communist Republic of Korea was formed in 1948. Since its formation, the country has gone through several republics. First, there was the Second Republic and Syngman Rhee

---

*This country profile was prepared by Ken Hasegawa, Andre Lambine, Helen Louie and Abraham Tokashiki, University of Hawaii, Manoa.

was elected the president. He was reelected for several terms until 1960 when he was forced to resign. During his presidency, the Korean War broke out in 1950. The war disrupted all aspects of Korean life. Despite US aid following the war, economic development in South Korea was slow. In 1961, a military coup ended the Second Republic.

Park Chung Hee's Third Republic was created in 1963. Park Chung Hee initiated many economic reforms. South Korea's economy was strengthened during his government. The country, though, became increasingly dissatisfied with Park's leadership and he was assassinated in 1979.

The next leader to emerge was Chun Doo Hwan. He established the Fourth Republic in 1980. However, once again, the people became dissatisfied with the government and mass protests led to democratic reform. In 1987, Roh Tae Woo was elected president. A new constitution was adopted in 1987 and put into effect in 1988. Under the new constitution, presidents were limited to one term of five years. In 1993, Kim Young Sam became the first civilian president in more than thirty years.

ECONOMY

South Korea's economy was traditionally based on agriculture. Starting from the 1960s, though, it shifted towards the production of labor-intensive goods, such as clothing and footwear. Currently, South Korea is experiencing another shift towards the manufacture of high-tech goods, such as electronics.

Since the 1960s, South Korea's economy has grown rapidly. Between the mid-1960s and late 1980s, the annual growth of the country's GDP was over 9 per cent. From 1989 to 1993, the GDP growth fluctuated between 5.1 per cent to 9.5 per cent. GDP growth in 1992 and 1993 was unusually low at 5.1 per cent and 5.5 per cent respectively. GDP growth for 1994 to 1996, however, is expected to rise above 7 per cent (Economist Intelligence Unit, 1994–95). In 1993, agriculture contributed approximately 8 per cent to the GDP; manufacturing contributed 30 per cent. In 1992, South Korea's GNP totalled US$296.349 billion. GNP per capita totaled US$6,790.

TRADE

South Korean exports have grown rapidly since the 1960s. Exports grew 27.2 per cent from 1965 to 1980 and from 1980 to 1988, they grew 14.7 per cent (Microsoft Corporation, 1993). In 1993, South Korea's main exports were machinery and transport equipment, textiles, clothing and accessories, and footwear. Main imports consisted of machinery and transport equipment, mineral fuels and lubricants, raw materials, chemicals, food and live stock.

Over the last few years, South Korean trade in the Asian region has been experiencing some significant increases. Trade with the North American region, primarily the US, is decreasing. Trade growth in the European region has been moderate. Despite decreasing trade with the US, the US is still one of South Korea's main trading partners. South Korea's other main trading partners include Japan, Hong Kong, Germany, Singapore, Saudi Arabia, and Australia. In terms of trade balances, South Korea experienced an overall trade deficit in 1993. Trade balances with the three Chinas (China, Taiwan, and Hong Kong), the ASEAN, and the US were positive, though. The South Korean trade deficit with Japan was approximately US$8.5 billion (Rich, 1995).

In the preceding sections, a brief overview of South Korea was given. Factors affecting South Korea's industrialization were presented, and current trends were discussed. In the following sections other important aspects of South Korea, such as government, *chaebols*, and labor will be examined in more detail.

GOVERNMENT AND ECONOMIC DEVELOPMENT

INDUSTRIALIZATION THROUGH EXPORT PROMOTION (1960s)

The economic transformation of the Republic of Korea began in the early 1960s with the policies adopted by General Park Chung Hee, who seized power in a 1961 coup. Unlike the Japanese supportive approach, Korea employed a more authoritarian, military-style leadership that stressed economic development through industrialization, strong government control, government-directed economic planning, economic growth was given highest priority over balanced/equitable distribution, and emphasis on exports (Soon, 1994, pp. 31–32). A key element of this strategy was the development of a series of five-year plans beginning in 1962 that directed state policies.

The Economic Planning Board (EPB), chaired by the Deputy Prime Minister, was responsible for developing and implementing the Five-Year Economic Development Plans, formulating national budgets, and executing all major economic policies. The Ministry of Finance (MOF) was responsible for overseeing the government's financial affairs and the direction of the entire economy through its control of fiscal policy, government-owned banks, foreign exchange transactions, and security markets. The government revised the Bank of Korea Act and confiscated the stocks of banks in order to place the central bank (Bank of Korea) and commercial banks under its direct control. President Park Chung Hee initially banned trade unions, and then allowed the creation of a new Federation of Korean Trade Unions (FKTU) under close government supervision.

Devastation from the Korean War left the country with a large pool of unemployed laborers and little capital for development. In order to overcome the disadvantage of small size, limited natural resources and to earn foreign currency, the government adopted a strategy of industrialization through export promotion. This outward-looking development approach initially focused on labor-intensive manufacturing exports (clothing, footwear, luggage, textiles, leather goods, and simple fabricated goods) in which Korea had a comparative advantage. Korean currency was devalued by almost 100 per cent during the period 1961–64 to make ROK's goods more competitive in the world markets. Preferential interest rates on working capital loans to exporters fell from 14 per cent in 1960 to 6 per cent in 1967 to encourage expansion in these sectors (Lin, 1993, p. 192). Other incentives given to exporters included tariff exemptions, rebates on imports used in production of exports, tax subsidies, establishment of free trade zones, reduced public utility charges, simplified customs procedures, and reduction of taxes. Companies that met or exceeded the Ministry of Commerce and Industry's (MCI) set export targets received more favors, while sanctions and tax investigations faced those that failed to meet their quotas (Cherry, 1993, p. 140).

Rapid growth in the light manufacturing sector absorbed large amounts of labor, encouraged rural-to-urban migration, and changed Korea from an agricultural society to a semi-industrialized country. ROK had insufficient domestic savings to fuel this explosive growth so it borrowed heavily from outside sources. In an effort to raise additional funds, the Foreign Capital Inducement Law (FCIL) was modified in 1966 to encourage foreign investors by removing the minimum requirement for Korean participation in equity capital and by granting national guarantees against the threat of default. Government consulted business during this process through monthly Export Promotion Council meetings, five-year planning sessions, and informal personal contacts (Koo, 1992). Various economic organizations and industry associations assisted state agencies by providing information on the state of the economy, assessing the impacts of different policies, facilitating coordination, and fostering cooperation.

HEAVY AND CHEMICAL INDUSTRIES STRATEGY (1970S)

In the early 1970s ROK's industrial policy shifted to the promotion of heavy and chemical industries (HCI). The 1973 Heavy and Chemical Industry Development Plan prioritized the development of capital-intensive and technologically sophisticated industries such as shipbuilding, industrial machinery, steel, nonferrous metals, electrical products, automobiles, and petrochemicals. To achieve the necessary economies of scale in a limited domestic market, the government permitted monopolistic production and maintained high protective barriers for a few conglomerates or *chaebols*. Public funds, such as employee pensions, and private savings were mobilized under the National Investment Fund. These funds and other preferential policy assets were then channelled into heavy industry projects at nominal (sometimes negative in real terms) interest rates (Lin, 1993, pp. 193–194).

Under the 1972 Emergency Decree on National Security, unions were required to secure government approval before engaging in wage negotiations. The Labor Dispute Adjustment Law was suspended and replaced by direct government intervention in all labor disputes (Cho, 1994). Government actions often favored the interests of the businesses over the rights of the workers. Another component of the third Five-Year Plan (1972–1976) was to promote the development of the rural sector by launching the *Saemaul* (New Community). This program successfully boosted the productivity and income of farming and fishing families, but the price support element of the plan was a major contributor to Korea's chronic deficits (Cherry, 1993, p. 141).

These policies led to severe economic inefficiencies such as sectorial imbalances which diverted resources from other labor-intensive industries; concentration of economic power into large oligopolistic business groups; increases in non-performing government-directed bank loans; underestimation of the importance of technical and managerial expertise; requirement of heavy borrowing from external financial markets; and a rapid expansion of money supply which led to high inflation (Lin, 1993, p. 195). This resulted in the deterioration of Korea's export competitiveness, a slowing down in the overall growth of the economy, and an aggravation of income distribution inequalities. Thus, the stage was set for the adoption of major policy reforms in the succeeding years to correct these deficiencies.

LIBERALIZATION AND REFORM (1980s)

Under the government of President Chun Doo Hwan, efforts were made to initiate policy reforms aimed at liberating the markets from government intervention, stabilizing the economy, and strengthening market competition. In response to this new leadership, the Korean government undertook adjustment measures seeking to regain growth momentum, reduce the inflation rate, and improve the balance of payments position. Tight fiscal measures and conservative monetary policies were implemented to promote price stability. Greater market competition was encouraged through the privatization of five major commercial banks, reduction of administrative price controls, and enactment of new laws for monopoly regulation and fair trade (Lin, 1993, p. 196). Government began to phase out industry-specific support systems, including preferential interest rates and other industry-oriented financial facilities. The 1981 Anti-Monopoly and Fair Trade Act was enacted to eliminate monopolistic practices such as cartel arrangements and pricing. A managed flexible arrangement replaced the fixed exchange rate system and many trade barriers were reduced to impose international competitive pressures that compelled a greater need for domestic productivity.

Changing social and political conditions that led to a full democracy in 1987 forced the government to modify plans in order to meet the growing demands of the general public. In response to these new realities, the state revised the sixth Five-Year Plan (1987–1991) to reform land tenure, liberalize financial transactions, reduce the power of the conglomerates, improve labor-management relations, increase social welfare, expand the public health-insurance program, and implement an extensive pension system (Soon, 1994, p. 53).

CURRENT AND FUTURE CONDITIONS

The principal goal of the latest Five-Year Plan (1992–1996) is to pursue an advanced economy and society heading towards national reunification. It seeks to strengthen the competitiveness of industry by reorganizing the educational and human resource development system to develop the required technical skills; promoting technological development and innovation; furnishing and expanding the infrastructure; and raising the efficiency of business management and industrial structure by dispersing ownership of conglomerates. Inequities and imbalances in economic growth are corrected by restructuring regional and coastal areas to cope with further agricultural liberalization; alleviating the housing shortage; curbing land speculation; protecting the environment; improving social security by expanded coverage to farmers and fishermen; and promoting Korean culture. ROK strives to internationalize its economy by liberalizing its financial system; deregulating interest rates, foreign exchange, and foreign investment in capital markets; reducing government intervention in private economic activities; privatizing state-run and invested enterprises; opening service and agricultural markets to international competition; and providing the basis for national reunification through economic cooperation with North Korea (Soon, 1994, pp. 56–58).

Korea plans to spend US$52 billion during the period 1992–2001 to restructure its agricultural sector and establish processing plants. Land reforms that permit larger private landholdings of up to 100 hectares will allow for increasing economies of scale in farming. ROK has also launched an ambitious 10-year, US$120 billion plan to upgrade its infrastructure in areas such as roads, railways, ports, sewage facilities, and energy. Some of the major projects include establishing a high-speed rail link between Seoul and the southeastern port of Pusan; restarting work on the Yongjong international airport west of Seoul near Inch'on Harbor; and building nine nuclear power plants by the year 2001 with another nine to be constructed between 2002–2006 (Stewart, 1994, pp. 47–52).

Recent government policies are encouraging businesses to make the transition towards high-technology, high value-added areas such as electronics and semiconductors. Technological cooperation among government, private enterprises, research institutes, and universities in R&D, as a share of GNP, is expected to rise from 0.86 per cent in 1980 to 4 per cent by 1996. Various tax incentives are given to firms that invest in R&D and obtain new technologies. Government-sponsored manpower training programs are tailored to meet specific industrial needs (Lin, 1993, p. 201).

Current president Kim Young Sam implemented a major anti-corruption campaign aimed at removing the inefficient dishonest practices of the former regimes. Many politicians, generals, and intelligence officers were removed from their positions. A real-name financial system was instituted that banned all financial transactions involving false names in order to prevent the keeping of money obtained through illegal activities, hiding political contributions from big business, and avoiding taxes. False name accounts were estimated to involve between US$15–40 billion, or about 5–10 per cent of the entire deposit base, and about 30 per cent of the total value of the stock market (Stewart, 1994, p. 30).

Although Korea continues to liberalize its markets, the legacy of a strongly government-directed economy still prevails throughout its society. Intellectual property rights are only valid if registered with the appropriate Korean agencies such as the Patent Bureau or Council of Copyrights. Starting in 1994, foreign companies were finally given permission to acquire land for business purposes and to construct industrial parks. The limits on foreign stock ownership in the domestic market has only gradually been increased to 15 per cent in 1995. FCIL still restricts foreign investment in industries that are public services; hazardous to health, social morality or environment; receiving special government support; large consumers of energy or dependent on imported raw materials; highly extravagant consumer-oriented industries; related to farming or fishery; in early stages of development; and others stipulated in the Regulations. It also completely prohibits foreign investment in public administration, education, religious activities, and arts (*ibid.*, p. 157). Many foreign investments still require prior authorization under the Foreign Capital Inducement Act (FCIA). The Foreign Exchange Reform Plan seeks to scrap the Foreign Exchange Management Act by relaxing foreign exchange regulation, expanding outbound portfolio investment by institutional investors, allowing overseas branches to borrow foreign funds to finance overseas business, and simplifying documentation required to buy, sell, and remit foreign currencies. But it still limits the amount of foreign currencies that domestic firms can hold.

Governmental power has been decreasing over the years as it gradually phases in the various reforms. In 1994 the two most powerful agencies, the Ministry of Finance and the Economic Planning Board, were merged to create a combined Finance and Economy Ministry (Sohn, 1995). Its ability to direct and even destroy uncooperative business firms through credit rationing has deteriorated significantly as the *chaebols* gain greater economic clout.

The Chaebol

Introduction

Chaebols are huge business conglomerates that have come to dominate the modern South Korean economy. Their importance to the country's economy is demonstrated by the fact that in 1993, turnover from the five largest *chaebols* alone equalled approximately two-thirds of South Korea's GNP (McGrath and Mi-Young, 1994). Table 1 below provides data on the four largest *chaebols*, including the internal ownership ratio which is defined as the equity interests held by family members of conglomerate founders and affiliated companies ("Top Chaebols Continue Their Business Expansion," 1994, p. 43).

Table 1 South Korea's Big Four *Chaebol*

Company	1994 Sales US$ (billions)	Number of Subsidiaries	Internal Ownership Ratio	Main Businesses
Samsung	63	50	48.9	Electronics, automobiles, shipbuilding, aerospace, machinery
Hyundai	63	49	61.3	Automobiles, shipbuilding, electronics, construction, machinery
Lucky-Goldstar	48	53	37.7	Petrochemicals, electronics
Daewoo	40	25	42.4	Automobiles, shipbuilding, electronics, construction

Sources: "Top Chaebols Continue Their Business Expansion," 1994, p. 43 and Nakarmi, 1995, p. 79.

History of the Chaebol

In contrast to Japanese *keiretsus* such as Mitsubishi, Mitsui, and Sumitomo that can trace their origins to 18th Century *zaibatsus*, the history of the *chaebols* is relatively short. For example, Daewoo, the fourth largest *chaebol*, was only founded in 1967 and was able to grow in size by aggressively taking over smaller companies (*Asia Money*, 1994, p. 39). Daewoo is an extreme case of newness though, as the foundations for most chaebols were laid during the colonial period (1910–45) when the Japanese controlled most the country's factories and plants. With liberation in 1945, Koreans who had worked for these Japanese companies were allowed to purchase ownership rights. Although some companies, such as Samsung, were able to develop a dominant presence in a number of industries during the period between liberation and the military coup in 1961, many of today's *chaebols* existed only as small companies before the Korean War and began their ascent to large conglomerate form during the post war period of economic growth (Cherry, 1993, pp. 221–222).

The *chaebols* came of age particularly under the export-led economic growth policies of President Park Chung Hee (1961–79) who favored the development of large enterprises.

These economic policies have already been discussed at length, but to review, the government used access to credit (often at negative or zero real interest rates), export promotion and domestic market protection, tax and infrastructure policies, and restrictions on foreign investment, to encourage the *chaebols* to focus on export-led growth, and during the 1970s, moved aggressively into capital-intensive heavy industries such as steel, petrochemicals, shipbuilding, etc. The government also assisted the *chaebols* in suppressing labor, thereby keeping the wages low (Bello and Rosenfeld, 1992, pp. 34–37, 51–55).

The *chaebols* emerged more powerful than ever in the 1980s because of the deepening of heavy and chemical industries (HCI) drive of the 1970s. The HCI drive, by channelling massive amounts of capital to the *chaebols* at the expense of small- and medium-sized businesses, allowed the conglomerates to grow in size to the point that they could effectively put a stranglehold on the economy. While the government maintains great influence over economic life, the *chaebols* are no longer junior business partners of the government (as they effectively were under the Park regime), but are now on a much more equal footing. *Chaebol* power has been furthered as they have gained more direct influence over financial institutions. Although the *chaebols* are forbidden from owning banks, by 1992, the top 30 had managed to gain control of an estimated 50 per cent of the country's non-banking financial institutions, decreasing their reliance on the government for credit (Bello and Rosenfeld, 1992, pp. 59–71; Cherry, 1993, p. 225).

CHARACTERISTICS OF THE *CHAEBOL*

The major characteristics of the *chaebol* are described below (Cherry, 1993, p. 223 unless otherwise noted). It should be stated that while these characteristics describe the prototypical *chaebol* that has emerged out of South Korea's period of rapid economic development, the *chaebols* are increasingly involved in the process of changing and evolving their structures to compete successfully in the competitive global economy. These changes will be described later. The traditional *chaebol* is characterized by:

(i) FAMILY-CONTROLLED OWNERSHIP AND MANAGEMENT. The ownership ratios in Table 1 show that even in the largest conglomerates, the founding family retains large equity control. "Management by family" remains a strong tradition, with overall management of the group or individual subsidiary companies passed on to sons or sons-in-law.

(ii) AN AUTHORITARIAN MANAGEMENT STYLE. The chairman of the conglomerate, usually the founder or his close relative, has traditionally acted as a father figure in the Confucian tradition, with almost unchallenged power to dictate the group's activities. At Samsung, for example, all employees are required to read a little booklet containing the collected thoughts of Chairman Lee Kun-hee, son of the founder Lee Byung-chul. The thoughts of Chairman Lee for remaining competitive in the global economy range from the mundane to the bizarre as exemplified by the following passage: We should develop our own special language with a unique vocabulary ... that can be understood only by Samsung employees, a language that others outside of the group cannot understand (McGill, 1994, p. 98).

(iii) A WIDE RANGE OF BUSINESS ACTIVITIES. *Chaebols* are both vertically integrated and broadly diversified into many unrelated lines of business. For example, a report recently issued by the government showed that the largest 30 *chaebols* on average are composed of 21 companies involved in 20 major business lines (Nakarmi, 1995, p. 80).

(iv) A CLOSE RELATIONSHIP WITH THE GOVERNMENT. *Chaebol* ties with the government have already been discussed in the previous section on government economic policies.

Comparisons are often made between the *chaebols* and Japan's *keiretsus*. Like *keiretsus*, cross-holdings, cross-guarantees, cross-subsidization, and exchange of management personnel have been key techniques used to hold subsidiary companies together. However, family-controlled ownership and management in the case of *chaebols* has resulted in conglomerates whose component companies are more closely knit together and less independent than their professionally-managed *keiretsu* counterparts. Another major difference between the two types of business structures is that while *keiretsus* include banks and other financial institutions among their subsidiaries, *chaebols* have had to depend mostly on the government for financing. These distinctions may be blurring somewhat though, as the *chaebols* begin to decentralize their decision making and add financial institutions into their structures (Cherry, 1993, pp. 223–225; Nakarmi, 1995, p. 80).

COMPETING IN THE GLOBAL ECONOMY IN 1995 AND BEYOND

The *chaebols* are currently under intense pressure to change their business structures and practices. Beginning in the late 1980s and early 1990s, public and government sentiment began to turn against the *chaebols*. Whereas the *chaebols* were once seen as the vehicles for economic growth, they have come under criticism for their overly close relationship with the government and the resulting massive benefits they have received. Many believe the *chaebols* have become too large and powerful and have taken advantage of a protected domestic market to pursue reckless diversification and real estate speculation rather than invest resources to become competitive in the global economy.

Consequently, the government has taken reverse to a number of schemes to force the *chaebols* to decentralize their management, loosen the grip of the founding families, and abandon weak business lines in order to focus on a few core businesses. It is limiting access to new credit to three designated core businesses per conglomerate; withholding government approval of new business ventures to subsidiaries in which the founding family's direct or indirect holdings are 8 per cent or less; and banning subsidiaries from investing more than 40 per cent of their equity capital in another company in the group. The government plans to further cut this cross-ownership ratio to 25 per cent later this year to reduce the *chaebols*' ability to prop up unprofitable subsidiaries (Cherry, 1993, pp. 224–225; Nakarmi, 1995).

The real impetus for change, however, is coming from market forces. The *chaebols* must reorganize themselves to compete successfully with American, Japanese, and European multinationals both abroad and in the South Korean market, where there is an increasing trend towards deregulation and liberalization in the wake of GATT; and the government's desire to win membership in the Organization for Economic Co-operation and Development by 1996. While the global trend among multinationals in the 1980s and 1990s has been to get rid of unrelated businesses and focus on core strengths, the *chaebols* find themselves with an overly broad product mix that has reduced their competitiveness and made them too sluggish to compete in the fast-paced international economy. Typically, the *chaebols* are strong in one or two industries, such as Samsung in semiconductors and Hyundai in shipbuilding and autos, while they remain little more than subcontractors to foreign multinationals in other lines of business. They are profitable in many businesses only because they have been able to function as monopolies or oligopolies in the home market. They are overburdened with debt because of past government polices, spending on average, more than 5 per cent of total turnover on debt financing compared to only 2 per cent for Japanese and 2.5 per cent for Taiwanese companies. Unlike other multinationals, they have failed to invest heavily abroad in order to take advantage of cheap labor and skirt trade barriers. Currently, less than 5 per cent of their assets are outside of Korea (McGrath and Mi-young, 1994, pp. 47–51; Nakarmi, 1995). To rectify this situation, the *chaebols* are attempting to restructure themselves on a number of fronts. These changes are summarized in Table 2.

LABOR

OVERVIEW

The primary source of Korea's growth was labor. The government has been able to carry out its development policy unconstrained by a shortage of labor, and firms have been able to carry out their plans, taking low wages for granted. This is now changing. There have been a rising number of labor disputes since 1987, and over the last several years the wages have increased dramatically. Productivity has not followed the rapid increase of wages, and there has been a move from manufacturing jobs to construction and service sectors with better working environments. Many manufacturing firms have, therefore, started to experience shortages of labor, despite higher wages (Soon, 1994, p. 83).

In the late 1980s, the total labor force was estimated at 17.3 million. Of this figure, some 20 per cent were engaged in agriculture, 34 per cent in industry, and 46 per cent in services. The Federation of Korean Trade Unions is the principal labor organization with a membership of more than 1.5 million.

The enactment of the Special Measures for Safeguarding National Security Act in 1971 made union actions practically illegal. Once a labor union action took place, the government intervened automatically, and the agreement dictated could not be discussed. In December 1986, the government liberalized labor union activities (*ibid.,* p. 103).

PRODUCTIVITY

In 1960, when the student revolution broke out, the fully employed labor force was only 57 per cent of the potential workforce. The 1960s and 1970s were influenced by heavy investments in light industries. Many firms invested by importing capital and technology from abroad. However, several bottlenecks like shortages of skilled labor, technological know-how, and managerial capability appeared in the economy. These factors influenced

Table 2 Restructuring of Big Four *Chaebol*

Actions	Examples
Reducing the number of companies/subsidiaries	Samsung plans to cut its units from 50 to 24. Hyundai will merge and divest, reducing its companies from 50 to 23. Lucky-Goldstar is planning to merge several companies. Daewoo will merge and divest, leaving it with 14, down from 22.
Reforming management	Samsung is decentralizing authority, giving more power to individual CEOs, and reducing the chairman's clout. Hyundai will give more authority to professional managers. Daewoo companies will be run independently of the group's chairman, who will concentrate on managing its auto unit. Lucky-Goldstar plans to end the Confucian-based personnel management under which seniority was important. Job performance will now be the key.
Going international	Samsung plans to set up integrated electronics facilities in China and Mexico. It will also tie up with Western companies in semiconductors, computers, and telecommunications. Hyundai will invest $4 billion by the year 2000 in autos, telecom, and semiconductors. Daewoo will pursue autos and electronics. Plans to set up large electronic plants in Poland, Brazil, and Vietnam; auto parts plants in China; auto-assembly plants in Romania and Uzbekistan. Lucky-Goldstar Electronics will increase its share of overseas production by setting up plants in emerging countries; acquire foreign technology and companies.
Ownership and control	Samsung, Hyundai, and LG are gradually reducing founding family ownership by making more companies public. Daewoo is already largely in the hands of professional managers.

Source: Adapted from Nakarmi, 1995, p. 79.

the productivity negatively, but it still increased from year to year. The improvement of productivity came from improvement in the quality of workers in terms of knowledge, skill, and siginificantly, the willingness to work. Earlier, the workers had experienced dim prospects, so the worker had really strong incentives to work harder and longer. The new focus on education in the 1950s had created a generally highly literate force versed in the knowledge their work required. The country is now changing industries, and a focus on education is necessary, so the future industries will not suffer the same bottlenecks as did the industries in the 1970s (Soon, 1994, p. 84).

WORKING HOURS. The work week in Korea does not limit itself to 40 hours. In 1990, workers had to put in 50-hour weeks on average, compared to 41 in Japan, and 46 in Taiwan. They have traditionally worked the longest week of all the newly industrializing Asian economies and in most other developing countries. In countries like Japan and Taiwan, working hours have declined with rising income, but this has not happened in Korea, because the real wages have remained relatively low (Soon, 1994, p. 93).

LABOR DISPUTES. There were a total of 3,749 labor disputes, in 1987 which works out to an average of 10.27 per day. The reason for these disputes was the unleashing of pent-up grievances long suppressed by discipline and regimentation (Wilkinson, 1994). Higher wages were achieved, but inflation also increased, and many Koreans today look upon the many strikes as an expensive lesson, and that is part of the reason why the number of disputes has gone down. Other reasons are that the workers feel that they are now properly represented, and that the quality of work has improved. The general public has grown tired of the radical methods of changing things; violent labor and student movements do not have public support anymore.

The movement within the labor force has also been described as the "3D syndrome"; there is a tendency of workers to avoid Difficult, Dangerous, and Dirty jobs. The government has tried to give incentives against this, such as exemption from military service.

FOREIGN WORKERS. The 3D syndrome, and the movement of workers away from the manufacturing industry has brought foreign workers to the country. A current estimate is 100,000 workers from different countries in Asia. They earn 50 per cent of what the Korean workers do. Twenty thousand trainees have also come in, and they earn half of what the foreign workers do. Because of the wage differences, many of the foreign workers run away and work in the "black-market" in Korea. They are brought to the country to help out on the shortage of labor but are often treated badly. Since they get the 3D jobs, many get injured or even die while working. Until last year they did not have medical insurance, or money, so they could not take care of themselves. All foreign workers now have health insurance, even if they are illegal entrants (Yoo-Lim, September 1994, p. 28).

MANAGEMENT SUCCESSION PLANS OF SMALL COMPANIES

Over 50 per cent of the successors of current company's CEO come from the family (Yoo-Lim, October 1994, p. 43).

THE FUTURE

TECHNOLOGY

The country is moving into a new major industry, namely technology. Labor force and know-how are somewhat limited and the country must, therefore, focus on education in the appropriate fields to avoid the problems it experienced in the 1970s with its heavy and chemical industries. Japan leases out its low-end technology and produces its high-end technology itself. The majority of Koreas technology is leased from Japan and the country must develop some of its own by increasing R&D expenditure to be able to compete in the high-end technology areas.

US spends 21 times more in R&D than South Korea, Germany 7 times more, and Japan 13 times more (Economist Intelligence Unit, 1994–95, p. 26).

REUNIFICATION

South Korea is too poor for reunification and many people are afraid of the economical consequences if this should happen too soon. The cost of reunification in the year 2000 is estimated by the Ministry of Finance to be a total of US$980 billion. The recent unification of Germany has also made the people more aware of the economical, and other, problems created in the process of joining two countries.

POLLUTION

The rapid growth of the country has resulted in high pollution in the area. China and Russia have also used the surrounding sea to dump everything including nuclear waste and heavy metals. The number of fish species the oceans host has fallen from 141 to 24. The cost of cleaning up Korea itself will be high, and Korea has already offered money to its neighbors to help them clean up. Stricter pollution laws in Korea have caused the move of some factories to China, so some of the pollution from China is actually from South Korean-owned plants (Economist Intelligence Unit, 1994–95, p. 30).

INFRASTRUCTURE

There have been several accidents caused by failures in building constructions and poorly developed infrastructure. The country's infrastructure has not been developed well enough and Korea must invest to obtain country-wide improvement. The construction industry is one of the major export earners for Korea and the poor quality of the home sites can cause problems for this industry abroad (Economist Intelligence Unit, 1994–95, p. 14).

REFERENCES

Asia's Ruling Families, *Asia Money,* October 1994, pp. 38–39.
Bello, Walden and Stephanie Rosenfeld, *Dragons in Distress: Asia's miracle economies in crisis,* San Francisco: Institute for Food and Development Policy, 1992.
Cherry, Judith, *Cassel Business Briefings: Korea,* New York: Cassell, 1993.
Cherry, Judith, *Republic of Korea,* New York: Cassell, 1993.
Cho, Lee-Jay and Yoon Hyung Kim (Ed.), *Korea's Political Economy,* Boulder: Westview Press, 1994, p. 627.
Economist Intelligence Unit, South Korea, North Korea, *EIU Country Report 1994–95,* New York.
Koo, Bon Ho, *Sociocultural Factors in the Industrialization of Korea,* San Francisco: International Center for Economic Growth, 1992, p. 20.
Lin, Tzong-biau and Chyau Tuan (Ed.), *The Asian NIEs: Success and Challenge,* Hong Kong: Lo Fung Learned Society, 1993.
McGill, Peter, Tomorrow Belongs to Lee, *Euromoney,* October 1994, pp. 98–99.

McGrath, Neal and Ahn Mi-young, Colossal Change Awaits Chaebol, *Asian Business,* November 1994, pp. 47–51.

Microsoft Corporation, South Korea, *Microsoft Encarta,* 1993.

Nakarmi, Laxmi, South Korea: A flying leap toward the 21st century? *Business Week,* March 20, 1995, pp. 78–80.

Rich, Robert G., Jr. and L. Gordon Flake, Selected Economic Data, *Korea Economic Update,* March 1995, pp. 2–3.

Sohn, Jie-Ae, The Global Team, *Business Korea,* January 1995, pp. 33–34.

Soon, Cho, *The Dynamics of Korean Economic Development.* Washington, DC: Institute for International Economics, 1994.

Stewart, Peter, *Korea: The next step,* London: Euromoney Publications, 1994.

Top Chaebols Continue Their Business Expansion, *Business Korea,* July 1994, pp. 43–44.

Wilkinson, Barry, The Korea Labor "Problem," *British Journal of Industrial Relations,* September 1994, p. 342.

Yoo-Lim, Lee, Illegal Foreign Workers Get Shortchanged in Korea, *Business Korea,* September 1994.

Yoo-Lim, Lee, Family Ties Come First, *Business Korea,* October 1994.

SUGGESTED FURTHER READING

Das, Dilip K., *Korean Economic Dynamism,* Hong Kong: Macmillan Academic and Professional Ltd., 1992.

Kang, T.W., *Is Korea the Next Japan?* New York: The Free Press, 1989.

Kwack, Sung Yeung (Ed.), *The Korean Economy at a Crossroad,* Westport: Praeger Publishers, 1994.

Nakarmi, Laxmi and Joan Warner, Two Tigers Sharpen up Their Markets, *Business Week,* October 24, 1994, pp. 50–51.

Privatization Program Comes Under Fire, *Business Korea,* August 1994, pp. 32–33.

Sang-Yun, Kang, Korea's International Competitiveness Plunges, *Business Korea,* October 1994, pp. 26–27.

Sohn, Jie-Ae, Korea's Big Rush Abroad, *Business Korea,* December 1994, pp. 30–32.

South Korea: Can Korea Change? *Business Asia,* January 31, 1994, p. 16.

South Korea, *KCWD/Kaleidoscope,* [n.p.]: ABC-Clio, Inc., 1995.

South Korea, *Walden Country Reports,* [n.p.]: Walden Publishing Ltd., 1995.

Stevenson, Mark, And for My Next Miracle, *Canadian Business,* January 1995, pp. 75–81.

CASE TWENTY

Daewoo: The Favored Korean Chaebol*

Daewoo and Its Chairman

The Daewoo Group, South Korea's third largest business conglomerate, is in the midst of a campaign to become a truly global enterprise by the start of the new century. Its VISION 2000 strategy has set a goal of attaining sales of US$177 billion by the year 2000, more than a threefold increase in five years.

The sales target total consists of US$74 billion from trading, US$28 billion from electronics and telecommunications, US$30 billion from motor vehicles, US$18 billion from heavy industries and shipbuilding, US$18 billion from construction, US$7 billion from financial services, and US$2 billion from hotels.

To achieve this target, Daewoo is pushing to develop a worldwide network of 660 offices and plants in over 160 countries around the world—including 430 sales subsidiaries, 130 manufacturing subsidiaries, 30 technical and design R&D centers, and 70 local branch offices.

And to foster competitiveness and efficiency, Group founder and Chairman Kim Woo-Choong, 59, who has overseen managerial operations of all 25 principal group companies, will focus his managerial role mainly on overseas automotive manufacturing and sales. In early 1995, 11 new chairmen were given full managerial responsibilities for major group companies including Daewoo Corporation, Daewoo Electronics Co., Ltd., Daewoo Heavy Industries Ltd., Daewoo Motor Co., Ltd. and Daewoo Telecom Ltd.

---

* This case was prepared by Lane Kelley, Professor in the Department of Management and Industrial Relations, College of Business Administration, University of Hawaii at Manoa, for the purpose of class discussion rather than to illustrate the effective handling of management/administrative problems.

Chairman Kim says, "Around the world, national economic policies and international accords such as the new WTO are stimulating trade as never before. A genuinely global economy is emerging, and this means exceptional opportunities for all the companies of the Daewoo Group."

Daewoo is Korea's, and one of the world's, fastest growing company. Daewoo has grown at an annual average rate of 30 per cent in the last decade. In 1995, Daewoo's total sales grew to US$51.2 billion, an impressive 43.4 per cent increase over 1994 sales.

Daewoo, which means "great universe" in Korean, started as a garment exporting firm with five employees in 1967. It has grown to become one of the world's largest enterprises, with more than 191,000 employees worldwide engaged in trading, construction, shipbuilding, and in the manufacturing of motor vehicles, heavy equipment, machine tools, home appliances, electronics products, computers and telecommunications equipment. It also runs hotels and provides financial services.

In the January 5, 1987 issue of *Fortune* magazine, Daewoo's charismatic founder and chairman, Kim Woo-Choong, was selected by the magazine as one of "The Year's 50 Most Fascinating Business People." In June 1984, he had also been awarded The International Business Award which was presented by King Carl Gustaf XVI, to honor "an entrepreneur who had contributed to the idea of free enterprise." His firm, Daewoo, founded in 1967 with an initial investment of US$10,000 is now one of the largest business groups in the world, ranked 34th by *Fortune* magazine.

Chairman Kim is also popular with the general population of Korea and its government. Ask the secretaries of Korean business firms who is their most respected business leader and the answer would be unanimous: Chairman Kim. The Korean government have, on several occasions in the past, approached him to take over troubled business firms.

Daewoo and Kim are one and the same to the people of Korea. He is usually described as an authoritarian leader. He has rationalized his leadership style because of the entrepreneurial, high growth, status of the company. He has the reputation of a dedicated, hardworking leader who works 16-hour days, 365 days a year. "Other than hard work, I have no hobby," he says. Like most Koreans, he is very nationalistic and this strong nationalism seems to be a result of their history—especially their recent history. Korea was conquered and controlled by the Japanese from 1910 to 1945. The country has a long history of also having been attacked by the Chinese, Japanese, and Mongols. The Korean people's resentment towards the Japanese is still in evidence. This is manifested in business as a struggle to excel in their competition with Japanese firms. Kim Woo-Choong was a teenager during the Korean war and when his father was taken away by North Korean soldiers, never to be seen again, he took on the responsibility of supporting his family by selling newspapers. His entrepreneurial spirit was evident even then as he developed strategies to outsell the other newsboys. He is still known as a strong marketer.

CURRENT SCENARIO

Daewoo was established by five enterprising young men in 1967 and today it is the parent of 25 affiliates with over 190,000 employees (108,000 overseas). This Korean *chaebol* has a worldwide network of over 116 branch offices, trading in more than 3,000 products in more than 165 countries. Its initial business activities were concerned with manufacture and export of textile and garments but it has diversified into construction, financial services, shipbuilding, and the manufacture of automobiles, home appliances, and telecommunication devices. In the past, the Daewoo Group consistently accounted for more than 10 per cent of Korea's exports. The major activities of the group are:

GENERAL TRADING. As a trading company, Daewoo Corporation exports products manufactured by its affiliates and other prominent Korean manufacturers. Bilateral and trilateral trade programs, special trade projects, plant exports, international resource development, joint ventures, overseas investments, and import programs are some of its activities.

RESOURCE DEVELOPMENT. As one of the corporation's important international activities, resource development programs were originally aimed at securing the stable, long-term flow of energy sources to Korea; but Daewoo has, as part of these efforts, gone beyond sourcing supplies and into resource development programs in bituminous, uranium exploration, and other international resource development projects.

The corporation is also promoting new projects including import and domestic sales of sulfur and magnesite, oilfield development, and overseas oil refining projects.

CONSTRUCTION PROGRAMS. Active in a host of domestic and international construction and construction-related programs, Daewoo Corporation was selected by the Korean government in 1986 as an outstanding contractor for its contributions of excellence to Korean construction. The corporation's construction division is intensifying its port and harbor construction, military construction and plant construction projects in an effort to bolster its organizational base. The division is also making preparations to enter into North American construction markets as a major step in increasing international recognition, reliability and technology. The division received US$2.06 billion in new international orders in the first half of 1996.

CUSTOMER SERVICE NETWORK. Daewoo Corporation conducts extensive domestic sales operations, and has a network of 5,500 sales offices nationwide. These sales offices provide consumers with a broadening range of Daewoo Group products as well as imported goods and products by other renowned Korean manufacturers. This network is recognized for speedy, efficient sales programs and services in providing consumers with quality products at reasonable prices.

DAEWOO GROUP

The Daewoo Group has a somewhat unusual ownership structure. The ownership share of founder W.C. Kim and his family appears to be 41.8 per cent, but 40.74 per cent is owned by affiliated companies and the Daewoo Foundation. The share directly owned by the founder and his family is thus only 1.06 per cent, which stems entirely from 7.45 per cent ownership in the Choongbook Bank. The founder and his families do not own any stock of any other affiliated companies listed on the Korean Stock Exchange. This is a truly exceptional case of ownership structure among Korean *chaebols*.

Basically, Daewoo Foundation owns the stocks of Daewoo Corporation, which, together with the foundation, owns the stock of affiliated companies in the group. With Daewoo Foundation and Daewoo Corporation as intermediary ownership mechanisms, Daewoo's ownership structure is considered as Type II in a pure form with W.C. Kim owning 26.9 per cent of Daewoo Trading Company (now Daewoo Corporation), which owned the affiliated companies. But in 1980 during the political transition following the assassination of President Park, Kim donated most of his holdings to Daewoo Foundation, which took his place as the legal owner of the group. Such an ownership structure can hardly be found in other Korean *chaebols*.

EARLY HISTORY

Daewoo's initial business was the export of tricot fabrics to Singapore and Indonesia. Its export sales grew from US$580,000 in 1967 to about US$4 million in 1969. His next challenge was the US market and Daewoo built one of the largest textile manufacturing plants in Korea so that they could deal with the large clients like J.C. Penneys and Sears and Roebucks. Daewoo experienced great success in the US market but correctly foresaw the climate of protectionism, which resulted in the installation of an import quota on textiles. Since the allocation of the quotas in Korea was based on recent export performance, Daewoo was in a very advantageous position because it had basically gone for market share rather than profits. It was awarded 30 per cent of Korea's quota.

In the next few years Daewoo became one of Korea's most profitable firms. The resulting profits and a new stock issue in 1973, which was sold at a premium of over 300 per cent of par value, gave them the funds to go on an acquisition drive. It acquired 14 companies and took major positions in two others. It now was in the manufacturing and trading textiles, leather goods and other light industry products and banking and financial businesses. In 1975, Daewoo was designated a general trading company by the Korean government and this provided special access to export financing, which was a major problem at that time because of the closed Korean financial markets.

In 1976, Kim was approached by the government's Korean Development Bank to take over the struggling Hankook Machinery Ltd., a major manufacturer of industrial machinery, rolling stock, and diesel engines. Under Japanese, and later Korean, ownership it had not shown a profit over a period of 38 years. Kim worked around the clock, often sleeping on the factory floor. In the first year, he turned its operations around to break-even status; and showed a profit the following year. His reputation and, just as important, his relationship with the government were now assured.

In 1978, Kim was again approached by the government to take over an ailing shipyard, Okpo Shipbuilding Company, which was close to bankruptcy. It was one-third the way to completing the largest dry dock in the world. The dry dock was completed in 1981, and started operating profitably in 1983.

Another firm acquired in this period was Saehan Motor Company, which was a 50-50 joint venture with General Motors. With this Daewoo entered the automobile industry.

KOREA AND THE AUTOMOBILE INDUSTRY: THE 1990S*

In seeming disregard of warnings from Western car makers about overcapacity in the world auto industry, Korean producers are expanding assembly capacity at a rate reminiscent of the startling growth of the Japanese industry in earlier decades. The second largest Korean car manufacturer, Kia, has announced that it plans to start assembly of four-wheel drive sport/utility vehicles in Germany—the vehicles will be assembled by Karmann, the German automotive engineering group. A Korean car to be manufactured by a German firm is quite a turnaround for a country whose cars have worn the label of poor quality. This is indicative of Korean manufacturers' latest move marking Korea's rapid advance into world auto markets.

Supported by the rapidly growing and until now highly protected domestic market, Hyundai, Kia and the third largest Korean car maker, Daewoo, are determined to break into the industry's front ranks. Exports, to developing regions and North America and Europe, are growing as is the scope of plans for foreign assembly plants in many different countries as the following sections will describe. At a time when other major Asian manufacturers are downsizing, Korean firms are expanding production capacities. Hyundai Motor, the leading South Korean car maker, plans to increase vehicle production capacity by 60 per cent to 2 million units by the year 2000 from the present 1.25 million, according to Mr. Se Yung Chung, the group's chairman. It is planning to build more foreign production sites to reinforce its presence in overseas markets, he says, with manufacturing facilities in North America, Europe, Southeast Asia and the Middle East. Individually, Hyundai, Kia and Daewoo are all voicing the ambition of becoming the world's top 10 producers, an aim that would mean dislodging the likes of Mitsubishi, Mazda, Chrysler and Fiat.

The threat of increasing Korean automobile exports allied with the high barriers to foreign car imports, which accounted for well below 1 per cent of domestic sales, are pushing the issue of Korean expansion towards the top of European car makers' agenda.

During one month of 1994, the major automakers—Hyundai, Kia, Daewoo, Asia, and Ssangyong—raised exports to nearly 40,000 cars, 6.6 times the figure of the same period a year earlier. Korean exports are actually widely dispersed in international markets:

- With a 317 per cent jump to US$229 million, Germany sprang up from Korea's ninth largest market in 1991 to third in 1992. In the Middle East, Iran was the sixth largest importer.
- Chile, 20th biggest importer of Korean vehicles in 1991, jumped to 10th in 1992 with exports growing 367 per cent to US$70 million.
- In fourth place, Taiwan imported US$111 million worth of Korean cars, up 16.7 per cent, followed by Australia with US$90 million of Korean auto imports, up 39.8 per cent, in fifth place.
- Britain was seventh with shipments rising 4.5 per cent to US$93 million.

---

* This section is adapted from the articles, Korean Auto Exports, *The Korean Times,* February 27, 1993, pp. 1–4 (supplement) and John Burton and Kevin Done, Risky Manuevers in the Fast Lane, *Financial Times,* April 28, 1994, p. 15.

- Italy made eighth for buying the greatest number of cars, vans, and buses, with its imports reaching US$101 million, up 68.5 per cent.
- Greece ranked ninth with Korea's exports growing 23.2 per cent to US$68 million.

According to statistics from the Trade-Industry Ministry, the automobile industry took a 4.2 per cent share of the nation's economic development in 1981 with the portion rising to 6.4 per cent in 1989. In 1980, the car industry accounted for 3.31 per cent of the nation's total manufacturing production and 0.7 per cent of its global exports.

As the industry is now engaged in fierce economic competition, Korea and advanced countries are stepping up efforts to strengthen the international competitiveness of their car industries, since automobiles is the largest item in world trade. In 1990, the global trade of cars amounted to US$250 billion, 8 per cent of all merchandise exchanges.

In 1991, Korea was the ninth largest car maker in the world, producing 1.498 million units. Among the top 10 automakers were all the members of the G-7—the United States, Japan, Germany, France, Italy, Canada and the United Kingdom.

Japan topped the list with production of 13.242 million units, followed by the United States (8.806 million), Germany (5.015 million), France (3.610 million), Spain (1.932 million), Italy (1.877 million), Canada (1.876 million), the Commonwealth of Independent States (1.845 million), Korea and the United Kingdom (1.454 million).

Although Korean car makers are striving hard to expand their production facilities and catch up with their counterparts among the advanced nations, they are faced with many internal problems. First, they are finding it difficult to secure land and funds for the expansion of their production facilities. Specifically, they are restricted in floating corporate debentures and must use special foreign exchange for the purchase of foreign machinery due to the government's strict monetary policy. Second, lack of infrastructure such as paved roads is hampering their development. Lastly, the levy of heavy taxes on car owners hinders the expansion of their domestic sales. Koreans pay 1,213 times more taxes than Americans at the time of their car acquisition, while Japanese and Britons pay 1,744 times and 903 times, respectively, more than Americans. Korean car makers are calling upon the government to remove such obstacles immediately to boost their facility expansion so that they can compete with their counterparts in rich countries on an equal footing in the near future.

DAEWOO DRIVES OFF THE BEATEN TRACK*

Kim Woo-Choong, head of South Korea's Daewoo Group, had travelled a long way to look at what might be his auto factory of the future. Aboard a helicopter in Tatarstan, Russia, some 19,000 kilometers from Daewoo headquarters in Seoul, Kim flew over the plains of the autonomous republic along the Volga River in February 1992. Tatarstan Deputy Prime Minister M.M. Kasnulin pointed out the site for their proposed US$1 million joint venture: a brand new factory built next to a former Soviet missile plant. The Koreans were elated

---

*This section is based on the article, Daewoo Drives off the Beaten Path, *Business Week*, June 28, 1993, pp. 33–34.

to be getting a nearly completed plant. "Think about the money we'll save," says Yoo Ki-Bum, president of trading company Daewoo Corp., who accompanied Kim on the trip.

An article in *Asia Business* (July 1993) described Daewoo as the first Asian multinational company to make major investments in Myanmar—in sectors such as consumer electronics, garments, and retailing—"despite the country's economic backwardness and pariah political status." Also, the Vietnam government has given its approval for a US$170 million joint venture with Hanoi Electronic Corp. to produce cathode ray tubes for television sets, a 70 per cent stake in Orion picture tube and two smaller but significant ventures.

The proposed Tartarstan project is one of many new cooperative projects Chairman Kim has been nurturing lately in countries long ignored by most auto makers. For Daewoo, Korea's fourth-largest *chaebol,* or conglomerate, the strategy marks a sharp departure from Kim's grand plan to make the US$2.4 billion Daewoo Motor unit a major player in lucrative North American markets. That effort has now been changed, partly because Daewoo is restricted by their previous relationship with General Motors over the LeMans series. Instead, Kim is betting the future of Daewoo Motor on the fast growing but unpredictable markets of the developing world. If his plan works, other Korean companies could follow his lead, in effect carving out a new industrial strategy for their country. It is still not certain if Kim can pull it off. But some experts at least are giving him the benefit of the doubt. Says Y.S. Chang, a consultant with Organizational Dynamics Inc. in Burlington, Massachusetts: "Kim brings modern technology to the middle of nowhere, and he'll take something that particular country has in surplus and use his trading company to sell it." The Daewoo Group, for instance, has a consumer electronics plant in Myanmar and a tire factory in the Sudan. By striking such deals, Kim is seeking to have an edge over other international competitors, who are more reluctant to wheel and deal in undeveloped and unproven markets.

Chairman Kim's plan does not lack for ambition. By the year 2000, he wants Daewoo Motor Co. to become a global manufacturer, increasing production nearly fivefold, to 2 million vehicles. Half of them will be manufactured overseas. China will be the key. Currently, Daewoo is working hard to win Beijing's approval to build a US$1 billion plant in the northeast just across the Yellow Sea from South Korea. Kim came a step closer to realizing the China project when Chinese Foreign Minister Qian Qichen visited Seoul in May 1993. The diplomat took time off from discussions with South Korean officials to tour a Daewoo automobile facility.

Winning approval from Beijing may take months. In the meantime, Daewoo has plenty of other partners. In Uzbekistan, a US$600 million joint venture will begin production of 200,000 cars. Kim has also cut a deal with Tehran to establish an assembly plant in Iran. Shortly after his helicopter ride over Tatarstan, Kim signed a memorandum of understanding with the local government. Kim has also met with Peruvian President Alberto Fujimori, Vietnamese Prime Minister Vo Van Kiat, and Philippine President Fidel Ramos about setting up plants in their countries.

Kim needs the Third World leaders' markets as much as they need his plants. That's because Daewoo has nowhere else to turn. An ambitious partnership with General Motors Corp., through which Daewoo had once hoped to enter North America, collapsed in 1992. The plan originally called for the two companies to cooperate on the LeMans, a car designed in Germany by GM's Opel unit, produced in Kim's state-of-the-art plant in Pupyong, South Korea, and sold through the vast network of GM's Pontiac Division. But while the Koreans wanted to gain market share in the US, Daewoo officials say GM was more interested in sales in Korea. In September 1992 GM finally sold its 50 per cent stake in Daewoo Motor back to the group. Under the terms of the "divorce," Daewoo is permanently banned from selling the LeMans in the US and was forbidden from exporting the car elsewhere until 1995. "The problems with GM prevented us from making any effort to export Daewoo cars, let alone win market share," says Kim.

After the end of their joint venture with GM in 1992, Daewoo suffered losses for three years; but in 1995 its sales totaled US$4.49 billion and its net profits were US$13.6 million. Daewoo Motor is running third in the overall domestic market; but in passenger cars, it is second to Hyundai and leading Kia Motors.

Daewoo has long been the pioneer among Korean companies in building trade ties. As an example, long before the 1992 formalization of relations between Seoul and Beijing, Daewoo set up a US$10 million refrigerator plant in China. At present, Daewoo has 27 planned or on-going projects, valued at over US$900 million—the most of any Korean company.

Interestingly, legal sales only began in China in August 1993. On the legal side, Daewoo sold only 111 cars in China in 1992, but after legalization, sales have taken off. In the first four months of 1993, the company's direct exports to China rose to 1,649 cars. By the end of 1993, direct Korean exports to China totaled about 30,000 vehicles, with Daewoo shipping more than one-third or 12,000 units. Even more cars entered illegally: an additional 50,000 Korean-built cars were smuggled into China.

Daewoo appears to be hedging its China bet with a new $2.2 billion plant and state-of-the-art testing facility, under construction in Kunsan, Korea, on the west coast—a very short distance from China.

If the Chinese balk at letting Kim assemble cars on the mainland, he hopes to set up assembly in Korea some 640 kilometers by sea from China's Shandong province. He would then use Chinese suppliers of labor-intensive parts and ship them to Korea for final assembly. With Chinese content in its cars, Daewoo can be expected to have an easier time exporting to China.

Partly because of the smuggling, the pressure is building on Beijing to open its doors. The demand for cars and the new affluence in China's coastal provinces mean Beijing will have little choice but to allow manufacturing or permit more legal imports. The Chinese government already has moved to meet consumer demand by slightly increasing its auto imports while cracking down on smuggling. But that may not be enough to stop the illegal traffic in Korean cars. Demand for them is especially keen as the high yen has put the Japanese at a disadvantage.

Overall, Kim is targeting countries that either already restrict Japanese imports or fear becoming too dependent on Japan. He argues that his strategy will pay off over the long term, as the economics of doing business in obscure places changes. "Countries like Uzbekistan have enough purchasing power and resources to buy cars," says Kim. Marketing costs are lower because advertising needs are much reduced.

Daewoo's strategy basically is to avoid as much competition as possible. Its reliance on OEM left it with strong manufacturing capabilities but no strong models of its own. Will third world markets be profitable? "You don't make as much profit by selling cars in the US or Europe as you do in selling to developing countries," says Daewoo's Yoo. Targeting developing countries may look less attractive to Koreans than a First World strategy. But if he succeeds, Kim will change a lot of minds.

Daewoo Motor Co., Ltd., managed independently since ending a 14-year joint venture with General Motors of the United States in 1992, recorded sales of US$4.5 billion in 1995. It produced 446,214 passenger cars (1.5 liter to 3.2 liter models), 3,996 heavy trucks and 4,500 large buses. In addition, Daewoo Heavy Industries Ltd. built 65,806 mini-cars, vans and trucks (powered by 800 cc engines). About half of total auto production was exported to 150 countries.

Daewoo's new plant at Kunsan, southwest of Seoul, which will have an annual production capacity of 300,000 passenger cars and 12,000 commercial vehicles, will begin operation towards the end of 1996. Daewoo is also operating and constructing overseas production bases in Uzbekistan (200,000 units), Romania (200,000 units), Poland (220,000 units) and India (210,000 units), as well as in the Czech Republic, Iran, the Philippines, Vietnam, Indonesia, and China to bring total global production capacity to two million units annually, half overseas, by the year 1998. This would place Daewoo among the world's top 10 automakers.

To globalize its technology and R&D, Daewoo Motor has expanded its automotive technical center in Pupyong, near Seoul, into a general research complex and has established overseas R&D facilities in Britain and Germany. To achieve its ambitious goals for the automotive business, Daewoo plans to invest US$11 billion in capital investment over the next five years.

Daewoo is equally ambitious in the electronics business, as it plans to invest a total of US$43.9 billion by the year 2000 to become one of the world's three largest manufacturers of consumer electronics products and home appliances, with annual sales of US$10 billion.

Daewoo's aim is to capture between 10 to 20 per cent of the world electronics market in its six core product areas: televisions, VCRs, refrigerators, washing machines, microwave ovens and color computer monitors. With expansion into new business areas, Daewoo Electronics forecasts that it will become one of the world's top five electronics manufacturers with total annual sales of US$50 billion by the year 2010.

Since its founding in 1967, Daewoo has pioneered the international market for national economic development and strengthened international economic cooperation. As a result of these overseas experiences, Daewoo formulated the gobalization strategy in March 1993. As of March 1996, it has developed an international network of over 400 sites around the world that include sales and production subsidiaries, research centers and branch offices. It will continue to make qualitative, as well as quantitative, investments into this network; and by the year 2000, it expects to have a global network of over 1,000 sites, including about 650 overseas subsidiaries. The following, extracted from an internal progress report, describes the accomplishments of Daewoo's global strategy:

The demise of the cold war has prompted restructuring of the international order, which is now centered on fierce economic competition. We are witnessing the emergence of a truly global economy; yet at the same time, we are witnessing seemingly contradictory phenomena, such as the formation of regional blocs, greater protectionism, and the decline of domestic industrial competitiveness.

As a result, we deemed it inevitable that business would have to set the firm foundation for global cooperation.

Against such a background, we realized that we would have to go beyond a simple import-export system and establishment of overseas production bases. The times call for integrated, flexible managerial strategies for total globalization, and to create a new type of business, based on localization of management, in order to strengthen international competitiveness.

As of the end of June, Daewoo had a total of 403 sites in its global network, including 277 overseas subsidiaries. Our overseas employees now total more than 100,000.

The number of overseas subsidiaries is growing rapidly; from only 58 in 1992, to 86 in 1993, 155 in 1994 and 277 as of June this year. As this globalization program continues to mature, we expect to have a total of 650 overseas subsidiaries by the year 2000.

In addition, to meet demands in emerging markets, Daewoo is establishing new sales subsidiaries in less-developed markets and strengthening marketing activities there to become a market leader.

By region, major investments are centered in Eastern Europe including Poland, Hungary and Romania; the CIS nations; China, India and Vietnam in Asia; Mexico in the Americas; and the Sudan in Africa.

In Eastern Europe, which is one of the most important strategic regions, we have become a major foreign investor, particularly in Poland and Romania.

Daewoo's major investments in Poland include auto production plants, Daewoo Motor Polska and Daewoo-FSO, and a large electronics production complex.

In Romania, we have the Rodae Automobile production plant.

We are also involved in a commercial vehicle production project in the Czech Republic, and in a number of finance ventures in Hungary.

In the CIS, we have a large production plant in Uzbekistan for our Cielo subcompact and our Tico mini-sedan. We expect to increase our sales throughout the CIS through auto sales subsidiaries in Kazakhstan and Azerbaijan.

In Russia, we have expanded our merchandising network and are rapidly set to do extensive business. We are reviewing potential projects in the Ukraine and other CIS nations as our global network grows.

In Asia, we see the greatest market potential in China, India and Vietnam, markets which we actually entered some time ago and where we have established prominence. We are also expanding our Asian network through various projects in other nations as well.

In China, we are Korea's largest investor, with more than 30 on-going projects, including cement, bus, excavator, and electronic component production; in telecommunications, and in transportation. We plan to add auto production in the future.

India is also important to our globalization program, and major projects there include DCM-Daewoo auto production, an electronics complex, and CRB Securities. We are promoting more than 10 additional projects in India, including $1.5-billion build-own-operate thermal investments with $5 billion in sales.

Daewoo is the largest foreign investor in Vietnam, a nation we consider core to our Southeast Asian activities. Our 14 on-going projects include auto production, a home appliance production complex, a television tube plant, the Daeha Business Center in Hanoi, industrial complex development in Saidong, oil exploration, banking, agrochemicals and light industry.

We are ready to invest an additional $2 billion in Vietnam, in projects ranging from rolling stock to highway construction.

To counteract the formation of regional blocs, we are expanding our production bases in specific areas to avoid tariffs. In Mexico, we are expanding our electronics production facilities to serve all the Americans. We are also developing a global trade and electronics sales network throughout the Americas, and we expect to enter the North American automobile market in 1997.

In Europe, we have concentrated home appliance and electronic consumer goods in three nations—Northern Ireland, France and Poland—and are pushing forward so that a plant can produce 500,000 motor vehicles per year at facilities in Poland, Romania and the Czech Republic. We are expanding sales throughout Europe with our network of 19 auto and 10 electronics sales subsidiaries.

In addition, we have automotive and electronics research facilities in England, Germany and France. These facilities afford us the opportunity to absorb the latest in advanced technology. And they will play an integral part in fully localizing our interfaced European network of research, production, finance and sales facilities.

In the Americas, we are concentrating our investments in Mexico, particularly in electronics. We already have a home appliance production complex and an electronic component plant in operation, and are building a television tube production facility.

In Africa, we established a base in the Sudan several years ago, and we are using this as a springboard to the rest of Africa. In the Sudan, we are operating a tire plant and textile plants, other light industry subsidiaries, and a guest hotel.

Based on results so far, I am pleased to say that we have set a firm foundation for global market systems, particularly in the fields of motor vehicles and electronics.

Our network of motor vehicle production facilities now includes plants in 10 nations—some of which I have already mentioned—which will provide us with one million vehicles annually.

Also, our Daewoo Worthing Technical Center in England and our Munich Technical Center in Germany work in coordination with our Technical Center in Pupyong, Korea, as part of our growing global network to develop advanced auto technology. Our sales subsidiaries in Western Europe are setting the pace for sales in nations there.

In electronics, we plan to capture a 10 percent share of the world market in six product categories, becoming one of the world's top three manufacturers. We have already established regional headquarters in Europe and the CIS, and plan more in other strategic regions.

We have already set up three major production complexes, in Vietnam, Poland and Mexico, and have established a firm foundation for a global network that includes over 30 production and 28 sales subsidiaries.

We expect to be producing more than 60 percent of our electronics products at overseas sites by the year 2000.

We now have a Global Telecommunications Network that links Seoul headquarters and over 400 overseas sites to provide the latest in all types of relevant business and trade information. This network will continue to grow along with our global network of overseas sites.

APPENDIX

Table 1 Worldwide Car Production

	Actual				Forecast			
	1989	1990	1991	1992	1993	1995	1997	1999
Japan	9,052	9,947	9,753	9,378	8,497	8,824	9,235	9,391
US	6,967	6,294	5,687	5,937	6,135	6,981	6,927	7,142
Germany	4,563	4,660	4,659	4,863	3,753	3,850	4,412	4,939
France	3,408	3,294	3,187	3,325	2,854	2,987	3,268	3,337
South Korea	**856**	**964**	**1,128**	**1,255**	**1,498**	**1,962**	**2,389**	**2,638**
UK	1,299	1,295	1,236	1,291	1,375	1,551	1,983	2,186

Table 2 Daewoo Electronics: Profile

Country	Items	Annual Capacity ('000)	Year Founded	Year of Operation	Investment Ratio (%)
China	Home refrigerators	300	1987	1988	50
France	Microwave ovens	300	1988	1989	66
UK	VCRs	500	1988	1989	100
Myanmar	TVs	250	1990	1991	55
	Audios	160			
	Home refrigerators	20			
Mexico	Color TVs	500	1990	1991	100
France	Color TVs	400	1992	1993	100
Vietnam	Electrical home appliances	1,000	1993		65
Uzbekistan	Color TVs	100	1993		50
	Audios	100			
	Air-conditioners	100			
	Heating devices	200			

Table 3 World's 25 Largest Motor Vehicle Producers, 1989 (all monetary data in US$, millions)

Rank	Company	Country	World Market Share (units)	Automotive Revenues	Total Revenues	Total ('000)	Auto (%)	Truck (%)	Net Earnings	Capital Expenditures	R&D
1	General Motors	US	17.7	99.7	126.9	7,946	74	26	3,831	7,386	5,248
2	Ford	US	14.6	76.8	96.1	6,336	70	30	4,259	6,695	3,100
3	Toyota	Japan	9.4	53.8	63.3	4,115	76	24	2,836	3,273	3,709
4	Volkswagen	W. Germany	6.6	34.4	34.4	2,948	93	7	921	2,434	1,111
5	Nissan	Japan	6.4	36.4	37.8	2,930	77	23	945	1,222	1,564
6	Chrysler	US	5.4	30.8	34.9	2,382	48	52	629	1,531	954
7	Fiat	Italy	5.4	26.4	37.9	2,436	90	10	2,453	2,612	1,306
8	Peugeot	France	4.6	22.8	23.9	2,216	88	12	1,518	1,872	546
9	Renault	France	4.2	26.4	27.2	2,053	80	20	1,451	1,616	468
10	Honda	Japan	4.0	25.2	26.5	1,960	86	14	945	1,222	1,564
11	Mazda	Japan	2.8	14.5	17.1	1,460	74	26	189	655	545
12	Mitsubishi	Japan	2.7	16.7	16.7	1,335	55	45	167	873	836
13	Hyundai	S. Korea	1.9	3.9	5.6	819	89	11	67	NA	NA
14	Suzuki	Japan	1.7	7.3	7.3	875	33	67	73	436	218
15	Daimler-Benz	W. Germany	1.7	29.8	40.5	803	67	33	1,317	2,910	2,646
16	Daihatsu	Japan	1.4	5.1	5.5	600	38	62	49	305	182
17	Fuji-Subaru	Japan	1.2	5.0	5.4	530	65	35	44	393	218
18	BMW	W. Germany	1.2	14.0	14.0	523	100	0	460	1,058	661
19	Rover Group	Britain	1.1	5.6	5.6	535	90	10	105	328	NA
20	Volvo	Sweden	1.0	11.0	14.1	465	87	13	793	971	955
21	Isuzu	Japan	0.8	9.6	9.6	590	19	81	124	313	291
22	Kia Motors	S. Korea	0.7	1.1	2.7	412	67	33	41	NA	NA
23	Daewoo Motors	S. Korea	0.4	NA	NA	NA	NA	NA	NA	NA	NA
24	Lada	Russia	0.3	NA	NA	NA	NA	NA	NA	NA	NA
25	Saab-Scania	Sweden	0.3	6.0	6.9	138	74	26	495	575	493

Daewoo Corporation—Balance Sheets, 1992–95 (in million won)

Assets	1995	1994	1993	1992
Current assets				
Cash	496,384	270,791	473,961	462,801
Marketable securities, at cost which approximates market	130,676	67,767	170,338	60,308
Trade notes and accounts receivable	2,498,811	2,008,196	2,060,341	1,867,114
Less: allowance for doubtful accounts	7,675	5,866	6,034	5,374
Net trade receivables	2,491,136	2,002,230	2,054,307	1,861,740
Other receivables	284,230	145,076	159,834	107,978
Inventories	1,480,462	1,438,012	1,090,189	1,091,090
Prepayments	938,366	588,410	516,555	465,097
Other current assets	192,352	125,659	135,736	110,689
Total current assets	6,013,606	4,638,045	4,600,920	4,159,703
Investments				
Affiliated companies	1,476,853	1,291,803	1,126,290	1,110,552
Other investments	78,872	62,705	66,755	63,611
Total investments	1,555,725	1,354,508	1,193,045	1,174,133
Property, plant and equipment				
Land	127,591	90,342	78,065	67,887
Building and structures	268,424	239,176	132,799	80,076
Machinery and equipment	561,667	583,591	559,594	527,915
Construction in progress	36,336	20,868	6,951	17,948
	994,018	933,977	817,409	693,826
Less: accumulated depreciation	470,369	448,656	447,563	380,419
Net property, plant and equipment	523,649	485,321	369,486	313,407
Other assets	649,655	638,689	449,421	525,786
	8,742,635	7,116,563	6,663,232	6,173,029

Daewoo Corporation—Balance Sheets, 1992–95 (in million won) (cont.)

Liabilities and stockholders' equity	1995	1994	1993	1992
Current liabilities				
Short-term loans	1,895,116	1,605,766	1,962,993	1,557,378
Current portion of long-term debt	434,994	285,390	114,231	326,480
Trade notes and accounts payable	1,570,085	1,155,670	1,035,300	1,193,347
Other payables	271,920	258,313	106,190	127,077
Income taxes	4,375	1,799	5,423	3,453
Deposits and advance receipts	504,708	214,204	229,632	227,682
Accrued expenses	145,485	74,223	68,281	87,444
Other current liabilities	–	–	247	15,699
Total current liabilities	4,826,683	3,595,365	3,522,050	3,572,870
Long-term debt	2,148,768	3,595,365	1,474,749	973,233
Deposits and advance receipts, non-current	146,392	119,774	184,874	291,046
Retirement and severance benefits	159,177	122,227	101,537	85,832
Foreign currency translation gain	–	–	–	9,219
Total liabilities	7,281,020	5,690,411	5,283,210	4,922,981
Stockholders' equity				
Common stock of 500 par value: Authorized 200,000,000 shares; issued 113,096,623 shares in 1995 (worth W5,000 par value), 107,725,338 shares in 1994 (worth W5,000 par value), 104,038,024 shares in 1993, 88,056,024 shares in 1992	565,483	538,627	520,190	440,285
Revaluation surplus	–	–	160	7,673
Capital surplus	446,542	452,554	424,112	371,845
Appropriated retained earnings	454,823	439,093	406,468	394,401
Unappropriated retained earnings	60,867	45,734	44,452	40,994
Total stockholders' equity	1,461,615	1,426,152	1,380,022	1,250,048
Commitments and contingencies	–	–	–	–

Daewoo Corporation—Balance Sheets, 1992–95 (in million won) (cont.)

	1995	1994
Sales	15,024,667	10,528,648
Cost of goods sold	13,948,542	9,643,271
Gross profit	1,076,125	885,377
Selling, general and administrative expenses	566,314	388,054
Operating income	509,811	497,323
Other income (deductions)		
Interest income	123,963	103,434
Interest expense	(563,099)	(496,560)
Gain on sale of marketable securities and investments, net	36,826	31,061
Gain on disposition of property, plant and equipment, net	4,765	5,534
Exchange and translation gain, net	18,621	27,284
Dividends	8,121	3,982
Other, net	(62,191)	(108,664)
	(432,994)	(433,929)
Earnings before income taxes	76,817	63,394
Income taxes	16,515	15,267
Net earnings	60,302	48,127
Earnings per share in won and US$	548.24	447.51

CASE TWENTY-ONE

SSANGYONG CEMENT INDUSTRIAL COMPANY LIMITED*

HISTORY

In May 1962, Ssangyong Cement Industrial Co. Ltd. was founded and established as the parent company of the diversifying group of Ssangyong and has since become the main driving force behind the group's expansion and growth. In addition, coinciding with Korea's First Five Year Economic Development Plan** in 1962, Ssangyong Cement was able to contribute to the rapid growth of the Korean cement industry and hence has helped to boost the economy into a fast-growing Newly Industrializing Economy (NIE).

The company began production at its Yongwol plant in 1964, with an annual production capacity of 408,000 tons. With continuous expansion and facilities rationalization programs, Ssangyong Cement presently boasts a remarkable domestic annual production capacity of 15 million tons of clinker with the addition of two other production plants at Tonghae and Mungyong. (Table 1 traces the major events in Ssangyong Cement's 30 years of existence.)

Establishing itself in the domestic market was not the only consideration as Ssangyong Cement wanted to build its presence in the international arena as well. It first ventured overseas with export of cement of Vietnam in 1964. Subsequently, the company expanded its export markets throughout Southeast Asia and the Middle East during the 1970s, and Japan and the USA in the 1980s. It soon became the leading cement exporter in Korea.

---

* This case was prepared by Young-Chul Chang, Department of Organisational Behaviour, Faculty of Business Administration, National University of Singapore.
** The First Five Year Economic Plan in 1962 was aimed at enhancing export as well as to stimulate domestic industrial investment. It stressed import substitution and primary goods export in order to alleviate the serious deficit.

Table 1 Ssangyong Cement: 30-Year History

Year	Month	Major Events
1962	May	Ssangyong Cement Industrial Co. Ltd. was established.
1964	April	Completed the Yongwol plant with a capacity of 408,000 tons a year.
	July	Labor union was founded.
	December	Korea exported bagged cement to Vietnam for the first time.
1965	July	Began ready-mixed concrete production.
1967	October	Completed Kiln 3 of the Yongwol plant.
1968	October	Completed the Tonghae plant with a capacity of 1.7 million tons a year.
1973	April	Established Youngpyeong resort.
	July	Hosted the inaugural meeting of ACPAC (Asian Cement Producer's Amity Club).
	November	Established Ssangyong Cement (Singapore) Ltd.
1975	January	Acquired Taihan Cement Co. Ltd.
	May	Listed on the Korea Stock Exchange.
	December	Established the Research Center.
1976	September	Adapted a Management Information System for the first time in Korea.
1980	April	Completed the 5.6 million tons expansion of the Tonghae plant.
1981	November	Awarded the grand prize of National Quality Management.
1983	July	Ssangyong Cement (Singapore) Ltd. was listed on the Singapore Stock Exchange.
1984	May	Developed new ceramics.
1987	April	Provided operation and maintenance services to Suez Cement Co. in Egypt (till March 1989).
1988	August	Awarded the grand prize of National Productivity.
	October	Established Ssangyong Cement (Pacific) Ltd.
1989	February	Established CenCal Cement Co.
1991	January	Reorganized corporate structure into divisional system.
	May	Acquired Riverside Cement Co. completed the ferrite magnets production plant in Pohang.
	November	Issued US$70 million CBs on the European Monetary Market.
1992	February	Awarded the grand prize for creating a rewarding workplace.
	May	30th anniversary of Ssangyong Cement.
	August	Completed NSP work on Kiln 1 at the Tonghae plant.
1993	March	Won the First Gold Tower Industrial Peace Award. Completed the ALC production plant in Asan. Entered the Housing Construction Business
	July	Expanded the second Research Center.

It did not stop there. In order to provide for a potential over-capacity situation, Ssangyong Cement constantly worked towards exploring new export markets. The company is also continuing to expand its distribution network in Japan, its major overseas market, and actively marketing products in Southeast Asia, a fast growing region. As a result, in 1993, its exports amounted to 1,955,740 tons, which is 71.2 per cent of Korea's total cement exports since its inception 30 years ago.

COMPANY PROFILE

With accumulated technology and expertise in the cement industry, Ssangyong Cement rises to be the largest manufacturer of cement in Korea. It controls about 30 per cent of the domestic market. Its business can be divided into three major divisions: cement, remicon, and other products, which account for 67.5 per cent, 23.0 per cent and 9.5 per cent respectively of its total sales in 1993. Most products are distributed to the domestic market, as only 5.0 per cent of total sales were from exports in 1993. In the cement division, Ssangyong Cement can produce 14.0 million tons of cement annually at its 3 main plants and 16 other plants. The main production facility is the Tonghae plant which has an annual production capacity of 11.5 million tons. Also, Ssangyong Cement was the first manufacturer of remicon in Korea.

As Ssangyong Cement established itself in the cement industry, it began to diversify into related sectors, namely ready-mixed concrete, ferrite magnets, fine ceramics, and other new building materials. In addition to Auto-claved Light-weight concrete (ALC), these sectors form a natural synergy.

Other diversifying efforts include the acquisition of Yongpyeong Resort from Ssangyong Engineering & Construction Co. in 1973 with which Ssangyong Cement made its first move into the leisure industry. The resort includes ski slopes, golf courses, hotels and condominiums. Currently, Ssangyong Cement has four overseas branch offices, one each in Tokyo, Singapore, Los Angeles, and San Francisco.

Finally, a peek at the economic performance of Ssangyong Cement. Table 2 below shows the financial highlights as revealed in its 1993 annual report.

Table 2 Economic Performance of Ssangyong Cement (in million won)

Indicators	1993	1992	1991	1990	1989
Net sales	952,648	911,625	815,177	713,933	609,150
Net income	27,135	35,846	29,253	30,420	37,105
Total assets	1,883,324	1,801,264	1,612,690	1,338,895	1,248,965
LT liabilities	726,50	771,536	618,505	492,004	494,316

Source: Ssangyong Cement Industrial Company Ltd. (Korea), *Annual Report,* 1993.

Over the past few years, Ssangyong Cement has also received the following foreign and domestic awards and certifications. They are:

1. *Grand prize award for creating a rewarding workplace*: Ssangyong Cement won this prestigious award due to its efforts at promoting a corporate culture of cooperation between labor and management and respect for the individual.
2. *The First Gold Tower Industrial Peace Award*: Ssangyong Cement earned the newly designed "The First Gold Tower Industrial Peace Award" in March 1993. This award is

for outstanding efforts in a number of areas—minimal industrial accidents, outstanding employee benefits, and ideal labor-management relations based on labor-management efforts for industrial peace. For a period of 30 years, Ssangyong has not had a single labor-management strife. This is the very fruit of traditional Ssangyong emphasis on the importance of overall harmony and total harmonization of efforts.
3. *The ISO 9002 Quality System Certification*: This award was presented to Ssangyong Cement (Singapore) on March 1, 1993 for its high quality management and assurance. This internationally renowned certificate only serves to confirm the high quality standards of Ssangyong's products, enhancing Ssangyong's reputation as a quality producer.

In November 1992, Ssangyong Cement began a "customer satisfaction role playing program" in an effort to discover customers' needs and to obtain their comments, so that the company can constantly upgrade its products and services. To instill "the customer is the highest priority" mentality into the employees' minds, posters that carry this theme are displayed and relevant training and education programs were conducted to reinforce this philosophy companywide.

In December 1992, the company created a Customer Service Department to better serve its customers by addressing their complaints and providing solutions to their problems.

THE MANAGEMENT'S PHILOSOPHY

FOUNDER'S PHILOSOPHY: COUNTRY'S DEVELOPMENT

Since the company's establishment in 1962 by Mr. Kim Sung-Kon, Ssangyong Cement has spearheaded the construction of the nation. This focus on the country's development has been the founder's philosophy. During the 1960s, Korea was an underdeveloped country, badly in need of foundations for growth. This in turn translated into a high demand for the infrastructure and materials for construction. This, coupled with the natural resources of Korea and Mr. Kim's philosophy, all interacted and matched to create a strategic fit. Unlike other **chaebols**, Ssangyong Cement has never diversified into consumer products as they feel that these industries do not contribute directly to building the country's foundations for further growth.

In addition, since its very inception, Ssangyong Cement has been designated as the core business area of the Ssangyong Group. As a result, a lot of companies like Ssangyong Engineering & Construction, Ssangyong Oil Refining, and Ssangyong Paper have been founded to support its growth to become an integrated material-maker.

The shift from light industry to heavy industry in 1975 marked a major turning point in the structural transformation of the Korean economy. Increasingly Korea approached the forefront of world leadership in manufacturing many products. Moreover, there was a significant trend to venture into the advanced sectors, symbolized by the emphasis on electronic products and semiconductors.

The helm of the Ssangyong Group passed from Kim Sung-Kon to his elder son Kim Suk-Won in 1975. The contrast between these two personalities and generations is reflected in the peripheral ventures pursued by them. The elder Kim's extra-business endeavors were recreational. In sharp contrast, the second generation Kim ventured on his own to construct Korea's first ski resort in Yongpyeong, which began operations in 1975.

Kim Suk-Won's tenure has also resulted in a qualitative transformation. From 1975 to 1987, the gross turnover of the Group increased from $164 million to $4.7 billion, a 29-fold increase, and its total assets jumped from $222 million to $4.9 billion. In short, Ssangyong Group's aggressive expansion into heavy industries and other sectors of the Korean economy has dramatically changed its constitution. This is illustrated by the relative decline of the cement company. Whereas it had accounted for 80 per cent of the Group's total assets in 1975, it controlled a mere one-sixth by 1987. Nevertheless, the mainstay of the Ssangyong Group continues to be Ssangyong Cement Industrial Co.

Another dramatic change occurred in the process of generational shift at the top. The founder, Kim Sung-Kon was widely regarded as an autocratic leader, considered typical of those who created *chaebols* in Korea. However, his son believes in bottom-up planning. This is seen especially in the formal adoption of "Management by Objectives" (MBO) in the 1970s. Along with the concept of MBO, the concept of QCC was first introduced in 1975 and has spread to most of the cement companies by 1979.

The three guiding mottos of Ssangyong Group are harmony, reliability, and innovation. Among these, harmony is considered to be the most critical. This is reflected symbolically in the Ssangyong Group's symbol, the ascending dragons. "The driving force of the ascending dragons is harmony as is the main philosophy of the Ssangyong management." In keeping with this philosophy, the company has always treated all its employees as part of the family and as such, they all love the company and never want to leave.

Customer Satisfaction

The Ssangyong management philosophy is devoted to satisfying their customers' needs—always lending an ear to the voice of their customers—and has worked hard to satisfy their needs through better quality and a variety of services. To Ssangyong Cement, customer satisfaction means that no matter how good a product may be, if the customer is not satisfied with it, it will not be chosen. It means that Ssangyong will operate on the basis that it is the customers who determine the market, and will continue to promote this management philosophy in the years to come.

All these efforts began in 1989 when three corporate concepts—"Reliability, Innovation, and Harmony"—were introduced. Top priority is accorded to reliability, thought, and winning the trust of its customers is Ssangyong's highest goal.

Vision and Strategy

In 1990, Ssangyong Cement articulated its vision and long-term strategy in terms of the New Strategy for Prosperity toward the 21st Century (NSP). The vision is to accomplish the goal of super-excellence in the 21st century by reaching the sales volume of 2 trillion won (1 trillion won from existing businesses and 1 trillion won from new businesses).

This vision is the inspiration that drives the formulation of Ssangyong Cement's strategy. Ssangyong strategy has a hard and a soft aspect. The hard strategy involves upgrading the existing business through securing advanced facilities/equipments, maintaining market dominance, product differentiation, capitalizing on the developed technologies, maximizing the utilization of Yongpyeong resorts and strengthening the new businesses through linking the raw materials industry and processing/assembly industry, expanding the business of construction materials, and developing high value-added products. The soft strategy includes establishing a quality management system, strengthening the companywide cooperation system, implementing customer-satisfaction management practices, upgrading the quality of human resources, establishing employee welfare system, and developing a productive labor-management relationship. These strategies reflect Ssangyong Cement's willingness to transform the company from a conservative to a more entrepreneurial organization by AD 2000.

MANAGEMENT STYLE AND PRACTICES

MANAGEMENT STYLE

SUCCESSION. Family members are the obvious and most favored candidates for succession to top management positions. This is reasonable as the family members are insiders and, therefore relatively, have more loyalty and trustworthiness than outsiders. Moreover, coming from a rich family, they are more likely to have had better and higher education. However, Ssangyong Cement does employ a number of professional managers for their expertise, education and knowledge, which it needs for facing competition in this aggressive age.

DELEGATION OF AUTHORITY. As top management needs to take strategic decisions that will guide and shape the company's future, they cannot attend to everything themselves. Thus they delegate authority to the lower management and employees to decide certain matters, depending on the levels of importance of the issues. For instance, a purchasing executive who despite his best efforts, cannot obtain the contract price laid down by top management, may use his discretion to finalize the contract at the lowest price he can get.

DECISION MAKING. There are basically 28 boards of directors in this large organization. Each individual director covers two or three departments which have their own meetings. Although separated by this departmentalization, in line with Ssangyong Group's philosophy, each department cooperates with the others on a daily basis to fulfill the organization's goals.

Every quarter, the company rents a hotel conference room, where all the important people in the company (approximately 300) like the chairman, president, all directors, and department and section chiefs gather and report on their three-month results. There is also an open exchange of opinions and criticisms among all those present such that the section chiefs can directly question the directors.

The company practices target operation and it requires the various departments to submit a five-year future operation or business plan. This proposal must be thoroughly researched and is submitted to top management for approval and discussion. One practice of Ssangyong Cement is the setting of high target. For example, when the actual production capacity is only 900,000 tonnes, the target set will be at 1 million tonnes. This is to create pressure for the departments to do their best and strive to attain the seemingly impossible.

RULES AND REGULATIONS. Although like all other companies, Ssangyong Cement has strict rules and regulations; they are applied in the light of the company's mottos. This can be seen from the fact that in the past, the management personnel did not punch time-cards while the rest had to, thus implying an unequal two-tier system that favored the management. The time-card system has now been scrapped to reflect top management's trust in the employees, regarding them as family members. Another example is that the white helmets with red band for the management staff and yellow helmets for all employees, has now been replaced by white helmets for all. This is to stress the equality in status of all employees, regardless of position.

HUMAN RESOURCE MANAGEMENT

RECRUITMENT AND SELECTION. The Ssangyong Group, on a yearly basis, recruits 700 new graduates out of 3,000 applicants. The first screening is done through reviewing the applicants' resume as a result of which about 1,500 applicants are eliminated. Next, the 1,500 successful candidates are required to sit for an examination in Kookmin University and the top 700 qualified candidates are then selected.

Basically, Ssangyong Group employs only competent university students for their management team as the nature of a manager's job requires incumbents with a good education.

In addition, employees have to have the right attitude because Ssangyong Cement stresses on collectivism and as such looks for team players rather than individual performers. Employees are expected to work closely together to achieve the organization's goals. This means that individualistic behavior and attitude are not tolerated.

TRAINING AND DEVELOPMENT. In Korea, the training programs for new entrants are very tough. This is to broaden their minds and hearts which Ssangyong Cement demands from and strongly inculcates in its employees.

The training lasts for three months in a special institute. During this period, they travel overseas to the various subsidiaries around the world so as to familiarize themselves with all the company's operations. Upon arrival, they are handed assignments which they are required to accomplish within a short time. In fact, in 1993, new college graduates were sent to Japan and Singapore for an eight-day training program. This gave them an opportunity to visit the company's overseas operations, tour outstanding local corporations and to experience the local culture. This is done with the aim of developing employees with the international perspective necessary for the company's international operations.

The Korean style for training new employees is not very appropriate in Singapore due to the shortage of manpower and a difficult local culture. Ssangyong Cement (Singapore), therefore, sends its local workers to Korea in the autumn. These personnel could be from any level in the company and they tour Ssangyong Cement's Tonghae plant and research centers. Upon returning, they have to submit a report and if they have any good ideas they can submit them for implementation.

Ssangyong Cement has always emphasized the continuous training and development of its employees. In fact, 37.5 per cent of its employees have received some form of overseas training. One of the methods the company employs is job rotation: The employees are divided into engineers and non-engineers. The employees in each category stay in the same position for three to four years and are then shifted to another department. This is to provide a general orientation of the company for the employees. However, the employees in the two categories cannot be rotated interchangeably, for their focus and job are of different nature.

INCENTIVES. Ssangyong Cement adopts a standardized reward system. To motivate and reward their best performers, Ssangyong Cement holds an annual top award session—"Best in Ssangyong." The candidates are recommended by their managers and the best are subsequently selected by a committee. This award ceremony is held at the beginning of the year in Seoul and involves all Ssangyong Cement's subsidiaries worldwide, including Singapore. The recipients who have received the award have it recorded in their personal file, and in addition, automatically receives a one grade promotion. Another form of incentive is a yearly holiday on wedding anniversaries.

PROMOTION. Ssangyong Cement adopts an appraisal system whereby those not meeting the standards are warned first and if there is no improvement, are penalized. This takes the form of denial of promotion and reduction of salary.

As a basis of promotion, Ssangyong Cement uses both age (in terms of length of service) and performance. This is to encourage employees to be loyal to the company and also to put in a good performance. Employees who have good job performance and long service in Ssangyong, are then rewarded accordingly.

RESEARCH AND DEVELOPMENT

Ssangyong Cement, due to its superior production capacity, enjoys a commanding position in the cement market and responds to its customers' needs with diverse, high quality products. It produces a variety of cements used in construction projects, especially where specialized properties are required. Some of these products are super-high early strength cement, ultra-rapid hardening cement, sulphate-resistant cement, non-explosive demolishing agents, and soil stabilizers. Ssangyong Cement is in the process of consolidating production facilities for specialty cement at the Mungyong plant and its research center continues to strive for product diversification and quality improvement.

In line with developments in building technology and the increasing durability of building structures, Ssangyong Cement produces about 200 types of ready-mixed concrete including underwater concrete, shrinkage-proof concrete and fiber-reinforced concrete to meet customers' diverse demands. Furthermore, to focus on product differentiation and to raise the superiority of Ssangyong's concrete, in 1992 the company began to supply color concrete, which is color permanent, thereby changing the old concept that "concrete is gray." This clearly represents the technological superiority of Ssangyong Cement.

In 1983, Ssangyong Cement put the knowledge accumulated in the R&D of inorganic materials to use and entered the fine ceramics business, a high-tech materials industry. Since then, Ssangyong Cement has achieved tremendous growth in the cutting tools and engineering ceramic sectors. In fact, they have received awards for the superior quality of their products. "Cermet," which was developed through the use of TiC and TiCN, is a new product with a broader range of applications than currently existing ceramic cutting tools.

Ssangyong Cement entered the ferrite magnets business in 1988 with an investment in the latest facilities to produce and supply ferrite magnets for use in speakers, automobiles, mini-motors and medical equipment. Ssangyong Cement is planning to develop its advanced materials division into a principal, strategic business by focusing on R&D and analyzing market-based information to actively develop new, high value-added products. It is, in fact, strengthening R&D of electronic ceramics and biotech materials to ensure a broad range of products and high quality production in the ceramics sector. As for its ferrite magnets, it will continue to expand its range of existing products.

To compete more effectively in the 1990s, Ssangyong cement began its autoclaved light concrete and building materials business as a step towards diversification into related business areas. This is done with help from Hebel International GmbH & Co., a German company well known for the world's best ALC processing technology. ALC is substantially superior to general concrete in terms of weight, heat-resistance and suspension, usage, outstanding sound absorption and resistance to humidity. All these qualities make it a promising building material of the future.

With a view to becoming a high-tech materials maker of the 21st century, Ssangyong Cement took the initial step towards this goal in 1975 with the establishment of its research center, the first for a private corporation in Korea. The research center is well-recognized for its high level of success in inorganic materials research and employs a staff of 200 highly trained researchers who actively conduct research in cement, fine ceramics, building materials and other areas. The R&D efforts to develop new products are so successful that many of its products are the exemplar of the industry. The importance Ssangyong Cement attaches to R&D is evident from the fact that it plans to increase its R&D investment to 3 per cent of sales to make greater strides not only in cement production but also in next generation technology areas like electronic ceramics, bio-ceramics, building materials, and environmental science.

Last year, Ssangyong Cement (Singapore) also provided a US$400,000 grant to the National University of Singapore's Faculty of Engineering to fund joint research into a more durable cement. A memorandum of understanding has been signed with NUS' Department of Civil Engineering for joint exploration of the potential of Portland Blast Furnace Slag Cement (PBFSC).

Overseas Business

Ssangyong Cement (Singapore) Ltd.

As noted in Table 1, Ssangyong Cement extended its operation to Singapore and set up Ssangyong Cement (Singapore) Ltd. in 1973. It was formed as a joint venture with two local partners, namely DBS and Afro-Asian. This joint venture was listed on the Singapore Stock Exchange in 1983 and was judged in Korea as one of the most successful cases of overseas direct investment by a Korean company. This has turned out to be a profitable venture.

The firm's turnover increased by 15 per cent to S$159.3 million while the consolidating profit before tax recorded an increase of 26 per cent to S$31.9 million. The chairman, Mr. Lee Sung-Won attributes these improvements to the "ability of the management and staff to respond to the needs of the market in their businesses, and at the same time focus management in the areas of cost control, improved productivity and R&D programs." The overall performance of Ssangyong Cement (Singapore) over the past few years is shown in Table 3.

Table 3 Overall Performance of Ssangyong Cement (Singapore)

	1993	1992	1991	1990	1989	1988
The group turnover (all figures in S$'000)	159,337	139,048	125,688	64,427	42,703	30,314
P/L before tax	31,899	25,241	17,616	7,027	2,462	176

Source: Ssangyong Cement (Singapore) Ltd., *Annual Report*, 1993.

Basically, the business of Ssangyong Group in Singapore can be divided into two parts: construction materials and high technology operations. Figure 1 depicts an overview of the group structure.

The Singapore plant is actually a "processing station," i.e., it processes into cement clinker shipped from Korea to Singapore. The final product is then exported to the nearby countries. Singapore was initially chosen for its strategic geographical location.

CenCal Cement Company

In 1989, the company established CenCal Cement Company in the northern California port of Stockton, with five silos capable of storing a total of 40,000 tons of cement to secure a stable supply of cement in the US market. This move also helped Ssangyong to establish northern California as a strategic export market.

Riverside Cement Company

In May 1991, Ssangyong Cement acquired a 50 per cent stake in Riverside Cement Company, located in the suburbs of Los Angeles, which is capable of annually producing 1.2 million tons of portland cement and 110,000 tons of white cement. Through this joint venture,

Case Twenty-One

Ssangyong Group Structure

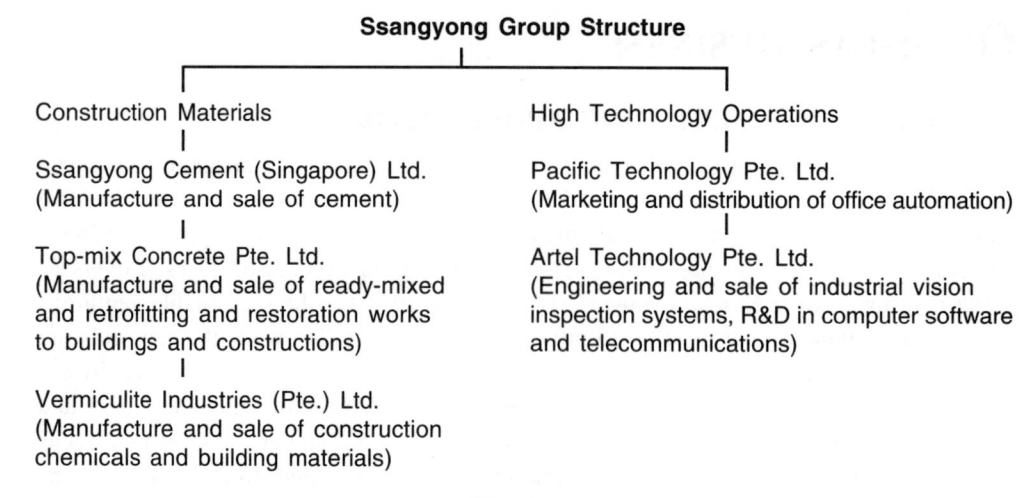

Construction Materials
- Ssangyong Cement (Singapore) Ltd. (Manufacture and sale of cement)
- Top-mix Concrete Pte. Ltd. (Manufacture and sale of ready-mixed and retrofitting and restoration works to buildings and constructions)
- Vermiculite Industries (Pte.) Ltd. (Manufacture and sale of construction chemicals and building materials)

High Technology Operations
- Pacific Technology Pte. Ltd. (Marketing and distribution of office automation)
- Artel Technology Pte. Ltd. (Engineering and sale of industrial vision inspection systems, R&D in computer software and telecommunications)

Figure 1

Ssangyong Cement has expanded its production and distribution facilities overseas, thus opening up a new avenue in the company's strategy for internationalization.

SHANGHAI BAO LONG BUILDING MATERIALS PLANT

Ssangyong Cement (Singapore) also acquired a 60 per cent stake in the Shanghai Bao Long Materials Plant which will produce and market 600,000 tons of ordinary and portland cement in its first year. The plant is expected to double its capacity in the subsequent years. According to analysts, Bao Long's planned initial output represents about 60 per cent of Ssangyong's Singapore operations and could add a hefty 50 per cent to Ssangyong Cement (Singapore's) pre-tax profits when it starts operation by mid-1995. Prospects for the Shanghai plant are very promising, with some US$40 million worth of infrastructure projects due to be launched in the city.

ONODA COMPANY

Ssangyong Cement has recently signed an initial cooperation agreement with Japanese cement maker Onoda Cement Company. The agreement calls for the two companies to exchange personnel for joint development of cement production technology, invention of materials, and recycling of industrial wastes. The companies would also share one another's licenses, help sales in Japan and South Korea, and seek joint development in other countries.

NEW ENGINEERING BUSINESS DIVISION

In December 1992, Ssangyong Cement launched its new Engineering Business Division which will provide technical and other consulting services for cement plants. At present, it is bidding for projects in Southeast Asia. Ssangyong Cement plans to concentrate on developing this division to secure orders for plant and engineering services on a turnkey basis.

NEW BUSINESS AREA

Ssangyong Cement also made solid progress in new business lines which serve as cornerstones for their plans to become a world-class corporation in the 21st century. In ferrite magnets, fine ceramics and other new business divisions, strong marketing efforts have helped to improve sales of such new materials.

FINE CERAMICS

Ssangyong's fine ceramic is a new material developed by the accumulated high technology of Ssangyong Cement. Its mechanical and chemical stability is very good and these properties include the ability to withstand heat, wear, and thermal shock in high temperature ranges. Ssangyong fine ceramics has, through strict material selection and quality control, established a strong reputation in the machine and automotive industries. In fact, in 1993, sales in the fine ceramics sector amounted to 3.8 million won, an increase of 56.4 per cent over the previous year. A list of the fine ceramics products, their properties and applications, is given in Table 4.

FERRITE MAGNETS

Ssangyong Cement also made great strides in the field of ferrite magnet development. Ferrite magnets are widely used in the electronics industry for products such as loudspeakers, DC motors and microwave ovens. Using its authorized know-how and technology, Ssangyong Cement is able to produce high-quality products conforming to rigid standards of perfection. At present, it produces two main types of magnets, the SBM and the SSM, and aims to be soon recognized as a world-class manufacturer of all varieties of magnets.

AUTOCLAVED LIGHTWEIGHT CONCRETE (ALC)

As a step towards diversification into related business areas, Ssangyong Cement developed its ALC business with assistance from Hebel International GmbH & Co., a German company known for the world's best ALC processing technology. ALC is a light prefabricated building material which has better heat resistance, outstanding sound absorption, and humidity control abilities than normal concrete. ALC can be used for residential, commercial, and industrial building construction and can be applied in interior/exterior walls, floors, and roofs. An ALC manufacturing plant has already been set up in Asan, South Chungchong province, and the annual production capacity is projected to be 165,000 cubic meters with a sales growth rate of 25 per cent by the year 2000.

YONGPYEONG RESORT

Yongpyeong Resort, which opened in 1975, is located at an 11 million square meter site on Palwang Mountain. It is a four-season resort with ski slopes and golf courses in addition to roomy lodging facilities and various sports facilities which include a bowling center, swimming pool, tennis and racquet ball courts and a discotheque. At present, Yongpyeong Resort is

Table 4 Ssangyong's Fine Ceramics Fields of Application

Material	Property	Application
Alumina system cutting tool (Al_2O_3 + TiC)	For high speed cutting using the property of high temperature strength Excellent property of wear resistance to the high hardness material	Light roughing and finishing of steel or cast iron Machining of high hardness material and workpiece which is hard to machine
Silicon nitride system cutting tool (Si_3N_4)	Excellent toughness and thermal shock resistance For wet machining	Roughing of cast iron Interrupted cutting Milling
Zirconia (ZrO_2)	The highest toughness and strength among the ceramic materials Bright luster of diamond crystal Because of non-magnetism, it does not have a bad effect on the magnetic memory tape It is possible to measure the oxygen partial pressure	High class watch case Decoration accessory Ceramic adjuster–TV screen control driver Cutter Oxygen sensor
Silicon nitride (Si_3N_4)	Excellent strength and wear resistance in the high temperature range The best thermal shock resistance among the ceramics	Engine parts Jig and fixture parts in the high temperature High temperature or wear-resistant parts
Silicon carbide (SiC)	Excellent anticorrosion in the chemical system Excellent hardness or wear resistance Frictional resistance is the best in the dynamical contact parts	Mechanical seal Wear-resistant or anticorrosion parts
Alumina (Al_2O_3)	Good hardness or wear resistance in the low temperature range Excellent accuracy of dimension at any condition	Pump cylinder, bushing Physics and chemistry parts Electronic or semiconductor parts

constructing a variety of leisure facilities and developing more events and activities. To promote more recreational activities and raise the level of national culture, they annually sponsor the Yongpyeong Summer Music Camp and Festival and the Yongpyeong Cup International Alpine Ski Games.

Sales of 19 million won were recorded for the year 1992 and Ssangyong Cement is actively marketing the resort to tourist groups from Taiwan, Japan, Singapore and China. In 1990, the resort established a reciprocal relationship with Grindlewald, a renowned resort in Switzerland as part of its continuing efforts to provide better services and facilities to its guests.

SWOT Analysis

Strengths

STRONG CUSTOMER ORIENTATION. Ssangyong Cement's management philosophy is built on satisfying customers' needs. Their main concern is the welfare of customers and all decisions are centered on customer satisfaction.

Their efforts in customer satisfaction, which began with the realignment of their internal management systems, are reflected through direct contact with their customers. In meetings with customers, they listen to the needs of their customers in order to meet and exceed the latter's expectations. Suggestions concerning improvements on problems pointed out by customers from orders to final delivery are incorporated systematically and consistently, not only in R&D, technology, production, and distribution, but also throughout the management structure. Besides, each business office of Ssangyong Cement holds annual get-togethers with its customers so as to let them become familiar with the company's operations.

GOOD LABOR-MANAGEMENT RELATIONSHIP. By respecting the unique characteristics of each employee and creating an environment in which employees can freely utilize their abilities and creativity at an optimum level, Ssangyong Cement promotes cooperation between the individual and the organization. The concept of *Inhwa* at Ssangyong has created a corporate culture which encourages employees to actively create new ideas. Also, in order to ensure smooth flow of communication within the company, Ssangyong uses advanced management techniques and a variety of cross-communication systems that include a junior board, a suggestion system, small group activities, and a counselling system. To meet the needs of the employees, the company provides household and educational financing and gives employees access to leisure resorts and club organizations.

GOOD ECONOMIC PERFORMANCE. As noted above, the 1993 economic performance of both Ssangyong Cement (Singapore) and Ssangyong Cement (Korea) was good. It is worthy to note that Ssangyong Cement (Korea) attains such good results at a time when the Korean economy was going through a depression in 1993.

QUALITY MANAGEMENT. With increasing emphasis on the importance of quality management, Ssangyong Cement (Singapore) has become one of the leading Ssangyong Group companies and also the first Asian cement manufacturer to receive the international standard ISO 9000 Series certification. This ISO 9000 Series was established in 1987 by the International Standard Organization for quality management and quality assurance.

The acquisition of the ISO 9000 certificate on March 1 will not only bolster international recognition of Ssangyong Cement Singapore's quality products, but would also lead to increased sales on both the Singapore domestic and export markets.

VERTICAL INTEGRATION. With its integration into related sectors, Ssangyong Cement has gained greater control in its operations and can remove volume constraints imposed by the size of the cement industry. It will also reap economies due to sharing of operations, functions and technological know-how. An entry barrier is thus erected in that any new entrants must face a cost disadvantage unless they also enjoy the benefits of integration.

WEAKNESSES

SOME UNDESIRABLE PERSONNEL PRACTICES. As the Group refrains from laying off or retiring old workers whose productivity is low, it may end up with a larger than necessary workforce and thus not only incur additional costs but also adversely affect the upward mobility of its more competent staff. This may result in demoralization of the employees and increase personnel turnover. Like other *chaebols,* first preference is given to the founder, Kim Sung-Kon's family members and relatives for the top management positions. This practice may breed inefficiencies and grievances as competent people would not be allowed to aspire to the key positions.

RIPPLE EFFECT. By investing in too many interrelated sectors, Ssangyong Cement may render itself vulnerable to the negative ripple effect caused by a single undesirable happening in one of the sectors which could eventually affect other related businesses as well. For instance, a drop in sales of cement, could lead to a drop in the sale of paper products for packaging of cement, transportation and others.

JOB ROTATION. Employees at Ssangyong Cement are given a new job responsibility after they have been three or four years in one job. Although this practice enables the staff to have a better grasp of the overall operations of the company and also introduces job variety, it also breeds "Jacks of all trades but masters of none." In addition, this is a kind of lateral transfer; instead of promotion and movement up the corporate ladder; the staff keep moving from one department to another with no significant increase in job responsibilities. This also implies that they will take longer to move up the corporate ladder. Hence, this may affect the employees' morale and reduce their motivation to work hard.

OPPORTUNITIES

REGIONAL ECONOMY. The Asia-Pacific region has been growing rapidly over the last few years. The 1993 GDP growth rates forecast for many countries in this region depict a rosy picture: e.g., Indonesia 7.0 per cent, Thailand 8.0 per cent and Taiwan 8.5–9.0 per cent. More foreign direct investments will be expected in this region, especially when governments of some developing countries like China, Vietnam and India strongly encourage foreign companies to bring their capital and expertise into those countries to boost their economic growth. As a result, many construction projects will be anticipated for building factories, office buildings and developing various infrastructures. With the establishment of the AFTA (ASEAN Free Trade Area) by the year 2008, there will be a significant increase in export activities in the ASEAN region. Finally, opportunity also exists for exploiting the Asia-Pacific market, by either using existing facilities or opening more offices and subsidiaries in the region.

STABILIZING KOREAN ECONOMY. The Korean economy is set on the path of recovery, following a relatively slow growth of 4.7 per cent in GNP and the problem of inflation in 1992. The Korean government has stepped in to revive the stagnant economy and is now liberalizing its economy for greater foreign investment.

All these efforts, coupled with the decision to open the economy to foreign investors will eventually restore foreign investors' confidence, and hence, attract them to set up operations in Korea. The greater volume of foreign direct investments may then result in more construction projects in the form of building, factories and plants.

DESIRE FOR MORE LEISURE. As a country becomes more wealthy and advanced, its people start to desire more leisure. After the Koreans, who are known for hard work and conscientiousness, have reaped the fruits of their labor they would naturally wish to slow down their work pace to enjoy life. Hence, there will be a greater demand for recreational facilities in Korea as well as in other parts of the world.

Therefore, after the first step into the leisure industry by buying Yongpyeong Resort, Ssangyong Cement can consider exploring other aspects of the leisure industry and also extending its resort facilities to other more affluent countries.

RISING EDUCATIONAL STANDARDS. Korea is known for its huge pool of educated labor. In recent years, the educational standards have risen further and more talent is available to be groomed to take on the managerial role in an organization. This is indeed good news for companies who want to expand globally but lack the necessary managerial supports.

The rising educational standards have also produced more trained personnel in key areas like engineering, computer electronics, etc., who are essential for the development of indigenous technology.

THREATS

POTENTIAL OVER-CAPACITY SITUATION. As a result of the expansion programs adopted by the main manufacturers, an excess capacity situation is imminent in the Korean Cement industry. As the cement industry as a whole is growing slowly, it may not readily absorb any excess capacity and prices may be depressed, leading to much reduced profit margins. For firms that are not cost efficient, this may result in heavy losses.

LABOR SHORTAGE. This is a situation that is evident in both Singapore and Korea. For Korea, where there is a persistent drain of home-grown talent to foreign countries, the labor shortage is even more serious. As a result, many companies in Korea experience frequent cases of job-hopping as the demand for skilled labor exceeds supply. In the context of Singapore, the Ssangyong Cement (Singapore) operation is inclined towards low skills, and manual and hard work puts off many potential employees. Consequently, Ssangyong Cement (Singapore) relies heavily on foreign workers and this means a high implication of foreign labor laws on its operation.

CRITICISM AGAINST *CHAEBOLS*. The Korean *chaebols* have been accused of corruption, exploiting labor, banning labor movements colluding with politicians, and contributing to an unequal distribution of wealth. Now, even the government who had helped the *chaebols* to gain their present status, are reducing their support to the *chaebols*.

TOUGHER FOREIGN COMPETITION. First, more foreign competitors are becoming bigger and stronger as a result of mergers and acquisitions. Secondly, grouping of nations by regions as seen in the integration of the EC and North American trade blocs, has resulted in greater protectionism and trade barriers. Thirdly, more foreign companies now have easier access to the liberalized Korean market and are competing with indigenous companies in the domestic market. Lastly, some developing nations like China, India and Vietnam, which offer attractive incentives to foreign investors and have an abundant supply of relatively cheap resource, pose a threat to the competitiveness of Korean companies.

LABOR STRIFE. Korea has been plagued by a growing labor strife. More workers are protesting for higher wages and better employee benefits. For example, on July 7, 1993, 60,000 workers of the giant Hyundai group went on strike to demand higher pay and better working condition and this set off a ripple effect where other Hyundai subsidiaries encountered a similar situation. It would appear that the companies may have to concede to the workers' demands and will, as a result, have to shoulder a greater cost burden that will cause their products to be less competitive when prices are raised to absorb the cost increase. Alternatively, they may have to lay off workers to contain the cost thus resulting in unemployment.

FUTURE PROSPECTS

Prospects for the cement industry in 1995 may be the same as they were in 1994. In contrast to 1992, which had the Korean economy suffering from inflation and depressed market conditions, 1993 and 1994 showed signs of recovery due to the Korean governmental effort to stabilize and liberalize the economy. Many national projects such as the continuous housing projects (500,000 new units each year), and the new international airport, will help to accelerate the growth of this industry. In fact, the GNP growth rate for 1994 showed a more promising rate than the growth in the previous years (1992–1993) (see Table 5).

However, the government's recent attempts to liberalize the Korean economy and promote the growth of small and medium enterprises in Korea has meant a significant decrease in government support for the *chaebols*. An outcome of this may be that the *chaebols* will have to be self-reliant and strive to be more efficient and effective, in order to compete with the strong foreign firms.

This means that Ssangyong Cement should now concentrate on investment in existing businesses rather than in new ventures for consolidation is the key to increased competitiveness in the 21st century. To preempt foreign competition, Ssangyong Cement should improve its productivity and reduce its production costs in order to be cost effective. It should also expand its overseas operations and exploit opportunities like the booming construction industry

Table 5 Principal Economic Indicators

	1994	1993	1992	1991	1990	1989	1988
GNP growth rate (%)	8.5	5.6	5.0	9.1	9.6	6.9	12.0
Per capita GDP (US$)		7,466	7,007	6,757	5,883	5,210	4,295
Unemployment rate (%)	2.0*	2.8	2.4	2.3	2.4	2.6	2.5
Growth rate of wages							
Nominal (%)			15.2	17.5	18.8	21.1	15.5
Real (%)			8.4	7.5	9.4	14.5	7.8

*As of November, 1994.
Source: The Bank of Korea, *Monthly Statistical Bulletin*, December 1994.

in China. As already stated, with developing countries liberalizing their economies, there will be a rush of foreign investors leading to a high demand for construction projects like housing, office and plant premises and supporting infrastructures. In other words, there would be a boom in the demand for cement and cement-related products, which would be a golden opportunity for Ssangyong Cement. A more customer-oriented focus is also now essential to satisfy the various needs of the customers with respect to changing building technology. Besides, only by meeting customers' needs through better services, differentiation of products and high product quality can Ssangyong Cement hope to survive against its foreign competitors.

Ssangyong Cement will continue to diversify into related businesses like ceramics and specially concrete to capitalize on the expertise developed for the cement industry. This diversification will in turn generate future growth for the company as cement is basically a maturing and saturating industry. Moreover, to be constantly ahead of its competitors, Ssangyong Cement has directed its efforts towards the developments of innovative products such as colored concrete and ALC to meet the new needs of the construction industry.

This commitment to engage in focused and motivated R&D in construction materials has given Ssangyong Cement the competitive edge in the regional construction industry and many of its products have become the industry standard.

CASE TWENTY-TWO

Samsung Electronics Company Limited*

History: The Early Years

The history of Samsung Electronics starts in 1938 when its founder, Lee Byung-Chull, set up a small firm in Taegu with an initial investment of $2,000 and some 40 employees. The company grew rapidly by actively engaging in trade with partners in Manchuria and Beijing and later by venturing into manufacturing. In 1948, it moved its headquarters to Seoul and expanded its scope of activity to include Southeast Asia and the United States. Samsung began to build up its manufacturing capacity in earnest eight years after the end of the Korean War, and led the national postwar efforts for economic reconstruction by carrying out ambitious projects in key industries and diversifying its range of business lines. As such, Samsung has taken firm root as a nationally based corporation.

From 1969 to 1991

Samsung Electronics is the leading maker of consumer electronics in Korea in terms of annual turnover and exports. Although it currently has four major product divisions, it was first founded in January 1969 as a producer of consumer electronics and industrial appliances only.

The move into the industry took place at a time when electronics was the leading new-growth business of the day. This was in line with the government's Second Five Year Plan (FYP) whose major policy directions included laying the foundation for industrialization,

---

* This case was prepared by Chang Young-Chul, Department of Organisational Behaviour, Faculty of Business Administration, National University of Singapore.

improving the balance of payments position, creation of employment and improving technology and productivity.

In the 1970s, the electronics subsidiaries rapidly diversified the product line and enhanced the technological expertise. Samsung began fabricating silicon wafers in 1974 and producing electro-guns for cathode-ray tubes (CRTs) the following year. In 1975, the company went public and was listed with a paid-in capital of 3 billion won. In 1978, it established its first overseas sales subsidiary, Samsung Electronics America, Inc. Before the decade was over, the company was also developing or manufacturing video-cassette recorders and integrated circuits for TVs and telephone exchanges.

In 1980, emphasis was placed on Research and Development (R&D). Samsung Electronics opened its research and development institute for consumer electronics in that same year. Some of the major achievements in this area include the following: it developed the 1M DRAM the following year. The 64M DRAM was developed in 1992. This achievement in DRAM technology was of major significance as it is a very important factor that contributed to Samsung's worldwide recognition by showing that it has reached the international leading ranks in this technology. In addition, the sophistication of this in-house chip technology enabled the production of application of specific integrated circuits (ASICs) and microprocessors used in a wide variety of consumer and electronic products.

In November 1988, Samsung Electronics merged with Samsung Semiconductor & Telecommunications (SST). SST was originally acquired from Korea Telecommunications Co. and was renamed in December 1982. This merger brought the company much-needed semiconductor profits, but also a high debt burden from the heavy capital and R&D investments the new divisions needed. It also created a mega-enterprise that proved increasingly difficult to navigate through the troubled waters of a global recession.

As a start to steadily building up an overseas production presence and to cope with worldwide protectionist trends, Samsung Electronics established consumer electronics plants in Portugal in 1982. Later in 1990, this move was continued by the construction of overseas subsidiary plants in Hungary and Spain, and Malaysia in 1991. To augment its growing presence in export markets, it has set up regional offices in the US, Europe and Asia.

CURRENT SCENARIO (1992–93)

Samsung Electronics had an impressive US$7.74 billion in net sales and US$4.56 billion in exports in 1992. Its revenue growth rate is estimated by company officials and securities analysts to be about 15 per cent. Its four major product divisions—consumer electronics, information systems, semiconductors and computers—account for 58 per cent, 16 per cent, 21 per cent and 5 per cent of the total sales respectively. The company has fourteen technical collaboration agreements with foreign companies and employs 43,559 persons.

As of December 31, 1991, Samsung Electronics' major shareholders are: Samsung Life Insurance (9.7 per cent), Lee Kun Hee and others (6.6 per cent) and Samsung Co. Ltd. (3.8 per cent). Its major holdings are Samsung Electro-Mechanics (18.2 per cent), Samsung Heavy Industries (34.4 per cent) and Samsung Credit Card (52.6 per cent). As such, the Samsung Group's ownership is that of mutual possession, in which the owner and/or his relatives own the core company and/or some kind of foundation, which in turn owns other affiliated enterprises. These enterprises can possess each other's stocks.

Previously, Samsung Electronics was jointly run by four presidents, each presiding over one of the four autonomous divisions. In December 1992, the four divisions were merged to reduce redundancies and to reap the advantages of forging cross-divisional links in product design and production. The former president of Samsung's semiconductor business, Kim Kwang-Ho was appointed president of all four operating divisions. The choice of Kim implies that Samsung will focus more attention and more of its resources on the semiconductor division.

Although the four divisions are now merged, this change has only been very recent and for most of the time, the company has been operating as four separate divisions. Therefore, knowledge of each division would give a better understanding of the company.

CONSUMER ELECTRONICS DIVISION

Just as Samsung Electronics is the flagship of the Samsung Group, its consumer electronics division is the major contributor to the company's sales. The consumer electronics division still accounts for over half of the company's sales. Sales amounted to US$3.85 billion and US$4.24 billion in 1991 and 1992 respectively. Its major product lines include: audio/video equipment, home appliances, heating and cooling machines, business machines and factory automation equipment. Through the years, it has climbed to the second position in the world market for colour TVs and VCRs. It has a commanding 14 per cent share of the global microwave oven market, a 10 per cent share of the world VCR market, and 6 per cent of the colour TV market. About 52 per cent of its sales are accounted for by its domestic market. However, as demand on world markets for consumer electronics made in Korea has been declining, profitability margins have narrowed to the vanishing point.

INFORMATION SYSTEMS DIVISION

The major product lines of this division are switching systems, fibre optic communication systems, telecommunication equipment, home and office automation equipment, and integrated telecommunication systems. Its sales were US$1.07 billion and US$1.50 billion in 1991 and 1992 respectively, with almost equal weightage of exports and domestic sales. Its major success was the time division exchange (TDX), which was purchased by Korea Telecom for the nation's public telephone network. Overseas TDX customers include Russia, Poland, Hungary, Nicaragua, and the Philippines. A TDX manufacturing plant will be built near Moscow under a joint-venture scheme and the TDX will account for a quarter of all electronic switching systems to be installed under an ambitious ten year modernization program of Russia's telecommunications network. The company is also the world's leading producer of monitors.

SEMICONDUCTOR DIVISION

Samsung Electronics' move to acquire this semiconductor business was perhaps to backward integrate and to develop its own indigenous products. Once known for making copycat versions of other companies' products, Samsung Electronics now sells its expertise in computer memory chips to Japan. Although this division was merged into the company only in November 1988, Samsung Electronics' current profitability is mainly dependent on it. It already contributes some 20 per cent to the company's annual sales and has had some tremendous successes that gave Samsung worldwide recognition. Samsung Electronics has secured a leading position for itself on the global DRAM market by all criteria—technology, quality and market share. The company also made other impressive achievements in other memory devices and packaging of semiconductor devices. Its 1991 sales amounted to US$1.37 billion of which 94 per cent is contributed by exports. In 1992, the Semiconductor division reported 25 per cent sales growth to US$1.7 billion. DRAMs account for about 70 per cent of the division's revenue.

COMPUTER AND SYSTEMS DIVISION

This youngest division was established in 1989, following the computerization age. Its sales were US$352 million and US$323 million in 1991 and 1992 respectively, and though it has made some notable achievements like a pen-based PC, RISC workstations and the TICOM supermicrocomputer, it is still incurring losses. Its annual losses are estimated to be anywhere between US$25 and US$40 million. However, Samsung is determined to secure and maintain a strategic position in this business sector.

Its advantage lies in its extensive network linking Samsung R&D teams with national research institutes and R&D centres overseas, such as research facilities at Samsung Software America (SSA) and the Personal Computer R&D Center in the US. This network provides an invaluable means for evaluating customer demands and rapidly changing market trends. However, Samsung has yet to overcome its weakness in software design. It is addressing this problem by adopting a total solutions approach to the company's development efforts that incorporates hardware, software and systems integration. Over the next two years, the company will design and produce some 250,000 personal computers for IBM.

In sum, 1992 sales revenue of Samsung Electronics shot up by 17 per cent to US$7.76 billion on the strength of impressive growth in export sales, particularly to such newly emerging markets for the company as China, Eastern Europe and South America. It should, however, be noted that Samsung Electronics' greatest strengths lies in two high-tech areas: semiconductors and telecommunications. According to economy analysts, Samsung Electronics will not only record rapid growth in sales but it will also show great improvement in profits because of the recent boom in semiconductors and other electronics fields.

SAMSUNG'S MANAGERIAL REFORM

Over the years, Samsung has become a mega-enterprise, and along with it came all the bureaucracies. In the past, a manager at Samsung Electronics tried to order some equipment, seeking the approval of his superior. This upward approval seeking took months and eventually reached the chairman-cum-founder Lee Byung-Chull. Before the approval was given, Lee died and was succeeded by his son, Lee Kun-Hee. The younger Lee was so appalled by this bureaucratic nonsense that he decided to launch management reform forthwith.

Now, Lee's orders to his to executives are: Get off managers' backs and let them make their own decisions on purchasing, product design and marketing. Basically, the management reform involves decentralizing decision making to the lowest possible levels so that the company can be more flexible and responsive to the environment.

Lee wants Samsung to be a nimble world competitor able to survive in this dynamic environment. He hopes to do this by grafting modern Western management practices onto the group's Confucian hierarchy. He adds that the group's goal of becoming the tenth largest conglomerate in the world and the fifth largest electronics player by the turn of the century depends on this radical reform, which is dubbed the Second Foundation. The nation's international competitiveness may also be at stake, as other South Korean firms will be watching closely to see if Samsung stumbles by introducing Western management practices.

Samsung is now in the early transition phase of this revolution. It is definitely not easy to implement this structural change as there are multiple obstacles and resistance that must be cleared first. It also involves a lot of risk.

First, South Korea's strong Confucian culture perpetuates an authoritarian management style that often stifles innovation and creativity. This top management was trained by the late chairman Lee to emulate the Japanese system, not innovate. It also makes it very difficult for the Samsung people to accept new, radical Western management practices. For example, recently Samsung's working hours were changed to 7 am to 4 pm, so that the people may complete their work earlier in the day and be more efficient by avoiding the rush-hour traffic jams. However, contrary to the seemingly beneficial effects such a change would bring, the Samsung people were used to starting slow in the day and becoming more productive in the late afternoon, working late into the night. Now that they are forced to go home at 4 pm, they do so without completing their work. Essentially, their working practices and style are deep-rooted and it will take much time and effort to effect the new practices.

Another difficulty of implementing such decentralization lies with the power held by the group's secretariat. This has been the nerve centre of the conglomerate, and is famed for leading the group into myriad new and untried business fields with scant regard for local or international market conditions. Such top-heavy management structure also hinders productivity and competitiveness. For example, a former Samsung executive said that the key factors of control are money and manpower, yet these have not been surrendered by the secretariat to individual companies. As a result, every decision that involves these two factors has to be approved by the secretariat. The time needed for this approval greatly slows down the decision making and affects the flexibility with which the individual companies can react to the environment. Despite Lee's calls for empowerment, the secretariat's grip on group companies remains formidable.

Now, although managers are empowered, there is no commitment from the top to support these reforms. Managers seeking to act independently often face resistance, even when their suggestions are good and have been sanctioned by senior management. The secretariat is also responsible for reviewing new investments for feasibility, and then pooling financial resources for investment. However, innovative ideas bubbling up from the bottom of the company are studied for years. By contrast, business plans developed by the secretariat in response to those of local competitors are acted upon quickly, often with disastrous consequences. For example, line managers' proposal in late 1989 to merge the four divisions of Samsung Electronics was only implemented three years later in December 1992, as it was delayed by the search for consensus at the top. The merger allowed special teams from the semiconductor division to be placed in every part of the company to coordinate the production of ASIC chips which are integral to the electronics business. Now, Samsung is behind world leaders in ASIC chips, but if the secretariat had listened to the line managers, they would have had a headstart.

Many comments have been made about Samsung's lack of leadership. Some people have attributed Samsung's current state of uncertainty during this stage of transition to Lee's unconventional management style. This is of course, debatable. Lee is an unconventional boss—he stays at home most of the time and delegates to his managers far more authority than is usual in Korea. He insists that the presidents of Samsung's 25 companies make their own decisions and asks that his 700 senior management understand his management philosophy—to think creatively about the future and grab the opportunities. His comments are philosophical and he does not make decisions, so the chairman's office interprets for him and all executives avoid responsibility, seeking consensus instead. The result is a corporate gridlock at the top as executives pursue consensus, and confusion below as line managers struggle to be innovative while adhering to the demands of the group's still hierarchical Confucian corporate culture. Samsung line managers complain that they are overwhelmed with work related to all of the on-the-spot decisions they are now expected to make on top of the traditional reports they still must pass up the hierarchical chain of command.

Although this structural reform has the potential to make Samsung a fiercer competitor in the global economy, its implementation needs stronger leadership in terms of provision of clear, concrete guidelines and objectives to managers instead of mere, vague philosophical ideas. With time, a strong leadership is necessary to uproot old and inculcated habits and put into place what seem to be very radical ways of doing things. For a start, at least, people need to be told where to go and how to do things as well as the benefits of doing so.

The challenge now is to mesh independent-minded managers with the traditionally authoritarian style of decision making in South Korea. Samsung needs to overhaul the conglomerate's rigid hierarchical structure to enhance competitiveness without losing the strong corporate teamwork. In essence, Samsung cannot readily imitate the Japanese, Taiwanese or US management styles because of its strong Korean culture. It needs to develop an original Korean management innovation team. Dr. Cho Yeong Dok, a leader of the team, thinks that the two-way exchange of information through team leadership is a way to rid the group of authoritarianism while enhancing consensus-oriented decision making. This meshes the group's Confucian traditions with the new independence given to line managers. Dr. Cho also thinks that the key to these management reforms is the concept of "professionalism".

Professionalism involves empowering lower-level managers by giving them more responsibility and promoting them on the basis of performance instead of seniority. Currently, this is still a very radical idea in South Korea. Only about 10 per cent of Samsung management promotions are done on a non-seniority basis. Professionalism also means no support staff which leads to a flatter hierarchical structure. This would force the white collar managers to improve their productivity. One of the tools used to encourage professionalism is an in-house management process called the Ace Professional Quality (A-Pro-Q) which was launched in April 1992. Its goal is to get senior management to grant young executives more decision making autonomy.

MANAGEMENT PHILOSOPHY OF SAMSUNG ELECTRONICS

Shortly after his appointment of Samsung Electronics in December 1992, Kim Kwang-Ho established a new managerial platform (see Appendixes 1 and 2). This new management philosophy is in line with the management reform at the group level. On top of internal management practices, Mr. Kim Kwang-Ho also said that the new Samsung Electronics should be quality- and customer-oriented in order to compete. The following are the key issues emphasized in his management reform declaration:

PRODUCT COMPETITIVENESS. Samsung Electronics stresses two main objectives. First, they aim to increase their sales in high profit products. Second, they want to create first-class products in the world. This objective is in recognition of the fact that sales and profits increase with high quality products. Samsung Electronics hopes to have at least one world-class product from each division. If this can be successfully accomplished, each division will be profitable and self-reliant. Dependency on the semi-conductor division can thus be reduced.

To achieve product competitiveness, the company is emphasizing quality instead of short-term profits. At Samsung Electronics, product quality is supported by the use and development of computer-aided design, manufacturing and engineering systems. Data on consumer taste and the operating environment in which the product will be used are incorporated into the product design.

MANAGEMENT EFFICIENCY. Three "S"s characterize how Samsung Electronics should be managed: simple, slim and speedy. Market-oriented management is to be practised which means that the company's focus should be on market demands and at the same time, employees are given authority and support to solve problems as they appear. It also means more autonomy for decision making. All obsolete regulations and practices should be done away with. Employees are encouraged to be creative, challenging, united with a "can-do" spirit, and unafraid of mistakes and failures. They should act and execute, not just think at the desk.

Mr. Kim Kwang-Ho also wants to make the company slimmer to consolidate the divergent divisions and make decisions faster. However, his new plan to reorganize the company into larger departments will not result in layoffs. Excess managerial manpower will be used to form special task forces under his personal command. Potential tasks for these forces include handling the US dumping charges, and searching out new markets and investment opportunities.

Self-reliant technology. Samsung Electronics stresses the importance of securing basic core technology and enhancing it by the synergy effect of merging essential element technology. Mr. Kim Kwang-Ho recognizes that developing own indigenous technology is a definite positive NPV investment. He once said that real cooperation is a give-and-take relationship. Only when one has some technology to give will one have power. At the same time, technologies that are mutually beneficial would greatly speed up their product development to give them an edge over their competitors.

A new star. The concept of company-before-self is emphasized. Everything should be done with the entire company's success as the primary consideration. Employees are thus urged to be industrious, sincere, loyal and frugal. Internal cooperation should be placed prior to individual tasks.

Customer orientation. In an environment where customers have endless choices and their bargaining power is increasing, customer satisfaction seems to act as the most reliable measure of one's success. As a result, Mr. Kim Kwang-Ho stresses the importance of customer satisfaction. The company should provide the customers with anything they want, accepting any requests while solving internal problems without any excuses.

Relationship with vendors. Samsung Electronics want to develop and maintain a common growth relationship with their vendors. They want to ensure their vendors as much growth as they deserve, and to provide the outstanding ones with finance and management know-how. A good relationship with suppliers can bring about benefits such as dependable and good quality supplies, reduced demands, contributions to product developments and easier implementations of new practices (e.g., JIT).

Implications on Human Resource Management

The emphasis on the above objectives has implications on the company's human resource management. Firstly, the selection criteria will undergo a change. Higher-skilled employees are needed to operate the sophisticated machinery needed to produce the high quality products. Continuous training needs to be emphasized so that skills will not become obsolete. There will also be increased demand for engineers and R&D personnel. Now, it also needs people who are dynamic, creative and independent as opposed to the type who need to work under an authoritarian management style.

Certain changes must be made to the corporate culture for the philosophies to be successfully implemented. Firstly, quality must be inculcated into the company's culture. Quality Control Circles (QCC) or other problem solving task groups may be set up to involve the employees in the efforts to improve them and to improve quality. This sort of participation may increase their commitment. In addition, quality needs to be defined from the customers' perspective, since ultimately, they will be the judges. Hence, the company needs to be outward looking and receptive to consumer needs. This customer orientation will help to produce products that the market wants.

Secondly, top management must be dedicated and willing to delegate both responsibility and power to the lower rungs of the hierarchy, as the traditional authoritarian style of management will not nurture and allow the self-management concept proposed in the management reform.

Thirdly, there must be dedication to creativity and innovation from the top. The corporate culture's emphasis on R&D needs to be increased. Communication channels should also be improved to encourage ideas to emerge from the lower levels. Top management must also change their attitude to be more receptive to suggestions from below.

"This is not my company, but our company", the idea advocated by Chairman Lee, needs to be a driving force in the company's culture. The employees need to feel they own the company so that they will be committed to it and will be willing to put it before themselves. This idea of ownership serves to encourage initiative as well as self-management.

IMPLICATIONS ON STRATEGIC FOCI OF SAMSUNG ELECTRONICS

RESEARCH AND DEVELOPMENT STRATEGY

Samsung Electronics recognizes that R&D is the single most factor critical to the company's future growth. They believe that technology is the key to innovating products that can better meet the unique needs and desires of consumers in different markets. Therefore, one of the main aims of Samsung's R&D strategy is to replace 40 per cent of their entire product line each year with new products. This ambitious commitment to R&D is the foundation of their competitive edge in the world market.

As such, they have invested a huge amount of money as well as manpower in R&D. In 1992, Samsung Electronics invested US$600 million (8 per cent of revenue) into R&D. At the same time the company employed about 12,000 engineers and researchers, which is more than a quarter of their total workforce, in R&D activities.

Samsung Electronics currently has twelve R&D centres worldwide, including six in Korea that deal exclusively with each of the four major business areas: computer systems, consumer electronics, semiconductors, and telecommunication systems. The other six R&D centres are in Japan and the United States.

Research for basic or core technologies is done by the Samsung Advanced Institute of Technology in Korea. Application technology and mid-term projects are pursued by research centres associated with the company's four business sectors. Following this, the research team attached to each division unit will help to develop and fine-tune manufacturing and production technologies. This three-tier R&D structure integrates the company's research activities smoothly, resulting in a consistent flow of new and better products.

All Samsung's research centres at home and abroad are equipped to conduct independent projects, although more often than not, they work together. For example, for Samsung's new pen-based PC, product planning and prototyping were performed at the US R&D centre while teams in Korea were in charge of design revisions and the production process.

Samsung also offers its own graduate level courses in science and engineering in addition to working with leading universities at home and abroad to provide advanced training for their employees. These innovative programmes are tailored to provide Samsung research and engineering personnel with additional training to improve their skills and promote greater creativity.

Samsung no longer want to be known as producers of cheap copies. They want to innovate rather than imitate. As such, most of their R&D has been focused on developing new products rather than improving their speed of production. Being aware of the Japanese technological prowess, Samsung realize that to make themselves known in the international market, they need to be first in introducing new things to consumers. Therefore, they have decided to concentrate on technologies that allow them to leapfrog ahead of their formidable competitors.

In 1992, Samsung invested a total of 1.05 trillion won into its R&D. This figure has been projected to go up to 1.15 trillion won in 1993, a 10 per cent increase. This implies that Samsung Electronics would also have a higher budget for their R&D activities in 1993.

Strategic R&D Activities

Semiconductors. One of the main areas of research was in semiconductors. In 1991, Samsung became the first company in the world to ship commercial samples of a 16-megabit DRAM, a semiconductor device capable of holding 16 million bits of data on a single chip. In 1992, the company overtook the top spot as the world's leading supplier of 1M and 4M DRAM. At the same time, Samsung also developed a fully operational 64M DRAM test chip in which no other chip manufacturer, including Japanese competitors, has yet developed.

High definition TV. Samsung Electronics also embarked on the development of HDTV technology. This research required an investment of US$25 million and about 80 research personnel. In April 1993, this investment paid off when Samsung Display Devices (SDD) announced the development of a picture tube for HDTV. Being involved at the early stages of HDTV commercialization will definitely put them in a position to be world HDTV market leader.

Digital video disc recorder. Over the last three years, Samsung has also been heavily involved in the development of a digital video disc recorder, investing about US$60 million over this period and deploying about 60 researchers for this project. This video disc recorder is able to put an entire movie into a 5.25-inch disk and retrieve massive amounts of information required for interactive multimedia products. If the product is successful, video recorders and laser disc players will become obsolete.

Others. Other areas in which Samsung electronics has been looking into include products for integrated services digital network (ISDN), artificial intelligence (AI) robots and terminals, opto-electronic devices, and voice recognition computers.

All these strategic activities have also resulted in many indirect benefits for Samsung Electronics. Shorter development cycles, new manufacturing processes, higher standards of quality and stronger business partnerships all owe a considerable debt to Samsung Electronics' continuing R&D efforts. All these factors are crucial for success in the electronics industry.

CONSUMER RESEARCH. Product development is driven by consumer demand. As such, each business unit develops its own value engineering product plan (VEPP). This plan starts with extensive grassroots feedback from customers. From this feedback, product concept engineers work together with lifestyle and cultural researchers to pinpoint consumer needs and to promptly reflect those needs into their new products.

The Life and Cultural Research Centre was created in part to analyze the way consumers use the company's products. The Life Soft Centre in Los Angeles, California, was the first such research centre. Samsung Electronics plans to establish four more Life and Cultural Research Centres in other strategic cities around the world.

In addition, a Design Centre has been established and is being operated in Frankfurt, Germany. Their ultimate goal is to improve the quality of life by introducing products better suited to the wants and lifestyles of consumers in different markets. This helps Samsung to develop products that provide superior functionality at less cost.

GLOBALIZATION STRATEGY

Samsung Electronics believes that internationalization of its various business lines is best pursued through partnership with local companies that are well respected in their local or national communities. Samsung's joint ventures are based on complementary strengths and mutual trust. In order to work better with their overseas partners, Samsung's employees possess detailed knowledge of the communities they serve. Samsung Electronics sends over 200 employees annually from its Korea offices overseas for training as international marketing specialists and to better familiarize themselves with local market conditions. At the same time, the company also hires a large number of employees from the local communities.

STRATEGIC ALLIANCES. In December 1992, Samsung formed an alliance with its arch rival Toshiba, the world's largest DRAM maker to establish a new type of chip called flash memory as a de-facto industry standard. This product aims to replace hard-disc drives in the market. This alliance was formed because Samsung needed Toshiba's technology and patents while Toshiba could benefit from Samsung's tremendous power in the production and distribution of the product. Samsung sought a licence to start producing 16-megabit flash memories in 1994.

Samsung has also developed a new colour video printer with Kodak. This product is able to turn sharp picture from TV screens in a shorter time than competing Japanese printers. Samsung is now making a version for Kodak which they sell under their own brand name. This is one of the promising products which Samsung hopes will change the customers' impression that their products are just low-cost copies.

With regard to HDTV, Samsung has agreed in principle to collaborate with General

Instrument, the American company that first devised digital TV broadcasting. Together, they would be better able to set the standards for the industry.

Other successful partnerships over the years include projects with Hewlett-Packard of the United States for personal computers, Sequoia of the United States for system integration and General Electric for satellite communication. They have also joined with Motorola in developing a palm computer on which users can write with an electric pen and send messages by wireless.

According to the president of Samsung Electronics: "Real cooperation is a give-and-take relationship. Now we have some technology to give, and we have some power." In other words, for a business partnership to be successful, each must have something to offer so that they can take advantage of each other's relative strengths. By bringing together different competitive advantage in an international partnership, they can create a competitive force greater than the sum of the partners.

OVERSEAS PRODUCTION. Samsung Electronics operates offshore manufacturing plants in twelve countries worldwide, producing a wide range of products from colour TVs to semiconductor chips.

After the cold war, business activity with the former East Bloc countries expanded at an exponential rate. Samsung Electronics wasted no time in setting up a joint venture TV plant in Hungary and a joint TDX venture in Russia. Recently, Samsung Electronics has also concluded an agreement with Calex of Czechoslovakia for manufacturing refrigerators and compressors.

A colour picture tube plant in eastern Germany has also been resurrected recently by Samsung Electronics. The company intends to invest US$120 million over the next few years to raise the plant's annual output to 2.5 million units. This plant would then be able to supply tubes to their colour TV plant in Hungary.

To maintain their position as a champion maker of commodity chips, second only to Toshiba, Samsung is expanding their production capacity by entering into a joint venture with Texas Instrument (TI) to set up a plant in Porto, Portugal, for the production of semiconductor chips. In addition, the company has also been making semiconductors at a plant outside Moscow.

With the cost of labour rising so rapidly in Korea, Samsung has also made plans to set up a US$54 million manufacturing plant in Tianjin to produce VCRs. This would allow them to tap China's vast pool of cheap labour as well as its huge market.

On-site manufacturing makes it possible to better identify consumer needs and to reflect those needs, in new products designed for local markets, quickly. Other obvious advantages of localized manufacturing include faster delivery times and reductions in delivery and other related costs.

INTERNATIONAL MARKETING ACTIVITIES. Samsung Electronics currently have 37 branch offices and 18 sales subsidiaries worldwide. In 1992, the company stepped up efforts to strengthen their international marketing network. First, they acquired Prostar Telecom Inc.

which will function as the marketing company for telecommunications systems sold in the US and secondly, they formed a new joint venture marketing company in Japan with local partner Tomen Electronics to boost their semiconductors.

Samsung Electronics is also planning to set up a dealer network in the Commonwealth of Independent States (CIS). This network would be spread over ten locations, the first of its kind in the CIS. According to the Head of Samsung Electronics' operations, this should greatly enhance their distribution and marketing operations in the Commonwealth.

As for their advertising and promotion, Samsung Electronics has plans to consolidate its US$100 million global marketing and promotion budget with the aim to become one of the world's top five consumer electronics marketers by the year 2000. In the last few years, Samsung electronics has engaged firms like Saatchi and Saatchi Advertising and Bozell. The company feels that a global public relations and advertising campaign would be better for their product and their brand name as Samsung is the same wherever you go.

Besides their marketing network, Samsung Electronics has a global after-sales network to ensure customer satisfaction with their products. This network consists of 17 service centres and over 10,000 service agents and authorized representatives in 86 countries. Service/parts centres are located in each geographical region to ensure ready access to supplies of replacement parts. Training programmes for service personnel are provided by the headquarters as well as local sites to guarantee continued improvement in the quality of after-sales service. Through their efforts, Samsung Electronics has achieved rapid diversification of its markets. In the past, the company relied on Europe, the United States and Japan for over 70 per cent of their sales revenue. However, dependence on these three markets has declined significantly as a result of successful penetration of new markets in central and South America, Africa, the Middle East and the former East bloc countries.

FUTURE PROSPECTS

The alliance with Toshiba for making flash memory chips offers great potential for the company. Toshiba estimates that the market would be worth 300 billion yen (US$2.4 billion) by 1995 and would reach 1 trillion yen by the turn of the century. Therefore, dominating the market together with Toshiba would ensure Samsung Electronics a large piece of the pie.

Samsung's breakthrough in the development of HDTV would also pay handsomely in the years to come. The annual world market for imaging devices is expected to exceed US$54 billion by the year 2000, with HDTV making up 60 per cent of this figure. As such, being the first company outside Japan to achieve success in this field, Samsung Electronics is now in an excellent position to take advantage of this high growth market.

Due to the difference in broadcasting formats in US and Europe, it is very difficult to come up with a HDTV for a widely accepted broadcasting standard. US and Europe are now developing their own broadcasting formats, but they lag behind in the development of HDTV technology. However, the picture tube has nothing to do with the broadcasting standard and can be used with any type of format. Hence, once the US or Europe come out with their own HDTV versions, Samsung will be ready to export their tubes to the world market along with the Japanese.

Samsung Electronics has also found many opportunities in the CIS. They expect sales revenue to surpass US$100 million in 1993 with purchases of TV and video cassette recorders accounting for more than 75 per cent of the sales. This is a 100 per cent increase over the 1992 sales revenue.

Samsung Electronics has also been able to buy more brain power for the money they are paying by hiring Russian scientists to work in their labs. These Russian scientists are the solution to the difficulty of obtaining technology since the Americans want too much money for its technology and the Japanese will not part with it at any price. Now, Samsung has a chance to hire top-class talent for next to nothing. The Russians are renowned for their world-class laser technology which contributes significantly to the R&D for Samsung Electronics. Furthermore, Samsung needs to only pay them US$100 a month each. Compared to their previous income of US$15 a month, this is considered a vast improvement by them.

Besides, Samsung Electronics also acquired the entire semiconductor laser production process technology from Russia for a mere US$500,000. Considering that a piece of semiconductor production equipment can cost several million dollars, this was certainly a tremendous bargain for the digital video disc recorder which they hope to bring to the market in 1995.

With this import of technology as well as the know-how at low cost, Samsung is able to further narrow the gap that separates them from their Japanese rivals. At least seven other Japanese companies are known to have developed systems based on this same technology but have yet to demonstrate a working prototype, which Samsung has already done. Therefore, Samsung hopes to leapfrog their competitors with the introduction of the digital video disc recorder. They plan to have a very wide distribution for the product and to price it under US$500. This their competitors would find very difficult to match.

Samsung's daring race for super growth is much more than an empty slogan. They are now a company that can compete against anyone anywhere in the world. The changes in their management philosophy have set them on the right path to meet the challenges in the 21st century. Their emphasis on R&D will certainly pay off in the next few years where they will start setting industry's standards instead of following standards set by others.

APPENDIX 1

PRESIDENT'S MANAGERIAL PLATFORM*

NEW SAMSUNG ELECTRONICS: QUALITY AND CUSTOMER ORIENTED, ACTIVE

1. Product Competitiveness
- Sales increase in high-profit products
- Creation of the first-class products in the world

2. Management Efficiency
- 3S (simple, slim, speedy)
- Market-oriented self-management

3. Self-Reliant Technology
- Securing basic core technology
- Enhancing the merging synergy effect of complex essential-element technology

4. New Start
- Company, instead of me or our section, goes first and foremost
- Industrious, sincere and frugal

---

* Internal source, Samsung Electronics Co. Ltd., Singapore branch office.

APPENDIX 2

PRESIDENT'S MANAGEMENT REFORM DECLARATION*

1. **We provide our customers with anything they want.**
   - We accept any requests by our customer, while solving internal problems without any excuses.
   - We make our customer satisfied with our heart as well as our product.
   - We place internal cooperation ahead of individual tasks.
2. **We see, hear and solve problems on the spot.**
   - Authority on the spot, support on the double.
   - Slim, simple and speedy.
3. **We create world-class products with our spirit in it.**
   - We place quality prior to short-term profit.
   - Each division creates, at least, one world-class product.
   - We compete in the world, equipped with know-how of management and technology.
4. **We grow together with our vendors.**
   - We ensure our vendors as much growth as they deserve.
   - We provide our outstanding vendors with finance and management know-how.
5. **We sweep all obsolete regulations and practices, armed with can-do spirit.**
   - Creative, challenging, fair, all together, in high spirits, we ceaselessly pursue ways to clear obstacles on the road.
   - We challenge, not afraid of mistakes and failures.
   - We act and execute, not just thinking at the desk.

---

* Internal source, Samsung Electronics Co. Ltd., Singapore branch office.

SUGGESTED FURTHER READINGS

Better Than You Might Except, *Korean Economic Report*, February 1993, pp. 67–70.
Business Korea Yearbook 1992/93, Samsung Electronics Co. Ltd.
Gadacz, O., Samsung Surprise: Could shift $100M, *Advertising Age,* January 19, 1993.
Grane, G., One Head is Better Than Four, *Economic Report,* January 1993, p. 43.
In a League of Their Own, *Korean Economic Report*, July 1993, pp. 44–45.
Johnstone, R., Quick as a Flash, *Far Eastern Economic Review*, January 7, 1993, p. 57.
_____, Russian Bargins, *Far Eastern Economic Review,* April 15, 1993, p. 44.
Kraar, L., How Samsung Grows So Fast, *Fortune*, May 3, 1993, p. 17.
Lilley, J., Dancing with the Bear, *Far Eastern Economic Review*, May 10, 1993, p. 56.
Lindorff, D. and L. Curry, The Korean Tiger is Out for Blood, *Business Week*, Vol. 8, May 31, 1993, pp. 18–19.
Nakarmi, L., A Peace That's All Dividend, *Business Week,* September 7, 1992, p. 24.
Nakarmi, L., R. Brady, and L. Curry, Can Korea Unite and Conquer? *Business Week*, October 26, 1992, pp. 22–24.
Nakarmi, L. and R. Neff, Samsung: Lee Kun-Hee's management revolution, *Business Week,* February 28, 1994, pp. 34–37.
New Whiz Kids on the Bloc, *Business Korea*, February 1993, pp. 67–70.
Paisley, E., Innovate, Not Imitate, *Far Eastern Economic Review,* May 13, 1993, p. 64.
_____, Time to Focus, *Far Eastern Economic Review,* April 8, 1993, pp. 60–61.
Paisley, E. and S. Awanohara, Tying the Knot, *Far Eastern Economic Review,* January 7, 1993, pp. 56–57.
The High Price of Protectionism, *Korean Economic Report*, March 1993, p. 68.

Brochures from Samsung Group & Samsung Electronics:
Office of the Executive Staff of Samsung Group, *The World of Samsung,* 1992.
Public Relations Office, Samsung Electronics, *Creativity and Innovation*, July 1993, p. 45.
Samsung Newsletter, Vol. 15, No. 5, May 1993, p. 11.

CASE TWENTY-THREE

LUCKY-GOLDSTAR INTERNATIONAL CORPORATION—DIVERSIFICATION AND GLOBALIZATION*

HISTORY

Lucky-Goldstar International Corporation, the trading arm of the Lucky-Goldstar Group, is one of Korea's major general trading companies (GTC).

During World War II, Koo In-Hwoi, the founder of Lucky-Goldstar Group, made tooth powder for Koreans to use in place of salt. In 1947, he established the Lucky Chemical Co. (now Lucky Ltd.) to make facial cream and later detergent, shampoo, and Lucky toothpaste. The company soon became Korea's only plastics maker.

To facilitate his company's imports and exports, Koo established a trading company during the dawn of Korean industrialization in 1953. The company was registered under the name of Lucky Industrial Ltd., the forerunner of present-day Lucky-Goldstar International Corporation. It carries out the international trading activities of Lucky-Goldstar Group.

In an effort to boost the economy through exports, general trading companies were established by the Korean government in 1975. To qualify, a company had to have at least seven export products spread over 10 markets, to maintain a minimum of 10 overseas branches and to have a minimum of US$2 million in capital. The GTC received several benefits, both tangible and intangible. These included access to highly subsidized trade financing, preferential treatment in industrial policy, regular direct access to the President and considerable public status. The government's intention was to create a handful of powerful trading houses along the lines of Japan's *sogo shosha* to serve as an "export window" for the Korean economy.[1]

---

*This case was prepared by Chang Young-Chul, Department of Organisational Behaviour, Faculty of Business Administration, National University of Singapore.

In 1976, the company (it was named Bando at that time) went public and was listed with a paid-up capital of 1.2 billion won. Since it fulfilled the criteria, it was designated a general trading company. In 1984, the company's name was changed to Lucky-Goldstar International Corporation (LGI) and its paid-up capital had increased to 30 billion won. Over the years, LGI has developed business relationships in more than 100 countries. It has over 40 overseas branch offices including six subsidiary companies which operate in Africa, South America, North and Central America, the Middle East and Europe.[2]

LGI contributes a substantial portion of Korea's overall export volume. In 1991, the company registered sales of approximately US$4.9 billion, with exports accounting for US$3.6 billion of the total.[3]

COMPANY PROFILE

CORPORATE MISSION

LGI's mission is to lead the globalization process of the Lucky-Goldstar Group and to establish and maintain its reputation as an integrated global corporation.

VISION. "Benefit to customers by the talented" and "a global enterprise trusted by the customers" are LGI's corporate guidelines as well as its long-time vision for the 21st century.[4]

MANAGEMENT PHILOSOPHY

In steering its international activities for almost 40 years, LGI has been guided by the Korean concept of *Inwha* or harmony. This is also the group's management philosophy. Being consistent with the group's management spirit, LGI places great emphasis on harmony as well as human-oriented management.

At the heart of the philosophy are two key concepts. First is the concept of creating value for the customer. Since customers are the reason Lucky-Goldstar exists, management must always make decisions with the goal of creating value for them in mind. This involves avoiding any actions which may negatively affect customer satisfaction and consistently providing a high level of service. Second is the concept of management based on the principle of respect for the individual. Since the creation of value depends on employees, management must always provide an appropriate workplace atmosphere. This includes respecting the individuality of all employees, ensuring they know their mission and tasks in the value-creation process, equipping them both mentally and physically to successfully complete their responsibilities, and fairly evaluating and compensating them for their work.

LGI's management firmly believes that it must offer the highest quality services to its clients and engage in business relationships which are not only beneficial to the company, but to its clients as well. This principle has been the guiding influence on all of LGI's business strategies and goals. The management believes it could establish a reputation of reliability and trust through creating convenience to its clients and instilling the spirit of professionalism in its employees.

BUSINESS ACTIVITIES

Through the use of capable, professional staff in a worldwide network of over 40 branch offices, LGI oversees foreign investment and resource development, offshore and counter trade, financing, information and technology transfer, and the domestic marketing of a variety of products.

TRADE. Trade is LGI's most basic function and involves the related fields of import, domestic sales and distribution, export, offshore trade, counter trade, and technology transfer.

IMPORT. Along with distribution, import is among LGI's most strategic activities. LGI's import activities are aimed at supplying vital items such as raw materials and natural resources, industrial materials and parts and a variety of consumer goods to the Korean market.

LGI provides the nation with the raw materials and natural resources it lacks, including nonferrous metals, raw materials for the production of textiles and chemicals, timber, pulp, grains, minerals, and energy resources.

DOMESTIC SALES AND DISTRIBUTION. Through its network of 200 sales outlets and over 1,300 supermarkets of its affiliate, the LG Mart Co. Ltd., LGI's distribution activities have increased dramatically each year. In order to meet the growing demand for fashion garments, sporting and leisure goods, seafood, petrochemicals and a variety of other merchandise, LGI continues to invest in the expansion of its distribution network and its warehousing facilities. The company has recently expanded its VAN (Value Added Network) System and, in cooperation with LG credit card, is expanding its marketing activities to include such services as car loans, factoring and consumer instalment financing.

EXPORT. LGI brings four decades of experience to bear on all of its activities in the export field, earning for the company an international reputation as a global trader. LGI has greatly expanded its base of operations, maintaining 34 branch offices and 6 foreign subsidiaries around the world.

Through its solid foundation built on an unmatched network of professionals, LGI exports tens of thousands of different products to more than 100 countries. As a member of the Lucky-Goldstar Group, LGI receives support from group companies which deal with various other fields. The group is able to provide a complete line of quality products, all of which are available to LGI at a moment's notice.

OFFSHORE TRADE. As one of the leading GTCs in Korea, LGI has extended its geographic range beyond the traditional hub of Korea to major business centers such as New York, Tokyo, Frankfurt, London, Singapore, and Hong Kong, where its locally incorporated subsidiaries conduct offshore trade activities independently of the parent company in Korea.

LGI promotes the offshore trade of raw materials, industrial facilities and finished products that result from its foreign investment and international project activities. LGI experts in this field handle garments, polypropylene, PVC resin, power distribution facilities, and crude oil through the company's global network of subsidiaries.

COUNTER TRADE. In response to increasing worldwide demand for counter trade services, LGI has organized a team of professionals in this field to handle the complex transactions involved in barter, counter-purchase, buy-back and offset activities.

LGI's counter trade activities are based on a mutual benefit concept. As a pioneer in the field of counter trade in Korea, LGI accommodates a wide variety of needs and successfully promotes the international exchange of goods and services. The company's record of success in the area of counter trade stems from its considerable expertise in information gathering and data analysis, organization and financing carried out by an extensive worldwide network.

TECHNOLOGY TRANSFER. LGI is also involved in many technology transfer arrangements, recommending advanced foreign technology, exporting domestic technology, supporting the export of Korean manufacturing facilities, mediating in international joint venture activities, and introducing new products to the domestic market. The company's activities in this field are backed by technological information provided by its overseas network of specialists and by 39 R&D centers: one each in Ireland, Germany, and Japan, 5 in the US and 31 in Korea.

FINANCING

Based on its experience in conducting traditional financing activities such as import and export financing, payment risk management, and custom-tailored financing arrangement, LGI has branched out into a diversity of more sophisticated activities in this field.

LGI's more advanced financing services include: interest rate and currency swaps; foreign exchange exposure management; financial futures and options on futures; overseas project financing through equity participation and joint venture and plant export financing.

LGI dispatches specialists in foreign exchange and financing to form an international network with the combined expertise to assure effective risk exposure and financial management. Working closely with their business counterparts, the LGI team of professionals in this field have achieved remarkable successes in meeting the specific financial requirement of all LGI clients.

LGI has also successfully expanded its international investor-base and gained wide recognition in the international financial market through its US$45 million US commercial paper issuance program launched in 1985 and its US$90 million Euro-commercial paper facility launched in 1987, and 1989.

Through its participation in the international capital market, and with the use of the various financial instruments which are available in the market, LGI continues to satisfy its ever-expanding domestic and overseas funding requirements.

INFORMATION

Like trade and financing, the gathering, analysis and distribution of information are among the most important functions of a GTC, and this is becoming increasingly vital as the world's economic structure shifts from "hard" to "soft" industries and as services begin to account for a greater portion of the world's industries.

LGI's broad and diverse information network is responsible for keeping the company and its clients up-to-date on what is happening in the vast world of business. With offices based in the Lucky-Goldstar Twin Towers, Korea's first intelligent office building designed by Skidmore, Owings & Merril of the United States, LGI has access to an advanced communication system complete with LAN and its own specialty network, facilitating the fast and accurate gathering, analysis, and distribution of vital information. Database sources include a variety of domestic and overseas research centers such as the Stanford Research Institute, LGI worldwide offices, LGI clients, and a wide selection of international publications.

To systemize its overseas information network, LGI's overseas market was subdivided into five regional headquarters. Financial and commodities specialists closely monitor hourly developments in futures and spot markets around the world.

In the domestic market, LGI's Fashion Division expanded its VAN system, adding national consumer credit sales network in cooperation with LG Credit Card Co. Ltd.

LGI provides product, market, futures trade, industrial technology, resource, price, financing, and foreign exchange information to each of its clients according to their specific needs.

As the world's information technology develops at an increasingly rapid pace, LGI maintains its position at the leading edge, maximizing its capacity to gather and manage the flow of information through state-of-the-art office automation systems, and to provide efficient international data exchange and data analysis through its extensive on-line system.

System Technology Management Corp., a joint venture between Lucky-Goldstar and Electronic Data Systems (EDS), strengthens LGI's information service, providing computer system integration, computer networking services, information technology and information-related software development.

FOREIGN INVESTMENT

As world trade practices become more complex and increasingly competitive, Korean firms are expanding into other markets through direct foreign investment activities. Foreign investment ensures the nation a constant supply of foreign resources, raw materials for national production, and a variety of advanced technologies.

From its humble beginnings as a consumer of foreign capital and technology, Lucky-Goldstar has come of age in the 1980s as an exporter of capital and technology through foreign investment. LGI is expanding its role as a window to the world and in coordinating the group's advancement in international business.

LGI's foreign investment activities primarily focus on the following three categories: investments in the company's overseas marketing network, investments in manufacturing facilities through joint ventures, and investments in resource development projects.

In a joint venture with Philips and others, LGI is involved in the development of sources of crude oil in Indonesia, Egypt, Papua New Guinea, UAE and Colombia, working in cooperation with companies from Japan, Italy and Australia.

LGI has also invested considerable amounts in the production of toys, garments, imitation crab-meat and containers in China, Thailand and Malaysia.

Current expansion plans include LGI investments in the development of sources of non-ferrous metals such as copper and aluminum, as well as coal and oil, in such resource-rich areas as Los Pelambres in Chile.

Project Organization Activities

Through the systematic coordination of all its services and activities, LGI has been able to serve as an organizer for a number of major projects, applying the accumulated expertise gleaned from its extensive experience in product trading, and from collaboration with such affiliates as Lucky Engineering, Lucky Development, Goldstar, Lucky Ltd., and Lucky Insurance.

An active member of project tenders, LGI successfully links small and medium-sized companies together to accomplish business projects of global scale and scope. The company provides a start-to-finish synthesis of all of its services in this field.

LGI plays a central role as an organizer in multiparty projects. NPC, a VCMPVC resin plant constructed and in operation under a joint venture agreement between Lucky Ltd. of Korea and SABIC of Saudi Arabia, is a representative example of LGI's organizing expertise. For this project, LGI acted as organizer between the joint venture partners, provided direct investment funding, and continues to participate in the project, distributing the product to countries throughout Asia.

Other major project organizing achievements include power distribution facilities and a carbon rod plant in Bangladesh, a dyestuff plant in Iran, a carbon black plant in Indonesia, an imitation crab-meat and sorbitol plant in Thailand, and a PVC sheet plant in Malaysia.

Corporate Structure

Under the current leadership of its CEO, the company's business is divided into nine major divisions: chemicals and plastics, food, resources, metals, electronics, machinery, general merchandise, textile and fashion, and information and communication.

Chemical and plastics. LGI's chemicals and plastics division is backed by over 40 years of experience accumulated through the Lucky-Goldstar Group activities in this field. The division stands ready to offer its customers a full range of high quality chemical and plastic products.

Food. With 15 years of accumulated experience in food-related industries, the LGI food division has put in great effort to create ample benefit for customers by sourcing and supplying excellent food products and resources while capitalizing on its financial, trading and marketing capabilities.

Not only long-term contracts with reliable sources, but overseas direct investments are also very active ventures for the stable procurement and development of quality products. The division is making remarkable strides to cooperate with specialized overseas and Korean partners by taking advantage of their own expertise such as a cattle-feeding project in Australia, and a joint venture factory of *surimi*-based seafood in Thailand.

Resources. As a result of Korea's dynamic economic growth and its increasingly high standard of living, the national demand for energy and mineral resources continues to rise sharply. Through its affiliation with the Honam Oil Refinery and the Lucky Metals Corp., both affiliates of the Lucky-Goldstar Group and national leaders in their fields, LGI's resources division plays a major role in Korea's trading activities in these industries.

Through the division, LGI supplies the Honam Oil Refinery with imported crude oil and exports a large portion of the refinery's 380,000 barrels per day (BPD) of petroleum products. To meet increasing domestic demand for petroleum products, the division also imports such products as naphtha LSWR and carbon black feedstock.

In addition to this offshore trade of crude oil and petroleum products, LGI also provides international bunkering services for ships flying foreign flags calling at Korean ports.

The division imports steaming and cooking coal from Australia, South Africa, China, etc., and supplies it to domestic power plants, steel mills, cement plants and cogenerating power plants at various industrial complexes. Other division activities include the supply of imported anthracite for household fuel and coke for the metallurgy industry.

METALS. LGI's metal division offers services for a variety of transactions involving nonferrous raw materials, refined metals, scraps and semi-products. Metals handled by the division include aluminum ingots, copper cathode, lead ingots, nickel and tin, as well as such precious metals as gold, silver, platinum and palladium.

In addition to the import, export and domestic distribution activities in this field due to its close affiliation with the Lucky Metals Corp. (LMC), formerly Korea Mining and Smelting Co. Ltd., a co-member of the Lucky-Goldstar Group, Lucky Metals Corp. is a longstanding national leader in its field.

ELECTRONICS. To assist the nation in maintaining its competitive edge in the strategic field of electronics, LGI's electronics division is stepping up its efforts to expand the scale and scope of its activities, focusing its considerable energies on the diversification and upgrading of its product line.

The division exports a wide range of consumer electronics including audio and video equipment and home appliances, C&C equipment including computer hardware, software and peripherals, various telephones and answering devices, parts and components for the telecommunication industry and such industrial electronic products as PABXs, TDXs and a variety of cables and wires. Through its export activities, the division is diversifying its line of high-quality products, fostering international cooperation in strategic projects, and investing in technology transfer and joint venture agreements.

MACHINERY. LGI's machinery division provides a full range of services to meet the demands of clients in worldwide industries. From machined components and industrial machinery, to such services as feasibility studies, turnkey plant installation, distribution and financing, the division is capable of satisfying every requirement of today's industrial society.

The division has led the nation in activities aimed at promoting the domestic production of a wide range of industrial machinery, the export of manufacturing facilities, and the import of high-tech equipment from abroad. These activities have succeeded in supporting a diversity of Korean industries along the road to development.

GENERAL MERCHANDISE. In keeping with Korean market trends based on government's relaxing of import restrictions, LGI's general merchandise division is placing great emphasis on increasing imports and domestic sales, as well as on such activities as offshore trade, and transactions with such strategic markets as those of the socialist countries. This shift in focus away from export activities is based on extensive market research and data analysis.

LGI's general merchandise division is known for its reliability in securing major foreign suppliers and well-qualified domestic agents. Building stone, for example is purchased from diverse suppliers in the United States, Spain, and Italy. The division also exports sporting goods, household products and toys under its own brand name to Russia, Japan and other countries.

The division's major import line includes partial board, timber, MDF, stone and precious metal. Its major export line includes products such as sporting and leisure goods, construction materials, rubber products, plastic products and a variety of miscellaneous items.

TEXTILE AND FASHION. LGI's textile division has contributed greatly to the development of the Korean textile industry, turning out high-quality garments for distribution in Korea and around the world.

As the export volume of textiles continues to increase at a rapid rate, the division's emphasis is shifting away from garments and toward fabrics and raw material. In order to meet the demands of the volatile world fashion market, the textile division has become the first Korean manufacturer of fabrics carrying its own designs. Exports of these fabrics have already reached a total sales volume of US$80 million in the United States alone. This remarkable success can be attributed in part to the staging of "Texibition," LGI's fabric shows held twice a year in New York.

The division also leads the nation in imports and exports of cotton fabric, cotton and silk yarn, and raw cotton. A division's subsidiary deals only in raw cotton, and the division has obtained an import license from China giving it exclusive rights to distribute Chinese silk yarn and fabrics in Korea.

The division also operates clothing manufacturing facilities at home and abroad. LGI's Bando House of Fashion is the national leader in the fashion industry and the first to introduce ready-to-wear fashions in the Korean market. LGI has its own factory producing jacket knit coats in Indonesia.

INFORMATION AND COMMUNICATION DIVISION. The division handles the import and export of C&C equipment including computer hardware, software, parts and components for the telecommunication industry. It is also involved in turnkey plant projects and installation of telecommunication equipment.

Environmental Factors and Their Implications

Domestic Market

The inauguration of a civilian government committed to economic reform and deregulation has contributed to the gradual recovery of the Korean economy. During the first quarter, the new government cut regulated interest twice and announced the 100-day Economic Revitalization Plan which includes a set of policy measures to expedite economic recovery.[5] The lowered interest rates were expected to boost investment by Korean companies and corporate earnings in 1993. The economy grew 5.1 per cent in 1993—high by the standards of the industralized world, but dismal in comparison with the double digit figures posted by Korea during much of the previous decade. The Bank of Korea forecasts GNP growth in 1994 of 6.3 per cent.

Implications. With the economy on the path of recovery, this is good news for LGI's domestic sales and distribution. With its extensive network of sales outlets and supermarkets, it will be able to profit from the increase in domestic demand brought about by the economic recovery. LGI should take this opportunity to further expand its distribution network and make a stand in the domestic market. This is in line with the company's wish of shifting emphasis away from the export function.

However, foreign competition is quite intensive in certain product areas.[6] The electronics industry especially has been suffering from long-standing slow domestic sales, due to tough competition from imported products. In the case of car audio products in particular, Japanese brands have been penetrating the domestic market. They have regained their price competitiveness through technical innovation and overseas production in factories in Southeast Asian countries.[7]

Recent developments in the foreign exchange markets, however, may open up an opportunity for LGI. The yen's recent and continual appreciation has caused many of LGI's Japanese competitors to raise the prices of their products.[8] LGI could take this opportunity to try to increase its market share in both the domestic and overseas market. This is a short-term advantage that LGI could use to gain new customer loyalty.

Export-Oriented Economy

According to a recent GATT report, Korea moved up one place to become the world's 13th largest exporting country. Exports of US$77 billion grew 0.1 per cent to account for 2.1 per cent of the world's combined export volume. The total value of export (FOB) in the first quarter of 1993 rose 7.5 per cent to US$18.24 billion.[9] In late April (1993), the government revealed a draft of the new Five-Year Economic Plan (1993–98), which indicates the government's determination to implement structural reform of the Korean economy to attain advanced country status.[10] Under the plan, the Korean economy is projected to grow at an average rate of 7 per cent in 1993–98 and per capita GNP is forecast to rise from

US$14,506 in 1998. Exports are also projected to grow at an average annual rate of 11.6 per cent. The government feels that economic growth led by domestic demand is not appropriate for the Korean economy, which can't help but depends on foreign countries for raw materials. Export-oriented economic growth is thus indispensable at least until the external balance settles down in a surplus trend.[11] In fact, the Korean economy recorded a trade surplus of about US$2 billion, compared with a 1992 deficit of US$2.1 billion, mainly due to brisk exports in 1993 of autos, electronic goods and machinery (cf., *Business Times*, March 16, 1994, p. 13).

IMPLICATIONS. The new government's action shows that it recognizes the importance of the country's export industries and thus the roles played by the GTCs in fueling the economic growth of the country. LGI should make good use of the various measures introduced in the 100-Day Plan and the new Five-Year Economic Plan to assist it in its business activities. Included in the plans are interest rate reductions, deregulations of business activities, new public projects and assistance in technological developments, which will greatly help LGI in its various business functions of trade, financing, foreign investment and project organizations, etc.

MAJOR MARKETS

As a higher-wage, medium technology nation with an export-oriented economy geared toward the US, Japan, and the EC, the last three or four years have not been easy for Korea. The share of Korea's export to its three major markets fell to 47.2 per cent in the first quarter of this year, marking the first decline below 50 per cent. As recently as 1990, these major markets took up nearly 70 per cent of Korea's exports.[12]

For the US market, things may be starting to look up—or at least not getting any worse—as the US economy is showing some signs of recovery which is expected to boost exports of automobiles, semiconductors, and home electronics.

For the EC markets, the outlook is more gloomy. Export to the EC sank to 10 per cent from 12 per cent during the four months compared to the previous year with the export of iron and steel products falling by more than 70 per cent in the first months of 1993. In the coming months, export of electronic products to Europe is likely to be hit hard, as the EC is about to commence anti-dumping investigations of Korean color TVs with more than 18-inch screens, condensers and satellite video receivers. Final or preliminary rulings against compact disc players and car audio sets are due soon as well. With dumping charges, electronics exports to Europe are falling sharply.

As for the Japanese market, export to Japan fell from negative 2.2 per cent in 1991 to negative 6.6 per cent for the first five months compared to last year. Such decline might be slowed in the coming months as the Japanese yen appreciates, making Korean imports cheaper and more competitive in the Japanese market.[13] However, in the long term, export of light industrial goods is likely to be substituted by cheaper imports from developing countries resulting in further decline in this and other markets.

IMPLICATIONS. To overcome the slump in exports, most electronics companies are changing their overseas strategies to avoid dumping and quota regulations The three electronics giants—Samsung Electronics Co., Goldstar Co. and Daewoo Electronics Co.—have decided to focus on merger/acquisition activities and seek cooperative ties with local partners for sales networks.[14] LGI has a great role to play in these mergers/acquisitions and cooperative tie-up activities. Its information gathering and analysis function will be of vital importance in assessing such overseas ventures. LGI, being the Lucky-Goldstar Group's window to the world, will have to make full use of its financing, foreign investment and project organizing expertise and skills to carry out these new global strategies in the developed countries for the group.

EMERGING MARKETS

Korean exports to less developed countries, particularly China and Southeast Asia, rose by 22.2 per cent last year. The trend of exports to these countries will continue because these countries need a great deal of facility goods and materials such as steel, chemical goods, machinery and intermediary goods. Taking the region as a whole, East Asia, without Japan, has replaced the US to emerge as the largest market for Korean goods. Since 1988, exports have grown 25.5 per cent a year to reach 30.4 per cent of Korea's overall export in the first four months of this year compared to just 23 per cent for the US.

ASIA PACIFIC. Fueled by a modestly accelerating world economy, economic growth in the Asia-Pacific region is forecast to average 7 per cent per annum during 1993 and 1994, according to the *Asian Development Outlook 1993*, a report compiled by the Asian Development Bank (ADB). Imports in the region are also expected to grow over the next two years due to trade liberalization and large investments in infrastructure.[15]

CHINA. Direct exports to China totalled US$2.65 million last year, when the two countries established diplomatic relations, up 165 per cent from 1991. The rapid growth in trade was attributed to the booming Chinese economy and tariff reductions in preparation for China's joining the General Agreement on Tariffs and Trade. In the first quarter of this year, the People's Republic of China emerged as Korea's third largest trading partner and most popular destination for new investment. Conversely, Korea has become China's fifth largest foreign investor and the country's sixth largest trade partner, as Korean exports to China jumped 162 per cent in the first quarter of 1993. Government officials projected a 70 per cent growth in bilateral trade for the entire year of 1993.

Korean exports are led by steel and steel products, petroleum, synthetic fibers, textile fibers and filaments and yarn. Steel products surged a tremendous 352.6 per cent to US$355 million in the first quarter of 1993. Bolstered by the flood of Korean investment into China, general machinery exports climbed 93.3 per cent. The economic boom in China will continue in 1993 and 1994 with the double-digit growth rate maintained although it will slow somewhat because of bottlenecks in transportation, energy and raw material production and because of inflationary pressure.[16] In February 1994, the Korean government unveiled a package of measures designed to further boost its already booming bilateral trade with China and strengthen economic cooperation, under which Korea hopes to build bilateral trade from US$8.9 billion in 1993 to US$28 billion in 1997.

IMPLICATIONS. To fuel the tremendous economic growth of China and the developing countries in the Asia-Pacific region, there is a great demand for infrastructure-related products including transportation, energy and raw material. Korea is also likely to receive a massive diversion of Chinese business from Japan. Although the Chinese will still need Japan for certain high-tech inputs, as the country tries to modernize and diversify its industrial base, Korea is likely to emerge as its key supplier of capital and intermediate goods (including building materials such as steel, industrial machinery, engineering services, commercial vehicles and ships).[17] LGI should make good use of this golden opportunity to make available its services to these growing economies. It has both the necessary experience (accumulated through projects undertaken in the Middle East and Latin America) and support of other companies in the Lucky-Goldstar Group to cater to the needs of infrastructure building and support.

With such booming economies comes greater demand for consumer goods. LGI has already established branch offices in Beijing, Guangzhou and Shanghai and established Goldstar as a well-known household brand in China and other developing countries. East Asia, especially China, offers it the opportunity to diversify from its traditional markets of the US, Japan and the EC where it is facing both economic and legal/political problems with its exports.[18]

VIETNAM. Full diplomatic ties were restored with Vietnam in December 1992 and Premier Vo Van Kiet visited Seoul in early 1993. Even before the US-led embargo on Vietnam was lifted, Korean companies were quietly making inroads into Vietnam as early as four years ago. The Vietnamese are cheaper to employ, hardworking and very skilled with their hands. They are also eager to do business with Korean companies, which they view as a potential source of technologies and skills suitable to the present development of the country. Hanoi hopes to follow the same path towards industrial development as did Seoul. There are some problems however, the most common being the rampant corruption and the usual bureaucracy associated with Communist countries, and the lack of infrastructure. Vietnamese government officials say Korea has more to offer them than Japan, whose technologies too are generally expected to expand with a South Korean consulate-general opening in Ho Chi Minh City in June 1993 to serve the needs of the more than 600 Korean businessmen now stationed in the city. Laws related to direct investment by foreigners are also being revised in a government effort to improve the business environment. Hanoi will also encourage Laos and Cambodia on the path to full ties with Korea.[19]

IMPLICATIONS. Many Korean companies, particularly Samsung and Goldstar, have already scored well with Vietnamese consumers. In the future, Korean companies are expected to do well in oil exploration and construction. The Vietnamese government is urging businessmen to invest in the manufacturing sectors such as machinery, shipbuilding and petrochemicals; and infrastructure projects such as harbor, road, airport and communications projects.

LGI already operates technical support centers in Hanoi and Ho Chi Minh City to back up maintenance and repair of telecommunication facilities. These centers are also aimed at training Laotian and Cambodian engineers before Goldstar advances into these neighboring countries. Goldstar invited some 70 Vietnamese technicians to Korea for training recently. During the next five years, the company plans to invite another 100 Vietnamese technicians for training in Korea.[20]

As the Southeast Asian markets develop their potential, LGI plans to set up a joint venture in Vietnam aiming at not only the local market but also the neighboring countries. With all these advantages, LGI should manage to perform successfully in this vital market of the future which is not only full of potential, but can serve as a valuable starting point to equally promising, but untapped markets in the region.

KOREA'S LIGHT INDUSTRIES

The most critical problem facing Korean exports is the rapid decline of light industrial exports, such as textiles and footwear. It is going to be very difficult in the future for these exports to recover because cheap goods from less developed countries are taking Korea's products off the market. From a negligible 0.6 per cent growth in 1991, exports shrank 1.9 per cent in 1992 and further by 7.9 per cent in the first quarter of 1993 compared to 1992.[21]

Many Korean firms are looking to China as an offshore base for manufacturing in such labor-intensive industries as textiles and footwear, but the Chinese are not usually willing to allow such manufactured products into their domestic market; the items are re-exported instead, competing with similar industries employing Koreans at home. This results in a growing demand (from China) for tanned leather and textile fibers, filaments and yarn, an intra-industry division of labor, in which Korean light industrial inputs are ferried back and forth across the Yellow Sea for processing and assembly. The finished products are re-exported, pricing light industrial goods made solely in Korea out of both third markets and the domestic market. This is known as the boomerang effect, with the textile and the toy industries being the hardest hit.[22]

IMPLICATIONS. Korea can no longer compete in terms of price with developing countries in light industrial goods so it must diversify its export markets for capital and intermediate goods. It will also have to develop items that meet the needs of developing countries and effectively differentiate its products. In the long run, the light industrial sector has to develop into a leaner and meaner sector which can earn more foreign exchange with higher value-added, specialized products on a reduced production scale than the present fragmented setup of low-technology industries.[23]

The light industries under LGI (e.g., textile and fashions) will inevitably suffer the same fate as the rest of the industry. Thus, LGI must seriously look into dualizing its production by producing cheaper items abroad and high value-added items at home. To maintain its market share of light industrial products in both the domestic and export markets, it must look for quality products with high value added that are differentiated from the cheaper products of developing countries.

The resultant increase in demand for light industrial input and intermediate products is also an opportunity not to be missed. Amid gloomy projections for the overall textile sector, only synthetic fiber production is projected to be positive. The rise in synthetic fiber output is due to brisk production of polyester and acrylic fiber. LGI's expertise in the offshore trade of raw material should come in handy with this boom in demand.

ECONOMIC PLANS

The government announced the 100-day economic plan during the first quarter of 1993 and a draft New Five Year Economic Plan in April. In the first plan, some of the issues raised are: reduction of interest rates and implementation of public projects, strengthening of small businesses' competitiveness, expanding investment for technological development and easing regulation on business activities. In the second plan, the New Five Year Economic Plan stresses the need for structural reform of the economy. The major areas of reform are financial liberalization, promotion of the *chaebols'* specialization and government support for technological development.[24]

IMPLICATIONS. These restructuring and economy-boosting measures have both positive and negative effects on LGI. In the financial liberalization measures, the central bank terminates all loans to big enterprises for the expansion of export facilities at the end of June, and in allowing greater autonomy in fund management, reduction of non-performing loan, greater credit control and supervision and liberalization of foreign exchange control, the *chaebols* and their subsidiaries could be hurt.[25] However, favorable measures like liberalization of foreign exchange controls help. Beginning in April, Korean trading companies with annual exports of more than US$100 million were allowed to possess foreign exchange up to US$100 million. Previously, only eight GTCs were allowed to hold a maximum of US$10 million in foreign exchange. Under the relaxed foreign exchange control system announced by the Ministry of Finance, the 136 qualified traders are also able to invest their foreign exchange holdings in financial assets, including securities.[26]

The government also plans to open completely domestic markets to direct foreign investment within five years. A detailed liberalization program for foreign investors, including the gradual lifting of restrictions now applied in one form or another on 224 business lines, will be worked out for implementation.[27] This poses a serious threat to LGI's domestic market share. As foreign investors get a foothold in the market, the competition for a piece of the local market share will definitely intensify. LGI would do well to boost its local sales network and get ready to defend its market share.

SMALL AND MEDIUM ENTERPRISES (SMEs)

Shortly after his inauguration in February 1993, President Kim Young-Sam told a meeting of *chaebol* chairmen that they would have to start dealing fairly with SMEs; delaying payments to SME contractors for up to a year after receipt of deliveries would no longer be tolerated.[28]

A 1.42 trillion won assistance fund for SMEs was formed in spring to help structure small- and medium-sized companies, especially manufacturers, and will be increased to 2 trillion won by 1998.[29] Corporate tax and business income tax levied on small- and medium-sized companies will be reduced by 20–40 per cent over the next two years. The economic planners are convinced that SMEs hold the key to Korea's future prosperity. In 1991, SMEs accounted for 40 per cent of the nation's total export. The government will select and choose the very promising firms and provide assistance and support only to selected SMEs. Korea has a relatively weak parts and components sector, so that a lot of technology-intensive parts have to be imported, mostly from Japan. Core components such as liquid crystal displays, charge-coupled devices and multi-layer PCBs are still missing. In order to upgrade the electronics industry, the critical point is to develop and enhance SME parts suppliers.[30]

IMPLICATIONS. A vast majority of SMEs depend on the large firms for their survival. Goldstar Co. alone has about 2,000 to 3,000 SME subcontractors. The government's move shows the importance it places on the SMEs. This time it is not only doing lip service, but backing up its words with funds and legal supports.[31]

It will be advantageous for LGI to cooperate with the SMEs as now some of them will be very well positioned to take advantage of the government's offers and incentives. This will result in making them better equipped to take on foreign competition. LGI with its expertise on project organizations and venture capitalization could tap these potentials in the SMEs.

Should the SMEs manage to achieve what the planners envisioned, they would also provide very strong products for LGI to export to other parts of the world. Less reliance on costly Japanese input will also enable local products to be produced more cheaply and they would be better able to compete on price with the Japanese in the global markets. It will also be less tied to the state of the Japanese economy and supply fluctuations.

OVERSEAS INVESTMENT

The government is currently simplifying complicated screening procedures for overseas investment in communist countries. Korean companies will be given a freer hand to invest directly in these countries. Currently, any direct investment exceeding US$5 million in socialist or former socialist countries is subject to review by related government ministries and the interagency Northern Economic Policy Working-level Committee. After passing these hurdles, investors must still get approval from the Bank of Korea. According to a new ministry plan, direct overseas investments with a total project cost of less than US$5 million and net overseas investment of under US$1 million, will not have to undergo government inquiries into their sources of capital and the project's viability. These criteria have often been arbitrarily applied by screening officials to approve or block planned investments without any discernible pattern. That, in turn, has elicited complaints from small-scale investors, who represented 81.6 per cent of total investment application in 1992. The new rules also free large investments of more than US$30 million from the obligation of conducting feasibility studies in advance of their investment.[32]

IMPLICATIONS. The current change in policies, although not drastic enough to really affect the GTCs, indicates the direction that the government will take. This is a good sign as it shows that the government recognizes both the importance of export and the "opening" of communist or former communist countries. Further actions in the future will consolidate its presence in these countries so as to properly take advantage of any future opportunities.

The measures announced, however, have helped many SMEs to invest abroad. This could lead to a flood of competition in these potential markets while at the same time, LGI's project-organization activities could be stepped up to take advantage of these new inflows of investment funds in the developing countries. Its expertise and experience would be well sought after as SMEs normally could not go it alone in these overseas ventures due to size limitations and uncertainty or lack of experience with the host countries.

LABOR

Korea has become a high wage society which resulted in some of its products becoming uncompetitive in the world market, most notably the light industrial products. Prospects for exports will depend on the growth of world trade and on the international competitiveness of Korean products, which may improve as inflation and wage increases are contained and industrial restructuring progresses.[33]

Another serious problem is a severe labor shortage that is preventing some industries from developing. The labor shortage was approximately 300,000 people for all industries in 1992 and is still increasing in large numbers.[34] The situation becomes more severe when it comes to the textile industry which needs at least 30–50 per cent more people in order to operate properly. Demographic changes and more years in school have resulted in far smaller cohort groups of young workers to cope with this severe shortage. Firms have adopted more capital- and technology-intensive production processes and higher value-added products, and they are shifting production to lower wage countries. The economy as a whole is experiencing a sectorial shift to more sophisticated industries, especially services.

IMPLICATIONS. The implication is that LGI's export structure will change dramatically in the near future as the nation's competitiveness changes. From an estimate released by the Minister of Trade, Industry and Energy, export of heavy industrial goods will increase to 75 per cent from the current 61.4 per cent while light industrial goods will decrease from 34.4 per cent to 25 per cent by 1998. The figures also show the changes in export structure over the years since 1986. Technology-intensive and capital-intensive products are targeted to increase to more than 80 per cent in 1998 while labor-intensive products will decrease to 20 per cent or less from the current 36.1 per cent.[35]

LGI should position itself to take advantage of this shift, anticipating the changes before they take place. It should shift its emphasis along the same lines as the economy, developing its expertise in the area of technology- and capital-intensive product lines while increasing or decreasing emphasis on exports of the more labor-intensive products.

The labor trend also points to a shift of labor-intensive manufacturing to other developing countries and developing more knowledge-based industries within the country. Again LGI's expertise in project organization and foreign investment would be of use. It should also place greater emphasis on its business of transfer of technology and knowledge as the country begins its shift towards high-technology and knowledge-based society. Sourcing for appropriate technology and the gathering and analysis of information will be of even greater importance than before.

TECHNOLOGY

For Korea to sustain high economic growth despite the external and internal challenges, technology development is considered a top priority. Without upgrading technology and restructuring towards technology-based and knowledge-intensive industries, Korea will find it increasingly difficult to compete in the world market. This issue is being addressed by the government and the private sector, but a potentially difficult period of adjustment may be encountered as restructuring efforts will have to be pursued in tandem with the main objective of macroeconomic stability.[36]

On the other hand, current Korean technology is cheaper and less advanced than the Japanese, making it better suited to the needs of developing countries like Vietnam, Laos, Cambodia, China, and countries in the Middle East and Latin America.[37]

Technology transfer is developing into a major business as the various developing countries of the world require technology from others to help them to progress at greater speed and scale. China is trying to attract capital- and technology-intensive investments in exchange for offering foreign firms a market share, tempting firms with pipedreams of its elusive "market of 1.2 billion." But at the same time that China is taking an increasingly assertive position on technology transfer, the Korean government is seeking to retain its technological edge by becoming increasingly selective and cautious in technology transfer, especially to second-tier NIEs (newly industrializing economies).

IMPLICATIONS. These needs of technology transfer are good news as LGI has been in this field for a long time. It could tap its extensive worldwide network to acquire the necessary technology for the country's needs, benefiting both the manufacturer and its more competitive exports in the future.

China and Korea both possess medium technology, but China's strength lies in textiles, petrochemicals and chemicals; while currently, Korea's medium technology centers on the automobile, shipbuilding and electronic appliance sectors. China has a very large, diversified industrial system which can produce advanced goods with cheap labor, so its technological level will quickly improve and might overtake Korea if Korean firms do not improve on the R&D front. Towards this end, the government is increasing its funding for R&D and simplifying procedures for the application for such funds.

The transfer to Korea of technologies not yet commercialized in China will be another aim. China has high technology in the aerospace and military-related industries, which Korean companies need. The ability to tap this technology and put it to commercial use will generally benefit the company.

STRATEGIC ORIENTATIONS

GLOBALIZATION

Beginning with the export of plastic household goods in 1953, LGI began to build up the Lucky and Goldstar brand names which are now well-recognized in countries around the world. Through its well-established international network, LGI has helped the Lucky-Goldstar group to achieve a remarkable international presence in four short decades. LGI continues to lead the globalization process of the Lucky-Goldstar Group and plays an important role in the group's development into a global organization.

TAPPING OPPORTUNITIES FOR GROWTH WORLDWIDE. LGI plays an active role in developing new markets and tapping opportunities worldwide. To increase international exposure and foster growth, LGI has made inroads into those emerging markets.

On the heels of a major television deal with Romania in 1990, LGI landed a US$9 million contract in late 1991 to supply 3,900 color television sets to Czechoslovakia. Activities in the Middle East have been brisk and in February 1992, LGI won two major telecommunication cable projects. A US$33 million deal was signed with Syria, many of the company developments were close to home in Asia. In April 1991, LGI participated in a consumer product exhibition. The company established an office in Ho Chi Minh City in advance of the exhibition to coordinate future expansion into Indo-China. Southeast Asia is also a source of projects. In March 1993, LGI accepted a US$60 million order from the Port Authority of Singapore (PSA) to construct container crane facilities. LGI won the contract over 14 other crane manufacturers, including Mitsui and Mitsubishi of Japan as well as leading Germany and Italian corporations.[38]

In addition, LGI established overseas branch offices in Beijing, Guangzhou and Shanghai. This enables the company to penetrate China's market, which is one of the fastest growing economies in the world.[39]

By actively searching for new opportunities and markets, LGI ensures growth and prosperity. The experience gained in developing these new markets also enhances LGI's competitiveness. LGI will continue to make contact with these emerging markets not only for practical business but also for the betterment of its corporate image.

MAKING PROGRESS THROUGH COOPERATION. Entering alone into overseas markets is not always the best policy. For this reason, LGI has chosen to set up joint ventures with local partners around the world, to the mutual benefit of both parties.

In 1991, LGI joined a three-party joint venture in a 24000 TEU container factory. The company will export materials and parts for the containers to China as well as export the finished containers from China. In another joint venture, LGI's general merchandise division entered into a joint venture with China National Electronics Import and Export Corporation to produce quality plush stuffed toy.

Through joint ventures, LGI could gain access to technology of strategic fields from its partners. LGI could also enter into projects which require high setup cost and might have appeared unfeasible to set up on its own.

MAKING STRIDES IN THE INDUSTRIAL WORLD. While concentrating resources on emerging markets around the world, LGI has not neglected operations in the industrialized world. The company will continue to reinforce its solid footing in these markets. In countries such as the United States, Germany, Britain, Sweden, Norway, Finland and Japan, LGI's products have gained great recognition and received favorable ratings. This could be partly attributed to its considerable efforts directed at promotional activities in these markets. LGI is actively involved in trade exhibitions and trade shows to create international awareness of its products. An example is the staging of "Texhibition," LGI's fabric shows held twice a year in New York.

FUNCTIONAL DIVERSIFICATION

The management feels that it is important to strike a balance between exports, imports, and domestic sales. However, most GTCs have been overdependent on exports since the export growth was the major target and the reason for existence.[40]

As far as LGI is concerned, the role of a GTC is not limited to exports. It involves activities like imports, distributions, domestic sales, finance, information, and investment in foreign countries as well. LGI is trying to strengthen these areas by adapting some measures such as the linkage of exports and imports, securing long-term import sources, enriching information systems and stock sales in the domestic market.

LGI is moving away from export-oriented business management. The company will diversify its business by expanding imports and domestic marketing, and participating in new projects such as overseas resource development, investment in sophisticated industries and joint venture abroad. Besides export/import businesses, LGI will seek diversified business operations combining raw materials, technology and plant facilities, through counter purchase or package deals. Direct exports will be increased to improve the company's profitability and it will advance into value-added high-technology industries.

PROCURING NATURAL RESOURCES OVERSEAS. For a country like Korea with poor natural resources, securing a stable supply of resources in the long term is very important in anticipation of possible price hikes in the future. Therefore, LGI will pursue counter trade with resource-rich countries and actively participate in resources development projects in joint ventures with foreign firms to realize a stable supply of energy sources.[41]

LGI aggressively expanded its activity in overseas oil exploration and production since it participated in Adang Block oil field in Indonesia in 1984, and is currently involved in exploration projects widely distributed in the Pacific Rim. It also acquired an equity interest in Khalda field, Egypt, with daily production of 28,000 BOPD. LGI's goal is to secure its equity oil from worldwide production equivalent to 10 per cent of daily capacity of Honam Oil Refinery by the year 2000. As to mining projects, LGI is participating in the development of the Enham Coal Project in Queensland, Australia and the development of the Los Pelambres project in Chile with a view to supplying copper concentrates to Lucky Metal Corporation.[42]

GREATER EMPHASIS ON IMPORTS OF HIGH QUALITY AND HIGH-TECH PRODUCTS. LGI intends to intensify its import activities in the area of technology-intensive products, industrial products and industrial materials and parts such as factory automation equipment, CAD and

CAM systems, computer and communication equipment, and precision measuring and testing for the advancement of Korea's industrialization efforts.

The increasing standard of living in Korea has also led LGI to increase the import of internationally renowned brands of fashion garments and accessories, foodstuffs and household goods. All these efforts will prepare LGI for the 21st century, an era of quality and technology.

INCREASING PARTICIPATION IN THE INTERNATIONAL FINANCIAL MARKETS. As the company increases its international commitments, it requires more funds to finance its activities. LGI's financial function is becoming more important as international trade develops a more complex finance role. LGI will further expand its role in international financing by issuing commercial papers or international bonds abroad and swap transactions. This would enable LGI to gather funds for its overseas projects on a stable, long-term basis.

EXPANDING DOMESTIC AND OVERSEAS MARKETING CAPABILITIES. LGI's distribution activities have increased dramatically each year. To facilitate its marketing activities, LGI continues to invest in the expansion of its distribution network and its warehousing facilities. To further strengthen its marketing capabilities, LGI has established a strong sales network consisting of a professional sales force. This sales network is not only for trading activities but also for gathering market information. These strategic moves enable LGI to improve its competitiveness in both domestic and overseas markets.

OEM (original equipment manufacturer) arrangement used to be very popular and has benefited many Korean manufacturers who produce for other established brand names in the developed countries. However, this has become a great disadvantage today when the company tries to establish its own brand name in these markets. Korean products are traditionally viewed to be of lower quality and even though this is no longer true, the image remains. Thus, LGI is working very hard to re-establish its brand name in these markets. It has also realized the importance of establishing its brand name and is making sure that the mistake is not repeated in the emerging markets. The Lucky-Goldstar brand is very popular and represents quality products in new markets like Vietnam and China due to the effort of LGI in this area.[43]

RELOCATION OF LABOR-INTENSIVE MANUFACTURING FACILITIES. The rising wages in Korea have caused Korean-made products to become less competitive. In order to maintain its global competitiveness, LGI has shifted some of its labor-intensive facilities to countries which provide cheap labor.[44]

Towards this end of dualizing its production capabilities by producing labor-intensive products overseas and value-added products at home, LGI has invested in manufacturing facilities for the production of toys, garments, imitation crabmeat and containers in China, Indonesia, Thailand and Malaysia. These places provide LGI with an abundant supply of cheap labor which allows its products to be produced at a low cost, thus maintaining its competitiveness.

Recommendations

Strengthen domestic market share. In view of the domestic economic recovery and the more intensive competition due to market liberalization, it is advisable for LGI to strengthen its position in the domestic market.

Product differentiation. In order to compete effectively in the developed countries, LGI has to pursue a strategy of product differentiation as the traditional price competitiveness is no longer a strength in the face of competition from developing countries. It must concentrate its attention on brand name, design and quality perception-building which were previously neglected under the OEM arrangement.[45]

Market diversification. LGI should attempt to diversify away from the traditional markets of the US, Japan and the EC. Currently there is heavy reliance on these markets resulting in overdependence on their economic performance. When these economies "catch a cold," LGI's export performance will "catch the flu." There is also a trend towards greater protectionism in these markets resulting in greater difficulty operating there.

Establish presence in emerging markets. LGI's experience in Vietnam and China has shown that it is very important to have first mover advantage in new markets. Thus, it should ensure that its presence is established in the emerging markets of the world. Being the first big player in the market normally results in market leadership in subsequent years when the market is more open and attractive for other investors.

Light industry/infrastructure development. Looking at the competitive structure in the world today, Korea has lost its cost competitiveness in light industrial products. Thus, LGI should move away from the export of light industrial products and towards the export of raw materials and intermediate products such as raw cotton, cotton fabric, cotton and silk yarn and synthetic fiber. These products are needed by the light industries (e.g., textiles) of developing countries while Korea has the technology to produce them at much lower cost. With the growing number of developing countries opening up their markets and trying to build up their infrastructure, LGI should use these opportunities to put its expertise in these areas to good use, helping these countries develop their plants and machinery, resources and raw material extraction, communication and transportation, etc.

Functional diversification. In view of the changing global competitive strategies of Korean firms, LGI should diversify away from its emphasis on export in order to take advantage of these changes. Its experience and expertise developed over the years as a GTC will enable it to assist firms in their mergers/acquisitions and cooperative ties with foreign companies. This is likely to develop into a major business function in the coming years as foreign direct investment grows in importance.

R&D/TECHNOLOGY TRANSFER. Investment in research and development might not seem very appropriate for a GTC, but looking at it from another angle, the results of such R&D could be well utilized by its trade partners benefiting both the manufacturers and LGI as its exports gain competitive advantages from advancement in technology. The government is also showing greater concern in this area and has provided incentives that firms can use in further R&D efforts.

Technology transfer is fast becoming a very strategic business. Sourcing for the appropriate technology from abroad and transferring needed technology to developing countries is growing in importance and is an area where LGI can make good use of its existing worldwide information gathering network.

COOPERATION WITH SMEs. SMEs are gaining importance and with growing government support, selected SMEs could prove to be very successful in the future. However, they lack the extensive resources and network to effectively expand their operations both within and outside their countries. LGI could assist them in their ventures and in the process build up goodwill with both the government and the SMEs, forming cooperative ties that might prove useful in time to come.

DEVELOP HUMAN RESOURCES. At LGI, two people are chosen each year to study in the Soviet Union, Taiwan or China. The course usually lasts nine months to a year. The purpose is to nurture talented employees for international business. Trainees are encouraged to pick up both language skills and the local culture. It must be realized that human resource is very important especially for a GTC like LGI with operations all over the world. The need to develop executives who are "multi-cultured" cannot be over-emphasized.

FUTURE PROSPECTS

LUCKY-GOLDSTAR'S VISION 2000

The goal of Lucky-Goldstar's Vision 2000 is to make Lucky-Goldstar one of the world's finest business groups as it moves into the 21st century and beyond.

LUCKY-GOLDSTAR INTERNATIONAL'S ROLE

GLOBALIZATION. The future market should be the entire world, but to be more specific, there will be two markets: the developed and the developing countries. The two economies must be approached with different strategies.

For the developed countries, the concentration would be on differentiating Korean products from those made by developing countries, which means that products must be of better quality and high value-added with better after-sales service, since prices cannot be competitive. For developing countries undergoing industrialization, export of intermediate goods and parts will be increased to meet subsidiary demands.

FUNCTIONAL DIVERSIFICATION. Many Korean firms are expected to continue to invest overseas. The motivations for foreign direct investment have become diversified and even multipurpose. Traditionally, import quotas imposed by the advanced countries have been the most significant reason for foreign direct investment, as in the textile industry.

Recently, however, increasing pressures for market expansion and technological development have resulted in many projects in North America. In the future, with market experience, many Korean firms are expected to increase their range of activities and establish new plants in other areas of the world.

LGI has a crucial role to play in this development towards globalization. Its project organization, financing, foreign investment, information gathering and analysis activities will grow into functions just as important as its export and import activities.

ESTABLISHMENT OF OWN-BRAND EXPORTS. LGI will seek to establish its own-brand exports, moving away from OEM arrangements with established brands. At the same time, it will seek to localize its operations from R&D to production to management, as it moves to become an inside player in major world markets.

AUTONOMOUS STRATEGIC GROUPING. Business functions and divisions will be organized into autonomous strategic groupings where management authority and its accompanying responsibilities will be placed in the hands of managers so that they can better analyze and understand particular markets. This is to be carried out with the intention of increasing cooperation, reducing duplication of functions and activities, and boosting managerial efficiency.[46]

ULTIMATE GOAL. The ultimate goal and the vision for LGI's future is to create value for the customer. Through innovations in products, services and organization, LGI prepares itself to meet the needs of the consumers around the world, both today and tomorrow.[47]

ENDNOTES

1. Trade Shows in Beijing and Seoul, Pace Accelerates for Economic Cooperation, *Business Korea,* April 1991.
2. *Business Korea Year Book,* 1992/93, p. IV-673.
3. *Ibid.*
4. Lucky-Goldstar International Corp., *LGI—A world of business for the business world.*
5. South Korea Government, *Investing in the Pacific,* 3rd quarter 1993, pp. 33–35.
6. Lucky-Goldstar Hits Australian Coal Jackpot, *Business Korea,* April 1985, p. 70.
7. 1993 Business Outlook, *Economic Report,* January 1993, pp. 47–54.
8. *Supra* note 5.
9. Hopes Run High, *Business Korea,* July 1993, pp. 37–45.
10. Korea's Five Year (1993–97) Financial Reform Plan, *Korean Quarterly Review,* 1993, 3rd quarter.
11. Building a Firm Foundation for Exports, *Business Korea,* July 1993, pp. 45–46.
12. *Supra* note 9.
13. *Supra* note 9.
14. *Supra* note 7.
15. Trade Blocs and Exports, *Economic Report,* May 1993, p. 39.

16. Chai, Denise, The Proverbial Double-Edged Sword, *Business Korea,* July 1993, pp. 56–61.
17. *Ibid.*
18. Korea Keeps China's Open Doors Ajar, *Asian Finance,* March 1991, pp. 16–18.
19. A New Deal for Hanoi, *Economic Report,* June 1993, pp. 12–13.
20. Long Distance on a Ho Chi Minh Trail, *Economic Report,* May 1993, p. 51.
21. *Supra* note 9.
22. *Supra* note 9.
23. *Supra* note 11.
24. *Supra* note 10.
25. *Supra* note 10.
26. South Korea Government, *Investing in the Pacific,* 2nd quarter 1993, pp. 35–37.
27. *Supra* note 10.
28. "Big Money" on the Wheel of Politics, *Economic Report,* June 1993, pp. 34–36.
29. Sohn, Jie-Ae, Small but Strong Government, *Business Korea,* June 1993, pp. 16–18.
30. *Supra* note 28.
31. Good Neighbors, *Economic Report,* May 1993, pp. 20–21.
32. *Supra* note 10.
33. *Supra* note 11.
34. *Supra* note 7.
35. *Supra* note 9.
36. R&D is the Key, *Economic Report,* May 1993, pp. 36–38.
37. *Supra* note 19.
38. *Lucky-Goldstar Monthly Bulletin,* May 1993.
39. Cho, Dong-Sung, *The General Trading Company: Concept and strategy,* Lexington Book, 1987.
40. Lucky-Goldstar, Multilateral Functions Essential for Survival, *Business Korea,* December 1985, pp. 78–80.
41. GTCs Face up to New Set of Challenges, *Business Korea,* December 1984, p. 64.
42. General Trading Companies Running for Cover, *Business Korea,* September 1991, p. 28.
43. *Supra* note 20.
44. *Supra* note 11.
45. *Supra* note 11.
46. *Supra* note 4.
47. *Supra* note 4.

COUNTRY PROFILE

SINGAPORE: ASIA'S BRAVE NEW WORLD*

HISTORY

Singapore was a flat, swampy island inhabited by a small Malay community when the British East India Company purchased it in 1819, mainly due to the efforts of Sir T.S. Raffles. Under Raffles, the island developed rapidly and in 1832, it became the center of government for the newly created Straits Settlements Colony. Despite the construction of a massive naval base and extensive fortifications after World War I, the Japanese occupied Singapore in 1942, during World War II. This event weakened British control and Singapore became self-governing in 1959.

Lee Kuan Yew of the People's Action Party (PAP) was selected as the first Prime Minister of Singapore. Under his leadership, which spanned the next 31 years, the country witnessed remarkable economic development and modernization. On September 16, 1963, Singapore joined with Malaya, Sarawak and Sabah to form the Federation of Malaysia. However, due to tensions between Malays, who were dominant in the federation, and ethnic Chinese, who were dominant in Singapore, an agreement was made under which Singapore became a separate nation on August 9, 1965.

CULTURE

DEMOGRAPHICS

Singapore is a multiracial society that consists mainly of four groups—Chinese, Malays,

---

* This country profile was prepared by Licie Fok, Luke Yeh, Michele Young, and Nathan Yuen.

Indians, and Eurasians. Chinese make up the majority with 77.7%, followed by Malays at 14.1% and Indians at 7.1% (Craig, 1993, pp. 95, 145, 193).

The various religious groups in Singapore can be categorized by ethnic groups too. Chinese are predominantly Buddhists, Taoists and Christians. Malays are Muslims who follow the prophet Mohammed, the founder of Islam. And Indians are primarily Hindus (Layton, 1990, p. 61).

The national language of Singapore is Malay. Among the other three official languages, Mandarin is spoken by Chinese, Tamil by Indians, and English is the main language used in business and commerce. Most of the population is bilingual or multilingual (Layton, 1990, p. 71).

POPULATION

There are approximately 2.92 million people living on the peninsular island of Singapore, which is 626 square kilometers or 242 square miles. This translates into approximately 4,600 persons/square kilometer.

Singapore's government is very active, not only in the traditional political sphere but also in the economy and in social and family matters. Since 1959, the government had encouraged family planning with the slogan "Two is enough." They raised hospital delivery fees and taxes on families with more than three children. In 1987, a New Population Policy was introduced since the old policy had worked so well that the number of births was not matching the number of deaths (replacement level). Therefore, the government changed its slogan to "Three is better," or "Have three, and more if you can afford it" (Milne and Mauzy, 1990, p. 12). The government gave tax rebates for the third child, tax reductions for the wife's earned income, subsidies for child-care centers, provisions for priority registration at Primary I entrance level for children in three-child families, and priority in obtaining larger government flats (*ibid.*, p. 11). Reproduction was particularly encouraged among the better-educated and wealthier groups. It was thought that this group would produce more intelligent and productive children. Disincentives were given to low income groups with low levels of education; for example, hospitals fees were raised.

To encourage well-educated people to meet socially, the Social Development Unit (SDU) was established by the government. This is a modern matchmaking service that organizes events and activities, such as cruises and dances, for university graduates to meet. There is also a Social Development Section for non-graduates with the same purpose. Since it began in 1985, there have been 4,000 marriages (Layton, 1990, p. 54).

EDUCATION

The government recognized very early on that its most valuable resource as well as asset is its people. Therefore, a free and effective education system was implemented. Students in Singapore are required to learn two languages: English and the mother tongue such as Mandarin, Tamil or Malay.

The government is moving towards privatization of schools where schools will have more autonomy and greater curriculum freedom, a better student-teacher ratio, and control over the hiring of teachers (Milne and Mauzy, 1990, p. 21). Education is not compulsory in Singapore. On average, a child will receive 10 years of formal education. There is an extensive examination system that regulates "movement" through the education system. The students are "streamed" into two groups: those that will advance to universities (bilingual) and those that will attend vocational training (monolingual) (*ibid.*, p. 22).

There are two universities: the National University of Singapore and the Nanyang Technological University. The government's goal is to have 10 per cent of the high school population go directly into the workforce and the rest attend universities and vocational schools (EIU, 1996, p. 20).

The government offers vocational and professional educational training. The Economic Development Board offers assistance for new companies in training and incentives. There is also a National Productivity Board which is a "collaboration among government, employers, unions, professional associations and academia" (*Training & Development*, 1994, p. 56). This board focuses on training for the existing workforce. The Institute of Technical Education concentrates on vocational education.

Moral education is taught in schools in the student's mother tongue (*Economist*, 1994, p. 39). The idea is to counteract any harmful Western ideas that students may learn from Western culture and business.

About 20 per cent of the population is under 20 years of age. Its workforce is intelligent, well skilled, English-speaking and literate (approximately 90 per cent). Hewlett-Packard and Motorola are examples of two companies who have capitalized on Singapore's workforce (Engardio et al., 1994, p. 112).

BUSINESS ETIQUETTE

Handshaking is common during introductions; however, a woman should not shake a Muslim man's hand since it is against his religion to touch a person of the opposite sex. It is safe to shake a person's hand if it is offered first.

Business cards are an important practice. When exchanging cards, hold the card with both hands and turn the card so that the recipient is able to read your name. Study the card for a few moments and look back at the person, smiling, then put the card away (Craig, 1993, p. 76).

Gifts are encouraged, especially small gifts from your country or hometown. These should be wrapped in good luck colors—Chinese like red and pink which symbolize happiness and joy rather than white, blue or black which symbolize death. Gifts are not usually opened in front of the giver.

Open disagreement and criticism are not acceptable behaviors when dealing with Singaporeans as they cause them to lose face. They also work in a hierarchy where the senior person receives the most respect. Also, humility and modesty are valued traits (Craig, 1993, p. 89).

GOVERNMENT

BACKGROUND

Since 1959, the island has been ruled by the People's Action Party (PAP). The PAP was headed by Lee Kuan Yew and he continues to be a prominent figure in Singapore's history and its future. He handed over the Prime Ministership to Goh Chok Tong on November 29, 1990, but remains in the cabinet as a senior minister.

The two main opposition parties to the PAP are the Singapore Democratic Party (SDP) and the Workers' Party. They are still in the process of putting their houses in order after being hit by leadership crisis and financial woes. The PAP has only token opposition.

Singapore's government policy actively encourages private enterprise and foreign investment. The government in the past has been very active in investing in new economic activities such as the widely acclaimed Singapore Airlines. The government has shifted its emphasis in manufacturing away from labor intensive processes to capital intensive high technology industries such as information technology industries and microelectronics. Labor intensive manufacturing industries have been encouraged to shift their operations to neighboring regions such as the southern part of Malaysia and the Riau Islands of Indonesia. The government has also emphasized the development of services such as banking and finance, telecommunications, information, and distribution and warehousing. The development of the country as a key regional center for banking and finance is one of the government's highest priorities.

The government directly holds stakes in individual companies from high-tech defense contractors to low-tech service industries. The government indirectly holds stakes in firms through a number of agencies. The Government of Singapore Investment Corporation (GIC) is principally responsible for investing Singapore's large foreign reserves overseas. Temasek Holdings keeps important stakes in the banking, shipping and engineering sectors. Singapore Technologies tends to concentrate on high technology or defense-related activities. The government control over utilities is in the broadest sense. This control will not be threatened by recent part-privatization of Singapore Telecom and the Public Utilities Board. The government's Housing and Development Board and the Jurong Town Corporation control land and housing developments.

The complex web of government involvement in industry and the secretive nature of some of its agencies have an advantage. The government is able to encourage the development of certain industries, without the competitors knowing exactly what is going on. A disadvantage of this involvement is a belief that government-linked firms enjoy substantial advantages in the domestic market, which may discourage the development of privately owned firms.

The government developed a strategy to build and maintain foreign confidence so that multinational corporations would find Singapore suitable for investment. The strategy included the following steps:

1. Industrial and political stability would be improved.
2. Infrastructure facilities would be developed further.
3. Inducements would be offered to foreign investors in priority industries.
4. Key state-owed boards and enterprises would be established to direct the economy.
5. Investment climate would be good and it would be promoted at all cost.

Lee Kuan Yew

Because of the able leadership of Lee Kuan Yew, Singapore has a per capita GNP higher than its colonizer Great Britain. It has the world's busiest port, is the third largest oil refiner, and a major center of global manufacturing and service industries. This prominence has taken place within one generation. After 31 years of strict rule under Lee Kuan Yew, the former colonial outpost has been transformed into a major metropolis. Westerners describe him as having a tough autocratic style who uses the power of media to influence the populace. He is also seen as being responsible for Singapore's amazing economic growth, its spotlessness, its low crime rate, and its political stability. Lee thinks the American society is far too permissive, without moral or ethical standards, and this accounts for much of its crime, violence and ineffective schools. He feels Americans have lost their self-reliance, depending on the government to solve all their problems.

Lee Kuan Yew is the perfect example of Asian patience coupled with an ability to take the long-term view. He believes that in time the USA will return to its old virtues, that China will move away from communism, and that most of the world's dangers will be overcome. He finds some attractive and some unattractive features about the US. His likes are the free, easy and open relations between people, regardless of social status, ethnicity or religion. Lee finds guns, drugs, violent crime, vagrancy, and unbecoming behavior in public—in sum, the breakdown of civil society in America—unacceptable.

Lee travels often to East Asian capitals, from Beijing to Hanoi to Manila, dispensing advice on how to achieve economic growth while retaining political stability and control. Most recently, Lee Kuan Yew was the featured speaker at the inaugural meeting of the International Confucian Association, held in November 1994 in Beijing. Lee is recognized as the most vocal advocate of "Asian values."

Policy/Regulation

The caning of American teenager Michael Peter Fay in May 1994, after he was convicted of vandalism, created a rift in Singapore-United States relations. Fay was arrested with eight other expatriate teenagers. He was sentenced to six strokes of the cane, fined S$3,500, and jailed for four months for vandalizing two cars with spray-paint and for acts of mischief, including throwing eggs at a car, damaging the front door of a vehicle, and keeping stolen items. The caning was reduced to four strokes following an appeal to President Ong Teng Cheong. This case snowballed into an issue that engaged politicians, the public opinion and the media in both countries. President Bill Clinton described the caning as excessive, declaring that it would be a mistake for Singapore to cane Fay. Parts of the US media condemned the sentence and asked major American companies doing business in the republic to pressure Singapore. But the public opinion in the US supported the caning.

The government monitors and initiates controls on the population size of Singapore. As of 1991, the annual rate of increase was 2.1 per cent for the total population. This was a direct result of government-sponsored family planning programs. If this trend continues, the population will start to decrease after peaking at 2.9 million around the year 2010. In the light of this, the government is now encouraging citizens to have more children. The government's aim is to increase the population to four million while maintaining the current racial balance.

Automobile usage is discouraged by the government. A new car incurs import duties of 45 per cent of its value plus an additional registration fee at 150 per cent of its value. Car ownership can easily cost more than US$100,000. The alternative to car ownership is the city's Mass Rapid Transit system which encompasses a 41-mile route, above and below the ground with 42 stations. The transit system has a capacity of a million passengers per day and links the city's major housing estates with the central business district and industrial areas.

There are fines for offenses such as jaywalking, smoking on elevators or buses, littering, spitting, and leaving stagnant water under potted plants where mosquitoes can breed. The 1989 Clean Public Toilet Law fines a person up to US$300 for failing to flush toilets in restaurants, theaters or department stores.

Breaking Singapore's laws concerning drug dealing results in execution, as does the possession of a gun. Pornography is outlawed, the government censors movies, radio, television and all printed media. Speeding truck drivers are self-incriminated because trucks must have roof lights which blink when the vehicle exceeds the speed limit. The result of these seemingly restrictive laws is a city-state with virtually no homelessness, poverty, unemployment, drugs, or gang violence.

ECONOMY

ECONOMIC INDICATORS

	Average					Projected
	1983–1990	1991	1992	1993	1994	1995
Real GDP (%) change	6.8	6.7	5.8	9.8	10.1	7.5–8.5
Inflation (%)	1.3	3.4	2.3	3.4	3.3	3.1
Money supply (%) change	13.0	12.4	8.9	8.5	NA	NA
Current account balance ($, billion)	0.5	3.3	2.9	1.9	NA	NA
	Dec 31, 1992		Dec 31, 1993		Jun 1, 1995	
Exch. rate (S$: US$)	1.64		1.61		1.39	

Sources: Nilsson and Schuster, 1994, p. 2; Chuang, 1995, p. 1.

GROWTH

Over the past two decades, Singapore has mostly enjoyed the best of both worlds—strong economic growth and modest inflation. Singapore attained its initial economic success as a result of its strategic geographical location and excellent deep water harbor. Singapore's continued strong growth has been fueled by, among other things, political stability, a sound infrastructure, the ability to attract foreign investment, a strong currency, and the promotion of the country as a premier international financial center. Attracting foreign investment has meant providing an array of tax incentives as well as permitting foreign ownership of companies in Singapore.

Economic growth for 1995 is forecast to be strong again at around 8 per cent, albeit lower than the previous year (Chuang 1995, p. 1).

FUTURE ECONOMIC GOALS

DEVELOPING SINGAPORE AS A PREMIER FINANCIAL CENTER. A major policy objective of Singapore's government is to develop Singapore as a premier international financial center, once control of Hong Kong reverts back to China. The policy places special emphasis on promoting the development of more sophisticated fee-based financial services such as fund management, risk management, capital markets, financial and commodity futures, financing third-country trading, and reinsurance and captive insurance.

DEVELOPMENT OF HIGH-TECH INDUSTRIES—TELECOMMUNICATIONS. The Singapore government, in its efforts to attract foreign capital, is placing emphasis on technology intensive industries. A case in point is the growing telecommunications industry. The government is in the process of breaking the monopoly of Singapore Telecommunications Ltd. over the local telephone market. A major step towards that goal was taken in May 1995, when the government granted cellular phone and paging licenses to new competitors. These contracts were awarded to consortia of Singaporean and foreign companies. Analysts predict the penetration rate for cellular phones to be as high as 25 per cent by the end of the century. Nearly 30 per cent of Singaporeans already carry pagers, and growth is expected at around 20 per cent over the next three years (Mark, 1995b, p. 26).

ISSUES AND CONCERNS

THE ROLE OF GOVERNMENT. The government has been very much involved in Singapore's economic development and management. This has been exemplified by the government's selective encouragement of individual industries (such as electronics, financial services and telecommunications), along with its active role in attracting foreign investment and fostering foreign trade. To its credit, the government has been quite successful in its interventionist policies, as demonstrated by the country's strong economic growth. However, there is concern that continued intervention may ultimately impede the country's economic development. An area in particular is the financial services industry. Some critics question whether Singapore's tight controls on information and intolerance of public criticism of government policies will prevent the country from truly becoming a premier financial center.

THE COLLAPSE OF BARINGS. A recent incident that has focused much attention on the Singapore financial markets was the collapse of Barings plc in February 1995. The incident left unsettled obligations totaling 127 million Singapore dollars, raising concerns about whether Singapore's financial markets have adequate controls and risk management systems. With its financial reputation at stake, Singapore has announced measures to increase controls, which include new restrictions to prevent traders from settling their own accounts and mandatory licensing of futures traders.

SUSTAINING GROWTH. There is concern about whether Singapore can continue such rapid economic growth. Recent external factors which may have adversely affected the economy are rising US interest rates and the sharp rise of the Singapore dollar against the US dollar. As of May 1, 1995, the Singapore dollar had appreciated by more than 5 per cent since the beginning of the year. Both trends may potentially hurt Singapore's export competitiveness. Ironically, it has been Singapore's relatively strong currency which has been a key ingredient to the country's economic success, by curbing the demand for imports and hence helping to keep inflation in check.

INDUSTRIES

The contributions of some of the industries in Singapore in 1991 were: manufacturing, 27.3 per cent of GDP; banking and financial services, 26 per cent; and commerce and trade, 15.7 per cent (Price Waterhouse, 1993, p. 5).

MANUFACTURING

Like many developing Asian countries, Singapore began its rise to prosperity with a concentration of low value-added manufacturing such as textiles. As the country developed into the distribution and financial center of Southeast Asia, along with Hong Kong, it upgraded its manufacturing base into high-value-added, primarily high-tech products (*East Asian Executive Reports,* 1994, p. 8).

Unlike any other Asian country, however, Singapore offered unheard of incentives for multinational corporations (MNCs). Thus, it is now the manufacturing home for over 400 MNCs. To support its manufacturing base and to attract MNCs, Singapore has over 200 commercial and merchant banks, more than 100 insurance companies and nearly 30 finance firms to assist new businesses (*East Asian Executive Reports,* 1994, pp. 14, 16).

Manufacturing is the primary engine of Singapore's economy, with the electronics industry being the largest component. Singapore is the leader in manufacturing disk drives and is fifth in the manufacturing of semiconductors (*ibid.*, p. 14).

With the rising cost of doing business in Singapore, low-technology industries are relocating to Malaysia (Montagu-Pollock and Hoon, 1995, p. 3). In order to keep its manufacturing base from neighborhood countries with lower labor costs, Singapore has been implementing an ambitious automation drive. Singapore's strategy is to retain its position as the hub for new technology, techniques and business practices, thus raising its own productivity and standard of living (*East Asian Executive Reports,* 1994, p. 8).

Other major areas of manufacturing include oil refining, chemicals and pharmaceuticals. In 1995, the USA remained the largest foreign investor, with commitments totaling US$1.48 billion, mainly in electronics, petroleum and industrial chemical industries. With commitments of US$1.5 billion, the European Union countries (principally the UK, Germany and the Netherlands) were the second largest investor, with commitments largely designed to upgrade existing facilities in the semiconductor, petroleum and petrochemical industries. This forced Japan to third place in the investment league: most of its US$1.2 billion of investment commitments were destined for the electronics sector (EIU, 1996, p. 16).

Foreign Investment Commitments in Manufacturing, by Origin	(S$ million)		
	1993	1994	1995
USA	1,452	2,452	2,076
Japan	779	914	1,153
EU	806	893	1,511
Total (including others)	**3,177**	**4,327**	**4,852**

Source: Ministry of Trade and Industry, Singapore, *Economic Survey*.

A key factor in the growth and strength of the manufacturing sector has been Singapore's ability to attract multinationals to invest capital and establish regional operational headquarters. Foreign investors account for roughly two-thirds of the country's investments and capital expenditures in manufacturing.

According to the First Quarter 1996 EIU *Country Report*, the electronics industry set the peace for manufacturing growth. Output of computer peripherals and telecommunications equipment increased sharply. Such growth also meant increased demand for the fabricated metal products sector which manufactures precision metal components, as well as a greater need for plastic products to be used as components and packaging materials (EIU, 1996, p. 16).

Selected Industries	1993	1994	1995
Electronics and components	22.8	21.7	19.2
Electrical machinery	3.6	10.7	4.9
Petroleum products	14.7	2.4	− 2.1
Machinery (including oil rigs)	− 5.3	21.1	11.9
Other metal products	4.0	11.5	15.7
Printing and publishing	8.6	7.6	4.2
Paints and pharmaceuticals	3.2	3.4	0.4
Transport equipment	− 0.8	7.0	1.2
Industrial chemicals and gases	4.9	18.8	1.0
Manufacturing	10.2	13.0	10.3

Source: Ministry of Trade and Industry, Singapore, *Economic Survey*.

Beginning in 1996, the Economic Development Board (EDB) will be focusing on the following projects: wafer fabrication plant, biotechnology joint venture, agrobiology business park, a new petrochemical project, and the upgradation of aerospace capabilities (EIU, 1996, p. 17).

BANKING AND FINANCIAL SERVICES

Formal development of the banking and financial services industry began in the 1970s with the establishment of the Monetary Authority of Singapore (MAS). MAS is responsible for the administration and management of Singapore's financial system, at the heart of which are the Singapore International Monetary Exchange (SIMEX) and the Stock Exchange of Singapore (SES). SIMEX is a financial futures market, and is presently the world's third largest foreign exchange market, with an average daily turnover of US$85 billion (*Euromoney*, 1994, p. 29). SES is Asia's first fully computerized stock market, the measuring index for which is the Strait Times Industrial Index.

COMMERCE AND TRADE

With very few natural resources, Singapore relies heavily on foreign trade. To foster foreign trade, Singapore operates as a free port with virtually no import or export duties on raw materials, equipment or products. Japan, the United States, Malaysia, the People's Republic of China and the countries of the European Community account for two-thirds of Singapore's foreign trade. Singapore is a member of the Association of Southeast Asian Nations (ASEAN), and cooperates under the ASEAN Preferential Trading Arrangements (APTA). Under APTA, more than 15,000 items produced by member countries are subject to a 50 per cent concession of the prevailing import duty (Price Waterhouse, 1993, p. 15).

TOURISM

Singapore has become a popular tourist destination. In 1993, it had 6.4 million visitors, more than twice the resident population, which positively affected Singapore's economic growth. In 1992, Singapore had 181 visitors daily per square mile of land. Earnings of S$8.5 billion in tourism receipts ranks it second in Asia in 1992. Approximately 180,000 workers were employed in 1992 in the tourism and hotel industry, accounting for 13.4 per cent of the workforce. To accommodate the 10–15 per cent increase in tourists per year, the hotel industry has expanded rapidly, almost doubling in the number of available rooms in the last 10 years (Khan et al., 1995, pp. 64–65).

EMPLOYMENT PATTERNS

There is a shift from a domestic workforce to a global workforce due to market economies, steady improvement in education and decades of overseas training by multinationals in fields ranging from product development to finance and architecture. These jobs were once reserved for Western white-collar workers (Engardio et al., 1994, p. 112). Global workers are becoming more accessible worldwide due to telecommunications advances. An example of a company taking advantage of this workforce is Motorola, Inc. Its paging-device plant in Singapore boasts 75 local engineers and a new US$35 million building dubbed the

"Motorola Innovation Center." One product developed entirely by Singapore engineers is the Scriptor pager (*ibid.*, p. 115). The government's focus to develop highly skilled English-speaking workers has obviously paid off as this example demonstrates. In addition, the shortage of English-speaking workers in Hong Kong has given Singapore an edge over Hong Kong in providing skilled workers for the service sector (*Business Asia*, 1995b, p. 12).

Singapore's only natural resource, viz. its labor force, is also its greatest liability. The shortage of skilled workers and higher production and operating costs are causing concern among manufacturers. Singapore cannot sustain the high wage growth of recent years, an average of 8 per cent per annum, without causing inflation. The government's decision to raise civil service and ministerial salaries sharply could send the wrong signals to the private sector and can only aggravate the wage increase (*Business Asia*, 1995a, p. 11).

Small- and medium-sized enterprises (SMEs) are important in Singapore's economic development. However, surveys show that SMEs are not viewed favorably as MNCs or as self-employment. Several reasons cited were pay, fringe benefits, career prospects, and marketability. The government and SMEs face the challenge of making employment opportunities more attractive (Teo and Poon, 1994, pp. 20, 24).

Singaporeans are not willing to work in other countries due to their "well-regulated lifestyle" and "their children's education" (EIU, 1996, p. 20). In order to make working abroad more attractive, the government has provided the following incentives: "cost-of-living allowances (typically between S$2,000 and S$6,000 per month); transfer and disturbance allowances; clothing allowances; medical benefits; housing subsidies often accompanied by utility benefits; and cars" (EIU, 1996, p. 20).

FUTURE PROSPECTS

THE GOVERNMENT'S PLANS

EDUCATION. In 1991, the Government of Singapore published a book entitled *Singapore: The next lap*, which outlined their plans for Singapore's growth for the next 20–30 years. A country with no natural resources, the government has wisely recognized that its people are Singapore's most precious resource. Therefore, education will be a primary focus of the government. Every effort will be made to improve the quality of education for all Singaporeans. The *first step* will be to encourage greater flexibility in the running of schools and greater diversity of programs to promote innovation and progress. *Second*, specialized programs will be developed to encourage students with exceptional talents in the arts, music or languages. In addition, students with learning disabilities will be given special attention. *Third*, innovative programs will be refined to encourage continuing education for workers. *Fourth*, the new National Institute of Education (NIE) will provide training programs for teachers as well as conduct research in education. *Fifth*, better facilities and buildings will be built and current schools will be upgraded. *Finally*, the government will raise its financial commitment to education from 4 per cent to 5 per cent of GDP. An Edusave account will be opened for every Singaporean school child between the ages of 6 and 16. An annual sum will be contributed to each account to be used for school-related fees.

POPULATION. The government will be keeping an eye on the size of Singapore's population. Concerned with an anticipated low replacement level, the government will continue to encourage the creation of larger families and attract new talent to Singapore.

A CITY OF CULTURE AND GRACE. Now that Singaporeans enjoy one of the highest standards of living in the world, the government will be turning its attention to cultural, recreational and sporting activities. To encourage the development of cultural activities, the National Arts Council was set up to oversee and encourage cultural activities. In addition, the Singapore Arts Centre is to be completed in the next few years. An arts belt will be created from a large part of the Civic District, and existing theaters and concert halls will continue to be upgraded.

To encourage a healthy interest in physical activities, the government will utilize the mass media to encourage mass participation and excellence in sports. Newly revised physical education and extracurricular activity programs will give school children the chance to participate in sports and develop their skills. Access to sports facilities such as swimming pools, tennis courts, golf courses and stadiums will be made easier. The Southern Islands will be developed into recreational resorts.

POTENTIAL CONCERNS

LEADERSHIP. With Lee Kuan Yew still in the government picture, it is not difficult to foresee that conflicts between Lee and Goh Chok Tong will arise. It is evident that these two gentlemen have very different styles of leadership. Lee is more autocratic and extremely strict about adherence to government policies. Goh, on the other hand, seems to be more liberal, even asking the public to voice their opinions on the government (Nonis, 1991, p. 64).

Another scenario to consider is the death of Lee Kuan Yew. If this were to happen, will the current government be strong enough to continue to guide Singapore to future success or will internal conflicts break the back of the PAP?

Finally, public discontent with Singapore's strong government policies is increasing. The younger generation is better educated, more worldly, and less inclined to conform to current government controls.

WORLD RELATIONS. As already mentioned, Singapore's greatest resource is its people. Therefore, Singapore needs to develop and maintain relations with other countries and international companies who need a trained and educated workforce. Apart from its participation in ASEAN, it can be predicted that Singapore will independently further its relationship with other European and North American countries and, more specifically, with companies that operate in these areas.

Another relationship to consider will be with Hong Kong in anticipation of 1997 when Hong Kong reverts to China. If Singapore lures Asians with skills that it needs, then it can accomplish two of its goals at once: improving the current Asian talent pool and increasing the population.

CONCLUSION

A single-party government is both Singapore's asset and its curse. The government's ability to plan for the future and predict future needs and wants of its people is a great strength. It has put Singapore in a position to continue its upward growth and allow this country to be flexible enough to overcome any barriers and meet obstacles head on. For example, Singapore can mobilize an army of 250,000 in less than 24 hours. On the other hand, the strong hand of government also stifles public imagination, creativity and innovation.

Under Goh Chok Tong's slightly more liberal leadership, it is possible that a balance between strong government and public expression may be obtained. One thing is for sure, though, Singapore can only succeed if a torch of solid leadership is passed on from one generation to the next.

REFERENCES

Bloomber News, Singapore Invests $1 billion in Manufacturing, May 17, 1995.
Business Asia, The Rich Get Richer, January 30, 1995a.
Business Asia, English Skills in Hong Kong: Not so well spoken, August 28, 1995b.
Chuang, P. Ming, Singapore's Economic Growth Slows to 7.2% in 1st Quarter, *Bloomberg News,* May 17, 1995.
Craig, JoAnn Meriwether, *Culture Shock! Singapore,* Singapore: Times Books International, 1993.
East Asian Executive Reports, Selling Automation Equipment and Robotics in Singapore, February 15, 1994.
Economist, Teaching Asia to Stay Asian, October 8, 1994.
Economist Intelligence Unit (EIU), *Country Report: Singapore,* London, 1995.
Economist Intelligence Unit (EIU), *Country Report: Singapore,* London, First Quarter 1996.
Engardio, Pete and Rob Hof, et al., High-Tech Jobs All over the Map, *Business Week,* November 18, 1994, pp. 112–115.
Euromoney, Looking Offshore for Inspiration, September 1994.
Khan, Habibullah, Phang Sock-yong, and Rex Toh. The Multiplier Effect: Singapore's hospitality industry, *Cornell Hotel & Restaurant Administration Quarterly,* February 1995, pp. 64–69.
Layton, Lesley, *Cultures of the World: Singapore,* Singapore: Times Books International, 1990.
Mark, Jeremy, Singapore's Stable Market Induces Analysts' Snores, *The Asian Wall Street Journal Weekly,* May 1, 1995a.
Mark, Jeremy, Singapore Licenses for Cellular-Phone, Paging Services Offer New Opportunities, *The Asian Wall Street Journal Weekly,* May 13, 1995b.
Mark, Jeremy, Singapore Awards Mobile Phone Licenses to Competitors of Singapore Telecom, *The Asian Wall Street Journal Weekly,* May 15, 1995c.
Milne, R.S. and Diane K. Mauzy, *Singapore: The Legacy of Lee Kuan Yew,* Boulder, CO: Westview Press, 1990.
Montagu-Pollock and Hoon Lim Siong, The Dilemma of Growth, *Asia Money,* September 1995, pp. 3–9.
Nilsson, Erik and Richard Schuster, *Pacific-Asia Report,* Scotiabank, Economics Department, August 1994.
Nonis, George, *Hello Chok Tong, Goodbye Kuan Yew,* Singapore: Flame of the Forest, 1991.
Price Waterhouse, *Doing Business in Singapore,* 1993.
Reed, Stanley, China: Move Over, Karl Marx—Here Comes Confucius, *Business Week,* May 29, 1995.

Silverman, Gary, Blame Washington, *Far Eastern Economic Review,* January 12, 1995, p. 25.
Tan, Su Yen, Young and Free Spending, *Singapore Business*, September 1994, pp. 18–22.
Teo, Hee Ang and James Poon Teng Fatt, Career Choice of Undergraduates and SMEs in Singapore, *The International Journal of Career Management,* 1994, pp. 20–26.
Training & Development, Best-in-the-World Practices, June 1994, pp. 52–57.
Turnbull, C.M., *A History of Singapore: 1819–1975,* Singapore: Oxford University Press, 1977.
US Department of Labor, *Employment and Training Administration,* Issue 9, Summer 1993.
Vasil, Raj, *Governing Singapore*, Singapore: Reed International Books, 1992.
Weinberger, Caspar W., Singapore, *Forbes*, May 9, 1994.
Zakaria, Fareed, Culture is Destiny—A conversation with Lee Kuan Yew, *Foreign Affairs,* March/April 1994.

SUGGESTED FURTHER READING

Baranthan, Joyce, Has Singapore Got What It Takes to be a Finance Powerhouse? *Business Week,* March 20, 1995, pp. 54–56.
Barber, Noel, *The Singapore Story*, Great Britain: William Collins Sons, 1978.
Economist Intelligence Unit, *Singapore*, London, 1995.
Far Eastern Economic Review, Singapore, *Asia 1995 Yearbook.*
Government of Singapore, *Singapore: The next lap*, Singapore: Times Edition, 1991.
Mini-Dragons: Singapore, New York: Ambrose Video Publishing, 1990.
Oei, Anthony, *What If There had been No Lee Kuan Yew?* Singapore: Reed International Books, 1992.

CASE TWENTY-FOUR (A)

SINGAPORE AIRLINES: IN PURSUIT OF EXCELLENCE*

The airline industry is, by its very nature, a service industry and, in a free market, the success or failure of an individual airline is largely dictated by the quality of the service it provides. As with most service industries, the consumer's preference is influenced by the expectation of value (or quality) for money; and being satisfied the first time around, he becomes a repeat customer.

In markets where open competition is allowed free rein, important quantitative factors—network, frequency, and capacity—are often equal vis-a-vis the competition. In such a situation, quality of service is of paramount importance. Thus, a standard of service "that even other airlines talk about" has been the overt reason for SIA's success as a regional and intercontinental carrier (J.Y.M. Pillay, Chairman, Singapore Airlines, in *The Pursuit of Excellence: An island and its airline,* SIA publication).

The charm of the Singapore girl, flying in "the world's most modern fleet" has put Singapore Airlines among the world's top dozen airlines in just 12 years.

If anyone ever doubted that Singapore Airlines had become, through a combination of ambition, efficiency and shifting geographical fortunes, a legitimate star among the world's airlines, these doubts were dispelled at the Paris Air Show (1983). There, at a show generally lacking earth-shaking commercial developments, Singapore Airlines announced that it

---

* This case was prepared by Dr. Gan See Khem, School of Management, National University of Singapore, for the purpose of class discussion. Any use or duplication of the material is prohibited, except with the written consent of the School.

Copyright © 1985, School of Management, National University of Singapore, Kent Ridge, Singapore.

would be buying a total of 16 new-generation aircraft—4 Boeing 757-200s, 6 Boeing 747-300s, and 6 Airbus A310-200s. In an era when nobody seems to be actually buying any aircraft—when any new aircraft order seemed to be tied to a leasing arrangement, a buy-back or some other episode of creative financing, the Singapore announcement was astounding, and had the Paris crew talking for the rest of the week.

One out of every 81 people in Singapore works for Singapore Airlines. The SIA Group, which includes Singapore Airlines, Airport Terminal Services, Singapore Airport Duty-Free Emporium, Singapore Aero-Engine Overhaul, Singapore Aviation and General Insurance, and Tradewinds Private Limited, is one of the country's largest employers (over 15,500 people, of which 10,000 are employed by the airline) and its revenues account for 3.5 per cent of the country's gross national product—the highest percentage for any airline in the world. The airline brings 41.2 per cent of the 2.4 million tourists to Singapore each year.

HISTORICAL OVERVIEW

The airline industry in Singapore began operations in 1947 with thrice a week flights from Singapore up the Malay Peninsula to Kuala Lumpur, Ipoh, and Penang. These early flights, on a twin-engined Airspeed Consul, carried only five passengers, and inflight refreshments consisted of a flask of ice water replenished at each stop. By 1955, Malayan Airlines was flying Douglas DC-3 aircrafts, and the routes had been extended to Jakarta, Medan, Palembang, Saigon, Bangkok, Borneo, Rangoon, and Brunei. Comet jets were introduced in 1962. In 1963 it was renamed Malaysian Airways Limited and owned by BOAC, Qantas and some others.

A major change in the airline occurred in 1966 when the governments of Malaysia and Singapore acquired majority control of the company, which was then renamed Malaysia-Singapore Airlines Ltd. (MSA). Routes were expanded to Taiwan, Japan, and Australia. Boeing 707s and Boeing 737s were introduced to replace the Comets. With the introduction of the Boeing aircraft, MSA began a program of substantially upgrading cabin services.

MSA expanded to Europe, and in the 1960s, Singapore was rapidly becoming a major hub of airline traffic in Southeast Asia. However, by 1971 it was an open secret that the two partners, Malaysia and Singapore, had developed divergent objectives for the airlines. Specifically, Malaysia wished to maintain a substantial domestic operation connecting the remote areas of that country. Singapore, an island of less that 250 square miles, had no interest in such an operation. The Singapore government saw the airline as an investment in a portfolio held by the republic. The operation of the airline through the Singapore hub certainly supported the objectives of the republic to expand its role as a center of trade and communication in the region.

On October 1, 1972, MSA ceased to exist and was replaced by Malaysian Airline System (MAS) and Singapore Airlines (SIA). All of the Boeing jets in the MSA fleet and most of the international routes were retained by SIA. The Re-formation Agreement of 1972 awarded SIA most of their (MSA's) international routes. Historical accounts noted that Malaysia at that time was interested in regional needs, adhering more to an "import substitution" policy for development; but Singapore's economic policy had evolved since 1967 (when the

Malaysia-Singapore common market plan was abandoned) to an export-oriented strategy. By 1981, 70 per cent of ticket sales for SIA flights were outside of Singapore.

OWNERSHIP

SIA was incorporated in 1971 as a subsidiary of Temasek Holdings (Pte) Ltd. The authorized capital was Singapore $200 million as S$1 shares. The issued capital was S$116 million. Fully 98.1 per cent of the shares were owned by the Singapore government.* At that time the issued capital and reserves totalled S$220 million. Temasek, Singapore's largest corporation at that time, was wholly owned by the government and was part of the Ministry of Finance. Although Temasek generally did not interfere in the decisions of SIA or its other subsidiaries, it monitored decisions concerning shareholder matters. The means of control was primarily through appointment of company directors. There were also periodic reviews of past performance and future plans of selective companies, through meetings and reports. Equity capital or shareholders loans were provided where required for the development of approved projects.

Temasek compiled monthly and quarterly financial statements from companies in the group. As a "private exempt" company Temasek itself was not required to submit financial reports to the Registry of Companies. Therefore, its consolidated statements were not available to the public.

J.Y.M. Pillay was the chairman of the board since the inception of Temasek in 1974. The board consisted of senior civil servants. At the founding of *Singapore Airlines (SIA)* in 1972, then Prime Minister Lee Kuan Yew delivered the following welcome address: *SIA* has been founded to serve the public and to make profit—and not for prestige reasons. The Prime Minister added that if the company is unable to make a profit, it will be closed down.

The government authorities to which SIA report are the Department of Civil Aviation (DCA), Ministry of Communications, and the Ministry of Foreign Affairs. However, SIA's only formal reporting requirement is to Temasek. Besides, SIA consults with DCA and the Ministry of Communications on matters involving airport management. It communicates with the Ministry of Foreign Affairs on any matters involving international relations such as air service agreements. Charges by other airlines about the Singapore government providing subsidies and other market support to its own airlines abounded. However, in the airline industry, major logistical decisions, on routings and traffic rights can only be negotiated on a government to government level.

Today's SIA seems generally to operate free from government interference, according to most observers. There is certainly little doubt that the airline is capable of standing on its own. It has a highly acclaimed management team and a very successful record of performance. The board of directors at SIA is composed almost entirely of senior members of the civil service and statutory bodies. In reply to a question concerning the government's role, SIA's

---

*Through the staff share-holding scheme, the shares owned by Temasek had dwindled to 85 per cent in the early 1980s.

Director of Planning described the company's planning as being no different from what is done anywhere else.

> It's a symbolic process, neither initiated nor guided by the government, directly or indirectly. Of course, I can't say if particular civil service members of the Board have their own or the government's needs in mind as they contribute to the planning process. But there's no apparent evidence of it.

However, there were some noteworthy instances where the government intervened in SIA, or on its behalf. When Australia's International Civil Aviation Policy (ICAP) announced a fare structure favoring its own airlines in 1979, negotiations at a ministerial level resulted. ASEAN made a united stand, speeches were made on the floor of the United Nations, and in June 1981 Australia dropped its ICAP entirely.

MISSION AND CORPORATE OBJECTIVES

The set of corporate objectives that was adopted at the incorporation of Singapore Airlines manifested a concern for its nationalistic accomplishments. The objectives were stated as:

- Be a flag carrier of Singapore.
- Seize every opportunity to expand provided that return is adequate.
- Provide safe, convenient, and economical air services to the public.
- Promote the growth of the Republic's economy and tourist trade.
- Invest in businesses related to the air service industry.

In the nine years since 1972, SIA revenue had grown seven times, production multiplied 6.9 times and staff productivity increased fourfold (see Exhibit 1). However, this period of rapid growth was greatly threatened by the onslaught of the second oil crisis and the recession that ensued. The severity of the worldwide recession and its impact on the airline industry prompted SIA's management to critically address the issues that will be facing them in the turbulent 1980s.

A corporate planning committee was formally established to formulate organizational goals and objectives to meet the challenges of the 1980s. The committee members comprised senior executives from marketing, commercial, engineering and corporate affairs. A consultant group, Cresap, McCormick, and Paget, was invited to participate and guide the process.

In early 1982 the following statement was made known to the public and staff:

> *MISSION*
>
> Singapore Airlines is engaged in air transportation and related businesses. It operates worldwide as the flag carrier of the Republic of Singapore, aiming to provide services of the highest quality at reasonable prices for customers and a profit for the company.

Singapore Airlines: In Pursuit of Excellence

Exhibit 1 Singapore Airlines—10-Year Statistical Record

		1982–83	1981–82	1980–81	1979–80	1978–79	1977–78	1976–77	1975–76	1974–75	1973–74
Financial											
Total revenue	($, '000s)	2,620,600	2,524,350	2,287,068	1,887,962	1,480,772	1,142,472	876,317	707,545	549,614	398,044
Total expenditure	($, '000s)	2,574,700	2,498,705	2,269,090	1,876,673	1,420,921	1,092,973	833,040	666,135	509,162	356,683
Profit after tax	($, '000s)	104,800	104,814	94,840	68,352	39,080	37,791	23,871	30,818	35,352	23,261
Internal funds											
generated	($, '000s)	952,000	863,131	702,997	430,890	315,831	263,613	211,473	154,714	136,968	106,690
Capital disbursement	($, '000s)	386,200	421,081	932,139	1,152,600	739,619	446,975	149,965	53,785	189,241	180,089
Unit cost	($/t-km)	0.69	0.71	0.74	0.70	0.62	0.62	0.61	0.61	0.58	0.53
Yield	($/t-km)	1.05	1.04	1.12	1.03	1.02	1.05	1.03	1.02	1.06	0.99
Breakeven load											
factor	(%)	65.8	68	66	68	60	59	59	60	55	54
Production											
Network size	(km)	223,563	217,802	183,104	172,822	168,448	138,973	89,408	95,924	90,144	83,181
Distance flown	(km, '000)	68,920	66,939	68,174	70,622	60,282	47,247	41,788	38,266	34,818	32,525
Time flown	(hours)	92,548	90,141	93,115	96,630	83,791	68,719	62,281	58,082	51,785	47,715
Available capacity	('000 t-km)	3,614,521	3,338,206	2,923,274	2,537,770	2,049,971	1,567,112	1,267,212	1,064,446	853,816	649,557
Available passen-	('000										
ger capacity	seat-km)	24,810,000	23,966,100	21,024,700	17,321,500	13,918,200	11,169,800	9,410,800	7,969,800	6,199,386	4,814,186
Traffic											
Passenger carried	('000s)	4,559	4,517	3,932	3,491	3,025	2,571	2,210	1,904	1,551	1,333
Passenger carried	('000s pas-										
	senger-km)	18,081,300	17,922,100	15,182,200	12,807,300	10,209,800	8,233,000	6,675,400	5,450,014	4,133,529	3,416,360
Passenger load											
factor	(%)	72.9	75	72	74	73	74	71	68	67	71
Goods carried	(t-metric)	121,704	107,986	92,373	92,197	75,370	52,239	44,768	37,417	24,202	20,835
Goods carried	('000 t-km)	753,985	679,749	551,556	557,551	452,714	275,393	193,799	156,153	113,52	81,151
Mail carried	('000 t-km)	23,512	21,148	19,454	14,220	12,210	10,938	12,606	9,734	7,068	6,274
Total load carried	('000 t-km)	2,478,723	2,385,332	2,011,529	1,792,320	1,435,408	1,066,826	838,423	681,042	509,912	406,968
Load factor overall	(%)	68.6	71.5	69	71	70	68	66	64	60	63
Staff											
Strength average		10,655	10,449	10,226	10,058	8,800	7,461	6,895	6,444	5,550	4,906
Revenue per											
employee	($)	245,950	241,588	223,652	187,707	168,270	153,126	127,095	109,799	99,030	81,134
Available capacity											
per employee	(t-km)	339,232	319,474	285,867	252,314	232,951	210,040	183,787	165,184	153,836	132,403

Case Twenty-Four (A)

CORPORATE OBJECTIVES
To maintain the highest level of safety.
To deliver the highest quality of customer service.
To generate earnings which provide sufficient resources for reinvestment and satisfactory returns to shareholders.
To adopt human resources management practices companywide that attract, develop, motivate, and retain good and loyal employees.
To maximize the utilization and productivity of all resources.

These objectives were translated into more specific and tangible corporate goals. By 1982, SIA had formally established a corporate planning section. A hint to some of the rationale for the change was contained in a later (June 1983) speech by Deputy Chairman Lim Chin Beng, to wit: "SIA is run as a commercial enterprise and not as a prestigious flag carrier." Chairman J.Y.M. Pillay disclosed that Singapore Airlines had one goal for the future: survival.

PERFORMANCE RECORDS

SIA has maintained its consistent climb up the world aviation ladder in both passenger and freight carriage according to the annual Air Transport World's ranking of the world's largest airlines in 1982.

In terms of total revenue passenger-kilometers (RPKs) performed, SIA was ranked 13th in the world (see Exhibit 2). In freight, SIA has broken into the ranks of the top 10 carriers in the world. The top six positions in the Air Transport World listing for Revenue Passenger-Kilometers performed were held by US carriers, four of them, domestic US carriers. The only Asia/Pacific carrier ranked ahead of SIA was Japan Air Lines, which was (as of 1982) the fourth largest international airline behind Pan Am, TWA and British Airways. SIA's passenger load factors had been consistently above 70 per cent for the greater part of the past 10 years. The break-even load-factor, was an average of 65.8 per cent for the past few years. This figure was considerably lower than most international airlines.

Productivity is SIA's catchword in its drive for excellence. SIA's employee productivity measured against the number of CTKs produced, is one of the highest amongst international airlines (see Exhibit 3).

SIA intrinsically believes in being slim and trim. Staff recruitment is tightly controlled and is closely related to capacity growth rates. Staff made surplus through technology are either retrained or redeployed or induced to leave through generous redundancy schemes.

One part of SIA's advantages for several years had been low labor costs, only 16 per cent of total costs compared to 42 per cent for US carriers and 35 per cent for members of the International Air Transport Association (IATA). It should be noted that part of this superior productivity came from the fact that SIA operated relatively "young aircraft." But in 1981 there were strong signs that salary expectations among Singapore's workers were rising.

Exhibit 2 The World's Top 25 Airlines in 1982 (passenger-km)

Rank	Airline	RPKs (millions)
1	United	62,965
2	American	49,747
3	Pan Am	45,943
4	Eastern	42,059
5	TWA	41,082
6	Delta	39,280
7	British Airways*	37,010
8	JAL	32,925
9	Air France	27,288
10	Northwest	25,846
11	Air Canada	21,866
12	Lufthansa	21,718
13	Singapore	18,161
14	Continental	18,128
15	All Nippon	17,435
16	Iberia	15,948
17	Qantas	15,384
18	Republic	14,852
19	Western	14,308
20	Alitalia	12,562
21	Swissair	11,893
22	SAS	11,046
23	CP Air	10,655
24	US Air	9,923
25	Cathay Pacific	9,269

Note: Data could not be obtained from KLM and Saudia, which normally would rank in the top 25.
*Estimated data.

Exhibit 3 CTKs/Employee (1982–83)

1973–74	132,403
1974–75	153,836
1975–76	165,184
1976–77	183,787
1977–78	210,040
1978–79	232,951
1979–80	252,314
1980–81	285,867
1981–82	319,474
1982–83	339,232

Note: Lufthansa (1982): 209,075, CTKs/employee;
Swissair (1982): 170,221, CTKs/employee;
KLM (1982–83): 256,120, CTKs/employee.

Passenger Feedback

SIA has become something of a legend when it comes to inflight service. In a recent survey of international top bankers, a frequent traveller said, "When it comes to service, my only criticism is that SIA does not have enough routes. I wish they flew everywhere."

In the most recently published INTRAMAR study (1982) of airlines operating in the Asian region, SIA was rated on top of 52 competitors in measures of all the "dimensions of airlines" as perceived by travellers. These were:

- Service and performance
- Esteem and preference
- Airline image
- Awareness and familiarity
- Advertising recall

Ratings were published triannually and were generally regarded as a standard of reference by the travel industry. In the "service" rating, considered the most important dimension, SIA had been first since 1973. The survey noted: "This is the first time in the 18-year history of INTRAMAR that any airline has emerged in first place in all five of the measurements."

SIA was also ranked very highly in a survey conducted in the United States by the esteemed financial publication *Institutional Investor* in 1983. The survey found SIA second to Swissair and ahead of Lufthansa. According to the report, these top three carriers finished ahead of the rest by a conspicuously wide margin, putting them in a very special class by themselves. Significantly, SIA gained the highest marks for any airline in terms of service (see Exhibit 4).

Competitive Environment

In the recessionary times of the early 1980s the sensitivity of international competitors to any perceived advantage held by particular participants was especially marked in the airlines industry. Singapore Airlines was one of the few international carriers to be consistently profitable through the recession, in an industry in very dire straits. US airlines reported a net operating loss of $500 million for the first quarter of 1982, and had not made a profit since 1979. Members of IATA lost $1.7 billion on international routes in 1981. The industry sentiment seems to tilt towards *"protectionism."*

The beginning of the harsh 1980s had been a testing time for SIA. In its rise to prominence, SIA had incurred the wrath of such heavy weights as Qantas and Lufthansa. Resentment of SIA seems to be rooted in the fact that it was able to offer lower fares than other western airlines and still made a profit. Critics contended that SIA could offer "economic fares" because of low wages, government effectiveness in keeping labor unrest under control, and government subsidies.

Exhibit 4   International Airlines Rankings (1983) Accorded by *Institutional Investor*

1	Swissair
2	Singapore Airlines
3	Lufthansa German Airlines
4	Cathay Pacific Airways
5	Japan Air Lines
6	Air France
7	Scandinavian Airlines
8	British Airways
9	Qantas Airways
10	Pan American World Airways
11	KLM Royal Dutch Airlines
12	Finnair
13	Varig Brazilian Airlines
14	Thai Airways International
15	Trans World Airlines
16	American Airlines
17	Alitalia Airlines
18	British Caledonian Airways
19	Malaysia Airlines
20	Gulf Air

SIA began the 1980s by being accused by the Australian front of poaching on the market share of Australian domestic airlines on the Kangaroo route (Australia-Singapore-London). SIA was accused of practising what in effect amounts to the "sixth freedom" without prior agreement with the Australian government. This indirect carriage of air traffic was technically the most controversial. The so-called "sixth freedom" carriage occurred when "a carrier, whose home country is a direct transit point of air transportation, participates in such air cargo on both the stretch to and the stretch from its home country." This is described as "interlining." It was claimed that these practices by SIA seriously undermined the marketing efforts of Qantas and British Airways.

SIA had been accused of unfair practices by several competitors. Pan Am filed a complaint with the US Civil Aeronautics Board that SIA was subsidized by the government and engaged in below-cost pricing. SIA was not alone here, other Asian airlines had also been mentioned. SIA's success had led to regulatory trouble from the US government with which Singapore maintains bilateral airline agreements. When SIA filed to increase its flights into Los Angeles via Tokyo from three to five a week, three US airlines reacted quickly to try to prevent it. Pan Am even asked Washington to repeal its aviation agreement with Singapore, calling SIA "an exceptionally aggressive and well-financed national airline [that] can only work against long-term US interests." SIA replied that "the fault lies with the US airlines that they cannot exploit effectively the opportunities available" and argued that Pan Am was trying to create a "monopolistic regime" because of this inability "to thrive in open competition." The US Civil Aeronautic Board deliberated on SIA's application for more than two years. Under the Singapore-US bilateral agreement, SIA has the right to operate an unlimited number of services to a variety of destinations in America.

British Airways and Cathay Pacific expressed concern about SIA's plans to route some of its proposed extra services to the United States through Hong Kong. After several rounds of talks with the US Civil Aeronautics Board, over a period of two years, SIA has finally got its two additional flights to San Francisco. But in order to do this, SIA has had to sacrifice its services from Hong Kong to Bangkok and Tokyo and accept a quota on the number of passengers on flights between Hong Kong and Taipei.

During 1981 another storm was gathering, where Lufthansa singled out SIA as the "market leader" among other airlines that were selling tickets below officially approved prices. As a 3rd and 4th Freedom operator, SIA competes in the German market with not only Lufthansa but also KLM, Swissair, Air France and Sahara. SIA stopped discounting, but complained that the market cannot be controlled against other discounters. Lufthansa still pointed to SIA's transgressions, that it was "flooding nearby markets." SIA implicity confirmed this charge by responding that this occurred because fares were lower outside Germany. (Other airlines were also discounting outside Germany.) The argument continued, affecting the "air services agreement" negotiations for German access rights—which were scheduled for May 1982, but the local news reported on 19 May: "A Department of Civil Aviation official said yesterday: 'We reached no agreement on anything!'" Later meetings in November 1982 also failed, and the disagreement continued through 1983. Such conflicts hampered foreign sales operations and route development.

Another dimension in SIA's competitive environment comes from airline originating in the Asia-Pacific region. In 1981, there were reports that the competitive services of Cathay Pacific and Thai Airways International were improving rapidly. Malaysia Airlines and Philippine Airlines were watched with some concern, since their service measures might be skewed by their domestic operations. There were reports that Malaysia Airlines was improving rapidly and was ordering B-747 aircraft which would be more competitive with SIA's offering. Philippine Airlines had installed new management, and the airline was committed to an announced strategy of service improvement. There had been reports to SIA management that the service on board Philippine Airlines' new B-747 aircraft was excellent. SIA's share of traffic in and out of Singapore was excellent and the market share was increasing in several markets, but the Director of Marketing was still concerned about softness in some of the markets where the emerging airlines of the region were reproducing a very successful version of the SIA service strategy.

FLEET ACQUISITION AND OPERATIONS

From MSA (Malaysia-Singapore Airlines), the joint airline of what was once the federation of Malaysia and Singapore, SIA inherited a head office building, a hangar, a number of overseas offices, a fleet of five Boeing 707s and five Boeing 737s, an overseas route network, and, above all, an intact, organic body of employees.

SIA undertook an aggressive growth and equipment program in hand almost immediately after the reorganization. One decision was to acquire two Boeing 747 "jumbo jets" which went into SIA's service in 1973. This was the first of many bold fleet re-equipment decisions. Thereafter, the fleet size of the airline started to grow rapidly (see Exhibits 5A and 5B).

Singapore Airlines: In Pursuit of Excellence

Exhibit 5A New Aircraft Deliveries (1973–83)

Year	B-747-200	B-747-300	DC10-30	A300	B-727
1973	2				
1974	1				
1975	1				
1976	1				
1977	2				3
1978			2		3
1979	4		4		4
1980	7		1		
1981				3	
1982				3	
1983		4		2	

Exhibit 5B Aircraft on Order (1984–88)

Year	B-747-300	A310	B-757
1984	2	2	4
1985	3	4	
1986	2		
1987	2		
1988	1		

SIA's fleet in 1983 comprised 17 B-747s, 8 A300s and 2 B-727s. By 1985, the average age of SIA fleet was 28 months, the lowest in the world.

The justification for these major airline purchases was as follows:

1. SIA was able to exploit its traffic rights which helped to stimulate traffic enabling the airline to expand at a rate of between 25–30 per cent a year throughout the 1970s.
2. SIA needed to invest in the latest technology to support its claim of high service standards. It has since been part of SIA's strategy to maintain a youthful fleet with the lowest operating costs. The two fuel crises in 1973 and 1979 vindicated these "bold" decisions, since the new aircraft proved to be an excellent hedge against fly-away inflation.
3. The major purchases were made at the bottom of the business cycle and best deals were therefore struck. With the carefully phased-out delivery of these aircraft, SIA could take advantage of any upturn in the economic cycle when demand for additional capacity was strong.

By April 1988, SIA's fleet is expected to consist of the following aircraft:

      9 B-747-200B
    14 B-747-300SUD
      6 A310
      4 B-757

SIA intended to have the new Boeing 747-300s flying 75 per cent of its US west coast routes by 1984. Subsequently, flights were planned for Australia and the long haul to London. These new aircraft increased profitable high-yield seating, with 42 seats in business class and 40 seats in first class. They were predicted to add additional freight revenue and reduce fuel costs. SIA was spending $18 million annually on fuel for each 747 in the fleet. The new aircraft were expected to reduce fuel consumption by 5 per cent.

SIA capitalized merchandizing the spacious first class cabin and the secluded upper-deck business class section to high-yield customers. They were proud of the large airy environment created by removing the circular staircase from the rear of the first class cabin. The business class section on the upper deck was the aircraft's biggest treat and would hold the greatest potential for increasing revenue along those routes where it was flown.

In 1983, Europe was still the bigger market for SIA (accounting for a third of its revenue with sales of $534 million), the United States was the fastest growing. It was in second position accounting for 20 per cent of SIA revenues. The others were North Asia, Southeast Asia and Southwest Pacific in that order. After more than two years of consolidation, during which SIA did not open a single new route, it started a new round of route inauguration in 1983. These were flights to Brisbane, Adelaide in Australia, Male in the Maldive Islands and Jeddah in Saudi Arabia. It also negotiated for traffic rights to Vancouver in Western Canada. SIA and the Civil Aviation Administration of China were ready to start the China-Singapore air link. SIA planned to operate twice weekly flights to Canton.

In 1972, SIA operated scheduled services to 22 cities and had 48 overseas offices. By 1984, SIA was operating to 40 cities and had 82 overseas offices.

ORGANIZATION AND MANAGEMENT

Mr. J.Y.M. Pillay has been at the helm of SIA since its incorporation in 1971. Mr. Pillay was born in the Malay Straits on March 30, 1934. He went to London University, where he was awarded a B.S. degree with first class honors. The Chairman of Singapore Airlines is a modest, unassuming mechanical engineer who has been able to guide his company to year-to-year profits, even during periods when most of the world's airlines were big money losers.

J.Y.M. Pillay gives credit for his airline's success to his management team—"I get good people to help me and then I let them do their job," he said in a recent Washington interview.

The Deputy Chairman of SIA, Mr. Lim Chin Beng has also received international recognition for his role in the successful performance of SIA. The leadership of SIA has often been described as being not only capable but aggressive.

Pillay and the management of Singapore Airlines felt strongly that the key to success was value or quality for money. Pillay summarized the SIA management style to deliver this quality in six points:

1. SIA is, above all, a democratic organization—not in the sense of one-man, one-vote, but in the sense that it is not authoritarian, autocratic, or paternalistic organization.

2. Despite the size of the Group, SIA strives to create the smallest possible units to carry out required tasks.
3. There has to be delegation of authority down the line.
4. SIA tries to create an environment in which responsibility within the authority delegated, can be exercised effectively at all levels.
5. Training and retraining is an unwavering object of the Group.
6. Because of the tightly integrated nature of our operations, there is no question of one department being more important than another.

The essence of SIA corporate philosophy is dedicated teamwork and the pursuit of excellence in every sphere of the group's activities. SIA's organizational structure is rationalized on functional lines in accordance with the needs of managing a wide variety of specialized functions (see Exhibit 6). Members of the board of directors were drawn from the civil service and the National Trades Union Congress. There are nine functional divisions, each overseen by a director. Each division is responsible for a wide range of more specific functions which are designated as department. Each department is managed by a manager. The complex nature of the airline business necessitates a wide range of organizational units to be established. For example, the director of engineering has over 20 managers reporting to him. In order to ensure coordination, directors meet regularly in formal committee meetings.

The need for precision and coordination in the task of running an airline, coupled with the large size of the organization has made SIA a task-oriented organization. In March 1984, a summary of the findings of an American consultant, Professor Karlin, made headlines in the local press. "Behind the sweet smile of the Singapore girl is a bunch of sombre, isolated and somewhat autocratic bosses."

There were suggestions that SIA staff has often expressed grouses over various management decisions. For all its projection of success, SIA scored poorly in management-employee relations. The airline appears to suffer from "insufficient communication, too little emphasis on people issues and too much emphasis on task issues." But the fact that Professor Karlin's report was brought up for discussion at the SIA bi-annual business meeting suggests that the management is giving it some weight.

SIA's management is attempting to correct the situation. Trying to change the management's image among employees is not an easy thing. SIA's management is backing up its efforts with more concrete action. For a start, it is decentralizing its personnel functions and sending 800 supervisory staff for training in human relations. The company has also focused attention on creating a better environment for improving staff and management relations through what it calls "people-centered management practices." The airline has asked the National Productivity Board to train some of its supervisory staff to start QC circles to encourage participative management at grassroot levels. The company has also implemented the "staff suggestion scheme" which has been widely practiced by Japanese companies.

Of all the major and well-established airlines in the world, SIA has one of the youngest management teams. The average manager is in his late 30s, with the executive directors only three or four years older.

Case Twenty-Four (A)

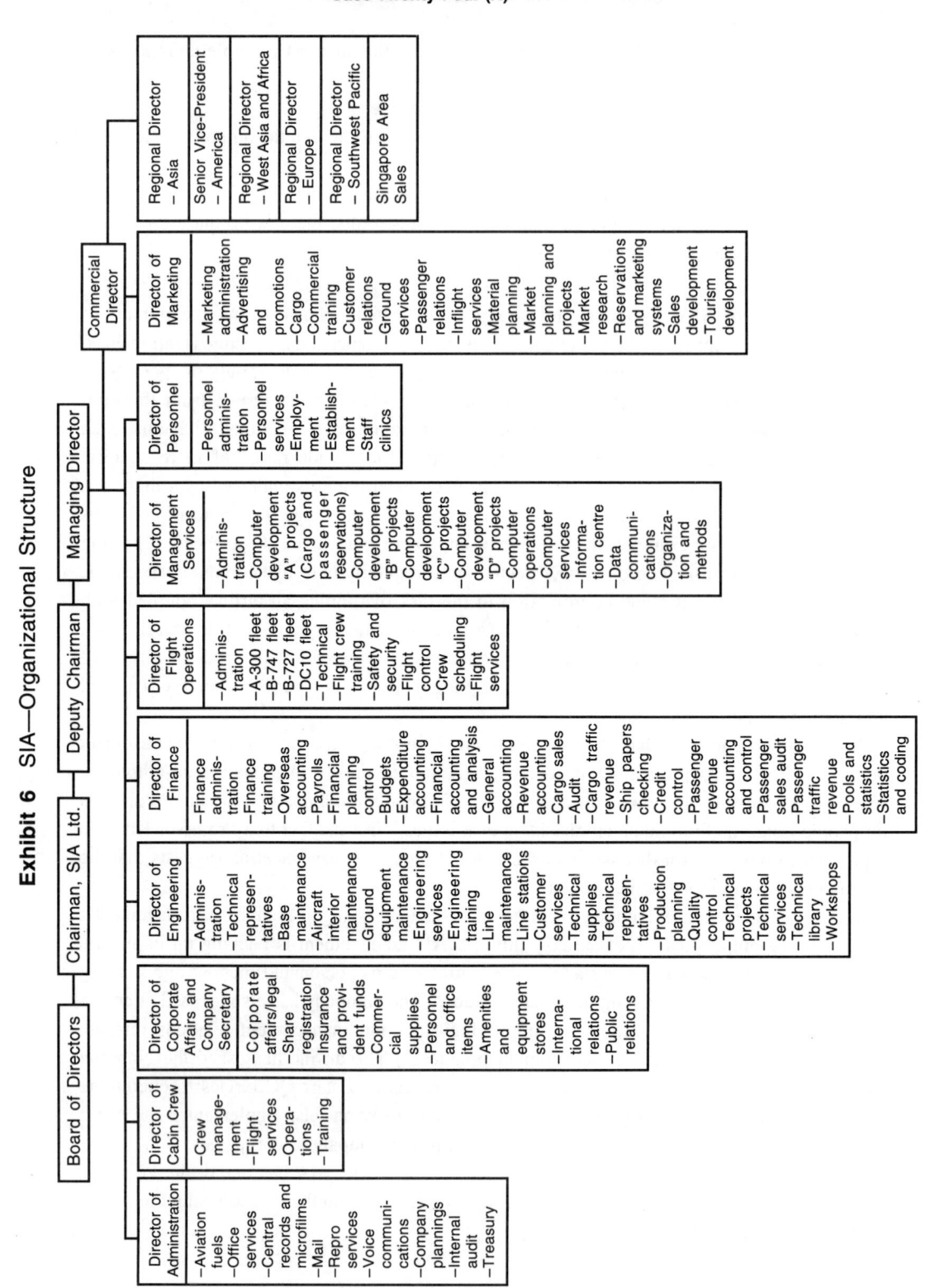

Exhibit 6 SIA—Organizational Structure

Board of Directors
Chairman, SIA Ltd.
Deputy Chairman
Managing Director

Director of Administration
- Aviation fuels
- Office services
- Central records and microfilms
- Mail
- Repro services
- Voice communications
- Company plannings
- Internal audit
- Treasury

Director of Cabin Crew
- Crew management
- Flight services
- Operations
- Training

Director of Corporate Affairs and Company Secretary
- Corporate affairs/legal
- Share registration
- Insurance and provident funds
- Commercial supplies
- Personnel and office items
- Amenities and equipment stores
- International relations
- Public relations

Director of Engineering
- Administration
- Technical representatives
- Base maintenance
- Aircraft interior maintenance
- Ground equipment maintenance
- Engineering services
- Engineering training
- Line maintenance
- Line stations
- Customer services
- Technical supplies
- Technical representatives
- Production planning
- Quality control
- Technical projects
- Technical services
- Technical library
- Workshops

Director of Finance
- Finance administration
- Finance training
- Overseas accounting
- Payrolls
- Financial planning control
- Budgets
- Expenditure accounting
- Financial accounting and analysis
- General accounting
- Revenue accounting
- Cargo sales
- Audit
- Cargo traffic revenue
- Ship papers checking
- Credit control
- Passenger revenue accounting and control
- Passenger sales audit
- Passenger traffic revenue
- Pools and statistics
- Statistics and coding

Director of Flight Operations
- Administration
- A-300 fleet
- B-747 fleet
- B-727 fleet
- DC10 fleet
- Technical
- Flight crew training
- Safety and security
- Flight control
- Crew scheduling
- Flight services

Director of Management Services
- Administration
- Computer development "A" projects (Cargo and passenger reservations)
- Computer development "B" projects
- Computer development "C" projects
- Computer development "D" projects
- Computer operations
- Computer services
- Information centre
- Data communications
- Organization and methods

Director of Personnel
- Personnel administration
- Personnel services
- Employment
- Establishment
- Staff clinics

Commercial Director

Director of Marketing
- Marketing administration
- Advertising and promotions
- Cargo
- Commercial training
- Customer relations
- Ground services
- Passenger relations
- Inflight services
- Material planning
- Market planning and projects
- Market research
- Reservations and marketing systems
- Sales development
- Tourism development

- Regional Director – Asia
- Senior Vice-President – America
- Regional Director – West Asia and Africa
- Regional Director – Europe
- Regional Director – Southwest Pacific
- Singapore Area Sales

Singapore Airlines: In Pursuit of Excellence

FINANCE

SIA has made extensive acquisition of new aircraft in recent years. The management planned to use internally generated funding plus some additional commercial loans for a large part of the payment, but would also need to issue shares to keep its debt/equity at an appropriate level. Part of the internal finance would come from the group's reserves and the sale of old aircraft. This was explained by a company spokesman.

> *Total investment in new aircraft for April 1981–March 1986 is S$3 billion. Add Changi Airport Development and other requirements, and it becomes $3.6 billion. Cash flow is expected to be S$2 billion (S$1 billion from sale of old aircraft), so S$1.6 billion comes from reserves, borrowing and equity.*

The debt-equity ratio at March 1981 was 3.1:1, but the company hoped to reduce that to 1:1 by 1986. The need for financing caused widespread speculation that SIA would "go public," but the company announced that it planned to raise S$400 million by offering new shares only to its present owners. The company asserted that "there is no question of subsidy since the shares were offered at a price determined by the net tangible assets of the company.

SIA Annual Reports gave some information on debt, shown in Exhibit 7. The airline, manifesting management's incessant concern with outside suspicions of unfair government support, gave credit to the company for the low interest charges, saying:

> *Fortunately, due to our excellent credit rating and our excellent record of consistent profitability, we have been able to get favorable financing to finance our huge capital expenditure ... Our Treasury Department has done a good job in ... concluding a number of favorable loan agreements.*

Concerning government guarantees of debt, the Singapore government had guaranteed US Eximbank loans because that was an Eximbank requirement. SIA also revealed (through a rebuttal by Mr. Pillay filed against charges of government subsidy in the US House of Representatives) that the government had also guaranteed certain bond issues, but had charged a service fee that raised the effective interest rate to what "any private corporation with an excellent credit rating" would pay.

A further feature of the 1983 aircraft purchase financing is leasing. SIA has entered into leveraged leasing deals with two banking houses, Bankers Trust and Citibank Grindlays, for the purchase of two 747-300s. Company officials and some of SIA's bankers are confident that SIA's gamble with the historic fleet acquisition program will pay off handsomely in the long run though the short-term cost could be a sharp reduction in the substantial profit increases of recent years.

Throughout the debate about funding requirements, there was no suggestion that the dividend rate might be reduced. The company announced in early 1982 that "the dividend

Exhibit 7 Singapore Airlines Group: Loan Negotiated

Interest	Amount ('000,000)	Creditor
1978–79		
8.25*	US$157.8	Japanese consortium (lease financing)
8.0**	US$222.8	Eximbank
NA	S$300.0	POSB and other Singapore banks
0.125% above 6-mth Libor*	US$150.0	British bank consortium (International Westminister, Morgan Grenfell, etc.)
NA	US$8.3	Export Development Corporation of Canada
1979–80		
Under 10%**	US$230.0	European bank consortium
9.75%†	S$120.0	Consortium of Singapore interest (80% from DBS) arranged by Morgan Grenfell (lease financing)
NA	S$350.0	Singapore bank consortium
July 15, 1982		
under 10%**	US$199.0	European bank consortium including London branches of some Singapore Banks; through European Export Credit Scheme
December 18, 1982††		
NA	S$88.0	Consortium of Singapore interests, arranged by Morgan Grenfell (lease financing)

* SIA: Billion dollar injection of public funds to head off competition, *Insight*, April 1982, p. 14.
** Company publications.
† *Business Times*.
†† *Business Times*. (The interest charge was known to be favorable because the investors had full tax benefit from depreciating new aircraft while providing only 20 per cent of the financing. DBS provided 80 per cent, with the largest part of the levered (20 per cent) portion provided by Keppel.)

rate for the next few years is expected to continue at a respective 15 per cent, despite the downturn in the fortunes of the airline industry."

The strong Singapore dollar in the 1980s became the bane of Singapore Airlines. It reported staggering foreign exchange losses when its foreign earnings were converted back into Singapore dollars. In the year 1982–83, the loss was $207 million. The half-year loss for the latest six months in 1983 was a staggering $108 million.

SERVICE DIFFERENTIATION

"How many ways can an airline differentiate itself?" SIA managers asked themselves when they began their determined attack on the intercontinental competition in 1973. The product differentiation SIA focused on was inflight service. The strategy was summarized by the manager of Inflight Services, when she was serving as SIA's advertising manager.

What we needed was a "unique selling proposition."

Happily we found it. Or perhaps I should say we found her because the "Singapore Girl" has become synonymous with Singapore Airlines.

SIA is an Asian airline, and Asia has a long tradition of gentle, courteous service. The Asian woman does not feel she is demeaning herself by fulfilling the role of the gracious, charming, helpful hostess. What we hope to do is translate that tradition of service into an inflight reality.

SIA capitalized on oriental charm with stewardesses of Chinese, Malay, Indian, and Eurasian ethnic backgrounds. They were costumed in a specially designed version of the graceful Malay *sarong kebaya,* designed by Pierre Balmain. Passengers were treated to some of the best food on any airline, and as one observer commented, "It is served with lots of warm smiles, warm towels, and attention to detail." SIA had more cabin staff per seat than most other airlines and provided first, business, and economy class passengers cocktails, French wines and inflight motion pictures at no charge.* Managing Director Lim felt strongly that "once a passenger pays for his or her ticket, there should be no more charges on the airplane." This philosophy partly explains the fact that SIA has deliberately stayed out of the industry association IATA. The principal disagreement lies in the ceilings imposed by IATA on inflight services.

SIA executives frequently stated that the airline's cabin crews were the vital ingredients of its highly differentiated inflight service. The strategy of the company was to provide passengers an experience of gracious service reflecting warmth and friendliness but maintain an image of authority and confidence in the minds of the passengers. As noted by Pillay, "good inflight service is important in its own right and is a reflection of the attention to detail throughout the airline."

Mr. Chew Choon Seng, Director of Marketing noted:

To back up intensive investments in aircraft of the latest design, not to mention computer complexes and engineering facilities, we spend a lot of time, money and effort in training, developing and motivating staff to give of their best in serving the customer.

PRICING

Historically, the determination of international air fares and air freight rates had been abdicated by governments in favor of the industry association, IATA. Critics often referred to IATA as a fare-fixing cartel and until deregulation took place in the US, it even enjoyed anti-trust immunity.

---

* See D. Wykoff, Singapore Airlines, HBS Case Services 0-682-044, for a more thorough treatment of the service strategies of SIA.

SIA operates outside the IATA ambit and has been advocating the benefits of the market forces in the pricing of air travel. The company's flexible pricing strategy allows it to relate various factors in determining its price structure. These are costs, expected volume of the traffic to specific destinations, and competition from industries competing for the customer's dollar. SIA has been innovative on pricing aimed at stimulating new markets.

In 1979, it took the lead in introducing a Round-the-World fare in conjunction with Trans-World Airline (TWA). By that time, a round-the-world flight routing was a prestige exercise no single airline could indulge in. The tie-up with TWA, which had a network complementary to SIA's, was a logical move especially if a special promotional fare was introduced. The round-the-world fare was an instant success and today many more airlines between themselves have followed suit.

PROMOTION

Perhaps the most universally recognizable element of SIA promotion was the "Singapore Girl." The "Singapore Girl," an idealized version of the SIA flight stewardess, had become the focus of the company's advertising program. SIA used very high-quality photography in the ads, and the stewardesses were always the central feature of the photograph. By contrast, Swissair, the consistently number one in international airline rankings, has focused on the aircraft and engineering and maintenance crews in its advertising.

By 1983, SIA advertisements whilst still featuring "Singapore Girl" was increasingly focusing on SIA's new assets: the most modern fleet in the world. The campaigns then featured the new technological wonders of the "Big Top." The small figure of the "Singapore Girl" was still there, perched on the winds of the new aircraft. Today, the term "Big Top" playfully coined by SIA staff is not only used in its promotional campaign, but is almost a generic name for this line of aircraft.

International Research Associates (INRA) conduct surveys in the Asia-Pacific area every three years. One topic studied by INRA is advertising recall. Going by the results of the 1982 INRA survey, SIA's advertising campaign is more likely to capture the imagination of larger proportion of frequent travellers throughout the Asia-Pacific region than the advertising of any airline (see Exhibit 8).

Exhibit 8 Advertising Recall in 12 Asia-Pacific Cities (per cent rank)

	1982	1979	1976	1973
SIA	49 (1)	50 (1)	32 (1)	21 (3)
Cathay Pacific	39 (2)	40 (2)	29 (2)	10 (7)
Japan Airlines	29 (3)	31 (4)	21 (5)	28 (2)
Thai Airways International	24 (4)	23 (6)	13 (8)	10 (7)
British Airways	21 (5)	21 (7)	16 (7)	21 (3)
Average index for all airlines	6.7	9.6	8.8	NA

Reappraisal

Though the SIA services had continued to receive excellent reviews, SIA management was carefully reappraising them in 1981. While most of the measures top management watched, appeared to be in line, there were serious questions being raised about the service strategy of the 1980s.

An innovative idea used by many airlines in the late 1970s was the "executive" or "business" class. SIA responded to the competition by offering the business class in its B-747 Trans-Pacific flights. However, the concept of business class presented marketing problems for SIA. Adding more services and amenities would blur the image of SIA's first class offering. Advertising business class seemed to detract from both first and economy classes. This distinction was further confused when SIA allowed economy passengers to be upgraded to business class in case of overbooking.

SIA had instituted some new organizations to work on inflight improvements. In July 1981, the Inflight Service Task Force (ISTF) was formed to monitor the total service package and to develop ideas to improve services. SIA was preparing, as an innovation, to introduce jackpot (slot) machines in August 1981 on selected B-747 flights in the Trans-Pacific market. The February 1981 news release about the jackpot machine test had already produced national publicity in the United States as well as attention in media throughout the Far-East.

The company also initiated inflight service survey to monitor passenger satisfaction during flight. The response from these questionnaire surveys provided valuable input for service standards maintenance at SIA.

Future Outlook

Singapore Airlines faced crucial years in the 1980s as the airline industry prepared to battle a host of unprecedented problems.

In painting the scenario of the difficult times ahead Mr. J.Y.M. Pillay, SIA Chairman, cited the following problems:

- The alarming and continuing fuel price increase
- Heavy interest payments on new aircraft as well as SIA's projects at Changi Airport
- Stagnating yields which reflect an environment of slower market growth and fierce competition
- The development of high risk new routes like the Trans-Pacific

These factors have adversely affected the company's financial performance system-wide. In a review of the airline's performance it is noted that although the total flown revenue rose by 20.4 per cent it is still below budget.

In the light of these developments, SIA has decided to moderate its expected rate of expansion. SIA's management is showing signs of mellowing its call for total deregulation. According to informed sources, SIA is now seriously considering trade association membership of IATA. There is a need for SIA to shed its 'maverick' image. One stumbling block is SIA's refusal to toe the IATA line by severing its close ties with non-IATA affiliated travel agents. However, it appears that some compromise is in sight.

BIBLIOGRAPHY

Asia Travel Trade, 1980–1982.
Business Times, Singapore.
Chew, Choon Seng, An Asian Approach to International Marketing: The SIA experience, in Tan Chin Tiong and Gan See Khem (Eds.), *International Business in the Asia Pacific Region: Trends and prospects for the 80s' Singapore,* National University of Singapore, 1984.
Euromoney, 1983.
Far Eastern Economic Review, 1982–1984.
Institutional Investor, 1983.
Journal of Commerce, "Transportation" section, 1982.
Loi, Hai Poh, Airlines in ASEAN: A case study of regional air transportation, Department of Geography, National University of Singapore, 1981.
Lyon, Mark, *Splashy Singapore Airlines, Airline Executive*, July 1983.
Outlook, House newspaper of the SIA Group, 1980–1984.
Pacific Asian Trade Association Annual Conference Proceedings.
Sikorski, Douglas J., Singapore Airlines: A case study of public enterprise in international competition, Working Paper No. 33, School of Management, National University of Singapore, March 1983.
Singapore Monitor, 1983.
Singh, Darshan, SIA: A case study, Department of Political Science, National University of Singapore, 1982.
Straits Times, Singapore.
Summary of speech by the Prime Minister at the Singapore Air Transport Workers Union silver jubilee dinner held on July 16, 1972.
Wyckoff, D. Darye, Singapore Airlines, Harvard Business School case, 1981.

CASE TWENTY-FOUR (B)

SINGAPORE AIRLINES—AN UPDATE*

It is now the mid-1990s, and time for an updated look at Singapore International Airlines (SIA). A public company listed on the Singapore Stock Exchange, an enterprise accounting for 3 per cent of Singapore's GNP, and 54 per cent held by the Singapore government through its holding company Temasek, Singapore Airlines has come upon difficult times as have other major airlines and companies around the world.

Its parent, SIA Group, includes not only the airline, but also SIA Engineering Company, Singapore Airlines Terminal Services, SilkAir (a small regional carrier formerly known as Tradewinds), SIA Properties, and Singapore Flying College. These subsidiaries account for about 10 per cent of the Group's revenues.

The situation is expressed clearly in SIA's 1992–93 Annual Report:

> *The difficult trading conditions of the preceding two years continued to plague the airline industry....*
> *Revenue for (SIA) expanded just 2.4 per cent, to S$5.1 billion....*
> *Aviation analysts, surveying the carnage in the industry, are sunk in despair. Their dejection contrasts poignantly with the euphoria that animated the industry in the latter part of the 1980s.... the industry indulged in an orgy of aircraft ordering (but) SIA's policy of steady growth had deterred it from cavalierly accumulating aircraft (so) we are under no pressure now to scale back on fleet-expansion plans....*

---

*This case was prepared by Neil Holbert, then Senior Lecturer in the Department of Marketing, Chinese University of Hong Kong. He is currently Assistant Professor of Marketing, The American College in London.

The aggregate cost of ... (SIA's) capital investments is (about) S$2 billion a year. Because of pressure on profits, that scale of investment has made deep inroads into our cash reserves (which) dropped from S$1.9 billion to S$1.3 billion during the year. It was the second consecutive year of (such) fall.... It is possible that, in a few years' time, we shall have to incur debt....

Pressure on margins will remain until a rising tide lifts the entire industry to a more even balance between demand and supply.

SIA now has a fleet of 60 planes: 20 B747-400s (the "Megatop"); 11 B747-300s (the "Big Top"); 3 B747-300 Combis; 2 B747-200s; 14 A 310-300s; 5 A310-200s; 4 B747-200 freighters; and 1 B737-300 freighter. On order are 36 more planes, with options for yet another 34.

Its average age of five years makes SIA's passenger fleet among the youngest, and its list of destinations (68, in 40 countries) could make a good international test ("Where is each city?") for a geography student:

Adelaide, Amsterdam, Athens, Auckland, Bandar Seri Begawan, Bangkok, Beijing, Berlin, Bombay, Brisbane, Brussels, Cairo, Calcutta, Christchurch, Colombo, Copenhagen, Dallas/Ft. Worth, Darwin, Delhi, Denpasar, Dhahran, Dhaka, Dubai, Durban, Frankfurt, Fukuoka, Guangzhou, Hanoi, Hiroshima, Ho Chi Minh City, Hong Kong, Istanbul, Jakarta, Johannesburg, Karachi, Kathmandu, Kota Kinabalu, Kuala Lumpur, Kuching, London, Los Angeles, Madras, Madrid, Male, Manchester, Manila, Mauritius, Melbourne, Nagoya, New York, Osaka, Paris, Penang, Perth, Port Moresby, Rome, San Francisco, Sendai, Seoul, Shanghai, Singapore, Surabaya, Sydney, Taipei, Tokyo, Vancouver, Vienna and Zurich.

In the six months ending September 30, 1993, the following flight increase occurred:

- to Taipei, increased from 17 to 19 flights a week
- to Nagoya, increased from 4 to 5
- to Hong Kong, raised from 24 to 26
- to Australian cities, flights increased from 21 to 23
- to Chinese cities, enhanced from 8 to 12 flights; in addition, SilkAir flies twice weekly to Kunming and Xiamen

Strategy also always involves looking outward as well as inward. In international terms, SIA tried for a stake in Qantas, the airline of Australia, but Australia wanted a non-Asian partner for Qantas. SIA's strategic alliance with Swissair and Delta—through a swapping of shares—was an instrument to help SIA reach out to a broader world ambit. These three carriers are also experimenting with marketing and scheduling integration, as is, by the way, Hong Kong's Cathay Pacific, and its partially controlled China-flying partner Dragonair. In a further international move, SIA has recently taken a 40 per cent stake in the Cambodian airline, Royal Air Cambodge. SIA believes that, as things stabilize in Cambodia, that country will have great tourist and business potential.

Undoubtedly, the SIA image continues to inspire. And indeed, its continuing profitability (though off in 1993) is more than admirable in a world of airline profit turbulence. But then, as *Asian Business* noted in May 1992.

> *Making profits in Asia used to be about ramming down costs and keeping the factory humming 24 hours a day. Not any more. If stormy economic conditions have taught Asian companies one major lesson, it is that they must add value to their products—or risk losing competitiveness.*

While "value-added" is a vital strategic notion, it is not especially clear exactly what it means. It can mean offering a brand name so strong that, in a world of private labels, generics, and knockoffs, the consumer will find "added value" in the reputation of the brand, and be "loyal" to it (whatever that means)—and at a premium price. "Value-added" can also mean taking unrefined pieces and adding skilled (or whatever) labor to it so as to put the pieces into a name-centered non-parity product league of its own—that is, work it into a more "marketable" (promotable) shape, and clawing out the added value in a new integral Utility of Form, as the economists would say. What could all this "value-added" thinking mean to an airline? It may well start with that very "image" component.

An image must reflect reality: it must be a picture in the mind's eye that translates into the reality of effective scheduling and good service and all the rest. Yet the image does exist also by itself, as a clue to a much-desired relationship between "customer" and "product": it's an airline "for me," one that represents things I like, want, and am comfortable with.

And for many, the "Singapore Girl" image on television and in print—for nearly 20 years now, to the tune of S$750 million, with another S$100 million added this year—stands for just about the best job in airline advertising anywhere and any time: clear, consistent, and charming.

> *Such a gentle way about you*
> *All around the world*
> *Wouldn't go away without you*
> *My Singapore Girl.*

This song, sung to a soul beat, showing the sloe-eyed Singapore stewardess in her *sarong kebaya*, could well be considered sexist and even demeaning by contemporary Western PC ("politically correct") standards. (After all, there was revulsion in America many many years before when stewardesses for another airline coyly noted in advertising: "We move our tail for you.") Still, after a period of SIA advertising featuring the Big Top aircraft, Singapore Girl, in late 1993, is back. (Also in the advertising nowadays is an emphasis on SIA's premium "Raffles" Class service.) Indeed, Singapore Girl is the first commercial figure to be displayed at Madam Tussaud's wax museum in London. And only 6–8 applicants out of 100 ever get to be a Singapore Girl. And only one company got to be number one in a poll for the Most Admired in the region. It was SIA, and it was in *Asian Business'* 1992 poll (May 1992, pp. 24ff.). The top ten in descending order were:

1. SIA
2. San Miguel Corp.
3. Singapore Telecom
4. McDonald's
5. Samsung Bank
6. DBS Bank
7. Cathay Pacific
8. Astra International
9. Thai Airways International
10. Sony Corp.

That same article continued like a paean. SIA, it said:

> ... *places massive emphasis on activities and policies that bring it admiration. It enjoys strong customer loyalty. It makes a significant contribution to the local community. It has a highly motivated workforce....*
>
> SIA's senior managers, who are mainly ex-civil servants, have been with the airline since it was founded in 1972.
>
> (Says) Michael Tan (SIA's deputy managing director [commercial]): "The whole company works in the same direction. We are pretty democratic, and we can agree or disagree freely on tactics. We encourage staff to come forward with new ideas, and don't build internal walls. But our main goal is clear—how best to satisfy our customers." ...
>
> SIA has set standards for in-flight service that have since become the industry norm. It was one of the first airlines to give away drinks and headsets, install beds in first class, and give economy class passengers a choice of menu.... It recently began offering first-class passengers a choice of Dom Perignon or King champagne.
>
> It is also equipping its aircraft with telephones, to enable passengers to make long-distance calls while on the move—another first.
>
> "We have to be creative and innovative continuously," (says Michael Tan): "It's not easy maintaining our number one position. We have nobody to chase after but ourselves. We can't allow complacency to creep in."

What of the very latest numbers, and what of the future? The numbers for 1992 and 1993 are shown in Exhibits 3 and 4 in the Appendix.

Simply put, for SIA traffic was up (10 per cent), but operating profit was down (32 per cent). In golf, the professionals say: "You drive for show and putt for dough," and as a former China Airlines chief said: "International is for show and regional is for ... dough."*

And SIA—like its competitors—certainly relies on Asia traffic more than on any other area, as the Table 1 shows:

Table 1 Airlines' Revenue for 1992 by Area (per cent)

	Cathay Pacific	China Airlines	Malaysia Airlines	Singapore Airlines	Thai Airways
Asia	69	64	42	40	36
Europe	19	5	22	27	38
North America	5	26	7	21	12
Australia/New Zealand	7	2	9	12	7
Domestic		3	20		7

Source: *Far Eastern Economic Review*, August 26, 1993, p. 44.

That same piece continues:

> ... demand is burgeoning for airline seats. But almost all the demand is for heavily discounted economy class seats. That poses a dilemma for Asian airlines: Can they hope to maintain a "boutique" approach—excellent service for a high price—when just about everybody wants low-cost flights? Or, to put it more bluntly, can they win back the "right" passengers?
>
> Business travel has not picked up appreciably since the Gulf War in early 1991 ... Many companies, hit by the world recession, have simply cut back on travel. Some first class travellers have shifted back into business class while a lot of business class passengers have moved back to economy class.
>
> So will everybody shift forward again when there's an economic upturn? Don't bet on it, advises Sheldon Kasowitz, an analyst at Jardine Fleming in Hongkong. "The 20 per cent-plus operating margins for Singapore Airlines and Cathay are over," he says. "Revenues and yields are dictated by global trends."
>
> Kasowitz says some travellers will once again fly first class when the world economy brightens. But he doesn't accept the "boutique" approach to pricing for air travel. "It's bound to get more like a commodity," he says. "Most of us want reasonable comfort at a reasonable price."

Yet, Asian airlines are still making money, as illustrated in Table 2, which is more than can be said for many of the world's carriers (see Table 3). Indeed SIA led them all in profits in 1992.

---

* *Far Eastern Economic Review*, August 26, 1993, p. 44.

Table 2 Ten Leading Airlines: Profits for 1992

Airlines	Net Profit (US$, millions)
SIA	518.5
Cathay Pacific	391.5
British Airways	309.8
China Airways	143.3
Thai Airways	120.4
Qantas	106.6
Southwest Airlines	103.6
Swissair	80.4
Air New Zealand	61.8
Malaysia Airlines	57.5

Source: *Far Eastern Economic Review*, August 26, 1993, p. 44.

Table 3 The Big Money Losers of 1992

Airlines	Net Loss (US$, millions)
Delta Airlines	564.8
American Airlines	475.0
Iberia Group	418.4
United Airlines	417.0
Northwest Airlines	405.1
US Air Group	404.5
Varig	380.3
Air Canada	373.9
TAP-Air Portugal	(Estimate) 370.0
Japan Airlines	349.3

Also, as SIA's latest numbers suggest, even Asian regional carriers are having trouble. The same *Far Eastern Economic Review* article noted that despite the region's prosperity, Asian carriers are being buffeted by what SIA Chairman J.Y.M. Pillay terms the "carnage in the industry."

The prolonged recession in Europe and North America is forcing companies to keep a much tighter rein on travel costs. The result is that First class and Business class travel gets the chop. In addition, the industry is suffering from a surfeit of seats because of all the aircraft ordered during the travel boom of the 1980s. And global fare wars are wreaking havoc on airlines' profitability—while giving consumers a bewildering choice of bargain fares.

Some Asian airlines thought the region's dynamic growth would help shield them from all this. Indeed, air travel is booming in Asia; Boeing forecasts 8.5 per cent annual growth until 2000, far faster than in Europe or North America. But a severe economic downturn in

Japan has kept many people there at home. Double-digit inflation in Hongkong is boosting airline costs and fierce competition is forcing some major Asian players to offer the once unthinkable frequent-flyer programs.

SIA, Hongkong's Cathay Pacific Airways and Malaysian Airline System have started a joint program called "Passages"—but only for First class and Business class passengers. Free travel will also be available through hotel chains, while credit card companies will be taking part.

For the foreseeable future Asian airlines are likely to do much better than their European or North American rivals, but that may not be much consolation. Says Jardine Fleming's Kasowitz: "It's a terrible business."

Is it?

APPENDIX

Exhibit 1 SIA Group: Balance Sheet for Fiscal Years Ending March 31 (in S$, millions)

	1989	1990	1991	1992	1993
Current assets	2,627	3,048	3,400	3,278	2,511
Fixed assets	4,165	4,749	5,201	6,175	7,181
Long-term investment	**67**	**439**	**458**	**522**	**588**
Total assets	6,857	8,236	9,059	9,975	10,250
Current liabilities	1,768	1,825	1,945	2,051	2,075
Long-term liabilities	**642**	**518**	**450**	**421**	
Total liabilities	2,410	2,342	2,395	2,472	2,075
Net cash	1,126	1,676	2,038	1,881	1,344
Ratios					
Current ratio	1.49:1	1.67:1	1.75:1	1.60:1	1.21:1
Current assets/liabilities	1.09:1	1.30:1	1.42:1	1.32:1	1.21:1

Note: In some cases, sum of items may not add up to total due to rounding.

Exhibit 2 SIA Group: Profit and Loss for Fiscal Years Ending March 31 (in S$, millions)

	1989	1990	1991	1992	1993
Total revenue	4,566	5,093	4,948	5,421	5,648
Total expenditure	**3,573**	**3,854**	**3,997**	**4,446**	**4,749**
Operating profit	994	1,239	951	976	899
Surplus on sale of aircraft and spares	96	195	208	129	42
Share of profits of associated companies	1	2	2	4	4
Profit before tax	1,091	1,435	1,161	1,109	945
Profit after tax and minority interests	985	1,201	912	928	851
Per share data (S$)					
Earnings before tax	0.88	1.15	0.91	0.87	0.74
Earnings after tax	0.80	0.96	0.72	0.72	0.66
Dividend	11.3	17.5	20.0	22.5	22.5
Dividend cover (times)	10.4	7.9	5.1	4.6	4.1
Ratios					
Return on shareholders' fund (%)	27.0	25.0	15.6	14.0	11.6
Return on total assets (%)	14.9	15.9	10.6	9.8	8.4
Revenue per employee (S$ '000)	266	270	240	248	244

Note: In some cases, sum of items may not add up to total due to rounding.

Exhibit 3 SIA Group: Profit and Loss for Six Months Ending, September 30, 1993 vs. 1992 (in S$, millions)

	1992	1993	Change 1993 vs. 1992 (%)
Revenue	2,753	3,035	+ 10
Expenditure	2,276	2,637	+ 16
Operating profit	477	398	− 16
Profit before tax	498	424	− 15
Profit after tax and minority interest	446	391	− 12
Earnings per share (S$)			
Before tax	38.9	33.0	− 15
After tax	34.8	30.5	− 12

Exhibit 4 Singapore Airlines: Profit and Loss for Six Months Ending, September 30, 1993 vs. 1992 (in S$, millions)

	1992	1993	Change 1993 vs. 1992 (%)
Revenue	2,533	2,726	+ 8
Expenditure	2,174	2,482	+ 14
Operating profit	359	244	− 32
Profit before tax	428	338	− 21
Profit after tax	400	333	− 17
Passenger seat factor (%)	72	72	
Cargo load factor (%)	64	71	+ 7
Passengers carried (million)	4.3	4.7	+ 10
Cargo carried (million kg)	188	235	+ 24
Yield (S$/load/tonne-km)	83	76	− 8

CASE TWENTY-FIVE

KAO IN SINGAPORE*

As he sat at his desk on the evening of April 16, 1980, Toshio Takayama pondered uneasily over what he should do about Kao Singapore Private Limited, where he was the newly appointed director and representative of the Japanese parent, Kao Corporation. Kao was the leading soap and toiletries manufacturer in Japan (see Exhibits 1 and 2 for data on Kao and its position in the Japanese economy).

In September 1974, after Kao and its former agent in Singapore decided to terminate their business arrangements, Kao Singapore had been set up to take over the distribution of Kao products in Singapore. At that time, Kao sales in Singapore were only about S$2.4 million a year.** By 1979, sales had grown to S$4.5 million; however, the Singapore operation had never made money. Already by 1976, cumulative loss was exceeding equity. Nevertheless, the Japan head office continued to hope that Singapore could be made into a model international operation. Hence Kao Singapore was sustained through repeated injections of equity in 1977 and 1989. In addition, bank loans fully guaranteed by the parent were arranged to overcome cash flow difficulties (see Exhibits 3A to 3D for financial data on Kao Singapore).

Before Takayama was assigned to the Singapore Company, he had had an interview with his mentor, Kozaburo Sagawa, who was then senior managing director of Kao Japan and chairman of Kao Singapore. Sagawa had stressed:

The Singapore market, though small, is ideal to be a model international operation.

---

* The case was written by Professor Joseph D'Cruz as a basis for class discussion rather than to illustrate either effective or ineffective handling of an administrative situation. Copyright © 1989 by IMEDE, Lausanne, Switzerland. Not to be used or reproduced without permission.

** In 1980, Singapore $1 = US$0.4670 and ¥105.54.

Exhibit 1 Growth of Japanese Economy and Total Advertising Expenditures, and Kao Japan's Advertising Expenditures

	Japan						Kao Corporation				
	Nominal GNP		Ad. Expenditure		Net Sales			Ad. Expenditure			
Year	(¥, billions)	Growth Rate (%)	(¥, billions)	Growth Rate (%)	(¥, millions)	Growth Rate (%)	(¥, millions)	Growth Rate (%)	% of Sales	Rank in Ad. Expenditure
1965	33,602	13.3	334	−4.3	32,813	17.0	2,894	19.3	8.8	NA
1966	39,509	17.6	383	14.7	39,230	19.6	3,982	37.6	10.2	NA
1967	46,239	17.0	459	19.9	43,691	11.4	5,264	32.2	12.0	NA
1968	54,761	18.4	532	15.8	45,435	4.0	5,688	8.1	12.5	7
1969	64,920	18.6	633	18.9	50,179	10.4	6,223	9.4	12.4	8
1970	75,152	15.8	756	19.5	57,708	15.0	7,169	15.2	12.4	9
1971	82,806	10.2	787	4.1	66,131	14.6	8,920	24.4	13.5	5
1972	96,539	16.6	878	11.6	83,785	26.7	12,419	39.2	14.8	2
1973	116,679	20.9	1,077	22.6	116,189	38.7	14,791	19.1	12.7	2
1974	138,156	18.4	1,170	8.6	142,057	22.3	12,804	−13.4	9.0	4
1975	152,209	10.2	1,238	5.8	146,917	3.4	13,910	8.6	9.5	2
1976	171,153	12.4	1,457	17.7	161,056	9.6	17,742	27.5	11.0	2
1977	190,035	11.0	1,643	12.8	186,753	16.0	17,858	0.7	9.6	2
1978	208,781	9.9	1,846	12.4	214,264	14.7	20,431	14.4	9.5	2
1979	225,453	8.0	2,113	14.5	245,698	14.7	21,243	4.0	8.6	2
1980	245,163	8.7	2,278	7.8	252,438	2.7	22,052	3.8	8.7	2
1981	259,669	5.9	2,466	8.2	280,628	11.2	26,612	20.7	9.5	3
1982	272,383	4.9	2,627	6.5	305,551	8.9	27,963	5.1	9.2	2
1983	284,058	4.3	2,782	5.9	330,612	8.2	28,361	1.4	8.6	3
1984	303,020	6.7	2,915	4.8	369,812	11.9	30,718	8.3	8.3	1
1985	320,775	5.9	2,983	2.3	405,709	9.7	32,026	4.3	7.9	1
1986	334,026	4.1	3,052	2.3	441,172	8.7	35,430	10.6	8.0	1

Sources:
1. Data on GNP: Economic Planning Agency, Japan, *National Economic Accounting Annual Report*, Tokyo.
2. Data on total Japanese advertising expenditures: Dentsu Incorporated, *Dentsu Japan Marketing/Advertising Yearbook*, Tokyo, Japan.
3. Kao figures: Company records.

Exhibit 2 Kao Corporation: Balance Sheet, Profit and Loss Account
(as of 31 March)

(in yen millions)	1976	1977	1978	1979	1980	1981
Current assets	36,605	39,415	54,379	62,998	74,042	74,384
Fixed assets	40,154	40,944	46,687	67,193	108,407	97,866
(Tangible assets)	(31,540)	(31,714)	(36,732)	(50,213)	(84,281)	(70,609)
(Investments, others)	(8,614)	(9,230)	(9,955)	(16,980)	(24,126)	(27,257)
Total	76,759	80,359	101,066	130,191	182,449	172,250
Current liabilities	40,752	41,784	53,777	65,882	78,093	69,953
Long-term liabilities	12,897	7,667	13,271	25,216	56,330	48,845
Shareholders' equity	23,110	30,908	34,018	39,093	48,026	53,452
(Common stock)	(3,632)	(4,400)	(5,397)	(6,165)	(7,479)	(7,749)
(Legal reserves)	(4,261)	(9,229)	(9,377)	(11,538)	(16,790)	(19,731)
(Retained earnings)	(15,217)	(17,279)	(19,244)	(21,390)	(23,757)	(25,972)
Total	76,759	80,359	101,066	130,191	182,449	172,250
Net sales	146,917	161,056	186,753	214,246	245,698	252,438
Ordinary profit	4,422	6,127	7,377	9,797	8,835	8,880
Income before tax	4,243	5,988	7,089	9,269	8,149	9,233
Income after tax	2,059	2,749	2,930	3,304	3,619	3,885

Exhibit 3A Kao (Singapore) Private Ltd.—Sales Amount by Product Category

(Unit: S$, '000)	Sep. '75–Dec. '75	Jan. '76–Dec. '76	Jan. '77–Dec. '77	Jan. '78–Dec. '78	Jan. '79–Dec. '79	Jan. '80–Dec. '80
Toilet soap		29	14	28	106	310
Shampoo and other hair-care products	211	359	431	945	1,878	2,980
Laundry detergent	818	2,082	1,248	1,249	1,664	1,717
Other detergents	5	14	249	389	805	769
Others	6	33	25	31	44	60
Total	1,040	2,517	1,967	2,642	4,497	5,836

Exhibit 3B Kao (Singapore) Private Ltd.—Sales Contribution by Product Category

(Unit: %)	Sep. '75–Dec. '75	Jan. '76–Dec. '76	Jan. '77–Dec. '77	Jan. '78–Dec. '78	Jan. '79–Dec. '79	Jan. '80–Dec. '80
Toilet soap		1	1	1	2	5
Shampoo and other hair-care products	20	14	22	36	42	51
Laundry detergent	79	83	63	47	37	30
Other detergents	0.5	0.5	13	15	18	13
Others	0.5	1.5	1	1	1	1
Total	100	100	100	100	100	100

Exhibit 3C Kao (Singapore) Private Ltd.—Balance Sheet (as of December 31)

(Unit: S$, '000)	1975	1976	1977	1978	1979	1980
Current assets	553	110	412	686	1,547	2,010
Cash	359	1	3	5	4	27
Trade debtors	123	43	141	298	873	994
Inventories	60	41	235	300	511	527
Others	11	25	33	83	159	462
Fixed assets	62	140	129	153	197	405
Motor vehicles	57	129	115	130	164	370
Others	5	11	14	23	33	35
Total	615	250	541	839	1,744	2,415
Current liabilities	547	516	774	924	1,821	2,345
Trade creditors	372	183	401	461	1,110	1,305
Bank overdraft		213	272	314	398	480
Others	175	120	101	149	313	560
Shareholders' equity	68	(266)	(233)	(85)	(77)	70
Share capital	100	100	300	600	600	600
(Revenue reserve)	(32)	(366)	(533)	(685)	(677)	(530)
Total	615	250	541	839	1,744	2,415

Exhibit 3D Kao (Singapore) Private Ltd.—Profit and Loss Account

(Unit: S$, '000)	Sep. '75–Dec. '75	Jan. '76–Dec. '76	Jan. '77–Dec. '77	Jan. '78–Dec. '78	Jan. '79–Dec. '79	Jan. '80–Dec. '80
Net sales	1,040	2,517	1,967	2,642	4,497	5,836
Cost of sales	842	1,609	1,275	1,669	2,575	2,934
Gross profit	198	908	692	973	1,922	2,902
Admin., selling expenses	83	432	619	848	1,121	1,609
Marketing expenses	151	774	271	315	844	1,121
Operating profit/(loss)	(36)	(298)	(198)	(190)	(43)	172
Non-operating profit/(loss)	(1)	(33)	33	43	41	(25)
Profit/(Loss) before taxation	(37)	(331)	(165)	(147)	(2)	147
Tax						
Profit/(Loss) after taxation	(37)	(331)	(165)	(147)	(2)	147
Depreciation charged for the year	3	30	38	48	65	123
Kao Japan's subsidy*			471	778	963	901

*For marketing activities not included in the above Profit and Loss Account.

The market is competitive, complex but manageable. We want to learn from this compact international operation and use the experience to develop our other larger international markets.

However, the current performance of our operation in Kao Singapore is far behind our expectations. We want to experiment, to lead and be profitable in this market. We want to turn Singapore into a model Kao international market which our other markets can emulate.

How to turn the Singapore operation into an international model had become Takayama's obsession. At the minimum, he knew that he must not only increase sales but also make the operation profitable. It was clear that Kao's problems in Singapore were not simple. There was severe competition from well-established multinationals like Proctor & Gamble, Colgate-Palmolive, and Unilever, as well as from local manufacturers. Furthermore, Singapore was one of the world's most open markets and hence had products from virtually every corner of the world.

Takayama found that Kao's product lines were usually concentrated in the high quality and relatively high priced end of the market, while the Singapore market in general tended to be dominated by a wide range of lower quality and lower priced products. Knowing Kao's tradition of positioning its products as market leaders, Takayama was reluctant to adopt a low price strategy in Singapore to achieve brand leadership. On the other hand, Takayama wondered how Kao could become a market leader in Singapore.

A proposal to launch Biore facial cleanser in Singapore lay on his desk. The proposal had been prepared by Chia Hock Hwa, the most senior local manager in Kao Singapore. Chia was pressing for an immediate decision on Biore. However, Takayama knew that the officials at the Tokyo head office would be firmly opposed to it.

KAO CORPORATION IN JAPAN

Founded in 1890, Kao Corporation* had developed into Japan's leading cleaning products company for the household sector. Its first product, Kao toilet soap** gave the Company its direction, which it continued to follow. Early efforts were focused on fats and oils (tallow and coconut oil), the basic raw materials of the soap industry. Thus Kao's interest in organic chemistry began. Progressively, Kao began to emphasize research in surface and polymer sciences because of the role surface tension played in soap chemistry and the detergent industry. More recently, the Corporation was engaged in research on skin physiology and other aspects to biological science, as part of an attempt to understand how the Company's products worked on the human body (see Exhibit 4 for details of R&D at Kao).

---

* The company changed from its former name, Kao Soap Company Ltd., to Kao Corporation in July 1982.

** This was a high quality soap which, when launched in Japan, was the only soap that could claim "so high in quality that it can be used to cleanse your face." In fact, in Japanese the word "Kao" means "face."

Exhibit 4 R&D at Kao Corporation*

Laboratories	R&D Activities
1. Wakayama First Laboratory	Fat and oil chemistry
	Organic chemistry
	Polymer science
	Manufacturing processes
2. Wakayama Second Laboratory	Special chemicals
	Lubricant additives
	Foundry chemicals
3. Tochigi First Laboratory	Biological science
	Skin physiology
	Organic chemistry
4. Tochigi Second Laboratory	Household products
5. Tochigi Third Laboratory	Hygiene products
	Technology of developing composite materials
6. Tokyo First Laboratory	Hair-care products
	Color science
	Fragrances and flavors
7. Tokyo Second Laboratory	Skin-care products
	Cosmetics
8. Kashima Laboratory	Fat and oil chemistry
	Edible oils and foods
	Fermentation and enzymes
9. Recording and Imaging Science Laboratories	Applied physics
	Information and electronic industries related products
10. Knowledge & Intelligence Science Institute	Computer science
	Information science
11. Production Technology Institute	Production technology systems
12. Kao Institute for Fundamental Research	Fundamental research in cooperation with domestic and foreign universities and research institutes

*Kao had 12 R&D laboratories with more than 1,700 researchers.

In Kao, senior managers went about the Company's business activities with an almost religious sense of dedication. This was reflected in the Corporation's slogan, "A Clean Nation Prospers." It was generally accepted that it was the duty of every Kao employee to "strive hard to create products that will truly benefit people in their everyday lives."

Fulfilling this mission required more than emphasizing R&D (Research and Development). Early in its development, Kao made the strategic decision to develop and produce in-house, wherever possible, the essential ingredients that would affect the quality of its products. The Corporation was not satisfied with merely mixing purchased raw materials to formulate finished products. Instead, it established laboratories to work on developing new materials which could be subsequently manufactured in the Corporation's own plants as the raw materials for its finished products.

This strategy of vertical integration was later extended into the marketing system. Many toiletries and cosmetics manufacturers in Japan tended to rely heavily on the country's multistate wholesaling system to place their products in retail outlets. Kao, however, worked through a network of wholesalers who distributed Kao products exclusively. In many ways, these wholesalers operated like Kao branches. In fact, Kao salesmen frequently worked from the wholesalers' premises. They would take orders for the wholesaler in addition to performing their regular jobs, which included promoting new products, doing administrative work with the trade (such as merchandising and handling complaints), and collecting information about competitors' activities. The close working relationship between Kao salesmen and wholesalers often strengthened the bonds between Kao sales managers and the owners/managers of the wholesalers. These exclusive Kao wholesalers were acutely aware of the advantages of distributing Kao products. They benefited not only from Kao's having wide product lines that were extremely popular with consumers, but also from the philosophy, style and management system at Kao. Thus they were very eager to cooperate with Kao. Unlike other wholesalers, they were totally dedicated to that one company.

When Kao introduced its integrated marketing intelligence system (MIS), designed to track sales by product, region and market segment, the wholesalers cooperated enthusiastically. They installed Kao data terminals in their offices and even allowed Kao salesmen to enter their own orders. The MIS was used both to monitor sales and market trends and as a tool for market research. Kao market researchers frequently visited retailers along with the wholesalers' salesmen to gather information directly from the trade. Kao was known to operate one of the most sophisticated trade intelligence systems in Japan.

Supplementing its trade intelligence, Kao developed an equally sophisticated system of consumer intelligence. An integral part of this system was a 24-hour "hot line" which consumers were encouraged to use if they had a complaint or any question about using Kao products. An on-line computer system assisted the hotline staff in answering queries. This system also recorded pertinent data from every call. Analysis of these data and other computerized data on market research served as the basis for monitoring consumer interests and identifying new product opportunities.

Managing Corporate R&D at Kao

Kao managers firmly believed that R&D was an important element in the Corporation's strategy. Kao operated 12 laboratories employing about 1,700 people (roughly a quarter of the total employees), who worked in many different areas of science and technology (see Exhibit 4). The Corporation had developed a number of organizational devices and management processes in its R&D activities.

An example of the unique R&D operating style was the monthly R&D conference, usually attended by all members of top management and key R&D staff. These informal meetings were conducted like university seminars. Researchers reported on studies in progress and presented the results of their projects. The theoretical and practical implications of the research findings were openly discussed by the participants. During these meetings, researchers received prompt feedback on their projects from other researchers. They also benefited from the advice and encouragement that members of top management offered on the commercial implications of their work.

All R&D meetings at Kao were "open door", i.e. any interested employee could attend. It was a strictly observed rule, however, that visitors never spoke unless asked for their opinion. It was not unusual to find employees from sales and marketing at R&D meetings. Occasionally, these employees even brought along outside visitors—suppliers, customers or academics. Visitors were often struck by the open and informal nature of these meetings. Kao managers felt that this informality encouraged individual creativity, a vital ingredient for maintaining the quality and momentum of the Company's R&D.

This practice gave Kao's R&D efforts tremendous flexibility and enabled the Corporation to undertake large-scale interdisciplinary projects. Furthermore, the projects were usually undertaken in spacious, open office research laboratories where scientists and engineers from various disciplines worked together daily in close physical contact with each other. Kao's top management considered this type of environment essential for its R&D activities as it facilitated integrated technological development.

The process of R&D was commonly referred to as "sowing seeds for improved products to better satisfy consumer needs." R&D was highly integrated with the Corporation's various other components, especially marketing. The Corporation's key technologies were continuously being applied in primary chemicals for new product development.

In developing and introducing new products, Kao closely observed a basic set of principles to ensure that the products would truly meet consumer needs:

1. Is the new product truly useful to consumers and society?
2. Is Kao's basic technology being fully utilized?
3. Is its performance superior to that of similar products made by competitors, both in terms of quality and cost?
4. Has the product recorded significant acceptance in consumer tests?
5. Has the marketing communication plan been effectively formulated, so that accurate information on the product's value is received by every participant in the distribution channel (from the Corporation to the consumer)?

Management would have to be fully satisfied with the responses to these questions before deciding to launch any product. Kao usually avoided the standard test marketing programs favored by its competitors before launching a new product. Instead, when basic requirements were fulfilled, Kao's products were often launched nationwide, mobilizing the entire salesforce and wholesaling network to achieve rapid distribution. National advertising would then quickly follow.

DEVELOPMENT OF BIORE IN JAPAN

The development of Biore, a non-soap facial cleanser, followed the typical strict but simple process of Kao's R&D. Its impetus came from analysing data received by Kao's consumer hot line (see Exhibit 5). These data showed that using soap to wash after removing facial

Case Twenty-Five

Exhibit 5 New Product Launch Plan for "Biore" Facial Cleansing Foam in Japan (Extract)

1. MARKET SITUATION
   (a) Products currently used for facial cleansing are cleansing cream, facial soap and toilet soap.
      The market shares of these products are 44, 31 and 25 per cent respectively. It is projected that the share of cleansing cream will grow considerably because of some changes observed in the facial cleansing habit of consumers.
   (b) The usage rate of cleansing differs among age groups:

Age group (year)	15–19	20–24	25–34	35–44	45–54	55–59
Usage rate	56%	70%	54%	48%	34%	28%

   Heavy users are the young 20s followed by high teens, and older 20s or young 30s.
   (c) What benefits do consumers expect to get from cleansing cream?

	15–24 years	25–39 years
• Gentle on skin/Less skin irritation by use	21%	34%
• No tight feeling/Feel moisturized after use	22%	23%
• Helps to prevent pimples	11%	2%

   Though a good cleansing ability is the common expectation, different age groups have different expectations.
      That is, high teens and young 20s expect gentleness on the skin and pimple prevention as well while the other age groups show higher expectation on gentleness even on delicate skin.
   (d) The market size of cleansing cream has been reported as follows:

1978	1979	1980
¥12 billion	¥13 billion	¥14 billion

   The total market size of cleansing cream and facial soap is estimated to be approximately ¥25 billion in 1980.
2. "BIORE" FACIAL CLEANSING FOAM
   (a) Biore performs differently compared to other existing facial cleansing products.
      It is gentle even on delicate skin. It does not leave a "tight" feeling but leaves a moisturised feeling even if it is repeatedly used in a day. It is also effective in preventing pimples.
   (b) Biore's main ingredient is MAP (Mono-Alkil Phosphate) which was developed by Kao's R&D.
      MAP is neutral and non-alkaline. It is totally different from soap. It is not harmful to the skin and is as gentle as water.
      MAP's cleansing ability is as good as that of soap. While cleansing by soap **washes away NMF (natural moisturising factor) of the skin, MAP washes off dirt** but retains NMF on the skin. This is why cleansing with soap leaves a "tight" feeling on the skin but not cleansing with MAP.
      Together with an antiseptic agent and an antiphlogistic agent, MAP also works effectively to prevent pimples.
3. "BIORE" MARKETING ACTIVITIES
   (a) To emphasize gentleness on the skin, less chances of skin troubles or irritation even with the frequent use of the product.
   (b) To create and encourage a new cleaner and gentler washing habit.

Exhibit 5 New Product Launch Plan for "Biore" Facial Cleansing Foam in Japan (Extract) (Cont.)

  (c) To achieve a good product distribution in the market and to secure a dominant position against existing competitors' products.

  Note: Almost all of existing competitors' products are packed in tubes or jars, and all are soap-based.

4. "BIORE" MARKETING ACTIVITIES
  (a) To launch the product in March 1980.
  (b) Media Advertisement:
   To start in April mainly using TV and magazines
   To target females in 20s who are heavy users of cleansing cream and high teens who are concerned with pimple prevention
   To promote brand awareness, explain product characteristics and encourage a new facial cleansing habit
  (c) Product Distribution:
   To achieve high product distribution, especially at self-service outlets and pharmacies. Targeted distribution ratio are 85 per cent and above at self-service outlets, 60 per cent and above at pharmacies and 50 per cent and above at other types of outlet
  (d) Product Sampling:
   To carry out a sampling program to the targeted user group, and encourage trial usage of the product

---

cosmetics, the conventional method used by Japanese women, was not really effective. Consumers were asking Kao for a product that would give a cleaner wash. Laboratory tests confirmed that soap was not efficient for thorough cleaning after removing make-up because the facial pores were often clogged with cosmetic pigments following the use of cleansing cream and paper tissues. Leaving pigments in the pores harmed the skin's natural mechanisms. Kao researchers concluded that a water-soluble product, gentle yet effective in cleansing delicate facial skin, was needed.

This challenge was solved by MAP, a neutral non-soap-based chemical developed by Kao's organic chemists. "Biore" was formulated with MAP and blended with a subtle flowery perfume specially developed by Kao's fragrance researchers to complement the product's image as a gentle facial cleanser. It was decided to package the product in a plastic tube to emphasize its quality image. Recommended prices for consumers were ¥300 for the 60 g size and ¥550 for the 120 g size, substantially higher than an equivalent amount of soap.

Kao considered two factors when developing its positioning strategy for Biore. One element was cleansing ability. Competitive products were cleansing creams, and facial and toilet soaps, mostly sold by cosmetic companies as part of a line of branded cosmetics. The second element was the prevention of pimples. Since this was one of Biore's claims, it had to compete with the drug products positioned for treating pimples and acne. The major product in this category was "Clearasil," an anti-acne cream marketed by Nippon-Vicks K.K., the Japanese subsidiary of Richardson-Vicks, a US-based multinational. Clearasil was marketed as a registered drug. Under Japanese law, registered drugs could be sold only through pharmacies. Hence, though Nippon-Vicks had extensive distribution of Clearasil at drug counters in retail outlets, its overall retail coverage was poor. Despite Clearasil's heavy advertising, its market share was small, as sales were limited to registered druggists only, where it had a dominant position.

Kao decided to avoid the constraints of a registered drug product. Biore was positioned as a skin cleanser that also helped to prevent skin problems rather than as a product just to prevent or treat acne and pimples. Advertising focused on the benefits of a clean face, emphasizing the importance of thoroughly cleaning the face after the superficial removal of make-up. This approach contrasted sharply with Clearasil's hard selling commercials that focused on pimple treatment. Biore's advertising also deliberately aimed to downplay the product's treatment role. Because Biore was not registered as a drug, Japanese law allowed Biore to have a significantly broader retail coverage than Clearasil. Biore was sold widely by conventional toiletries retailers as well as at self-service toiletry counters in pharmacies. The product was an instant success and a new category of facial cleansing cream was born.

KAO'S INTERNATIONAL OPERATIONS

Kao's first ventures outside Japan had been to look for raw materials. Coconut oil was an important raw material for many of the company's products such as soaps, shampoos and detergents. As it was important to have a reliable source of high quality coconut oil, a major subsidiary was set up in the Philippines to produce coconut alcohols and their derivatives. Later, other subsidiaries were established in Spain, Mexico and Indonesia to produce fatty acids, fatty amines and other raw materials. These chemical subsidiaries also benefited from Kao's R&D efforts in Japan. For example, Kao developed a species of more productive coconut plant which matured more quickly and produced fruit at a lower height. In Japan, Kao also conducted extensive R&D in natural fats and oils, using the results in its overseas operations.

Other subsidiaries were established in Taiwan, Thailand, Hong Kong, Malaysia, Indonesia, the Philippines and Singapore to produce and sell consumer products in overseas markets. While initial efforts in these countries were mainly to facilitate exports from Japan, Kao also emphasized the principle that subsidiaries' activities "contribute toward improving people's lives in the host countries." In every case, Kao tried to maintain close control of raw materials and the manufacturing process to ensure a consistently high quality product.

In 1980, Kao began to expand marketing operations to developed countries. Overseas branches were established in the US and Germany, and plans were being made to set up branches in other countries. Progress was deliberately slow, partly because Kao's philosophy was to investigate the local consumer habits before introducing any fundamental product in a developed country. For example, when introducing a shampoo, the structure and physiology of the people's hair would be carefully studied so that Kao's product formulations could be modified accordingly.

As the senior managing director, Kozaburo Sagawa was responsible for the major policy and strategy issues in Kao's international operation. At the same time, he was head of the household products division to which the international counterpart reported. Sagawa was a dynamic individual with a strong personality. Though some members of top management tended to be conservative in thought and action, Sagawa appeared to enjoy being different. He was known to use strong language and was reputed to have a fiery temper. However, he was generally respected for his creativity and ability to adopt a difficult course of action for the company's long-term benefit. For example, he received credit for the strong performance made by an unorthodox but successful joint venture business between Kao and Beiersdorf AG, a major German company. Sagawa had always been critical of Kao's foreign operations. Therefore, when international business was added to his portfolio, there was much speculation among Kao managers as to how he would improve things.

TAKAYAMA'S APPOINTMENT TO SINGAPORE

Sagawa was widely recognized as Takayama's mentor in the Company. Takayama had joined Kao in April 1967 after graduating from Tohoku University. His first assignment had been in the personnel department where Sagawa was director. Although Sagawa was a chemist by training and had been the Tokyo plant manager for six years, he had a keen interest in general management and particularly in strategic marketing. With his persuasive personality and strong interests in human relations, Sagawa had succeeded in injecting great dynamism into the personnel department.

Takayama, then a new employee, respected Sagawa not only because of his seniority but also for his dynamism. Sagawa often challenged, with great conviction, the wisdom of continuing traditional practices. Sagawa's revolutionary ideas occasionally caused interdepartmental friction as well as within his own department. However, his fine achievement record continued to earn strong support from most of his colleagues, particularly in top management. He aired his views openly and critically. He was hard on his staff, always demanding their best efforts in the shortest time. However, Sagawa had always been kindly disposed towards Takayama, perhaps because Takayama was then only a trainee, but perhaps also because his open and straightforward behavior was similar to Sagawa's. Takayama himself felt that it was his persistence and old fashioned patience that appealed to Sagawa.

In May 1968, Sagawa was appointed to the main board of the Corporation. Three years later, he was promoted head of marketing operations. In June 1974, Takayama was transferred to the chemicals division. He worked for another three years in the chemicals division, responsible for the accounting and financial functions of two subsidiaries within the division. In September 1976, Sagawa requested Takayama's transfer to the marketing division. Takayama was made directly responsible for a line of French perfumed soaps and fragrance products for which Kao then acted as the sole agent in Japan. For reasons not clear to anyone, Takayama reported directly to Sagawa. That was unusual, for Takayama's new role was of no particular significance, and his position in the management hierarchy was in fact considerably lower than the others reporting directly to Sagawa.

One day in February 1980, Sagawa called Takayama into his office. He explained that Kao's Singapore subsidiary was having problems. For the past four years, sales had been growing but, despite financial support from the head office, the business did not appear to be viable. He showed Takayama the following summary:

Case Twenty-Five

Kao's Operations in Singapore

(Unit: S$, '000)	1976	1977	1978	1979
Sales	2,517	1,967	2,642	4,497
Contribution margin	908	692	973	1,922
(per cent of sales)	(36)	(35)	(37)	(43)
Overhead	1,206	890	1,163	1,965
Operating loss	298	198	190	43
(per cent of sales)	(12)	(10)	(7)	(1)
Kao's subsidy in overhead		471	778	963
Actual loss	298	669	968	1,006
(per cent of sales)	(12)	(34)	(37)	(22)
Actual break even sales level	3,350	3,889	5,246	6,809
(per cent of actual sales)	(133)	(198)	(199)	(151)

Sagawa provided Takayama with more details:

> *Like Hong Kong, where we have been relatively successful, Singapore is a free and competitive international market. Because of Singapore's strategic position in the region, I want Kao to be successful there too. This can be done by applying correct marketing strategy and an appropriate management style.*
>
> *You may be too young (Takayama was then 35) to take charge of an overseas company. However, I have to send someone to replace the current manager and I want you to go there. I don't want to hear anything from you about accepting this job, but do ask your wife if she will go with you to Singapore. That's all.*

After seeing Sagawa, Takayama knew that his transfer to Singapore had been already decided. Sagawa was right. Not only was he young, he had never been outside Japan, let alone working in isolation in an overseas subsidiary. Though he was nervous, he felt he had to do what Sagawa instructed. Outwardly he appeared confident. Inside, he knew this confidence was only because he felt that he had Sagawa's support. He was amused that Sagawa had said he should consult his wife. She knew Sagawa well as she had previously been a secretary for a senior managing director in Kao. When Takayama mentioned the transfer to his wife, she calmly replied, "Is there a choice? If Sagawa-san says go, we have to go. Let's pack!" Next morning, Takayama sent a message to Sagawa, "My wife says 'yes'."

Three weeks later he was in Singapore tasting his first overseas posting as a director of Kao Singapore. In the months that followed, as he struggled to understand the various problems confronting the subsidiary, he often wondered how such a short simple meeting with Sagawa could have resulted in this dramatic change in his career and way of life.

When Takayama first arrived in Singapore, he knew that he faced a difficult situation. The outgoing Japanese director, Nagase, had reported regularly that sales were improving and that the operational activities were going well. However, the company was continuing to lose money, which was attributed to the high operational expenses. Although Nagase was eager to return to Japan and rejoin his family, he did spend a few days with Takayama to explain the Singapore crisis thoroughly. After Nagase's excellent briefing, Takayama felt that he understood the situation well, but he continued to feel uneasy since the reasons for these problems remained vague and confusing.

Before arriving in Singapore, Takayama had decided that, since this was his first working experience abroad, he should spend most of the first year observing and learning about the Singapore operation, its market and culture. When he had previously done business with the French in Japan, he had found it difficult to understand foreigners. He remembered the cultural differences between the French and the Japanese. Therefore, he assumed that the Singaporean way of thinking might also differ from the Japanese. Until he understood the local people, he felt that he should avoid speculating or imposing his ideas about what needed to be done. After meeting with Nagase, he felt even more strongly that his "observe first, do later" strategy was appropriate. With this in mind, he set about getting to know his local staff. He took an immediate liking to Chia Hock Hwa, a local manager. Board meetings with him were often "conducted" in the local "pubs."

Sagawa had told Takayama that he would be in Singapore around four years. However, given the Singapore situation, Takayama estimated that it would need at least six or seven years to achieve something worthwhile. It would take one year to understand, the next two years to plan and experiment, and the last three years to set up a strategic plan. Takayama explained:

> *I feel I should wait until the second or third year after I understand the local situation before trying out my ideas. At Kao, top management tends to say, "hurry up" or "do it now," but this Singapore situation reminds me of the old Japanese proverb, "Haste makes waste."*
>
> *However, I am aware of my responsibility at Kao Singapore. Although I prefer to be an observer for at least the first year, I am prepared to accept the full responsibility from my first day in charge if things don't go well.*

THE CRISIS OF KAO SINGAPORE

Kao's products had been sold in Singapore as early as 1965. At that time, Kao had appointed a sole distributor in Singapore—Boustead Trading Sdn. Bhd., then a major British-owned trading house with significant operations in Singapore and Malaysia as well as in several other Southeast Asian countries. Boustead had a strong network and considerable experience distributing consumer goods in these countries. In fact, when Boustead took on the Kao line, it was already representing P&G (Proctor & Gamble, a major competitor of Kao) besides other well-known brands such as Gillette, Ovaltine, Kellogg's and Del Monte. However, under Boustead, growth of Kao sales in Singapore was slow. In 1975, Kao and Boustead agreed to terminate their Singapore trading arrangement. This was partly because Bousted was increasingly being pressured by P&G to decide between the two competing companies. Boustead chose P&G as it had a much larger volume of business than Kao. Despite this decision, Kao and Boustead parted on friendly terms; in fact, the two companies continued their shampoo joint venture operation in Malaysia which had started in 1972.

Instead of appointing another agent, Kao decided to set up his own operations in Singapore. Chia Hock Hwa was hired to run the operation. Chia had previously worked for Boustead, where he was responsible for sales of Kao, P&G, and Gillette products in Singapore. Chia found Kao's corporate philosophy attractive and was interested in building the new business. He felt confident that with hard work and financial support from Japan, the Singapore operation could be made highly successful.

At the start, overall responsibility for the Singapore office was given to a Kao manager, a Japanese named Akimi Suzuki, who had been the director of a newly established Kao joint venture in Indonesia. To ease communication and accommodate his family, he had been technically based in Singapore, returning there once a month. For the rest of the time, he travelled throughout Indonesia.

When Kao's Singapore office commenced business, its major products were laundry detergents and a few shampoo items. Since detergents were bulky, transportation from Japan was expensive. To overcome this problem, Kao had made an arrangement with UIC (United Industrial Corporation), a local competitor in Singapore, to manufacture the Kao detergents for the Singapore market. Kao supplied or specified the raw materials and packaging, set quality standards and conducted regular quality checks. Despite difficulties of implementing this arrangement, Kao felt that it could be made to work well. This system enabled Kao to obtain detergents in Singapore at a lower cost than importing them from Japan. Another advantage was that Kao did not have to make investment in production facilities. Chia tried hard to convince the head office that Kao's detergent was not an appropriate product for the Singapore market even with this arrangement. He explained repeatedly that the Singapore market differed from the Japanese. In Japan, consumers had been using home washing machines for many years. They were quality conscious and willing to pay higher prices for better products. In Singapore, on the other hand, the market was acutely price-conscious. Machines in the home were still relatively uncommon and laundry was mainly washed by hand. Thus the market potential for high-priced, high quality detergents was limited. Despite vigorous marketing efforts, sales of detergent products in Singapore remained small. In a final attempt to increase the detergent business, Kao decided to launch a product at the lower end of the market. Sales increased somewhat, but the costs of selling grew even more rapidly.

At the same time, other non-detergent product lines were gradually being added, mainly hair-care products imported from Japan. Sales of these new products grew significantly. Kao Singapore consciously limited itself to those household and basic toiletry products that were well established in Japan. To expand this business, Chia was constantly looking to Japan for new non-detergent products. In late 1976, Kao was persuaded to provide some funds to help advertise some of the new products. Though sales of these products responded well to advertising, Kao's head office was really more interested in promoting detergent products. Instructions were often being sent to Singapore to push detergent products more aggressively.

As Kao's Singapore business grew, Japan felt that Singapore required a stronger senior management team than the existing arrangement. Accordingly, Teruyuki Nagase was sent from Japan in 1978 to be the full-time Japanese director. Nagase was new to overseas operations and was persuaded to operate the Singapore subsidiary along the line of the parent company in Japan. He emphasized detergents the same way as in Japan, obtaining more funds from Japan to advertise Kao detergent products. Chia managed to persuade Nagase to maintain the level of funds previously allocated for hair care products. Total sales then began growing significantly; profitability increases, however, came mainly from sales of hair care products. Sales of detergent products also climbed, but the expenses for detergent sales grew at an even faster rate. As a result, Kao Singapore continued to incur losses.

With the newly available funds from Japan for advertising and promotion, Chia regained his confidence and optimism about Kao's future in the market. However, he said:

> *We have got to be willing to do things differently. We are emphasizing the wrong products here. We must be sensitive to the environmental factors and move from a selling company to a marketing company. We must have a range of products that will give us steady growth based on both sales and profits.*

Chia made no effort to hide his dissatisfaction with the detergent product line. He repeatedly complained about its low-priced positioning. On the other hand, he admitted that the Singapore market was price-sensitive, and any attempt to move the Kao product line upscale was unlikely to be successful. Until laundry washing habits changed, high quality detergents would not have a chance, he reasoned. At the same time, Kao had no opportunity to become a low-cost producer in Singapore, because its detergents were being manufactured by UIC, the only viable local detergent manufacturer. Thus Kao's costs would always be higher than UIC's, which had its own brand in the market. Chia was firmly convinced that detergents could not provide the base for a successful Kao business in Singapore.

When Takayama came to Singapore, Chia explained to him:

> *We will never make it with detergents. If we want to lead and be profitable here, we have to think of something else or forget the whole thing.*

When Takayama reported this opinion to the head office, he received a sharp negative reaction:

> *Our company has been built on soaps and detergents.* That is the base of our business in Japan, and that should also be the base of our business in Singapore. It is not wise to change a corporate strategy that has been so successful. Instead, you must convince your people in Singapore to think correctly about the importance of detergents. Don't you understand your role in Singapore?*

---

* At that time, about one-third of Kao's total sales in Japan were in detergent products.

Case Twenty-Five

BIORE FOR SINGAPORE

On one of his frequent visits to the head office in Tokyo, Chia learned about the Biore development project at one of the open door meetings. Chia was fascinated by the Biore idea. He was convinced that he had found the product that could turn Kao Singapore around and give it a new direction. However, Biore had become a controversial product at Kao. In a company that had been built on soap, many were skeptical of a non-soap cleanser like Biore. Kao's long-time employees said:

> *All these years we have been telling our customers that they should use our high quality soap to clean their faces. Now, with Biore, we need to say soap is bad for the face. That's ridiculous. It is also extremely difficult to convince women to clean their faces with a chemical product in a tube.*

Chia obtained a sample of Biore. When he tried it in his hotel room in Tokyo, he was amazed by its cleansing action. He was deeply impressed and convinced that biore's unique properties would give Kao Singapore a real chance to develop and lead a new market. The more he studied the Biore proposition, the more he liked it. The Singapore market for cleansers was underdeveloped. There was only one major product sold as a facial cleanser—"Dearland." It was manufactured in Taiwan and imported into Singapore by a local company. On his return, Chia bought a tube of Dearland. When he tried it, he was pleased to find that Biore clearly seemed to be the superior product.

Chia particularly liked the Biore idea because he felt that the product was capable of satisfying a need, was effective and unique. He also realized that the product could be sold at a price high enough to sustain advertising. He said:

> *With the higher margin, Biore is capable of making a significant contribution to fixed operating costs. This could turn the Company into a profitable operation within a short period of time. In fact, Biore could also help project the Company from a completely sales-oriented organization into a more strategy-directed consumer marketing company.*

During his years working with Gillette and P&G, Chia had acquired various aggressive marketing tools that he was eager to use but could not because the margins in the detergent business were so low. He felt Biore would give him this opportunity.

THE DILEMMA. Takayama started at the proposal from Chia on his desk; it strongly recommended that Biore be launched in Singapore right away. Although he knew that Chia was right, Takayama remembered his decision to act only as an observer during the first year. He was also familiar with the attitude of the managers at the head office in Japan. Facial cleansers were still new in Japan and Biore was a new product category just created by Kao. The parent company had been built over the years on toilet soaps (launched in 1879), shampoos (1930s), detergents (1950s), laundry additives (1960s) and sanitary products (1975). Biore facial cleanser marked a challenging entry into the high value-added cosmetics business. That was not an easy entry in Japan, where the established competitors in cosmetics were strong and well entrenched. Kao managers felt that there was still much more to be learned about the facial cleanser business. Many regarded Biore as an experiment which could easily fail. The Biore product team, of course, was enthusiastic about their new product's prospects, sure that they had a winner. But they admitted that there were many uncertainties.

Takayama was at a loss about how to respond. He told Chia:

> We are not sure whether this new product will succeed or fail in Japan. If we fail in Singapore and they fail in Japan, we will be reprimanded for being impatient and not waiting for Japan's results to be known. If we succeed and they fail we will have to withdraw the product from the market any way, since it will be discontinued and no longer available. Introducing this product will work only if we all succeed, a situation that is uncertain at this point. The head office has instructed us to wait another two to three years. Furthermore, to launch this product now, we would need more advertising money from the head office. Even if we proceeded without their blessing, we would still have the problem of funds.

An integral part of Chia's proposal was his recommendation that Singapore should get out of the detergent business to free up the sales team for the Biore business. This recommendation was even more disturbing and Takayama knew that the response from the head office would be strong and sharp. Chia stubbornly upheld his stand. He told Takayama:

> Kao should get out of the detergent business in Singapore. We've not yet made and will never make a profit in detergents. Actually, we are only helping to build UIC's business. The opportunities for us here are in hair-care and cosmetic products, not detergents.

Takayama could see the merits of Chia proposal and was particularly impressed by Chia's calculations:

> If only 10 per cent of our sales in Singapore come from Biore, we will become profitable. For the same result, we would have to increase detergent sales six times.

Takayama also felt that this strategy might be the only way to fulfil Sagawa's goals to make the Singapore operation profitable and to start establishing Kao brands in leadership positions. On the other hand, he was afraid to take the risks that most of his colleagues in Japan were advising him to avoid. He knew that they were counting on him to proceed with building up the detergents business. Furthermore, he did not know the market well enough to be able to evaluate Biore's prospects in Singapore. Would Biore really do as well as Chia claimed?

As he pondered these questions, Takayama felt lonely and suddenly realized how much he missed his network of contacts at Kao. Takayama was well known and liked at Kao where so many different jobs had brought him into contact with a large number of people. After office hours, he had often met casually with his colleagues in bars and small restaurants. When something troubled him seriously, he would usually talk it over informally with several people. He had found that such dialogues helped him understand the various aspects of his problem and usually the appropriate solution would emerge.

In Singapore, Takayama was the only Japanese manager on the spot. He was alone with no opportunity to talk things over with his peers and superiors. It was then he realized why Sagawa had insisted that he take his wife to Singapore. Though she knew little about business matters, her support and confidence in him were comforting and he could talk to her in the traditional way. Even so, Takayama's confidence in himself was becomingly increasingly shaken. Having to decide about Biore was the major cause of his depression. He looked again at Chia's proposal for Biore. How should he respond to Chia? Should he stay with his original strategy merely to observe during the first year? Should he call Sagawa to ask his advice? Or was this the opportunity he should seize to make a personal impact in the Company? He noticed that his ashtray was filled to the brim and that he had run out of cigarettes. The time had come to act. He looked around the empty room and murmured to himself, "I will decide this by myself!"

When Takayama officially presented the plan for launching Biore in Singapore to his seniors in Tokyo, he was severely criticized:

> *You were sent to Singapore to teach the locals how to implement our corporate strategy. Instead, it appears that you have been convinced by them!*

Takayama decided not to start by defending the Biore plan; first he reaffirmed Singapore's commitment to detergent products as Tokyo had prescribed. He reassured his senior colleagues in Tokyo repeatedly that he had no intention of abandoning the detergent business in Singapore. He promised that he would continue to try hard to build up that business. Then he sought their understanding and support for Biore. As he had planned his presentation, he had asked himself many times, "How else can I accomplish what I feel is best? After all, what is my role supposed to be?"

CASE TWENTY-SIX

HAW PAR VILLA DRAGON WORLD*

In mid-May 1991, Mr. Goh, the General Manager of International Theme Parks Pte. Ltd. (ITP), was wondering how he should market Haw Par Villa Dragon World (HPVDW), a newly revamped world class Oriental theme park in Singapore, in order to achieve a higher level of growth. Apart from the fact that ITP was making a profit after eight months of operation, Mr. Goh was worried that the attendance rate for locals might drop after the novelty of the park had worn off. Nevertheless, he faced two important issues:

1. In the long run, what strategy he should adopt to maintain or increase the visitorship to HPVDW.
2. In view of the up-coming attractions, such as Bugis Square, Telok Ayer Market, Sentosa Underwater World, and Tang Dynasty Village, he wondered what actions he should take to maintain the competitive edge of the park.

With these issues in mind, he had several meetings with his managers, and together they came up with two possible alternatives:

1. Either to re-dress the theme park as a show park by adding more shows, or
2. To add more rides to the existing park, thus, slanting the theme park to an amusement park.

---

*This case was prepared by Ms. Clare Chow and Associate Professor Wee Chow Hou as a basis for class discussion rather than to illustrate either effective or ineffective handling of an administrative situation and may contain disguised information. Copyright © 1991, Faculty of Business Administration, National University of Singapore.

All monetary values are in Singapore dollars.

Mr. Goh was not sure which of the two alternatives would be the best way to promote Haw Par Villa Dragon World so as to increase the percentage of visitorship to the park. Mr. Goh had asked Mr. Lee, the divisional manager, and Mr. Sim, the entertainment manager, to look into these issues thoroughly.

Origin of Haw Par Villa

Haw Par Villa (HPV), also known as Tiger Balm Gardens, was built in 1931 by the Aw brothers as part of their private residence. The original HPV occupied an area of about 1.9 hectares. The design and construction of HPV was undertaken over a period of two years. The uniqueness of Haw Par's architecture was attained at considerable expense, of S$1.2 million in 1931, a huge sum at that time. HPV took its name after the Aw brothers, Boon Haw, the tiger (Haw), and Boon Par, the leopard (Par).

In 1937, the villa was opened to the public. The Aw brothers renamed the villa "Tiger Balm Gardens" after their flagship product, Tiger Balm, a Chinese herbal ointment. No admission charge was levied. Previously, the villa was opened to the public only once a year during the first three days of the Chinese New Year. The public was able to enjoy the myriad displays which portrayed the legends of Chinese mythology and ancient folklore. Most of the themes centred on filial piety, righteousness and obedience to authority which were the cornerstones of Confucian ethics. Apart from their sharp acumen for business ventures, another virtue of the Aw brothers was their generosity towards contributing to the public good. Thus, by opening the park to the public, they not only provided the masses a place to relax and enjoy themselves but also a conduit to promote Tiger Balm. Throughout the park, one could witness statues and figures holding the Tiger Balm ointment.

HPV was destroyed in World War II. After the war it was revamped in 1952 with an estimated cost of S$800,000. Two years later, the philanthropic Aw brothers dedicated the villa to the public domain. Since its inception, Haw Par Villa has remained a favourite attraction both to foreign and local visitors alike. Most guide books list the villa as a must-see showpiece.

In 1984, a survey conducted by the Singapore Tourist Promotion Board (STPB) placed HPV as the fifth most visited tourist attraction in Singapore. The redevelopment of HPV became a priority as its well-being was seen to play a vital role in the development of the tourist industry in Singapore. The following year, the villa was leased to STPB which in turn invited the private sector to submit proposals for the redevelopment of the park. In 1986, the redevelopment project was awarded to International Theme Parks (S) Pte. Ltd. on a 40-year lease.

Corporate Background

The new Haw Par Villa was developed by International Theme Parks (S) Pte. Ltd., a 75-25 joint venture between two local corporate giants, Fraser & Neave Limited and Times Publishing Ltd. Fraser & Neave Ltd., founded in 1883, has business concerns in beers, soft drinks, ice-cream, dairy products, packaging and property development. Times Publishing is a leading company in the publishing industry. For the fiscal year 1990, Fraser & Neave reported a profit of $54.3 million while Times Publishing Limited posted a profit of $45.4 million. The debut of HPVDW marked the entry of the two conglomerates into the leisure industry. Being the major investor, Fraser and Neave was appointed the managing agent of HPVDW.

International Theme Parks (ITP) was confident that HPVDW would continue to be profitable for the company. Since its opening, the daily attendance level was encouraging. Management realized that in order to maintain the current success, International Theme Parks had to constantly enhance the park's attractions. The design of the new HPVDW was undertaken by American Theme Park Consultant. It had several outstanding works to its credit, namely, Knotts Berry Farm in the USA, Lotte World in Korea and Expo '86 in Vancouver, Canada. Because of such creative influence, HPVDW had the ambience of a Disneyland with a generous dose of Oriental flavour, taking into consideration that the company, Battaglia Associates Inc., was itself an offshoot of Walt Disney Productions.

Incorporated in 1985, International Theme Parks had as at May 1991, a full-time cast of about 450. The term "cast member" and not the usual "staff" or "worker" is applied to all employees at the park. Mr. Lee, the divisional manager, explained that they chose to call their staff "cast" because every member of the company was "cast" to perform a task. The main idea was to promote HPVDW as a "show" rather than a "park". Thus, everybody involved in the day-to-day functioning of the park had a specific role to play, just as if they were performing in one of the various live shows staged. Most of the cast members were hired one month prior to the official opening of the park in October 1990. Members of the top management at HPVDW received training from major theme parks in the United States. Management felt that the training would provide them with some park experience.

NEW HAW PAR VILLA DRAGON WORLD

Singapore's first class theme park opened its doors on 2 October 1990. The newly revamped show park was named Haw Par Villa Dragon World. The appendage "Dragon World" is intended to distinguish the new park from its predecessor. Redeveloped at a cost of $80 million over a period of two years, the new HPVDW occupied an area of about 9.5 hectares and encompassed plots of land adjacent to the old park ground. Located in Pasir Panjang, along the West Coast of Singapore, it was five times larger than the original park. HPVDW was easily accessible by bus or taxi. There were ample parking facilities, with over 300 car park slots and 25 coach slots, directly opposite the main entrance. The car park charges were $4.00 per entry. The management of HPVDW was considering converting the present car park into a $20 million retail, food and beverage, and entertainment theme complex.

Being the only Chinese mythology theme and show park in Singapore, HPVDW attracted more then 4,000 visitors on its very first day. The major draw for visitors to HPVDW was the shows and exhibits on Chinese culture, history and tradition.

The high-tech park offered not only the unique displays reminiscent of the Aw brother's collections of immensely colourful statues and figures but included a selection of rides, shows and displays that truly distinguish it from other theme parks around the world. The visitors were greeted with bursts of colour from every possible source, even the footpaths and waste bins were brightly coloured. Live shows were staged at scheduled times, presenting Chinese mythology and legends with the aid of the latest electronic gadgetry, laser, smoke machines and stereo sound equipment.

The nine major attractions included three high-tech theatres with special laser, sound and visual effects, three open-air theatres for live performances, two fun rides and the Xu Mu Kong Plaza, a place where pugilists entertained visitors with stunts and dances.

The three high-tech theatres were:

1. Creation of the World
2. Legends and Heroes
3. Spirits of the Orient

The open-air theatres, mainly for live shows, were:

1. The South China Sea Amphitheatre
2. The Puppet Theatre
3. The Four Seasons Theatre

The two available fun rides in the park were the Tales of China boat ride—a leisurely cruise through the belly of the 60-metre long giant dragon sculpture, and the Wrath of the Water Gods ride, a faster paced ride.

The park operating hours were from 9:00 am to 6:00 pm daily. Sundays and public holidays were the most popular times for local visitors. Hence, in February 1991, the operating hours were extended to 10:00 pm on these occasions to give the public more time to enjoy themselves and also in part to ease congestion. The management was pleased that extending the operating hours had increased operating costs only marginally. The peak time for park attendance varied. On weekdays, the peak hours were between 9:00 am to 1:00 pm. On weekends, the peak hours were from 10:00 am to 2:30 pm. Hourly attendance figures were computed from ticket stub numbers as well as the turnstile counters.

As of May 1991, the entrance fees to HPVDW were $16.00 for adults and $10.00 for children between the age of 3 and 12 years. Children and babies in arms under three years of age were admitted free of charge. The entrance fees were inclusive of all rides and shows. When the public came to know about the $16.00 admission fee, the majority of people commented that the fee was too high especially when it was free of charge before the park underwent major expansion. The management responded to this price-sensitive group by explaining that the $16.00 included five shows and two rides. This averaged out to $2.29 per show or ride. Moreover, a survey conducted on park visitors showed that the vast majority considered the price of admission to be reasonable and most felt that they had got their money's worth. Tickets could be purchased at the entrance or at selected outlets.

Besides the rides and the shows, the park also provided food and beverage facilities, souvenir and gift shops, a hospitality centre, a lost and found centre, first aid stations and a "lost-parents" centre—the deliberate play on words here was designed to dispel the anxiety and fears most parents have when they lose contact with their children. This light-hearted approach was seen as congruent to projecting the park's image as a fun place to be in.

There were four major food and beverage outlets:

1. The Artisan Eating House
2. Bamboo Tea House
3. The Golden Nest
4. Water Gardens Seafood Palace

Both Western and Chinese cuisines were served in these four restaurants. The food was rated favourably by the visitors. The Water Gardens Seafood Palace was the only air-conditioned restaurant in the park. Refreshment kiosks or carts, which served drinks and light snacks, were located throughout the park.

Games stalls which were available at Xu Mu Kong Plaza were introduced in February 1991 as a new channel for revenue. These stalls featured the typical games of skill that one might find in any amusement park. Souvenir shops were present within the park grounds. These outlets sold gift items and handicrafts and formed an integral part of the park. Kiosks outside the main park ground also provided similar amenities. Some of these kiosks were concessioned to non-HPVDW retail owners. Even though the kiosks were rented out, ITP still maintained control over the kiosks in terms of pricing and sale of items.

HPVDW ATTRACTIONS

The Creation of the World Theatre had 3D multi-image and 2D mixed media presentations. It told the tales of earthly creations according to early mythology. It had a capacity of 240 seats and the whole show ran for 17 minutes.

The Legends and Heroes Theatre, which could accommodate up to 240 visitors, was a multi-image mixed media presentation. It featured a life-sized robotic old man figure who told the tales of past heroes and warriors. The length of the show was 18 minutes.

The Spirit of the Orient Theatre could entertain up to 500 visitors at a time with its 17-minute, multi-screen slide show presentation. It highlighted the stories behind many Chinese traditions and practices.

The Four Seasons Theatre was an open air theatre with a sitting capacity of 100. A story telling session conducted by four character actors, Spring, Summer, Autumn and Winter, lasted about 20 minutes.

The Puppet Theatre catered to younger visitors. The open-air theatre provided a 20-minute fully computerized puppet show.

The largest theatre in the theme park was the South China Sea Amphitheatre with a sitting capacity of 2,000. This was an open-air theatre with a huge sun shade. Live entertainment included cast members playing figures representing the elements of nature, such as Father

Sun, Mother Earth, Fire, Water, Wind and Cloud. Members of the audience were invited to come to the stage to mimic the actions of cast members and to put on impromptu shows. The response from the audience had generally been favourable. In addition, there were several park entertainers whose main duties were to delight and amuse visitors standing in line for the shows or rides. They include Jazzo, Da-Long, Toh Be and Lee Ming who mingled with visitors to delight and amuse, much in the same genre as the Mickey Mouse and Donald Duck characters that one might find at the Disney Theme Parks.

Of the attractions, the Wrath of the Water Gods flume ride and the Tales of China boat ride proved to be the most popular. The Tales of China boat ride took visitors on a 16-seater ancient Chinese boat-ride through the belly of a 60-metre long dragon. The journey lasted about 10 minutes, during which visitors would witness the adventures of the legendary Eight Immortals, the tale of Lady White Snake, and scenes from the fabled Ten Courts of Hell.

The Wrath of the Water Gods flume ride was a favourite with the young at heart. This was one of the most energetic rides available where riders literally plunged about 15 metres down a waterfall at its climax. The whole ride took about eight minutes.

Physical Constraints of the Park

For a visitor to enjoy all the attractions, the average length of time that he or she would have to stay was estimated to be about 4.3 hours. On weekends, due to the larger crowds the length of time spent queuing up increased. Hence, the total time a visitor needed to spend in the park also rose. According to the monthly financial report, the park had been attracting a capacity of between 2,000 to 7,000 visitors a day since its opening in October 1990. The average attendance was approximately 3,000 visitors per day. However, HPVDW could accommodate up to 7,000 visitors at any one time or an average of 12,000 visitors per day. During the 1991 Chinese Lunar New Year, an uncommonly large number of visitors boosted the daily attendance level to past the 17,000 mark. As the park capacity was 7,000 at any one time, entrance to the park had to be controlled. The park attendance capacity was constrained by the actual physical space available as well as the capacity of the kitchens to provide meals.

Mr. Lee had thought of having caterers to supply food on occasions when the park's kitchen capacities were exceeded. Aside from this option, he also considered tendering out the food and beverage outlets. However, he preferred the former because ITP could still exercise direct supervision to maintain food quality and customer services even though the latter option ensured a fixed income.

Target Market

HPVDW was designed to appeal to tourists as well as the locals. The local target market comprised families, younger generations and corporate groups. The business review report of ITP revealed the adult/child ratio as 9 to 1.

Singapore, despite its small population of slightly over 3 million attracted a record 5,322,854 foreign visitors in 1990. In 1990, the average visitor arrival on a monthly basis was estimated to be 440,000 (see Exhibit 1). The trend of visitor arrivals was increasing steadily. Realizing that Singapore had a large tourist market, Mr. Goh wanted to capture a substantial portion

Exhibit 1A Statistics on Total Number of Visitors (1981–90)

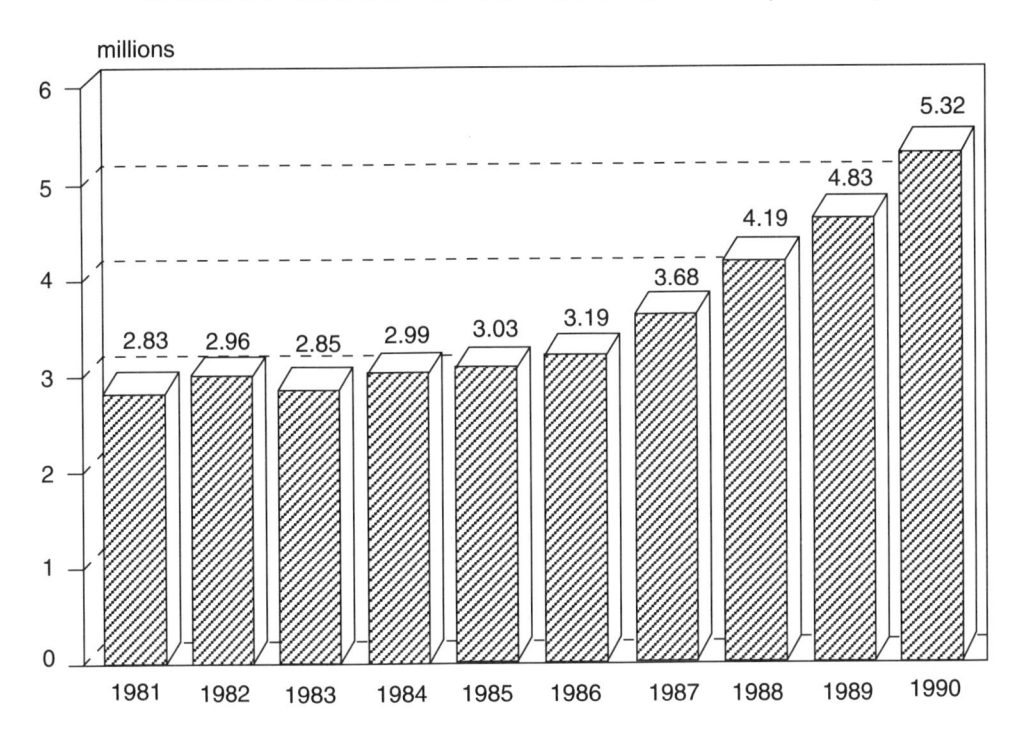

millions

Year	Visitors (millions)
1981	2.83
1982	2.96
1983	2.85
1984	2.99
1985	3.03
1986	3.19
1987	3.68
1988	4.19
1989	4.83
1990	5.32

Exhibit 1B Total Number of Visitors to Singapore from January 1990 to April 1991

	Total No.
1990	
January	433,549
February	425,093
March	445,492
April	430,812
May	410,356
June	409,917
July	409,917
August	474,880
September	492,569
October	435,285
November	448,583
December	488,784
1991	
January	432,286
February	363,560
March	403,170
April	418,318

of it. He also realized that once the local market was exhausted, the total park attendance rate would decline unless there were repeat visits or the tourist participation rate increased.

Exhibit 2 shows the tourist composition from the STPB annual report. The majority of the tourists were female, arrived by air, on holiday and stayed in hotels. By studying the characteristics of tourists, management hoped to market HPVDW more effectively.

Before the park began operation, ITP projected a visitor profile consisting of 60 per cent tourists, 30 per cent residents (who were either Singaporean or permanent residents of Singapore) and 10 per cent Malaysians. However, in mid-May 1991, the visitor profile, which was obtained from an in-park survey showed that it consisted of 30 per cent tourists, 60 per cent residents and 10 per cent Malaysians. Mr. Goh wondered why the tourists did not come to the park. He estimated that only 0.27 per cent of all tourists who arrived in Singapore had actually visited HPVDW. As yet, there was no evidence of repeat visits from the local residents. Management would also like to take advantage of the fact that the vast majority of tourists fell under the category of the free, independent traveller (FIT or non-group tours) as reported in STPB's survey. The detailed breakdown of visitor arrivals by purpose of visit and the Singapore tourist market is shown in Exhibit 2. ITP had conducted its own survey and discovered that 80 per cent of the visitors surveyed had reported satisfaction and had rated the park favourably. It also found that a larger percentage of foreign visitors had rated the park more favourably than their local counterparts.

PROMOTION

Management at HPVDW forecasted total attendance level to reach 1.7 million by the end of September 1991. To achieve this, conscious effort had been made to capitalize on the theme park's uniqueness in terms of the displays, rides and most importantly, the shows. Promotional programmes included press releases, advertisements in news dailies, travel trade magazines, lifestyle magazines and selected news agencies. To maximize its exposure to potential visitors, HPVDW, worked in close cooperation with other sectors of the tourist industry. Arrangements were made with as many as 61 hotels to advertise the attractions of HPVDW. Tour agencies also offer packages for tourists intending to visit HPVDW. Admission tickets were sold to tour agents at wholesale price who in turn sold their packaged tours, inclusive of transport from hotels to HPVDW, at a higher price.

However, unlike other tourist attractions, HPVDW did not offer incentives to tour guides. As a visit to the park usually took up more than half a day, it was commonly known that a substantial number of tour guides were reluctant to bring their clients to HPVDW.

In the local media, HPVDW was featured in "Variety Tonight", a regular TV show. Promotional advertisements were also placed regularly in the local English and Mandarin dailies. Extensive efforts were made to promote the park locally. Besides newspaper, television and radio advertisements, HPVDW was also involved in some community work. In December 1990, a total of 259 underprivileged children were invited to the park for a free visit. A taxi promotion scheme was introduced in February 1991 to motivate taxi drivers to bring passengers to the park. As the school June holiday was around the corner, ITP initiated a colouring contest for children.

Another scheme whereby special arrangements were made to cater to demands for "theme"

Exhibit 2 Summary of Characteristics of Visitor Arrivals from Major Countries (%)—January 1991

Characteristic	Total	ASEAN	Japan	India	Taiwan	Hong Kong	Korea	UK	Germany	Scandinavia	Netherlands	France	Australia	New Zealand	USA
Mode of arrival	100.00	100.00	100.00	100.00	100.00	100.00	100.00	100.00	100.00	100.00	100.00	100.00	100.00	100.00	100.00
Air	79.95	65.71	88.60	86.88	78.03	83.57	87.59	82.94	80.61	75.34	83.97	83.65	84.94	83.25	85.92
Sea	7.53	19.33	2.35	2.59	3.28	1.97	6.25	3.50	5.68	4.48	5.59	3.11	2.40	2.04	5.17
Land	12.53	14.96	9.06	10.53	18.69	14.46	6.16	13.56	13.71	20.17	10.45	13.24	12.66	14.72	8.91
Sex	100.00	100.00	10.0.00	100.00	100.00	100.00	100.00	100.00	100.00	100.00	100.00	100.00	100.00	100.00	100.00
Male	61.88	63.57	57.12	76.76	61.82	68.59	55.07	59.74	60.66	60.39	62.11	64.87	54.63	54.75	66.34
Female	38.12	36.43	42.88	23.24	38.18	31.41	44.93	40.26	39.34	39.61	37.89	35.13	45.37	45.25	33.66
Age group (years)	100.00	100.00	10.0.00	100.00	100.00	100.00	100.00	100.00	100.00	100.00	100.00	100.00	100.00	100.00	100.00
14 and below	5.75	5.64	3.06	6.08	3.99	3.53	3.78	5.65	2.44	4.20	2.67	4.96	13.13	9.99	4.75
15–19	2.66	2.97	1.61	2.17	1.12	0.91	0.99	2.01	0.88	2.00	0.77	1.32	7.80	6.31	1.31
20–24	8.61	10.86	8.90	9.37	6.25	6.32	3.87	7.14	5.84	12.08	6.24	5.20	8.92	10.62	6.15
25–34	26.14	29.57	21.39	35.48	28.27	34.60	16.04	23.83	28.97	27.87	25.24	28.07	19.91	26.31	21.28
35–44	24.15	27.69	21.10	25.14	28.65	29.94	25.65	18.88	21.67	16.84	19.12	25.75	22.31	19.64	23.93
45–54	17.32	14.18	20.40	11.90	14.41	13.52	24.52	18.79	23.46	20.22	21.33	18.16	17.87	16.04	20.37
55–64	9.93	5.70	16.00	6.42	10.43	7.50	18.42	14.08	10.63	10.75	14.91	10.15	6.75	7.44	12.14
65 & above	4.72	2.25	7.14	2.41	6.29	3.32	6.03	9.14	5.69	5.57	9.16	5.87	2.86	3.11	9.49
Not stated	0.71	1.14	0.39	1.03	0.58	0.36	0.70	0.48	0.42	0.47	0.57	0.53	0.45	0.55	0.57
Average age (years)	37.82	35.22	41.51	34.89	39.16	37.27	43.47	40.61	40.52	38.37	42.31	39.22	33.77	34.20	41.35
Purpose of visit	100.00	100.00	100.00	100.00	100.00	100.00	100.00	100.00	100.00	100.00	100.00	100.00	100.00	100.00	100.00
Holiday	61.94	46.31	87.78	43.33	65.64	47.46	72.86	67.56	68.61	75.61	61.39	58.04	67.50	62.48	45.03
Business	11.44	14.83	6.47	14.94	14.78	28.60	6.07	10.36	8.76	7.21	11.10	16.57	6.45	5.72	18.51
Business and pleasure	3.51	4.48	0.86	4.24	3.27	5.97	6.50	3.60	2.53	2.89	3.53	3.43	2.20	2.18	7.01
In transit	9.76	9.81	2.21	9.49	6.54	6.76	4.68	11.05	12.06	8.15	15.76	12.77	15.86	20.02	19.36
Convention	0.35	0.71	0.06	0.32	0.28	0.62	0.42	0.10	0.11	0.13	0.12	0.24	0.23	0.10	0.20
Official mission	2.85	3.90	0.32	9.65	1.76	5.16	1.41	2.54	1.06	1.49	2.43	1.75	3.37	3.84	4.24
Education	0.43	0.93	0.03	0.59	0.24	0.33	0.59	0.13	0.06	0.15	0.22	1.12	0.19	0.04	0.36
Others	4.79	9.71	1.10	7.73	3.05	2.84	3.87	2.34	2.73	2.39	2.61	3.21	1.93	2.81	2.65
Type of accommodation	100.00	100.00	100.00	100.00	100.00	100.00	100.00	100.00	100.00	100.00	100.00	100.00	100.00	100.00	100.00
Hotel	73.04	52.08	93.27	54.95	82.88	76.52	89.3	76.77	76.95	81.11	76.34	77.52	74.19	72.25	76.97
Residence of friends/relatives	12.25	20.40	2.02	26.50	7.71	15.79	3.33	12.72	5.91	6.84	10.11	9.85	14.77	16.51	13.03
Others	3.78	7.21	1.53	6.03	2.54	1.77	3.06	2.40	2.96	2.72	2.53	2.50	1.59	2.10	1.96
No accommodation required	5.84	10.09	1.78	3.82	2.35	3.18	1.74	1.23	7.49	5.91	7.76	5.50	7.82	7.20	6.08

Exhibit 2 Summary of Characteristics of Visitor Arrivals from Major Countries (%)—January 1991 (cont.)

Characteristic	Total	ASEAN	Japan	India	Taiwan	Hong Kong	Korea	UK	Germany	Scandinavia	Netherlands	France	Australia	New Zealand	USA
Frequency of visit	100.00	100.00	100.00	100.00	100.00	100.00	100.00	100.00	100.00	100.00	100.00	100.00	100.00	100.00	100.00
First visit	38.96	11.90	61.55	37.53	51.12	31.07	73.78	47.51	49.34	53.18	40.03	42.38	31.78	31.69	38.68
Re-visit	53.86	77.27	25.76	52.63	44.02	66.24	22.49	51.06	46.84	44.95	57.50	53.29	67.24	67.46	59.38
Travel arrangement	100.00	100.00	100.00	100.00	100.00	100.00	100.00	100.00	100.00	100.00	100.00	100.00	100.00	100.00	100.00
Package/group travel	26.79	7.32	75.53	13.60	38.55	17.10	74.12	8.22	21.66	18.44	12.97	17.10	8.83	8.35	13.05
Non-package/group travel	65.01	78.56	22.16	70.75	54.19	78.45	21.84	86.33	71.06	77.02	81.28	73.07	87.03	86.47	83.29
Length of stay (days)	100.00	100.00	100.00	100.00	100.00	100.00	100.00	100.00	100.00	100.00	100.00	100.00	100.00	100.00	100.00
Under 1	12.08	21.38	5.10	9.06	9.61	7.41	4.89	8.57	13.46	8.67	14.97	12.00	10.96	10.27	14.57
1	19.68	19.75	15.69	12.78	23.35	22.12	22.54	18.66	25.63	20.38	26.34	24.06	20.27	23.49	24.96
2	22.49	15.42	27.54	13.10	37.67	27.74	58.18	23.81	23.75	21.11	22.54	21.49	18.56	21.17	19.08
3	17.46	10.74	35.97	14.85	10.93	14.99	6.26	20.21	15.96	16.88	14.63	15.75	13.76	14.58	12.88
4	8.17	6.11	10.13	11.08	5.60	8.30	3.38	9.57	7.76	14.08	6.53	7.43	8.86	8.10	7.42
5	4.09	3.98	2.32	6.49	2.97	4.72	1.19	4.36	3.15	6.03	3.30	5.26	5.87	5.18	4.29
6	2.82	2.99	0.78	5.40	1.70	2.49	0.57	2.57	4.50	3.55	2.45	2.32	5.21	3.77	2.88
7	2.25	2.57	0.58	3.95	1.31	3.00	0.59	2.04	1.47	2.16	1.60	2.56	3.31	2.65	2.85
8–10	3.27	4.14	0.77	5.20	2.42	3.39	0.52	2.97	1.51	2.94	2.79	3.52	5.57	3.32	4.09
11–14	3.97	7.03	0.62	9.15	2.26	2.93	0.91	3.12	1.38	2.18	2.14	2.76	3.72	3.35	3.19
15–29	2.26	2.84	0.37	5.15	1.32	2.04	0.66	3.25	1.17	1.64	1.90	2.11	2.86	3.07	2.83
30 and over	1.46	3.06	0.13	3.78	0.85	0.86	0.30	0.86	0.27	0.37	0.81	0.75	1.06	1.05	0.97
Average length of stay (days)	3.44	3.87	2.64	5.20	2.76	3.30	2.18	3.48	2.64	3.24	2.84	3.17	3.79	3.48	3.31
	(3.81)	(4.53)	(2.69)	(6.13)	(2.97)	(3.57)	(2.27)	(3.84)	(2.76)	(3.41)	(3.09)	(3.43)	(4.15)	(3.85)	(3.65)

*Figures in parentheses denote the average length of stay computed using 30 days as cut-off point.

Source: *Annual Report* of the Singapore Tourist Promotion Board (STPB).

parties was also implemented. Some corporate customers indicated that they were interested in having parties in which their staff could be involved in some play or act, for example, dressing up in ancient Chinese costumes. ITP charged their customers for creating a unique theme party. There was a minimum requirement for a theme party, that is, at least 100 people and the charges ranged from $50.00 per person and above, depending on the client's requirements. Advertisements for this sort of service were placed in Teleview, a local information channel. HPVDW also advertised extensively overseas. STPB played a significant role in promoting HPVDW abroad. Apart from this, ITP sent several members overseas to market HPVDW. Recently, a giant poster featuring scenes of the park was erected at the Marriot Marquis Hotel in New York City, USA.

OTHER TOURIST ATTRACTIONS IN SINGAPORE

HPVDW faced competition from other tourist attractions in that all must vie for the limited time a visitor to Singapore had available to him or her. According to a 1990 STPB report, 55.15 per cent of all tourists visiting Singapore stayed for two days or less. The average length of stay for a tourist was 3.44 days. Management was aware of other new and old attractions in Singapore and had studied their marketing strategies in order to develop a competitive strategy.

The major competitors were:

TANG DYNASTY VILLAGE. A theme park highlighting the legends, folklore and tales of the Tang Dynasty. Developed at a cost of almost $70 million, it was scheduled to be opened in September 1991. It had already received publicity in the form of a newspaper write-up published in the *Sunday Times* on 3 February 1991. Tang Dynasty Village was the closest competitor on two counts. Firstly, it was located nearby and secondly, its theme focused on the Tang Dynasty period, which though not identical in nature, was nonetheless a subset of the legends, tales and mythology of ancient China that received close attention at HPVDW.

BUGIS SQUARE. This was in the initial stage of redevelopment in 1991 and used to be a favourite tourist hangout in the past. Whether or not it would regain its past popularity remained to be seen. Competition here, if any, would be during the evening hours of operation. Bugis Square hoped to rekindle the ambience of the 1950s and 1960s with its cabaret-style entertainment complete with hostesses. Also the Bugis of yesteryear was a showpiece of sorts, due in part to the special touch of its unforgettable transvestite population. These "Ladies of the Night" were a tremendous draw in the past and were considered as a "show" in their own right.

The redevelopment plans for Bugis Square included a mini-theatre with a capacity of about 150 seats and would feature shows unique to the Bugis subculture. Two to three shows per night were planned on two stages complete with spotlights. Other features included 105 stalls, hawker food, six retail shops and an English-style pub with a live band. It would appear that when completed, Bugis Square would be a major competitor to HPVDW in terms of the entertainment it had to offer, that is, shows, decor and cuisine sans the rides.

SENTOSA. A 375.5-hectare island that was a stone's throw from HPVDW was yet another competitor for the tourist's time, attention and spending power. As of 1991, Sentosa upgraded many of its facilities by putting in several million dollars' worth of renovation and new constructions. Last year, Sentosa received 2.62 million visitors of which 45 per cent were foreign visitors. At the end of 1990, local visitors recorded an increase of 12 per cent while foreign visitors had an increase of 41 per cent over the previous year. Their major attractions include a man-made swimming lagoon, an elaborate musical fountain, the Corallarium, Fort Siloso, the butterfly park, the wax museum, and the rare stone museum. Sentosa adopted a differential pricing scheme whereby the normal tickets, inclusive of ferry ride, musical fountain shows, unlimited monorail and bus rides, access to the lagoon and the playground, were $3.50 for adults and $2.00 for children under 12. There were additional charges for entry to major attractions. The normal ticket price was reduced to $3.00 for adults after 5:00 pm. The other type of ticket was known as the composite ticket. It was similar to the normal ticket but it included additional admission to the Pioneers of Singapore and Surrender Chambers, Corallarium, Nature Ramble and Fort Siloso. This type of pricing offered flexibility to visitors in selecting the choice of attractions in Sentosa. The ferry services at Sentosa began at 7:30 am and were available till 11:00 pm on four days each week and were extended to midnight from Friday to Sunday.

The Beaufort Sentosa Resort Hotel, a five-star hotel still under construction, would allow visitors to stay on the island after operating hours. To cater to this new presence, more late night activities were planned; for example, concerts, variety and fashion shows and others. All in, the projected increase to visitorship was estimated at about 12.3 per cent for 1991.

The latest attraction at Sentosa was the Underwater World, a place where one could get an undersea view of the marine life through a see-through tunnel. This viewing tunnel was one of a kind in this region.

JURONG BIRD PARK. The Jurong Bird Park, open daily from 9:00 am to 6:00 pm, was a 20-hectare park featuring more than 4,000 birds of over 400 species. It had the largest bird collection in Southeast Asia. The admission fee of $5.00 for adults and $2.00 for children covered admission to all the shows within the park. These bird shows were available daily. There was a tram ride, which cost $1.00 for adults and $0.50 for children, that took the visitors around the park. Jurong Bird Park's operation expense was subsidized in part by public funds and corporate donations. Hence, a more competitive admission price was possible.

SINGAPORE ZOOLOGICAL GARDENS. The Zoological Gardens occupied 28 hectares and were home to over 1,700 animals comprising more than 170 species. The enclosures within the gardens were designed to be as close as possible to the actual habitats of the animals. In 1990, pandas were brought from China on a promotional tour. The pandas' presence boosted the visitor attendance level to well over 200,000 representing a 46 per cent increase over the previous month. The admission fee for the zoo, which included primate, reptile, elephant and sealion shows, was $5.00 for adults and $2.50 for children. These shows were scheduled twice a day. The zoo was opened daily from 8:30 am to 6:30 pm, and it also offered other attractions such as tram rides ($2.50 for adults and $1.50 for children), pony rides and elephant rides. As with the Jurong Bird Park, the zoo was highly subsidized by public funds and corporate donations.

THE SINGAPORE SCIENCE CENTRE. The Science Centre had well over 500 exhibits covering the physical, life and health sciences. The admission prices of $2.00 for adults and $0.50 for children did not include shows conducted at the planetarium and the OMNI theatre, one of the few installations in the world capable of screening the panoramic omnimax movies. These movies were screened daily at noon, 1:30 pm, 3:00 pm, 4:30 pm, 7:00 pm and 8:30 pm. The planetarium operated at 10:00 am and 11:00 am daily.

THE BOTANICAL GARDENS. The botanical gardens covering 47 hectares consisted of almost half a million plant species ranging from orchids to trees. It was a natural habitat for plants. The garden was opened daily from 5:50 am to 1:00 pm, except on weekends when it was closed at midnight. There was no admission fee. Many tourists visited this garden to enjoy its natural beauty.

JURONG CROCODILE PARADISE. This crocodile park offered a showcase of 2,500 crocodiles and included crocodiles wrestling shows at 11:30 am and 3:00 pm. This farm was opened daily from 9:00 am to 6:00 pm. The admission fees were $4.50 for adults and $2.50 for children under 12 years of age. Besides this farm, there were two other crocodile farms in Singapore. The crocodile farm at Serangoon was the only farm that did not charge admission fee but it had no wrestling shows.

LITTLE INDIA. This Indian neighbourhood at Serangoon Road offered an insight to Indian culture, such as Hindu temples, flower garland vendors and shops selling Indian items and exotic Indian food.

CHINATOWN. Chinatown encompasses an area of about two square kilometres. Here, one might find the pre-war shophouses, some still engaged in trades reminiscent of years long past, such as Chinese traditional medical halls, Chinese handicrafts stores, old-fashioned tea houses, etc. Amidst the old and traditional, one could also find the modern and sophisticated. There were several shopping complexes in the area offering everything from compact disc players to stereo televisions. Prices in this district were usually not fixed and the shopper was expected to bargain for the best possible price, sometimes as much as 50 per cent off the original quoted price. If the tourist did not mind the shabby decor, Chinatown was probably the best place for bargain hunting.

The average length of stay for a visitor to enjoy all the sites varies among these attractions. These figures are shown in Exhibit 3.

Exhibit 3 Average Length of Hours Spent by a Visitor*

Attractions	Average Number of Hours Needed to Visit All the Sites
Tang Dynasty Village	NA
Bugis Square	NA
Sentosa	12
Jurong Bird Park	3½
Singapore Zoological Gardens	3½
Singapore Science Centre	2
Botanical Gardens	1
Jurong Crocodile Paradise	1
Chinatown	3
Little India	1½

* Data as provided by the Singapore Tourist Promotion Board (STPB).

These are just a few of the 40 local tourist spots that competed with HPVDW for the tourist's time and resources. As the tourist trade was extremely lucrative and contributed a significant percentage to Singapore's GNP, both the STPB and the EDB (Economic Development Board) were actively promoting Singapore's attractions in order to attract a larger number of visitors to the country. No particular bias was given to any of the attractions mentioned above and all were given equal promotional exposure.

PARK OPERATIONS

Visitor attendance levels of HPVDW were closely monitored. To keep track of the latest changes in its attendance level, HPVDW made use of an on-line reporting system. Through the use of such a system, management of HPVDW was provided with an up-to-date figure on park attendance. This attendance information was primarily used to ensure that the number of visitors within the park was within manageable levels so that the enjoyment of the shows and rides was not hampered by long queues. Whenever park attendance was high enough to warrant action, the message was relayed to all managers and key personnel, all of whom carry transceivers on duty. The managers were constantly moving within the park grounds and decided what action to take. For example, if they found that the queue of the Tales of China boat ride was longer then usual, they might call for pocket entertainments—impromptu shows—to be staged to relieve the visitors from the boredom of standing in line waiting to get onto the rides or shows.

Under the close supervision of the duty managers, park operations were kept running as smoothly as possible. There was a set of standard operating procedure manuals that the managers or supervisors could refer to if in doubt. These procedures detailed how a particular job or action was to be undertaken. For example, it was clear that all maintenance jobs were to be carried out at night after operating hours were over.

As the whole theme involved projecting the park as a show, interruptions or distractions were strongly discouraged. Therefore, all servicing, clearing and repair work were kept out of view and normally not done during park operating hours. In cases where work had to be done immediately or during operating hours, for example, repainting of statues, a sign was put up which read "Artists at work". Thus, a job was turned into a performance and the worker was presented as a cast member.

The main administrative building was located at the rear of the park grounds. The main building houses the administrative offices, staff canteen, restrooms, rehearsal halls, costume and props rooms and the computer facilities.

ITP was organized into two divisions and five departments. The divisions were the finance and administration division and the park operation division.

The five departments were:

1. Human Resource Department
2. Retail and Merchandise Department
3. Advertising and Promotional Department
4. Food and Beverage Department
5. Sales Department

Each of the divisions had a divisional manager who handled the day-to-day operation of its own sub-departments (see Exhibit 4). Each department had its own manager. Under the finance and administration division, there were two sub-groups: administration and finance, and purchasing. The administration and finance department was responsible for all administrative matters including all financial matters. The purchasing department secured

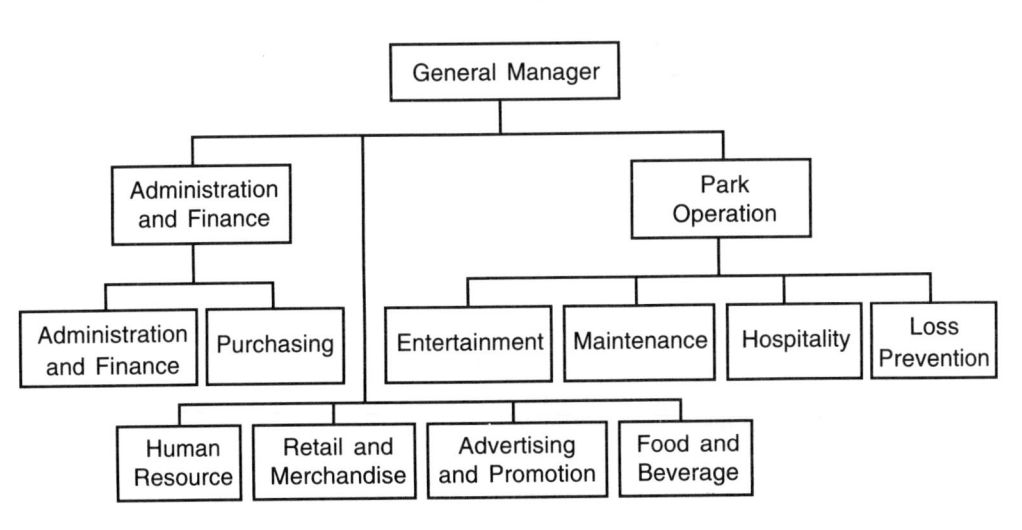

Exhibit 4 HPVDW's Organization Structure

```
                    General Manager
                   /               \
         Administration          Park
         and Finance           Operation
         /         \          /    |    |    \
Administration  Purchasing  Entertainment  Maintenance  Hospitality  Loss
and Finance                                                          Prevention
    |              |              |              |
  Human         Retail and    Advertising    Food and
  Resource      Merchandise   and Promotion  Beverage
```

all the material necessary for the functioning of HPVDW, such as office supplies, sourcing for goods, calling for quotations, and working closely with the administration and finance department in negotiations for supply contracts on all necessary purchases. The park operation division had four departments under its supervision. These were entertainment, maintenance, hospitality, and loss-prevention.

The entertainment department ensured that the shows and performances were carried out as scheduled. Details such as the availability of cast members, props, support staff, functionality of the equipment needed to stage the shows, were looked after by the entertainment manager. The most important responsibility here was to ensure that visitors got their money's worth in that a professional and efficient presentation of shows, displays and rides were accomplished with as little disruption and inconvenience as possible. The basic tenent at HPVDW was that the visitor was there to enjoy himself and that everything must be done to ensure that his visit was as memorable and pleasant as possible. Therefore, certain things had to be avoided at all costs, such as power failures, fused light bulbs, sound systems that did not work, queues that were too long, and shows that were cancelled because some cast members were late or not available. Management attempted to maintain a high degree of professionalism. However, certain things needed to be constantly monitored. The maintenance department had the responsibility of ensuring that park grounds were kept litter-free at all times. In fact, every employee, from kiosk helpers to divisional managers, helped to keep the park clean. The maintenance department was also accountable for the repairs of faulty equipment and making sure that every piece of equipment was performing efficiently.

The hospitality department handled visitors' queries, took care of missing person reports, maintained the theatre grounds, admission area, car park operation, rides operation, theatre operation, and looked after sale of tickets.

The loss prevention department was responsible for both internal as well as external theft investigations. Fire prevention and safety measures also fell under the jurisdiction of the loss prevention department.

The radio control room was under the supervision of the park operation division. From this room, the operator monitored, executed and coordinated messages sent by cast members to one another. It could be described as a message service centre. From this location, the status of the attendance level was collected. Three forms of abbreviations were used to record park attendance level. These were:

1. PAE—Park attendance entrance
2. PAL—Park attendance left
3. PAS—Park attendance status

These hourly reports gave management an up-to-the-minute picture of the attendance level, such as in the past hour, how many visitors had entered the park (PAE), how many had left (PAL) and how many were still in the park (PAS).

Key personnel within the park stayed in constant contact with each other through the use of transceivers. These "walkie-talkies", each costing about $1,000, allowed their users to communicate with each other. Conversation through the transceivers was kept short and to the point. After several months, there evolved a certain convention involving the use of call-signs. For example, the duty manager was referred to as "Happy Dragon" over the airwaves. Grammar and syntax were not usually a high priority when conversing. Rather, the main point was to get the message across as quickly, clearly and with as few words as possible. As at 1991, there were 53 sets of transceivers available for staff use.

Cast Members

As of May 1991, the park had 39 full-time performers and was expanding this pool of performers. The majority of the performers hired by HPVDW had singing and/or acting experience. In fact, most were hired only after they had passed an audition whereby their skills and talents were tested. Once hired, HPVDW provided the coaching necessary for these performers to polish up their acting abilities. The successful performers were put through a series of dance, song and acting classes. HPVDW aimed to have a performer mastering all the roles so that he or she could be called upon to assume any role whenever needed. HPVDW enlisted the aid of professional artists to coach some of its performers. These professionals were also involved in the selection process. Successful applicants were awarded generous remuneration, vacation and medical benefits plus insurance coverage.

Financial Performance

ITP was not subsidized by public funds. It was fully self-funding and as such, profitability was an important issue. The performance of the company was measured by its per capita spending and per capita cost. The per capita cost was defined as the total operating cost divided by the total number of visitors. The per capita spending was defined as total visitor spending over the total number of visitors. Total visitor spending included the admission fee plus all sales from the souvenir and games stalls, and car park collections and food outlet. The operating expenses consisted of fixed and variable costs. Up to May 1991, the average per capita spending was greater than the estimated per capita cost.

Mr. Lee was satisfied that the per capita spending and cost met his projected figures. According to its internal findings, management affirmed that locals tended to spend less on souvenirs, food and beverages. Another source of revenue came from sponsorships. The Spirits of the Orient Theatre was sponsored by Kodak and the flume ride was sponsored by Fraser and Neave. Sponsors got to have their sponsorship announced at the beginning of each sponsored show. ITP planned to have more corporate sponsors for its other attractions in the future.

ITP reported that its current operating costs were 20 per cent below its budgeted costs for fiscal year 1991. Mr. Lee was not sure whether this indicated insufficient spending or efficient cost control. Mr. Lee would prefer to have a high variable cost than a high fixed cost because variable cost varied with the attendance level. The expenses incurred by each department were used to calculate its per capita expense, that is, expense over total number of visitors. Using the figure for the per capita expense, Mr. Goh could have better control over the operating expense for each department. The performance of a department was evaluated on its per capita expense. Also, from the data available to him, Mr. Goh could identify which show, exhibit or kiosk was making a profit and which was operating below its per capita expense.

Major Management Concerns

There were several issues which management were determined to resolve. Many of these issues were teething problems, that is, the park being quite new, certain unforeseen matters were discovered that needed attention. First, visitors complained about the weather and indicated that the park should do something to alleviate visitors' discomfort from the scorching heat or the occasional downpour. Management was looking into the possibility of installing a fogging system to cool the entire park. Trees were being planted to provide shade but these would take time to grow. There were several instances where visitors demanded a refund because of heavy rain that resulted in the cancellation of some shows. The South China Sea Amphitheatre had a giant canopy to provide some protection against the sun. To render quality customer service, management implemented a pilot scheme in January 1991 whereby 5,000 umbrellas were purchased for use by visitors during adverse weather. After three months, they discovered that only 10 per cent of the 5,000 umbrellas were returned. The visitors just kept the umbrellas when they left the park.

The second major concern of the park was in the recruitment of talented performers and instructors to join its ranks. HPVDW has found that good performers and instructors were hard to come by in Singapore. Unlike other establishments, HPVDW paid its performers overtime compensation according to the National Wage Council (NWC) guidelines. Its basic pay was also very competitive. One reason for the lack of suitable applicants could be that movie companies and TV stations offer their actors and actresses wider audience coverage and exposure. Currently ITP experienced a high turnover rate for part-timers. Mr. Lee wondered how he could resolve this problem.

Decision to Add More Shows or More Rides

The management at HPVDW felt strongly that the success of the park depended primarily on its "product contents." By this, they meant that for HPVDW to continue to attract visitors, there must be a certain element of fluidity, or change. The emphasis therefore was on the live performances and shows as opposed to static displays or rides. In addition, the life span of a ride was normally three to five years. Furthermore static displays involving statues provided very little flexibility. These statues, like the rides, could neither be easily moved from their locations nor could their contents be changed. Thus, it was believed that the success of HPVDW was contingent upon its "product" design. Since there was more flexibility involved in changing shows and performances than to change the rides or statuary displays, management was highly confident of the success of HPVDW as a show park. Currently, there were five scheduled shows in five different theatres. The times for the theatre shows were fixed whereas the show times for the live performances varied for obvious reasons. The schedule for the shows was updated as and when necessary and distributed to visitors at the entrance to HPVDW.

After seven months of operation, none of the live shows were changed. Management had not established the life span of a particular show since the opening of HPVDW. However, management was aware that to attract repeat visitors, the shows had to be varied periodically. Thus, in February 1991, two new shows were staged in conjunction with the Chinese Lunar New Year. Management was pleased with the response because the park attracted more than 4,000 visitors to the park during that period. At present, all shows were performed in English. Local senior citizens were disappointed that all the shows were in English as the majority of them could not understand the language. The shows were choreographed in such a way as to involve as much audience participation as possible. The costumes were deliberately designed to be colourful and vibrant. The songs and musical scores were a unique blend of Western and Oriental sounds. All shows, musical scores and park characters were copyrighted and specially tailored to the park's theme.

Mr. Lee had also looked into contracting shows from abroad and had sent Mr. Sim to China to look into the feasibility of getting shows from there to perform locally. The shows from China would be in Mandarin (Chinese language) and these shows would have a mixture of acrobatics, opera and plays. The type of shows in Beijing was more traditional than in Shanghai. As such, Mr. Goh wondered to what extent they should maintain the degree of Chinese tradition. HPVDW found it more cost effective to produce the shows in-house than to contract outside performers. The cost of producing a live show in-house ranged from $5,000, for a simple show with four performers, to $200,000 for a full scale live show with special effects. However, management was concerned about the fact that there were relatively few experienced and talented performers and instructors in Singapore.

With all the information collated by both Mr. Lee and Mr. Sim, Mr. Goh had to carefully consider the alternatives that were available. Apart from this issue, Mr. Goh had to decide whether he should keep the park just as it was or if he wanted change, what sort of changes were appropriate so as to ensure the continual success of the park.

INDEX

abandonment, 73
acquisition of firms, 72
activity ratios, 56
adaptive control, 102
adhocracy, 19
allowance, 61
analytical framework, 27
anti-trust legislation, 39
ASEAN, 33
Asia-Pacific, 28
asset utilization, 56
assets, 56
autocratic states, 4

backward integration, 61
balance sheet, 56
bankruptcy, 58
bargaining power, 41
bland strategy, 19
borderless, 15
Boston Consulting Group, 64
    growth-share matrix, 74–76
brand names, 61
brand strategy, 19
break-even analysis, 58
bubble economy, 73
bureaucratic organizations, 34
business-level strategies, 74
business portfolio models, 74
business strategy formulation, 78–83
buyer concentration, 42

capacity, 21
capitalism, 13
capitalist, 30

cash flow, 56
categorization of market structure, 38
centralization, 49
chaebols, 5, 86, 97–98
chain, 7
China, People's Republic of, 30
Chinese family business, 53
Chinese strategies, 84
clan control, 105
collaborator approach, 94–95
colony (Hong Kong), 5
combinations of strategy alternatives, 74
commander approach, 94–95
Communist gerontocrats, 13
Communist Party (China), 32
comparative advantages, 39
compensation benefits, 63
competitive advantage, 6, 47
competitive edge, 60
competitive forces, 78
complex conditions, 35
complexity, 35
concentration, 71
concentric diversification, 72
conceptual framework, 27
conceptualizations, 39
conciliatory mode, 8
confrontation, 6
Confucian, 13
Confucianism, 54
conglomerate, 49
conglomerate diversification, 73
constraints, 20
consumption, 37
contingency plans, 106

Index

continuation strategy, 90
control process, 100
core competencies, 47
corporate culture, 49
corporate identity, 17
corporate resources, 49
cost centres, 106
cost of funds, 58
cost leadership, 78–79
cottage industry, 13
credit terms, 61
creditors, 58
crescive approach, 94–95
critical success factors, 48
culture, 11
current ratio, 56
customer analysis, 60
Czepiel, 14

debt/equity ratio, 56
decentralization, 89
declining stage, 36–38
Delpphi technique, 35
demand, 35
demand curves, 40
democracy, 3
demographic factors, 28
deregulation, 18
determinants of capacity, 63
DHL, 9
differentiation, 39, 80–81
disclosure, 58
discount, 61
Disney, 9
distinctive competencies, 14, 48
distribution channels, 37, 60
diversification, 49
diversification strategy, 72–73
diversity, 35
divestiture, 73
dividend policy, 58
divisional organizational structure, 92
downsizing, 19
dumping, 28
durability, 3
dynamic conditions, 35
dynamism, 34

earnings after taxes (EAT), 57
earnings before interest and taxes (EBIT), 56
East vs. West, 2

economic miracle, 13
economies of scale, 39
egalitarian, 24
embargo, 34
embryonic stage, 37
entrepreneurial style, 38
entrepreneur's dream, 22
entry barriers, 41
equity joint venture, 98
European Economic Union (EU), 33
execution, 20
exhortative states, 4
exit barriers, 43
experience curve, 17
exports, 28
external environment, 27

face, 2
familism, 16
feedback, 20, 100
feedforward, 101
financial ratio, 56
focus, 81–83
focus groups, 35
formal organization, 92
formalization, 49
4 M's, 63
four-petal model, 52
4 P's, 60
franchises, 38
freewheeling, 5
frequent flier programme, 42
functional approach, 27
functional strategy formulation, 83
future-oriented, 35
futurism, 13

gap analysis, 102
General Agreement on Tariffs and Trade (GATT), 34
General Electric strategic planning grid, 76–78
generic corporate strategy, 71–74
geographic dispersion, 49
global competition, 19
government intervention, 16
grand strategy, 19
gross domestic product (GDP), 48
groupism, 4
growth stage, 36–37
growth-share matrix, 74–76
growth strategies, 49, 71–72
guanxi, 2, 84

Index

hahk-yun, 98
harmony, 4
hongs, 5, 50
horizontal (lateral) integration, 72
human rights, 34

imitation, 48
implementation control, 102
imports, 28
inbound logistics, 65
income statement, 56
income taxes, 44
industry, 34
industry analysis, 44
industry attractiveness, 77
industry growth rate, 75
Industry Life Cycle, 36
inflation, 48
inflexibility, 17
information technology, 8
infrastructure, 66
initial stage, 37
interactive process, 55
interlock, 5, 18
intermediaries, 61
internal customers, 20
internal environment, 27
Internal Factor Evaluation Matrix, 64
internal factors, 55
interweave, 18
introduction stage, 36–37
inventory turnover, 56
investment intensity, 59
inwha, 98
ISO 9000, 64

Japanese strategies, 85–86
ji-yun, 98
job descriptions, 63
joint ventures, 15, 94
just-in-time (JIT), 63

keiretsu, 4, 51, 61, 85
kinfolk, 54
Korean strategies, 86–87

laissez-faire, 30
leadership, 62
leadership styles, 38
learning organization, 89
leverage, 56

liabilities, 56
licences, 72
liquidation, 73
liquidity, 56
list price, 61
little dragons of Asia, 5
logo, 18
long-range planning, 70
loyalty of consumers, 37

macro environment, 28
management information system (MIS), 64
market attractiveness, 15
market niche, 39
market segment, 40
market stretching, 38
marketing mix, 60
Marks & Spencer, 14
matrix, 49
matrix organization, 92
maturity stage, 36–38
megatrends, 13
Ministry of International Trade and Industry (MITI), 30
mission, 8
mission statement, 70
mobility barriers, 41
modernization, 5
MOFERT, 32
molecular arrangement, 50
monopoly, 38
Most Favored Nation Status (MFN), 33
multinational corporations (MNCs), 84

national character, 11
Neo-Confucianist, 2
nepotism, 98, 99
net present value (NPV), 106
network (*keiretsu*), 61
new entrants, threat of, 41
newly industrializing countries, 64
niche marketing, 17
non-intervention, 5
North America Free Trade Agreement (NAFTA), 33

objectives, 47
oligopoly, 39
opportunities, 47
order, 2
 divisions, 92
 simple, 49, 91

Index

organizational strategy formulation, 71–74
organizational structure, 49, 91
original equipment manufacturers (OEM), 94
outbound logistics, 66
overall cost leadership, 78–79
ownership, 30

Pacific Rim, 39
package, 60
pan-Asian, 14
patents, 38
paternalistic ethos, 63
paternalistic states, 4
people-based competencies, 63
perfect competition, 38
peripheral vision, 17
perpetuation, 21
personal selling, 60
place (channels of distribution), 60
political actions, 28
political agency, 32
political systems, 4
Porter, Michael, 41
portfolio management, 72
portfolio theory, 17
post-action control, 101
power-oriented, 52
practicality, 14
premise control, 102
price, 60
price fixing or collusion, 39
pricing strategies, 61
primary activities, 65
privatization, 32
privileges, 21
procurement process, 66
product, 60
product life cycle, 61
Profit Impact of Market Strategy (PIMS), 59
profit margin, 56
profitability, 21, 37
promotion, 60
protectionism, 28
publicity, 60

quotas, 38

radical reassessment, 21
radical strategy change, 90
reappraisal, 20
recurring costs, 37

redirectional change, organizational, 90
re-engineering, 21
regional synergies, 14
regulations, 38
relative market share, 75
reliability, 3
representative office, 22
resources of a firm, 47
responsibility centres, 106
restructuring, 74
retail chains, domination of, 42
retrenchment, 74
return on investment (ROI), 57
right-sizing, 89
ringi-sho, 96
Ringi system, 96
rivalry, 38, 41
    intensity of, 43
routine strategy change, 90

S-curve, 36
sanctions, 13
scenarios, 13
secondary activities, 65
7-S framework, 52
shake-out stage, 37–38
skills inventories, 63
socialist, 30
Sogo shasha, 61
Sony, 11
South Korea, 30
sovereignty of Hong Kong, 5
specialization, 92
St. Michael (brand name), 14
stages of life cycle, 36–38
State Enterprises (of China), 30
static environment, 34
stockholders, 58
stockholding, 12
strategic alliances, 15
strategic audit, 107
strategic business unit (SBU), 19, 49
    cash cows, 76
    dogs, 76
    problem child, 76
    question marks, 76
    stars, 76
strategic concepts, 17
strategic control, 100
    process, 100
strategic goals, 16

Index

strategic groups, 39
    identification of, 40
strategic intent, 24
strategic philosophy, 14
strategic planning, 70
strategic planning grid, 76–78
Strategic Planning Institute, 59
strategic surveillance, 102
strategic thinking, 19
strategy, 7
strategy formulation, 62, 83
strategy implementation, 62, 89
    collaborator approach, 94–95
    commander approach, 94–95
    crescive approach, 94–95
strengths of business, 47, 77
subcontracting, 94
substitutes, threat of, 41
subsystem, 92
Sun-tzu, 24
sunset industry, 74
supportive states, 4
switching cost, 43
SWOT analysis, 47
synergy, 18, 64
systems, 52

tactical objectives, 16
tactics, 18
Taiwan Aerospace, 32
tariff, 33
technological factors, 28
telecommunications, 22

temporal factors, 48
territory (Hong Kong), 5
theory building, 39
time-binding, 24
tobagi, 98
total quality management, 3
trade blocs, 33
trade concession, 34
trading companies (*sogo shasha*), 61
turbulent stage, 37–38
turnaround, 74

uncertainty, 23
Uruguay round (GATT), 34

value-added, 79
value chain analysis, 47
value-creating activities, 47
vertical integration, 49, 72
virtual corporation, 21
vision, 7

warranties, 61
weaknesses of a firm, 47
West vs. East, 2
what-ifs, 13
wholly owned operations, 94
working capital, 56, 58

Yaohan Department Store, 10

zaibatsu, 51
zero-based budgeting, 89